P9-CBS-691

THE
ABC-CLIO
WORLD HISTORY
COMPANION TO

Capitalism

THE
ABC-CLIO
WORLD HISTORY
COMPANION TO

Capitalism

Larry Allen

ABC-CLIO

Library of Congress Cataloging-in-Publication Data

Allen, Larry.
   The ABC-CLIO world history companion to capitalism / Larry Allen.
   p.   cm.
   Includes bibliographical references and index
   ISBN 0-87436-944-4 (alk. paper)
   1. Capitalism--History. I. Title.
HC79.C3A45 1998   98-3908
330.12'2--dc21   CIP

02 01 00 99 98   10 9 8 7 6 5 4 3 2 1

ABC-CLIO, Inc.
130 Cremona Drive, P.O. Box 1911
Santa Barbara, California 93116-1911

This book is printed on acid-free paper.
Manufactured in the United States of America

Contents

Preface

The British prime minister Benjamin Disraeli advised, "Read no history: nothing but biography, for that is life without theory." Contemporary economics, which is highly theoretical and makes use of impersonal facts and statistics, rarely turns to history, and even more rarely to biographies, to gain new insights and answers to problems. After teaching economic theory for 20 years, however, I often observed that economic events often outsmarted our formulas, creating a skepticism that opened my mind to different approaches. I began collecting material and making notes, which have found their way into this book, out of my own curiosity about new knowledge and perspectives that could be gained when economics is studied shorn of mathematical formulas, theoretical diagrams, and statistical studies.

To study economics without theory, one has to turn to economic history, not withstanding Disraeli's advice not to read history—economic history is economics without theory. That is not to say that this book does not have any theory in it. I wrote the book as the history of the development of capitalism, as seen through the eyes of one trained in economic theory rather than history, and chose the topics and their treatment accordingly. Nevertheless, there is not a underlying theoretical theme that pervades this book.

While occasionally making use of thought-stirring ideas to enliven the subject matter, I put the emphasis on descriptions that let the events speak for themselves.

The purpose of this book lies in the synthesis of existing knowledge, and not in the economic analysis of particular events or problems. Economic analysis, aided by computers that can process the most advanced mathematical and statistical models, has discovered a prodigious amount of knowledge about how economic systems function. The sense of power from our ability to manipulate the economy has even led some economists to talk about fine-tuning the economy. This knowledge, which gave us an added sense of power over our economic environment, came from studies in highly specialized fields of economics, but it has done little to enlarge a total perspective that can enrich our ability to formulate purposes, values, and goals. It might have even made us a little careless of these things. This book strives to bring to readers the background and enlarged perspective that will help them think about current economic issues involving purposes, values, and goals, and brings to bear on these issues a total vision of a capitalist economy evolving in a historical context.

The librarians at the Mary and John

Gray Library on the Lamar University campus deserve my hearty appreciation for tireless assistance in helping me assemble materials for this book. They always made the task of finding a particular book or reference much easier than I expected. Also, I owe a special debt of gratitude to Dr. Ron Fritze, Professor of History at Lamar University. Dr. Fritze's encyclopedic knowledge enables him to shed light on any subject brought to his attention—a trait that I often made use of while writing this book. After helping me formulate the original idea for this book, he patiently advised me along the way. A word of appreciation is due Todd Hallman, the acquisitions editor at ABC-CLIO, who guided me through this project. Mr. Hallman could always be counted on to mix a good bit of praise with his suggestions of how material should be presented.

Introduction

Capitalism is an economic system in which the means of production are privately owned. The means of production include arable land, natural resources, transportation and communication facilities, factories, machinery, warehouses, etc. The owners of these resources are guided by their own self-interest in deciding how to deploy them. The system is spared from being a recipe for rewarding greed and selfishness by competition among sellers for the consumer's dollars, among employers for the best workers, and among consumers for the best products. In the purest forms of capitalism, the government enforces fair dealing and adjudicates disputes, but plays a modest role, never playing favorites in the struggle for economic survival.

Capitalism can be interpreted as a system of rewards and penalties for producing and conserving goods and resources. The price of a product is a reward to the producer for producing it, and a penalty to the consumer for consuming it. Owners of private property are rewarded with higher property values when property is conserved and used wisely, and are punished with lower property values when property deteriorates.

The energy devoted to the pursuit of profit is either dissipated in a self-canceling competitive process, or becomes a powerful inspiration for innovation and invention. With the spread of capitalism, inventions began to multiply at an accelerated rate, rendering obsolete and destroying industries that were not yet old, and creating new industries.

In the fifteenth century, capitalist interests and institutions began to dominate the social and political life of the Italian city-states. The merchant princes of these cities rivaled in political power and social prestige the landed aristocracy of the hereditary feudal societies. Maritime city-states have been a popular haven for capitalism, as can be seen in the thriving commercial activity of present-day Hong Kong. Peter the Great laid out St. Petersburg with the purpose of making it the Venice of the North. England, a relatively small country geographically, was the first nation-state to exhibit a capitalist pattern of economic development. From England, capitalism spread to the larger nation-states of Europe.

The New World clearly gave the advantage to capitalist organization and private initiative. European countries that historically depended upon government initiative for economic development, that is, Spain and Portugal, were the first to discover and trade with the New World, but their government-directed policies failed to stimulate economic development at a rate commensurate with boundless supplies of natural resources. The colonies of England, a country with strong capitalist traditions, exhibited the rapid economic development that was possible with the virtually unlimited supply of natural resources.

At the end of the eighteenth century, a torrent of rational critique of society pulled down what remained of the tradition-bound, highly regulated feudal and mercantile societies in England and France, beginning the era of laissez-faire capitalism.

The American and French revolutions were symptomatic of this process. However, the same aggressive rationalism in social thought, which had served as a midwife to capitalism and had swept away feudalism, turned its penetrating scrutiny to capitalism itself in the nineteenth century.

Even the critics of capitalism marveled at a transformation of material life that raised the hope of unlimited progress. In the *Manifesto of the Communist Party*, written by Karl Marx and Friedrich Engels, one reads what the capitalist class had contributed to human progress:

> It has been the first to show what man's activity can bring about. It has accomplished wonders far surpassing Egyptian pyramids, Roman aqueducts, and Gothic cathedrals; it has conducted expeditions that put in the shade all former migrations of nations and crusades.... Its rule of scarce one hundred years has created more massive and more colossal forces than have all preceding generations together.... [W]hat earlier century had even a presentiment that such productive forces slumbered in the lap of social labor?

Capitalism boasted of great achievements, but also aroused deep resentment and discontent. Both the achievements and the discontent can be traced to the role of economic inequality in the capitalist system. According to John Maynard Keynes, in *The Economic Consequences of Peace*,

In fact, it was precisely the inequality of the distribution of wealth which made possible those vast accumulations of fixed wealth and of capital improvements which distinguished that age from all others. Herein lay, in fact, the main justification of the Capitalist System.... The immense accumulations of fixed capital, which, to the great benefit of mankind, were built up during the half century before the war [World War I], could never have come about in a Society where wealth was divided equally.... In the unconscious recesses of its being Society knew what it was about. The cake was really very small in proportion to the appetites of consumption, and no one if it were shared all around, would be much better off by the cutting of it. Society was working not for the small pleasures of today but for the future security and improvement of the race,—in fact for "progress."

Keynes, who belonged to the upper income echelons of British society, could afford to accept with equanimity the social and economic inequality that the impoverished and unemployed working classes found unreasonable. The working classes, seething with a white-hot hatred for an impersonal factory system that swallowed their wives and children, as well as themselves, developed a compensating vision of a utopia. This utopia was not a land of milk and honey, where all their basic appetites and instincts were satisfied, but a land where everyone was equal. In the words of the French libertarian socialist Pierre Joseph Proudhon, written about 1848, "The enthusiasm which possesses us, the enthusiasm for equality is an intoxication stronger than wine, deeper than love; a divine passion and furor which the delirium of Leonidas, of St. Bernard, or of Michaelngelo, can never equal."

Reconciling the working classes with capitalism was one of the main accomplishments of the twentieth century. The spread of the voting franchise to universal male suffrage allowed the propertyless workers to vote, leading to the enactment of legislation that protected the rights of workers to unionize and protect themselves. The further extension of the voting franchise to universal suffrage, male and female, strengthened the forces of humanitarian reform. Economic reforms designed to strengthen the hand of workers and low-income families in the democratic capitalist countries, accompanied a deep disillusionment over failure of socialist societies to rid themselves of inequality and provide rising living standards. Disillusionment over socialist experiments, combined with improved economic conditions for workers, brought a more harmonious relationship between capital and labor in capitalist countries.

Karl Marx argued that capitalism would self-destruct because of an internal contradiction between the desire to keep wages low and the drive for higher production. In such a system, production tends to race ahead of demand, causing periodic crises. According to Marx, in one of these crises, the working classes would seize political power, spelling the end of capitalism. Capitalism may contain an internal contradiction that could lead to its own destruction, but not the one Marx envisioned. On the other hand, capitalism leads to constantly rising living standards, and the enjoyment of greater amounts of leisure. Even in the wealthiest capitalist societies, however, economic insecurity remains a fact of life, and a rapid fall from riches to rags becomes a fate worse than death. (Stock market crashes and farm foreclosures are known to cause people to take their life.) As people become more affluent in every other aspect of their lives, this kind of pressure in the capitalist system may cause more resentment. Rising living standards do not provide any relief from economic insecurity and pressure, which helps to fuel much of the criticism associated with capitalism.

The pages that follow trace the evolution of capitalism, starting with the highly regulated, tradition-bound medieval economy, rising to the apex of laissez-faire capitalism in the nineteenth century, and ending with contemporary capitalism as influenced by the challenges of socialism, environmental degradation, and pleas for more social justice. Chronologically, the book covers the period from a.d. 1450 to the present. Since it is impossible to see all sides of capitalist development from just one angle, this book proposes to portray its development from the perspective of specific laws, government policies, events, and ideas that have made a difference. In keeping with the economic interpretation of history, which makes underlying economic realities, rather than heroic personalities, the deciding factors in historical evolution, individual personalities are represented to a lesser extent. Each law, policy, event, or idea is discussed as a contribution to the future development of capitalism, or, in some cases, as a temporary reaction. Laws and policies are explained in relation to the best economic thinking at the time of their enactment, and the wisdom of policies and laws are also examined in light of contemporary economic thinking. Where possible, discussions of important events, such as the Great Depression of the 1930s, throw light on the dynamic processes of capitalism as they are currently understood, and the adaptations capitalism has made to avoid repetitions of similar events.

In the name of fairness, the voices of the great critics of capitalism, such as Karl Marx, are given their turn to speak, as are the great admirers, such as Adam Smith. The ideas of these thinkers generated much of the social and political thought that became a shaping force in the development of capitalism. Individual entries in this dictionary are intended to stand on their own merits, each looking into the nooks and crannies of capitalism, and studying it from various viewpoints. The book, taken from start to finish, gives the subject matter vision, by drawing all these various threads of capitalist development together into a unified perspective.

Age of Steel (1854–present)

The development of processes to mass-produce steel opened fresh horizons for the Industrial Revolution. Steel is a hardened metal that is more durable and malleable than iron. Heavier machinery, faster spinning wheels, and more powerful engines put demands on metals that iron struggled to meet. After 3,000 years of the Iron Age, some observers saw mankind entering an age of steel. Steel became such an important industry in the twentieth century that low-income countries regarded a domestic steel industry as a status symbol.

Sir Henry Bessemer received credit for first developing a process for mass-producing steel from pig iron, an innovation that came to be known around the world as the Bessemer process. In his autobiography, Bessemer told how he was developing rotating projectiles for the French military when he saw a need to mass-produce steel. Rotating projectiles improved accuracy, but demanded stronger cannons. In January 1854, he applied for a patent in England on a new process for producing steel. William Kelley developed the process separately, in the United States, and received a patent in 1857. Others gave the process necessary fine-tuning, but Bessemer was an experienced inventor who managed to control his invention. Bessemer also patented much of the equipment that went with the process. Even in the United States, where Kelley had the process patented, steel producers had to pay Bessemer royalties for the use of his machinery. Patent disputes in the United States might have cost Kelley some of the credit he deserved for developing the process.

The new process was soon put to use manufacturing steel rails for railroads. Wrought-iron rails were normally replaced at six-month intervals, and, on occasion, at three-month intervals. Steel rails were known to last 17 or 18 times as long as wrought-iron ones. For the remainder of the nineteenth century, steel rails accounted for most steel production. The Bessemer process deserves much of the credit for worldwide extension of the railroad system. However, despite the advantages of steel over iron, steel production did not overtake iron production until 1886.

Like the Industrial Revolution, the age of steel came first to England, which dominated the export market for steel until the end of the nineteenth century. England contented itself with using the original Bessemer technique, but Germany was aggressive at adopting improvements. In 1878, Great Britain supplied 69 percent of the world export market for steel, compared with 22 percent for Germany. By 1895, Great Britain's share had fallen to 57 percent, Germany's share had risen to 22 percent, and the United States accounted for 2 percent of world exports of steel.

The United States became a major steel producer after the discovery of one of the world's largest reserves of iron ore deposits in the Lake Superior region. However, this ore was not suitable for the Bessemer process. In the 1860s, patent protection was awarded to an open-hearth furnace method of steel production that was more adaptable to the iron ore deposits discovered near Lake Superior. By 1908, open-hearth steel production exceeded Bessemer steel production, and the United States joined the ranks of the world's major steel producers. On the eve of World War I, Germany accounted for 39 percent of the world's steel exports, Great Britain accounted for 30 percent, and the United States accounted for 18 percent. The United States emerged from

World War II as the biggest steel producer in the world.

During the twentieth century, the steel industry became the cornerstone of industrial and military might in the United States. Perhaps the greatest contribution of the steel industry to lifestyles was the all-metal automobile. The development of methods to stamp sheets of steel into shapes made the modern automobile design possible. In addition, the internal combustion engine owed much of its endurance and practicality to steel.

The steel industry laid the foundation for a new industrial structure. New factories had to be built, and new capital had to be raised, to produce automobiles, agricultural implements, and military hardware. In capitalist countries, market forces had to be counted on to supply the steel that an economy needed at full levels of employment. After all, a bottleneck in steel production could bring economic expansion to a halt. Goods made from steel are very durable, and do not wear out or need replacement on a regular basis. If consumers repaired durable goods in a recession, instead of replacing them, the economy collapsed into a major depression. However, despite such added complexities of the age of steel, modern capitalism has maintained a long-term record of economic growth that other economies could not match.

See also Railroads.

References Fisher, Douglas Alan. *The Epic of Steel* (1963); Warren, Kenneth. *World Steel: An Economic Geography* (1975); Warren, Kenneth: *Triumphant Capitalism* (1996).

Agricultural Adjustment Act of 1933 (United States)

The Agricultural Adjustment Act was the New Deal's answer to a mounting farm crisis that had been worsening for a decade. In 1931, the price of cotton stood at 5.7 cents per pound, compared with the 41.7 cents per pound that it sold for in 1920. By 1932, the value of farm output had fallen by 60 percent within three years. An epidemic of farm foreclosures swept the nation, as farmers defaulted on mortgages and taxes.

Some farmers reacted with anger and recklessness. In several midwestern states, barricades went up, blocking trucks on the way to markets, and milk and produce were dumped. Striking dairy farmers in Wisconsin provoked a tear gas and bayonet attack from the National Guard. Armed farmers met eviction notices with threats against public officials. Groups of farmers intimidated bona fide bidders at foreclosure auctions and purchased property at low prices, returning it to the bankrupt owner.

In May 1933, Congress enacted the Agricultural Adjustment Act, on the recommendation of President Franklin D. Roosevelt, and in response to rising violence in rural areas. The act was based on the assumptions that agriculture suffered from overly abundant production, and that the key to raising farm prices and incomes lay in restricting production. The ideas of restricting productivity and government controls met with some criticism and skepticism in Congress, but not sufficient to delay passage of the bill. The bill enabled the Agriculture Adjustment Administration (AAA) to sign production limitation contracts with farmers, which subsidized farmers for not producing.

Since the bill passed after spring planting, farmers were forced to plow up crops that were already in the ground. A severe drought did enough damage to the wheat and corn crops to remove any need for deliberate destruction. Cotton farmers plowed up 10 million acres of cotton, and hog growers destroyed 6 million piglets. When American people reacted with confusion and anger to the destruction of food in a time of soup lines and unemployment, the government made some effort to distribute pork to hungry relief recipients. By mid-December 1933, farm prices were up from 50 percent to 68 percent of parity. The slaughter of piglets raised the price of hogs 15 percent.

The influence of large commercial farms made itself felt in the formulation of

AAA policy. Tenants and sharecroppers did not share in the subsidies for not producing. Many plantations took land out of cultivation and forced sharecroppers out of farming. The New Deal undertook very limited efforts to assist tenant farmers and sharecroppers in acquiring their own land.

In 1936, the Supreme Court ruled against the constitutionality of the AAA, because of a tax on food processors that financed the program. Congress reacted by passing the Soil Conservation and Domestic Production Act, which pursued the same production-restricting policies as the AAA, in the name of soil conservation. It withdrew land from cultivation and introduced grasses and legumes that enriched the soil and combated erosion. In 1938, Congress passed a second Agricultural Adjustment Act that provided benefits for voluntary acreage reductions.

The programs of the two AAAs achieved some success in reinvigorating agricultural income, which had fallen from $79 billion in 1929 to $39 billion in 1933, but rose to $66 billion in 1939.

The AAA represented the kind of blunt, forceful intrusion into the market system that should never be necessary, according to the textbook operation of the capitalist system. Perhaps because of attachment to family farms as a lifestyle choice, falling incomes in the 1920s failed to reduce the number of farmers sufficiently, and government had to take direct action to reduce production.

See also Great Depression.

References Biles, Roger. *A New Deal for the American People* (1991); Hamilton, David E. *From New Day to New Deal* (1991).

Agricultural Revolution

Agricultural revolution usually refers to the rapid spread of scientific farming practices and improved organization that made English agriculture famous in the latter half of the eighteenth century and early part of the nineteenth century. This time frame is unnecessarily simplistic. The beginning of the period of infinitely expanding agricultural production probably started in the middle of the seventeenth century, and the rapid mechanization of agriculture began in the mid-nineteenth century. Nevertheless, the last half of the eighteenth century saw an outpouring of agricultural literature on improved farming techniques. By then, books sold at cheap prices and farmers were more literate. One farmer whose writings helped popularize new methods of farming was Thomas Coke. Between 1717 and 1821, Coke's farm attracted visitors from all parts of the country, who came to observe his methods. King George III developed a model farm at Windsor using the new techniques of farming.

The application of new knowledge to agriculture touched several areas. Improvements in crop rotation, adapted to particular soils and climatic conditions, increased the productivity of the soil. One well-publicized system of crop rotation, the Norfolk system, rotated crops through a complete cycle of wheat, turnips, barley, and clover. The cultivation of new grasses and other new crops raised the level of animal nutrition, increasing the production of meat and milk. Farmers also learned how to improve the soil by marling, manuring, and draining. Marl was a mixture of clay and lime, or chalk and lime, which improved the moisture content of light soil, and made heavy soil easier to work. Inexpensive materials were developed to improve drainage sys-

Cyrus Hall McCormick's reaper, invented in 1847, revolutionized agriculture by increasing the amount of land one person could farm.

tems: Good drainage was often necessary for the new farming methods. Farm implements also entered a phase of improvement and innovation.

Livestock breeders experimented with crossbreeding to improve meat, milk, and wool production. They discovered that specific diets for animals could produce special qualities in animal products. Hobby-farming aristocrats sought out pedigree breeders for animals with those special qualities.

Enclosures consolidated strips of scattered fields, increasing the size of farming operations. The advocates of progressive farming saw small farmers as resistant to progress. A new phase of the agricultural revolution began after 1850. Reapers, steam-powered threshing machines, and horse-drawn cultivators increased the amount of land one person could farm.

Increases in agricultural productivity reduced the share of the population needed for food production, and made more of the population available for the production of manufactured products. Industry recruited new workers from agriculture, who were not subject to guild regulations. As industries and cities grew, farmers turned to producing for profit, rather than producing for their own consumption. The income of farmers fueled the market for manufactured products.

See also Enclosures.

References Addy, John. *The Agrarian Revolution* (1972); Mingay, G. E. *The Agricultural Revolution* (1977).

Airline Deregulation Act of 1978 (United States)

The Airline Deregulation Act of 1978 freed airlines to compete on the basis of fares and choice of routes. Since the creation of the Civil Aeronautics Board (CAB) in 1938, airline fares had been set by government regulation. In addition to fixing fares, the CAB granted airlines permission to introduce service on a route already served by other airlines. The reasons favoring regulation of the airlines lay in the deflationary forces of the De-

pression. In the minds of many, the price system became a euphemism for cutthroat competition. For growth in the fledgling airline industry, prices had to be maintained at a profitable level.

By a grandfather provision, the 16 airlines in existence in 1938 kept the routes they had been serving. These routes became the trunks. Before the passage of the Airline Deregulation Act, the CAB had effectively barred new airlines from entering markets on major routes. Because of mergers, the number of airlines providing service on the trunks fell from 16 to 11. The major airlines who served the trunks met with difficulties and hindrances in obtaining permission to serve additional routes. To obtain permission to add a new route, an airline had to show that the public interest would be served, and that carriers already serving that market would not be harmed. On occasion, the CAB granted a lucrative route to a carrier suffering financial difficulties. Unofficially, the CAB set limits on the number of carriers allowed in each market. The CAB was generous in granting permission to service small communities, where volumes were low.

The prime concern of the CAB in setting fares was the profitability of the airline companies. Fares were set across the board, based upon cost per passenger mile, rather than upon a market-by-market basis. The fares approved by the CAB favored short routes over long routes, encouraging the provision of service to small communities. The long routes earned fares above cost, subsidizing the cost of short routes. In practice, extra profits on long routes went to pay for amenities to passengers, and for extra flights. The CAB approved fare increases to pay the cost of fewer passengers per flight on long routes.

In the mid-1970s, the regulation of the airline industry drew fire from critics in academia and government. Intrastate carriers in Texas and California were free from the CAB's regulatory authority. These companies charged lower fares in comparable markets and earned profits. In 1976, the CAB began to grant carriers more flexibility to offer discount fares to special groups of customers, such as those who buy tickets 30 days in advance. Airline companies were facing competition from charter companies. In 1977, the CAB made it easier for carriers to enter new markets, and the airlines prospered under the new ground rules.

The Airline Deregulation Act ratified the deregulation begun by the CAB. Competition brought lower fares and the safety record of the industry withstood close scrutiny in the face of new competition. The smaller communities lost jet service in many cases, and competition pushed some companies to bankruptcy. Braniff Airlines was one of the trunk companies who filed for bankruptcy. Many companies struggled to find ways to lower labor costs. Continental Airlines filed for bankruptcy to abrogate its labor contracts, reorganizing itself as a low cost carrier.

The airline industry is a textbook case of government regulation protecting the industry instead of the consumer. The fall in fares in the aftermath of deregulation strengthened the conviction among many policymakers and economists that price regulation is a poor substitute for price competition.

See also Deregulation of Trucking.

References Kaplan, Daniel P. "The Changing Airline Industry." *Regulatory Reform: What Actually Happened?* (1986); Winston, Clifford. "Economic Deregulation: Days of Reckoning for Microeconomists." *Journal of Economic Literature* (1993).

Alkali Acts (England)

The Alkali Acts represent the first effective air pollution legislation in England, the birthplace of the Industrial Revolution. In 1863, the first Alkali Act was enacted on a five-year trial basis. The act was renewed on a permanent basis in a second Alkali Act passed in 1868. Subsequent Alkali Acts expanded the coverage of industries and types of emissions, and stiffened the standards for atmospheric emissions.

By the mid-nineteenth century, the areas surrounding areas Widnes, St. Helens, the Mersey, and Tyne, usually clothed in rich, green vegetation, bore a marked resemblance to a lifeless industrial wasteland. The culprit was neighboring plants producing alkali. One description painted the environmental damage in these words:

> The sturdy hawthorene makes an attempt to look gay every spring; but its leaves...dry up like tea leaves and soon drop off. The farmer may sow if he pleases, but he will only reap a crop of straw. Cattle will not fatten...and sheep throw their lambs. Cows, too,...cast their calves; and human animals suffer from smarting eyes, disagreeable sensations in the throat, and irritating cough, and difficulty breathing.

The process of producing alkali at that time caused the emission of hydrogen chloride gas, which combined with the moisture in the atmosphere to produce clouds of hydrochloric acid that descended upon the surrounding area. Alkali manufacturers tried to improve the situation by building taller chimneys, which only caused the damage to spread over wider areas.

Common law held out little promise of remedying the grievances of surrounding land owners, because of the expense and the difficulty of tracing the damage to one particular manufacturer. Court judgments against manufacturers rarely afforded sufficient compensation to surrounding landowners, and seldom caused a discontinuance of the polluting process.

Before taking action, the House of Lords formed a select committee to study the problem, which took evidence from eminent scientists and manufacturers. This committee found that condensing hydrogen chloride gas before it left the chimney was scientifically and economically feasible. Armed with this knowledge, Parliament passed the first Alkali Act.

The act created the position of inspector, a civil servant who monitored emissions from the alkali works, and who had the power to seek civil damages against offenders. Alkali manufacturers shared in drafting the legislation, and cooperated with its enforcement. Most manufacturers met the effluent standards required by the act before it was officially enforced.

Laissez-faire capitalism held the allegiance of the best thinkers and government officials of the age when Parliament enacted the Alkali Acts, an important departure from the principles of laissez faire. Air pollution was one problem that could only be attacked with heavy-handed government intervention. The Alkali Acts were successful within their limited scope, but England continued to suffer from an excess of coal smoke. With the passage of the Clean Air Act of 1956, England launched an aggressive, comprehensive program for cleaning up the air.

References Clapham, J. H. *An Economic History of Modern Britain* (1930); Macleod, Roy M. "The Alkali Acts Administration, 1863–1884: The Emergence of the Civil Scientist." *Victorian Studies* (1965).

An anarchist poster invites working men to a meeting that would end in the Haymarket riot in Chicago on 4 May 1886.

American Federation of Labor

A list of the most powerful and influential labor federations in American history would show the American Federation of Labor (AFL) at the top. Unlike earlier federations of nineteenth-century America, the AFL survived the pitfalls of success, and became the driving force behind the political offensive of labor in the twentieth century.

In 1881, a group of insurgent craft unions of the Noble Order of the Knights of Labor, along with some independent national unions, formed the Federation of Organized Trades and Labor Unions (FOTLU), which became the American Federation of Labor in 1886. The membership of the Knights fell from 700,000 in 1886 to 200,000 in 1890. The Knights tried to embrace too many disparate groups, and were prone to militancy.

Samuel Gompers served as the first president of the AFL. He opened an office on East Tenth Street in New York,

and earned a salary of $1,000 per year that was paid when union finances permitted. One of the AFL's first victories was a strike of the Brotherhood of Carpenters and Joiners for an eight-hour day. The strikers claimed moderate success. The AFL put a two-cent levy per head on federation members to raise a strike fund for the carpenters. Typical of the AFL, its strategy singled out one craft to be the thin edge of the wedge for winning an eight-hour day, rather than organize a general movement. By 1892, about 40 national unions were affiliated with the AFL. Between 25 and 30 of the member unions belonged in the dues-paying category, and sent delegates to an annual convention. In 1897, the AFL moved its offices to Washington, D.C. On 4 July 1916, President Wilson officiated at a dedication of a new office building for the AFL, and declared that in the future no president of the United States could ignore organized labor.

The philosophy of the AFL is what distinguished the organization from its European brethren, and its predecessors in the United States. In the words of Samuel Gompers, the AFL stood for "pure and simple unionism," which meant championing the rights of skilled workers to bargain collectively with employers, using the power of monopoly control of skills. Craft unions controlled the supply of skilled labor with apprenticeship regulations and restrictions on immigration. Unlike trade unions in many European countries, the AFL kept its distance from socialist doctrines, and refused to use labor's political muscle to advance utopian schemes for reforming society. Also, the AFL stood against formation of a labor party in the United States. British unions formed the British Labor Party, and the German unions were affiliated with a specific political party. The AFL's principle of nonpartisan politics proposed "to defeat labor's enemies, and to reward its friends."

One of the most notable tactics of the AFL was the boycott of employers who refused to bargain with unions or to settle strikes. On its "We don't patronize" list, the AFL published the employers that members should boycott.

At the beginning of World War I, much of the propaganda in the world labor movement put the blame for the war at the feet of the capitalist economic system. Gompers resisted pressure to denounce the war, and brought the AFL around to support preparation for war, and when war came, the AFL supported it. In turn, Gompers won an increasing voice for labor in the counsels of government. The AFL sank its roots deep into America's sociopolitical structure during World War I. It membership reached a peak of 5 million in 1920.

By 1930, the membership in the AFL had fallen to 3 million. During the 1930s, employers launched an effective counterattack against unions, and the AFL's tradition of craft unionism became a hindrance to the exploitation of opportunities to organize unskilled workers in large industries. In 1935, a Committee for Industrial Organization was expelled from the AFL and became a rival federation—the Congress of Industrial Organization. In the late 1930s, the AFL began actively organizing industrial workers, increasing its membership from 2.9 million in 1937 to 4.2 million in 1940. During the post-World War II era, labor again found itself on the defensive in the political sphere. To strengthen labor's political stance, the AFL and the CIO officially merged to form the AFL-CIO in 1955.

The history of the AFL exhibits the successful adaptation of the trade union movement to a capitalist society in which class consciousness has not formed, and the propaganda of class warfare falls on deaf ears.

See also Knights of Labor, Boycotts, Danbury Hatters Case.

References Cartter, Allan M., and F. Ray Marshall. *Labor Economics: Wages, Employment, and Trade Unionism* (1967); Lorwin, Lewis L. *The American Federation of Labor* (1970).

American Revolution
See Class Struggle, Constitution of the United States, Hyperinflation of the Continental Currency.

American Telephone and Telegraph Monopoly
In the late 1950s, American Telephone and Telegraph (AT&T) commanded a monopoly position in the telephone industry, subject to Federal Communication Commission (FCC) regulation. AT&T was the parent company, and its wholly-owned subsidiaries were the regional Bell telephone companies, Western Electric (an equipment manufacturing company), and Bell Laboratories.

The origin of the AT&T monopoly lay in the original Bell patent that gave Bell companies a monopoly on local phone service between 1876 and 1893. After the patent rights expired, other local service companies arose to compete with the Bell companies for the provision of local telephone service. The Bell System stood above the other local telephone companies, because it was the only company with a unified, interconnected long-distance system. The Bell System's own cutting-edge technology preserved its monopoly on long-distance service. Through price competition and acquisition of independent local telephone companies, the Bell System maintained control of about 80 percent of local phone service.

AT&T's monopoly was not part of a planned public policy for the development of the telecommunications industry. After AT&T's long-distance service came under regulation of the Interstate Commerce Commission in 1910, and then the FCC in 1934, government regulation acted to preserve the existing structure of the industry. The regulatory authorities allowed neither the Bell companies nor the independent companies to encroach on each other's territory.

At the end of World War II, AT&T's

Alexander Graham Bell inaugurates the New York-to-Chicago long-distance telephone line.

control of telecommunications appeared to be watertight, but cracks in the armor came to light in two areas. One was AT&T's insistence that its customers use only AT&T equipment; the second area was microwave technology, which was unpatented, because it originated in World War II defense research.

The FCC found it difficult to uphold AT&T's requirement that its customers use only AT&T equipment. AT&T wanted to disallow the use of reasonable accessories under this rule. In the 1960s and 1970s, the FCC chipped away at AT&T's control over the use of non-AT&T equipment. It opened up competition on the switching equipment for private business use (PBXs). The FCC then faced a new issue: How to prevent AT&T from using profits from its monopoly on long distance to undercut competitors on the equipment side of the business? In 1981, the FCC forced AT&T to establish Western Electric as a separate unregulated business owned by AT&T.

For long-distance service, the competition horse got out of the barn in 1969, when the FCC granted a request to Microwave Communications Incorporated (MCI) to provide communication between St. Louis and Chicago. MCI had flung down a challenge that struck at a weak point in the pricing structure of the AT&T monopoly. First, AT&T had kept rates up on high-volume connections, such as St. Louis and Chicago, to hold rates down on low-volume routes. Second, AT&T used profits from its long distance to subsidize the costs of providing local telephone service. Therefore, local phone service was priced artificially low. MCI wanted to serve only the high-volume routes, and to connect to AT&T's local terminals, where rates were artificially held down. The introduction of competing long-distance services mandated an overhaul of the telecommunications system.

By 1974, 36 separate companies had filed suit against AT&T under the Sherman Antitrust Act. That same year, the Justice Department filed suit against AT&T for monopolizing the telecommunications business. In a negotiated settlement, AT&T divested itself of its regional operating companies, such as Southwestern Bell. These companies became independent, stand-alone, corporations. In addition to its long-distance service, AT&T retained Bell Labs and Western Electric. Divestiture meant the end of long-distance revenues subsidizing local telephone rates. It also precluded the use of profits from the regional operating companies, which were still publicly regulated monopolies, to subsidize the competitive businesses. Long-distance service and telephone equipment became competitive businesses.

In this new competitive environment, AT&T was able to maintain about a 70-percent market share in the long-distance business. In 1996, AT&T spun off Western Electric and Bell Labs as an independent company called Lucent Technologies.

The history of AT&T illustrates the positive side of monopolies in a capitalistic context. First, the lucrative profits generated by monopolies provide the financial resources to undertake research and development that are necessary for progress. Second, monopolies only exist at a point in time. If competitors producing identical products make no headway, technology will in time either render the monopolist's product obsolete or create a close substitute.

See also Patent System, Sherman Antitrust Act of 1890.

References Brock, Gerald W. "The Regulatory Change in Telecommunications: The Dissolution of AT&T." *Regulatory Reform: What Actually Happened?* (1986); Garnet, Robert W. *The Telephone Enterprise: The Evolution of the Bell System's Horizontal Structure, 1876–1909* (1985); Temin, Peter, with Louis Galambos. *The Fall of the Bell System* (1987).

Amsterdam Exchange

Exchanges in the Low Countries (Belgium, Luxembourg, and Netherlands) were originally called bourses. In the fourteenth century, Bruges could boast of having the most active European exchange and money market. The term "bourse" arose from an inn of the same name near the consular offices of Genoa, Venice, and Florence. The van der Beurzes family ran the inn. From Bruges, the name spread to exchange and money markets on the European continent. Today, the major stock exchange in France is the Paris Bourse.

By the sixteenth century, Antwerp outshone Bruges as a trading and financial center. Antwerp built the famous New Bourse in 1531. An inscription on the New Bourse read, "For the use of merchants of whatever nation or tongue." The merchants of Amsterdam met in the open spaces before building their own bourse in 1613. The architecture of the Amsterdam Bourse followed the model of the Antwerp Bourse. All commercial activities in Amsterdam except the grain trade took place in the bourse. A separate corn exchange existed for grain. By 1612, Amsterdam kept 300 brokers with 600 employees busy.

The charter of the Dutch East India Company, financed by transferable shares of stock, brought a new trading innovation to the Amsterdam Bourse. Up until 1670, only the stocks of the two Dutch India companies (East and West) traded on the bourse. The year 1672 saw the first public funds quoted, when Dutch governments floated wartime loans to fend off a French invasion. In the latter part of the seventeenth century, the bourse was the scene of trading in shares of big companies and in the public debt of the Estates-General, the towns and provinces of the United Provinces, and the British government. In 1750, the daily prices of the stocks of three Dutch companies and three English companies were quoted, in addition to 25 Dutch public funds and 13 foreign loans.

Techniques of speculation in futures reached a high level of development on the Amsterdam Exchange. Most of the futures speculation was in commodities, but futures contracts were traded for the stock of the Dutch East India Company, as well as for the shares of the great English companies. Several bans on futures speculation in commodities and securities were ignored. The stock in the West India Company was never traded in futures, probably because of a ban.

All accounts on future deals were settled at first on a special day of each month, and later on a special day of each quarter. On the settlement day, the winners could cash in their profits. The losers could take out bonds to finance losses and remain in the market until the next settlement day. Amsterdam traders well understood speculating with small amounts of capital. What we now call bulls were called lovers, and bears, as we now call them, were known as counterminers. The tulip mania speculation climaxed in 1637, giving the modern world the first example of financial euphoria leading to a crash.

In the eighteenth century, the Amsterdam Exchange lost its position of preeminence in European finance to London. Bouts of overspeculation sapped the public's confidence. Amsterdam did not have discounting banks that could provide funds to help weather the financial stress of economic crises. In 1763 and 1772, deflation and bank failures dealt heavy blows to the Amsterdam stock market.

See also Bank of Amsterdam, Dutch Capitalism, Tulipmania.

References Braudel, Fernand. *Civilization and Capitalism*, Vol. 3 (1984); Ehrenberg, Richard. *Capital and Finance in the Age of the Renaissance* (1928); Houte, J. A. van, *An Economic History of the Low Countries, 800–1800* (1977); Israel, Jonathan I. *Dutch Primacy in World Trade, 1585–1740* (1989).

Anglo-French Commercial Treaty of 1786

The Anglo-French Commercial Treaty of 1786 briefly liberalized trade between England and France, just prior to the French Revolution. Some critics of the treaty claim it caused the economic crisis in France that sparked the French Revolution.

Mercantilist trade theory reigned in Europe during the seventeenth and eighteenth centuries. This theory favored high tariff walls to protect domestic industry from foreign competition. Between high tariffs, trade reprisals, and periodic wars, trade between France and England slowed to a trickle. The thinking of the best economists of the time, including Adam Smith, unveiled the errors in a mercantilist system that discouraged mutually advantageous trade. For the first time, the ideas of free trade were rearing their head. The Physiocrats, the first school of economic thought associated with laissez faire, rose to influence in the councils of government in France, and Adam Smith published his book favoring laissez faire in 1776.

After the War of American Independence, England and France entered into negotiations to lower trade barriers between the two countries. These negotiations led to the signing of the Anglo-French Commercial Treaty of 1786, also called the Eden Treaty, after William Eden, who negotiated for the English. Under the treaty, England exempted French shipping from enforcement of its navigation acts. In return, France lifted its prohibitions on the importation of English goods. The treaty provided that each country charge the other for linens no more than what the Dutch paid each country for the same commodity. The treaty levied a modest 12-percent ad valorem tax on imports of cotton, hardware, chinaware, pottery, and glassware. This portion of the treaty clearly favored the English, who were farther along in the Industrial Revolution and could produce manufactured products cheaper. France received important concessions on its exports of wines, brandies, and olive oil. The English ban on the importation of French silks remained in place. Silks were the only industrial good France could export to England at a profit.

The treaty obviously favored English industrial interest and French agricultural interest. French imports of English manufactured goods rose from 13 million livres in 1784 to 58.5 million livres in 1787. French industrialists keenly felt the blow. The years 1787–1789 saw one of the worst depressions of eighteenth century France. Many textile districts experienced a 50-percent reduction in the number of looms employed. More than half of their workers were turned out of doors. Bankruptcies mounted. The crises in the State's finances forced the king's hand and he called the Estates General. The grievances aired before the meeting of the Estates General condemned the Anglo-French Commercial Treaty. The Bureau of Commerce, a government agency, put the blame on the Treaty for the industrial depression.

The Estates General was followed by a second revolutionary congress, the Legislative Assembly, which was followed by a third congress, the Convention. The Convention declared war on England on 1 February 1793, and annulled the Anglo-French Commercial Treaty. A few months later it prohibited the importation of a great number of English manufactured goods. French trade policy remained protectionist throughout most of the nineteenth century. France flirted briefly with trade liberalization under Napoleon III, but returned to strong protectionism up to World War I.

Another century would pass before ideas of free trade would gain ascendancy in trade policy. Countries discovered that whatever advantages protectionist policies held out to domestic industry, these advantages were often canceled out in retaliatory measures. Critics of capitalism found trade wars a cause of wars between capitalist countries. A major push to liberalize European trade policies came after World War II, and led to the creation of the European Common Market, of which France is a member.

See also Continental System, French Revolution and Napoleon.

References Ashley, Percy. *Modern Tariff History: Germany, United States, and France* (1970); Bancroft, Shepard. *France: A History of National Economics, 1789–1939* (1964); Lefebvre, Georges. *The French Revolution*, Vols. 1–2 (1969).

Anglo-French Commercial Treaty of 1860

The Anglo-French Commercial Treaty of 1860 marked a sharp break with protectionism in European trade policy. England had begun liberalizing trade policy as early as 1825. The treaty of 1860 called for fewer concessions from England, whose trade policy reflected the spirit of free trade. For France, the treaty opened a new era of trade policy that was free from prohibitive tariffs and that was moderately protectionist.

The treaty granted a most-favored-nation treatment to both nations, and left each nation free to grant most-favored-nation status to other nations. The next decade saw France sign similar treaties with other principal European countries. Belgium signed a treaty with France in 1861; Prussia in 1862; Italy in 1863; Switzerland in 1864; Sweden, Norway, the Grand Duchy of Mecklenburg, Spain, and the Netherlands in 1865; Austria in 1866; and Portugal and the Papal States in 1867. The treaty with Prussia was extended to all the states of the Zollverein in 1864. France put continental Europe on a path of free trade that lasted until the 1880s.

The first diplomatic effort to reduce trade barriers between England and France led to the Anglo-French Commercial Treaty of 1786. With the conclusion of the treaty of 1786, both countries appeared to stand on the threshold of an era of free trade. French industry, however, entered into a significant slump and the governing bodies of the French Revolution cut short this European experiment with free trade. The French governments stood staunchly on the side of protectionism until the government of Napoleon III. His government began reducing trade barriers in specific industries in 1853. Before the treaty of 1860, French tariffs on manufactured goods ranged in the 50- to 100-percent range. The government prohibited the importation of some goods, such as iron castings. The tariff on unbleached cotton yarn fell 300 to 400 percent. Imports of steam engines and loco-motives paid a 50-percent import duty.

The provisions of the treaty gave France five years to reduce all tariff rates to a maximum of 25 percent. England lifted the import duties on nearly all French goods. The most important ex-ception, wine and spirits, remained sub-ject to import duties, but at lower rates.

Industrial production in France showed no signs of economic crisis, such as fol-lowed the treaty of 1786. Prices leveled off and stabilized, perhaps because of im-port competition. French industry re-ported a significant drop in the number of handlooms in operation. From 1860 until 1864, in France, the number of industrial steam engines in use rose from 178 to 242. Manufacturing efficiency benefited from the stimulus of foreign trade.

The treaty remained in force until 1881. Most European countries, including Russia, joined the free-trade movement until the 1880s, when the tide began to turn in favor of protectionism. By 1892, France had swung around to protectionism again. England kept faith with the princi-ples of free trade until the Depression of the 1930s. The spirit of free trade, how-ever, bypassed the United States, where civil war put a heavy burden on public ex-penditures. The aftermath of the Civil War left the U.S. government in need of tax revenue, but significant tariff reform was avoided until the eve of World War I.

After World War II, the free-trade movement received fresh momentum. The trade wars of the Depression had been self-defeating, and the recent world war reminded nations of the importance of avoiding economic policies that lead to tensions. Periodically, the world's trading partners conduct multilateral negotiations to reduce trade restrictions.

See also Anglo-French Commercial Treaty of 1786, General Agreement on Tariffs and Trade.

References Ashley, Percy. *Modern Tariff History: Germany, United States, and France* (1970); Louis, Arthur. *The Anglo-French Commercial Treaty of 1860 and the Progress of the Industrial Revolution in France* (1971); Price, Roger. *The Economic Modernization of France* (1975).

Anti-Socialist Law (Germany)

The anti-socialist law of 1878 banned the Social Democratic Party and its press in Germany. The Social Democratic Party was composed almost exclusively of workers. The law did not specifically target trade unions, who were hit very hard by this legislation. The Social De-mocratic Party had been active in orga-nizing unions, and the structure of unions made them vulnerable to the law. The Prussian high court held that trade unions were political associations, and the gov-ernment squashed unions on the slightest suspicion of involvement with the Social Democratic Party.

The German chancellor, Otto von Bis-marck, took political advantage of two at-tempted assassinations of William I to call elections for the Reichstag and launch a campaign against socialism. This strategy weakened the dominant National Liberal Party, as Bismarck expected, and left the Reichstag without a majority party, but right after the election the Reichstag en-acted the anti-socialist law, specifically called A Law Against the Dangerous Ac-tivities of the Social Democracy. Bismarck claimed that unions devoted only to im-proving wages and working conditions would be exempt from this law. In prac-tice, however, the law was used against unions.

The Tobacco Workers Union dissolved within two days of the passage of the law. Glass workers, carpenters, metal workers, shoe workers, and miners lost their unions. Within a short time, 17 national unions and 18 local organizations fell victim to the new law. More than 1,500 socialists were arrested, and many others were harassed or exiled. Fourteen papers were suppressed.

The Social Democratic Party moved its activities and press to Switzerland and continued to play a leadership role in German trade unions. Unions operating strictly upon a local basis dodged the law. With the antiunion leadership from the government, many employers turned to repressive tactics against unions, and, in

1886, an amendment banning strikes was added to the law.

The anti-socialist law was due to expire in 1890. The new kaiser, Frederick III, felt conciliation was the best approach for dealing with the Social Democrats, but Conservatives wanted to extend the law without alteration. When the National Liberals insisted on amending the law, the Conservatives, aided by the radical opposition, voted the attempt down. A new general election was called for February 1890. The parties aligned with Bismarck suffered a major defeat, and he resigned in March. The government disavowed the law in September 1890.

The Social Democratic Party survived the anti-socialist law. The votes of Social Democrats increased from 493,000 in 1878 to 1,427,000 in 1890. Trade unions in Germany developed under stern repression, compared to the unions in the United States and Britain. This repression may have helped to make the German unions highly centralized, disciplined, and politicized organizations. It may also have made Germany fertile soil for the spread of communists and socialist ideology. After 1890, trade unions gathered strength in Germany.

See also Combination Acts, Le Chapelier Law, Revolutions of 1848.

References Foster, William Z. *Outline of the History of the World Trade Union Movement* (1956); Rimlinger, Gaston V. *Welfare Polic and Industrialization in Europe, America, and Russia* (1971); Sheehan, James J. *German Liberalism in the Nineteenth Century* (1978).

Antwerp Bourse

At the end of the 15th century, Antwerp replaced Bruges as the crossroads of trade in northern Europe. In 1531, Antwerp's bourse moved into a splendid new building, which became a model for structures in Amsterdam and England. Henry II of France conceived, but never carried out, a plan to build at Lyon a bourse on the architectural plan of Antwerp's. Antwerp could boast of the first international, or world, bourse. Although Antwerp's bourse preceded the era of speculation in shares of stock, commodities and bills of exchange traded on the bourse, and governments floated loans to finance national debts.

Traders at Antwerp were no strangers to speculation, particularly in East Indian spices. A syndicate of pepper merchants monopolized the supply and possibly rigged the price on the bourse. Still, random factors, the uncertainties of war and peace chief among them, drove the market on a course of wide fluctuations, creating an unparalleled opportunity for speculation. Traders judged the temper of the bourse by the price of pepper. Trading became risky business for anyone, and particularly for those who could not track the market on an hourly basis.

One person, Christopher Kurz, claimed to have worked out an astrological system for predicting prices on Antwerp's bourse. Merchants of the first rank read and made notes on his commercial reports based on his astrological system. He claimed his system enabled him to forecast, a fortnight in advance, the prices of pepper, ginger, and saffron. Apparently, his clients were not wholly enthusiastic. In a letter, he discussed the application of his system to the bills of exchange market:

> As ye have often noted in my writings to you how great an alteration is there here day by day in bills on Germany, Venice, or Lyons, so that in the space of eight, ten, 14, or 20 days and with other folk's money, a man may make a profit.... On these also have I my experiment so that I may foretell not only from week to week the tightness or ease in money, but also for each day and whether it shall be before or after midday. I have, however, nigh forgot this again, since I have found you so reluctant.

In the foreign exchange market, speculators in Antwerp used a trading tool called wagers. One speculator would wage (bet) that the exchange rate at a fair in Antwerp would be at a 2-percent premium or discount. Another would wage that the discount or premium would be 3 percent. The speculators pledged to pay each other the difference, according to the result. The same type of speculation probably took place in commodities, also. The Netherlands government outlawed these wagers in 1541.

Governments kept agents in Antwerp to float loans, bonds, and annuities. Sir Thomas Gresham represented the English government, and Antwerp's bourse inspired him to build the Royal Exchange in London. The king of Portugal and the king of Spain borrowed on the Antwerp market. Governments paid higher interest rates than merchants at the time. The market in government securities entered into a boom in the 1550s, which ended when the Spanish government suspended interest rate payments and became effectively bankrupt. This event shook the foundations of Antwerp's bourse, and marked the end of rapid economic growth in Antwerp. A Spanish army later invaded Antwerp. Bourses in Amsterdam and England became the chief beneficiaries of the decline of the Antwerp Bourse.

See also Antwerp Capitalism, Financial Crisis of 1557.

References Ehrenberg, Richard. *Capital and Finance in the Age of the Renaissance* (1928); Houte, J. A. van. *An Economic History of the Low Countries, 800–1800* (1977); Van Der Wee, Herman. *The Growth of the Antwerp Market and the European Economy* (1963).

Antwerp Capitalism

Referring to the prosperity of Antwerp in the early sixteenth century, Philip II of Spain wrote in a memorandum: "No one can dispute, they say, that the liberties granted to the merchants is the cause of the prosperity of this city." During that era, Antwerp stood at the crossroads of world trade in Europe.

Antwerp got its start by holding fairs twice a year, attracting merchants from England, Italy, and the Hansa towns. Fair towns temporarily lifted restrictions on foreign merchants while the fairs were in progress. Then Antwerp began to trade outside the season of the fairs, with merchants keeping booths open year-round. England particularly made use of Antwerp for its cloth trade. Growth in the availability of standardized products encouraged year-round trading, enabling merchants to look only at samples or models of products, and to buy for future delivery. As trade grew in Antwerp, fairs became less important, and Antwerp evolved from a fair town to a bourse town.

After discovering the sea route to the East Indies, the Portuguese crown acquired a near-monopoly on the spice trade. It sold the spice cargoes to a few large syndicates. who concentrated the spice trade in Antwerp to maintain monopoly prices, making Antwerp the center from which spices were marketed throughout the rest of Europe. Silver was more valuable than gold as a medium of trade with Asia, and Antwerp was situated close to the silver mines of upper Germany. The world market for tropical products beat a path to Antwerp.

Perhaps Antwerp's greatest contribution to capitalist development lay in the area of mercantile freedom. Most cities placed restrictions on foreign merchants: For example, in Venice, transactions by foreign merchants had to go through a special government office; in other cities, foreign merchants had to go through a native middleman. Trade in money and precious metals was subject to severe restrictions in many cities and countries, requiring, among other things, a sworn money changer. In Antwerp, any burgher could act as a foreign exchange dealer, and the natives demanded no special privileges, though many of them did act as commission brokers for the less-mercantile companies. The profession of the commission broker owes it origin primarily to Antwerp. The great merchant companies maintained their own offices and marketing facilities, and foreign merchants stood on equal footing, regardless of their country of origin. Foreign merchants were free to enter and leave Antwerp.

Antwerp was the first city to boast of an international bourse. In 1531, it dedicated its new bourse to "the use of business men of whatever nation or language." Trading in futures became a popular form of speculation on the Antwerp Bourse, and Antwerp also became the headquarters of the European capital market. Cities and states went to Antwerp to float bonds and arrange loans. The Spanish crown borrowed and defaulted on bonds and loans floated on the Antwerp exchange.

Antwerp's career as a commercial center came to an end in 1576, when unpaid Spanish troops sacked the city. The nerve center of world trade migrated from Antwerp to Amsterdam, but Antwerp's innovative mercantile freedom inspired a valuable idea that continued to work itself out in the development of capitalism.

See also Antwerp Bourse, Financial Crisis of 1557.

References Houte, J. A. van. *An Economic History of the Low Countries: 800–1800* (1977); Van Der Wee, Herman. *The Growth of the Antwerp Market and the European Economy* (1963).

Asian Capitalism

In the latter half of the twentieth century, Asian capitalism budded into fully modernized industrial economies in Japan and the so-called Four Little Dragons—South Korea, Taiwan, Hong Kong, and Singapore. Japan and the Four Little Dragons stand in the ranks of economic miracles, achieving staggering economic growth rates.

Japan served as the prototype for the Asian capitalistic model. It ruled South Korea from 1905 until 1945 and Taiwan from 1895 until 1945, and was the reigning Asian industrial power when the Four Little Dragons evolved into full-fledged capitalistic economies. From 1955 until 1975, these countries reported GNP growth rates ranging from 7.8 to 9.5 percent, and per capita GNP grew in the 5-percent range. Although Japan continued to register significant growth after 1975, the Four Little Dragons replaced Japan as the Asian economic miracle in the 1980s.

Before Britain turned Hong Kong over to China on 1 July 1997, that colony was reported to be the only known case of a colony having a higher per capita income than its mother country. Manufacturing exports drove the economies of the Four Little Dragons, and, to a lesser extent, Japan. Aside from Hong Kong, governments played an influential role in shaping economic development of these countries. Except for government involvement in education, these countries bear little resemblance to the modern welfare state found in Western societies. A mix of high savings rates, low taxes, and a strong work ethic is a common denominator of Asian capitalism.

Japan pioneered the paradigm for Asian capitalism. After the Meiji Revolution, the Japanese government sent a mission of selected government officials on a tour of Western countries. President Grant entertained the emissaries in the United States. Britain and France received the emissaries with interest, but Bismarck's Germany made the most favorable impression. Bismarck recommended that Japan generate as much of its own capital as possible, minimizing dependence on foreign capital, and not let the parliament encroach on the power of the emperor.

Geopolitical factors may share a portion of the credit for the rapid growth of these countries. Japan, South Korea, and Taiwan were strategic locations for the United States during the Korean War, and U.S. involvement in South Korea and South Vietnam acted as an economic spur to the entire region. Some theorists contend that these countries promoted domestic economic growth as a means of avoiding foreign domination. Japan obviously felt threatened by the forcible entry by the United States, and the Four Little Dragons felt menaced by Communist China.

Although the spirit of capitalism has helped shape and mold the economic institutions of the area, the spirit of laissez faire, excepting Hong Kong, has not made itself felt. Japan took the lead, followed by Korea, Singapore, and Taiwan, in fostering a close working relationship between business and government. In Japan, the Ministry of International Trade and Industry counsels businesses, formulates industrial policy, and is credited with much of Japan's economic miracle. Korea has most closely followed the Japanese model, emphasizing close ties between business and government.

Since the publication of Max Weber's book, *The Protestant Ethic and the Spirit of Capitalism*, scholars have looked for cultural traits that may contribute to economic development. Japan and the Four Little Dragons may owe some of their economic success to specific values of Chinese culture. The emphasis on discipline, delayed gratification, and practical knowledge, rather than abstract theorizing, may have helped create the kind of attitudes and values that prevailed in the early phase of western European capitalism. Communal solidarity, as opposed to the maximum development of the individual, has remained a strong force in Asian capitalism.

Perhaps because government assisted in the entrepreneurial function, these societies stood less in need of the colossal entrepreneurs of nineteenth-century American capitalism. Hong Kong, however, received a strong impetus from an indigenous entrepreneurial spirit, and its colonial government took a laissez-faire stance on economic development. Only in the 1990s did the government of Hong Kong talk of developing an industrial policy.

Singapore and Hong Kong are city-states reminiscent of Venice and Amsterdam in the early days of capitalism. They practice free trade, building a prosperity dependent on the rest of the world remaining open to trade. The division of the world into trading blocs, such as the European Union and the North American Free Trade Agreement, would spell trouble for the continued growth of these economies. Singapore shares with Hong Kong the conditions of a city-state, but, unlike Hong Kong, the government of Singapore took an active interest in developing Singapore manufacturing. The countries of Asian capitalism do not fit neatly into one formula.

The future of Hong Kong's economy hinges on how well it meshes with the socialist economy of China. The market reforms of the Chinese government hold out some promise that Hong Kong can continue to prosper as a world city, emphasizing finance and commerce, as China increases manufacturing output. Financial markets in Asia, however, were depressed in the last half of 1997. Fallout from the Tokyo Bubble, rising costs of production, and the change of government in Hong Kong may put a brake to the phase of supernormal growth among the Four Little Dragons.

Asian capitalism broke the bonds of mass poverty faster than any other type of economic system found in Third-World countries. Asian capitalism, treated as a distinct brand of capitalism, merits serious study to unlock its secrets, and bears watching in the future.

See also Bank of Japan, Confucianism, Meiji Era, Tokyo Bubble, Unequal Treaties, Zaibatsu.

References Berber, Peter L. *The Capitalism Revolution: Fifty Propositions About Prosperity, Equality, and Liberty* (1986); Chiu, Stephen W. K., K. C. Ho, and Tai-lok Lui. *City States in the Global Economy: Industrial Restructuring in Hong Kong and Singapore* (1997).

Bank Charter Act of 1844 (England)

The English Bank Charter Act of 1844 signals a turning point in the evolution of paper money. That act took the first step in giving the Bank of England a monopoly on the issuance of bank notes (paper money). In the early 1800s, bank notes from a multitude of commercial banks circulated as money in England, France, the United States, and other countries.

Sir Robert Peel was prime minister at the time Parliament passed the Bank Charter Act of 1844. Before the passage of that act, Peel had told his cabinet that he shared the views of David Ricardo, who had concluded that the issuance of currency should be a monopoly of the government, with the profits accruing to the government. In Peel's words, if he was "about to establish in a new state of society a new system of currency..., a board would be constituted, independent of Government but responsible to Parliament, charged with the issue of paper, convertible into gold, to be a legal tender." In reality, Peel chose a more moderate course that made use of existing institutions.

Important provisions in the Bank Charter Act are paraphrased as follows:

1. The note issue department of the Bank of England became separate and distinct from other departments. The bank removed it to a different building.
2. The Bank of England was required to hold gold bullion equal in value to the volume of its bank notes issued in excess of £14 million. The government debt secured most of the first £14 million.
3. The Bank of England was required to stand ready to redeem its bank notes into gold at the rate of £3, 17s. 9d. per ounce of gold.
4. The creation of new banks with the privilege to issue bank notes was prohibited.
5. Banks currently issuing bank notes continued to issue notes as long as their total notes in circulation never exceeded their average for the 12 weeks preceding 27 April 1844.
6. If a bank became insolvent, it lost its right to issue bank notes.
7. If a bank stopped issuing notes for any reason, it could never again put notes into circulation.
8. If two or more banks combined and ended up with more than six partners, the new bank could not issue bank notes.
9. The Bank of England was allowed to issue new bank notes backed by securities up to two-thirds of the value of discontinued country bank notes.

As intended, the act gradually centralized the issuance of bank notes in the hands of the Bank of England, which, by World War I, held a monopoly on the issuance of bank notes. The monopolization of the issuance of paper money allowed the monopolizing entity to control the money supply. This control seemed necessary to maintain the value of money, which is the same as avoiding inflation. The act helped bring stable prices, but the government was forced to suspend it in major financial crises. Suspensions occurred in the financial crises of 1847, 1857, and 1866. The act's restrictions on issuance of bank notes hampered the Bank of England from serving as a lender of last resort in crises.

The Bank of France acquired a monopoly on the issuance of bank notes in 1848. The United States established a uniform national currency in 1864, by placing a tax on the issuance of state bank notes, effectively forcing them into retirement. Today, the Federal Reserve System enjoys a monopoly on bank note issue. The provisions of the Banking Charter

Act requiring the convertibility of bank notes into gold have not survived into modern practice. The gold-standard provision prevented the note-issuing bank from injecting liquidity into the financial system in a crisis.

See also Federal Reserve System, Greenbacks.

References Davies, Glyn. *A History of Money from Ancient Times to the Present Day* (1994); Powell, Ellis. *The Evolution of the Money Market, 1385–1915* (1915).

Bank of Amsterdam

The Bank of Amsterdam, established in 1609, rose to fill a key role in European and even world monetary affairs in the seventeenth and eighteenth centuries. The bank hardly matched the description of anything we now call a bank: It seldom made loans, and the exceptions that proved the rule were loans to Dutch municipalities and to the Dutch East India Company.

Banks of the small Italian city-states of Venice and Genoa supplied the model for the Bank of Amsterdam. The circulating currency of the small city-states subsisted partially in their own coin, and partially in the coin of neighboring states. Often, the currency that poured in from trade was clipped and worn, and foreign bills of exchange paid in this currency were of uncertain value. These small city-states sought to remove this inconvenience by requiring that foreign bills of exchange above a certain amount be paid in transfers between accounts in a bank, rather than in domestic currency. A special bank, enjoying the full backing of the government, was established to handle these transactions.

Before 1609, Amsterdam saw its currency depreciate 9 percent below the value of money fresh from the mint. The merchants of Amsterdam ran short of good money to pay their bills of exchange, and the Bank of Amsterdam was created to relieve this problem. It accepted deposits of currency. Worn, clipped, and diminished currency, whether foreign or domestic, was accepted at face value, along with good currency. The bank deducted a small recoinage fee and a management fee from currency deposits, and credited the balance to the customer's account. This money of account at the bank was called bank money, and it never suffered any kind of debasement. Its value was the same as money fresh from the mint. Along with the establishment of the bank came the legal requirement that foreign bills of exchange drawn on Amsterdam be paid in bank money. This legal requirement applied to bills of exchange equal to, or above, 600 guilders.

The Bank of Amsterdam also took deposits of bullion. In return, a customer received a receipt for a stated amount of bullion valued in bank money, and a credit of bank money on the customer's account equal to the value of the bullion. The receipt entitled the customer to buy back the bullion with bank money at the price stated on the receipt. The bank charged a modest fee for, in effect, storing the bullion for its customers. If a customer defaulted on the storage fee, the ownership of the bullion reverted to the bank. This bullion was sold as part of the bank's profit. The bank money was much more convenient to handle than bullion, and just as good in the eyes of European bankers. Because of its great deposits of coin and bullion, the bank became a part of the reserves of the monetary system of Europe, and a source of regulation.

Since the Bank of Amsterdam was not a lending institution, it maintained stores of currency and bullion to redeem all of its outstanding bank money. Bank money was superior to currency, and was valued at a premium by merchants. A portion of the bank's income came from its ability to sell bank money at one price in currency, while buying it at a lower price.

In the 1780s, wartime difficulties forced the bank to underwrite loans to merchants in difficulty. The bank's reserves dropped substantially below its outstanding bank money, and the public became cautious. When the French invaded the Netherlands in 1795, caution turned to panic, and the bank's position became untenable. In 1802, the bank reopened with the aid of a forced loan, but it was not particularly successful. In 1820, the bank was liquidated.

See also Bills of Exchange, Dutch Capitalism, Medici Bank.

References Braudel, Fernand. *Civilization and Capitalism*, Vol. 3 (1984); Houte, J. A. van. *An Economic History of the Low Countries, 800–1800* (1977); Israel, Jonathan I. *Dutch Primacy in World Trade, 1585–1740* (1989); Smith, Adam. *An Inquiry into the Nature and Causes of the Wealth of Nations* (1776).

Bank of England

The Bank of England is the central bank of the United Kingdom. The bank has the sole authority for issuing paper money, acts as the government's bank, serves as a banker's bank for commercial banks, and manages monetary policy.

The Bank of England received its

The Bank of England as it appeared in the late eighteenth century, from a woodcut by B. Cole

charter from Parliament in 1694. England was then engaged in a costly war with France, and the government needed money. The Bank of England came into being to meet this need. Parliament imposed a duty on tonnage, with the proceeds earmarked for the benefit of such persons as should voluntarily advance money to the government. The government planned to borrow £1.2 million at 8-percent interest. To help raise this sum of money at a moderate rate of interest, Parliament granted the subscribers to the loan the privilege of pooling their funds and incorporating themselves under the name of the Governor and Company of the Bank of England. The debate in Parliament raised quite a howl. One member charged that the bank "would encourage fraud and gambling and thus corrupt the morals of the nation."

The original charter was good for ten years. The bank had the right to trade in gold and silver bullion, and in bills of exchange. The charter prohibited the bank from selling merchandise, excepting what had been held as security for loans. The bank could issue bank notes equal in amount to its capital. The charter put the management in the hands of a governor, deputy governor, and 24 directors, elected yearly by the stockholders.

The charter was always renewed, usually in return for a loan to the government, often at lower interest rates. In 1709, the bank's charter was renewed with the provision that no other joint-stock company with more than six partners could issue bank notes. This was the provision that eventually gave the Bank of England a dominant position in the issuance of bank notes. In 1751, the bank took over the administration of the national debt. By 1780, the bank had a virtual monopoly on the issuance of bank notes in London, and smaller banks began the practice of keeping deposits in the Bank of England, so the bank began to act the part of a central bank.

Just as the bank was conceived to raise money to fight a war, the wars with revolutionary France and Napoleon brought on a particularly innovative period in the development of the bank. It was forced to accommodate the financing needs of the government to any amount, but not without protest from the bank's directors. The bank began issuing notes in much smaller denominations. In 1797, the bank suspended the convertibility of its bank notes into specie. An act of Parliament approved the suspension. Government borrowing had weakened the bank's reserve position, and bank note holders were making a run on the bank. The value of the bank's notes stood up well, partly because the government accepted them at par value in all payments. In 1812, the government made the bank's notes legal tender for all payments, and the country banks began to hold the bank's note as reserves for their own issues.

In 1821, the bank resumed convertibility of its bank notes into specie. The bank's notes grew in acceptability relative to gold, and the country banks found the notes just as useful as gold for managing a cash drain. The country banks began to look to the Bank of England to loan them funds in a liquidity crisis. In 1833, the government again declared Bank of England notes legal tender for sums above £5, so long as the notes remained convertible. As the bank's notes replaced gold as the circulating medium, the bank became the major holder of gold reserves.

The Bank of England resisted the pressure to become a lender of last resort in financial crises. The bank remained free to compete with other commercial banks, but the effects of such competition were destabilizing. After the crash 1847, the bank began to accept its role as a lender of last resort, and to use adjustments in its bank rate of interest to stabilize money markets. The bank discovered that adjusting its bank rate to compete with other banks destabilized markets.

In the years prior to World War I, the bank developed its method of using the bank rate of interest and open market operations to regulate interest rates. The bank came to see itself as the custodian of the gold standard. During the war, the government outlawed the export of gold. The bank supported the restoration of the gold standard after the war. This goal required high interest rates to prevent a drain on gold reserves, but this was a policy out of step with the needs of the time. In 1931, Parliament passed the Gold Standard (Amendment) Act, suspending the gold standard. The bank was never quite the same again. The government had given the bank very little guidance as to what policies to initially follow after the suspension.

During the interwar years, the bank's policies came under closer scrutiny, with more criticism. The Macmillan Committee in Parliament inquired into the full range of activities of the bank. Economist John Maynard Keynes summarized the criticism: "that the methods of Central Bank monetary management deserve an adequate trial...that it would be rash to estimate in advance what would prove possible until the policy had received an actual trial."

The success of the government-directed war economy led a new Labor government in Parliament to embark upon a program of nationalization of major industries after World War II. Controversy over the policies of the Bank of England before the war made it an obvious target. It was nationalized in 1946, and brought under the authority of the Exchequer, or British treasury.

See also Bank of France, Central Banks and Free Banking, Federal Reserve System.

References Gilbart, J.W. *The History, Principles, and Practice of Banking* (1968); Macaulay, Thomas B. *The History of England from the Accession of James II*, Vol. IV(1849–1861). Sayers, R. S. *The Bank of England, 1981–1944* (1976); Smith, Vera C. *The Rationale of Central Banking* (1936).

Bank of France

The Bank of France is the central bank in France, comparable to the Bank of England, or to the Federal Reserve System in the United States. Central banks regulate interest rates, credit conditions, and money supply. They can serve as a lender of last resort in financial crises.

When Napoleon took the reins of power in 1799, the French government, in the throes of revolutionary turmoil, had lost credibility in financial matters, and the government of Napoleon faced difficulty in discounting government bonds. In 1800, Napoleon created the Bank of France to help with this problem. It was capitalized at 30 million livres. Three years later, the 30 million livres became 30 million francs. After the disaster of John Law's bank (1716), the term "bank" had fallen into disrepute and disappeared in the names of French financial institutions, until the Bank of France. The Caisse des Comptes Courants, a Paris discount bank that issued bank notes (paper money), dissolved and merged its capital into the Bank of France.

The financial capital for the Bank of France came partly from the capital of the dissolved Caisse des Comptes Curants, partly from public subscriptions, and partly from the government. The stockholders elected a governing committee. In 1802, the other chief note-issuing bank in Paris, the Caisse d'Escompte du Commerce, merged unwillingly with the Bank of France. In 1803, the government granted the Bank of France the exclusive privilege to issue bank notes in Paris, and other note-issuing banks in Paris had to withdraw their bank notes before a certain date. The government had to approve the opening of any new note-issuing banks in the provinces.

From the beginning, Napoleon wanted the Bank of France to discount government debt at the lowest possible interest rates. In 1804, the bank caved in and issued too many bank notes, amid rumors that Napoleon had shipped the metallic reserves to Germany for military purposes. The bank had to partially suspend specie payments, and its bank notes depreciated 10 to 15 percent, but the bank, rather than the government, took the blame for the crisis. In 1806, the gover-

nance of the bank underwent a major overhaul: A government-appointed governor and two deputy governors replaced the committee elected by stockholders. Another partial suspension of convertibility came in 1814.

Napoleon emphasized low interest rates as a means of softening the blow of the continental blockade. He pressured the bank to keep its discount rate in the 4- to 5-percent range, a practice the bank continued until midcentury. He also encouraged the bank to act as a lender of last resort.

The Bank of France took advantage of its authorization to set up branch banks in the provinces. These branch banks were unsuccessful at first, despite regional monopolies on note issuance given these banks. A few private banks opened in the provinces, but they were subjected to strict regulation and were often unprofitable. By 1840, private banks began to be a threat in the provinces. Between 1841 and 1848, the Bank of France opened 15 branch banks in the provinces. After 1840, the government refused to grant charters for new private banks with authority to issue bank notes.

In the political crises of 1848, the government counted on the Bank of France for financial support. The public, remembering the assignats of the Revolution, began to hoard specie. The government protected the bank by making its bank notes legal tender, and by putting a limit on the number of bank notes the bank could issue. The Bank of France now achieved a clear advantage over the private provincial banks, whose bank notes were only legal tender in their respective regions. The private provincial banks merged with the Bank of France, and the Bank of France acquired a nationwide monopoly on the issuance of bank notes.

The Bank of France kept its discount rate fairly constant until the 1850s. It then began the practice of adjusting its discount rate to regulate the flow of specie. An increase in the discount rate could halt a specie outflow. In 1857, the bank became exempt from the usury law setting a 6-percent ceiling on interest rates.

By 1900, the Bank of France had offices in 411 French towns, and it had as many as 120 full branches. This compares with just eight branches for the Bank of England. The Bank of France played a much greater role in the French money and banking system than the comparable Bank of England played in the British system, but the tight control the Bank of France held over the development of banking in France may have inhibited French economic growth in the nineteenth century.

The French government relied heavily on borrowing and bank-note issue to finance World War I and World War II. Bank notes increased 400 percent between 1940 and 1945, but controls suppressed the inflation until 1944. The government nationalized the Bank of France in 1945. Inflation grew to acute levels in the 1950s.

Napoleon's preference for centralization and government control set an influential precedent. Central banking became a publicly regulated activity in most countries. The Bank of France tended to err on the side of inflation, which may have reflected its subjection to the government.

See also Bank of England, Central Banks and Free Banking, Federal Reserve System, First Bank of the United States, Second Bank of the United States.

References Davies, Glyn. *A History of Money* (1994); Kindleberger, Charles P. *A Financial History of Western Europe* (1984).

Bank of Japan

Three decades before the United States created the Federal Reserve System, the Japanese government established the Bank of Japan on the European model of central banks. Japan is the first non-Western country to consciously transform its economy into a developed capitalistic system. Feudalism was still a fresh memory when the Japanese government created a central bank.

After the Meiji Restoration in 1868, the government launched Japan on an intensive path of westernized economic development. The new government found gold, silver, and copper coins circulating alongside paper money issued by feudal lords and merchants. Like previous revolutionary governments, including the Continental Congress of the United States, the Restoration government turned to the issuance of inconvertible paper money to finance government spending. In 1877, the government issued another round of inconvertible paper money to suppress a rebellion, and, until 1881, inflation surged.

To meet its currency and inflation difficulties, the Japanese government studied European and American models. In 1872, Japan had adopted a national banking system patterned after the banking system in the United States. These banks held government bonds as collateral for bank notes. The government's inconvertible paper currency could be redeemed in government bonds. The system broke down after the government allowed national banks to issue inconvertible bank notes in the late 1870s.

In 1881, the minister of finance visited Europe to study central banking systems. The National Bank of Belgium had been created in 1850, and appeared to the Japanese as the most advanced institution of its type. The United States had no central bank, and the Bank of England had evolved over nearly two centuries, without a written constitution. In the words of a Japanese prime minister, "After careful study and comparison of the central banking systems we found the Bank of Belgium was peerless..., consequently it was decided to adopt the Belgium system."

The Bank of Japan Act of 1882 led to the establishment of the Bank of Japan. The bank was organized as a private joint-stock company, with the government furnishing half of its capital. The governor of the bank and the other officers received appointments from government officials, who also supervised the policies and administration of the bank. The treasury exerted strong influence on the operations of the bank. The bank was set up to serve as the fiscal agent for the government, stabilize seasonal and regional fluctuations in the flow of funds, finance international trade, and hold specie reserves. The bank held a monopoly on the issuance of bank notes, and served as a lender of last resort to other banks. In 1897, Japan went on the gold standard, making the bank notes of the Bank of Japan fully convertible into gold.

In 1868, precious-metal specie accounted for 75 percent of the money supply. By 1881, that percentage had decreased to 20 percent. Bank deposits accounted for 7 percent of the money supply when the Bank of Japan was formed; by 1914, this percentage had grown to 44 percent. Japan's economy became highly monetized, complete with bank notes and bank deposits.

The process that led to the formation of the Bank of Japan reveals something of the method that lies behind the Japanese economic miracle. Today, Japanese commercial banks are among the largest in the world.

See also Bank of England, Bank of France, Central Banks and Free Banking, Federal Reserve System, Meiji Era.

References Davies, Glyn. *A History of Money* (1994); Cameron, Rondo, et al. *Banking in the Early Stages of Industrialization* (1967).

Bank of Venice

Compared to other banks, the history of the Bank of Venice is the most revealing of the forces that led to the creation of public banks. It also reveals the roles these banks played, and the needs they met in early capitalist development.

In 1171, the government of the Republic of Venice extracted forced loans of specie from wealthy citizens. The government kept a record book that showed the amounts the government owed individual citizens, who otherwise had no bonds, IOU's, or other certificates of indebtedness in their hands. The government paid its citizen creditors 4-percent interest per year, but did not pay down the principal. The citizens of Venice began exchanging ownership of these government obligations to transact business. They found that money transactions settled by entries in books were much more convenient than coined money transactions, particularly when sizable amounts were involved. The citizens of Venice soon voluntarily deposited specie with the bank, and accepted book-entry deposits that could be transferred to other depositors in any amount.

As early as 1374, a committee of scholars proposed the formal organization of a public bank, but no action was taken until 1587, when the government established the Bank of Venice as the Il Banco dell Piazza del Rialto. By then, other Italian cities had already established public banks, diminishing Venetian claims of priority in the history of banking. The credit for the first beginnings of modern banking practices, however, belongs to Venice.

The Venetian practice of banking on the security of government loans proved its worth by surviving into the modern period. Today, in the United States, the Federal Reserve System issues federal reserve notes, and deposits at Federal Reserve Banks, and holds government bonds as securities against these notes and deposit liabilities.

See also Bank of England, Venetian Capitalism.

References Kindleberger, Charles P. *A Financial History of Western Europe* (1984); Knox, John Jay. *A History of Banking in the United States* (1903).

Bankruptcy Act of 1705 (England)

The Bankruptcy Act of 1705 recognized the concept of the honest bankrupt. Before the act of 1705, English bankruptcy law targeted debtors who purposely sought to evade or defraud creditors. The early law protected the rights of creditors to seize property of defaulting debtors, and to demand an inequitable distribution of assets among creditors. Concealment of property and other fraudulent activities drew criminal penalties. In England, defaulting debtors faced imprisonment until the mid-nineteenth century.

To finance growing trade with a distant New World, capital had to be available on terms agreeable to borrowers and lenders. The risk of failure was high, and these early trading entrepreneurs sought relief from the rigors of bankruptcy laws that gave creditors the power to ruin debtors for life. According to a pamphleteer writing in 1734:

> In a Trading Country, those who have become insolvent, by pursuing Projects, or by any other Losses incident to Trade, ought to be gently dealt with; so even this of venturing another Man's Money upon a reasonable Project, or Scheme of Trade, ought not to be looked on as a very gross Fault.

The act of 1705 sheltered bankrupt traders and merchants from the harsher consequences of bankruptcy, including imprisonment for debt, and included provisions enabling a bankrupt individual to start afresh. The act bore a faint resemblance to class legislation, since it was intended to cover wholesalers and manufacturers, rather than retailers and artisans. In the words of Sir William Blackstone, retailers and artisans "take the consequences of their own indiscretion..., for the law holds it to be an unjustifiable practice, for any person but a trader to encumber himself with debts of any considerable value."

The act protected traders and persons with debts equal to or exceeding £100. It called for a bankrupt to surrender his estate for the satisfaction of his creditors. When four-fifths of the creditors, in number and share of debt, agreed with the settlement, the bankrupt was discharged from his debts. If creditors received a minimum of eight shillings on the pound, the debtor retained 5 percent of the realized estate to start afresh.

The practice of restricting the protection of bankruptcy legislation to the trading class appeared less reasonable to future generations. When the new federal government of the United States tried to enact bankruptcy legislation on the English model, the former colonists objected to a practice that gave speculators and promoters more protection than small farmers. Congress passed a law based on the English practice in 1800, but repealed it in 1803. Future bankruptcy legislation in the United States expanded coverage to all debtors. England extended the coverage of its bankruptcy laws to all debtors in 1841.

The bankruptcy legislation aided the development of a culture of enterprise in the early development of capitalism. Improving technology and new discoveries increased the sheer magnitude of business undertakings. As financial capital grew in abundance, governments sought to lift a bit of the risk burden from the risk-taking entrepreneurs.

See also Bankruptcy Act of 1898, Bankruptcy Act of 1978, Bankruptcy Acts of 1543–1624, Imprisonment of Debtors.

References Coleman, Peter J. *Debtors and Creditors in America: Imprisonment for Debt and Bankruptcy, 1607–1900* (1974); Daunton, Martin. *Progress and Poverty: An Economic and Social History of Britain, 1700–1850* (1995).

Bankruptcy Act of 1898
(United States)

Modern bankruptcy law in the United States dates from the Bankruptcy Act of 1898. Congress revised the bankruptcy laws substantially after 1898, but this act introduced important principles of bankruptcy law that shaped subsequent legislation. Before the Bankruptcy Act of 1898, Congress enacted several short-lived bankruptcy laws that invariably met with strong opposition from various quarters before Congress repealed them. The act of 1898 was the first bankruptcy act to command the acceptance of the majority of the political and economic interests of the country. The act was workable, and it endured.

Despite the belated success of the U.S. Congress in framing a bankruptcy law that met the needs of the country, the issue of bankruptcy laws rose to importance before the Constitutional Convention. Bankruptcy law varied between states, and business interests called for a uniform bankruptcy law. Article 1, Section 8 of the Constitution bestows upon Congress the power to establish "uniform laws on the subject of bankruptcies throughout the United States...," and Article 1, Section 10 says that no state can pass a "law impairing the obligation of contracts."

Congress debated bankruptcy law every year from 1789 to 1800, when the first bankruptcy law squeaked through Congress by the slenderest of margins. This law restricted relief to the commercial classes, covered debts incurred before the law was enacted, and provided that only creditors could initiate bankruptcy proceedings. Farmers and mechanics raised a howl against privileged treatment. Those with claims on the assets of insolvent merchants often felt short-changed. Insolvent farmers and mechanics received no protection, and either gave up all they owned, or faced debtors' prison. The electorate thought the law fostered speculation and defaults, and Congress repealed the law in 1803.

The bankruptcy issue lay dormant for 38 years, before Congress acted again with the passage of the Bankruptcy Act of 1841. Creditors and debtors supported the passage, and, a year later, the repeal, of this legislation. After the courts and lawyers took their share of a bankrupt's assets, creditors averaged 10 cents on the dollar. Debtors complained that assets protected from creditors by state laws were fair game under the federal law.

Congress made another trial of bankruptcy law with the enactment of the Bankruptcy Act of 1867. This law was amended three different times, before Congress abandoned it in 1878. Creditors were displeased that the law exempted property protected from creditors by state laws. They also observed that legal and administrative costs often left little of the

bankrupt's assets for creditors to claim. Debtors found fault that a single creditor could force a defaulter into bankrupt proceedings involuntarily.

Bankruptcy law became a permanent part of business law with the Bankruptcy Act of 1898. This act covered all debts, including those incurred before Congress enacted the law. Either the creditor or the debtor could initiate proceedings, and corporations, including national banks, had the same protection as individual debtors. Farmers and wage earners were spared the threat of involuntary bankruptcy forced by creditors. Property protected from the claims of creditors under state law enjoyed the same exemption under the new federal law. Insolvent debtors could have a grace period to reorganize their affairs and reach an agreement with creditors.

Bankruptcy laws in the United States were revised in 1938, 1978, and 1984. The growth of the corporation depersonalized many of the thorny issues that stood in the way of bankruptcy legislation in the United States. As business organizations grew ever more complex, it became important to established rules assuring equitable treatment for all creditors in the event of default.

See also Bankruptcy Act of 1705, Bankruptcy Act of 1978, Bankruptcy Acts of 1543–1624, Imprisonment of Debtors.

References Coleman, Peter J. *Debtors and Creditors in America* (1974); Gross, Karen. *Failure and Forgiveness: Rebalancing the Bankruptcy System* (1997).

Bankruptcy Act of 1978
(United States)

The Bankruptcy Act of 1978 substantially streamlined and expedited the bankruptcy process in the United States. Congress passed the first permanent bankruptcy act in 1898, and substantially revised bankruptcy law in 1938. The act of 1978 laid the foundation for current bankruptcy law, subject to modest refinement in 1984.

The Bankruptcy Act of 1978 is organized as eight odd-numbered chapters.

Congress deleted the even-numbered chapters that were part of the earlier act. Chapters 1, 3, and 5 outline various procedures that apply to the other chapters. Procedures for firm liquidation are the principle topic in chapter 7. Procedures for financially distressed municipalities are outlined in chapter 9. Chapter 11 has to do with reorganizing corporations that cannot meet their obligations. Procedures that apply to the adjustment of debts of "individuals with regular income" are explained in chapter 13. Chapter 15 sets forth the system of trustees appointed to administer the bankruptcy proceedings.

Chapter 11 is perhaps the most famous chapter, giving birth to the phrase "filed for chapter 11." Under chapter 11, financially troubled corporations receive protection from creditors while trying to reorganize on a profitable basis. The process begins when either the distressed corporation or its creditors petitions a bankruptcy judge for reorganization. A corporation that seeks protection on its own is a voluntary bankruptcy. An involuntary bankruptcy occurs when the creditors initiate the process. The management of the corporation may be put in the hands of independent trustees, or may remain with the corporation's officers.

A court-appointed committee of unsecured creditors, such as suppliers, employees, and commercial creditors, helps in the formulation of a plan for the retirement of debts. In a large corporation, secured creditors, such as banks, and stockholders may ask to have a hand in the process. A plan for returning to solvency might require liquidating certain assets, extending the payoff on loans, transferring ownership of stock to creditors, or merging with a profitable corporation. Total liquidation subjects the corporation to the provisions of chapter 7. Ultimately, a plan for reorganization must be approved by a simple majority of that class of creditors that holds two-thirds of the distressed corporation's debt. Creditors are split into two classes: secured and unsecured. Claims against the corporation are ranked according to certain principles. Administrative expenses are paid first, followed by unsecured claims, such as wages. After all other debts are paid, stockholders receive the remaining assets, if any.

U.S. bankruptcy laws have drawn fire from critics, who object to the use of bankruptcy laws to escape civil damages pending in court, or to abrogate collective bargaining agreements. Although these sorts of bankruptcy proceedings are in the gray area, they have been successful in a few instances.

Under current bankruptcy law in the United States, bankrupt individuals, or officers of bankrupt corporations, hardly face risks of debtors' prison. As the capitalist economic system has evolved, the burden of default risk has fallen to a greater extent on the creditors. The Bankruptcy Act of 1978 is a further step in simplifying the process for the debtors.

See also Bankruptcy Act of 1705, Bankruptcy Act of 1898, Bankruptcy Acts of 1543–1624, Imprisonment of Debtors.

References Gross, Karen. *Failure and Forgiveness: Rebalancing the Bankruptcy System* (1997); Spiro, George W. *The Legal Environment of Business: Principles and Cases* (1993).

Bankruptcy Acts of 1543–1624 (England)

England adopted its first statute of bankruptcy in 1543. The following 80 years saw three additional bankruptcy acts that either amended or replaced previous acts.

Prior to the bankruptcy statutes, a statute of 1352 gave statutory sanction to the practice of imprisoning debtors for private debts. The practice of imprisoning individuals who owed debts to the crown enjoyed a long history before 1352. Debtors avoided imprisonment either by fleeing, remaining housebound, or finding sanctuary in religious establishments. The purpose of the first bankruptcy act was to empower the state to seize debtors' assets and make sure the assets were distributed fairly to creditors.

The statute of 1543, entitled the Act

Against Such Persons As Do Make Bankrupt, began with the following preamble:

Where divers and sundry persons craftily obtaining into their hands great substance of other men's goods do suddenly flee to parts unknown or keep their houses, not minding to pay or restore to any their creditors their debts and duties, but at their own wills and pleasures consume the substance obtained by credit of other men, for their own pleasure and delicate living, against all reason, equity, and good conscience....

This statute designated the lord chancellor, the lord treasurer, the lord president, the lord privy seal, two other members of the Privy Council, and two chief justices to intervene on the side of the creditors. They could order the imprisonment of debtors and distribute debtors' assets to the creditors. In practice, a commission was formed to investigate the debtor's holdings and arrange for liquidation. Assets the commission could lay its hands on and sell included chattel, debts, goods, wares, merchandise, fees, lands, offices, and tenements. The act conferred upon the designated authorities the power to search, view, rent, appraise, or sell any of these assets to satisfy creditors.

A bankrupt individual received a summons demanding that he appear within three months "or as soon after as he conveniently may." This flexibility helped traders in remote locations, who needed time to respond in writing and arrange a voyage home. Bankrupt individuals could still avoid imprisonment by keeping to their house.

One object of the statute was to protect creditors from other creditors. Individual creditors could not negotiate individually with a debtor. Neither could the assets be distributed to creditors on a first-come, first-serve basis. Negotiations between the debtor and individual creditors were suspended, and the share of assets distributed to each creditor was based on the share of total debt owed to each creditor.

Third parties who took possession and concealed property of a debtor subjected themselves to a summons, and were required to disclose their holdings. A fine levied on a third party for such concealment could equal twice the value of the assets. The amount of the fine was distributed to the creditors. Creditors who sought individual preferences, or colluded with other creditors to arrange settlement outside legal procedures, also faced penalties.

Subsequent statutes passed in 1571, 1604, and 1624 refined the bankruptcy law and tried to close loopholes. The statute of 1571 made it more difficult to avoid bankruptcy by remaining at home. It also specifically authorized the formation of commissions to settle the affairs of bankrupt debtors. This provision strengthened the hand of the commissioners. The statute of 1571 specifically mentioned merchants and traders who buy and sell, as the individuals covered by the bankruptcy laws. The statutes of 1604 and 1624 did not mention merchants as the proper target of bankruptcy law. In 1621, Parliament considered a bill that called for corporal punishment under certain circumstances for bankrupt debtors. The statute of 1624 spared bankrupt debtors from corporal punishment or a felony charge, but sanctioned the use of force to open houses and shops.

Several decades and a revolution passed before England would again fine-tune bankruptcy legislation. The early bankruptcy laws were designed to protect creditors from fraudulent defaulters. The early stages of capitalism required as much protection as possible for creditors, to keep interest rates at reasonable levels. In the eighteenth century, England enacted bankruptcy legislation to protect honest bankrupt debtors. Discontent has accompanied bankruptcy laws up to the present day.

See also Bankruptcy Act of 1705, Bankruptcy Act of 1898, Bankruptcy Act of 1978, Imprisonment of Debtors.

References Jones, W. J. "The Foundations of English Bankruptcy: Statutes and Commissions in the Early Period." *Transactions of the American Philosophical Society* (1979); Pugh, Ralph B. *Imprisonment in Medieval England* (1968).

Banks

The term "bank" seems to have evolved from the bench of the money changers during the middle ages. Historically, some banks have principally held deposits of currencies from a wide range of countries, and facilitated payment in foreign trade transactions. The Bank of Amsterdam fell into that category. The Bank of Venice was formed when a group of the government's creditors combined and began using government debt as a means of payment in trade. The famous merchant bankers, such as the Rothschilds, acted mostly as brokers, marketing government and corporate securities to wealthy patrons. Central banks are bankers' banks, tracing their history from the Bank of England. These banks buy government debt, have a monopoly on the issuance of paper money, and often act as a lender of last resort to commercial banks. The term "bank" nowadays refers to these commercial banks.

Commercial banks in modern capitalist societies are financial intermediaries. They raise funds from one group of people (depositors), and they loan these funds to another group (borrowers). The claims that depositors have against banks are liquid, meaning that depositors can demand their money at almost any time. The claims that banks have against borrowers are considerably less liquid, allowing banks to reclaim money lent to borrowers only over a much longer span of time. If all depositors show up on a given day to withdraw all their money, theoretically the bank is then forced into bankruptcy, because the bank cannot immediately reclaim the money lent to borrowers. Much government regulation in banking strives to spare banks from this sort of thing happening.

A fundamental banking principle underlying modern banks is called fractional reserve banking. Banks operate on the principle that, in any given period of time, the bank will attract fresh deposits, and other deposits will be withdrawn. On balance, the fresh deposits and the withdrawn deposits cancel out, and the bank will maintain an average balance of deposits. This balance of deposits is money the bank has available to loan out. To avoid flirting with bankruptcy, however, banks hold back a certain fraction of deposits to cover themselves over periods of time when withdrawn deposits exceed fresh deposits. This fraction of deposits held back is called reserves. Banks are tempted to cut this fraction rather thin, because reserves earn no interest. These reserves, however, give the bank stamina to weather a crisis of confidence that causes masses of people to suddenly withdraw deposits.

Banking is one business in which a failure can do more harm to customers, the depositors, than to owners, making banks an excellent candidate for government regulation. Also, banks play a strategic role in the business cycle. During an economic downswing, banks have a natural tendency to become cautious, and to curb lending, sending the economy into a deeper trough. On the upswing, however, banks become more confident and generous in granting loans, perhaps sending the economy into an unstable boom. Government regulation strives to protect bank depositors from bank failures, and to force banks to become a stabilizing force, rather than a destabilizing force, in the economy.

See also Bank of Amsterdam, Bank of England, Bank of Venice, Central Banks and Free Banking, Depository Institutions, Deregulation and Monetary Control Act, Glass-Steagall Banking Act, Goldsmith Bankers, Medici Bank, Merchant Bankers, Swiss Banks, Wildcat Banks, World Bank.

References Baye, Michael R., and Dennis W. Jansen. *Money, Banking, and Financial Markets* (1995); Davies, Glyn. *A History of Money* (1994).

Baring Brothers and Company, Limited

Baring Brothers, the oldest merchant bank in London, has a history that stretches over 200 years. The bank has always been kept in the family, which is the oldest banking dynasty in Britain.

The Baring family first became acquainted with England as wool merchants in north Germany. Johann Baring visited England in 1717, decided to stay, married into a wealthy family, and became the founder of the Baring family in England. Two of his sons opened John and Francis Baring and Company in London, a company that began in the import and export business, and later expanded into merchant banking. Francis Baring made connections in the highest councils of the British government, counting among his friends William Pitt the Younger. In 1783, he opened a business in Philadelphia, and sent his son, Alexander, to America to investigate a land deal in Maine. Alexander returned to England with a wealthy American bride, and America became a major field of operations for Barings, which became the largest banking house in American before the Civil War. The administration of Thomas Jefferson engaged Barings to handle the financing for the Louisiana Purchase. Among Alexander's friends in America were John Quincy Adams and Daniel Webster.

John Baring retired in 1800, and John and Francis Baring and Company became just Francis Baring and Company. In 1806, the firm was renamed Baring Brothers and Company.

At the end of the Napoleonic Wars in 1815, Barings sponsored a loan of 315 million francs for the French government, allegedly prompting the Duc de Richeleu to say, "There are six great powers in Europe: England, France, Russia, Austria, Prussia, and the Baring Brothers."

The most famous merchant banking crisis in history was the Baring Crisis of 1890. Early in the nineteenth century, Barings began sponsoring Argentine loans. By 1890, Argentina had absorbed nearly half of Britain's foreign investment, most of which was arranged through Barings. The failure of Water Supply and Drainage Company to meet a contract agreement in Argentina, soon followed by a political revolution, left Barings with extensive holdings of unsalable financial assets. The Bank of England and other London banks, including the major merchant houses, supported Barings through the crisis, avoiding a major financial crisis. Barings was sufficiently shaken by the crisis to reconstitute itself as a limited company, protecting its owners with limited liability.

Governments now have their own banks to act as agents, and no longer depend on the services of merchant bankers like the Barings. Today, Barings deals with acceptance credit, new security issues, conventional banking services, and investment advisement services. Members of the Baring family have remained active in London financial circles. In 1966, George Rowland Stanley Baring became the one hundred thirteenth governor of the Bank of England.

Merchant bankers were perhaps the first to make commercial activity a path to social status comparable to the pedigreed nobility of feudalism. In the words of Walter Bagehot, "The merchant bankers go back to generations of merchant princes in Venice and Genoa who inherited wealth, power, and culture, and combined the taste of aristocracy with the insight and verve of businessmen."

See also Merchant Bankers; Morgan, John Pierpont; Rothschild Banking Family.

References Hidy, Ralph W. *The House of Baring in American Trade and Finance: English Merchant Bankers at Work, 1763–1861* (1949); Wechsberg, Joseph. *The Merchant Bankers*, 1966.

Bill of Conspiracies of Victuallers and Craftsmen of 1548 (England)

The Bill of Conspiracies of Victuallers and Craftsmen of 1548 stands as an early example of a law prohibiting worker combinations to raise wages or reduce hours. The legal status of worker combinations was somewhat murky at this point in English history, because the law upheld apprenticeship regulations and the government regulated wages. Parliament often heard complaints from workers about low wages. The Bill of Conspiracies of Victuallers and Craftsmen was probably directed at worker combinations that occasionally arose on a local basis, and which were of short duration.

The words of the act reveal something of what was happening at the time that provoked Parliament to take action. In the words of the bill:

Forasmuch as of late artificers, handicraftsmen and labourers have made confederacies and promises, and have sworn mutual oaths not only that they should not meddle one with another's work, and perform and finish that another hath begun, but also to constitute and appoint how much work they shall do in a day, and what hours and times they shall work, contrary to the laws and statues of this realm, and to the great hurt and impoverishment of the King's majesty's subjects: For reformation thereof it is ordained and enacted...that...if any artificers, workmen or labourers do conspire, covenant, or promise together, or make any oaths that they shall not make or do their works but at a certain price or rate, or shall not enterprise or take upon them to finish that another hath begun or shall do but a certain work in a day, or shall not work but at certain hours and times, that then every person so conspiring, covenanting, swearing or offending, being lawfully convict thereof by witness, confession, or otherwise, shall forfeit for the first offense ten pounds to the King's highness; and if he have sufficient to pay the same, and do pay the same within six days next after his conviction; or shall suffer only for the same offense 20 days imprisonment, and shall only have bread and water for his sustenance.

The bill goes on to specify that a person not able to pay a fine of £40 for the third offense would, among other things, lose one of their ears. More than 300 years elapsed before English law sanctioned trade unions. More than 200 years would pass before English workers, in the clutches of the Industrial Revolution, took those pioneering steps toward national trade unions that made them the trailblazers of the modern labor movement.

See also Combination Acts, Trade Union Act of 1871.

References Cole, G. D. H., and A. W. Filson, *British Working Class Movements: Selected Documents, 1789–1875* (1965); Webb, Sidney, and Beatrice Webb. *The History of Trade Unionism* (1920).

Bills of Exchange

Bills of exchange were an early financial innovation that replaced barter and movements of bulky quantities of precious metals in foreign trade. In the thirteenth century, Italian merchants, bankers, and foreign exchange dealers turned the bill of exchange into a powerful financial tool, combining short-term credit and foreign exchange transactions to facilitate foreign trade.

To see how a bill of exchange facilitated a foreign trade transaction, assume a Venetian merchant bought goods from a merchant in Flanders. The merchant in Flanders accepted a bill of exchange drawn on the Venetian merchant, who promised to pay an agent of the Flanders merchant in Venice at a certain date in the future, and in a certain currency. The bill of exchange allowed the Venetian merchant to accept delivery on the goods from Flanders, sell them, and take the proceeds to redeem the bill of exchange in Venice, probably in Venetian currency.

Bills of exchange were also instruments for foreign exchange transactions. Merchants in Italy and major trading centers in Europe bought bills of exchange payable at future dates, in other places, and in different currencies. In the example above, the Flanders merchant could sell the bill of exchange to an exchange dealer for currency of his own choosing. In turn, the exchange dealer could sell the bill of exchange to a merchant who planned to buy goods in Venice at the time the bill was due for payment.

Bills of exchange allowed bankers to evade usury laws by hiding interest charges in adjustments to the exchange rates that governed foreign exchange transactions. A banker in Florence might make an advance to an Italian merchant, and receive a bill of exchange payable at a future date to an agent of the bank in a foreign market. When the bill of exchange matured, the agent in the foreign market would draw another bill of exchange on the Italian merchant, payable at a date in the future at the Florentine bank that drew the first bill of exchange on the Italian merchant. The Italian merchant would be borrowing the use of money for the time it took for these transactions to be completed, and the interest would be embedded in the fees for handling the bills of exchange. Bills of exchange drawn only to grant credit were called dry bills of exchange.

Credit transactions involving bills of exchange are difficult to unravel and penetrate. Adam Smith, in the *Wealth of Nations*, acknowledged the difficulty of the subject of bills of exchange as credit instruments when he wrote:

> The practice of drawing and redrawing is so well known to all men of business that it may perhaps be thought unnecessary to give an account of it. But as this book may come into the hands of many people who are not men of business, and as the effects of this practice are not perhaps generally understood even by men of business themselves, I shall endeavor to explain it as distinctly as I can.

Smith goes on to describe a process in which bills of exchange are drawn, and then redrawn with interest charges added, turning the bill of exchange into a form of long-term credit.

Before the era of paper money, bills of exchange circulated as money substitutes, and minimized the need to move specie between countries. When London became the financial center of world capitalism during the eighteenth century, bills of exchange became less important as credit instruments. Uninfluenced by church doctrine toward usury, the London financial markets developed financial instruments clearly discounted at stated interest rates.

See also Genoa, Medici Bank.

References Davies, Glyn. *The History of Money* (1994); Homer, Sidney. *A History of Interest Rates* (1977); Kindleberger, Charles P. *A Financial History of Western Europe* (1984).

Bimetallism
See Gold Standard.

Bismarck, Otto Von
See Anti-Socialist Law.

Blacklisting
Blacklists enable employers to boycott, or refuse employment to, workers who had engaged in labor agitation, joined unions, or displayed other unwanted characteristics. Groups of employers not only agreed collectively not to hire blacklisted workers, but also pressured merchants to deny credit to such workers. In the United States, blacklists were a powerful weapon in the arsenal of antiunion tactics at the turn of the century.

One of the earliest instances of blacklisting occurred in Boston in 1832. A group of merchants and ship owners agreed to withhold employment to journeyman who joined unions, and to refuse patronage to any master mechanic who employed union members.

The use of blacklisting became widespread in railroads and mining. D. C. Coats, president of the Colorado Federation of Labor, testified in 1899 that:

> I know from personal experience that men are kept from positions in all parts

of the State of Colorado because of their connection with organized labor.... They (the employing class) practically have power to say that a man shall not have work; to destroy his credit with the merchants; to destroy or make valueless what little property he has; to separate him from his family and make him a wanderer upon the face of the earth.

Veterans from the strike of the American Railway Union in 1894 claimed to be victims of blacklisting for a number of years.

Charges of blacklisting were difficult to prove in court. In 1898, the Louisville Railroad was found guilty of belonging to a group of employers who agreed not to employ individuals terminated by a member of their group. In 1913, the Shoe Manufacturers' Association was convicted of blacklisting strikers. These blacklisted workers not only found themselves shunned by employers, but also merchants denied them credit.

The mechanism of blacklisting varied. Some employers made secret agreements not to hire a person without a specific type of recommendation from the previous employer. Sometimes employers supplied data sheets of workers to a central bureau for their industry. One organization accused of blacklisting was the Manufacturers' Bureau of Hartford County, Connecticut. This bureau served as an employment agency for 30 factories in the vicinity. Each applicant completed a comprehensive application card. The office kept a file on the workers after they found employment, and employers sent in information on each departing worker, including any reasons for dismissal. This bureau is reported to have been affiliated with similar organizations in New Haven, Springfield, Worcester, Boston, and New York.

These regional bureaus were associated with the National Association of Manufacturers, but the president of that organization disavowed any involvement in blacklisting. He described blacklisting as "cowardly oppression of the weak by the strong."

By 1911, 23 states and the federal government had enacted laws against blacklisting. Blacklisting had few public defenders, because it condemned individuals without trial or due process. The secrecy of blacklisting made it difficult to prove in court. Blacklisting eventually fell victim to widespread unionization, which made the practice unfeasible.

See also Boycotts, Yellow-Dog Contracts.

References Brooks, Thomas R. *Toil and Trouble: A History of American Labor* (1971); Laidler, Harry W. *Boycotts and the Labor Struggle: Economics and Legal Aspects* (1913).

Bond Market

Bonds are long-term credit instruments that bring borrowers and lenders together directly, rather than through financial intermediaries such as banks. To raise funds, a corporation or government sells a bond, essentially borrowing funds from whoever buys the bond. A new bond is sold for a face value, a certain rate of interest, and a maturity date. On the maturity date, the corporation or government that originally issued the bond redeems it at its face value. During the time the bond is outstanding, the bond's owner receives interest payments at scheduled intervals. The interest rate a bond earns as a percentage of its face value is fixed at the time the bond is issued. The time to maturity usually varies between five and 30 years.

Bonds may change ownership several times before maturity. Like corporate stocks, bonds are bought and sold in financial markets, and prices, particularly of long-term bonds, fluctuate with current interest rates. Secondhand bonds earning 10-percent interest will sell below face value, that is, at a discount, if currently issued bonds are earning 15-percent interest. Alternatively, a drop in current interest rates can lift the prices of older bonds issued at higher interest rates.

Since the early nineteenth century, agencies such as Moody's Investment Service and Standard and Poor's Corporation have rated bonds according to default risk. The higher the default risk, the higher the interest rate the bond must offer to attract investors. The safest bonds are rated triple A. Bonds rated triple B or above are considered investment grade. Double B or lower rated bonds are called junk bonds. During the 1980s, a strong market emerged for junk bonds, and these bonds played a major role in financing acquisitions and leveraged buyouts during the 1980s.

During the nineteenth century, the stock market stole much of the glamor of the bond market. However, the first assets widely traded on Wall Street were government bonds issued by various state governments. Beginning in the sixteenth century, government debt was widely traded in European financial markets. As warfare grew in cost, governments had to find more efficient means to raise funds, promoting the growth of financial markets. The techniques developed to market government debt paved the way for amassing the vast amounts of capital needed to finance the Industrial Revolution.

See also Financial Crisis of 1557, Financial Revolution, Interest Rate.

References Brigham, Eugene F. *Fundamentals of Financial Management* (1995); Van Horne, James C., and John M. Wachowicz Jr. *Fundamentals of Financial Management*, 10th ed. (1998).

Boycotts

In economics, boycotts are an organized effort to shun, and to persuade others to shun, business relations with a particular individual, business, or country. Boycotts have also targeted members of a race or religion, or products of a particular country. From the American Revolution to the American Civil Rights Movement in the 1960s, the boycott has served as a weapon of political and social protest.

Although boycotts have a long history, the term "boycott" is of relatively recent origin. In the latter nineteenth century, British landlords were evicting Irish farmers at a very high rate, averaging 500 per year between 1872 and 1877. After the famine of 1878, evictions accelerated, and the first half of 1880 saw more than 1,000 farmers evicted. The peasants formed a league to represent themselves.

One of the most despised of the retainers of the landlords was a Captain Boycott. In 1880, Boycott asked his tenants to harvest oats at approximately half the usual pay. His tenants refused to work for this pay, and Boycott, along with his wife and several relatives and servants, took to the fields to harvest the oats themselves. A few hours in the field exhausted them, and Boycott's wife pleaded with the tenants to finish harvesting, which they did. On rent day, however, the tenants were greeted with constables armed with eviction papers. The enraged tenants met in mass, and everyone present pledged to withdraw from relations with Captain Boycott and his family. The servants, herders, and drivers of Boycott also left. Boycott got his crops harvested at a cost several times their value. The social ostracism of Captain Boycott gave birth to the term "boycott" in its modern meaning.

Aside from the supporters of political and social causes, unions have made the most use of boycotts in modern history. The first wave of boycotts in the United States occurred in 1885, when *Bradstreet* gathered nationwide figures on the number of boycotts. The Knights of Labor organized most of these boycotts. In one instance, a barbershop was boycotted because it shaved scabs. In 1894, the American Railway Union boycotted all trains with Pullman Palace cars in tow, because the Pullman Palace Car Company refused to recognize the union. The courts issued an injunction against the leaders of the union for interfering with interstate commerce and the delivery of the mail. The American Federation of Labor made widespread use of boycotts, and published its infamous "We Don't Patronize" lists. In the *Danbury Hatters* case, the American Federation of Labor was held liable for civil damages under the

Sherman Antitrust Act. The Danbury Company sustained a nationwide boycott, because it refused to accept a closed shop.

The miners were involved in some of the worst abuses of boycotts in labor disputes. In the Anthracite Coal Strike of 1902, strikers threatened to boycott store owners who sold to scabs. They also forced a school board to dismiss a teacher because her brother, who was not living with her, went to work against the wishes of the strikers. A drugstore clerk found himself unemployed because his father was a scab.

After the *Danbury Hatters* case, labor unions lobbied to make unions exempt from the Sherman Act. The Clayton Act of 1914 was the first effort in this direction. The Taft-Hartley Act protected the right of unions to list products produced by employers with whom the union is engaged in labor dispute, but banned secondary boycotts (a boycott of one employer to force him to boycott or put pressure upon another employer with whom the union is engaged in a labor dispute).

English workers won the right to boycott in the Trade Disputes Act of 1906.

Outside of labor disputes, the courts have found boycotts illegal in the United States. In one important case, *The Fashion Originators Guild of America, Inc. v. Federal Trade Union*, the Supreme Court ruled against the Fashion Originators Guild of America (FOGA). This organization faced the problem of lower-priced copies of designs pirated from its members' original designs. Members of the FOGA agreed collectively not to sell to retailers who also carried lower-priced pirated designs. Over 12,000 retailers signed agreements not to sell pirated clothes. The Court held this agreement in violation of the Sherman Act.

Boycotts are against the spirit of free-enterprise capitalism. Because unions strive to raise the income of those earning incomes below average for a given society, they have often been exempted from laws against boycotts.

References Brooks, Thomas R. *Toil and Trouble* (1971); Laidler, Harry W. *Boycotts and the Labor Struggle: Economic and Legal Aspects* (1913); Waldman, Don E. *The Economics of Antitrust: Cases and Analysis* (1986).

Bretton Woods System

The Bretton Woods System was an international monetary system that governed exchange rate policies in the world economy during the post-World War II era, until 1971. The system took its name from Bretton Woods, New Hampshire, the site of an international conference of monetary officials that met in 1944, and negotiated the Bretton Woods System.

An exchange rate determines the conversion ratio at which one country's currency can be transformed into another country's currency. Put differently, it determines the price of a unit of currency, such as British pounds, in terms of another unit of currency, such as U.S. dollars.

For an individual country, exchange rates determine the cost of imported products to domestic consumers, and the price of domestic exports to foreign buyers. Economies rise and fall with changes in exchange rates.

Before World War I, the world economy was on a gold standard, which defined the value of each country's currency in terms of a fixed weight of gold, and which fixed exchange rates between currencies in the process. After World War I, governments returned to the gold standard, but results were unsatisfactory. The world economy abandoned the gold standard at the start of the Great Depression, and exchange rates floated freely, or with varying degrees of government involvement.

The Bretton Woods System held out the promise of combining the stability of fixed exchange rates with the flexibility of floating exchange rates. It created a system of adjustable peg exchange rates. Under an adjustable peg system, each country declared a par value of its currency in terms of gold, and committed itself to buying and selling foreign currency and gold reserves to maintain this par value in the foreign currency market. An individual country could not change the pegged value of its currency more than 10 percent, unless it had permission from the International Monetary Fund, a permanent international institution created by the Bretton Woods System.

In 1971, the Bretton Woods System came to an end, because the United States needed to devalue its currency. The United States experienced a considerable outflow of dollars relative to the inflow of dollars, because of foreign expenditures from the Vietnam War, and other obligations in foreign countries. By that time, however, most countries kept their currencies pegged to the value of the dollar, rather than the value of gold—a practice that crept into the Bretton Woods System, because gold monetary reserves were in short supply. In an effort to save the Bretton Woods System, the United States devalued its dollar relative to gold, but the outflow of dollars remained excessive. In 1973, the world economy went on a system of flexible exchange rates.

Perhaps the greatest accomplishment of the Bretton Woods System was the cooperation it fostered among trading partners in an important area of common interest. It also kept alive a vestige of the gold standard when gold monetary reserves were inadequate to support the growth in world trade and money supply. The end of the Bretton Woods System meant the end of the gold standard as a feature of the world capitalist system.

See also International Monetary Fund, World Bank.

References Acheson, A. L. K., et al. *Bretton Woods Revisited* (1972); De Vries, Margaret Garritsen. *Balance of Payments Adjustment, 1945–1986: The IMF Experience* (1987); Snider, Delbert. *Introduction to International Economics* (1975).

British General Strike of 1926

On 4 May 1926, the British General Strike began as a sympathy strike for miners who were locked out after a break-down in negotiations. It fell short of a real general strike, since only workers in basic industries, such as railwaymen, transport workers, iron and steel workers, builders, and printers, walked out. A full-scale general strike would involve a strike of all skilled and unskilled workers in society.

General strikes were usually organized to aid a revolutionary overthrow of government, or to force political changes, such as expanding the voting franchise to the working class. The idea of a general strike enjoyed some support as a means of preventing war. British unions, nonrevolutionary in character, were slow to accept the idea of a general strike. The growing influence of unskilled workers deserves much of the credit for making the general strike a more acceptable weapon in the arsenal of British trade union tactics. The British unions came to see the general strike as a means of showing sympathy or solidarity with fellow striking workers, rather than as a weapon of class warfare or revolution. The general strike was a way of compensating for the lack of clout that unskilled workers often had in strikes.

After the return to the gold standard at prewar parity, the British economy struggled against deflationary forces. In 1925, the mine owners asked for wage cuts and an extension to hours of work per day. The miners developed their slogan, "Not a penny off the pay, not a second on the day." There was talk among employers in all industries that wages were too high. The General Council of the Trade Union Congress promised to stand with the miners, and to call a general strike, if necessary. The government appointed a royal commission to study the problem and make recommendations. The government may have used the commission to bide its time and prepare for the strike. The commission's recommendations pleased neither party. The miners appealed to the Trade Union Congress for support. A conference of trade union executives led to a virtually unanimous vote favoring strike action in support of the miners. The government ended the negotiations suddenly, and, on 30 April 1926, the owners locked out the miners. The General Strike began on 4 May.

The leaders of the trade unions were apparently ambivalent about a general strike, and had been hoping for a negotiated settlement. Workers responded to the strike call en masse. The completeness of the work stoppage surprised everyone involved. The government organized a volunteer effort to transport food and necessities. Hundreds of workers met with arrest and imprisonment under the Emergency Powers Act. The unions faced a determined government under the leadership of Winston Churchill, who painted the strike as the beginnings of a revolutionary effort. The General Council of the Trade Unions Congress continued to search for a negotiated settlement. The miners stood intransigent, to the dismay of the General Council. On 12 May, the General Council called off the strike without prior consultation with the miners, the government, or the unions striking in support of the miners. The strikers were confused by the General Council's action, particularly when word spread that the miners were still locked out. The loss of the strike left the British trade union movement demoralized.

The miners stayed out on strike another six months. The fear of starvation had its way and the miners trickled back to work. The government repudiated the findings of its commissions on the mining industry, and gave the mine owners a free hand. Conditions worsened for the miners. The government passed the Trade Disputes and Trade Unions Act of 1927. This repressive union legislation remained in force until Parliament repealed it in 1946.

The weapon of the general strike wore too much of the aspect of a revolutionary action to be useful in societies that accepted the ideas of unionization and collective bargaining. It was more of a challenge flung down to society at large, than a means of applying pressure to particular employers.

See also General Strike, Syndicalism, Trade Disputes and Trade Unions Act of 1927.

References Cole, G. D. H. *A Short History of the British Working Class Movement, 1789–1947* (1948); Phillip, G. A. *The General Strike: The Politics of Industrial Conflict* (1976); Ridley, F. F. *Revolutionary Syndicalism in France* (1970).

Bruges (Low Countries)

In late-thirteenth-century Bruges, the front of the house of the Van der Buerse family became a gathering place for merchants wanting to strike business deals. From this accidental beginning, commodity and stock exchanges and money markets came to be known as bourses in Europe. Today, the Paris stock exchange is called the Paris Bourse. During the fourteenth and fifteenth centuries, Bruges was the center of trade for an area covering the Mediterranean, Portugal, France, England, the Rhineland, and the towns of the Hanseatic League.

In the late Middle Ages, Bruges, which shared in the thriving textile industry that had sprung up in the Low Countries, joined the cities that were on the fair circuit. Its advantages included the Zwin River, which opened Bruges to the North Sea, but it was shallow and in constant danger of silting up. Cargo arriving by sea had to be put in lighter ships and brought to Bruges. Outer harbors were built at Damme and later at Sluys to accommodate ships that needed deeper water.

Both the Hanseatic League and Italian merchants resided at Bruges. The Italians traded spices and pepper from the Levant for the products of the textile industry in the Low Countries. England exported its wool to Bruges, where it was used by the local textile industry, or reexported to other cloth-making towns. Portugal exported olives, figs, sugar, and cork to Bruges.

Several factors may have contributed to the end of Bruges's career as an international trading center. First, Bruges kept open access to the sea only by waging a constant struggle against silt building up in its harbor. Second, Bruges inherited many regulations from the medieval organization of trade, such as the requirement that all trade be conducted through brokers. Foreign merchants naturally sought freedom from burdensome regulations. Third, textile goods from England and the Mediterranean began to compete with textiles from Bruges. Last, Bruges was not a political or military power, and lost favor with the governing feudal power.

Antwerp displaced Bruges as an international trading center at the end of the fifteenth century, perhaps because of better access to the sea, and absence of regulations on foreign merchants, who left Bruges and took up residence in Antwerp. Although Bruges fell a bit short of the grandeur of Venice or Antwerp, the bourse in Bruges gave its name to bourses in Antwerp, Amsterdam, and other money markets and exchanges on the European continent. The history of Bruges is a reminder that economic prosperity tends to migrate from one geographical location to another. Of the cities in the Low Countries, Amsterdam outlived Bruges and Antwerp as a center of world trade, partially because its military power, particularly naval power, kept it independent of feudal governments.

See also Antwerp Bourse, Antwerp Capitalism, Hanseatic League.

References Braudel, Fernand. *Civilization and Capitalism*, Vol. 3 (1984); Houte, J. A. van. *An Economic History of the Low Countries, 800–1800* (1977).

Bubble Act of 1720 (England)

The Bubble Act of 1720, as its name implies, was a reaction to waves of speculation, or bubbles, in the market of stocks issued by joint-stock companies. In the late 1500s, the English crown began the practice of granting charters to joint-stock companies. The historic East India Company was founded in such a manner in 1600. These charters usually awarded the company a monopoly on English trade with a certain part of the world. The joint-stock companies were different from partnerships for this reason: Regardless of the debts or liabilities of the company, individual stockholders could lose no more than the amount paid for the stock. This protection for the investor was necessary to raise money for highly risky ventures, such as trading with a distant land. The chief purpose of the Bubble Act was to control the incorporation of new companies.

The ownership of shares of stock in a joint-stock company could be transferred to new owners without permission of other stockholders, and a market developed for trading in shares of stock. According to Walter Bagehot, "It was about the year 1688 that the word stockjobber was first heard in London. In the short space of four years a crowd of companies, every one of which confidently held out to subscribers the hope of immense gains, sprang into existence."

For example, shares were floated for a diving company that planned to recover precious effects from shipwrecks. The company announced that it had diving equipment resembling complete suits of armor, with helmet complete with one big glass eye, and fitted with pipe through which air was admitted from the surface. The whole process was exhibited on the Thames to a group of invited ladies and gentlemen who "were hospitably regaled, and were delighted by seeing the divers in their panoply descend into the river and return laden with old iron and ship's tackle." The methods of stockjobbers were sometimes less innocent, even bordering on criminality.

The government soon looked for ways to tame the excesses of speculation. As early as 1696–1697, the number of stockbrokers was limited to 100. The hype over the stock of the South Sea Company in 1720 engendered a frenzied wave of speculation in stock issues, and Parliament took action with the passage of the Bubble Act. The act made it illegal for a group of persons to act as a joint-stock company without receiving a charter confirmed by a private act of Parliament. It particularly made it illegal for those persons to offer for public subscription shares transferable by simple sale. The Bubble Act also made it harder to obtain a charter from Parliament. The act passed with the support of companies like the South Sea Company, who wanted fewer competitors for the public's money in the stockmarket.

The Bubble Act remained in effect until its repeal in 1825, when it was brought down by a chorus of harsh criticism. Economist Alfred Marshall commented on the negative effects of the act, including lowering the rate of investment, and sustaining the family-based business organization. You could say it held back the march of capitalism.

See also London Stock Exchange, South Sea Bubble.

References Bagehot, Walter. *Lombard Street* (1873); Daunton, M. J. *Progress and Poverty: An Economic and Social History of Britain, 1700–1850* (1995); Schumpeter, Joseph. *Business Cycles: A Theoretical, Historical, and Statistical Analysis of the Capitalist Process*, Vol. 1 (1939).

Buck's Stove and Range Case
(United States)

The *Buck's Stove and Range* case concerns the legal battles surrounding an injunction issued against prominent labor leaders for organizing a boycott against Buck's Stove and Range.

The clash between labor and the company began in 1906, when Buck's Stove and Range Company of St. Louis attempted to enforce a ten-hour day for metal polishers. Metal polishers had been working a nine-hour day without objection from the company. The polishers contended that their work was associated with a high incidence of lung disease, and that a nine-hour day was justified because of health risks. The Metal Polishers, Buffers, Platers, Brass Molders, and Brass and Silver Workers International Union of North America represented the polishers. The president of Buck's Stove and Range was J. W. Van Cleave, who was also president of the National Association of Manufacturers and the Citizens Industrial Alliance. Van Cleave seems to have been on a crusade against unions.

When the polishers walked out at the end of a nine-hour shift, the company fired the leaders of the walkout. When the company then refused to reinstate the fired employees, the polishers struck. The polishers union local in St. Louis picketed the company and organized a boycott in a short time. The St. Louis Trades and Labor Council stood with the polishers and supported the boycott.

In March 1906, the delegates at the convention of the American Federation of Labor (AFL) heard from the polishers union. Joseph Valentine, vice president of the AFL, inquired into the possibility of settling the matter and received notice that Van Cleave was not interested in negotiating the issue. Local labor leaders also reported that Van Cleave stood firm. In May 1907, Buck's Stove and Range was put on the AFL's "We Don't Patronize" list. In November 1907, Samuel Gompers, president of the AFL, sent a special plea to union members regarding the boycott. In his circular to local unions, he said:

> It would be well for you, as central bodies, local unions, and individual members of organized labor and sympathizers, to call on business men in your respective localities, urge their sympathetic cooperation and ask them to write to Buck's Stove Range Company of St. Louis, urging it to make an honorable adjustment of its relation with organized labor. Act energetically and at once....

In St. Louis, the local union organized parades that halted in front of stores selling Buck stoves. Speeches and posters told of the workers' grievances and urged shoppers to stay away.

On 18 December 1907, Justice Ashley M. Gould of the Supreme Court of the District of Columbia issued a sweeping injunction against the officers of the AFL. This injunction forbade the AFL officers from speaking, writing, printing, or distributing any word connecting Buck's

Stove with its "We Don't Patronize" list, or any other reference to a boycott of Buck's Stove. The February 1908 issue of the "We Don't Patronize" list omitted Buck's Stove, but a January issue had still shown it on the list. Gompers delivered speeches in Indianapolis and Boston denouncing the injunction. John Mitchell presided at a convention of the United Mine Workers that adopted a resolution to put Buck's Stove on an unfair list. On 23 December 1908, the court held Samuel Gompers, John Mitchell, and Frank Morrison, secretary of the AFL, guilty of contempt of court. Gompers received a one-year sentence for this offense. Mitchell was sentenced to nine months, and Morrison to six.

Although the sweeping nature of the injunction was toned down by an appeals court, the Supreme Court of the District of Columbia did not drop its proceedings for contempt of court. The injunction and the contempt cases went as one case to the Supreme Court of the United States. Meanwhile, Van Cleave had died, and the new management and the union settled their differences before the Supreme Court acted. After the settlement, the Supreme Court dismissed the injunction case and the contempt case, but left the Supreme Court of the District of Columbia free to act on the contempt case. The contempt case eventually came back to the Supreme Court. The union officers were saved from jail by the expiration of the three-year statue of limitations.

As a result of the *Buck's Stove and Range* case, the AFL abandoned its "We Don't Patronize" list. This brush with the reality of incarceration mobilized labor in the political field. With the passage of the Clayton Act of 1914, the unions achieved the first step in winning labor exemption from the use of legal injunctions. The Norris-LaGuardia Act of 1932 significantly restricted the use of injunctions in labor cases.

See also Boycotts, *Danbury Hatters* Case, Clayton Act of 1914, Norris-LaGuardia Act of 1932.

References Laidler, Harry W. *Boycotts and the Labor Struggle: Economic and Legal Aspects* (1913); Taft, Philip. *The A. F. of L. in the Time of Gompers* (1957).

Bundesbank
See Central Banks and Free Banking

Business Cycles
Business cycles are recurring fluctuations in economic activity. These cycles are usually not regarded as recurring at regular intervals, but there are theories of cycles that recur at certain intervals, such as every 50 years.

Business cycles have four different phases. The sinking phase is called a recession, and the recession bottoms out in a trough. From the trough the economy reverses the downturn and begins a recovery phase. The recovery climaxes in a peak, and at the peak the economy noses over into another recession. During the declining phase, production falls (particularly for durable goods, such as automobiles), inflation subsides or becomes negative, interest rates fall, unemployment goes up, and business failures increase. The onset of a recession is often signaled by a crisis in financial markets, i.e., a stock market crash. During the expansion phase, production increases, interest rates rise, unemployment falls, and bankruptcies diminish. As the economy reaches full employment, the inflation rate may rise sharply, signaling that supply can no longer keep pace with demand.

Technically, an economy is in a state of recession when Gross Domestic Product (GDP), a measure of aggregate output, drops for two consecutive quarters of a year. A depression is a prolonged and deep recession, but, unlike recession, it does not have a precise definition. During the 1890s and 1930s, the economies of the world experienced major contractions that were called depressions. During the Depression of the 1930s, the unemployment rate rose to 25 percent in the United States. By contrast, U.S. recessions during the post-World War II era have never seen unemployment rates above 12 percent.

Historically, business cycles may have been caused by variations in agricultural production, perhaps caused by weather. Modern capitalism, however, is mostly shielded from the effects of weather, and modern economists look for systemic causes in the capitalist system, such as waves of optimism or pessimism in the long-term expectations of the business community. Governments may also inadvertently play a role.

See also Kondratieff Cycle, Political Business Cycle.

References Bowers, David A. *An Introduction to Business Cycles and Forecasting* (1985); Moore, Geoffrey H. *Business Cycles, Inflation, and Forecasting*, 2nd ed. (1983); Schumpeter, Joseph. *Business Cycles: A Theoretical, Historical, and Statistical Analysis of the Capitalist Process*, Vols. 1–2 (1939).

Capital

Capital is the means of production in modern economic systems, encompassing factories, warehouses, building, transportation facilities, etc. It is one of the basic resources, along with labor, natural resources, and entrepreneurial ability, that must be cooperatively organized to produce goods and services.

Capital involves what is sometimes called round-about production, meaning that producers manufacture tools before they set to work to build goods. To understand what is meant by round-about production, consider a farmer who plans to raise a crop of cotton. The farmer could go to the field with a sack of seeds, dig little holes in the ground with his fingers, and bury the seed using his foot. Round-about production begins when the farmer decides to cut a stick of a certain length, sharpen one end, and use it as a farming implement. The more time the farmer invests in making farm tools before entering the field, the greater the degree of round-about production.

In modern industrialized societies, in which a complete automobile factory is erected before one automobile rolls off the assemble line, the degree of round-about production is extensive. Round-about production pays off in vast increases in production, but it requires a preparatory phase in which labor and resources are invested in producing goods that are not directly consumable, such as a factory.

Increasing the amount of capital per worker is considered the most direct means of increasing output per worker. Therefore, the accumulation of capital is the most essential element in the process of economic development. Capitalist societies such as Japan, relatively poor in natural resource endowment, achieve high living standards by accumulating large amounts of capital.

The distinguishing feature of the capitalist economic system is that the capital is neither owned by the workers, nor by the government, but is privately owned and operated for the profit of the owner(s). The ownership and management of capital became the chief source of income to a business class in the capitalist economic system. In the medieval guilds, workers owned their own tools and facilities; in modern socialism, governments own and operate the capital goods.

See also Factory System.

References Higgins, Benjamin. *Economic Development* (1968); McConnell, Campbell R., and Stanley L. Brue, *Economics*, 12th ed. (1993).

Carnegie, Andrew (1835–1919)

Andrew Carnegie consolidated a steel empire in the late nineteenth-century United States, before retiring and giving away much of his fortune for philanthropic purposes.

Born in Scotland in 1835, Carnegie emigrated with his family to the United States in 1848, settling in the Pittsburgh area. He remained a bachelor throughout his life, perhaps because his widowed mother asked him not to marry as long as she was living. He came to the iron and steel industry via the railroad industry, rising from a private secretary to superintendent of the Pittsburgh division of the Pennsylvania Railroad. He saved and borrowed to invest in a firm that built iron bridges. Later he infused his own capital into a firm engaged in building railroad-car axles. A merging of the bridge and axle firms created a new firm called Union Iron Mills.

From being one of four partners, Carnegie gained control of Union Iron Mills when he arranged to have a surrogate buy the stock of one of the partners.

Carnegie moved himself and his mother to New York, opened an investment firm, and, when not selling bonds, marshalled business for Union Iron Mills. Whenever Carnegie received word that other firms were expanding at the expense of Union Iron Mills, he expanded Union Mills.

When his partners proposed building a new plant based on the Bessemer process, Carnegie refused to join in. In the Panic of 1873, Carnegie's partners left Union Iron Mills, and Carnegie, having second thoughts, bought into the plant using the Bessemer process. In 1881, Carnegie bought control of a steel company in Homestead, Pennsylvania. The stock sold at bargain basement prices because of labor difficulties. When another company set up a plant in the same area and started underselling the Carnegie Steel Company, Carnegie circulated a letter to railroads charging that rails produced by the other company were unsafe. After the rival company lost much of its business,

Carnegie bought it out and began producing rails using the same, less costly technique.

In 1892, Carnegie sparked a bloody labor dispute in Homestead, when he cut wages at his plant, where workers were strongly unionized. Fourteen people were killed and 163 lay wounded before the bloodshed ended. The plant reopened as a nonunion plant, but the public bore a grudge against Carnegie over the episode.

By the turn of the century, J. Pierpont Morgan had organized a steel trust. Carnegie went into the expansion mode, but when the offer came to sell, he accepted, and his company became part of the giant United States Steel Corporation. He retired in 1900, at age 65.

At his death in 1919, Carnegie had given away 90 percent of his fortune. His most famous project was funding the construction of libraries in the United States and England. He was a follower of Herbert Spencer in economics and philosophy, and felt the spread of knowledge the only sure path for improving humankind.

Carnegie was the most literate of the capitalist moguls in the nineteenth-century United States, but he exhibited the same drive to control and dominate as the other capitalist entrepreneurs of the age. Many of the business practices of Carnegie and his rivals are now illegal. Nevertheless, the giant corporations born of the era of Carnegie and Morgan survived to set an example for the massive corporations of the twentieth century.

See also Entrepreneurship; Morgan, John Pierpont; Rockefeller, John Davison.

Reference Livesay, Harold C. *Andrew Carnegie and the Rise of Big Business* (1975); Wall, Joseph Frazier. *Andrew Carnegie* (1970); Warren, Kenneth. *Triumphant Capitalism* (1996).

Andrew Carnegie, 1896

Cartels

A cartel is a legal agreement among sellers in the same industry to regulate prices, restrict production and supply, divide market share, and undertake various cooperative initiatives. The members of the cartel remain independent entrepreneurs who unite by legal agreements to avoid competition for prices and territory.

In *The Social and Economic History of Germany from Wilhelm II to Hitler: 1888–1939*, W. F. Bruck wrote: "As far as modern cartels are concerned, they are a German invention...." In the latter nineteenth century, the economic forces favoring consolidation of industrial capacity made themselves felt in most industrialized countries. Just as the predominant form of consolidation in the United States was trusts and mergers, and, in England, the associations and unions (of manufactures), in Germany, the cartels were predominant.

The late 1870s saw the first significant growth in cartels in Germany, perhaps as a reaction to the depression following the crisis of 1873. One of the purposes of cartels was to short-circuit the ruinous and cutthroat competition that often reared its head in the midst of industrial depressions. The trend toward cartels received an important boost in 1879, when Germany raised higher trade barriers, to shelter domestic industry from world competition. Cartels enabled German industries to collectively raise domestic prices above world market levels, by prohibiting competition among German firms.

German cartels varied in the control they exerted over individual members. The "Produktion" cartels set production quotas for each member of the cartel and divided the market into regions served by different members of the cartel. The most advanced form of cartels was the syndicates, in which a general selling office processed the sales of individual members of the cartel and the profits were pooled. Some syndicates organized members from different stages of production of the same product. These syndicates controlled prices from the raw material stage to the stage of retail sale. An incomplete list of industries organized into cartels included coal, iron, steel, sugar, cement, alcoholic beverages, machine tools, and locomotives. The coal, iron, and steel cartels were industrial giants.

Cartels were known to set prices that allowed inefficient firms to survive that would not have survived in a competitive environment. More often, cartels shut down unprofitable plants, limiting production to the more efficient facilities. Cartels engaged in price discrimination, selling products in export markets at lower prices than in sheltered domestic markets. This practice led to the development of international cartels based upon agreements between cartels of several countries.

Before World War I, Germany never questioned the desirability of cartels. Industrial production in Germany grew at a heady pace, and Germany credited its industrial organization for the success of its products in almost every market. By the turn of the century, Germany surpassed England in pig-iron production.

German economists and theorists were much more sympathetic to monopoly than economists in the English tradition. They saw cartels as a manifestation of a stage of economic development in which planning began to replace free-market decision-making. Writing in 1938, Bruck wrote:

> From the theoretical point of view, the large-scale undertaking has the novel feature of organizing demand as well as supply. It is no longer a mere competitor with other undertakings of production on the supply side. It is the mark of a modern industrial state that the big undertakings of production have to create their own markets, with all the corollaries such as the financing of the producer and the consumer.

The Third Reich encouraged the formation of cartels, and made use of them for national planning, and for conversion to a wartime economy. Cartels were forbidden during Allied occupation, and domestic cartels were banned by legislation in 1957, but export cartels were exempted from the ban.

Cartels are still possible in international trade. The Organization of Petroleum Exporting Countries (OPEC) functioned as an effective cartel from 1972 until 1986, limiting the production of crude oil, and raising prices. Political turmoil within OPEC ended its effectiveness as a cartel.

The German cartels were regarded as a more coercive form of market domination than the trusts and holding companies in the United States. Since World War II, the trend in the capitalist world has been to promote competition at home and free trade abroad. Small companies are now seen as making a larger contribution to economic growth. Large companies have not always aged well in an environment of rapidly changing technology that puts a premium on flexibility and adaptability.

See also Holding Companies, Interlocking Directorates, Mergers, Totalitarian Monopoly Capitalism, Zaibatzu.

References Bruck, W. F. *Social and Economic History of Germany from William II to Hitler: 1888–1938* (1938); Edwards, George W. *The Evolution of Finance Capitalism* (1967).

Cavour, Count Camillo Benso di
See Unification of Italy.

Casa de Contratacion
See Spanish Colonial Empire.

Central Banks and Free Banking

Central banks serve as bankers' banks. They hold deposits of commercial banks, make loans to commercial banks, and can serve as a lender of last resort to commercial banks in financial crises. Typically, a central bank acts as the government's banker, and holds a monopoly on the issuance of paper money. The Federal Reserve System in the United States, the Bank of England, the Bank of France, and the Bundesbank of Germany are examples of central banks.

All advanced capitalist countries today have a central bank. A monetary system regulated by a central bank became the preferred form of monetary regulation in the latter part of the nineteenth century. The alternative to central bank regulation is what is called free banking. In the high tide of nineteenth-century laissez faire, central banks were not fully evolved, and free banking became a trend in capitalist countries. The United States abandoned the Second Bank of the United States and turned to a form of free banking.

Free banking denotes a banking system in which note-issuing banks are established according to the same principles that govern the establishment of any new business enterprise. The ability to start a new bank requires sufficient financial capital and public confidence to make the new bank notes acceptable to the public, and to help the new bank reach a profit-making scale of operation. A new bank need not clear any legal hurdles, such as charters or grants, which require a special act of government. Each bank issues its own bank notes, which it converts on demand into an acceptable medium of exchange, often, but not necessarily, gold. None of the banks issue notes bearing the status of legal tender, or in any way favored by the government. A bank's refusal to redeem its bank notes into an acceptable medium of exchange is equivalent to a declaration of bankruptcy.

The critics of free banking claim the system causes instability in the economy. In an economic upswing, banks have an incentive to make as many loans as possible and issue as many bank notes as possible. The loans stand an excellent chance of being repaid, keeping the bank in a position to redeem its bank notes. This expansion of loans and bank notes turns the upswing into an overheated boom and inflationary spiral.

In an economic downswing, on the contrary, banks find extending loans and issuing bank notes more risky, and curtail these activities according. This restriction on credit and money can push the downswing over the precipice of depression. Individual banks, driven by the profit motive in a free banking system, add to the severity of cyclical fluctuations.

Central banks seek the public interest, rather than striving to maximize profits. In a downswing, central banks supply more credit to the system, rather than less. In an upswing, central banks restrict the supply of credit. The monopoly on the issuance of bank notes and commercial bank reserve deposits gives the central bank control over the money supply, interest rates, and credit conditions. These can be adjusted countercyclically, to smooth out economic fluctuations.

In the twentieth century, the preference of central banking over free banking is dogma. Nearly all discussion weighing the relative merits of these two systems took place in a 40- to 50-year interval in the nineteenth century.

See also Bank of England, Bank of France, Bank of Japan, Federal Reserve System, Wildcat Banks.

References Mittra, Sid. *Central Bank Versus Treasury: An International Study* (1978); Smith, Vera C. *The Rational of Central Banking, and the Free Banking Alternative* (1936), Timberlake, Richard Henry. *The Origins of Central Banking in the United States* (1978).

Chapter 11 Bankruptcy (United States)
See Bankruptcy Act of 1978.

Chartist Movement (England)

The Chartist movement was a working-class political movement in the first half of nineteenth-century England. Although the agenda of the Chartists was chiefly political, the dismal economic conditions of the working class added much of the momentum.

The working class had aided the middle-class property owners in the movement to reform Parliament. Even artisans and craftsmen who enjoyed the right to vote before the reform found themselves among the disenfranchised working class. With the middle class and industrial capitalists pulled into the establishment, workers turned to unionization and cooperative societies to re-

form society. When this effort failed, the working-class struggle, shorn of its middle-class alliance, set to work to give the working class a voice in Parliament.

The Chartist movement began with the emergence of working-class societies in urban areas and industrial districts. In London, a group of workers formed the London Working Men's Association (LWMA), which sent out organizers and propaganda to principal areas, and soon working-class societies were springing up everywhere. In Birmingham, a remnant of the earlier reform movements reappeared to support a similar agenda. The Birmingham group was mostly a working-class organization with middle-class leadership.

In 1837, Francis Place arranged for a group of radical members of Parliament to meet with leaders of the LWMA, to draft a reform bill to be introduced in Parliament. What was drawn up became known as the People's Charter, which contained six points: (1) manhood suffrage; (2) vote by ballot; (3) annual Parliaments, annually elected; (4) abolition of the property qualification for Members of Parliament (MPs); (5) payment of MPs; and (6) equal electoral districts, reconstituted after each ten-year census. This charter gave the Chartist movement its name. All points, except the last one, were in the Birmingham Petition, which was submitted to Parliament by the Birmingham organization.

The Chartists held a convention in 1839 to organize support for the charter. The convention organized mass meetings in various areas to get signatures for a petition supporting their proposals. It made a vague effort to organize a general strike, including a run on the banks, if Parliament failed to approve their proposals. The government took a hard line, breaking up the mass meetings and arresting leaders. Parliament voted down the bill based upon the charter. The convention was powerless to organize a general strike; workers were already suffering from a trade depression. A small uprising in Newport brought a clash between soldiers and insurgents, in which a number of the latter were killed or wounded. After the Newport uprising, the government became more repressive toward the Chartist movement.

The Chartist movement, despite the imprisonment of many of its leaders, regrouped in 1840, with the formation of the National Chartist Association (NCA). Other splinter groups grew out of the Chartist movement, but only the NCA attracted a mass following. In 1842, another petition was presented to Parliament, but once again the Chartists received a rebuff. In protest, the Chartists encouraged a rash of strikes that were especially provoked by industrial depression and wage cuts. The government stationed troops to suppress the disturbances, and jailed many Chartist leaders. Starving workers submitted to employer demands for wage cuts.

From 1845 to 1847, the Chartist movement devoted itself to a land scheme that proposed to set up workers as small proprietary farmers. When revolutions broke out throughout Europe in 1848, Chartists launched an effort to organize a third convention and national petition. The convention planned a march to Westminister to deliver the petition to Parliament. In the event Parliament rejected their proposals, they planned to elect a National Chartists Assembly that would not dissolve until Parliament relented. Troops and artillery greeted the marchers, the petition was delivered to Parliament in a cab, and the marchers dispersed.

After 1848, the Chartist movement was a spent force, although the NCA held regular conferences until 1858. The working class continued to see itself as a special class created by the capitalist system. It searched for ways to improve its economic status. After the development of modern trade unions, the working class began to associate capitalism with progress for itself.

See also Class Struggle, Proletariat.

References Cole, G. D. H. *A Short History of the British Working-Class Movement: 1789–1947* (1948);

Goodway, David. *London Chartism, 1838–1848* (1982); Thomas, Dorothy. *The Chartists* (1984).

Child Labor Legislation (United States)

Federal child labor legislation, limiting the hours and ages of working children in industries related to interstate commerce, became part of the law of the land in the 1930s, which indicates that legislation in this area got off to a slow start in the United States.

Child labor itself did not get off to a slow start in the United States. A Virginia statute of 1646 cited the "laudable custom" in England of binding out children for work. The statute made mention of parents not making their children work. It ordered county commissioners to draft poor children between seven and eight years of age for work in the Jamestown public work house. In 1790, manufacturing pioneer Samuel Slater employed only children between seven and 12 years in his first Rhode Island factory. Alexander Hamilton's Report on Manufactures, referred to children who "are made more useful by manufacturing establishments than they otherwise would be." In 1869, an article in the New York Times noted that "a great multitude of the youth are growing up, stunted in body, and with not even the rudiments of school training, a prey to the insatiable requirements of industry and capital." By the turn of the century, 28 states had adopted some sort of child labor legislation. The state legislation was mostly ineffective. Cotton mills in the South were major employers of children. From 1870 to 1900, the number of employed children between ages 10 and 15 increased from 0.75 million to 1.75 million.

The federal government created the Child Labor Bureau in 1912. This was the first victory at the federal level for the National Child Labor Committee (NCLC), a group of social reformers spearheading the child labor movement. The bureau collected and disseminated information about child labor in the United States.

During Woodrow Wilson's administration, the NCLC and the Children's Bureau began pushing for child labor laws banning child labor in interstate commerce. Because of constitutional questions, Wilson at first gave only lukewarm support for child labor legislation. Just before his renomination as a presidential candidate, Wilson strongly endorsed a bill that passed both houses of Congress. This bill banned children under 14 from working in factories, workshops, and canneries. Children under 16 were banned from working in mines and quarries, and could only work eight hours per day between 7 A.M. and 7 P.M. Wilson signed the bill on 1 September 1916. A group of cotton mill owners challenged the constitutionality of the law, and, on 3 June 1918, the Supreme Court, in a 5 to 4 decision ruled the child labor law unconstitutional. According to the Supreme Court, the federal government was trying to use its power to regulate interstate commerce to regulate local labor conditions.

Congress passed a second bill in 1919 against child labor. This bill put a 10-percent tax on net profits of canneries, mills, and factories using child labor under conditions outlawed in the first bill. This bill met a similar fate at the hands of the Supreme Court; in an 8-to-1 decision, the Court held the law was an abuse of the power to tax.

The NCLC now turned its attention to the adoption of an amendment to the Constitution banning child labor. Congress approved an amendment to the Constitution, but states were slow to ratify it.

President Franklin Roosevelt favored child labor legislation, and, in 1938, Congress passed the Fair Labor Standards Act, which had provisions banning child labor. This act outlawed interstate shipment of goods originating from a point where children had been employed within the last 30 days. Children meant persons under 16 years in nonhazardous occupations and under 18 years in hazardous occupations,

as designated by the Children's Bureau. On 3 February 1941, the Supreme Court unanimously upheld the constitutionality of the Fair Standards Act.

The movement for a constitutional amendment lost momentum after the Supreme Court ruled in favor of the Fair Standards Act. In 1949, Congress strengthened and expanded the coverage of the provisions on child labor, specifically prohibiting the employment of child labor, rather than outlawing the shipment of goods produced by child labor. Commercial farms now came under the jurisdiction of the act.

Karl Marx, in *Das Kapital*, referring to the methods used in factories to evade the ban on child labor in the English Factory Acts, wrote: "Nothing is more characteristic of the spirit of capital than the history of the English Factory Acts from 1833 to 1864." The use of child labor justifiably drew protest of social reformers in the United States. It is one of the less edifying portions of the history of capitalism.

See also Factory Acts.

References Ensign, Forest Chester. *Compulsory School Attendance and Child Labor* (1969); Spargo, John. *The Bitter Cry of the Children* (1968); Trattner, Walter I. *Crusade for the Children* (1970).

Circumnavigation of the Earth

The first circumnavigation of the earth, besides giving practical proof of the size and roundness of the earth, achieved Columbus's dream of reaching the East Indies by sailing west. It was another act in the drama of European countries seeking direct trading routes to the East Indies. The one ship that completed the world-circling route returned with spices from the East Indies that paid the entire cost of the expedition. Such were the economic profits that inspired the heroic enterprises of the age of exploration.

The man credited with organizing the expedition was a Portuguese navigator disaffected from the Portuguese crown, because it refused his request for a better pension. Ferdinand Magellan had participated in the Portuguese expeditions that captured sea power from the Moslems in the Indian Ocean, and which gave Portugal a monopoly of the Indian spice trade with Europe. After 1494, a treaty between Portugal and Spain ceded to Portugal all new lands south of the Canary Islands and east of 46 degrees 37 minutes west longitude, further cementing Portugal's monopoly on the Indian spice trade. The treaty ceded lands west of this line of demarcation to Spain. Magellan went to Spain, renounced his nationality, and offered to lead an expedition to the Spice Islands on a western route around the southern tip of South America. Magellan's planned route would show that the Spice Islands lay on the Spanish side of the line of demarcation. The king of Spain ordered that five ships be fitted out for Magellan's service.

Magellan made his departure on 20 September 1519. He had five weather-beaten ships, barely seaworthy, manned by waterfront sailors of the lowest sort. Experienced sailors were loath to join such an expedition, with good reason—of the 270 men who began the expedition, only 35 would return. The expedition owed much of its success to the leadership, resourcefulness, and determination of Magellan, who nevertheless would become one of its casualties.

The expedition reached Brazil in October, and began sailing south along the coast of South America, entering the bay of Rio De Janeiro on 13 December. From March to August, Magellan wintered in the Port of St. Julian, where his leadership and resourcefulness were put to the test when crews of three of the five ships mutinied. Magellan quashed the mutiny, but one ship stole away to Spain, and another one wrecked on a reef. On 21 October, Magellan entered the straits now bearing his name, which opened into the Pacific. He sailed up the coast of Chile until 18 December, and then took a northwesterly heading across the Pacific. Magellan's iron will and determination now became a deciding factor as his crew battled scurvy and starvation on a dreary 99-day voyage that ended at Guam. On 6 March, Magellan departed Guam and sailed for the Philippines, where he hoped to reprovision his crew, and make ready for a landing in the Spice Islands. On 27 April 1521, Magellan was killed in the Philippines, while assisting a local ruler against neighboring enemies.

The expedition continued to Moluccas or the Spice Islands, which lie between the Philippines and Australia. The crew, now too small to man three ships, burned one of them. Loaded with spices, one ship set out to retrace its route back to Spain, but failed, and returned to the Spice Islands, where the Portuguese imprisoned its crew. Another ship, under the command of Juan Sebastian del Cano, continued on a course of circumnavigation, rounding the Cape of Good Hope, and arriving in Spain on 8 September 1522, after a voyage of three years.

The circumnavigation of the earth opened the world's trading ports to the spread of European capitalism. Coupled with the discovery of the New World, it propelled Western capitalism on a path of unlimited development that led to virtual domination of the world economy by the end of the nineteenth century. Access to world resources and markets created the favorable conditions in Europe for the technological and industrial development needed for the creation of a global economy.

Magellan's ship Victoria *completed the first circumnavigation of the world, but Magellan was killed during the voyage. Portraits of Magellan, Francis Drake, and two other explorers surround the ship.*

See also Columbus, Christopher; Da Gama, Vasco; Spice Trade.

References Joyner, Tim. *Magellan* (1992); Morison, Samuel Eliot. *The Great Explorers* (1978).

Civil Rights Act of 1964 (United States)

See Equal Employment Opportunity Commission.

Class Struggle

Karl Marx and Friedrich Engels opened chapter 1 of the *Manifesto of the Communist Party* with the sweeping statement, "The History of all hitherto existing society is the history of class struggles." Marx's theory became part of the allegedly scientific basis for socialism. In the latter portion of the nineteenth century, the class struggle became conscious of itself. Socialist and trade-union propaganda moved workers to action with assurance that they would be the victors and not the victims in the next class war.

Perhaps Marx and Engel's enthusiasm for the theory of class struggle helped infect the oratory of the whole working-class movement with stirring images that raised class consciousness, and stung proletarians into action. The enthusiasm in the *Manifesto* can move even a skeptic:

Freeman, and slave, patrician and plebeian, lord and serf, guild-master and journeyman, in a word, oppressor and oppressed, stood in constant opposition to one another, carried on an uninterrupted, now hidden, now open fight, a fight that each time ended either in a revolutionary reconstitution of society at large, or in the common ruin of the contending classes.... In the earlier epochs...we find...a manifold gradation of social rank.... In the Middle Ages, [we have] feudal lords, vassals, guild-masters, journeymen, apprentices, serfs.... The epoch of the bourgeoisie...has simplified class antagonisms.

Society as a whole is more and more splitting up into two great hostile camps, into two great classes directly facing each other—bourgeoisie and proletariat.... [I]n times when the class struggle nears the decisive hour...a small section of the ruling class cuts itself adrift, and joins the revolutionary class, the class that holds the future in its hands.

According to Marxist theory of capitalist development, the common denominator in the major revolutions of the modern era lay in the bourgeoisie (owners of capital) overthrow of the feudal nobility. The English Revolution of 1688, the American Revolution of 1776, the French Revolution of 1789, and the Japanese Revolution of 1868 fit the pattern of a bourgeois revolt against a feudal nobility in class warfare. Marx recast the American Civil War as class warfare that bourgeois capitalists waged against a slave-owning oligarchy of plantation owners who bore a marked political resemblance to feudal nobility. Toward the end of the nineteenth century, Marxists and socialists hoped for an international class war, cutting across national boundaries, that would end national wars, and lead to a golden era of peace. World War I put to rest the myth of an international class struggle. Most socialist parties and working-class organizations patriotically supported their national governments in that struggle.

The class struggle in capitalist countries failed to reach the apex of crisis that Marx predicted. Marx formed his theory of class struggle before the spread of the corporate business form, which diffused ownership, and before the rise of a large class of white-collar professionals that stood between unskilled workers and the owners of the corporations. Advanced capitalist countries also saw a decline in the percentage of workers that fall into the unskilled category. Society failed to split into two warring classes. A decline in the share of inherited wealth versus first-generation wealth may also have helped diffuse the class struggle. The idea of a united working class that brings about a revolution, and then runs a country, probably seems a bit frightening to a typical white-collar worker in modern capitalism.

See also Communist Manifesto, Paris Commune of 1871, Proletariat, Syndicalism.

References Dasgupta, K. *Phases of Capitalism and Economic Theory and Other Essays* (1983); Hamilton, Richard F. *The Bourgeois Epoch: Marx and Engels on Britain, France, and Germany* (1991); Marx, Karl. *The Class Struggles in France, 1848–1850* (1964); Marx, Karl, and Friedrich Engels. *Manifesto of the Communist Party* (1848); Yeo, Eileen, and Stephen Yeo, eds. *Popular Culture and Class Conflict, 1590–1914: Explorations in the History of Labor and Leisure* (1981).

Classical School of Economics

The classical school of economics supplied the theoretical rationale for laissez-faire capitalism. Characteristically, Britain, where the outlines of capitalism first emerged in a nation-state, was the birthplace and home to the classical school. Adam Smith laid the foundation of classical economics in his book, *An Inquiry into the Nature and Causes of the Wealth of Nations*, published in 1776. In the nineteenth century, British economists, particularly Thomas Malthus, David Ricardo, and John Stuart Mill, developed and elaborated the classical system, and brought it to maturity.

The classical school championed two principles that helped shape the development of the capitalist system, first in Britain, and later in the world. First, classical economists embraced economic man as a creature seeking his own self-interest, displacing altruistic principles of behavior. This vision of man was a major departure from the schools of economics that evolved from the theologians of the Middle Ages. Second, classical economists saw not conflict, but harmony, between private interest and public interest in most markets and industries. Therefore, not only did individuals seek their own self-interest, but society benefits when individuals are free to seek their own self-interest, without fetters from govern-

ment regulation. In the classical system, the self-seeking activities of individuals are distilled in a competitive process that cancels out everything not promoting the public interest.

Classical economists deducted several revolutionary principles from their theoretical system. First, classical economists advocated lifting tariffs and trade barriers in favor of policies of free trade. Although trade barriers may be well-meaning actions of governments to spur domestic economies, classical economist frowned on shielding economic activities from competition. In the classical system, economies should specialize in industries that are competitive in a world market based upon free trade.

Second, classical economists believed that economies have a natural tendency to operate at full employment. Depressions are aberrations fated to be temporary, probably caused by malfunctions in processes incidental to the basic capitalist economic system. Admitting the economic system is buffeted by shocks from various sources, classical economists emphasized the self-correcting characteristics of the economic system that enabled it to absorb shocks without long-term departures from full employment. Central to the vision of the economic system as a self-correcting system was the concept of Say's Law, named for its originator, Jean-Baptiste Say. According to Say's Law, "supply creates its own demand," rendering the economic system immune to the dangers of overproduction. Early economic theories placed the blame for depressions on excess production, relative to demand. Say argued that no one produces anything unless they want to consume something. When people produce something, they acquire the right to consume what they produced, or trade it, and consume other things of equal value. Therefore, the act of production signifies a desire to demand and consume. Classical economists also emphasized the role of interest rates and prices in markets that balance supply and demand.

The classical economists explained how laissez-faire capitalism works on paper. The Depression of the 1930s discredited classical economics, and economists and policy makers openly avowed the need to regulate the capitalist economic system. The prohibitive trade restrictions of the 1930s, however, backfired, vindicating the free-trade doctrine of classical economists. In the 1970s, the failure of government policies to cure the paradox of simultaneous inflation and unemployment further helped to rehabilitate classical economics, which has now re-emerged as the new classical economics.

See also Keynesian Revolution; Smith, Adam.

References Fitzgibbons, Athol. *Adam Smith's System of Liberty, Wealth, and Virtue: The Moral and Political Foundations of the Wealth of Nations* (1995); Heilbroner, Robert. *The Worldly Philosophers* (1953); McNally, David. *Political Economy and the Rise of Capitalism: A Reinterpretation* (1988).

Clayton Act of 1914 (United States)

The purpose of the Clayton Act was to exempt unions from antitrust action, and to close the loopholes in the antitrust legislation that allowed monopolistic business practices to continue. The Clayton Act prohibited interlocking directorates, horizontal mergers of competitors, and tying contracts. (A tying contract forces a customer to buy good X in order to obtain good Y.) It also banned price discrimination (charging different customers different prices for the same product), if the effect is to substantially lessen competition. Under the Clayton Act, purchasing the stock of another corporation can be illegal if it acts to lessen competition.

Although the Clayton Act was an important addition to the government's legal arsenal to fight monopolies, the leaders of the labor movement hailed it as labor's Magna Carta for its labor provisions. The Sherman Antitrust Act of 1890 outlawed all combinations in restraint of trade between states or with foreign nations. How Congress expected the new law to affect labor unions remained unclear. The U.S. Supreme Court interpreted union actions as violating the provisions of the Sherman Act. In the *Danbury Hatters* case (1908), the American Federation of Labor (AFL) was held liable for a triple damage award. The damage came from a nationwide boycott of a nonunion firm. In the *Buck's Stove and Range* case (1911), three officers of the AFL received a jail sentence for disregarding an injunction. The injunction was against the inclusion of the Buck's Stove Company in a "We Don't Patronize" list. The AFL officers never went to jail, but these convictions, and other court cases, persuaded the AFL to bring pressure to bear on Congress to exempt labor unions from the Sherman Act.

Section 6 of the Clayton Act stated:

That the labor of a human being is not a commodity or article of commerce. Nothing contained in the antitrust laws shall be construed to forbid the existence and operation of labor, agricultural, or horticultural organization, instituted for the purposes of mutual help, and not having capital stock or conducted for profit, or to forbid or restrain individual members of such organizations from lawfully carrying out the legitimate objects thereof; nor shall such organizations, or the members thereof, be held or construed to be illegal combinations or conspiracies in restraint of trade under the antitrust laws.

The Clayton Act tried to deal a blow against the use of injunctions against peaceful strikes and pickets. In the words of section 20 of the Clayton Act, "no restraining order or injunction shall be granted by any court of the United States" in labor cases "unless necessary to prevent irreparable damage to a property right...for which there is no adequate remedy at law...."

The Clayton Act failed to live up to its expectations. The courts could still decide what were the "legitimate objects" of labor unions, and they continued to apply the Sherman Act to union activities. In the 1930s, Congress passed additional legislation to exempt unions from antitrust laws, and to protect workers' right to organize. By the 1940s, the U.S. Supreme Court changed its interpretation of the law, and made less use of the antitrust laws to restrict union activity.

See also American Federation of Labor, Holding Companies, Interlocking Directorates, Mergers.

References Cartter, Allan M., and F. Ray Marshall. *Labor Economics: Wages, Employment, and Trade Unionism* (1967); Waldman, Don E. *The Economics of Antitrust: Cases and Analysis* (1985).

Clean Air Acts (United States)

Congress passed the Clean Air Act in 1963, and amended it in 1965, 1967, 1970, 1977, and 1990, reflecting a prolonged commitment to improving air quality standards in the United States.

With the Clean Act of 1970, the federal government launched its first broad assault on air pollution in the United States. The act put stringent pollution controls on automobiles sold after 1974, calling for a 90-percent reduction of emissions of hydrocarbons and carbon monoxide gas. To meet protests from automobile manufacturers, Congress later extended the timetable to 1981. Automobile manufacturers were obliged to grant 50,000-mile warranties for pollution control devices. The act also set forth national standards for air pollution, granting states four to six years to establish programs for enforcing compliance with national standards. Violators of air pollution standards faced criminal penalties, including fines up to $50,000 per day, and jail sentences up to two years. Under the act, citizens can sue polluters, including the U.S. government, in federal court, bringing to bear the full force of the law to stop industries from polluting the air.

The 1990 revision further widened the scope of the Clean Air Act. It called for passenger cars to emit 60 percent less nitrogen oxide by 2003, and to be manufactured with pollution-control equipment lasting ten years. Chemicals that endanger the ozone would be forbidden by the year 2000. Stricter regulations curtailed the emission of industrial pollutants associated with acid rain. The 1990 revision invested the Environmental Protection Agency (EPA) with responsibility for enforcing all air-quality standards, and empowered citizens with the right to sue the EPA for failing to enforce the law.

Strict adherents to the philosophy of laissez-faire capitalism placed the fault for air pollution on the failure of the market system to work in the absence of well-defined property rights. According to this line of reasoning, clean air was disappearing for the same reason the buffalo disappeared. Nobody owned the buffalo, just as no one owned the clean air; therefore, no one had a vested interest in preserving the value of either one. An owner of the clean air could either stop industries from polluting their property, or, more likely, charge industries for the privilege of emitting certain quantities of pollutants. Charging industries for pollution rights would lead to a market solution most closely representing the choices of society. Since private ownership of the air was not feasible, the only other alternative was government intervention, which was preferable to polluted air.

See also Environmental Protection Agency.

References Schnitzer, Martin C. *Contemporary Government and Business Relations* (1978); Spiro, George W. *The Legal Environment of Business* (1993).

Clean Water Act (United States)

The Clean Water Act of 1972 proposed to end the discharge of pollutants into all navigable waters by 1985. The act significantly expanded the more limited Clean Water Act of 1970, and has since been amended in 1977 and 1987. The Environmental Protection Agency (EPA), in cooperation with state environmental control agencies, bears responsibility for enforcement of clean water standards.

The act put water pollution control in navigable waters under federal jurisdiction. On learning of a violation, the EPA either directly orders compliance, or informs a state agency with enforcement powers. In the absence of compliance, the EPA can seek civil damages or criminal penalties. Civil damages were on the order of $10,000 per day, and criminal penalties included fines ranging between $2,500 to $25,000 per day, and up to one year imprisonment. Second offenses drew heavier fines and longer prison terms. To force compliance, citizens could bring suits in their own right in federal courts.

The act requires industrial polluters to measure and record discharges of pollution, and to monitor the outcomes of pollution control efforts. The EPA sets nationwide standards for industrial discharges from each type of industry. Each plant must have a permit from the EPA or a state agency, to discharge pollutants into bodies of water. Individual states identify the uses for bodies of water within their jurisdiction, and set clean water standards accordingly. Water used for swimming and commercial fishing must meet cleaner standards than water used only for transportation.

The finger of blame for extensive water pollution and air pollution can quite rightly be pointed at laissez-faire capitalism, which opposes government regulation on principle. The obvious failure of laissez-faire capitalism to achieve a socially optimal use of resources, such as clean air and water, can be attributed to a lack of well-defined property rights. According to this reasoning, unfettered capitalism produced inferior outcomes in these cases, because the water and air were not privately owned. If the water was privately owned, the owner could seek legal recourse against plants that discharged pollutants into water without permission. Owners of water resources could charge polluters according to the cost of the damage inflicted on the water, or the cost of cleaning up the pollution. The absence of property rights meant that market solutions between buyers and sellers were not feasible; therefore, the government had to step in and apply water-quality standards.

See also Environmental Protection Agency.

References Schnitzer, Martin C. *Contemporary Government and Business Relations* (1978); Spiro, George W. *The Legal Environment of Business* (1993).

Closed Shops and Union Shops
Under closed-shop agreements, workers must be members of a union in good standing, before an employer can hire them. The employer depends on the union to supply workers, and hires workers through the union. Most closed shops are found in the United States. Class consciousness and weak employer opposition to unions made closed-shop agreements less important in Europe.

Closed-shop agreements meet with less resistance in labor markets in which employers hire highly skilled workers on a temporary basis (for example, dock workers and construction works). The union hall becomes the source of skilled workers for employers, and a place for workers to seek employment.

The closed-shop gives unions the power to restrict jobs to union members. For instance, a union can force an employer to fire without cause an employee who has been expelled from the union. Hiring bosses have extracted kickbacks from workers in return for good jobs. Unions under closed-shop agreements sometimes have limited recruitment to friends and relatives of current members, practiced racial discrimination, and monopolized job opportunities. Unions under these agreements can favor some employers over others in the labor market, leading to employer monopolization of product markets.

Closed shops were outlawed in the United States with passage of the Taft-Hartley Act of 1947, but labor markets still function informally as closed shops in markets where both employers and employees find the arrangement beneficial.

Union shops are a different arrangement, and should not be confused with closed shops. Under this arrangement, a worker must join a union after a set probationary period, probably not over 60 days. The employer hires and trains workers, and decides which ones to keep beyond the probationary period. Unlike the closed shop, the employer does not choose new employees from a pool of current union members.

Critics of union shops argue that workers should not be forced to join, or to pay dues to private organizations with goals they may not share; workers should not have to join unions as a condition of employment. On the other side, unions argue that they must provide the same benefits of union representation to nonmembers as to dues-paying members. Therefore, a free rider issue arises in the absence of a union-shop agreement.

The Taft-Hartley Act made it an unfair labor practice for a union to force an employer to terminate an employee under a union-shop or closed-shop agreement. The only condition workers must satisfy is payment of union dues and fees. Worker compliance with other union by-laws or participation in union activities is not necessary to keep a job. The same act also enabled individual states to pass right-to-work laws that outlaw union shops within those states.

See also Taft-Hartley Act of 1947.

References Cartter, Allan M., and F. Ray Marshall. *Labor Economics: Wages, Employment, and Trade Unionism* (1967); Clark, Gordon L. *Unions and Communities Under Siege* (1989).

Cloth Trade

See Colbertism, Depression of Late Sixteenth Century, Fairs, Florentine Industrial Capitalism, Industrial Revolution, Merchant Adventurers, Weavers Act of 1555.

Club of Rome

The Club of Rome is an association of leading business executives, political figures, and scientists, including economists, geneticists, and sociologists, and it sponsors studies and encourages debate on the major problems facing the world, such as pollution, population, and development.

The club was formed in 1968, with its headquarters in Rome. Its founder, Aurelio Peccei, was head of an Italian management consulting firm, and much of the club's financial support comes from Italian businesses.

In the early 1970s, the Club of Rome gained worldwide notoriety in the wake of publication of *The Limits to Growth*. This book reported the results of a study that the Club of Rome sponsored. This study, using computer simulations of mathematical models of the world economy, suggested that population growth, pollution, and depletion of resources would bring economic growth to a standstill early in the next century. In the words of the authors:

If the present growth trends in world population, industrialization, pollution, food production, and resource depletion continue unchanged, the limits to growth on this planet will be reached sometime within the next 100 years. The most probable result will be rather sudden and uncontrollable decline in both population and industrial capacity.

Even under the most generous assumptions of technological advance and birth control, world industrialization depletes resources, induces a pollution crisis, and brings on a drop in food production within a century.

The Club of Rome, which was responsible for the policy commentary at the end of the *Limits to Growth*, succeeded in attracting an unusual amount of publicity to this work. Critics scoffed at the pessimistic outlook, recalling that past prophets of doom had been outwitted by the future, and that the same fate awaited the forecasts of the Club of Rome. Early in the nineteenth century, Thomas Malthus had predicted that rapid population growth would force the mass of the population to a subsistence living standard. Historians of thought suggested that doomsday prophesies tend to arise when food and raw material supplies are tightening, such as was the case in the early 1970s, when crude oil prices quadrupled within a year. Malthus's pessimism appeared at a time of pressure on food supplies.

Notwithstanding these reservations, the Club of Rome succeeded in propagating a thought-provoking vision of the world economy as one system, and encouraged long-range thinking about where the world economy is headed. Even critics of the Club of Rome's views favored efforts to encourage governments to pay less attention to immediate political pressures and more attention to long-range goals and consequences. It is a tribute to the accomplishments of the world capitalist system that thinkers now envision the world economy as one system with needs that require coordinated policies involving all the governments of the world.

See also Global Commons, Rio Declaration on Environment and Development, Stockholm Declaration.

References Cole, H. S. D., et al., eds. *Models of Doom* (1973); Meadows, Donella H., et al. *The Limits to Growth* (1972).

Cockayne Project (England)

From 1614 to 1617, Alderman Cockayne spearheaded a plan, with government aid, to change England from an exporter of unfinished white cloth to an exporter of finished, dyed cloth. The plan threw the English textile industry into a major contraction and failed to make England a player in the market for finished, dyed textiles.

In 1614, unfinished white cloth accounted for the vast majority of London's cloth exports, which were sent to Germany and the Low Countries to be dyed and turned into finished textiles. The next stage in industrialization in England appeared to be the development of a domestic industry devoted to dying and dressing white cloth.

The finished goods sold for about twice the amount of the white cloth, a significant value-added that, in the eyes of England's policymakers, was lost to other countries.

A regulated company, the Merchant Adventurers, by virtue of a royal charter, monopolized the white cloth export trade. Cockayne persuaded the crown to suspend the monopoly charter of the Merchant Adventurers, and to grant a charter to a new regulated company, the King's Merchant Adventurers with monopoly privileges to export dyed and finished textiles. A proclamation in July 1614 forbade the export of white unfinished cloth and established guidelines for the formation of the King's Merchant Adventurers, which was to have a monopoly on fully finished textiles. The English government was gambling that if Germany and the Low Countries were denied access to English white cloth, they would have to buy finished textiles from England.

In the words of one promoter of the project, "they cannot live without our cloth, albeit dyed and dressed in England." The members of the displaced Merchant Adventurers warned the government that English workmanship was below par in the area of finished textiles, and that English output of finished textiles could not handle a substantial increase in demand.

This gamble turned out a miserable failure. Many members of the Merchant Adventurers refused to join the King's Merchant Adventurers, leaving the textile trade undercapitalized. A Dutch edict banning the importation of dyed and finished cloth raised another barrier that the English never overcame. By 1616, from one-third to one-half of the English looms lay idle in some areas. Unemployment spread as the price of white cloth fell, along with customs revenue of white cloth exports. In December 1616, the English government lifted the ban on the export of white cloth and reinstated the Merchant Adventurers.

The Cockayne project taught England a valuable lesson about the international division of labor in a world capitalist economic system. The English specialization in the production of unfinished cloth and the Dutch and German specialization in the finishing process were based upon underlying economic realities independent of government policies. These underlying realities gave England a comparative advantage in the production of unfinished textiles, and the Dutch and German towns a comparative advantage in the final stages of production. England also learned that the rest of the world could live without its cloth, and that its ban on white-cloth exports only acted to expand production of these goods in other countries.

See also Merchant Adventurers.

References Bowden, Peter J. *The Wool Trade in Tudor and Stuart England* (1962); Supple, B. E. *Commercial Crisis and Change in England, 1600–1642* (1959).

Code of Commerce of 1673 (France)
See Colbertism.

Colbert, Jean Baptiste (1619–1683)
See Colbertism.

Colbertism (France)
Referring to Jean Baptiste Colbert (1619–1683), Voltaire wrote,

> If we compare the administration of Colbert with all the preceding ones, posterity will be fond of this man, whose body the frantic populace after his death would have torn to pieces. The French certainly owe to him their industry and their commerce; and consequently that wealth, the sources of which are sometimes diminished in war, but are always opened up again with an abundant flow in peace.

Colbert served as minister of finance under Louis XIV. Although he was a forceful practitioner of mercantilism in the narrow sense of emphasizing exports to accumulate precious metals, he became known for his thorough application of mercantilist policy to the regulation of domestic economic activity. The term "Colbertism" came to denote a system of promoting and regulating manufacturing. The system made use of subsidies and tariff protection to encourage the growth of domestic manufacturing. Detailed regulations of each industry set quality standards, and sometimes controlled prices. He also brought down some of the barriers to internal trade. Colbertism stood for the kind of state regulation that laissez-faire capitalism strove to overcome.

Colbert's policy emphasized manufacturing at the expense of agriculture. In 1672, the government issued an edict regulating the wholesale and retail markets for foodstuffs in Paris. Illegal acts cited by the edict included such things as mixing goods of different grades, increasing prices while a sale was in progress, withdrawing goods after a sale had begun, cornering a market, buying standing grain within 10 leagues of the city, selling grain of poor quality, and buying more than an allotted amount of grain. During shortages, a price ceiling held down the price of grain.

The government appointed a committee that, with Colbert's oversight, drew up the Code of Commerce (1673). The code laid down regulations for bankers, brokers, bookkeepers, and guilds. It regulated the formation of companies and partnerships, instruments of credit, the charging of interest, alienation of property, bankruptcy proceedings, and many other matters. Fraudulent bankruptcy became punishable by death. In 1675, a government edict lowered the ceiling on interest rates to 5 percent, because Colbert felt low rates of interest forced investors to put their money directly into business ventures.

Colbert took a personal interest in the needs of merchants and entrepreneurs. He would help secure capital for new business, help a merchant collect a debt in a foreign country, or help recover cargo from ships wrecked abroad.

The tariff became a weapon for promoting manufacturing. Colbert revised tariffs to reduce levies on imported raw materials, raise levies on the export of raw materials, reduce levies on exports of manufactured goods, and raise levies on the importation of manufactured goods. This tariff legislation helped embitter French relations with England and Holland. Some countries retaliated.

Colbert was the driving spirit behind the formation of the French East India Company. The king gave the articles of the company the force of law. The third article read "The shares of individuals were not to be seized by the king, even if they belonged to the subject of a nation at war with France." The formation of this company inspired one of the first nationwide stock-selling campaigns in modern history.

Colbert's methods of encouraging industries included tax breaks, export subsidies, and loans of capital without interest. His most important method was grants of monopoly in industries previously unknown in France. He felt that high-quality goods with refinement of design and finish would win foreign markets. In the name of quality, he established hundreds of regulations, even prescribing size, color, technical processes, types of dye, and hours and working conditions for individual industries. The government appointed inspectors and sent them into the field to see that firms were complying with industry regulations. Municipal officials were authorized to adjudicate disputes between inspectors and firms. Public shame was meted out for faulty workmanship. Colbert nationalized a tapestry factory in Paris and made it a model of method and management.

Colbert's massive system of state-regulated industry aroused the resentment of traders, merchants, and industry. The system began to stumble from self-strangulation, and the cry for laissez faire rose up nearly 100 years before Adam Smith. When Colbert died, there was no one of his caliber to replace him. France became bogged down with war. Instead of reforming the economy, the government raised taxes, and rapid growth came to an end.

See also Mercantilism.

References Cole, Charles Woolsey. *Colbert and a Century of French Mercantilism* (1964); Sargent, Arthur J. *The Economic Policy of Colbert* (1968); Trout, Andrew. *Jean Baptiste Colbert* (1978).

Colonial Policy

The colonial policy, or system, is the exploitative economic regulations that mother countries imposed upon colonies. Colonial economics sacrificed development to serve the economic needs of the mother country, and fit one of five classifications. First, the mother country often restricted the exportation of colonial goods to any country other than itself. For example, Spain monopolized the precious metal trade with her colonies. Holland monopolized the spice trade with the Dutch colonies. The English Navigation Acts prohibited the exportation of "enumerated goods" to any country but England. The list of enumerated goods included tobacco, sugar, cotton, dyewoods, indigo, rice, molasses, and other naval cargoes.

A second class of restrictions governed colonial imports from countries other than the mother country. By elimination of foreign competition in colonial markets, manufactured goods from the mother country were traded for colonial goods on the most favorable terms. England required that all foreign goods imported by a colony be transported on an English ship, and also had to be rerouted through an English port. The Tea Act of 1773, which inspired the Boston Tea Party, granted the East India Company a monopoly on the colonial tea trade. The Molasses Act of 1733 laid a heavy import duty on French West Indian molasses imported into the colonies.

A third class of restrictions prohibited the export of colonial goods to the mother country via a foreign port. The target of these restrictions was often competing ports in foreign countries. Mother countries wanted to attract the entire trade to their own country.

A fourth class of restrictions required that all trade with the colonies be conducted on ships built and owned by citizens of the mother country. These restrictions were the main thrust of the British and French Navigation Acts, not only giving the domestic shipping industry a monopoly, but also supporting an industry that was essential to national defense.

A fifth class of restrictions prohibited the colonial manufacture of products manufactured by the mother country. England forbade the manufacture of fur hats, woolen goods, and cast-iron goods. America was encouraged to produce pig iron for export to England, whose manufacturers wanted the business of casting it into pots, pans, and other manufactured goods.

In addition to these restrictions, colonies often depended upon some sort of forced labor. Slavery and indentured servitude were common examples.

In 1861, Herman Merivale, an authority on colonies, wrote, "The so-called 'colonial system' of trade...has been abolished piece by piece by this country [England], and is only partially maintained by foreign countries. But the subject, though practically out of date as regards ourselves, is not without its historical and philosophical interest."

The independence of the American colonies, the abolition of slavery in English and French colonies, and the triumph of free trade and laissez faire in England, all marked the end of colonialism to many observers in the mid-nineteenth century. Germany's Bismarck commented in 1868, "On the one hand the advantages that may lie in the trade and industry of the colonies with the home country are based to a large extent upon illusions. For the costs of founding, supporting and keeping the colonies are much bigger than the profit for the mother country, as the example of England and France proves."

Another argument against colonialism is that it is hardly just that the whole nation should pay for the advantage of some commercial and industrial enterprises.

The latter portion of the nineteenth century saw a passion for colonies infect the major Western powers, and the world entered another phase of colonial expansion that lasted until World War I.

The legacy of colonialism and imperialism left bitter feelings toward capitalism in many decolonized countries in the world. These countries laid the blame for their poverty at the feet of the restrictive colonial policies that were enacted in mother countries to favor capitalist interest. Many of the countries that turned to socialism and communism felt victimized by colonial policies.

See also Financial Imperialism, Iron Act of 1750, Mercantilism, New Imperialism.

References Atack, Jeremy, and Passel, Peter. *A New Economic View of American History from Colonial Times to 1940* (1994); Fieldhouse, D. K. *Economics and Empire, 1830–1914* (1973); Merivale, Herman. *Lectures on Colonization and Colonies* (1861).

Columbus, Christopher (1451–1506)

Christopher Columbus's expedition in search of a western sea route to China and Japan led to one of the great developments in the history of capitalism, the discovery of the Americas. The great critic of capitalism, Karl Marx, put it in these words: "Modern industry has established the world market, for which the discovery of America paved the way. This market has given an immense development to commerce, to navigation, to communication by land."

In the chapter on money in *Das Kapital*, Marx even found it useful to quote a letter Columbus wrote from Jamaica: "Gold is a wonderful thing! Whoever possesses it is lord of all he wants. By gold one can even get souls into Paradise."

In the fourteenth and fifteenth centuries, the Venetians conducted a profitable European trade in spices and other East India goods. The political alliances of the Venetians gave them a virtual monopoly on access of these goods through Egypt. Other European countries, wanting to share in these profits, sought to find a sea route to the countries where these spices and other goods originated.

Columbus conceived the most daring project for finding a sea route to China and Japan. Although the best thinkers, theorists, and navigators of the age agreed that sailing west should lead to the East Indies, Columbus had the boldness and resolution to act on this knowledge. He studied the works of scholars, including the ancient geographer Ptolemy, and read Marco Polo's account of travels in eastern Asia. After marshalling the evidence to support his "Enterprise of the Indies," as he called it, Columbus spent a decade persuading the rulers of Portugal and Spain to finance his expedition. Apparently, it was the confidence and certainty that Columbus exuded, rather than his logic, that brought around Spain's joint rulers, Ferdinand and Isabella, to financing his expedition.

Between 1492 and 1504, Columbus made four roundtrips to the Caribbean and Central America. On the third trip, he was returned to Spain in chains, when a new Spanish commissioner at Santo Domingo heard complaints about how Columbus had been administering the island. Columbus remained convinced that he had found the outer fringes of the East Indies. His authority on eastern Asia, Marco Polo, had written of the islands that separated the wealthy countries of Japan and China, where savages lived like beasts without rulers. Columbus continued to search for Japan and the Great Khan that ruled China. Columbus never saw the Pacific Ocean, but he found enough gold to keep Spain interested.

Spain sought to protect its interest by appealing to the Pope for exclusive trading privileges with its new discoveries. The Pope had already granted to Portugal monopoly privileges in the southeastern Atlantic, which embraced the whole western coast of Africa. The Pope divided Atlantic trade between Spain and Por-

Christopher Columbus is "greeted" by the natives of the island of San Salvador in the Bahamas in a 1594 engraving by Theodor de Bry.

tugal. All of the Caribbean and South America belonged to Spain's sphere of control, except Brazil, which fell to Portugal. Other European countries later denied the Pope's right to split the New World between Spain and Portugal.

The influx of gold and silver from the New World caused a price revolution in Europe, raising prices faster than wages, and promoting industrialization. New raw materials fed European industry, and new markets in the New World wanted European goods. Economic prosperity gravitated from the Mediterranean basin to western Europe. As trade grew, the middle-class owners of capital gained in strength relative to the feudal lords, dominating in time the governments of Europe. In America, the break with European traditions allowed capitalist institutions to develop from a clean slate, emphasizing competition rather than special privileges.

See also Price Revolution in Sixteenth- and Seventeenth-Century Europe, Spanish Colonial Empire.

References Davidson, Miles H. *Columbus Then and Now: A Life Reexamined* (1997); Morison, Samuel Eliot. *Admiral of the Ocean Sea: A Life of Christopher Columbus* (1942).

Combination Acts (England)

The English Combination Acts of 1799 and 1800 banned trade unions and trade union activity. At the time of their enactment, employers already had legal recourse against worker combinations. Existing common law forbade restraints on trade, and various acts of Parliament prohibited worker organizations for raising wages and reducing hours of work. Toward the end of the eighteenth century, Parliament frequently heard complaints from employers about worker organizations, and workers sometimes petitioned Parliament for help. Employers complained that the existing legal remedies were time-consuming and ineffective. Parliament passed several combination acts for specific industries before passing the comprehensive Combination Acts of 1799 and 1800, which put speedy justice in the hands of the employers by empowering local magistrates to hold immediate trials.

Development of machinery and the factory system congregated great numbers of workers. These workers owned neither raw material, tools, nor finished products, and had no control over processes of production. They were simply wage earners, manual workers who frequently found themselves in competition with children. Trade unions for skilled workers had a long history by the end of the eighteenth century, and the new class of unskilled workers sought to help themselves by forming combinations. With the French Revolution in progress and fresh in the minds of employers and government leaders, any sort of meeting and organization involving this new class of unskilled and discontented workers inspired fear and suspicion.

The amended Combination Act of 1800 began as follows:

BE IT THEREFORE ENACTED that from and after the passing of the Act all contracts, covenants and agreements whatever, in writing, at any time or times heretofore made or entered into, by or between any journeymen manufacturers or other workmen within this kingdom for obtaining an advance of wages of them or any of them, or any journeymen manufacturers or workmen, or other persons in any manufacture, trade or business, or for lessening or altering their or any of their usual hours of time or working, or for decreasing the quantity of work..., shall be and the same are hereby declared to be illegal, null and void, to all intents and purposes whatsoever.

The act then went on to outlaw various specific activities, such as giving money to support a worker combination, encouraging workers to combine or strike, attending a meeting to form a worker combination, or participating in a strike. The act also empowered justices of the peace to arbitrate disputes between workers and employers.

Some judges took to enforcing the new law with real heartiness. One judge was known as Bloody Black Jack. According to one observer, "No judge took more pains than did this judge on the unfortunate printers, to make it appear that their offense was one of great enormity, to beat down and alarm the really respectable men who had fallen into his clutches, and on whom he inflicted scandalously severe sentences." Sometimes workers were arrested and imprisoned for meeting, even though no dispute with employers was ongoing.

The burden of the acts fell particularly on new industries, such as textiles. In one case, employers ignored wage rates that justices had declared as fair in arbitration. When the workers struck to enforce the justices' ruling, the leaders of the strike found themselves arrested, drawing sentences ranging from four to 18 months for their crime. The acts succeeded in suppressing unions in textiles, mining, and other new industries, but the trade unions of the older skilled, handicraft trades survived the acts.

Francis Place, a master tailor, turned his successful business over to his son in 1818, and devoted himself full time to the repeal of the Combination Acts. His ally in Parliament was Joseph Hume. He arranged for workers to testify before a committee of inquiry in Parliament. Significant public opposition to the acts never arose, but Parliament repealed the Combination Acts in 1824, with little debate. Many employers and justices remained unaware of the repeal and continued to prosecute workers. When word spread of the repeal, workers greeted the news with a wave of strikes. Parliament amended the repeal in 1825, protecting the workers' right to collective bargaining, but imposing severe penalties against intimidation, threats, and obstruction. Strikes were still questionable actions.

The beginning of trade unionism as an organized movement can be practically dated from the repeal of the Combinations Acts. British workers, in winning the right to organize and bargain collectively, blazed a trail that workers in other countries would follow.

See also Grand National Consolidated Trade Union, Le Chapelier Law.

References Carpenter, Kenneth E., ed. *Trade Unions under the Combination Acts: Five Pamphlets, 1799–1823* (1972); Carpenter, Kenneth E., ed. *Repeal of the Combination Act: Five Pamphlets and One Broadside, 1825* (1972); Cole, G. D. H., and A. W. Filson. *British Working Class Movements: Selected Documents, 1789–1875* (1965); Webb, Sidney, and Beatrice Webb. *The History of Trade Unionism* (1911).

Commercial Revolution

The conquest of the sea, culminating in Columbus's discovery of America and Magellan's circumnavigation of the globe, set in motion a commercial revolution that took the nerve center of European trade out of the enclave of the Mediterranean Sea. The Atlantic displaced the Mediterranean area as the stage for international trade. The ocean voyages of the great navigators and explorers between 1420 and 1560 virtually quadrupled the navigable area of the planet.

Improvements in nautical engineering and navigation played a role in the commercial revolution. Bigger and faster ships, driven by more masts, and combining square-rigged and lateen sails, made ocean transportation more profitable. In-depth knowledge of winds and currents helped sailors find routes to distant markets. The compass and the astrolabe increased the confidence of sailors on long stretches beyond the sight of land, and the growth in knowledge put accurate maps and charts in the hands of sailors. Harbors built lighthouses to beacon distant ships home.

Western Europe steadily gained economic supremacy over the Mediterranean states. Reports tell that Lisbon's port at its peak in the 1540s was filled with ships. Antwerp's port in the 1560s saw 500 ships a day. The number of English ships doubled between 1588 and 1618. At mid-seventeenth century, the Dutch could boast of a fleet of ships quadruple in number the combined fleet of Italy, Spain, and Portugal. Many of the important innovations in capitalism would occur with a 500-mile radius of Belgium.

World trade stimulated the demand for European goods, creating a need for mechanical inventions to increase output. Traveling long distances required new sources of power. Long voyages were more risky and required amassing great quantities of capital. Capitalism had to create a new form of business organization, the joint-stock companies, with limited liability for investors, to finance foreign trade in this new environment. Precious metals from the New World poured into Europe to finance new business undertakings.

See also Columbus, Christopher; Da Gama,

Vasco; Portuguese Colonial Empire; Spice Trade.

References Clough, Shepard Bancroft. *European Economic History: The Economic Development of Western Civilization* (1968); Subrahmanyam, Sanya. *The Portuguese Empire in Asia, 1500–1700: A Political and Economic History* (1993).

Commodity Markets

Commodity markets are markets in primary products, mostly agricultural products and industrially used raw materials. Among the goods traded in commodity markets are cocoa, coffee, tea, wheat, rice, maize, cotton, coconut oil, sugar, bananas, natural rubber, copper, tin, iron ore, and petroleum. Advances in transportation during the 19th century acted to centralize commodity trading in major trading centers. The world's largest commodity trading centers are London and New York. In the United States, Chicago ranks second only to New York as a commodity trading center. Other big cities have commodity exchanges that emphasize commodities produced in surrounding areas. Rice is traded on the New Orleans Commodity Exchange, and wheat on the Kansas City Board of Trade.

Commodities may be purchased directly from a supplier, or may be purchased through a commodity exchange, which furnishes the physical facilities and rules for settling contracts. Members of the exchange conduct the trading in pits, or outside of a ring. Orders for the purchase of commodities are executed by openly crying out bids and offers. In spot markets, commodities are traded for immediate delivery, and, in futures markets, commodities are traded for delivery six months or a year later. The bulk of commodity trading in exchanges is for future contracts. Commodity markets are highly competitive, and prices can fluctuate wildly.

Commodity trade accounts for a significant share of international trade, because commodity exports are an important source of income to many of the low-income countries of the world. Brazil depends on coffee exports to the United States and Europe to earn foreign currency needed to pay for imports. Central America exports bananas for similar reasons, and many oil-exporting countries are solely dependent on oil to earn dollars.

Sharp gyrations in commodity prices put a severe burden on the less-developed economies of the world that are often highly dependent upon the export of one or two basic commodities. In the name of stabilizing prices of commodities, international commodity control agreements have been concluded between producing and consuming countries. The International Cocoa Organization and the International Sugar Organization are examples of organizations established by international commodity agreements. These organizations give consumers and producers equal voting rights, supporting the stabilization of prices at levels fair to producers and consumers. Some of these organizations maintain buffer stocks of commodities, and buy and sell commodities to stabilize prices. Other organizations make use of quota systems, which reduce the need for sharp fluctuations in prices to ration commodities. Australia successfully uses a quota scheme to stabilize the price of wool. Petroleum-producing countries stabilized the price of oil by forming an international cartel, the Organization of Petroleum Exporting Countries (OPEC). Consumers have no voice in this cartel, which tries to put quotas on oil production in order to push the price of oil to the level most profitable to the producers.

See also Futures Markets, Royal Exchange.

References Burns, Joseph M. A *Treatise on Markets* (1979); Daniels, John D., and Lee H. Radebaugh. *International Business* (1998); Nappi, Carmine. *Commodity Market and Controls* (1979); Ping, Martin J., ed. McGraw-Hill *Handbook of Commodities and Futures* (1985).

Communist Manifesto

Karl Marx and Frederick Engels wrote the *Manifesto of the Communist Party* to serve as the platform for the Communist League, a German workingmen's association that later became an international organization. It commissioned Marx and Engels to write the *Manifesto* in 1847. The original German version and the French translation were published in 1848, and the English translation became available in 1850. The *Manifesto* sums up the philosophical foundations of the communist movement, critiques bourgeois society, or capitalism, and calls for a program of action.

Chapter 1 begins by saying, "The History of all hitherto existing society is the history of class struggles." According to the *Manifesto*, capitalism has simplified this struggle by splitting society into just two classes, the bourgeoisie and the proletariat. The bourgeoisie, as the owners of capital, are the upper class of capitalism. The proletariat are the unpropertied

Title page of Karl Marx's Manifesto of the Communist Party, *written in 1848*

workers, who have mostly become unskilled appendages to machines. The proletariat, reduced to the same low level, unite to form a class peculiar to capitalism. In the proletariat, capitalism gives birth to the social seeds of its own revolutionary destruction.

Marx and Engels go on say that capitalism under bourgeois leadership can boast of significant accomplishments:

It has been the first to show what man's activity can bring about. It has accomplished wonders far surpassing Egyptian pyramids, Roman aqueducts, and Gothic cathedrals; it has conducted expeditions that put in the shade all former migrations of nations and crusades.... The bourgeois...has created more massive and colossal productive forces than have all preceding generations together. Subjection of nature's forces to man, machinery, application of chemistry to industry and agriculture, steam navigation, railways, electric telegraphs, clearing of whole continents for cultivation, canalization of rivers, whole populations conjured out of the ground—What earlier century had even a presentiment that such productive forces slumbered in the lap of social labor.

Despite its accomplishments, capitalism exhibits characteristics that promise a sudden and convulsive death:

It is enough to mention the commercial crises that by their periodical return put the entire bourgeois society on trial, each time more threateningly.... And how does the bourgeois get over these crises? ...by the enforced destruction of a mass of productive forces...by conquest of new markets, and by more thorough exploitation of the old ones. That is to say, by paving the way for more extensive and more destructive crises.

The proletariat, born of the capitalist process of displacing skilled workers with an army of unskilled machine operators working at subsistence wages, becomes an antagonistic social class. Its mission in history is to strike the death blow against capitalism and organize a new society.

The theory of the communists calls for the abolition of private property. In the first step of the revolution, the proletariat rises to political supremacy. Initially, "despotic inroads on the rights of property" will be necessary. In the early stages of the reorganization of society, Marx and Engels call for:

- Abolition of property in land and application of all rents of land to public purposes.
- A heavy progressive or graduated income tax.
- Abolition of all right of inheritance.
- Confiscation of the property of all emigrants and rebels.
- Centralization of credit in the hands of the state by means of a national bank with state capital and an exclusive monopoly.
- Centralization of the means of communication and transport in the hands of the state.
- Extension of factories and instruments of production owned by the state; the bringing into cultivation of wastelands, and the improvement of the soil generally, in accordance with a common plan.
- Equal obligation of all to work. Establishment of industrial armies, especially for agriculture.
- Combination of agriculture with manufacturing industries; gradual abolition of the distinction between town and country, by a more equable distribution of the population over the country.
- Free education for all children in public schools. Abolition of child labor in its present form. Combination of education with industrial production, etc.

The *Manifesto* eloquently echoes the voice of social protest that rose against nineteenth-century capitalism. Several of the proposals, such as public education, child labor, and income taxes, have been adopted in capitalist countries.

See also Class Struggle, Proletariat, Revolutions of 1848, Welfare State.

References Hamilton, Richard F. *The Bourgeois Epoch: Marx and Engels on Britain, France, and Germany* (1991); Marx, Karl, and Friedrich Engels. *Manifesto of the Communist Party* (1848); Raddatz, Fritz J. *Karl Marx: A Political Biography* (1979).

Company Towns

Company towns describe situations in which employees live in nearby company-owned housing, trade at company-owned stores, and share among themselves a community life that is often geographically isolated from other urban areas. Employer control may extend to virtually every aspect of community life. The salaries of ministers, teachers, and law-enforcement officials are often paid by the companies. If a minister or teacher criticizes company policy, or a law-enforcement official refuses to do the company's bidding, they find themselves without employment. Company towns date back to the eighteenth and nineteenth centuries in England, and have appeared in many countries. In the United States, however, company towns cropped up in greater numbers than anywhere else in the world. The abundance of natural resources in sparsely populated areas in the United States made company towns an ideal instrument of capitalist development. Mining and lumber interests, coal mines, and textile mills are well represented in the roster of employers organized around company towns.

The evaluations of company-supplied housing often brought good reviews from companies, and more skeptical assessments from critics. In 1900, the company housing in the camps of the Colorado Fuel and Iron Corporation was described in a book as "houses and shanties, barren little homes that reared their weather-beaten boards above piles of ashes and tin cans." In 1902, the same company, after renovating the company housing, described its houses as "model workingmen's dwellings, neatly painted, thoroughly sanitary, convenient, and home-like." Often a company town provided a hierarchy of housing. A superintendent, store manager, physicians, and other professionals lived in the best houses, foremen and middle level employees lived in a second tier of houses, and workers lived in the lowest grade of housing. Workers paid rent, usually on the low side, to live in company housing.

As much or more criticism has been lodged against company stores as company housing. Worker resentment against company stores inspired the line, "I owe my soul to the company store." Company stores commanded either a geographical monopoly or the most convenient location. When competitive stores were accessible, workers were forced to trade at company stores as a condition of employment. Critics of company towns have charged company stores with granting credit as a means of reducing workers to states of peonage. Company stores, charging monopoly prices, kept workers in debt, forcing them to hold on to jobs. These stores could deduct directly from worker's wages money owed to the store and could find out workers' wages before granting credit. Some companies issued script instead of money wages, which was accepted only at the company store.

The economics of company towns explains many of the more severe cases of labor exploitation in U.S. history. The labor disputes in Pullman, Illinois, and in the Colorado mining fields are two famous instances of destitute workers turning to violence. In the early company towns, before the advent of modern transportation and communications, workers faced monopolies in every market effecting their living standard. There was only one employer hiring labor, who also enjoyed a monopoly on housing, food, and other necessities. Employees were surrounded by monopolies on all sides. Company towns can hardly be ranked among the most handsome developments of capitalism, but they played a part in mobilizing labor, a resource in short supply in the early United States. Company towns, some of which are pleasant communities, remain a part of the economic landscape in the twentieth century, but now the trend is toward liquidating them.

See also Ludlow Massacre; Pullman Strike of 1894; Slater, Samuel.

References Allen, James B. *The Company Town in the American West* (1966); Lindsey, Almont. *The Pullman Strike* (1964); Tucker, Barbara M. *Samuel Slater and the Origins of the American Textile Industry, 1790–1860* (1984).

Confucianism

Economists and sociologists have tried to understand the role played by Confucian ethics and values in the legacy of economic backwardness of Asian countries, and in the more recent rapid development of Asian capitalism.

Max Weber, in his book *The Protestant Ethic and the Spirit of Capitalism*, advanced the idea that the Protestant religion and values created fertile ground for the development of capitalism. Weber claimed that the Protestant Reformation developed out of a spirit of rationalism in theological issues, and that this spirit of rationalism lies at the heart of the spirit of capitalism. Weber found the spirit of Catholicism less congenial to capitalism, and went on to compare European with non-Western cultures, concluding that the religion and values of India and China were harmful to the development of the capitalist spirit of rationalism. Weber's views have not gone unchallenged, particularly as Asian capitalism has shown its vitality in the post–World War II era.

Confucianism itself is a secular philosophy, and not a religion. Confucian ethics and values, however, are a common denominator in the various religions and sects in East Asia. Aside from the absence of the spirit of rationality, Weber contended that Hinduism and Buddhism were unfavorable to the indigenous development of capitalism, because of their otherworldliness. Confucianism is not otherworldly, but focuses on this world, and this is a necessary ingredient for the emergence of capitalism. According to Weber, the missing element in Confucianism is asceticism, and capitalism requires asceticism (capacity for delayed gratification) without otherworldliness. Confucian philosophy emphasizes self-development, but awards a very low status to commercial activities. The following words of Confucius, taken from *The Mansions of Philosophy* by Will Durant, give a bit of the flavor of the wisdom of Confucius:

> What constitutes the higher man? The cultivation of himself with reverential care.... The higher man seeks all that he wants in himself; the lower man seeks all that he wants from others.... He conforms to the path of the mean.... The higher man is anxious less he should not get the truth; he is not anxious lest poverty should come upon him.... He is distressed by his want of ability, not by other men not knowing him. The thing wherein the higher man cannot be excelled is simply this: his work, which other men cannot see.

Without question, Confucian-trained government officials were responsible for the isolationist policies of East Asian countries, initially resisting modernization along Western lines. The weight of tradition in Confucianism, and the worship of ancestors, acted as a further drag on modernization. Nevertheless, more recent thinking suggests that Confucianism has played a positive role in the development of Asian capitalism, deserving some of the credit for the rapid modernization of East Asia, compared to Third-World countries.

Although the Confucian leadership that the East Asian countries received from their governments hindered the early stages of capitalist development, Confucian values among the population at large may have acted as a positive force. A work force could hardly avoid improvement from the Confucian focus on the affairs of this world, and the belief in self-cultivation, discipline, hard work, frugality, and education. The Confucian commitment to family, political order, duty, and the avoidance of litigation could only help furnish a favorable backdrop for capitalist development. The argument that Confucianism played a positive role in Asian capitalist development assumes that much of the population absorbed and learned to live by Confucian principles, without ever receiving official training in Confucian philosophy.

The thesis that the Protestant ethic contributed significantly to capitalist development appeared at a time when Protestant countries were in the vanguard of capitalist development. Economic success in countries such as Japan, Taiwan, Korea, and Hong Kong has brought a sense of fresh confidence in the values of Confucianism.

See also Asian Capitalism, Puritanism.

References Berber, Peter L. *The Capitalist Revolution* (1986); Kyong-Dong, Kim. "Confucianism and Capitalist Development in East Asia." *Capitalism and Development* (1994).

Conglomerate

A pure conglomerate is a corporation formed from the merger of firms in unrelated industries. There are three basic kinds of mergers. Horizontal mergers are mergers of firms in the same industry, often for the purpose of regulating the market and restricting competition. Vertical mergers are mergers of firms engaged in different stages of production of the same product. An example of a vertical merger can be seen when a manufacturer of finished products merges with a raw material supplier, or with a chain of retail outlets. A third type of merger, the conglomerate merger, unites firms in unrelated or distantly related industries.

The Clayton Act of 1914 and the Celler-Kaufer Act of 1950 banned mergers that lessen competition. The courts invariably held horizontal and vertical mergers involving large firms a violation of these acts. Conglomerate mergers were the least likely to provoke a challenge by the Justice Department.

During the 1950s, the number of conglomerate mergers steadily mounted, and the trend reached its stride in the 1960s. By 1970, 88 percent of all mergers fit the conglomerate model, and were not confined to particular industries. Manufacturing, banking, insurance, retail trade, and service industries participated in the conglomerate movement.

International Telephone and Telegraph (ITT) was one of the first firms to successfully make conglomerate mergers the springboard to the ranks of giant corporations. The Justice Department brought suit against ITT to test the role of antitrust laws in regulating conglomerates. Before World War II, ITT was a modest telephone, telegraph, cable, and wireless utility confined mostly to the Caribbean. In the 1950s, the company expanded into the manufacturing of telecommunication and defense-related equipment. In the 1960s, the company entered upon a path of diversification through conglomerate mergers. It acquired companies in such diverse areas as automobile rental (Avis), hotels and inns (Sheraton), consumer finance and insurance (Aetna Finance), baking (Continental Baking), fire and casualty insurance (Hartford Fire Insurance), residential construction (Levitt and Sons), to name a few. Over 100 domestic and foreign firms were merged with ITT. By 1970, its utility operations, once the prime source of its revenue, generated only 4 percent of ITT's total sales.

In 1969, the Justice Department brought suit against ITT under the existing antitrust laws. ITT had led the conglomerate movement in the number of acquisitions, setting a well-publicized example of rapid growth through conglomerate mergers. The Justice Department saw ITT's accumulated mergers as a trend that would lead to greater concentration of control of manufacturing assets. It challenged three of ITT's acquisitions: the Grinnell Corporation, a manufacturer of sprinklers and power plant piping;

Canteen Corporation, a vending machine manufacturer; and Hartford Fire and Casualty. The government's case cited several instances in which competition was impaired because of reciprocity between different subsidiaries of ITT. The case never reached the Supreme Court. ITT agreed to divest itself of a number of its acquisitions in return for the Justice Department dropping the case.

Currently, conglomerate mergers are approved by the Justice Department before they are finalized. Conglomerate mergers are generally approved, in which case the Justice Department agrees not to bring suit. Conglomerates are not limited to American-based companies, but American antitrust law gave the impetus to the conglomerate movement.

See also Cartels, Corporation, Holding Companies, Mergers.

References Schnitzer, Martin C. *Contemporary Government and Business Relations* (1978); Sobel, Robert. *The Rise and Fall of the Conglomerate Kings* (1984).

Congress of Industrial Organizations

From the mid-Depression years through the end of World War II, the Congress of Industrial Organizations (CIO) aggressively organized industrial workers in the United States. It remained an independent federation of industrial unions until it merged with the American Federation of Labor (AFL) in 1955.

By the 1930s, industrialization in the United States had given rise to a great number of unskilled or semiskilled manufacturing workers who did not fit into any of the skilled trades represented in the AFL. Discontent and anger spread through the industrial workforce during the Depression. Despite federal legislation strengthening the hand of union organization activities, the AFL leadership exhibited neither initiative nor enthusiasm for organizing the industrial workforce.

John L. Lewis, president of the United Mine Workers, stood forcefully on the side favoring the organization of un-

Police attempt to control the crowd during the Republic Steel Strike in Chicago, 1937.

skilled, industrial workers. During a convention the AFL was holding in Atlantic City in 1935, Lewis jumped a row of chairs to punch William L. Hutcheson, who was silencing the vocal opposition of a group of industrial workers. Within a few weeks, Lewis drew together a group of industrial union leaders and supporters, and organized the Committee on Industrial Organization (CIO) as an insurgent organization within the AFL.

A bit of radical propaganda helped arouse the unskilled industrial workers, who were more receptive to extreme measures than craft workers. In the words of Lewis:

> Our self-governing republic is at the crossroads. Only a strong labor movement could resist corporate domination.... [W]hile organized labor is striving to endure its Valley Forge...these mercenaries of our dominant private banking groups...the real

rulers of America, are spending millions on false propaganda...for the purpose of betraying organized labor and democracy.

Toward the end of 1935, the executive council of the AFL met and demanded dissolution of the CIO.

The CIO targeted workers in rubber, auto, steel, and radio. An opportunity for the CIO to prove its mettle came in February 1936, when thousands of Goodyear workers struck in Akron, Ohio. When Lewis addressed a crowd of striking workers in Akron, he drew cheers for attacking not only Goodyear, but also the AFL. By 21 March, the CIO could claim its first victory. The CIO gathered momentum from AFL hostility, industrial workers' enthusiasm, and the rhetoric of Lewis.

The victories that made the CIO a credible movement were its organization of General Motors and U.S. Steel in 1937.

These victories sparked a wave of organizing activity among industrial workers. The AFL's hostility continued as the CIO gained more victories. In the spring of 1938, the AFL expelled the CIO and CIO unions. In November 1938, the CIO held its first convention as a separate organization, and changed its name to the Congress of Industrial Organizations. Lewis served as president until he stepped down in 1940. He quarreled with the leadership of the CIO in the 1940s, and the United Mine Workers, which had financed the CIO in the beginning, pulled out. Nevertheless, the membership of the CIO grew from 1.8 million in 1939 to 3.9 million in 1944. After Lewis, Philip Murray served as president until he died in 1952.

Labor in the United States emerged from World War II with a loss of political clout, as evidenced by the Taft-Hartley Act. Declines in CIO membership contributed to a general stagnation in union membership. In 1955, new leaders in the AFL and the CIO put their differences behind them, and merged the two federations, in the hope that a united front could more effectively stem the tide against labor. The AFL-CIO is the largest and most influential federation in the United States today.

In capitalistic societies, unskilled industrial workers are the most angry and militant members of the work force. In many countries, this group of workers has turned to revolution and socialism to obtain a redress of grievances. Although the CIO had a communist element, it remained committed to the basic principles of unionization espoused by the AFL.

See also Lewis, John L.; Unionization of the Steel Industry.

References Lichtenstein, Nelson. *Labor's War at Home: The CIO in World War II* (1982); Ziegler, Robert H. *The CIO, 1935–1955* (1995).

Constitution of the United States

The Constitution of the United States stands as a seminal document in the struggle for individual liberty and protection of the rights of the individual against the state. Several provisions of the Constitution show the power of capitalist economic interest at the time. According to Charles Beard's pioneering interpretation of the Constitution, the owners of capital instead of land (meaning public securities, shipping and manufacturing interest, and creditors) were adversely affected by the Articles of Confederation. For example, of the 55 members of the Constitutional Convention, no fewer than 40 had some investment in public securities, and 24 members were engaged in lending money for interest. About 11 members owned shipping and manufacturing investments, 24 owned slaves, and 14 owned lands for speculation. The debates of the members of the Constitutional Convention make numerous references to the importance of the protection of property and the need for a property qualification for voters. The Senate and the judiciary were seen as important institutions for protecting the rights of property from the popular vote.

Article 1, section 8 of the Constitution specifically gives Congress the power to (1) levy taxes, duties, and imposts, (2) regulate commerce with foreign govern-

A copy of the original Constitution of the United States

ments, (3) establish uniform laws on the subject of bankruptcies throughout the United States, (4) to coin money, and (5) to provide for calling forth the militia to suppress insurrections and repel invasions. Section 10 of the same article says that no state can coin money, make anything but gold or silver legal tender in payment of debts, or pass any law impairing the obligation of contracts.

These provisions of the Constitution gave the new federal government the power to enact tariffs and regulate foreign shipping, which protected domestic manufacturers and shippers. The power to tax gave the new government the resources to redeem its government securities, which were then circulating at substantially below par. Insurrections, such as Shay's Rebellion in 1786, against farm and home foreclosures, could be suppressed. The ability of states to come to the aid of debtors suffered a severe blow. The items cited in Section 10 above directly struck at the ability of states to relieve debtors through the inflation of excessive paper money, determining the legal tender medium for paying debts, or impairing the obligation of contracts. Power given to the federal government to establish uniform bankruptcy laws also spoke to this issue.

The federal government could protect western land from the threat of Indians.

An important question is whether the vote for ratification of the Constitution took place along the lines of economic interest. The evidence appears to be inconclusive on this issue.

References Alexander, John K. *The Selling of the Constitution: A History of Newspaper Coverage* (1990); Beard, Charles. *An Economic Interpretation of the Constitution*, 1913; Brown, Robert E. *Charles Beard and the Constitution: A Critical Analysis of "An Economic Interpretation of the Constitution."* (1956); *Constitution of the United States* (1789).

Consumer Product Safety Act of 1972 (United States)

The U.S. Congress enacted the Consumer Product Safety Act, after the findings of the National Commission on Product Safety revealed widespread risk associated with consumer goods. The National Commission on Product Safety reported that 20 million people per year sustained home injuries from the use of consumer goods, a number four times higher than injuries from highway accidents. Of this total, 30,000 injuries were fatal, and 110,000 led to permanent disability. The cost to the consumers exceeded $5 billion per year.

The act established the five-member Consumer Product Safety Commission (CPSC), with broad powers to force manufacturers to produce goods engineered for safety. One important function of the CPSC is to gather and disseminate information regarding hazards of consumer goods. The act requires manufacturers to test products for compliance with established safety standards, and to supply distributors with certificates certifying compliance with consumer product safety standards. Knowledge and descriptions of applicable safety criteria must be in the hands of manufacturers. Manufacturers must be able to provide technical data on the performance and safety of products, sometimes supplying this data with the purchase of consumer goods. The CPSC can require labels that inform consumers of the results of product tests.

The act requires manufacturers to come forth with information concerning product defects that may cause hazards or failures, and to meet applicable consumer safety standards. The CPSC can require manufacturers to recall products, refund purchase prices, publicize information about risks, or replace products with equivalent products that meet safety standards.

The list of goods that have been recalled as a result of actions of the CPSC includes football helmets, plastic-coated soft drink bottles, disposable lighters, toys, carpets, children's pajamas, Christmas tree lights, and televisions. The CPSC has issued safety standards for a number of goods, including baby cribs, bicycles, power lawn mowers, and matchbooks.

The work of the CPSC has drawn a fair amount of ridicule for some of its decisions. One wit quipped that hammers will soon be sold with warning labels cautioning buyers not to put their thumb under the head of the hammer when in use. The president of a vacuum cleaner company said that, in the past, "we wondered who in their right mind would try to pick up puddles of water with a vacuum cleaner. Now we caution, 'Don't pick up puddles of water with vacuum cleaner.'"

Government-mandated standards for manufactured products are not new. During the mercantilist era, governments established detailed standards for manufactured products, striving to build reputations of high quality for home products in foreign export markets. The principle concern of governments then was promotion of exports as a means of bringing in precious metals. The rise of laissez-faire capitalism swept away the mercantilist regulations, but the concern for protection of consumers has brought a new era in government regulation of manufactured consumer goods. As consumer goods became more complicated, markets could not always count on informed consumers weeding out unsafe products, as should happen in laissez-faire capitalism. Therefore, the government has assumed the task of collecting the vast amount of information needed to rid markets of unsafe consumer goods.

See also Food and Drug Act of 1906.

References Schnitzer, Martin C. *Contemporary Government and Business Relations* (1978); Starling, Grover. *The Changing Environment of Business: A Managerial Approach* (1984).

Continental System

The Continental System is the name given to the all-encompassing economic warfare that Napoleon waged against England from 1806 until his fall in 1815.

Napoleon launched the Continental System with the Berlin Decree of 21 November 1806, which established a blockade of the British Isles. British subjects faced imprisonment, with seizure of their merchandise, if they were found in a country occupied by French or allied troops. The decree further declared French and Allied ports were closed to ships arriving from Great Britain or her colonies. Ships using false documents to gain admittance into French and allied ports were subject to confiscation, along with the ship's cargo. The Decree of Milan of 17 December 1807 extended the Continental System by subjecting to seizure and confiscation any ship sailing from a British port or a port in a country occupied by British troops. Napoleon issued the Decree of Milan in response to British orders in council expanding the rights of neutral ships to trade with Britain, and forcing all ships carrying trade with continental Europe to stop first in a British port. The British also allowed goods to come into Britain duty-free, if the goods were to be held in warehouses and exported later. In 1810, Napoleon, unable to stop smuggling of banned goods, levied a tariff averaging 50 percent on all imported goods. To suppress smuggling, searches were conducted for British goods. In October 1810, bonfires of British goods lighted the skies in Bayonne, Nantes, Antwerp, Zurich, Civita Vecchia, Ratisbon, Leipzig, Konigsberg, and Memel.

The Continental System tried to shut Britain out of trade with continental Europe. Prussia, Holland, Spain, Italian cities, and Russia were expected to enforce the continental blockade. Holland was annexed to France after balking at strict enforcement of the blockade. Napoleon regarded the capitalist nation of Britain as a nation of shopkeepers, whose power would collapse under the pressure of the blockade. The Napoleonic Wars in Spain, and, later, in Russia, were efforts to force these governments to enforce the Continental System.

The strain on the British economy made itself evident in food riots, unemployment, wage reductions, and bankruptcies. Britain survived this ordeal for a variety of reasons. Control of the seas kept open the flow of imports, and the flow of exports to the colonies. Continental imports from Britain were strictly forbidden, but continental exports to Britain faced fewer restrictions. A war of liberation in Spain allowed Britain to ally itself with Spain, and to gain access to trade with Spanish colonies. British industry, freshly invigorated with the steam engine and other inventions, weathered the blockade, because of access to raw materials, colonial trade, and widespread smuggling.

The failure of the Continental System stands as a reminder that powerful underlying economic realities will assert themselves in spite of government decrees and regulations, and that governments are often unaware of the force and strength of these realities. Part of the appeal of laissez-faire capitalism is that governments find it virtually impossible to permanently suppress the fundamentals of economic markets. Related to the Continental System was the concept of the economic unification of Europe, which reached fruition in the European Economic Community organized in the post-War World II era.

See also French Revolution and Napoleon.

References Ellis, Geoffrey James. *Napoleon's Continental Blockade: The Case of Alsace* (1981); Rose, J. Holland. "The Continental System, 1809–1814." *The Cambridge Modern History*, Vol. 9 (1934); Schroeder, Paul W. *The Transformation of European Politics, 1763–1848* (1994).

Corn Laws (England)

The Corn Law of 1670 set up an inverse scale for taxing the importation of grain. When domestic grain prices dropped below a legal threshold, the duty on imported grain increased. The government established three tiers of legal thresholds. The minimum duty became effective when the price rose above the highest legal threshold. In 1689, the government incorporated an export subsidy into this scheme for regulating the domestic supply and price of grain. When the domestic price of grain dropped below a legal threshold, the government subsidized the export of grain.

This law held out the promise of smoothing out fluctuations in domestic grain prices. When the price of grain was low, the government levied extra taxes on the importation of grain into an already abundantly supplied market. In addition, government-subsidized exports of grain helped drain off excess supplies when prices were low. When prices were high, the government removed the export subsidy, and lowered the import duty. These actions helped increase domestic supply, and to lower prices, protecting consumers from high prices, and farmers from low prices.

The corn law enjoyed a reasonable level of acceptance until about 1750, when agricultural productivity fell behind population growth. As grain supplies tightened, export subsidies were seldom paid, and, on occasion, grain flowed in duty free.

In 1773, the government changed the thresholds, and banned exports when prices exceeded a certain level. At that time, the English government allowed a practice similar to the modern foreign trade zones in the United States. To accumulate surplus stocks of grain for future shortages, the government allowed grain to be landed duty-free. The grain could later be reexported without payment of an import duty. The duty was only paid when the grain was sold domestically.

In the latter part of the 1700s, the price of grain often rose to the level at which exports were banned. The corn law fell out of favor of the landed interest, who argued that the legal threshold levels should be adjusted to encourage more domestic production.

In 1815, the government adopted a revised corn law that favored the landed interest. The new corn law banned grain imports when the price dropped below a threshold price. Above the threshold price, grain was imported duty-free. Critics saw the new corn law as a means of preserving the high prices and rents of the Napoleonic Wars.

The corn laws represented the kind of market regulation that was out of step with the tide of laissez-faire capitalism sweeping the economic landscape in the nineteenth century. The industrial sector resented the corn laws as protectionist legislation for agriculture. They argued it made more sense to protect domestic manufacturers from foreign competition.

In 1838, the Anti-Corn Law League formed as a Manchester group devoted to the repeal of the corn laws. The organization grew to a nationwide organization, and, under the leadership of Richard Cobden and John Bright, became a driving force for the repeal of the corn laws.

Parliament abolished the corn laws in 1846, beginning an era of free trade in England's commercial policy. England remained committed to a policy of free trade until the Great Depression of the 1930s.

England was ahead of its time in its commitment to free trade. Since World War II, the major trading partners of the capitalist world have regularly held talks to lower trade barriers and move the world closer to free trade.

See also Anglo-French Commercial Treaty of 1860, Import Duties Act of 1932.

References Barnes, Donald G. *A History of the English Corn Laws* (1961); Daunton, Martin. *Progress and Poverty: An Economic and Social History of Britain, 1700–1850* (1995); Prentice, Archibald. *History of the Anti–Corn Law League* (1968).

Corporation

The corporation is the predominant form of business organization for large businesses. In dollar values, corporations account for about 80 percent of all business conducted in the United States. Corporations are owned by stockholders, who elect a board of directors to oversee the management of the corporation. The concept of limited liability in corporations means that individual stockholders are not directly responsible for the debts of the corporation. The maximum loss a stockholder can sustain is the purchase value of his stock.

The legal concept of the corporation in English law grew out of recognition of towns and cities, and the rights and privileges associated with residence. Thus, a community became a legal entity separate from its individual residents. Precedent for the English practice is found in Roman law and canon law, which suggests that monasteries and churches may have been the earliest corporations. The charters granted to communities assumed that these communities, as separate legal entities, would outlast the current residents, and even last indefinitely. The concept of limited liability began with the protection afforded the members of the governing boards of these communities.

The corporate form of business organization made its appearance on a significant scale in sixteenth-century England. The mercantile trading companies, such as the East India Company, needed to raise great sums of capital for risky ventures. The corporate form of business organization could best serve this need, because of the protection of limited liability. This early corporate form was called a joint stock company. The early joint-stock companies were established by either a royal charter or an act of Parliament. Adam Smith distinguished joint-stock companies from other partnerships, in the *Inquiry into the Nature and Causes of the Wealth of Nations*, in the following way:

[I]n a private copartnery, ...each member, however, may upon proper warning withdraw from the copartner, and demand payment from them of his share of the common stock. In a joint-stock company, on the contrary, no member can demand payment of his share from the company; but each member can, without their consent, transfer his share to another person, and thereby introduce a new member. The value of a share in a joint stock is always the price it will bring in the market.

Royal charters and acts of Parliament that granted joint-stock charters were expensive and required political connections. The Bubble Act of 1720 specifically outlawed companies organized as corporations without government-approved charters. Nevertheless, companies found ways to function as corporations in violation of the Bubble Act.

The Napoleonic Code of Commerce included a general provision for the organization of corporations. This was the first general law that provided for the creation of a corporation without requiring a special act of government. This code provided for two types of corporations, one with limited liability and one without. The principles of company law in this code spread to Belgium, Holland, Switzerland, Italy, Spain, Prussia, and the Hanse cities. Growth of the corporate form in France started slowly because it was hampered by strict government regulations.

After the American Revolution, state legislatures were eager to grant special charters of incorporation to encourage investment. Bribery sometimes paved the way for passage of these charters, and this drew the protest of reformers, who considered the charters special privileges favoring people with connections. In 1837, Connecticut enacted a statute that standardized the process for establishing a corporation, sidestepping the requirement of a legislative act. The formation of a corporation simply required that certain information about the corporation be filed with a state official. Other states followed the example of Connecticut. By the turn of the century, the United States was ahead of European countries in the development of the corporation.

In 1844, England repealed the Bubble Act, although the principle of limited liability was only accepted in 1855. The creation of a corporation became a matter of registering with the government. In 1867, France relaxed its strict regulation of corporations. After 1885, the corporate form of business organization grew rapidly in England and France.

Corporations enjoy important advantages over other forms of business organizations. The life of the corporation stands independent of the life of an owner or group of owners, and limited liability puts a limit on the amount of risk the owners (stockholders) must bear.

These characteristics enabled corporations to amass capital far beyond the resources of single proprietorships and partnerships, and to become vast business enterprises. The chief executive officers of large corporations were seen as modern-day counterparts of the feudal barons and lords of medieval times, and corporations as feudal kingdoms that needed the taming influence of strong central governments. In 1967, Anthony Jay, in a well-publicized book, *Management and Machiavelli*, took Machiavelli's description of the politics among the city-states, papacy, and feudal kingdoms of Renaissance Italy, and applied the same analysis to account for the behavior of corporate management.

In the eyes of some observers, bigness itself wears a sinister aspect as an issue in public policy. A chief executive officer of General Motors, the United States' largest corporation, once stated before a congressional committee that "what is good for General Motors is good for the country." Only about 20 nations in the world produce an annual output that exceeds General Motors' annual sales. These giant corporations exert vast political and cultural influence in society. Through planned obsolescence and advertising, they manage the demand for products as well as supply, and the managerial and technical elite that control these corporations do not always seek the best interest of stockholders. At least, that is what critics say. The potential for conflict between public and private interest led to suggestions that corporations should be socially responsible and practice good corporate citizenship, including community involvement and environmental responsibility. Business schools have added curriculum on business ethics to help future managers cope with the numerous ethical issues raised by the modern corporation.

The justification for bigness must rest with the superior efficiency of large-scale production over small-scale production, allowing the bigger companies to undercut and drive out or swallow smaller companies. Some critics claim that modern corporations have exceeded the optimal size for efficiency, and have become too big for effective management, and for flexibility in the face of a changing environment. A former General Motors president put the problem in these words, referring to GM's Chevrolet division: "Chevrolet is such a big monster that you twist its tail and nothing happens at the other end for months. It is so gigantic that there isn't any way to really run it. You just sort of try to keep track of it."

In the past two decades, the trend toward larger corporations might have run its course. In 1975, Fortune 500 and Forbes 400 companies employed about 19 percent of all U.S. employees. By the mid-1990s, this number had fallen to 9 percent. Once seemingly invincible giant corporations, such as International Business Machines, found themselves besieged by a new generation of smaller corporations inspired by entrepreneurial leadership, rather than administrative managers, and adaptable to rapidly changing technologies.

The corporation is a uniquely capitalist institution. Its purpose is to raise vast sums of capital to finance large-scale and risky enterprises. The vast size of modern corporations may have forced governments to become larger, to remain a regulating force in society, a trend not everyone thinks is in keeping with the spirit of capitalism. Nevertheless, the place of the modern corporation in contemporary capitalism remains undisputed. As a form of business organization it has no close rivals.

See also Bubble Act of 1720, Conglomerates, East India Company, Joint-Stock Companies, Multinational Corporations.

References Galbraith, John Kenneth. *Economics and the Public Purpose* (1973); Jay, Anthony. *Management and Machiavelli* (1967); McConnell, Campbell R., and Stanley L. Brue. *Economics* (1993); Novak, Michael. *The Future of the Corporation* (1996); Nussbaum, Frederick L. A *History of the Economic Institutions of Modern Europe* (1935); Roy, William G. *Socializing Capital: The Rise of the Large Industrial Corporation in America* (1996).

Credit

Credit allows households and businesses to buy things in the present, and to pay for them in the future. For every creditor there is a debtor, the borrower. A creditor gives up the option to buy present goods in favor of an option to buy future goods. A debtor gives up an option on future goods in favor for present goods.

To appreciate the value of credit in a capitalist economy, assume an imaginary family living in primitive conditions on the edge of a river. This family has to spend all of its time fishing with hooks to catch enough fish to survive. Further assume that this family has the technological sophistication to build a net, but it cannot spare the time without a member of the family starving. The family is held in primitive conditions, not by a lack of knowledge or industry, but by its inability to reduce its full-time fishing effort without facing starvation. If this family could strike a bargain with a neighboring family, who has spare fish, because they have no children left at home, it could substantially improve its living condition. A family who could spare one fish a day could loan fish to the family that needs it to reduce its daily fishing effort in order to build a net. After the net was finished, the borrowing family could easily repay the lending family the one fish a day for however many days it took to build the net, and throw in an extra fish per day as interest. If the borrowing family received one fish a day for a year on credit, it could repay its loan by giving the lending family two fish a day for a year, perhaps helping the lending family during its retirement years.

At times, there appears to be a secret

war between debtors and creditors in capitalist societies. A wave of unanticipated inflation, sponsored by government, is one way that debtors can cheat creditors, forcing them to accept money in repayment for loans that had lost their purchasing power. Bankruptcy laws can also tip the balance in favor of debtors or creditors.

Credit is one of those important conveniences of free enterprise that is necessary for households and business to act on their own initiative. Financial institutions that supply credit are one of the most essential elements of any plan to promote economic development and industrialization in capitalist societies. In the United States, land banks and the Small Business Administration are examples of institutions and programs established by the government to increase the availability of funds to sectors of the economy starved for credit.

See also Bankruptcy Act of 1705, Bankruptcy Act of 1978, Bankruptcy Acts of 1543–1624, Imprisonment of Debtors.

References Brigham, Eugene F. *Fundamentals of Financial Management* (1989); Spiro, George W. *The Legal Environment of Business* (1993).

Da Gama, Vasco (1460–1524)

Vasco Da Gama was a Portuguese navigator who explored the sea route from western Europe to India. Like Columbus, Da Gama conducted his expeditions at the end of the fifteenth century, but during the sixteenth century the economic ramifications of Da Gama's discoveries were much more immediate and far-reaching. While the Spanish mariners floundered in the Caribbean looking for the East Indies, Portugal opened trade with the real India.

Unlike Columbus, Da Gama benefited from the work of a long list of predecessors. For over a century, Portuguese navigators had been pushing farther south, down the western coast of Africa. In 1420, Henry the Navigator had established his nautical college at Sagres, on the southwestern tip of Portugal. At this college, Jewish and Moslem astronomers, geographers, and map makers collected and expanded the best nautical knowledge and thinking of the time. The college sent Portuguese mariners on expeditions into uncharted waters, mostly down the coast of Africa. In 1445, the Portuguese reached Cape Verde, and, in 1487, the Portuguese mariner Bartolomeu Dias rounded the southern tip of Africa, which Dias named the Cape of Storms, but which King John of Portugal renamed the Cape of Good Hope, because of the possibilities it opened for the future.

Portugal's eagerness for a sea route to India stemmed from a desire to break the monopoly of Venice on the spice and precious-stone trade with India and the East Indies. An all-sea route also freed trade in Indian spices and precious stones from heavy tolls that strangled overland trade. To complement its nautical explorations, Portugal had sent an overland emissary to India via Arabia to learn of the sea routes that carried trade from India to Africa. This emissary had reached the city of Calicut on the southwest coast of India, and found Arabian and Persian ships loaded with spices headed for the eastern coast of Africa.

Da Gama began his first voyage to India on 8 July 1497. Rather than hugging the western coast of Africa, he boldly took a southwestern heading, avoiding coastal squalls, and intercepting the westerlies that carried him to the Cape of Good Hope. His route remains the standard route for sailing vessels leaving western Europe for the Cape of Good Hope. Sailing around the Cape of Good Hope, Da Gama continued up the eastern coast

Vasco da Gama, the explorer who discovered the sea route to India, is shown dressed in traditional clothing in an undated drawing.

of Africa. At Mozambique, he found a Moslem city with a busy port of Arabian traders, but the local sultan was uninterested in trading. After recruiting a local pilot, he pressed ahead up the coast of Africa. Da Gama met with suspicion and hostility at Mombasa, but at Malindi he received a friendly reception. There, Da Gama had the good fortune to bring aboard one of the most learned and experienced pilots of the age. From Malinda, Da Gama sailed across the India Ocean to the southwestern coast of India, finally dropping anchor at Calicut, the city that the overland Portuguese emissary had reached.

At Calicut, Da Gama failed to strike a trading treaty, because his ships were loaded with wares not in demand in India. From Calicut, he returned to Portugal, sailing into the port of Lisbon in September 1499. He made two other voyages to India, the last as Portuguese viceroy, and he died in India in 1524.

By opening the sea route from western Europe to the East, Da Gama set the stage for the European conquest of the East Indies. Portugal destroyed Moslem sea power in the Indian Ocean, taking control of European trade with the East. Portuguese merchants established themselves as far east as the Moluccas, also known as the Spice Islands. Portugal became the first modern imperial power in Europe, and the quest for colonies became a trademark of European capitalism until the twentieth century.

See also Commercial Revolution, Spice Trade.

References Hart, Henry H. *Sea Road to the Indies* (1950); Subrahmanyam, Sanjay. *The Career and Legend of Vasco Da Gama* (1997).

Danbury Hatters Case (United States)

In the *Danbury Hatters* case, the U.S. Supreme Court ruled that boycotts violated provisions of the Sherman Antitrust Act, and that union boycotts to pressure employers to settle labor disputes were lawful reasons for employers to bring suits against unions. The Sherman Act provided for triple damages.

In 1897, the Brotherhood of United Hatters of America launched a nationwide campaign to organize all hatters into closed shops. In 1903, the struggle for the closed shop had succeeded in 187 firms, but 12 firms were holding out. The main weapon of the union in this struggle was the boycott. One company brought to terms with the use of the boycott was Berg and Company of Orange, New Jersey. After the union imposed its boycott, this firm's sales of hats decreased from 2,400 dozen to 500 dozen per week.

E. Lowe and Company, of Danbury, Connecticut, rebuffed the union's demand for a closed shop, and, on 25 July 1902, their workers walked out. The union paid a shipping clerk to reveal the names of the company's customers, and, to learn the destination of the hats, he rode the wagons, and watched the railroad station. He sent customers' names to the union, who sent representatives, or wrote letters, to firms buying Lowe's hats, urging them not to carry Lowe's hats. The union also placed advertisements of the boycott in trade and labor journals. The company's profits plummeted from a net profit of $27,000 in 1901 to a net loss of $17,000 in 1902. The year 1903 brought the company another loss of $15,000.

On 31 August 1903, Lowe and Company brought suit against the union and individual union members, under provisions of the Sherman Act. The company asked for triple damages on an amount of $84,000. The legal system took its time with the case. In 1907, Judge James P. Platt, of the circuit court in Hartford, asked the Supreme Court for a ruling to determine if the union's boycott met the criteria of a restraint on trade under the Sherman Act. Chief Justice Fuller ruled that the Sherman Act was applicable to the case.

The case went to trial on 13 October 1909. Judge Platt instructed the jury to rule against the union, and only to concern itself with the amount of the damage award. The jury held the union responsible for $74,000 in damages. Given triple damages, and adding other costs, the total judgment against the union rose to over $230,000.

The Court of Appeals of the Second Judicial District overturned this finding, arguing that Judge Platt had overstepped his authority when he instructed the jury to return a guilty verdict. The court of appeals also disagreed with the lower court's finding that every single member of the union was liable for decisions made by the leaders of the union. Lowe and Company appealed to the Supreme Court, which refused to hear the case.

The case went to trial again on 4 August 1912. Again a jury returned a guilty verdict, and assessed damages of $80,000 and costs. The total judgment against the union exceeded $240,000. In 1917, the Supreme Court heard the case, and upheld the judgment against the union. The Court also upheld the right of the company to hold individual union members liable.

The *Danbury Hatters* case was a major defeat of the unions. It meant workers put themselves at risk of a lawsuit by joining a union. Union leaders were also liable for civil damages sustained by companies targeted by union boycotts. The AFL convention of 1915 raised funds to pay for the award against the members of the Brotherhood of United Hatters of America. Unions also opened a political lobbying effort to exempt unions from the antitrust laws. The Clayton Act of 1914 tried to exempt labor, but was only partially effective. With the New Deal and the change in public perceptions of unions, labor finally won its exemption from the antitrust laws.

See also Boycotts, Clayton Act of 1914.

References Brooks, Thomas R. *Toil and Trouble: A History of American Labor* (1971); Laidler, Harry W. *Boycotts and the Labor Struggle: Economics and Legal Aspects* (1913).

Declaration of the Rights of Man and of the Citizen (France)

See French Revolution and Napoleon

Depository Institutions Deregulation and Monetary Control Act of 1980 (United States)

The Depository Institutions Deregulation Monetary Control Act of 1980 (DIDMCA) was the most important piece of banking legislation in the United States since the 1930s, but, in contrast, the DIDMCA signaled a marked shift in government banking policy toward a deregulated banking system.

One important provision of the DIDMCA authorized all depository institutions to offer Negotiated Order of Withdrawal (NOW) accounts. Before the DIDMCA, only savings and loans, credit unions, and other thrift institutions offered NOW accounts. These accounts are interest bearing savings accounts on which depositors write checks. The banking legislation of the 1930s forbade the payment of interest on checking accounts. In the 1970s, thrift institutions were faced with an outflow of funds, and, to make savings accounts at thrift institutions more attractive, banking regulators granted permission to let thrift depositors write checks on savings accounts that paid interest. In practical terms, the DIDMCA enabled all depository institutions, including commercial banks, to pay interest on checking accounts.

A feature related to the authorization of NOW accounts had to do with automatic transfer accounts. These accounts let commercial banks switch idle checking-account funds into savings accounts in which interest accrued. By the mid-1970s, technology had made switching an inexpensive procedure, but the courts ruled that the automatic transfer accounts violated the law against the payment of interest on checking accounts. The DIDMCA made automatic transfer accounts legal, further lifting restrictions on interest-bearing checking accounts.

The DIDMCA called for the formation of the Depository Institutions Deregulation Committee, composed of the heads of the Treasury Department, the Federal Reserve, Federal Depository Insurance

Corporation, and the Federal Home Loan Bank Board, along with the National Credit Union administrator. The comptroller of the currency served as a nonvoting member. The charge of this committee lay in overseeing the removal of interest rate ceilings on all deposits except business deposits at commercial banks. The DIDMCA also removed interest-bearing deposits from restrictions of state usury laws.

The DIDMCA freed from state usury ceilings residential mortgages and agricultural and business loans in excess of $25,000. It extended partial exemption to other loans made by state-chartered banks, and by insured savings and loans (S&Ls) and credit unions. States had to take action by 1 April 1983 to reinstate the applicability of state interest-rate ceilings on these loans.

Under the DIDMCA, federally chartered S&Ls received permission to make consumer loans, and to invest in commercial paper and corporate debt securities. Up to 20 percent of an S&L's assets could be committed to these uses. Credit cards and trust and fiduciary services also joined the range of services offered by S&Ls under the DIDMCA. S&Ls now competed with commercial banks in a wider range of areas.

Mutual savings banks with federal charters could also enter the market for business loans under the DIDMCA. Their investment in these loans was limited to 5 percent of their assets, and these loans could involve checking privileges with the business borrowers.

Before the DIDMCA, the Federal Reserve set reserve requirements of federally chartered commercial banks. Raising reserve requirements protected depositors (or the FDIC) by making bank assets more liquid and less risky. It also made them less profitable. State laws invariably demanded lower reserve requirements, as a percentage, for state-chartered banks. The DIDMCA put all federally insured depository institutions under the reserve requirement imposed by the Federal Reserve. This change increased the power of reserve requirements as a tool of monetary regulation, and leveled the playing field between federally chartered institutions and state-chartered institutions.

In capitalistic systems, competition insures efficiency, but is also associated with higher rates of business failures. The consumer is the clear beneficiary of competition in most industries, but, when a bank fails, the bank's customers suffer as much as the bank's owners. In the Depression of the 1930s, the government enacted laws to reduce competition between banks to stem the tide of bank failures. With the passage of the DIDMCA, Congress took an important step toward restoring competition to the banking industry.

See also Glass-Steagall Banking Act of 1933.

References Baye, Michael R., and Dennis W. Jansen. *Money, Banking, and Financial Markets: An Economics Approach* (1995); White, Lawrence J. "The Partial Deregulation of Banks and other Depository Institutions." *Regulatory Reform: What Actually Happened?* (1986).

Depression of the Late Eighteenth Century

Beginning in the 1760s, Europe struggled with economic depression for three decades. T. S. Ashton labels the years 1762, 1765–1769, 1773–1774, 1778–1781, 1784, and 1788 as depression years for the English economy. Recoveries reached mild peaks that led to financial crises in 1763, 1772–1773, 1778, 1783–1784, and 1788. The crisis-ridden depression struck France and her colonies a decade later, and otherwise extended to European colonies in the Caribbean, and to North America.

Economists often point the finger of blame for depressions to monetary disturbances. According to the monetary explanation, the substantial increase in gold production from Brazilian mines had brought the seventeenth-century depression to an end. From the beginning of the eighteenth century, Brazilian gold production climbed steadily at a rate of 1,000 kilograms annually, reaching a maximum of 15,000 kilograms per year between

1740 and 1760. Exhaustion of gold mines caused a sudden fall in gold production to 10,000 kilograms per year between 1760 and 1780. From 1780 until the end of the century, gold production averaged 5,000 kilograms per year. From 2.5 million British pounds in 1760, Brazilian exports of gold fell to less than 1 million in 1780. Worldwide production of gold revealed a similar pattern, dropping from 781,000 ounces per year between 1741 and 1760, to an annual average of 665,000 ounces per year from 1761 to 1780. Worldwide gold production continued to decline into the nineteenth century.

After 1775, more than a decade after gold production dropped off, silver production began to compensate for the loss in gold production. World silver production, averaging 14 million ounces per year between 1721 and 1740, climbed to 28 million ounces per year between 1781 and 1810. Adam Smith, in the *Wealth of Nations*, cited the growth of paper money, and the use of short-term credit to finance long-term projects, reflecting the pressure to find money substitutes.

While sputtering from one depression to another, the world economy in the late eighteenth century stood on the threshold of an era of unparalleled capitalist development. Much of the groundwork for the explosive modernization in the nineteenth century occurred just when the European economy seemed unable to shake off the downdraft of depression. The culture of the era was shaped by the Enlightenment, whose unbounded faith in reason envisioned the perfectibility of man. Economically, the steam engine, and other inventions that mechanized the textile industry, seemed to hold out the promise of unending progress. Captain Cook and others explored the Pacific, preparing the way for colonization of New Zealand, Australian, and the south sea islands. Politically, the American Revolution and the French Revolution freed the economies of those countries from the shackles of mercantilism and feudalism. Adam Smith published the *Wealth of Nations* in 1776, laying the intellectual foundations for the laissez-faire capitalism that would flower in the nineteenth century.

The Russian economist Kondratieff argued that major inventions tend to cluster in recessions, and are applied during the following recoveries. Although Kondratieff's theory is speculative, the late eighteenth century shows that the depression phase of capitalist economic cycles often involve creative preparations for the next level of capitalist development. The last quarter of the eighteenth century stands forth as one of the most remarkable eras in human history.

See also Constitution of the United States, French Revolution and Napoleon, Kondratieff Waves, Steam Engine.

References Ashton, T. S. *Economic Fluctuations in England, 1700–1800* (1959); Frank, Andre Gunder. *World Accumulation, 1492–1789* (1978).

Depression of the 1890s

Before the Great Depression of the 1930s eclipsed its predecessors, economic historians regarded the depression of the late nineteenth century as the great depression. Depression struck hard in the United States in the 1890s, but Europe had experienced only incomplete recoveries since the financial crisis of 1873. Prices trended downward from 1873 until 1896. In Britain, the price of wheat in 1894 stood at only 35 percent of its 1867 level. A book entitled *Made in Germany*, published in England in 1896, sounds a familiar refrain in times of depression:

> Take observations in our own surroundings.... You will find that the material of some of your own clothes was probably woven in Germany. Still more probable is it that some of your wife's garments are German importations: while it is practically beyond a doubt that the magnificent mantles and jackets wherein her maids array themselves on their Sundays out are German-made and German-sold, for only so could they be done.... The toys and the dolls and the fairy books....

Of major Western countries, only Britain resisted the temptation to enact stiffer trade barriers to combat economic depression during the latter portion of the nineteenth century.

The period from 1873 to 1896 was not one of continuous economic deterioration. The British economy entered a slump in 1873 that lasted until 1879. It then took a turn for the better until 1881, before sinking into depression again from 1882 until 1886. It sputtered back to life for four years, before succumbing to the final phase of depression from 1890 to 1896. After 1896, prices turned upward and business confidence returned.

The United States shared in the general trend toward falling prices through 1897. In Britain and Germany, the last phase of contraction lasted from 1890 to 1895: In the United States, it lasted from 1893 to 1897. A severe slump from 1873 to 1879 made itself felt in the United States, but a downturn in 1882 was of brief duration. After 1886, manufacturing output remained close to full capacity until 1893, when the United States entered the depression of the 1890s.

The first warning of trouble in the United States came on 20 February 1893, when the Philadelphia and Reading Railway Company went into bankruptcy. The stock market stayed afloat until May, when it faltered in what became known as the Panic of 1893. Bank failures and suspensions in 1893 beat all previous records. After bankruptcy overtook the Erie Railroad on 26 July, economic contraction routed the railroad industry. By mid-1894, more than one-fourth of the railroad mileage and capitalization in the United States was in receivership. The downward price spiral bottomed out in 1896, but the cost of living in 1900 stood below its level in 1890. The U.S. economy only returned to full capacity after 1900.

In the United States, no major reformation of the economic system followed the depression of the 1890s, as followed the Great Depression of the 1930s. The depression of the 1890s occurred within a framework of industrialization; the economy continued to grow despite falling prices and financial collapse. The depression did sow seeds of doubt about the wisdom of laissez-faire capitalism, and Germany introduced social insurance programs. In the United States, William Jennings Bryan made, in 1896, the first of three unsuccessful attempts to win the presidency, on a program of radical economic reform.

See also Depression of the Late Sixteenth Century, German Great Depression, Great Depression.

References Beales, H. L. "The 'Great Depression' in Industry and Trade." *Essays in Economic History* (1954); Hoffmann, Charles. *The Depression of the Nineties: An Economic History* (1970).

Depression of the Late Sixteenth Century (England)

The trade depression that began in the 1550s represents one of the earliest depressions that generated sufficient data to meet the needs of critical analysis. The general outlines of economic policy changes initiated to meet the challenge of depression can be identified.

The first half of the sixteenth century witnessed a boom in the textile industry. In 1550, English cloth exports stood at 150 percent of their value in 1500, but, for the rest of the century, annual exports of cloth remained at least 20 percent below the peak in 1500. During two catastrophic slumps, cloth exports dropped to 50 percent of their level in 1550. Relatively free trade, and a depreciating pound sterling had characterized the boom phase of the cycle. The depreciating pound made English exports cheaper in foreign markets. In 1551, the pound turned upward in value, and cloth exports nosed over and never saw the peak of 1550 until the next century.

The economic and social reaction to the developing depression reveals something of the phases of capitalist development. The English intensified their search for foreign markets. In 1551, they sent a ship to Morocco, and others to

Guinea in 1553. They opened up trade with Russia, and reestablished direct trade with the Levant. In light of an apparent overproduction in the cloth industry, the English government enacted a series of laws to restrict production. In support of government action, one observer noted that, when production entered a slump, "infinite nombers of Spynners, Carders, Pickeers of woll are turned to begging with no smale store of pore children, who driven with necessitie (that hath no lawe) both come idelie abowt to begg to the oppression of the poore husbndmen, And robbe their hedges of Lynnen, stele pig, gose, and capon, and leave not a drie hedg...."

When Parliament met in 1551, it enacted two pieces of legislation to combat the depression. The first set standards of quality for English woolens, and prevented manufacturers from cutting corners to hold cost down in the face of falling prices. The second piece of legislation prohibited individuals who had not served a seven-year apprenticeship from weaving broadcloth. This measure restricted production by forcing new recruits out of the cloth industry. In 1563, Parliament enacted the Statute of Artificers, which required apprenticeships in trade and industry, and identified the classes that apprentices could be drawn from. It fixed wages and prohibited the sudden termination of contracts between employers and employees.

Merchants also sought to maintain income in their profession by restricting entry. Only those who had served apprenticeships could engage in trade. To further restrict new competition, apprenticeships were only open to the sons of the wealthy. Later in the sixteenth century, Parliament began to grant patents of monopoly to joint-stock companies engaged in foreign trade.

Last, Parliament enacted its first Poor Law, to provide minimum subsistence and public work for the unemployed.

In the depressions of the 1890s and the 1930s, capitalist development turned away from competition. In the 1890s, cartels and trusts controlled industry output and prices, replacing competition among rivals with cooperation. The depression of the 1890s also intensified the competition for colonial markets. In the 1930s, governments enacted programs to achieve much the same purpose. The U.S. government oversaw the destruction of livestock in order to maintain prices, and also enacted acreage allotments. These same trends can be extracted from the economic and political data of the last half of the sixteenth century. Economic history in the late sixteenth century gives another example of how governments experiment with capitalist institutions when economic expectations are disappointed.

See also Old Poor Laws of England, Statute of Artificers of 1563.

References Fisher, F. J. "Commercial Trends and Policy in Sixteenth Century England." *Essays in Economic History* (1954); Palliser, David M. *The Age of Elizabeth: England under the Late Tudors, 1547–1603* (1992).

Deregulation

The advance agents for the capitalist revolution of the 1980s were the proponents of deregulation. The so-called cutthroat competition of the 1930s had encouraged government action to regulate prices, but the high inflation and slow growth of the 1970s cast a cloud of suspicion on the efficiency of regulated industries.

In the United States, some of the most liberal political figures joined in the chorus of government officials favoring deregulation of important industries. In the late 1970s and early 1980s, Congress enacted legislation that deregulated or partially deregulated airlines, trucking, banking, railroads, natural gas, and television broadcasting. In 1982, AT&T lost its monopoly of long-distance telephone service in an out-of-court settlement of a Justice Department antitrust suit. Price competition in long-distance service replaced the price charged by a government-regulated monopoly.

Critics of government regulation argued that regulatory bodies often fell prey to the industries they were supposed to regulate. In their eyes, these bodies more closely resembled machinery for legally fixing prices to please industry, rather than consumer-oriented bodies holding down prices.

The outcome of deregulation seemed to prove that the effect of government-regulated prices was to hold prices up, rather than down. Airline fares, long-distance rates, and freight rates fell in the wake of deregulation. The opponents of deregulation have not been completely satisfied, pointing to concerns that airlines are taking shortcuts in maintenance to cut cost in a competitive environment, and that long-distance service has suffered as more companies compete for long-distance customers.

The partial deregulation of financial institutions set the stage for an unpleasant and costly wave of bankruptcies among banks and savings and loan institutions. The government bailout of the savings and loan industry sapped much of the political support for further deregulation in the United States.

See also Airline Deregulation Act of 1978, Depository Institution Deregulation and Monetary Control Act, Deregulation of Oil Industry, Deregulation of Trucking, Savings and Loan Bailout.

References Stein, Herbert. *Presidential Economics* (1994); Weiss, Leonard W., and Michael W. Klass, eds. *Regulatory Reform: What Actually Happened? (1986);* Winston, Clifford. "Economic Deregulation: Days of Reckoning for Microeconomists." *Journal of Economic Literature* (1983).

Deregulation of the Oil Industry (United States)

As a worldwide market developed for crude oil, domestic regulation of the oil industry became impractical and counterproductive. In the late 1970s, the U.S. government took steps to dismantle much of the domestic regulation of the oil industry. The petroleum industry stands at the top of the list of the world's largest industries. Oil companies rank prominently among the ten biggest corporations in the United States.

Public regulation of the oil industry in the United States began in 1911, when the Justice Department won an antitrust suit against Standard Oil of New Jersey for monopolizing the oil industry. Aside from the Standard Oil antitrust suit, early regulation of the oil industry favored the producers. The Revenue Act of 1913 not only established the income tax on a permanent basis, but included a provision granting oil companies a depletion allowance equal to 5 percent of annual production. By 1926, the depletion allowance stood at 27.5 percent, where it stayed for 40 years. In 1935, Congress passed the Connally Hot Oil Act, which allowed state agencies to restrict and coordinate the production of crude oil. In Texas and Oklahoma, where the oil industry had a strong voice in state government, state agencies set the number of days per month a well could produce. These state agencies restricted crude oil production in cartel fashion before the Organization of Petroleum Exporting Countries gained control of the world oil market in the 1970s. In 1959, the U.S. government put in place restrictions that limited oil imports to a percentage of domestic production.

By 1970, inflation began to gain ground. The government began phasing out import restrictions and the oil depletion allowance, and, in 1971, President Nixon announced the imposition of price and wage controls to contain inflation. In 1973, the government lifted the general regime of price and wage controls, but continued the control of crude oil prices.

Government regulation of the oil industry swung around to favor consumers at the expense of producers. The Emergency Petroleum Act of 1973 created a two-tier system of domestic crude oil prices. After 1973, new oil, stripper oil, and imported oil were not subject to control, but the government held the price of old oil substantially below the market price of new oil. Roughly speaking, the quantity of oil that came from pre-1972 wells, up to the quantity actually pumped in 1972, was classified as old oil. Congress developed a complicated system to assure that individual refiners received their share of cheap old oil. Later Congress introduced a middle tier price on oil from wells that started producing in 1975 and 1976.

In 1981, the government decontrolled domestic crude oil prices. It imposed a windfall profits tax on the oil companies to capture the windfall profits accruing to the oil companies from the rise in domestic crude oil prices. The tax was to be phased out over a period of ten years. The windfall profits tax was really an excise tax on the old oil that now sold at unregulated prices.

The regulation of the oil industry is a reminder of what a tangled web governments weave when they first try to control prices. The costs of the inefficiency caused by the regulation of the oil industry outweighed the gains to consumers. As market solutions to economic problems grew in the favor of decision-makers and voters, the pendulum swung away from the type of complicated regulation found in the oil industry.

See also Great Stagflation of the 1970s, Oil Price Revolution.

References Crumbly, Larry, and Craig E. Reese, eds. *Readings in the Crude Oil Windfall Profits Tax* (1982); Hubbard, Glenn, and Robert J. Weiner. "Petroleum Regulation and Public Policy." *Regulatory Reform: What Actually Happened?* (1986).

Deregulation of Trucking
(United States)

The Motor Carrier Act of 1980 lifted much of the government regulation of the trucking industry. In the late 1970s, the Interstate Commerce Commission (ICC), acting on its own initiative, began to deregulate the trucking industry. Before deregulation, the ICC regulated freight and passenger rates for trucks and buses, and controlled entry to specific markets.

The history of regulation in trucking began with the regulation of the railroad industry. After the Civil War, the federal government significantly subsidized the construction of railroads. The government subsidies, coupled with a bit of euphoria from railroad companies, led to overexpansion and excess capacity in railroads. The railroad companies tried various price-fixing arrangements to avoid cutthroat competition, before rushing into the arms of government regulation. In 1887, with broad support from railroad companies, Congress passed the Interstate Commerce Act to regulate pricing and market entry in the railroad industry.

In the 1920s, rail carriers faced new competition from the trucking industry. At first, the railroad companies acted to force state regulatory commissions to extend regulation to the trucking industry. When the U.S. Supreme Court refused to uphold the authority of the state commissions, the ICC, railroad companies, and the state commissions waged a campaign to bring trucking under federal regulation. The trucking industry fought against regulation of its industry until the 1930s, when deflation raised the specter of price war in many industries. After the National Recovery Act failed the test of constitutionality, Congress passed the Motor Carriers Act of 1935, without opposition from the trucking industry.

The Motor Carriers Act of 1935 subjected the trucking industry to regulation by the ICC. Trucking firms had to receive an operating license from the ICC to serve a particular market. The ICC took a restrictive stance, and virtually prohibited new carriers from entering markets served by other carriers. Freight rates and passenger rates had to be filed with the ICC, and could be protested by other carriers. After 1948, Congress exempted trucking firms from antitrust laws when they agreed on rates in rate bureaus.

The trucking industry, including the Teamsters Union, became a staunch defender of regulation. Operating licenses in some markets sold for over $1 million, and members of the Teamsters Union enjoyed high wages. The regulatory process became an instrument for monopoly pricing and profits.

The ICC began loosening the regulatory strings in 1975, by restricting protests of rate filings. After the successful deregulation of the airline industry in 1978, the movement to deregulate trucking gathered momentum. The ICC began granting operating licenses more freely. The movement toward deregulation led to the adoption of the Motor Carriers Act of 1980. This act substantially reduced the power of carriers to protest rate filings by competitors, and required the ICC to reduce restrictions on the freedom of operation of trucking firms.

In the aftermath of deregulation, truckload rates fell about 25 percent, and less-than-truckload rates about 12 percent. The value of operating licenses dropped to negligible levels, and bankruptcies in the trucking industry increased significantly. Fears that deregulation would harm service quality and service to small communities turned out to be unfounded.

The case of regulation and deregulation of the trucking industry reveals how government regulation often serves the purposes of special interests. The recent deregulation of industries such as trucking shows a renewed faith in one of the cornerstones of capitalism—the free market. The search for market solutions to regulatory problems is one of the important trends in capitalistic countries today.

See also Airline Deregulation Act of 1978.

References Moore, Thomas Gale. "Rail and Trucking Deregulation." *Regulatory Reform: What Actually Happened?* (1986); Winston, Clifford. "Economic Deregulation: Days of Reckoning for Microeconomists." *Journal of Economic Literature* (1993).

Disimperialism

The two decades following World War II saw the virtual dissolution of the colonial empires, a process that has been called disimperialism.

At the end of World War II, the British, French, and Dutch held the three principle colonial empires that were the product of capitalist expansion. The British Empire was by far the most widespread, governing, either formally or informally, one-fourth of the world's population. The French and Dutch empires were substantially smaller, but nevertheless vast. Belgium boasted one colonial possession, the Belgian Congo, one of the wealthiest of the European colonies, and Portugal clung to Angola and Mozambique, the last remnants of its once far-flung colonial empire.

The British showed the path for peaceful dissolution of an empire without lasting psychological wounds to the mother country or to former colonies. Under the formula of the commonwealth, the British government granted sovereignty to self-governing dominions, and helped each colony develop properly constituted colonial governments capable of self-government. Britain converted a centralized empire into a free association of self-governing, or potentially self-governing, nations, held together by commercial ties, and attachment to the British crown.

Britain began the process for establishing independent governments well before World War II, with the Statute of Westminster of 1931, which empowered properly constituted governments of self-governing dominions to make laws and decisions as sovereign political entities.

Britain's largest colonial possession was India, which, in 1947, became two independent countries—India and Pakistan. Britain also held important colonial possessions in the Far East and Africa that also became independent nations. Britain remained in possession of a few small holdings, including Hong Kong, which, under agreement with the People's Republic of China, remained in possession of the British government until mid-1997.

Unlike Britain, France fought to maintain possession of its colonies, particularly in Indochina and Algeria, but without success. France suffered heavy military loses in Indochina, and had over 400,000 troops stationed in Algeria when it signed a peace agreement with Algerian leaders, making Algeria an independent republic.

The Netherlands tried to regain its control over the Dutch East Indies after the withdrawal of the Japanese occupation forces, until it became apparent that the Netherlands' military resources were inadequate to overcome the nationalist forces. In 1949, Indonesia became an independent nation, excepting Dutch-held West New Guinea, which joined Indonesia in 1962.

Germany and Japan lost their colonial possessions during World War II. During the postwar period, these countries enjoyed much faster growth than the colonial powers, which cast doubt on the concept that colonies were a necessary component of high living standards. While France coped with the demoralization and military costs of fighting foreign wars to maintain colonial possessions, West Germany, without colonies, was becoming the most prosperous country in Europe. Europe exhibited the unusual spectacle that countries without colonies were more prosperous than countries with colonies. Britain, France, and Holland shared in the economic boom of the 1950s and 1960s, in spite of losing their colonial possessions. Although colonial empires are no longer a necessary part of capitalist development, imperialistic aims can work through more subtle channels. The U.S. government has been accused of exercising more than its share of influence in Latin America and the Middle East, exhibiting a particularly strong interest in maintaining the flow of oil from the Middle East. The high price of oil suggests that imperialistic relationships are not nearly so strong as they were under colonial empires. Experiences with the Soviet empire taught the world that imperialist behavior is not the exclusive province of capitalism, but that socialist countries can also exploit less-informed peoples.

See also Colonial Policy, Financial Imperialism, New Imperialism.

References Lloyd, Trevor Owen. *The British Empire, 1558–1983* (1984); Strachey, John. *The End of Empire* (1960).

Dollar Crisis of 1971

In 1971, a dollar crisis led to a suspension of the convertibility of dollars into gold. Before the suspension, foreign official holders of dollars had been able to convert dollars into gold at the rate of $35 per ounce. Domestic holders of dollars had been unable to convert dollars into gold since the 1930s. The dollar crisis of 1971 began the final break with the gold standard in the world economy, although gold has remained an important component of international monetary reserves.

The Bretton Woods System, established in 1944, put the world on the gold standard for international purposes, requiring each country to define a par value of its currency in terms of a fixed weight of gold. As the system evolved, however, countries defined their currencies in terms of dollars, and the United States stood ready to redeem dollars into gold at the official rate for foreign official holders. The redemption of dollars in gold drained the U.S. gold stock from $25 billion in 1949 to $12 billion in the early 1970s.

As world trade grew in the post-World War II era, the rest of the world began to treat dollars as monetary reserves comparable to gold, compensating for slow growth in world gold mining. Principally because of worldwide military and political obligations, the United States ran what are called balance of payments deficits, infusing additional dollars into a world economy hungry for monetary reserves. A balance of payments deficit meant that the outflow of dollars from U.S. imports, and U.S. investment abroad, exceeded the inflow of dollars from U.S. exports, and from foreign investment in the United States.

After the mid-1960s, the U.S. balance of payments deficits grew because of Vietnam involvement and heavy investment abroad. The rest of the world saw that the U.S. gold stock was insufficient to redeem all foreign-held dollars in gold. Uneasiness about the dollar reached crisis levels in August 1971, forcing President Nixon to announce that the United States would no longer convert dollars into gold for foreign official holders. Between August 1971 and May 1973, world governments endeavored, without success, to save the Bretton Woods System, with a dollar devalued in terms of gold.

After 1973, the value of the dollar was no longer defined in terms of a fixed weight of gold, and other currencies were no longer defined in terms of dollars. The exchange rates between currencies floated freely, and world international trade was off the gold standard. Nowadays, governments manage the floating exchange rates, but currencies are not tied to each other in fixed exchange rates.

Some observers of world capitalism attributed the inflation of the 1970s to the collapse of the gold standard. Most economists attributed inflation to undisciplined monetary growth, perhaps aggravated by powerful corporations and unions pushing up wages and prices. As control over monetary growth brought inflation down in the 1980s, a connection between the gold standard and price stability seemed less necessary.

See also Bretton Woods System, Gold Standard.

References De Vries, Margaret Garritsen. *Balance of Payments Adjustment, 1945–1986: The IMF Experience* (1987); Snider, Delbert A. *Introduction to International Economics* (1975).

Double-Entry Bookkeeping

Double-entry bookkeeping is a way of tracking the impact of each commercial transaction on the financial condition of a business. The firm's business activity is recorded in the context of an accounting equation. This equation takes the form

Total assets =
Total liabilities + Owner's equity.

Each business transaction affects at least two separate accounts in such a way as to leave this equation in balance. For instance, the sale of goods for cash decreases the inventory account on the asset side by the amount of the sale. It also increases the cash account by an equal amount on the asset side. The cash could be used to pay off a liability, which would

reduce both sides of the equation.

Double-entry bookkeeping made its appearance in ledgers of Italian merchants in the thirteenth century. Its most famous elucidator, Luca Pacioi, was a mathematics professor at the University of Pavia, and a friend of Leonardo Da Vinci, who painted his portrait. He devoted chapter 11 of his *Summa di arithmetica, geometria, proportioni e proportionalita'* (1494) to an explanation of the double-entry method, possibly the earliest textbook treatment of the subject.

Each business should maintain two registers. One register maintains a chronological record of all transactions. The second register records each transaction twice. This register enables the merchant to make an exact calculation of where the business stood in terms of assets and debts.

Some historians and philosophers have seen the development of capitalism as an expression of the same underlying spirit of rationalism that also led to the modern state and modern science. Werner Sombart, a well-known student of capitalism, wrote enthusiastically, "Double-entry bookkeeping was born of the same spirit as the systems of Galileo and Newton.... One might already glimpse in double-entry bookkeeping the ideas of gravitation, the circulation of the blood and energy conservation." Oswald Spengler, in his book *The Decline of the West*, ranked Luca Pacioli with Christopher Columbus and Copernicus. Such thinkers often cite the development of double-entry bookkeeping as an expression of this rationalistic desire to find order in the universe. With double-entry bookkeeping, profits became an abstract concept. The firm became an independent accounting entity, of which the owner only supplied the capital. Bookkeeping made the firm an abstraction separate from the owner, paving the way for the concept of the corporation.

Sombart summed up this thinking when he wrote, "One can scarcely conceive of capitalism without double-entry bookkeeping; they are related as form and content. It is difficult to decide, however, whether in double-entry bookkeeping capitalism provided itself with a tool to make it more effective, or whether capitalism derives from the 'spirit' of double-entry bookkeeping."

The double-entry bookkeeping system did not spread rapidly, and the praise lavished on it as a stimulus to capitalism is probably overstated.

See also Corporation.

References Braudel, Fernand. *Civilization of Capitalism: 15th–18th Century* (1979); Gordon, Myron J., and Gordon Shillinglaw. *Accounting: A Management Approach* (1969).

Dow Jones Industrial Average (United States)

The Dow Jones Industrial Average (DJIA) is the oldest and most influential stock market barometer in the United States.

The DJIA was a brainchild of Charles Dow. Born in 1851, Dow turned to journalism as a career when he was 18, and wrote on Colorado silver mining. He later sought employment on Wall Street as a reporter on mining stocks. After he established his reputation as a financial reporter, he joined Edward D. Jones and Charles M. Bergstresser in founding Dow, Jones and Company in 1882. This company began publishing a daily financial newsletter for subscribers, and in 1883 added a two-page newspaper entitled *Customer's Afternoon Letter*. In 1889, the *Wall Street Journal* replaced the *Customer's Afternoon Letter*.

Dow first published a market average on 3 July 1884, in the *Customer's Afternoon Letter*. He selected the stocks of 11 companies for the calculation for this first average. Nine of the stocks were railroad companies, and two were stocks of industrial companies. The list of stocks expanded to 14 in February 1885, but the number of industrials remained at two: Pacific Mail Steamship and Western Union. Railroad stocks dominated the early Dow Jones market average, because they were more actively traded than other stocks. The number of stocks on the list was cut back to 12 in 1886, and remained at 12 until 1916. The composition of listed stocks changed, and the first all-industrial average was published on 26 May 1896. Dow died in 1902, but his industrial average continued. Apparently, his partners, Jones and Bergstresser, played no role in developing the DJIA.

Dow's method of calculating the DJIA consisted of an unweighted arithmetic mean. He added up the values of the 12 stocks and divided by the number of stocks. The only stock on the original list of industrials to remain on the list into recent times, without changing its name, is General Electric. The number of stocks in the DJIA expanded to 20 in 1916, and to 30 in 1928, where the number has remained, although the composition has changed.

The DJIA is still an unweighted average, but the divisor in the computation is adjusted for stock splits and changes in the composition of stocks comprising the DJIA. This approach gives more importance to the higher-valued stocks. Alternatively, companies with the smallest number of outstanding shares exert an equal influence with companies with the greatest number of outstanding shares.

Newspapers and major television news organizations report daily the closing value of the DJIA. Economists and forecasters regard the DJIA as a bellwether of future economic conditions. Lack of information prevents free markets from operating efficiently in capitalist economic systems. The more time buyers and sellers must invest in collecting information, the less efficient the market functions. The DJIA filled an important information gap in the operation of the stock market.

See also New York Stock Exchange.

References Stillman, Richard J. *Dow Jones Industrial Average: History of Its Role in an Investment Strategy* (1986); Wendt, Lloyd. *The Wall Street Journal: The Story of Dow Jones and the Nation's Newspaper*, 1982.

Dutch Capitalism

During the seventeenth century, capitalism flowered in Holland on a scale surpassing anything observed in the Italian cities. Contemporaries talked of the Dutch secret and the Dutch miracle that dazzled the world then, just as today the German miracle and the Japanese miracle evoke admiration in the post-World War II era.

The French finance minister and physiocrat Robert Turgot may have come close to the Dutch secret, when he wrote in the mid-eighteenth century of "Holland, Genoa and Venice, where the state is powerless and poor, although individuals are wealthy." In Europe, the first showcases of capitalism appeared in city-states where the hereditary feudal governments had lost their grip to the bourgeoisie, or middle-class capitalists. The Dutch merchant fleet played a powerful role in the Netherlands' 80-year struggle to throw off the Spanish yoke, eventually winning a victory over the Spanish navy, which, in Dutch history, ranks with England's destruction of the Spanish Armada. After Dutch independence, Dutch nobility continued to hold government offices, but shared political power with the business classes, who, in the absence of a major mobilization of public opinion, wielded political power in the urban areas. Unlike Florence, the proletarian class never made an organized bid for power, perhaps because the Netherlands led the world in wages paid to workers.

By the mid-seventeenth century, Amsterdam had become the headquarters of world capitalism. Amsterdam shared with Venice (occasionally cited as the birthplace of capitalism) a common fate—both cities were virtually covered with water. Perhaps this single geographical trait turned both cities to sea trade as a means of livelihood at an early stage of development.

After the discovery of the western route to the East Indies and the New World, Amsterdam—much more favorably situated than Venice—became a natural location for the world's transshipment trade, making Amsterdam the warehouse for the world's goods. Goods were shipped in from the rest of the world, and agents working on commission bought and sold goods for merchants in the major cities of Europe.

In finance and commodity trading, Amsterdam took its cue from Venice and Antwerp. The Bank of Amsterdam patterned itself after Venetian banking, transferring deposits between accounts, but abstaining from the issuance of banknotes. Vast reserves, and a reputation for stability, made the Bank of Amsterdam the world's bank. It was not formed as a lending institution, but later made loans to governments and sound joint-stock companies. The Amsterdam Bourse followed the model of the Antwerp Bourse. The fast profits of East India trading helped infect the bourse with a fever for wild speculation that eventually damaged public confidence, causing the Amsterdam Bourse to lose ground to the London exchange in the eighteenth century.

Like their predecessors in capitalist development, the Dutch developed export industries that led the world in sophistication. Before development of the steam engine in England, the Dutch stood unmatched in the application of labor-saving devices. The windmill powered sawmills, planing mills, fulling hammers, and water pumps. Dutch shipyards supplied the major powers of Europe, and Dutch industry exported salted herring and whale products to the rest of the world. Like Japan in the twentieth century, Dutch industry thrived on its command of raw materials afforded by worldwide commerce.

At the beginning of the sixteenth century, the feudal governments of Spain and Portugal had opened direct trade between Europe and the East Indies and the New World. These feudal societies controlled this trade for a century, but could not fully take advantage of opportunities ideally suited for private initiative. The contribution of the Dutch to capitalist development lay in bringing these foreign markets under the control of the most advanced capitalist economy of the time. In 1597, the Dutch first reached Bantam in the East Indies. By the mid-seventeenth century, the Dutch had ousted the Portuguese, and established for themselves a monopoly on trade with the East Indies. The Dutch put aside any thought of Christianizing the natives, and enforced a merciless political control aiming solely at managing production. To manage supply and maintain prices, they built or destroyed plantations, sold, warehoused, or burnt harvested crops, and restricted production to certain areas.

Amsterdam was last on the list of the empire-building cities that played leadership roles in the development of capitalism. From Amsterdam, the leadership of capitalist development passed to England, the first modern territorial state to become capitalist in character.

See also Amsterdam Exchange, Bank of Amsterdam, Dutch East India Company.

References Fernand Braudel. *Civilization and Capitalism: 15th–18th Century*, Vols. 1–3 (1984); Cox, Oliver C. *The Foundations of Capitalism* (1959); Israel, Jonathan I. *Dutch Primacy in World Trade, 1585–1740* (1989).

Dutch East India Company

The Dutch East India Company came into being in 1602 with a charter from the States-General, the parliamentary body of the Dutch Republic. The company rose out of a merger of smaller companies engaged in the India trade. It bore the aspect of a quasi-public company. The States-General ranked among the company's largest stockholders, and its directors came mostly from the membership of that body. The company received from the Dutch government monopoly trading privileges with the East. It began business financed with 6,600,000 florins of capital, 44 times greater than the English East India Company, which started in 1600.

Although the company's prime purpose was commerce, it enjoyed the rights of sovereignty in its trading territories. It could strike treaties, fight wars, erect forts, and appoint and dismiss governors. The authority of the States-General stood behind its actions, and its governors and administrative officials swore an oath of loyalty to the Dutch government.

The Dutch East India Company opened trade with Japan in 1610, and with Siam in 1613. Control of the Moluccas came in 1615, and Formosa in 1623. Java and adjacent islands became an empire of islands ruled from the Java city of Jakarta, renamed Batavia. During this period of rapid expansion, the stockholders earned a return on investment of 22 percent.

The governance of the Dutch East India Company fell short of the democratic practices of the modern corporation. The broad outlines of company policy were set by a 17-member directorate. The directors were elected by various local groups, and chambers of former companies merged into the Dutch East India Company. Ordinary stockholders could not vote directly for these directors. A governor-general administered the company, with substantial autonomy within the broad policies of the directors. This governor-general ruled as a potentate over Java, and he appointed regional governors who ruled the native princes.

The Dutch East India Company began as a trading company and sea power. In time, the company became less a trading company and more a government entity for Java and adjacent islands. Plagued with debt and corruption, the company lost its government charter in 1799. The Dutch government took possession of its territories and assumed all debts.

Joint-stock companies such as the Dutch East India Company are a unique invention of capitalism. They succeeded in amassing capital for risky ventures, and limited liabilities of the owners to the amount invested in the stock. The owners could lose their investment, but they did not face debtors' prison because of debts of the joint-stock company. From business ventures such as the Dutch East India Company was born the modern corporation.

See also Amsterdam Exchange, Dutch Capitalism, Joint-Stock Companies, Spice Trade.

Reference Cox, Oliver C. *The Foundations of Capitalism* (1959); Israel, Jonathan I. *Dutch Primacy in World Trade, 1585–1740* (1989); Parry, John W. *The Story of the Spices* (1953).

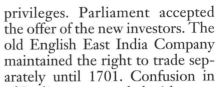

East India Company

The old English East India Company came into being with a royal charter granted by Elizabeth I in 1600. The charter gave the company an exclusive privilege, or monopoly, on foreign trade with India. Parliament never confirmed the exclusive charter, but that was not a major issue at the time, and the company enjoyed the freedom of monopoly trade, with little interference, for many years. The company began as a regulated company, with individual members sharing the ships for the first 12 voyages to India. In 1612, the company reorganized as a joint-stock company.

Adam Smith generally faulted exclusive trading companies for "negligence and profusion." In reference to the old English East India Company, he says their capital "was not so exorbitant, nor their dealings so extensive, as to afford ether a pretext for gross negligence and profusion, or a cover to gross malversation." He credits the company for carrying on a successful trade for many years.

As concepts of liberty came under closer examination, courts of justice had to consider whether a royal charter without confirmation from Parliament could bestow a monopoly or exclusive privilege. The decisions of the courts varied, and the old English East India Company met with less willingness from rivals to honor its monopoly position. Intruders multiplied, and the company fell on hard times. In 1698, Parliament received an offer of a loan to the government for £2 million at 8 percent, on condition that the investors receive a charter for a new East India Tea Company with exclusive privileges.

The old English East India Company countered with an offer to loan to the government £700,000 at 4 percent, nearly the full extent of its capital, for the same privileges. Parliament accepted the offer of the new investors. The old English East India Company maintained the right to trade separately until 1701. Confusion in the act of Parliament, coupled with overlapping membership between the two companies, kept the companies in a state of commercial rivalry for Indian trade. In 1708, Parliament amalgamated the two companies, and, beginning with 1711, fully established the new United Company in a monopoly of English trade with the East Indies. This company traded in cotton and silk goods, indigo, spices, and saltpeter. As trade in cotton goods declined in the mid-eighteenth century, the China tea trade became important.

Like other joint-stock companies, the East India Company, and later the United Company, maintained a military presence in trading areas. During the wars between England and France, the company became involved with the politics among the Indian princes, and used arms to acquire the revenues of a vast and extensive territory. The company reached the peak of its power. It gradually raised its dividend from 6 to 10 percent, and planned to raise its dividend to 12.5 percent, when the British government claimed its territorial acquisitions and associated revenue. After the company began paying the British government for rights to the territory, the company's finances began to show strain. According to Adam Smith, "The great increase of their fortune had, it seems, only served to furnish their servants with a pretext for greater profusion, and a cover for greater malversation, than in proportion even to that increase of fortune." After asking for a reprieve on its payments to the government, plus a government loan, the company became the subject of a Parliamentary inquiry. The Regulating Act (1773) and Pitt's India Act (1784) put Indian political policy into the hands of the British government, and the company lost its commercial monopoly in 1813. The company came to an end in 1873.

See also Colonial Policy, Joint-Stock Companies, Spice Trade, Statute of Monopolies of 1624.

References Philip Lawson. *The East India Company: A History* (1993); Smith, Adam. *An Inquiry into the Nature and Causes of the Wealth of Nations* (1776, reprint 1952); Webster, A. "The Political Economy of Trade Liberalization: The East India Co. Charter Act of 1813." *Economic History Review* (1990).

Economic Crisis of the Seventeenth Century

The sixteenth century opened when the New World and the all-sea route to the East Indies had just been discovered, ushering in a phase of rapid growth in world trade. Early in the seventeenth century, the growing European economy stalled out, and, for a half century, trade and industrial output either stood still or declined in the major economies of Europe.

The turning point in the economic cycle occurred around 1620, although one date cannot be pinpointed that fits all European economies. In 1610, Seville, Spain, which controlled trade with the New World, reported a peak in the tonnage of shipments arriving and departing. Tonnage stood at 87,048 in the 1560s, climbed to 273,560 in 1610, and subsided to 121,308 by midcentury. Similar figures for the Baltic trade suggest that the turning point occurred around 1620. The value of Danzig imports reached a peak in 1620, and dropped 75 percent by 1628. Venetian trade reached its peak around 1621. In Holland, wool production reached a peak in the decade 1621–1630, and saw slightly negative growth for the two following decades, before experiencing an upturn. Rotterdam ship construction climbed from 20 in 1613 to 30 in 1620, falling back to 23 in 1630, where it stood in 1650. In 1673, only 11 ships were constructed, and the number fell to five per year by the end of the century.

One explanation for the economic crisis of the seventeenth century lies in the monetary repercussions of the gold and silver shipments from the New World. The flow of gold and silver from the New World reached a peak at Seville between 1591 and 1600, and then declined gently until the crisis years of 1619 to 1622, when gold and silver imports dropped precipitously. The first 40 years of the seventeenth century saw a contraction in the issuance of money, restricting a necessary medium for trade and finance.

Another factor contributing to economic stagnation was a process in Europe called refeudalization. Signs of depression in agriculture appeared toward the end of the sixteenth century, leading to pauperization of peasants, and reductions in the number of freeholders. The bourgeois sought to join the ranks of the aristocracy, acquiring landed estates, and enforcing on the peasantry the privileges of feudal lords. Bourgeois farmers lost ground in a reversion to feudalism. Only England and Holland were spared the trend of refeudalization.

The economic and political warfare of the seventeenth century may have been the root cause of the economic doldrums. Long and frequent wars between France and Spain were destructive, engaging larger and more expensive armies. Spain placed an embargo on Dutch shipping from 1621 until 1647, and intimidated other Dutch trading partners. Maritime insurance soared as Spain harassed Dutch shipping with an aggressive raiding campaign. The disruption of shipping and shipping routes, the destruction of land wars, the tax burden, and drain on resources of maintaining vast armies and armadas, all acted as a drag to depress economic activity.

The Dutch–Spanish conflict was partly a conflict between feudalism and capitalism. Feudalism, embroiled in its own conflicts, lost out to the Dutch, who became the dominant players in world finance and trade in the second half of the seventeenth century.

See also Price Revolution in Sixteenth- and Seventeenth-Century Europe, Refeudalization,

Spanish Monetary Disorder and Inflation of the Seventeenth Century.

References Israel, Jonathan I. *Dutch Primacy in World Trade, 1585–1740* (1989); Ruggiero, Romano. "Between Sixteenth and Seventeenth Centuries: The Economic Crisis of 1619–1622." *The General Crisis of the Seventeenth Century* (1978).

Economic Recovery Tax Act of 1981 (United States)

In 1980, the new Republican administration of Ronald Reagan looked to supply-side economics for deliverance from the twin evils of unemployment and inflation, known as stagflation. According to supply-side economists, the secret cause of slow growth in the face of inflationary demand lay in the damage that high taxes wrought on incentives. The Economic Recovery Tax Act of 1981 sought to translate the principles of supply-side economics into action, significantly cutting tax rates to spur on economic growth. If we had followed the logic of supply-side economics to its merciless conclusion, we would have expected tax revenue to go up from a burst of economic growth, rather than fall from lower tax rates.

Supporters of the Economic Recovery Act of 1981 saw it as the biggest tax cut in the history of the United States. This tax law cut personal income taxes across the board by 25 percent over a two-year period. The first year of the tax cut saw the highest tax bracket decline from 70 to 50 percent, as an added incentive for savings. The law cut the maximum tax rate on capital gains to 20 percent. Capital gains are the profits from selling assets such as real estate, stocks, and other financial assets. For a profit to be regarded as a capital gain, the asset had to be held longer than one year. Under the act, 60 percent of the gain was exempt from taxation, and the remainder was taxed as ordinary income. By cutting the capital gains tax, Congress sought to spur the savings that the economy needed to finance faster growth.

As a further boost to savings, the act extended individual retirement accounts (IRAs), enabling individuals to exempt up to $2,000, and couples up to $4,000, from taxation, by forming tax-exempt independent retirement accounts. Interest earned from IRAs was also tax-exempt.

Since the major purpose of the tax cuts was to act as a stimulant for economic growth, business tax cuts were specifically targeted to accelerate investment spending in new plant and equipment. To achieve this purpose, the new tax law allowed businesses to write-off much faster the depreciation expenses of plant and equipment, significantly increasing the annual depreciation deductions for the calculation of profits. In addition, an investment tax credit of 10 percent was allowed on the purchase of new equipment, and an additional 6 percent credit was allowed for equipment written off within three years. Smaller corporations also received a significant cut on the corporate income tax.

Congress reduced estate and gift taxes by exempting estates valued at less than $600,000, which covered about 99 percent of all estates. The maximum tax rates on estates valued at over $5 million were scaled back from 70 to 50 percent over a four-year period.

The results of the Economic Recovery Tax Act did not quite live up to expectations. The economy soon plunged into recession, and annual deficits rose to unheard-of amounts. Sizable annual budget deficits have plagued the U.S. economy since the enactment of the Economic Recovery Tax Act. Soon after it became law, an influential officer in the government described the supply-side rationale for the tax cut as a "Trojan horse to bring down the top [tax] rates." Skepticism ran high on the new tax law, but the supply-side philosophy has remained an important element in taxing policy in the United States. In capitalist economic systems, perpetual war exists between the private and public sectors for the same pool of resources. By putting government spending on a diet, the Economic Recovery Tax Act reduced the growth of the public sector— a trend that will probably continue until the economy experiences a major deflationary crisis, such as in the 1930s.

See also Thatcherism.

References Kimzey, Bruce W. *Reaganomics* (1983); Stein, Herbert. *Presidential Economics* (1994).

Emancipation of the Serfs (Russia)

The process of emancipating the serfs in Russia began with the Emancipation Edict of 1861. This edict put an end to the landlords' authority over the serfs, but it left the serfs with something less than complete freedom, because local communes inherited part of the landlords' authority over the former serfs. Complete emancipation came in 1907.

Soon after the accession of Alexander II in 1855, the Russian government reached the decision to emancipate the serfs. The prime motivation lay in the profound humiliation the autocratic Russian government felt in the aftermath of defeat in the Crimean War (1853–1856), at the hands of the liberal governments of Western Europe. In the crisis of confidence that followed the war, serfdom became a symbol of Russia's backwardness. The landowning classes raised a howl against emancipation, and the provisions of the edict aimed to minimize the losses of the landlords.

The edict of 1861 conferred on the serf the status of a legal person who could own property, sue in courts, and vote in local elections. Two-thirds of the land was left in the possession of the landowners, and one-third became the property of the former serfs. Russia's landlords retained most of the pasture and woodland, and they received compensation for the third of land distributed to the former serfs, who paid for 20 percent of the value of the land, either directly with money, or with services to the landowner. The government compensated the landowners for the remaining 80 percent. The former serfs had to repay the government in redemption payments extended over 49 years.

The emancipation was less than complete because some of the landlord's authority over the serfs was entrusted to a commune. The commune held the title to the property that serfs received with emancipation. A former serf needed the permission of the commune to depart the area beyond a certain length of time, and these communes retained their historic authority to repartition land strips.

The economic condition of the serfs deteriorated after emancipation, adding momentum to the forces for revolutionary change in Russia. The redemption payments overburdened a peasantry that was already paying a high level of taxes. Before emancipation, serfs had paid rent to landlords with labor services. After emancipation, raising money to make redemption payments was difficult. Peasants, turning to village usurers to finance purchases of land, sunk into debt. Since the commune had the right to repartition land, individual peasant farmers had no incentive to undertake long-term improvements. The commune system of agricultural organization held back the industrious to protect the indolent, and inhibited economic progress. The loss of the use of much of the pasture and forest land added to the new burdens born by the peasants.

In 1891, the government reduced by one-fourth the amount of the redemption payments. The economic woes of the former serfs worsened, and the agitation of 1905 roused the peasants to action. After the spring thaw in 1906, peasants went on a rampage, looting and burning estates. To redress the peasant's grievances, the government ended the redemption payments, forgave past-due payments, and abolished the authority of the communes. Peasants were free to leave the communes and consolidate their holdings into individual farmsteads, and enjoyed complete freedom of movement. The government made money available to help peasants purchase land from landlords. It also helped peasants resettle in less-populated areas of the country.

After 1906, the economic condition of the peasants improved, but rural discontent remained a factor, and, in 1917, peasant violence erupted again. If Russia had moved less cautiously against serfdom, its later revolutionary chaos might have been avoided.

The nineteenth century saw Russia and the United States put an end to forced labor. Why did these two countries continue to use forced labor after it had been abolished in Europe? Perhaps because both countries controlled vast amounts of land. This land represented a constant enticement of the proverbial greener pastures to the rural agricultural work force. The agricultural economy particularly needs workers to remain at work during the harvest season. Whatever the reason, hardly any practice can be more contrary to the capitalist spirit than a system of forced labor, such as serfdom. Capitalism requires that resources be free to migrate to areas of highest productivity.

See also Enclosures, Slavery.

References Kolchin, Peter. *Unfree Labor: American Labor and Russian Serfdom* (1987); Pipes, Richard. *Russia under the Old Regime* (1974).

Employee Stock Ownership Plans (United States)

Employee stock ownership plans (ESOPs) issue company stock as part of worker compensation, giving workers a stake in the profitability of companies. ESOPs grew in popularity after Congress laid the foundation with the passage of the Employee Retirement Income Security Act in 1974. The Tax Reform Act of 1986 held out additional tax breaks for ESOPs, including incentives for estates selling stock to ESOPs, the use of ESOP dividends to repay loans, and lending funds to ESOPs. Through ESOPs, workers may own a token share or as much as 100 percent of a company. In most ESOPs, employees earn between 10 and 40 percent of the shares of stock in their company, and about one-third of all plans will eventually put a controlling interest into the hands of the employees.

To establish an ESOP, a company forms a trust fund that borrows money from banks and other financial institutions, to purchase stock. The company then makes contributions to the ESOP that are used to pay off the loan. The company may also make contributions of its own stock. The ESOP then allocates its holdings of stock to individual employee accounts, in proportion to employee salaries, seniority, or both. ESOPs that serve as retirement plans may diversify by investing in the stock of other companies. About 80 percent of all ESOPs have 75 percent of their capital invested in the stock of their own company.

Congress facilitated the development of ESOPs to encourage greater cooperation in the workplace. In the 1970s, clashes between labor and management seemed particularly counterproductive, in the face of fierce foreign competition and lagging productivity. Giving workers some of the incentives of owners makes them less distrustful of the profit motive. Studies indicate that ESOPs may deserve some credit for improving productivity and efficiency. One study of 238 companies, including 45 with ESOPs, reported that ESOP companies grew three or four times faster than non-ESOP companies. These results held, independent of the size of the company, or the size of the employee contributions, or the share of the company owned by the ESOP. For companies that had established ESOPs, growth rates were faster during the five years that followed the formation of the ESOPs, compared the five years that preceded them.

As modern capitalist societies become more affluent, a separate class supplying capital will appear less conspicuous. Workers who can afford to become stakeholders in companies may become less class-conscious, and identify more with their own company rather than with fellow workers in other industries.

See also Corporation.

References Alkhafaji, Abbass F. *Restructuring American Corporations: Causes, Effects, and Implications* (1990); Rosen, C., and K. Young. *Understanding Employee Ownership* (1991).

Employer and Workmen's Act of 1875 (England)

See Masters and Servants Acts.

Employer Liability and Worker Compensation (Germany)

Bismarck's Germany adopted the Employer Liability Act of 7 June 1871, which pioneered the enactment of legislation in the Western World to protect industrial workers from work-related injuries. This act held employers liable for industrial accidents if the employer was at fault, or if other employees were at fault for causing the worker's injury. Civil damages, medical costs, and burial expenses came within the guidelines of the statute. The act's major advance was the principle that the employer should be held liable if negligent workers caused injury to a fellow worker. The major weakness of the act was that injured workers had to sue for damages in the civil courts, and the burden of proof was on the injured worker or their survivors. The employers could deploy financial and legal resources to fend off suits from injured employees, who were without financial resources or experience with the legal system. Proving guilt on the part of an employer or fellow employees was difficult in purely accidental injuries, but the act was a good first start in accepting the principle that society owed protection to workers against accidental injury. In 1884, Germany enacted the Accident Insurance Law, which established insurance for a system of worker compensation. This system avoided the problem of proving guilt in the courts, and accepted the principle that workers deserve compensation for injuries or death at work.

Other countries followed Germany's example. England enacted a worker's compensation act in 1897. Before England enacted employer liability and worker's compensation laws, workers could sue for damages under English common law. Under common law, an employer was liable for negligence. An employer, however, was not liable for negligence of a fellow worker. Neither was the employer liable if the injured worker knew of the risks involved, or in any way contributed to the accident by his own negligence.

France enacted its first worker's compensation act in 1898. Russia enacted a system of worker's compensation in 1913, including a provision for maternity benefits.

In the United States, each state passed its own worker's compensation act; from 1910 to 1948, every state enacted worker's compensation legislation. The federal government passed worker compensation legislation for the District of Columbia, federal employees, longshoreman, and harbor workers. The provisions and kinds of injuries vary from state to state. In most states, the insurance is financed entirely by the employers. Some states run their own state insurance program, and others require employers to insure with private companies. Most state laws entitle a temporarily disabled worker to receive between 50 and 80 percent of their weekly wage. About half of the states provide lifelong disability for the permanently disabled.

Germany's history as a patriarchal society enabled that country to make important contributions to capitalism in the area of social legislation, including employer liability and worker compensation laws.

See also Social Insurance, Welfare State.

References Rimlinger, Gaston V. *Welfare Policy and Industrialization in Europe, America, and Russia* (1971); Spiro, George W. *The Legal Environment of Business* (1993).

Employment Act of 1946 (United States)

The Employment Act of 1946 marked an important departure from the philosophy of laissez faire in government policy. Rather than counting on natural forces to restore and maintain full employment, it placed the responsibility for achieving full employment on the shoulders of the federal government. The act read, in part,

> The Congress hereby declares that it is the continuing policy and responsibility of the federal government to use all practical means consistent with its needs and obligations and other essential considerations of national policy, with assistance and cooperation of industry, agriculture, labor, and State and local governments, to coordinate and utilize all its plans, functions, and resources, for the purpose of creating and maintaining, in a manner calculated to foster and promote free competitive enterprise and the general welfare, conditions under which there will be afforded useful employment opportunities, including self-employment, for those able, willing, and seeking to work and to promote maximum employment, production, and purchasing power.

The act devolved on the federal government responsibility for promoting maximum employment, production, and purchasing power. To assist the government in meeting these economic responsibilities, the act created the Council of Economic Advisors to advise the president, and, on the congressional side, the Joint Economic Committee. The Council of Economic Advisors consists of three members, who gather and analyze information on the state of the economy, and recommend economic policies to the president. The Council is required to publish annually an *Economic Report* describing its findings and policy recommendations to the president. The Joint Economic Committee consists of eight members of the House of Representatives and eight members of the Senate, and its task is to advise the Congress on the recommendations of the president.

The Employment Act of 1946 was adopted because policymakers and the public had lost faith in the ability of laissez-faire capitalism to maintain full employment. They feared that the depression levels of unemployment of the prewar years would return in a peace-time economy. The act put a premium on maintaining full employment, and did not mention price stability, an important area of government responsibility before the Great Depression. Far from depression conditions, the post-World War II economy was prosperous, and, by the 1970s, inflation was the principle economic problem. By the 1980s, the focus of government policy returned to maintaining price stability, or controlling inflation, and the Employment Act of 1946 had lost much of its influence on government policy.

See also Keynesian Revolution, Welfare State.

References McConnell, Campbell R., and Stanley R. Brue. *Economics* (1993); Stein, Herbert. *The Fiscal Revolution* (1996).

Employment Acts of 1980 and 1982 (England)

In Britain, high levels of inflation and unemployment during the 1970s raised questions about the abuse of trade union power in British society. Trade union aggressiveness and power were applied to wrench pay increases from employers that compensated for inflation and improved inflation-adjusted incomes. Margaret Thatcher came to power in 1979, and her government immediately made plans to reduce trade union power.

The Employment Act of 1980 banned secondary picketing, such as picketing one employer for engaging in business with another employer that is clashing with a union. The act also made unions subject to civil damages for secondary picketing and boycotts. Exposure to civil damages marked a significant shift in public policy, because the Trade Unions Dispute Act of 1906 had exempted union funds and union leaders from civil actions arising from industrial disputes.

Closed shops came under stricter regulations after the act of 1980. New closed shops required approval of 80 percent of the workers involved, or 85 percent of the workers voting. Workers became eligible for compensation when they lost jobs, owing to unreasonable exclusion from union membership under closed-shop conditions.

The act also made public funds available to pay for secret postal ballots in union elections. This provision was intended to increase the strength of moderate union members, who often failed to attend meetings to cast votes. The Thatcher government sought to increase the strength of rank-and-file moderates relative to radical activists.

The Employment Act of 1982 limited lawful labor disputes to disagreements between workers and their own employers regarding pay and working conditions. Labor disputes involving third-party employers were unlawful and exposed trade unions to civil damages. Trade union immunity from civil damages was further weakened by the act of 1982. The courts could also issue injunctions to halt unlawful industrial actions.

The act of 1982 brought closed shops under tighter regulations, including secret ballot reconfirmations at regular intervals. Nonunion individuals losing jobs unfairly under closed-shop conditions qualified for substantially improved compensation. Such individuals could only be dismissed with approval of 80 percent of the workers, or 85 percent of the voting workers in a closed shop. Dismissal elections required secret ballots.

The public in capitalist societies has historically shown support for measures to weaken the strength of trade unions that abuse their power. In Britain, the antiunion Trade Union Disputes Act of 1927 was passed in retaliation for the General Strike of 1926. In the 1970s, trade union power made itself evident in a struggle to maintain the purchasing power of wages in the face of rapid inflation, arousing public support for measures to curb that power.

See also Thatcherism, Trade Union Act of 1984.

References Dellheim, Charles. *The Disenchanted Isle: Mrs. Thatcher's Capitalist Revolution* (1995); McIlroy, John. *Trade Unions in Britain Today* (1988); Riddell, Peter. *The Thatcher Decade: How Britain Has Changed during the 1980s* (1989).

Enclosures

Enclosures put the use of agricultural land under the control of a private owner, depriving villages of communal rights, particularly for grazing and foraging for fuel. The great period of enclosure occurred in England prior to the Industrial Revolution, but enclosure has occurred in most European countries, often by government decree. The English experience shows the clearest example of capitalism's transformation of property rights in agricultural land use.

In medieval England, an open-field system of agriculture evolved in which members of a village enjoyed communal rights in the use of land. Individual peasants or tenants held scattered strips of fields, and communal controls decided what crops to grow, rotation periods, and times for planting and harvesting. Enclosures had the greatest impact on these communal rights. Fields were open for communal grazing on the stubble after the harvest and on the fallow. Communal controls prevented overgrazing. Beyond the open fields for growing crops lay the common waste, where livestock could graze. Some families held no land, but could still turn their livestock onto the open fields after harvest, or onto the common waste. The tightness of communal controls varied.

In certain geographical areas, enclosure happened because declining population reduced the pressure on land and the number of farmers. The remaining farmers consolidated and enclosed holdings. In some farming communities, owners reached a collective decision to consolidate holdings, often with a consensus of everyone with property or use rights.

Controversy arose when private acts of Parliament became the means for forcing agreements of enclosures when consensus was unobtainable. Between 1604 and 1914, Parliament approved 5,265 such acts; the years from 1750 to 1819 account for 3,828 of these acts. The rule was that the owners of 75 to 80 percent of the land had to consent before Parliament would act. Sometimes, landless families with a claim to common rights in land use would receive a small allotment at enclosure, but, more often, the landless families who foraged for wood and grazed livestock bore the greatest hardship from the enclosures. Often the village shopkeepers, blacksmiths, artisans, and traders fit into this category, and the enclosures marked their demise. Women's contribution to family income fell, since grazing the animals and foraging for fuel was an important part of their household responsibility. After enclosure, women were particularly prone to entering enclosed fields after harvest. What had been customary rights had become trespassing and theft. The courts, however, were slow to enforce the new property rights.

The General Report on Enclosures, made to the Board of Agriculture in 1808, argued that enclosures aided agricultural production and productivity. The report stated that after enclosure the owner was unfettered by custom and was free to adopt improved methods. Enclosures probably did lead to incremental improvements in methods, but they did not bring forth revolutionary changes in farming, or sudden gains in output. They created a more hierarchical rural society made up of large landed estates, tenant farmers, and a mass of landless laborers. Enclosure helped pave the way for the Industrial Revolution, because it reduced the number of people needed for food production, and made them available to work in the factories.

See also Agricultural Revolution.

References Addy, John. *The Agrarian Revolution* (1972); Daunton, Martin. *Progress and Poverty: An Economic and Social History of Britain, 1700–1850* (1995); Turner, Michael E. *English Parliamentary Enclosure: Its Historical Geography and Economic History* (1980).

English Usury Laws

In 1509, King Henry VII of England enacted a law against usury. In the words of David Hume, "Severe laws were made against taking interest for money, which was then denominated usury...which the superstition of the age zealously proscribed. All evasive contracts, by which profits could be made from the loan of money, were also carefully guarded against." In 1552, Edward VI followed up with another law against usury, defined as "taking any interest for money." Notwithstanding this law, a common interest rate of 14 percent was reported during that time.

Francis Bacon, writing in the early 1600s, cited arguments of his day against usury, which he defined as "interest, not necessarily excessive." It was said that "the usurer is the greatest Sabbath-breaker, because his plough goeth every Sunday...that the usurer breaketh the first law that was made for mankind after the fall which was...in the sweat of thy face shalt thou eat bread—not in the sweat of another's face."

Under the reign of Elizabeth I, the English government enacted a usury law in 1571 that condemned usury, but allowed a maximum of 10-percent interest to be paid. The wording of this law reflected the gradual change in the meaning of the word "usury" to refer to excessive interest.

The legal interest rate ceiling in England remained 10 percent from 1571 until 1624. From 1624 to 1651, the interest rate ceiling stood at 8 percent, and fell to 6 percent for the period 1651 to 1714. The interest rate ceiling did not apply on loans to the government. An amendment to the usury law in 1715 reduced the ceiling to 5 percent.

The maximum rate of 5 percent remained in effect through the eighteenth century. Adam Smith commented on it as being as proper as any other rate. The Napoleonic Wars exerted substantial upward pressure on interest rates, and by 1816 mortgage loans had become scarce. The many legal formalities of the mortgage business made evasion difficult. In 1818, the economist David Ricardo testified that the law was evaded "upon almost all occasions."

In 1833, Parliament exempted the Bank of England from the usury law for short-term money rates, enabling the bank to charge more than 5 percent. Parliament abolished the usury law in 1854. The tide of laissez-faire capitalism swept away the usury law in England, as it swept away many other government regulations.

See also French Usury Laws.

References Clapham, Sir John. *An Economic History of Modern Britain* (1951); Homer, Sidney. *A History of Interest Rates* (1977); Hume, David. *The History of England* (1754–1762, reprint 1985).

Engrossing and Forestalling Acts (England)

The engrossing and forestalling laws of sixteenth-century England were directed at the middlemen, who even in modern economies are often regarded as a source of unnecessary costs. In early English history, the middlemen in agriculture functioned barely within the bounds of respectability. In the words of Adam Smith, "In the years of scarcity the inferior ranks of people impute their distress to the avarice of the corn merchant, who becomes the object of their hatred and indignation."

Apparently, this hostility owed much to corngrain merchants, who contracted with some farmers to supply them grain at a set price over a number of years. In years of scarcity, the merchants sold grain at a premium over cost, earning them the public odium. In Smith's words, the trade of grain merchants "is abandoned to an inferior set of dealers; and millers, bakers, mealmen, and meal factors, together with a number of wretched hucksters, are almost the only middle people that, in the home market, come between the grower and the consumer."

During the reign of Edward VI (1547–1553), the English government enacted a law against engrossing and forestalling. An individual who purchased grain with the intention of reselling it was an unlawful engrosser. Forestallers were individuals who purchased grain with the intention of reselling it in the same market within three months. According to the law enacted under Edward VI, an individual purchasing grain for resale faced two months imprisonment for the first offense, along with the value of the confiscated grain. The second offense earned the individual six months imprisonment, and forfeited twice the value of the grain. For the third offense, the individual would be set in the pillory, face imprisonment for a time set by the king's pleasure, and suffer forfeiture of all goods and chattel.

Even the carriers of grain, called kidders, were subject to suspicion and regulation. An individual plying this trade needed a license certifying them to be of good character and fair dealing. Under statute of Edward VI, three justices of the peace had to approve the issuance of such a license.

This law strove to drive out the middleman, on the assumption that the grain could be purchased cheaper directly from the farmer. The farmer had to, at the same time, farm and exercise the trade of retail merchant. Smith complained that farmers were forced to keep a great part of their capital in the form of grain stored in granaries.

The law was later amended to permit engrossing when the price of grain dropped below pre-established threshold levels. At last, during the reign of Charles II (1660–1685), engrossing became legal, as long as the price of grain remained below a threshold level. Forestallers, reselling in the same market within three months, were still acting illegally.

George III (1760–1820) took further steps to repeal the ancient laws against engrossing and forestalling.

Laws against the activities of middlemen are strictly against the principles of laissez-faire capitalism. Modern capitalist societies have learned to accept middlemen as legitimate participants in the economy, who provide productive services that deserve to be rewarded. The inland corn laws were a product of a time when free markets were not well understood, and middlemen bore the brunt of the anger during times of shortages and inflation.

References Clapp, B.W., et al. *Documents in English Economic History* (1977); Smith, Adam. *An Inquiry into the Nature and Causes of the Wealth of Nations* (1776).

Entrepreneurship

The entrepreneur is the economics version of the great man in history. According to the great-man theory, historical events are determined by the actions and initiative of great men rather than impersonal social forces. A similar theory in economics holds that economic development comes from the actions, initiative, and creativeness of entrepreneurs.

Entrepreneurs marshal the resources and bear the risk to successfully market new products; introduce new methods of production; open new markets for existing goods and services; develop new sources of raw materials; or organize an industry along new lines, such as creating, or breaking up, a monopoly. Henry Ford stands out as the quintessential entrepreneur. He did not invent the automobile, but he envisioned the possibility of producing the automobile on a mass scale, and he acted on his vision.

Capitalism claims to be the economic system most successful in allocating entrepreneurial talents to productive activities. Before the rise of capitalism, economies received little benefit from the entrepreneurial talents of its participants. A story of ancient Rome tells of an inventor of unbreakable glass who shared the secret with the Roman emperor Tiberius, in anticipation of a reward. Tiberius, concerned about the impact of the invention on the value of gold, asked if anyone else was privy to this invention. After learning that no one else knew of the invention, Tiberius ordered the inventor beheaded. An entrepreneur would have marshaled the resources to put the invention into production. In ancient Rome, freed slaves conducted commerce and industry, and a potential entrepreneur suffered a loss of social status on entering

into commercial activity. Military activity, political involvement, or even corruption drew the entrepreneurial talents in search of wealth, power, and prestige.

In the Middle Ages in Europe, military achievement stood as the surest route to wealth and power, perhaps reflecting the importance of land in an agricultural society. Again, the pursuit of wealth and power led to unproductive forced appropriation of others' possessions, instead of productive entrepreneurial activity. Forced exchange of ownership of land and resources added nothing to the total output of the world economy.

In the latter part of the Middle Ages, a number of nonagricultural and nonmilitary activities began to turn handsome profits. Cities grew in size and independence with the expansion of international trade, creating opportunities in commerce, finance, and construction. Large cities, independent of feudal nobility, created the opportunity for the merchant and finance capitalists to acquire political power. The Medici banking family not only ruled the city of Florence, but sent one of its members to Rome to serve as Pope. As the cities came under the domination of the merchant princes, the social status of capitalist entrepreneurs grew accordingly.

When the use of water power began to replace animal or man power to operate mills, early in the fifteenth century, mechanical innovations and technological progress began to create a wide field of opportunities for innovating entrepreneurs. Instead of seeking wealth and power from military activity, the upper strata of society often sought grants of land or patents of monopoly from monarchs. This sort of political entrepreneurial activity was nonproductive, compared to the innovating entrepreneur, and business activity was no longer shunned.

A blow was struck to the power of monarchies in the eighteenth century, which gave birth to the Industrial Revolution, which is still in progress. The captains of industry and finance rose to a level of respectability and affluence unparalleled in human history. The eighteenth century also marked the beginning of an explosion in output in the world economy.

As societies moved away from pure capitalism in the twentieth century, new opportunities arose to attract entrepreneurial talents away from productive activities. At least some economists and political critics expressed this view. Unproductive entrepreneurial activities took the form of litigation, takeovers, tax evasion and avoidance, while careers in law rivaled careers in engineering and invention as the most likely path to wealth, power, and prestige.

Perhaps the most fertile country for studying entrepreneurship during the post-World War II era is Japan. The story of Soichiro Honda—who dropped out of school to race automobiles, attached motors to bicycles in war-torn Japan, and rose to become one of the world's foremost manufacturers of automobiles—is the stuff of which entrepreneurial legends are made, matching the industrial exploits of U.S. giants like Henry Ford. The founders of Sony also make an excellent case study of the role of entrepreneurial talent in economic development. The contribution of Japan's entrepreneurs helps account for Japan's rise from complete desolation during World War II to a world-class industrial power.

Several trends led to renewed interest in entrepreneurship in the 1980s. One factor was recognition of the growing and important role small businesses played in job formation. After the high levels of unemployment in the 1970s and early 1980s, governments sought means of encouraging enterprising activity, and of encouraging entrepreneurs. Small- to medium-size businesses, founded by fledgling entrepreneurs, were seen as the major source of future economic growth. Another factor was the rise of women entrepreneurs. Women, long frustrated by the glass-ceiling at major corporations, saw individual entrepreneurship as a career path that circumvented much of the inertia and rigidity of male-dominated corporations that were slow to change. An added factor stimulating interest in entrepreneurship was the number of contemporary entrepreneurs, born of the digital revolution, and earning a place among the great entrepreneurs in history.

See also Carnegie, Andrew; Ford, Henry; Rockefeller, John Davison; Whitney, Eli.

References Allen, Shelia, and Carole Truman, eds. *Women in Business: Prospectives on Women Entrepreneurs* (1993); Baumol, William J. "Entrepreneurship: Productive, Unproductive, and Destructive." *Journal of Political Economy* (1990); Gilder, George. *Recapturing the Spirit of Enterprise* (1992).

Environmental Protection Agency (United States)

The Environmental Protection Agency (EPA) is an independent agency within the executive branch that bears responsibility for enforcing environmental laws and regulations in the United States. The EPA administrator is the chief administrative officer for the organization, and reports directly to the president of the United States.

On 9 July 1970, President Nixon presented to Congress a plan reorganizing the environment-related agencies in the executive branch, and creating the EPA. Since neither House objected within 90 days, the plan became effective 9 September 1970. The newly organized EPA took over, from the Department of Interior, the Federal Water Quality Administration, and the Office of Research on Effects of Pesticides on Wildlife and Fish. From the Department of Health, Education, and Welfare, the EPA inherited the Bureau of Water Hygiene, the Bureau of Solid Waste Management, the National Air Pollution Control Administration, the Bureau of Radiological Health, and the Office of Pesticides Research. The Agriculture Department's Pesticides Regulation Division moved to the EPA. The Atomic Energy Commission contributed the Division of Radiation Standards. The Interagency Federal Radiation Council also joined the EPA. To head the new agency, President Nixon appointed William Ruckelshaus, a U.S. assistant attorney general, who had experience prosecuting water polluters at the state level.

The Nixon administration saw the EPA as a federal agency that would work to balance environmental goals with the goals of economic growth. The EPA, however, quickly established itself in the confidence of Congress, and became an advocate for environmental issues that had direct access to the president.

Perhaps because of his legal background, Ruckelshaus threw the weight of the organization into the work of enforcement, rather than into research and planning. The first 60 days saw a fivefold increase in the rate of enforcement actions undertaken on behalf of the environment. Ruckelshaus persuaded the Justice Department to sue Atlanta, Cleveland, and Detroit for illegal sewage discharges, and the Reserve Mining Corporation for dumping taconite filings into Lake Superior. The Justice Department also brought suit against Armco Steel Corporation for polluting the Houston ship channel, and Jones and Laughlin Steel Corporation and the Burton Oxygen Company for polluting the Cuyahoga river. These highly public initiatives won the EPA public support, which contributed to shaping the EPA as an advocacy agency for environmental issues.

At its inception, the EPA was chiefly an agency for protecting natural resources. Later it turned its attention to the problem of toxic substances, and shifted its emphasis toward protecting the health of people, rather than protecting the environment. The EPA is responsible for enforcing all major environmental laws, including the Clean Air Act, the Clean Water Act, and the Noise Control Act.

Disregard for the preservation of the environment is often counted among the failures of capitalism. According to critics, the logic of the capitalist system puts maximizing profits ahead of self-respecting environmental citizenship. In defense of capitalism, it can only be said that the communist countries have an environmental track record that is much worse. Governments in capitalist countries heard the voice of environmental protests, and enacted tough measures. In communist (Eastern bloc) countries, environmental protests fell on deaf ears, perhaps because the offending industries were government owned.

See also Clean Air Act, Clean Water Act.

References Edmunds, Stahrl, and John Letey. *Environmental Administration* (1973); Landy, Marc K., Marc J. Roberts, and Stephen R. Thomas. *The Environmental Protection Agency: Asking the Wrong Questions* (1990).

Environmental Regulation of Extraterritorial Resources

Environmental regulation acts to protect commonly held resources—resources that are not privately owned, and cannot be allocated optimally by the market system. Philosophers of capitalism can boast of how well the capitalist economy functions in the absence of government regulation. The history of the United States demonstrates, however, that regulations are necessary for the conservation of natural resources, which may be why the United States has been one of the more active countries pushing for protection of the natural environment. As the most highly developed of the New World countries, the United States has had wide experience with commercial exploitation of vast quantities of natural resources. In capitalist economic systems, resources not privately owned, and available on a first-come, first-serve basis, are invariably depleted to extinction. One must look no further than the American buffalo to learn what happens when capitalist enterprise, equipped with advanced technology, meets a resource owned in common.

The predicament of the great whales, facing extinction at the hands of commercial whalers, perhaps best symbolizes the global environmental issues that the nations of the world must wrestle with, and resolve, if environmental disaster is to be avoided. The epic struggle to save the whale has been a rallying point for activists concerned about the fate of the global environment, if the current pace of economic growth continues in the world.

In 1920, the first initiative for protecting whales came with the formation of the International Bureau for Whaling Statistics. All countries engaged in whaling were asked to collect data on their whaling operations and send them to the bureau. The League of Nations took up the cause of the whale, and the Convention for the Regulating of Whaling was signed in 1931. Twenty-four nations ratified the treaty, or voluntarily adhered to its provisions, but Japan and the Soviet Union abstained. In 1937 and 1938, a smaller group of nations signed an amended treaty that put teeth in the 1931 treaty, whose provisions were mostly good intentions.

In 1946, the United States sponsored an International Whaling Conference in Washington, D.C., which established a whaling code and created the International Whaling Commission (IWC), with authority to amend the code without formal conferences. The preamble to the agreement referred to "the interest of the nations of the world in safeguarding for future generations the great natural resources represented by whale stocks." The commission consisted of one member from each participating government. Its purpose was to develop an industrial code for the whaling industry that would protect whales from overexploitation. The IWC could issue regulations regarding open and closed waters, seasons, methods, and quotas. It could not put restrictions on the number or nationality of factory ships, whaling stations ashore, or quotas for specific nations. The code of the IWC could only be amended with three-fourths of its members, but most decisions required simple majorities.

The first three decades of the IWC saw little in the way of forceful action to spare the whales from shortsighted exploitation. The IWC was no match for the ingenuity

and stubborn persistence of the whaling industry. During the Stockholm Conference in 1972, which issued the Stockholm Declaration, environmentalists held a celebration of the whale, including a whale march into Stockholm. The whale became a symbol of man's shortsighted and greedy exploitation of commonly held resources. At the Stockholm Conference, the United States delegation pushed for a ten-year moratorium on commercial whaling.

During the late 1970s, the People's Trust for Endangered Species uncovered violations of the IWC's regulations, including Japanese-financed pirates operating under flags of non-IWC countries. Japan and the Soviet Union were most active in harvesting whales to the point of extinction. Agitation to protect whales reached a climax on 23 July 1982, when the IWC voted to place a five-year moratorium on commercial whaling. The vote was 25 to seven, with five abstentions. Although there is clearly a protectionist trend favoring the whale, the survival of the whale remains a matter of environmental concern. The history of whaling demonstrates, however, that capitalist countries have no monopoly on the urge to overexploit natural resources, since the Soviet Union was one of the major harvesters of whales.

In 1972, the U.S. government again took forceful action, with the enactment of the Marine Mammals Protection Act. This piece of legislation requires commercial fishing operations to adopt fishing methods that minimize the incidental slaughter of marine mammals, and is particularly targeted to protect dolphins. The act forbids individuals under United States jurisdiction from using fishing methods that are hazardous to dolphins. It also bans the importation of fish caught with fishing methods that are proscribed for individuals subject to United States jurisdiction. In the words of the act, the secretary of the treasury must "ban the importation of commercial fish or products from fish which have been caught with commercial fishing technology which results in the incidental kill or incidental serious injury of ocean mammals in United States standards." The main thrust of this act is to protect dolphins that are caught in nets of tuna-fishing operations. In the eastern Pacific, tuna fishers know that dolphins swimming on the surface are often a sign that a school of tuna can be found below the surface. Traditionally, tuna fishers cast nets that caught the dolphins and the tuna, and the dolphins rarely survived the ordeal. The Marine Mammal Protection Act provides that tuna be caught in nets designed to allow dolphins to escape.

The Marine Mammal Protection Act also provides that the secretary of commerce "require the Government of any intermediary nation from which yellowfin tuna or tuna products will be exported to the United States to certify and provide reasonable proof that it has acted to prohibit the importation of such tuna products from any nation from which direct export to the United States of such tuna and tuna products are banned under this section." Under the foregoing provision, the United States put restrictions on imported yellowfin tuna and tuna products from Mexico, Venezuela, and Vanuatu.

The United States has not been the only country to champion the cause of environmental issues at the global level. In 1992, Austria became the first country to require all wood products made from tropical timber to bear a label. In 1995, the Dutch government banned imports of tropical timber, except from sustainably managed forests, and the European Union banned the importation of all animal furs from countries that allowed the use of leghold traps. The importation of baby seal skins was banned in 1983, because of the brutal method of harvesting the seals.

International environmental regulation is a response to the problems created when technology races ahead and finds ever-more-efficient means of harvesting commonly held resources. Capitalism uses resources intelligently when the resources are privately owned, and are protected by the self-interest of the owner. The exploitation of commonly held re-sources requires intelligent purposes and thoughtful planning, which does not always keep pace with the multiplication of technological power. Whether it is senseless slaughter of dolphins, contaminating clean water, or polluting clean air, the profit motive drives businesses to minimize cost at the expense of society, or marine mammals. These are instances in which laissez-faire capitalism breaks down, which is why governments are clamping down on these activities against the current trend in favor of deregulation.

See also Global Commons, Rio Declaration, Stockholm Declaration.

References Caldwell, Lynton Keith. *International Environmental Policy* (1990); Nanda, Ved P. *International Environmental Law and Policy* (1995); Nash, Roderick. *The Rights of Nature: A History of Environmental Ethics* (1989).

Equal Employment Act of 1972 (United States)

See Equal Employment Opportunity Commission.

Equal Employment Opportunity Commission (United States)

Congress established the Equal Employment Opportunity Commission (EEOC) to administer the provisions outlawing employment discrimination in the Civil Rights Act of 1964. The five members of the EEOC are appointed by the president, with the approval of the Senate. Each member serves a term of seven years. The EEOC presently administers all the equal employment activities of the federal government.

The Civil Rights Act of 1964 made a comprehensive attack on discrimination and opened up equal access to public facilities, banned voter registration tests that discriminated, and withheld federal money from segregated programs and organizations. It also outlawed employment discrimination. Section 703 of Title VII of the act reads, in part:

(1) It shall be an unlawful employment

practice for an employer:

(a) to fail or refuse to hire or to discharge any individual with respect to his compensation, terms, conditions, or privileges of employment, because of such individual's race, color, religion, sex, or national origin;

(b) or to limit, segregate, or classify his employees or applicants for employment in any way which would deprive any individual of employment opportunities or otherwise adversely affect his status as an employee, because of such individual's race, color, religion, sex, or national origin.

Before the Equal Employment Act of 1972, the EEOC lacked the enforcement powers to make itself felt. In the act, Congress conferred on the EEOC the authority to file law suits, make rules and regulations, and call for reporting. EEOC field offices receive complaints from dissatisfied workers, collect information from concerned parties, and try to achieve conciliation. If the EEOC field office decides that the employee has a legitimate complaint, and the employer will not come to a settlement, the case is forwarded for legal action. If the EEOC takes an employer to court and wins, the court may force the employer to (1) award back pay, (2) put an end to testing programs, and immediately promote the disgruntled employee(s), (3) award seniority retroactively, and/or (4) establish an affirmative action program.

Affirmative action plans first became an EEOC requirement in 1974. Affirmative action requires employers to take positive steps to employ and promote groups who have been past victims of discrimination. Affirmative action takes on the task of correcting past wrongs, rather than only prohibiting discrimination in the future. The positive action marks a significant departure from the passive approach of Title VII of the Civil Rights Act.

The EEOC has set forth implementation and evaluation guidelines for affirmative action programs. Perhaps the most important component of the evaluation process is the utilization analysis. This analysis compares the age, sex, and race composition of a firm's work force with the composition of the labor force in the area. If important targeted groups are not sufficiently represented in the firm's work force, the firm is expected to set numerical hiring goals.

The EEOC and affirmative action overturned much of the social conditioning that prevented women from becoming airline pilots or car salespersons. In the capitalist system, free labor markets and the profit motive should have made a place for the discriminated groups, who were crowded into a small number of professions and occupations. If certain groups can achieve the same productivity for less pay, then profiting-seeking firms should hire them, bidding up their wages. Old prejudices, however, die hard. The federal government had to take action to assure equal economic opportunity, and equal pay for equal work.

References Burstein, Paul, ed. *Equal Employment Opportunity* (1994); Spiro, George W. *The Legal Environment of Business: Principles and Cases* (1993).

European Union

The European Union (EU) evolved from a common market of European nations officially established on 1 January 1958. A common market is a higher form of economic integration than either a free-trade area or a customs union. It removes tariffs on trade between member countries and applies a common external tariff to goods from nonmember countries. Unique to a common market, as opposed to a free-trade area or customs union, is the elimination of legal barriers on the flow of capital and labor between member countries.

The European Common Market evolved out of the European Coal and Steel Community (ESCS), which six European countries established with the Treaty of Paris in 1951. The original six countries (Belgium, France, West German, Italy, Luxembourg, and the

Netherlands) formed the ESCS to coordinate production and distribution of coal and steel within the member countries.

In 1957, the six countries took another step toward economic integration when the Treaty of Rome established the European Economic Community (EEC). The same six countries signed another Treaty of Rome that year that established the European Atomic Energy Commission for coordination of research and management in that field. Both treaties became effective 1 January 1958. These two treaties and the earlier Treaty of Paris supplied the principles for the constitution of the EEC.

The stated objective of the new organization was the formation "of an integrated market for the free movement of goods, services, capital, and people...." In 1967, the EEC changed its name to the European Community (EC). The membership grew from the original six countries: Denmark, Ireland, and the United Kingdom joined in 1973, Greece in 1981, and Portugal and Spain in 1986, increasing the number of countries in the EC to 12.

The vague outlines of a supranational political organization could be seen in the institutions of the EC. Leadership came from the European Commission, an executive body responsible for implementation of the treaties. A council of ministers, made up of the political leaders of member countries, served as the decision-making body on community-wide matters. Voters in member countries elected representatives to a European Parliament. The number of representatives from each country was allocated proportionally, by population. The European Commission evaluated proposals received from the European Parliament. A European Community court of justice hears disputes, and interprets the constitution. By 1968, the EC had abolished tariffs on trade between member countries and had erected a common external tariff.

Trade within the EC countries expanded rapidly in the 1960s, and member countries enjoyed faster-than-average growth rates. The stagflation that plagued the world economy in the 1970s and 1980s, however, took its toll on the European economies. Prolonged inflation and unemployment spawned a period of reexamination of the trade practices and rules of the EC. The European Commission issued a policy paper that cited a number of restrictive, nontariff, trade practices still impacting internal EC trade. These practices included such things as delays and administrative burdens at frontiers for customs purposes, and differences in technical regulations between countries. Government purchases exhibited a strong bias toward domestic companies, excluding other EC suppliers. Different value-added tax rates between members of the EC also distorted trade by blurring differences in true cost of production. The policy paper identified 282 proposals, which, if implemented by member countries, would remove the remaining barriers to free trade in the EC. The European Commission set a target date of December 1992 for the implementation of the proposals, giving rise to the phrase "Europe 92." Although the proposals have been approved by the European Commission and are ready for national approval, they have not been implemented by all 12 members. The establishment of a single European market is regarded as an ongoing process.

In December 1991, leaders of the EC met in Maastricht, the Netherlands, and drew up the Treaty of Maastricht. This treaty changed the name of the EC to the European Union (EU), and established a target date of 1999 for the establishment of European monetary union, with a common currency and a European central bank. The treaty also made proposals for expanding the EU into a political union. All member countries had approved the treaty by 1993.

Austria, Finland, and Sweden joined the EU in 1995. The countries of Eastern and Central Europe are the next likely candidates for membership in the EU. The EU is an important manifestation of the free-trade trend in the post-World

War II era. The subsequent development of other trading blocs, such as the North American Free Trade Association, has led to a fear that the world economy will splinter into trading blocs. These trading blocs could raise trade barriers between blocs, plunging the world into another era of protectionism.

See also North American Free Trade Agreement, Zollverein.

References Appleyard, Dennis R., and Alfred J. Field Jr. *International Economics* (1992); Daniels, John D., and Lee H. Radebaugh. *International Business* (1998); Hackett, Clifford P. *Cautious Revolution: The European Community Arrives* (1990).

Excess Profits Tax

Taxes on excess profits are intended to capture for society's benefit profits arising from sources that society refuses to sanction. For example, war profiteering certainly belongs on the list of profits that raise the ire of society. In the words of Franklin Roosevelt after the outbreak of World War II, "No American has the moral right to profiteer at the expense either of his fellow-citizens or of the men, women, and children who are living and dying in the midst of the war in Europe."

The state of Georgia made one of the earliest efforts to raise revenue from an excess profits tax. The time was 1863, and Georgia imposed an excess profits tax to pay for war pensions. Georgia's tax defined excess profits as profits in excess of an 8-percent return on capital, and these excess profits faced a graduated tax rate ranging from 5 to 25 percent. The tax was soon repealed.

World War I popularized the excess profits tax. The demands of financing the most mechanized war in history strained public resources as they had never been strained before. Socialist propaganda saw war-profiteering capitalists sparking wars, and profiting from them. At first, munitions manufacturers were the sole target of the excess profits taxes, but, as the war continued, the United Kingdom and the Scandinavian countries extended the tax to all industries. The example was conta-

gious, and soon Austria, the British Empire, France, Germany, Hungary, Italy, Japan, the Netherlands, Russia, Spain, Switzerland, and the United States imposed excess profits taxes.

In the United States, excess profits were profits in excess of normal profits, which equaled a set exemption of $3,000, plus 8-percent rate of return on capital invested in the business. In 1918, graduated rates on excess profits ranged from 30 to 65 percent.

The excess profits tax was a striking success for the duration of the war, but profits fell after the war ended, and businesses searched for ways to elude the excess profits tax. In 1921, Arthur Mellon, then secretary of the treasury, first talked of reducing tax rates to raise government tax revenue, a subject now known as supply-side economics. In the words of Mellon, "By cutting the surtaxes in half, the Government, when the full effect of the reduction is felt, will receive more revenue from the owners of large incomes at lower rates of taxes than it would have received at the higher rates."

The first Mellon tax cut of 1921 rolled back the high marginal rates on regular income and repealed the excess profits tax of World War I. Most other countries had repealed the excess profits tax by the end of 1921.

Heavy taxation of excess profits returned with the onset of World War II. In the United States, the Second Revenue Act of 1940 taxed excess profits on a graduated scale ranging from 25 to 50 percent. The tax rate on normal profits rose to the record high of 24 percent. High tax rates on corporate profits continued until the supply-side tax cuts of the 1980s.

In 1980, the U.S. government imposed a windfall profits tax on crude oil. This tax proposed to capture the profits domestic oil companies would earn after the government decontrolled the price of oil. If the price of oil held in domestic reserves rose to the world market price, American oil companies would experience a windfall gain. Although the tax was called a windfall profits tax, it was actually an excise tax levied on oil discovered before price deregulation. The excise tax equaled the difference between the price before controls were lifted and the new market price. The tax was to be phased out, no later than 1991.

Capitalistic economic systems only endure excess profits taxes when citizens feel threatened by war. In peacetime, corporations defeat the purpose of excess profits taxation. Instead of reporting excess profits, businesses purposely increase expenses by acquiring airplanes, yachts, resort facilities, etc. Although these goods are counted as business expenses, they are really consumer goods for employees.

See also Deregulation of the Oil Industry, Income Tax, Oil Price Revolution.

References Atack, Jeremy, and Peter Passell. *A New Economic View of American History from Colonial Times to 1940* (1994); Crumbly, Larry, and Craig E. Reese, eds. *Readings in the Crude Oil Windfall Profits Tax* (1982); Curran, Kenneth James. *Excess Profits Taxation* (1943).

Expropriation

Expropriation refers to government confiscation of private property, with or without compensation. In theory, expropriation and nationalization are identical, but in practice expropriation more often refers to the forced confiscation of foreign-owned property.

Latin America furnished numerous instances of expropriation during the mid-twentieth century. From 1936 to 1938, the government of Mexico confiscated plantations, ranches, and holdings of Sinclair Oil Group, and of Standard Oil Company of New Jersey. Between 1959 and 1960, Cuba, as part of a communist revolution, confiscated property owned by U.S. citizens. Between 1959 and 1962, the Brazilian government confiscated holdings of American and Foreign Power Company, and of International Telephone and Telegraph. The Argentine government took over properties of Standard Oil Company of New Jersey, and of ten other oil companies, in 1963. In 1969 and 1971,

the Bolivian government targeted property of Gulf Oil and United States Steel for expropriation. The Peruvian government was actively engaged in expropriation between 1969 and 1974: Industries and a sugar plantation belonging to W. R. Grace were confiscated. Agricultural estates, mining interests, and smelters were expropriated, along with the property of nine other countries. Between 1971 and 1973, the Chilean government confiscated properties of United States copper companies, and property of International Telephone and Telegraph.

Latin American governments practiced expropriation, because of widespread feelings that foreign investments were contributing to poverty in host countries, rather than assisting in economic development. Also, intellectual elites in Latin America worried about the effects of foreign intrusion on Hispanic culture. Critics pointed out that expropriation substantially damaged the climate for foreign investment in host countries, and often put property in the hands of inexperienced government workers who could not manage the property as efficiently as the private owners. Compensation for expropriation, which was invariably tardy when it did occur, drew resources away from other economic development projects.

The resurgence of capitalism in the 1980s, coupled with the failure of socialist economies, brought new respect to foreign investment as a vehicle for economic development. Now, less-developed countries, more eager to attract foreign investment, shy away from any sort of confiscation or expropriation. Furthermore, a policy of expropriation was always isolationist, making expropriation even less attractive today, after the burst of growth in international trade in the 1980s and 1990s.

See also Nationalization, Private Property.

References Baklanoff, Eric N. *Expropriation of U.S. Investments in Cuba, Mexico, and Chile* (1975); Ingram, George M. *Expropriation of U.S. Property in South America: Nationalization of Oil and Copper Companies in Peru, Bolivia, and Chile* (1974).

Factory Acts (England)

The Factory Acts were a series of nineteenth-century acts of Parliament designed to improve hours and working conditions in English factories. By 1800, the factory system, aided by the development of the steam engine, was in full production. Children accounted for two-thirds of the employees in some factories, and orphanages sent children to factories to reduce the burden of poor relief on local parishes. One factory agreed to take some idiots, along with a fixed allotment of normal children. Sixteen-hour days were common. The brutal exploitation of children aroused sympathy among ministers and social reformers.

Parliament passed the first Factory Act in 1802. This act established a 12-hour workday for children, and outlawed night work, in stages, by 1804. The act also required whitewashing of walls, proper ventilation, education, and religious training. Employers rose in a chorus of disapproval, and the act was never enforced.

In 1819, Parliament again addressed the problem of child exploitation. The Factory Act of 1819 forbade the employment of a child under nine in cotton mills. Children under 16 could work a maximum of 12 hours between 5:00 a.m. and 9:00 p.m. Twice a year, the walls and ceiling were to receive a cleansing. Each mill was to post a copy of the act, and violators could pay penalties between £10 and £20.

In 1825, a proposal to limit the workday to 11 hours failed. Parliament did pass an act banning the employment of children between 8:00 p.m. and 5:00 a.m., and during meal times. The act set a nine-hour workday for children on Saturday. The parents also had to certify the ages of children. Mill owners, and their fathers and sons, were ineligible to serve as magistrates in cases under the act. A bill with provisions similar to existing factory acts, but requiring employers to keep stricter records, failed to pass Parliament in 1831. A watered-down version passed, but was restricted to the cotton industry.

The year 1833 saw the passage of a major factory act, although reformers were disappointed, because the punishment clauses were weakened before passage. The act established, within six months, an eight-hour day for children under age 11. Within 18 months, children under 12 came under the eight-hour-day rule. Within 30 months, the eight-hour limitation became effective for children under 13 years. Persons under 18 were not to work more than 12 hours per day. Work between 8:30 p.m. and 5:30 a.m. was forbidden for persons between nine and 18 years of age. Permanent factory inspectors would monitor compliance with the act. In the words of no less of an authority than Karl Marx, in *Das Kapital*, "The normal working day for modern industry dates only from the Factory Act of 1833, which included the cotton, wool, flax, and silk factories."

Employers found ways to evade the act. A complicated relay system moved children from one work station to another; it was impossible for a factory inspector to establish how long they had worked. Parliament passed a new factory act in 1844. This act put women on the same footing as persons under 18 years of age. Women were now under the 12-hour restriction. The maximum hours for children under 13 decreased to six and a half hours. A complicated set of rules, including the use of a public clock, struck at the relay system employers used to evade the restrictions on hours of work.

In 1847, Parliament passed another factory act that reduced the maximum number of hours to ten per day for young persons under 18, and for women of all ages. Males were not subject to any of the restrictions on hours.

Working-class agitation in 1848 brought down a stiff government reaction. The Factory Act of 1850 relaxed the ten-hour restriction, and avoided the issue of the relay system. Additional acts were passed in 1856, 1860, 1864, 1867, 1874, and 1878. These acts expanded the coverage to additional industries and addressed safety issues, such as the fencing of machinery. Employer resistance to acts softened. The act of 1878, called the Factories and Workshop Act, consolidated factory law into one act. This act extended the regulations to virtually all manufacturing industries, and reinstated the ten hour day.

The Factory Acts were adopted during the time when the tide of laissez-faire capitalism swept away many of the economic regulations from the mercantilist era. People were hesitant to treat labor as another commodity. Karl Marx's *Das Kapital* quoted freely from the reports of the factory inspectors. In the exploitation of children, capitalism showed what the force of unfettered competition can do. The regulation of hours and working conditions became part of the legal environment of modern capitalism.

See also Factory System, Industrial Revolution.

References Thompson, Maurice W. *The Early Factory Legislation* (1972); Ward, J. T. *The Factory Movement, 1830–1855* (1962).

Factory System

The factory system replaced cottage industry with centralized large-scale production in one location. The heart of the factory was a single source of power that drove and synchronized a system of specialized machines. The first factories were often close to a source of water power. The development of the steam engine accelerated the concentration of production in factories, and left factories free to locate near to raw materials.

The first industry that evolved into a continuous process driven by a centralized power source was silk throwing. Between 1718 and 1721, Thomas Lombe erected a mill at Derby. Nevertheless, the silk industry was slow to adopt the factory system. In 1835, there was only about 1,750 power looms, compared to a total of 40,000 looms in Britain. At the turn of the nineteenth century the textile industry became highly mechanized. Cotton textile mills, powered by steam engines, began to replace hand-loom weavers, creating the first signs of the social problems associated with industrialization.

Various theories are put forward to account for the rise of the factory system. In the textile industry, technological advances had developed machines driven by water. Rotary power from steam engines became available in the 1780s. Also, the factory system reduced the transportation cost associated with the putting-out system, and aided in the production of a standardized product.

One group of theories attributed the development of the factory system to nontechnological reasons, citing the need to discipline factory workers who were prone to work less as wages increased. One writer in 1704 observed that "there is nothing more frequent than for an Englishman to work until he has got his pocket full of money, and then to go and be idle, or perhaps drunk, till 'tis al gone." Another writer, in 1774, commented that "everyone but an idiot knows that the lower classes must be kept poor or they will never be industrious." The factory system was a means of maintaining discipline over workers whose income allowed them to afford more leisure.

The factory system increased worker productivity by disciplining workers in the use of time. It was said that Richard Arkwright, one of the pioneers of the factory system, "had to train his work people to a precision and industry altogether unknown before, against which their listless and restless habits rose in continued rebellion." Workers may have resented the

Child labor and hazardous working conditions were common in nineteenth-century factories and mills.

loss of control over their lives. Workers faced fines, sometimes amounting to a good portion of a day's pay, if they were not at their station when the bell sounded the beginning of a shift. At one mill, it was a rule that "any person found from the necessary place of work, except for necessary purposes, or talking with anyone out of their own Ally, will be fined 2d for each offense." Some of the early factories used family units in the factory to maintain discipline. Children worked, with parents in supervisory situations. Sometimes, the parent was paid on a piecemeal basis.

During the nineteenth century, the plight of the factory workers, many of whom were women and children, drew protest from social reformers. The English Parliament passed several factory acts to improve the conditions of the workers. Karl Marx devoted a good bit of space to describing the ill effects of the factory system, in *Das Kapital*. In the words of Marx, "Every organ of sense is injured in an equal degree by the artificial elevation of the temperature, by the dust-laden atmosphere, by the deafening noise, not to mention danger to life and limb among the thickly crowded machinery, which, with the regularity of the seasons, issues the list of killed and wounded in the industrial battle."

The eight-hour day, abolition of child labor, and government regulation of the work environment improved the conditions of factory workers significantly in the twentieth century.

See also Child Labor Legislation, Factory Acts, Industrial Revolution, Putting-Out System, Steam Engine.

References Daunton, Martin. *Progress and Poverty: An Economic and Social History of Britain* (1995); Mantoux, Paul. *The Industrial Revolution in the Eighteenth Century* (1961); Tucker, Barbara. *Samuel Slater and the Origins of the American Textile Industry* (1984).

Fairs

At the dawn of the capitalist era, fairs made an important contribution to growth of international trade. The great international fairs grew in popularity during the medieval period. They were congregations of merchants from the major cities in Europe, and emphasized wholesale, rather than retail, trade. Merchants might keep booths permanently reserved, and wool, woolen cloth, and eastern products led the list of commodities traded at fairs. Some towns became fair towns, and held as many as four fairs per year. Antwerp began as a fair town, but the fair activity evolved into a year-round event, lifting Antwerp, for a brief while, to leadership in international trade and finance.

Local feudal governments usually offered special inducements to attract foreign merchants to a fair. Foreign merchants received guarantees of safe conduct, even if their home country was at war with the country hosting the fair. The confidentiality of business papers also received protection. Governments provided that the goods of merchants who died while a fair was in progress would be returned to the merchant's heirs. Exemption from taxation was another important attraction for foreign merchants. Tax exemptions were reserved for merchants who neither lived nor owned property in the host town. Free trade prevailed during fairs, and foreign money circulated freely. To expedite the settlement of transactions, fairs often established procedures for setting foreign exchange rates, and for settling accounts at the end of fairs. Fairs also put in place procedures for rapidly adjudicating commercial disputes.

Geneva, Lyon, Bruges, and Antwerp were important fair towns at the beginning of the capitalist era. Mercantile freedom, and settlement of transactions involving international trade, rank among the important contributions of fair towns to capitalist development. The techniques for promoting trade developed in fair towns spread to nonfair towns. The sack of Antwerp and the rise of Amsterdam to leadership of world capitalism marked the end of the fair town as a factor in the development of capitalism.

See also Antwerp Capitalism, Bruges.

References Braudel, Fernand. *Civilization and Capitalism*, Vols. 1–3 (1984); Cox, Oliver C. *The Foundations of Capitalism* (1959).

Fascist Capitalism (Italy)

If socialism is the antithesis of capitalism, fascist capitalism is the antithesis of laissez-faire capitalism. Benito Mussolini came to power as head of the Italian government in 1925, and his government soon launched Italy on a drive for fast, forward economic development. Fascist governments later came to power in Central and Eastern Europe, Japan, and Latin America and Spain. Countries making a bid for rapid modernization turned to fascism, resorting to strong-handed government intervention to accelerate economic development.

Characteristic of fascism was one of its early watchwords in Italy—productivity. To improve productivity, the Fascist government at first pursued policies to attract foreign investment and promote foreign trade, liberalizing tariffs and taxing rules for foreign investors. It also abolished commissions that regulated prices. To aid in the control of inflation, the government in 1926 gave the Bank of Italy a monopoly on the right to issue bank notes.

The Fascists developed a network of labor and employer organizations that kept labor and capital under tight control. Thirteen trade unions and organizations represented the nation's industrial interests, six for workers, six for employers, and one for professional people. Strikes and lockouts were prohibited, and the government made itself the final arbiter in labor–management disputes. Only members of Fascist labor unions could find work, and all workers had to pay dues to Fascist labor unions. Employers were organized by industry.

The Fascists undertook programs developing infrastructure, reorganizing public finances, and creating jobs with public works. Perhaps partially because of the philosophy of national pride that permeated Fascist politics, Mussolini insisted on the stabilization of the Italian lira at a high exchange rate. Because of a tight money policy, which reduced the money supply and the availability of credit, the Italian lira finished the year 1927 at record levels. The restrictive monetary policies necessary to stabilize the lira at the high rate, however, plunged the Italian economy into a deflationary depression. A highly valued lira made foreign imports cheap, and Italian exports dear in foreign markets, substantially reducing the demand for Italian manufactured goods.

The Italian economy had begun to recover from the depression caused by the stabilization of the lira, when the stock market crash in the United States marked the beginning of a worldwide depression, sending Italy into a deeper deflationary spiral, and spawning a burst of bankruptcies. To stem the tide of depression, the Fascist government intervened on a massive scale, bailing out failing private enterprises, encouraging the formation of cartels, raising tariffs on imported goods, and creating financial institutions to meet the needs of faltering businesses. In 1933, the government created the Istituto per la Ricostruzione Industriale (IRI) to raise capital for three of Italy's largest banks, whose major holdings of industrial securities had lost much of their market value. The IRI accepted these securities in exchange for cash, and became a major government holding company, making the Italian government the owner of a system of state enterprises. The IRI survived into the post-World War II era, and, in the 1980s, began a program to privatize firms in nonstrategic areas that had been acquired in government bailouts.

Fascism as a form of government conducive to economic development lost much of its prestige in the post-World War II era. Fascism had emphasized the development of military power and the acquisition of colonies, a pattern that had been followed by England and France. Both Germany and Japan, shorn of fascism, with its armies and colonies, experienced rapid economic growth during the post-World War II era, costing fascist economic policies much credibility.

See also Great Depression, Totalitarian Monopoly Capitalism.

References Clough, Shepard B. *The Economic History of Modern Italy* (1964); Gregor, James. *Italian Fascism and Developmental Dictatorship* (1979).

Federal Deposit Insurance Corporation (United States)
See Glass-Steagall Banking Act of 1933.

Federal Reserve System

The Federal Reserve System is the central banking system for the United States, and dates from the passage of the Federal Reserve Act of 1913. Most countries have only one central bank, such as the Bank of England, or Germany's Bundesbank. The Federal Reserve System makes up a system of 12 regional central banks, which are banker's bankers. They hold deposits of commercial banks, make loans to commercial banks, and can serve as a lender of last resort to commercial banks in an economic downturn. The term "Reserve" in the title refers to the role central banks play in determining the liquidity of commercial banks. Central banks use their power to manage the growth rate and elasticity of the money supply with changing economic conditions. Actions of central banks directly affect interest rates and credit conditions. Regulation of interest rates, credit conditions, and money supply comes under the heading of monetary policy.

The United States was slow to adopt the concept of a central bank as a system of monetary control. The early years of the Republic saw the creation of the First Bank of the United States (1791–1811). Congress chartered the Second Bank of the United States in 1816. These two banks, similar in structure, were early experiments in central banking, but were unpopular. President Andrew Jackson vetoed the renewal of the charter of the Second Bank of the United States, citing the excessive power of nonelected officials who set bank policy. The U.S. government owned one-fifth of the bank stock, which gave it minority representation on the board of directors. Fear of East Coast domination of the banking industry helped undermine support for the Second Bank of the United States.

Recurring money panics and financial crises plagued the decentralized and unregulated banking system of the latter 1800s. Public officials came to see the necessity for overcoming the political objections of a central bank. The political objections came from several directions. Government officials felt that the banking industry could not be trusted to regulate itself. The banking industry felt that elected politicians lacked the necessary knowledge to regulate banking, and were often irresponsible in financial matters. In addition to the distrust between leaders in banking and elected politicians, there was distrust between regions of the country. Many regions presumed a central bank would be located in New York City, and would unduly subject regional economies to Wall Street domination. These contending forces helped shape the Federal Reserve Act of 1913, which created the Federal Reserve System.

To diffuse the fear of Wall Street domination of banking, the Federal Reserve Act created a system of 12 regional central banks. The Federal Reserve Bank of New York is the most important for policy purposes, but there are Federal Reserve Banks in Boston, Philadelphia, Atlanta, Cleveland, St. Louis, Kansas City (MO), Richmond, Dallas, San Francisco, Chicago, and Minneapolis.

Like the First Bank and Second Bank of the United States, the Federal Reserve Banks are privately owned. Private ownership helped appease the banking industry, which felt that the banking industry can best be regulated by knowledgeable bankers. Commercial banks in each district who are members of the Federal Reserve System own the stock in the regional Federal Reserve bank. Membership is a requirement for all banks with national charters.

The final authority for monetary policy rests with the board of governors of the Federal Reserve System. The president of the United States makes appointments to this seven-member board, subject to the approval of the Senate. The seven board members serve 14-year terms, staggered so that one member's term expires every other year. This constant rotation on the board dilutes the power of any one president to put a political bias in the board. Congress set up the board to be independent of either the banking industry or elected politicians.

Usually, monopoly privileges are against the spirit of capitalism, but a monopoly can always maintain the value of its product by controlling its supply. Since maintaining the value of money is equivalent to preventing inflation, modern capitalist countries have opted to give a central bank, such as the Federal Reserve System, a monopoly on the privilege of issuing paper money, as a built-in guard against inflation.

See also Bank of England, Bank of France, Central Banks and Free Banking.

References Board of Governors of the Federal Reserve System. *The Federal Reserve System: Purposes and Functions* (1984); Schlesinger, Arthur M., Jr. *The Age of Jackson* (1945); Timberlake, Richard Henry, *The Origins of Central Banking in the United States* (1978).

Felipe Gonzalez and Spain's Capitalist Revolution (Spain)

Like Francois Mitterrand of France, Felipe Gonzalez, the leader of the Spanish Workers' Socialist Party, came to power in a democratic election, as a member of a socialist party. His party had never been in power before the election of 1982, and was without experience designing and implementing economic policies. The failure of Mitterrand's liberal policies in France may have been a factor in turning Felipe Gonzalez and his party to conservative, free-market policies.

During the 1970s, Spain's economy bore all the earmarks of stagflation, including high unemployment and inflation, bank failures, balance-of-payments deficits, slow growth, and low investment. Felipe Gonzalez's government imposed a restrictive monetary policy, slowing money supply growth, and lowering inflation. A key reform in the battle against inflation was ending the role of the Bank of Spain in financing public sector deficits, requiring instead that budget deficits be financed by the sale of government securities. To dampen the wage–price spiral that added momentum to the inflation process, the government brought employer associations and unions to an agreement to limit the growth of salaries and wages. Both public deficits and unemployment remained stubbornly high throughout Gonzalez's first term, which ended in 1986.

In 1983, the acquisition of private firms in financial difficulty had accounted for 70 percent of the deficit of the National Institute of Industry, reflecting the policy of the democratically elected governments of the United Democratic Center between 1977 and 1982. The new government of Felipe Gonzalez slowed the pace of the acquisition of private firms, and encouraged privatization. To increase efficiency, private firms benefited from new tax provisions allowing accelerated depreciation.

To promote economic development, Spain had traditionally imposed protectionist trade policies that shielded domestic industry from foreign competition. The high rate of business failures brought to light the need of an export market for domestic industry. To help in this area, Gonzalez's government pursued a policy of depreciating Spain's currency, which made Spain's goods and services cheaper in foreign markets. His government also worked to integrate Spain's economy into the European economy, leading to Spain's membership in the European Economic Community in 1986, which required that Spain phase out protectionist trade policies.

The last half of the 1980s heard talk of

Spain's economic miracle. Between 1986 and 1989, Spain's annual rate of economic growth exceeded the average in the European Economic Community by 1.5 percent. Although unemployment rates remained roughly double the average for the European Community, employment in nonagricultural sectors rose 24.7 percent between 1985 and 1990.

Spain shared in the capitalist revolution of the 1980s, which manifested itself worldwide, from the conservative economic policies of Ronald Reagan and Margaret Thatcher, to the collapse of the command economies of Eastern Europe and the Soviet Union. Spain saw that its industry needed to market products in export markets, requiring the peak of efficiency that can only be guaranteed by the rigors of the market system.

See also European Union, Mitterrand's Capitalist Revival, Thatcherism.

References Harrison, Joseph. *The Spanish Economy: From the Civil War until the European Community* (1995); Lieberman, Sima. *Growth and Crisis in the Spanish Economy in 1940–1993* (1995).

Finance Capitalism (Germany)

Finance capitalism refers to a form of capitalism in which banks become a major force in coordinating and promoting industrialization and economic development. It reached its fullest expression in nineteenth-century Germany. The same trend was evident, but much weaker, in Britain, France, and the United States.

In Germany, the rise of joint-stock banking coincided with rapid industrialization. Banks in England and Italy had developed as institutions for financing international trade. Banking in Germany developed to meet the financing needs of large-scale industry. The German banks combined deposit banking with speculative investments in industrial ventures. When a customer opened an account at a bank, he agreed to buy his stock investments from that bank. Often the bank required the customer purchasing stock to sign an agreement authorizing the bank to act as a proxy at stockholder meetings.

Banks bought up the new issues of stock and placed them on the market, often reserving the right to convert long-term industrial loans into shares of stock and debentures, and dispose of them on the stock market.

Banks enjoyed wide control over their industrial customers. Industrial enterprises were dependent upon banks for short-term and long-term capital. Banks not only held large blocks of stock, but controlled the stock proxies of bank customers; therefore, bankers could justify wide representation on directorates and supervisory boards. They had ready access to what is now called insider information.

Big banks encouraged the formation of cartels and syndicates to coordinate prices and marketing among firms in the same industry. They used their power over customers to consciously regulate industries, preventing price competition and encouraging cooperation among competitors. Big banks regulated the stock market by selling their own holdings in booms, and purchasing stock to avoid panics.

The big German banks grew in power to become almost states within a state. They planned and implemented their own economic policy and served as politico-economic instruments of the German government.

German banks in the latter portion of the nineteenth century took on much greater risks than their sister institutions in Britain and the United States. The unique role played by German banks may help explain the rapid industrialization experienced by Germany after unification in 1871. Bankers such as J. P. Morgan rose to prominence and power in the United States during the same period, but never wielded the influence of the German bankers. The rapid economic growth achieved by Germany prior to World War I seemed to make finance capitalism the wave of the future, but the concentration of economic power and the lack of competition associated with finance capitalism proved unpopular in more democratic countries. These traits may also have harmed efficiency in the long run. Even today, however, Germany's central banking system is the most influential and respected in Europe.

See also Merchant Bankers; Morgan, John Pierpont.

References Bruck, W. F. *The Social and Economic History of Germany from Wilhelm II to Hitler, 1888–1938* (1962); Edwards, George W. *The Evolution of Finance Capitalism* (1967).

Financial Crisis of 1557

Bankruptcies of the Spanish crown precipitated the financial crisis of 1557, which had widespread repercussions. The sixteenth century saw the development of two international bourses for contracting financial transactions. Antwerp had become an important capital market, because of its role in the international trade for commodities. The French kings saw the advantage that the Hapsburgs enjoyed by having a privileged access to the capital market of the Antwerp Bourse. Lyon grew into a rival international capital market, primarily as a policy of the French crown. Ready supplies of large amounts of capital were necessary for the conduct of war. Methods of taxation and other sources of revenue were too slow, inflexible, and primitive to meet these needs. Kings had learned that debasing coinage was a barbaric financial expedient.

From about 1542, credit dealing with European monarchs became big business on the bourses of Antwerp and Lyon. The major borrowers were the French, Spanish, and English crowns. Monarchs kept special financial agents in these cities to facilitate borrowing funds and floating of loans. Thomas Gresham represented the English crown in Antwerp.

In 1542, war broke out between Charles V (emperor of the Holy Roman Empire) and Francis I (king of France), dramatically increasing the demand for armaments. Charles V floated loans in Antwerp and Francis I in Lyon. Public loans had always paid higher interest rates than commercial loans at that time. Liquid money flowed into Antwerp and Lyon from all over Europe. The debt instruments were called the King's Bonds, Court Bonds, or Bonds of the Receivers General.

In 1552, Charles V again waged war against Francis I. A credit boom began on the bourses of both Antwerp and Lyon. All Europe was seized with a mania for investing in loans floated by these governments. England was also borrowing funds. Referring to the Lyon Bourse, the eminent political philosopher, Jean Bodins, remarked, "Everyone ran to it as to a fire." Interest rates were double digit. Loans were secured by various sources of government revenue, and by expected arrival of precious metals from the New World.

In 1557, a new war erupted between Spain and France. Charles V's son, Philip II, faced the prospect of suspending interest payments on loans to the Spanish crown. As a Catholic king, he consulted his theologians. They suggested that the credit agreements entered into by the Spanish crown were usurious, and therefore Philip II was not obliged to repay them. Philip II settled upon a less drastic step, forcing the holders of short-term obligations, earning 10- to 14-percent interest, to consolidate them into perpetual rentes (bonds that pay interest into perpetuity, rather than maturing at a set date) at 5-percent interest. The creditors could accept this choice or lose everything. France I, in the same year (1557), announced he could pay interest only on part of the debt. Mutual bankruptcy brought Spain and France to the peace table. Interest rates soared beyond 15 percent. Bonds sold at heavy sacrifices. The Spanish monarchy wobbled from one bankruptcy to another into the middle of the seventeenth century.

The capital markets of Antwerp and Lyon never recovered from the wars and bankruptcies of the sixteenth century, but they pioneered in the amassing of capital from every corner of a world market. Capital could be raised in these markets at interest rates half the levels in other markets.

See also Antwerp Bourse.

References Ehrenberg, Richard. *Capital and Finance in the Age of the Renaissance* (1928); Hauser, Henri. "The European Financial Crisis of 1559." *Journal of Economics and Business History* (1930).

Financial Imperialism

Under so-called financial imperialism, imperialistic countries make use of surplus capital to gain informal control over other countries for commercial and political advantages. In debtor–creditor relationships, creditors often impose requirements upon debtors as conditions of extending loans. In the late nineteenth century, weak, corrupt, and tottering governments in the Middle East and Far East needed capital from Europe, and European governments put themselves in a position to control the ability of these governments to raise capital in Europe. In return, European governments imposed reforms on these governments to insure loan safety, extracted commercial concessions, and furthered strategic political aims. According to Count St. Maurice, an exponent of the theory of financial imperialism, "a political protectorate succeeds the economic protectorate, and the debtor country sooner or later becomes the prey of its creditors. In this fashion are the modern conquest of the great powers prepared and executed."

A simple and uncomplicated example of the practice of financial imperialism can be seen in the financial history of the constitutional monarchy established by the Young Turks in 1908–1909. In 1910, the new government sent David Bey, Young Turk minister of finance, to Paris in search of a loan. At first, French financiers were cold to his proposals, but he finally arranged a loan from the Credit Mobilier of Paris. The loan, however, needed the approval of the French government, to be quoted on the Paris Bourse. In 1880, an executive decree had given the French minister of finance the power to prohibit the negotiation of foreign loans. The French government required: (1) more guarantees for the security of the loan, (2)

fiscal reforms to end recurring budget deficits, (3) a share for French industry of any part of the proceeds of the loans spent on materials from foreign countries, (4) the settlement of a political dispute of long standing. To satisfy the second condition, the French government wanted two French citizens stationed in the Turkish Finance Ministry, with real power to supervise its activities. Turkey rejected the terms of the loan, but this episode rather starkly brings into relief the imperialistic fusion of finance and politics.

The British government developed special relationships with banks in areas where it sought political influence. In Turkey, the British government encouraged British financiers to form the National Bank of Turkey. The president of the bank wrote to the British foreign minister, "The National Bank was founded with your strong encouragement, on the ground, as stated, that the prospects of the regeneration of Turkey and the progress of British interest there, depended upon the establishment in Constantinople of British Finance...."

The British government facilitated the development of the Imperial Bank of Persia with the sanction of a royal charter. This charter helped the new bank to attract British investors. In 1903, the British minister to Persia wrote to the Foreign Office, "The more we get her into our debt, the greater will be our hold and our political influence over her government.... Once the day of liquidation comes, the greater Persia's financial obligation to us...the stronger will be our moral claim to an authoritative voice in the settlement."

When other British financiers tried to compete with the Imperial Bank, the Foreign Office took sides, observing that the Imperial Bank "has always acted most loyally with the Foreign Office...."

In China, the British government did not participate in the formation of the Hong Kong and Shanghai Banking Corporation. Instead, it formed an exclusive relationship with this bank, and used it to control China's access to loans from Europe. As in Turkey and Persia, financing the central government was important. The Chinese government owed a war indemnity from a war with Japan. When the Chinese government sought a third loan to pay part of its indemnity, the English minister wrote to the British Foreign Office that "politically the power supplying this loan will have great leverage for influencing Chinese internal affairs."

Whether European governments followed the path of capital to other parts of the world, or whether capital followed the influence of European governments, remains a question in the philosophy of economic history. Critics of capitalism often see European governments as passively acting to safeguard European financial capital in foreign countries. Others say that European governments learned to "jingle their purse, rather than rattle their saber," to achieve political objectives. Certainly, the practices of financial imperialism induced a negative reaction to capitalism in countries where it was practiced.

See also Colonial Policy, New Imperialism.

References Blaisdell, Donald C. *European Financial Control in the Ottoman Empire* (1966); McLean, David. "Finance and Informal Empire before the First World War." *Economic History Review* (1976).

Financial Panic of 1857

The financial panic of 1857 was the first financial crisis that took on the aspect of a worldwide phenomenon. The origin of the crisis remains a subject for debate: The Crimean War ended in 1856, and the United States enacted a new tariff on 3 March 1857, which lowered duties on many articles, and expanded the list of free goods. A parliamentary inquiry in Britain brought to light more than the usual amount of fraudulent stock and other financial abuses.

The crisis seems to have begun in the United States. Railroad stocks and bonds had replaced government securities and bank stocks as the most popular securities for speculation. Continued investment in new railroad lines had reduced the profits

from some of the older lines, and immigration from the East was trailing off. The prices of railroad securities leveled off in mid-1857 and turned downward. In August 1857, the Ohio Life Insurance and Trust Company failed. The company's New York office had overinvested in railroad stocks, and one-fourth of its capital was invested in a single, faltering railroad company. This failure is often credited with causing depositors to withdraw funds from New York banks. Several railroads defaulted, including the Illinois Central, the Fort Wayne and Chicago, the Erie and the Pittsburgh, and the Reading lines. Western land values collapsed.

The end of the Crimean War may also have played a role, because the price of wheat began falling with the end of that war. The falling wheat prices may have put western farmers in a liquidity crunch, causing a drain on deposits from the eastern banks, and reducing speculation in western land.

The New York banks refused to rollover loans to brokers, causing a panic in the securities markets. The solvency of New York banks came into question as securities held as collateral dropped in value. The run on the New York banks began in mid-October: Half of the specie held by New York banks was withdrawn between 10 October and 14 October. New York banks suspended specie payments, and the scramble for specie led to a wave of bank suspensions, particularly in eastern states.

In 1856, more than one-fifth of British exports went to the United States. American securities were widely held in Britain, and trouble in Britain began after bad news arrived from United States. By 27 October, the Borough Bank of Liverpool and at least two large Scottish mercantile houses failed. Scottish banks either failed or suspended payments of specie. The British government suspended the Bank Charter Act of 1844, which required the Bank of England to maintain gold bullion reserves for all bank notes issued above a legal maximum. Serving as the lender of last resort, the Bank of England shipped gold to Scotland to ease the banking crisis. George Peabody and Co., an American banking and mercantile company, also obtained assistance from the Bank of England.

The financial crisis spread to Scandinavia, and then to Hamburg. Germany's fledgling banking industry saw many failures. The Bank of France raised its discount rate to prevent an outflow of gold, and securities prices in France fell.

The banking crisis proved temporary in the United States. Most American banks resumed specie payments in 1858, but trade and industry only recovered after the beginning of the Civil War.

The panic of 1857 was apparently propagated throughout the world economy by the financial system. A less likely possibility is that major economic fluctuations are a worldwide phenomenon that does not emanate from any one country. Learning how to use government economic policy to stabilize the capitalist economic system, to avoid crises, has been a preoccupation in the twentieth century.

See also Financial Panic of 1873, Stock Market Crash of 1929.

References Calomiris, Charles W., and Larry Schweikart. "The Panic of 1857: Origins, Transmission, and Containment." *The Journal of Economic History* (1991); Powell, Ellis T. *The Evolution of the Money Market: 1385–1915* (1915).

Financial Panic of 1873

The financial panic of 1873 marked the beginning of a deflationary trend in Europe and the United States that lasted until 1896. The Vienna stock market crashed in May 1873, halting the outflow of capital from Central Europe to the United States, whose railroad issues had been popular in German and Austrian stock markets. Financial panic began in the United States in September. England dodged the financial crisis, but nevertheless shared in the world industrial depression that followed.

The end of the 1870s saw a resurgence of restrictive trade barriers in response to poor economic conditions in many countries.

Railroad development boomed in the years immediately before the panic of 1873. U.S. railroad mileage doubled between 1866 and 1873. Russia had 12,000 miles of railroad come on line since 1868. Austria increased its railroad mileage from 2,200 to 6,000 miles between 1865 and 1873. The expansion of railroads, and cheaper steam transportation over water, acted to substantially increase the world's supplies of food and raw materials. Agricultural prices suffered from deflation to the end of the century.

Railroad expansion in the United States overshot the mark. Because prospects for immediate profits were low from new railroads built in sparsely populated areas, these companies had difficulty selling stock, and turned to banks and insurance companies for loan financing. When the railroads began defaulting on loans in 1873, the banks ran into difficulty. On 18 September, one of the nation's most established financial institutions, Jay Cooke and Company, failed when New York banks refused to extend additional credit. A run on banks began, and the stock market closed for ten days, because unloading stocks overburdened the system of selling by certified checks.

The Treasury injected added liquidity into the system by purchasing treasury bonds, and reissuing $26 million in greenbacks. The United States did not have a central banking system, at that time, to act as lender of last resort. New York banks made use of the New York Clearing House, which issued loan certificates against bonds, to add liquidity to the banking system.

The financial crisis manifested itself in Germany, where the corporate form of business organization was just gaining acceptance. In June 1870, Prussia could boast of 410 incorporated businesses. By the end of 1874, the number had increased to 2,267. Bank formation had become a virtual mania; 107 banks were created between 1870 and 1872, in Germany. Many of these banks did not survive the crisis of 1873.

The lull in railroad building threw the world into an industrial depression that lasted to the end of the decade. Finding ways to moderate sharp cyclical fluctuations associated with capitalism became a major focus of government policy in the twentieth century. The United States established a central banking system, and increased the size of its public sector, to smooth out cyclical fluctuations.

See also Depression of the 1890s, German Great Depression.

References Kindleberger, Charles P. *A Financial History of Western Europe* (1984); Myers, Margaret G. *A Financial History of the United States* (1970).

Financial Revolution (England)

The Glorious Revolution of 1688 brought William of Orange to the throne, who allegedly brought with him from Holland the knowledge of how to run a government that was deep in debt. The rapid innovations in public finance in the six decades after 1688 bear the marks of a revolution, in the eyes of some scholars. Referring to the system of public finance developed during that era, P. G. M. Dickson wrote,

> The rise of this system in the six decades before the Seven Years War was rapid enough, and important enough in both its main and secondary effects, to deserve the name of the Financial Revolution. Its effects on the country's life, social attitudes, and historical development resemble on a smaller scale those of the Industrial Revolution that followed it, and which it arguably helped to make possible.

Before the Financial Revolution, the English government issued a variety of obligations against itself in the form of sailors' tickets (scripts), army debentures, and, particularly, wooden tallies. The wooden tally ranks among the most unique forms of public debt to survive into the era of capitalist development.

The tally was a wooden stick notched with a code showing the amount of money the government owed. The government paid bills in tallies. The tally was split, and the government kept a smaller part, called the foil. These tallies circulated similar to money, but at discounts of between 20 and 30 percent, until the Bank of England began to make loans on them. When a tally was presented to the government in payment of an obligation, the government matched the two pieces and destroyed them, canceling the government obligation.

In addition to issuing these government obligations, the government could contract loans from private sources, always with the expectation that the loan would be repaid at a set date, but the government was often not timely in paying off its loans.

The essential features of the Financial Revolution lay in the development of long-term and short-term financial instruments that paid interest from dedicated sources, the emergence of financial markets that traded in these securities, and the establishment of the Bank of England. Parliament took the step to create a national debt in 1693 and 1694 by authorizing the issuance of lifetime annuities, sometimes stretching up to three lives, and by the floating of tontine loans. Tontine loans paid interest to a group of investors, who continued to divide the interest payments among the surviving investors. The government's obligation expired at the death of the last living investor. Parliament granted a charter for the Bank of England in April 1694, principally to raise funds for the government. This bank, holding government securities as collateral, issued bank notes, and made cash advances to the government. In April 1696, Parliament authorized the Exchequer (treasury of the British government) to issue short-term securities called Exchequer Bills. These bills also paid interest from dedicated sources.

The development of financial securities that were transferable, and could be traded, substantially increased the attractiveness of loaning funds to the government. These financial securities made safe investments for merchants and insurance companies, who often needed to convert investments into cash on short notice. Financial assets began to compete with land as an important means of holding wealth.

Some cynical observers saw the formation of a national debt as a means of securing public support for the government. Those who own government obligations automatically have a vested interest in the survival of the government, and see the necessity for collecting taxes.

With added efficiency in the system of pubic borrowing, England raised its public borrowing as a share of government expenditures from 31.4 percent in 1702–1713 to 39.9 in 1776–1783, enabling England to compete militarily with France, a much larger country. One authority even attributes the start of the French Revolution to the fiscal disarray of the French monarchy. Aided by the Financial Revolution, capitalist England survived the challenges flung down by France and other European powers, and rose to dominate colonial trade during the nineteenth century. The Financial Revolution also led to the development of financial markets that financed the Industrial Revolution.

See also Bank of England, Public Debt, South Sea Bubble.

References Dickson, G. M. *The Financial Revolution in England: A Study in the Development of Public Credit, 1688–1756* (1967); Kindleberger, Charles P. A *Financial History of Western Europe* (1984).

First Bank of the United States

The First Bank of the United States served as the U.S. government's bank from 1791 until 1811, and was the closest thing to a United States central bank during that time. The First Bank received its charter from the national government in 1791, when President George Washington signed the bill authorizing its incorporation. The First Bank of the United States was a brainchild of Alexander Hamilton, who saw such a bank as a means of raising short-term capital for the government. The government also wanted a bank to handle bills of exchange needed for making payments to foreign holders of the national debt. Hamilton promoted the bank as a means of increasing the bank notes in circulation. He patterned the First Bank after the role the Bank of England played in the English economy and government finance.

Hamilton's *Report on a National Bank* went to Congress in December 1790. The proposal drew fire from critics, who saw the bank as a monopoly sanctioned by Congress. As the debate on this issue waned, constitutional questions arose that were to haunt the bank for the duration of its life. The Constitutional Convention of 1787 had chosen not to give Congress the power to grant charters of incorporation, and the Constitution was silent on the subject.

The bill for the charter passed by a two-to-one vote in the House, and by a majority vote in the Senate, but Washington balked at signing the bill. When Thomas Jefferson, and others, urged Washington not to sign, Hamilton wrote a very able paper in defense of the First Bank, and Washington signed the bill chartering the bank.

The charter authorized a capital stock of $10 million. The U.S. government purchased one-fifth of the stock, paid for by a loan from the First Bank. The remaining four-fifths was opened for public subscription. Public subscribers could pay one-fifth in specie and four-fifths in government obligations. Within an hour, the bank was fully capitalized. Foreigners eventually held much of the stock. The charter prohibited the bank from trading in anything other than bills of exchange, gold and silver bullion, and goods held as security for defaulted loans. Only Congress could authorize the bank to make loans in excess of $100,000 to the U.S. government, to any state government, or to purchase any of the public debt. The total debt of the First Bank could not exceed its capital and money held on deposit.

The First Bank made Philadelphia its headquarters. Over Hamilton's opposition, the bank set up branches, one as far away as New Orleans. Commercial loans accounted for most of the bank's lending, and the bank served some of the functions of a central bank. At that time, bank loans were paid out in bank notes, convertible into specie on demand. The bank held the commercial banks accountable by presenting to them their bank notes for redemption in specie. This practice particularly helped control the issuance of bank notes by country banks, which was necessary to avoid inflation. The First Bank's role in controlling the issuance of bank notes won the support of the large commercial banks.

The charter for the First Bank came up for renewal in 1811. Constitutional issues and foreign ownership cost the First Bank much of its support in Congress. The vote for rechartering the First Bank failed by one vote in the House. The vice president broke the tie in the Senate by voting against the First Bank.

The United States was slow to accept a central bank. The Federal Reserve System was the first central bank in the United States to establish itself in the confidence of the voters. Central banks seem a necessary institution in capitalist countries for controlling inflation and counteracting cyclical fluctuations.

See also Bank of England, Central Banks and Free Banking, Federal Reserve System, Second Bank of the United States.

References Myers, Margaret G. *A Financial History of the United States* (1970); Timberlake, Richard H. *The Origins of Central Banking in the United States* (1978).

Florentine Industrial Capitalism

In the fourteenth and fifteenth centuries, the Italian city of Florence developed a capitalistic economy that bore an uncanny resemblance to modern capitalism. Among the similarities to capitalist societies evident in Florence were the rise of a business class to political power at the expense of the land-owning aristocracy, class warfare between an urban proletariat and the business class, the growth of export manufacturing, imperialism, and close collaboration between banking and industry.

The textile industry made up the industrial base of the Florentine economy, employing about 25 percent of the work force. Much of the work was organized in factories, with merchant capitalists supplying raw materials and machinery, and workers engaged in specialized tasks. Some processes were still at the handicraft stage, and merchant capitalists shuttled unfinished goods back and forth from factories to homes, until the product was finished.

Guilds achieved a degree of power and organization not seen again in European history. Merchants, manufacturers, bankers, professional groups, and skilled workers belonged to the greater guilds that stood at the apex of guild hierarchy. At the base of the guild pyramid were the minor guilds, which embraced butchers, bakers, blacksmith, carpenters, etc. Below the guilds were unions of industrial workers, and below the unionized workers were thousands of unorganized day laborers.

Following a pattern found in the history of modern capitalist states, the worker class made a bid for political power, after the business class had supplanted the land-owning aristocracy as the dominate political force. In 1345, ten labor leaders were executed for organizing the lower paid workers in the woolen industry. Foreign workers were imported to break the unions. In 1368, another working-class rebellion met with defeat. In 1378, however, the wool carders, led by Michele di Lando, staged a working-class rebellion that seized control of the levers of government, and established a dictatorship of the proletariat. The proletarian government legalized the unions of the lower-class workers, enacted a moratorium on debts of wage earners, and cut interest rates of wage-earner debts. Business leaders locked out workers, persuaded landowners to cut off the food supply, and hired strongmen to overthrow the proletarian government.

About 80 of the larger businesses in Florence also conducted banking business. The great bankers were members of the wool guilds, encouraging close cooperation between the international bankers and the textile trades. The Medici banking family were engaged in manufacturing silk and woolen goods, as well as in import–export trade in spices, almonds, and sugar. Great bankers, such as the Medici, opened offices in the major capitals of Europe, handled papal finances, and loaned money to governments and princes in return for trade concessions.

The drama of capitalist development played out in Florence would recur again as capitalist institutions spread to larger countries. With the discovery of the New World and the unification of small states in Europe, the size of capitalist economies grew larger, but the pattern of development remained similar to the one exhibited by Florentine capitalism. Put differently, the future history of capitalism could be interpreted as the results of applying the Florentine model of capitalism on a grander scale.

See also Class Struggle, Medici Bank, Paris Commune of 1871, Proletariat.

References Cox, Oliver C. *The Foundations of Capitalism* (1959); De Roover, Raymond. *The Rise and Decline of the Medici Bank, 1397–1494* (1966); Kline, Samuel. *The Laboring Classes in Renaissance Florence* (1980).

Food and Drug Act of 1906 (United States)

The Food and Drug Act of 1906 was the first important consumer protection legislation in the history of the United States. It provided for the creation of the Food and Drug Administration (FDA), which remains a major enforcement arm of the federal government's laws regulating food processing and drug manufacture and marketing. The enactment of the Food and Drug Act marks the waning of the nineteenth-century ideal of laissez-faire capitalism, voiced by Jefferson as "That government is best that governs least."

Massachusetts can lay claim to the first general food law in the United States, enacted in 1784. In the 1800s, other states enacted various measures to protect consumers in this area. Virginia passed a law in 1848, and Ohio in 1853. In 1850, California, one year after the gold rush, enacted a pure food and drink law. But state laws were ineffective in regulating food and drugs sold in interstate commerce.

The growth of large processing plants, and mass production and distribution, brought new health hazards from consuming food produced in unsanitary conditions, and which was sometimes purposely adulterated. Milk was often diluted with water, and chalk and plaster of Paris improved the color of milk from diseased animals. Fruit rotted on the shelves and spoiled meat awaited unwary consumers. Canned food was not always safer. American soldiers during the Spanish-American War died from eating canned meat that was decayed. Between 1879 and 1906, Congress considered over 100 food and drug bills.

In 1906, Upton Sinclair published *The Jungle*, which depicted unsavory processing in the meat-packing industry along the following lines:

It was only when the whole ham was spoiled that it came into the department of Elzbieta. Cut up by the 2,000-revolutions-a-minute flyers, and mixed with half a ton of other meat, no odor that ever was in a ham could make any difference. There was never the least attention paid to what was cut up for sausage; there would come all the way back from Europe old sausage that had been rejected, and that was mouldy and white—it would be dosed with borax and glycerine, and dumped into the hoppers, and made over again for home consumption. There would be meat that had tumbled out on the floor, in the dirt and sawdust, where the workers had tramped and spit uncounted billions of consumption germs. There would be meat stored in great piles in rooms; and the water from leaky roofs would drip over it, and thousands of rats would race about on it. It was too dark in these storage places to see well, but a man could run his hand over these piles of meat and sweep off handfuls of the dried dung of rats. These rats were nuisances, and the packers would put poisoned bread out for them, they would die, and then rats, bread, and meat would go into the hoppers together.

After reading *The Jungle*, President Theodore Roosevelt launched an investigation of the meat packing industry. The public was equally aroused, and a food and drug bill that had stalled in Congress suddenly took on new life and became law as the Food and Drug Act of 1906.

In addition to providing for the establishment of the FDA, the act banned adulterated and misbranded foods and drugs that traded in interstate commerce. The use of decomposed or diseased animal or vegetable substances in food processing was made illegal, as were additives that were harmful to the health of consumers. The act also banned the use of artificial coloring and coating for the purpose of concealing the true condition of foods. The labels of drugs could not bear false and misleading claims of effectiveness, and foods had to be properly labeled, including the correct weight. Violators faced criminal penalties, and repeat offenders could serve prison sentences.

Since the passage of the Food and Drug Act of 1906, Congress has enacted a rather impressive list of legislative measures to strengthen it and expand its coverage. The activities of the FDA now include such things as protecting consumers from exposure to radiation from medical x-rays, color televisions, and microwave ovens. The FDA administers a federal law that prohibits the use of food additives that cause cancer in animals or humans. Pharmaceutical manufacturers must obtain FDA approval before marketing new drugs, which the FDA tests against manufacturers' claims for curative power and safety for human use.

The philosophy of laissez-faire capitalism frowns on government regulation, because it allows governments to play favorites in the struggle for economic survival. Governments can reward friends who own regulated businesses by letting up a bit on the regulation. It can punish enemies by subjecting their businesses to stringent enforcement of regulations. Despite the risk of partiality, government regulation appears virtually indispensable in certain areas, particularly those touching on the health and well-being of consumers.

See also Consumer Product Safety Act of 1972.

References Schnitzer, Martin C. *Contemporary Government and Business Relations* (1978); Spiro, George W. *The Legal Environment of Business* (1993); U.S. Food and Drug Administration. *Milestones in Food and Drug Law History* (1974).

Ford, Henry (1863–1947)

By fully exploiting, and improving on, assembly-line techniques of mass production, Henry Ford brought the ownership of an automobile within the reach of Americans with modest incomes.

On 30 July 1863, Ford was born to a farm family of Irish immigrants near Dearborn, Michigan. He early demonstrated an aptitude and interest in farm machinery and mechanical gadgets, such as clocks and watches, and left school at the age of 15 to become a machinist's apprentice in Detroit. He spent his spare time tinkering with mechanical devices, particularly internal combustion engines. In 1899, he gave up his position as chief engineer of the Edison Company of Detroit to form, with a number of associates, the Detroit Automobile Company, a manufacturer of custom automobiles. He left this company to build and drive racing automobiles, where his success brought the kind of credibility he needed to attract partners for a major undertaking. In 1903,

Ford launched the Ford Motor Company, with the aid of 12 partners who together put up $28,000.

Parts for the Ford cars were subcontracted by several suppliers, and Ford Motor Company rented an assembly plant for $75 per month, and hired ten assemblers for $1.50 per day. The new company tried to produce 10 cars per day, and faced stiff competition from numerous new companies entering the automobile manufacturing business.

After Ford bought out five of his partners, giving him controlling interest in his company, he designed the Model T for mass production. He described it as an automobile for the "great multitudes." His remaining partners considered the venture a major risk. In 1909, the price of a Model T was slightly less than $1,000. With improvements in mass production, the price fell to $295, before the model was discontinued two decades later. It was the only car that Ford Motor Company produced. In 1914, Ford Motor Company produced 250,000 Model Ts, which accounted for 45 percent of all the automobiles produced in the United States that year.

In 1914, Ford created a sensation in American industry by announcing that Ford would pay a wage of $5.00 a day, and would adopt the eight-hour day. Since the going wage rate at the time ranged between $2.00 and $3.00 per day, workers lined up outside the gates at Ford waiting for a chance to earn $5.00 per day. Ford explained the move by saying, "We wanted to pay these wages so that the business would be on a lasting foundation. We were building for the future. A low wage business is always insecure.... The payment of $5.00 a day for a eight-hour day was one of the finest cost-cutting moves we ever made."

An engineering report at the time stated, "The Ford high wage does away with all the inertia and living force resistance.... The workingmen are absolutely docile, and it is safe to say that since the last day of 1913, every single day has seen major reductions in Ford Shops' labor costs. With the new wage absenteeism fell 75 percent."

Ford eventually bought out the other stockholders and made Ford Motor Company a family business. The other stockholders had successfully taken Ford to court for not distributing cash surpluses as dividends. Ford was skeptical of bankers and Wall Street, and preferred to finance expansion with capital generated internally.

Ford Motor Company grew to become one of the "Big Three" automobile manufacturers in the United States. By the time he died on 7 April 1947, Ford had seen the automobile transform American life.

Henry Ford is a fine example of the capitalist entrepreneur. He did not invent the automobile, nor did he invent the assembly line. Nevertheless, he saw the opportunity to produce the automobile inexpensively by producing it on a mass scale, using an assembly line, and he saw that people would buy it in great numbers if the price was low enough. By improving on the assembly line methods of Eli Whitney, Ford made automobiles affordable to the lowest third of income earners in the United States.

See also Entrepreneurship; Factory System; Whitney, Eli.

References Batchelor, Ray. *Henry Ford, Mass Production, Modernism, and Design* (1994); Gelderman, Carol. *Henry Ford: The Wayward Capitalist* (1981); Mankiw, Gregory. *Macroeconomics* (1992).

Foreign Aid
See Marshall Plan.

Free Trade
See Classical School of Economics, Cockayne Project, Continental System, Corn Laws, Depression of the 1890s, Judaism and Capitalism.

French East India Company
See Colbertism.

French Revolution and Napoleon

Never in the history of one country have the institutions of capitalism asserted themselves so forcefully in the face of medieval traditions, customs, and laws as during the French Revolution. Amid the chaos of the Revolution, General Napoleon Bonaparte seized power in a military coup (1799), and began the process of restoring order to the government and economy of France, until he was militarily defeated at Waterloo in 1815. From the viewpoint of capitalist development, Napoleon's government can be regarded as an extension of this process. In the words of Karl Marx, one of capitalism's harshest critics,

> Napoleon established throughout France the conditions that made it possible for free competition to develop, for landed property to be exploited after the partition of the great estates, and for the nation's productive powers of industrial production to be utilized to the full. Across the frontiers he made a clearance of feudal institutions, in so far as this was requisite to provide French bourgeois society with a suitable environment upon the continent of Europe.

In the early stages of the French Revolution (1789–1791), the National Assembly abolished the feudal system, manorial jurisdictions, and privileges of the nobility. Ecclesiastical tithes likewise came to an end in 1791. Some of the rights associated with particular pieces of land survived until 1793, when the National Convention ended them. The Declaration of the Rights of Man and of the Citizen (27 August 1789) stated that "private property is an inviolable and sacred right."

Government impediments to the conduct of business were swept away: Regulation and inspection of industrial products fell by the wayside. Privileged companies, such as royal manufacturers, lost their grants. One law (March 1791) declared guilds and workingmen's associations illegal and held that everybody now was "free to do such business and to exercise such profession, art, or trade as he may choose."

The National Assembly struck down the internal tariffs and controls that acted as a constriction on the flow of trade inside the borders of France. Laws forbidding the free circulation of goods internally came to an end. The National Assembly invited the Academy of Sciences to make recommendations for a unified system of weights and measures. A new tariff boundary at the foreign border protected French goods from foreign competition. Funds earmarked for charity and unemployment relief paid for the repair of roads, whose conditions had deteriorated.

In January 1791, the National Assembly passed a patent law. This law protected inventors for a maximum of 15 years, giving them the exclusive right to market their inventions. The Mining College (1793) and the Polytechnic (1794) came into being for the education of government engineers.

The Revolution abolished the French slave trade in 1793 and a year later freed the slaves in French colonies, and devolved upon them the full rights of citizenship. Napoleon later reestablished slavery in the colonies.

Napoleon's reformation of the law, the

Liberty Leading the People, *by Eugene Delacroix (Louvre collection)*

Napoleonic Code, ratified many of the economic reforms of the Revolution. French citizens continued to enjoy the freedom to enter any trade or profession. Associations of workers, collective bargaining, and strikes were alike illegal in the eyes of the law. Artisans were required to have identity cards, after 1803. The activities of the working classes aroused the close scrutiny of the police. Courts of law took the word of the employer in questions of wages paid to workers. An edict of 1806, authorizing the conciliation councils, put the employer representation on such councils in the majority.

Napoleon's government supported a society for encouraging industry that paid prizes for inventions and technical improvements.

One of Napoleon's greatest achievements in economic reform was the establishment of the Bank of France. This bank became the central bank for France. The new bank was capitalized at 30 million franks, 5 million of which came from the French government. The bank served as the fiscal agent for the government, holding deposits for the government, and dispersing dividends on government loans. The bank held a monopoly on the issuance of paper money in Paris.

Napoleon turned his attention with good effect to the neglected national system of transport. Under his decree of 1811, the construction and maintenance of main arteries became the responsibility of the central government. Local authorities assumed similar responsibility for the secondary roads. Military needs inspired some of the internal improvements, which did not detract from their usefulness to the economy.

Napoleon's continental blockade closed all the ports and coasts on the European Continent to British goods, and gave French goods a privileged position in markets on the continent, but this was more a measure to bring Britain to terms than an economic measure to protect French industry. Nevertheless, the continental blockade was a vast departure from the Anglo-French Commercial Treaty of 1786, signed on the eve of the Revolution. This treaty, which liberalized trade between the two countries, had drawn strong criticism from French manufacturers.

The experience of the French Revolution planted the idea in the French working classes of redressing their grievances through political revolution. They set to work to overthrow the business classes, just as the latter had overthrown the hereditary aristocracy. That is, workers emphasized mobilizing a political movement to overthrow the government, rather than negotiating with individual employers for better pay, hours, and working conditions. As a result, unions of the English and American model were slow to develop in France.

Under Napoleon, the French business classes consolidated their gains from the French Revolution. Subsequent governments followed Napoleon's example of maintaining tight control over working-class agitation. Unions were only legalized at the end of the nineteenth century. Napoleon's wars, and emphasis upon military spending, acted as a serious drag on the French economy, costing him support for his government. His centralized approach to government, however, shaped such organizations as the Bank of France, which influenced central bank development worldwide. Aside from a brief interlude under Napoleon III, France continued, throughout the nineteenth century, to shield domestic industry from foreign competition with high tariffs.

See also Bank of France, Continental System, Hyperinflation of the French Revolution, Le Chapelier Law, Livret.

References Clough, Shepard Bancroft. *France: A History of National Economics, 1789 to 1939* (1964); Henderson, O. *The Industrial Revolution in Europe, 1815–1914* (1961); Lefebvre, George. *The French Revolution*, Vols. 1–2 (1964); Schroeder, Paul W. *The Transformation of European Politics, 1763–1848* (1994).

French Usury Laws

Usury laws either ban the payment of interest on loans, or put a legal ceiling on interest rates. Historically, the medieval Catholic Church frowned on charging interest. As late as 1950, Pope Pius XII felt it necessary to declare that bankers "earn their livelihood honestly." In the late medieval period, the Church began to accept certain forms of credit that involved the payment of interest of up to 5 percent.

In the earliest period in French history, the crown often borrowed through forced loans at zero interest. Businesses found ways to work around the Church prohibition on interest.

In 1311, Philip the Fair (IV) drew a distinction between usury and trade loans made at fairs. He set a maximum of 2.5 percent for commercial loans between fairs. The annualized rate of this maximum added up to about 15 percent. During the same year, the legal pawnshop maximum stood at 21.66 percent. Later, this maximum rose to a high of 173.33 percent; in 1361, it stood at 86 percent. Apparently, the tax coffers benefited from the pawnshop loans; therefore, rates varied, depending upon the needs of the national budget and public opinion.

The French crown aided the growth of a competitive credit market in Lyon, by setting a private loan limit of 15 percent in that city. In 1522, Francis I floated (as opposed to forced) private annuities, called rentes, at 8.33 percent. In 1597, Henry IV forcibly reduced the rate to 4 percent. In 1551, he sold 12-percent bills, which at one point were discounted to yield 28 percent. These bills returned to par. In 1557, under the pressure of a financial crisis, Henry IV suspended payments and the government's credit deteriorated.

In 1601, Henry IV issued an edict putting a 6.25-percent legal ceiling on interest rates. The reasons that prompted this edict are unclear, but his government was active in promoting commerce, which may have been the justification. The edict was widely disregarded. Under the regime of Cardinal Richelieu, a royal edict (1634) further reduced the legal rate of interest to 5.55 percent, citing evil effects of high interest rates: They allowed people to live on interest income, instead of engaging in commerce.

During the time of Jean Baptiste Colbert, Louis XIV issued a royal edict (1665) lowering the maximum interest rate to 5 percent. Colbert also felt low interest rates gave investors an incentive to directly finance business and commercial activities. He saw high interest rates as a cause of unemployment and retarded trade. He is reported to have said that "a banker should behave toward a finance minister like a soldier toward a general." Apparently, the 5-percent maximum was not strictly enforced. The government sometimes paid more. The maximum was later raised to 5.55 percent on all loans, except those contracted at the fairs at Lyon. The edict also declared that all promises to pay higher rates were null and void.

The discussion at the time of Louis XIV's edict of 1665 is revealing. Louis XIV felt pangs of conscience for sanctioning the payment of interest, given the attitude of the Church. Before issuing the edict, he held an informal meeting with five of the most learned doctors of the Sorbonne, to discuss the matter. The dean of the faculty spoke first, and said that such a weighty matter should be discussed at a meeting of the whole faculty. The faculty took up the subject in the light of Scripture, writings of Church fathers, the decisions of various councils, and decrees of Popes. One of the doctors reported their findings, saying, "No doctor of the Sorbonne could approve the proposition that one could take interest on money or set the rate thereof."

In 1766, a law attempted to lower the interest rates from 5 to 4 percent, but it was not obeyed. Interest rates remained in the 5-percent range until the French Revolution, when interest-rate ceilings were abolished. The assignats, the fiat paper money of the French Revolution, originally paid 5 percent.

The practice of setting interest-rate ceilings fit with the mercantilist philosophy of a highly regulated economy. According to the principles of laissez-faire capitalism, interest rates, like other prices, should be set by supply and demand. The view has survived into the modern era that low interest rates contribute to economic prosperity. The proper method of securing low interest rates, however, is to provide for an ample supply of credit, rather than putting a legal lid on interest rates. The ample supply of credit must come from savings, rather than printing up new money, which can cause inflation.

See also Colbertism, French Revolution and Napoleon.

References Cole, Charles Woolsey. *Colbert and a Century of French Mercantilism* (1964); Homer, Sidney. *A History of Interest Rates* (1977).

Fugger Family

The Fugger family stands as an outstanding example of the merchant princes that emerged in the early phase of the evolution of capitalism. The Fugger family not only became the wealthiest family in fifteenth- and sixteenth-century Europe, but showed how to translate access to financial capital into political power.

Johannes Fugger began life as a weaver's son, twice married the daughters of masters of the weavers guild, and rose to become a successful textile merchant. He left a small fortune at his death (1409). His seventh son, Jakob, learned the goldsmith's trade, married the daughter of the mint master, and carried on the family business. At his death (1469), he was the seventh wealthiest citizen in Augsburg. Three of Jakob's sons, Ulrich, Georg, and Jakob II, took up the family business. They expanded into international trade, and made loans to feudal princes in Germany, Austria, and Hungary.

Jakob II applied himself to learning the cutting-edge techniques of business management, including double-entry bookkeeping. He entered into agreements with other firms to fix prices of various products. In 1498, Jakob II and his brothers, in cooperation with Augsberg merchants, cornered the market on Venetian copper. Through intermarriage, the family became party to a cartel to mine the silver and copper deposits of Hungary. The purpose of the cartel was to fix prices as high as possible. By 1501, the Fuggers could boast of a vast, far-flung mining operation, with mines in Germany, Austria, Hungary, Bohemia, and Spain. Textiles, manufactured or imported, remained a part of the family business. They also dealt in silk, velvet, furs, spices, citrus fruits, jewelry, and munitions.

The Fuggers made direct loans to Charles V and his family, usually secured by revenue from mining operations. Fugger loans helped Charles V (then Charles I, King of Spain) become Emperor of the Holy Roman Empire. Jakob II wrote to Charles in connection these loans,

It is well known that your Majesty without me might not have acquired the Imperial honor, as I can attest with the written statement of all the delegates.... And in all this I have looked not to my own profit.... My respectful re-

Jakob Fugger, member of the German family of financiers and merchants, from an engraving by Hans Burgkmair

quest is that you will graciously...order that the money which I have paid out, together with the interest on it, shall be returned without further delay.

When Charles V was at war with Francis I of France, the Fuggers backed Charles, and the Genoese banks backed Francis I. By 1540, the Fuggers were raising funds on the Antwerp Bourse, and relending them to Spain. In 1557, Philip II, son of Charles, suspended payments on his debts, and forced the Fuggers to consolidate his debts in a long-term loan. This loan was made at 12-percent interest, and was secured by tax receipts from the Netherlands. Bankruptcy became a regular occurrence for the Spanish crown, a total of six times between 1557 and 1647. The third bankruptcy in 1596 ruined the Fuggers.

Jakob Fugger II committed nearly every one of the sins attributed to the early capitalists. He practiced usury, and urged Charles V to rescind or amend laws against usury. In 1540, Charles V issued a decree that allowed a maximum of 12-percent interest. Fugger cornered markets to raise prices, violating the church doctrine of the just price. Last, he loaned money to kings to finance wars. His business practices drew scathing criticism from Martin Luther.

See also Financial Crisis of 1557.

References Durant, Will. *The Reformation* (1957); Homer, Sidney. *A History of Interest Rates* (1977); Kindleberger, Charles P. *A Financial History of Western Europe* (1984); Matthews, George T. *The Fugger Newsletter* (1959); Strieder, Jacob. *Jacob Fugger the Rich, Merchant and Banker of Augsburg* (1931).

Futures Markets

Futures markets are markets in which contracts are traded for future purchases and sales of commodities or financial claims. In a futures market, Quaker Oats can buy a contract for the delivery of oats six months or a year in the future, locking-in the future price of oats, avoiding the risk of unanticipated changes in the price of oats. Futures contracts are traded only in organized exchanges, such as the Chicago Board of Trade. Futures contracts are also traded to lock-in future interest rates, stock prices, and foreign currency exchange rates. Grains, feeds, livestock, industrial raw materials, precious metals, foods, Treasury bonds, and foreign currencies are typical of the real and financial assets traded in futures markets.

Futures markets began as far back as the tulipmania speculation in Holland, early in the seventeenth century. The volatility of commodities prices, interest rates, and foreign exchange rates in the 1970s and 1980s led to renewed interest in futures markets, and to the creation of futures markets in new areas. From 1991 through 1995, the Chicago Board of Trade approved new futures contracts for 85 different commodities and financial assets. On the list of new futures contracts were black-tiger shrimp, Brazilian bonds, recycled plastic, electricity, and milk. Only 20 percent of these newly approved futures contracts were successful.

Closely related to markets for futures contracts are markets for options. An option contract confers the right to buy or sell a real or financial asset over a range of time. Options come in two varieties. A call option confers the right to buy a real or financial asset at a prescribed price over a range of time. A put option confers the right to sell a real or financial asset at a prescribed price over a range of time. Although the parties to futures contracts are obligated to buy and sell at the contract prices, the owners of options have the option to buy or sell, which they may or may not exercise. Trading in options has often been regarded as pure gambling, and, during the 1920s, the Chicago Board of Trade banned trade in options, but, in the 1980s, trading in commodity options returned. Options are also traded for Treasury bonds, foreign currencies, and stock market indices.

See also Amsterdam Exchange, New York Stock Exchange, Sir John Bernard's Act, Tulipmania.

References Ferris, William G. *The Grain Traders* (1988); Keown, Arthur J., et al. *Foundations of Finance* (1998).

General Agreement on Tariffs and Trade

The General Agreement on Tariffs and Trade (GATT), an organization of the world's major trading partners, holds multilateral negotiations to lower trade barriers. The organization began in 1947 as an agreement among 29 countries to engage in negotiations to ease trade restrictions. Now, GATT can claim close to 100 members, plus another significant group of nonmember countries, who participate in the negotiations without having joined the organization. In addition to sponsoring multilateral negotiations, GATT acts as an ongoing organization that oversees the trade policies of its members.

The first round of trade negotiations, held in Geneva in 1947, succeeded in negotiating mutually acceptable reductions in trade barriers. Memories of the destructive trade barriers raised during the Depression were still fresh during these negotiations. The next three rounds (Annecy, France, 1949; Torquay, England, 1951; Geneva, 1956) met with less success. Another round of negotiations, held in Geneva in 1956, called the Dillon round, after the then-U.S. secretary of the treasury, also failed to impress observers.

Growing interest in the United States for access to the European Common Market led the U.S. government to push for more progress in reducing trade barriers. The enactment of the Trade Expansion Act of 1962 gave the U.S. president the authority to negotiate tariff reductions on the order of 50 percent. One provision of this act authorized the president to negotiate reductions across the board, rather than item by item. This provision enabled broad categories of goods to be treated as one item for negotiation, and it also provided that U.S. workers, who were displaced by foreign imports, could qualify for special assistance, such as extended unemployment compensation and help for retooling.

The Trade Expansion Act helped launch a new round of negotiations between 1962 and 1967, called the Kennedy Round. Seventy countries entered into these negotiations, which achieved, on average, a 35-percent reduction in tariffs on manufactured goods. The reductions were widespread, with 64 percent of manufactured goods seeing some reduction in tariffs.

As tariff rates came down, attention turned to nontariff barriers, which countries appeared to have been imposing in greater numbers, to offset the effects of tariff reductions. The Tokyo Round of trade negotiations took place between 1974 and 1979. The preliminary meeting was held in Tokyo in 1973, but the multilateral negotiations were held in Geneva. Again, Congress authorized the U.S. president to agree to substantial reductions in trade barriers. The Tokyo Round reduced tariff rates on manufactured goods by 33 percent, to be phased in over eight years, and produced agreement on a code of behavior with respect to nontrade barriers. This round of negotiations accepted the concept that less-developed countries should be exempted from reciprocity in tariff reductions. After these negotiations, the average tariff rates on manufactured goods for major trading partners ranged from a 2.9-percent low for Japan to a 6.3-percent high for West Germany. Tariff rates in the industrialized world are now at historically low levels.

The latest round of multilateral negotiations, which lasted from 1986 to 1990, started in Punta del Este, Uruguay, and became known as the Uruguay Round. This round began with a very ambitious agenda, but did not lead to important agreements that liberalized trade. Reducing tariff rates on agricultural products, and reducing nontrade barriers, ranked high in priority for this round of negotiations. The United States wanted more worldwide protection for its patents and copyrights.

In 1776, Adam Smith, in *An Inquiry into the Nature and Causes of the Wealth of Nations*, wrote of the advantages of free trade. In the post-World War II era, the nations of the world have shown sustained commitment to freer trade. For the first time since Adam Smith wrote his classic work in economics, free trade may be the wave of the future.

See also Anglo-French Commercial Treaty of 1786, Corn Laws.

References Appleyard, Dennis R., and Alfred J. Field, Jr. *International Economics* (1992); Daniels, John D., and Lee H. Radebaugh. *International Business* (1998).

General Strike

A general strike is a widespread work stoppage, affecting most of the major industries in a nation, region, or locality. It should leave society in a state of economic paralysis. A general strike may develop out of working-class sympathy for workers in conflict with a particular firm or industry. The British general strike of 1926 began as a sympathy strike for locked-out coal miners. General strikes have been used as a weapon to gain political reform, such as constitutional government or universal suffrage. The Russian general strike of 1905 led to the creation of an elected representative body called the Duma. A general strike may signal the first stages of a revolutionary overthrow of society, such as erupted at the beginning of the Russian Revolution of 1917. The Polish union Solidarity made use of general strikes as a weapon against a communist government.

The idea of a general strike as a flexing of proletarian muscle can be traced to the French Revolution. Maribeau reminded the Third Estate that the people produced everything, and that their power would be evident if they became motionless. In 1832, William Benbow outlined a proposal for a general strike in a pamphlet with the suggestive title of *Grand National Holiday and Congress of the Production Classes*. After Louis Napoleon's coup d'etat of 1851, Giradin, a French publicist, summed up the idea of a general strike:

> Let merchants cease to sell, the customers to buy, the laborers to work, the butchers to slaughter, the bakers to bake, let everyone cease to work, even the national press; let Louis Napoleon find neither compositor to set up Le Moniteur, nor printer to run it off, nor a bill-poster to put it up! Isolated, solitude, emptiness all around this man! With nothing but folding arms around him, he must fall. Let us organize the universal strike!

Fresh momentum for the concept of a general strike came from the United States in 1886. In Chicago, a general strike became part of the agitation for the eight-hour day. This strike culminated in the Haymarket Riot and a bomb explosion that killed several policemen and workers. When word of these activities reached Europe, interest in the general strike revived.

The literature of the French labor movement fully developed the theory of the general strike as a weapon in the class struggle. Although the general strike was touted in French working-class agitation as an effective measure, France never saw a general strike put into action. General strikes broke out in Belgium in 1893 and 1902, in Russia in 1905, and in Sweden in 1909. General strikes played an important role in Germany after World War I.

Nationwide general strikes sparked the Russian Revolution of 1905. These strikes grew out of industrial grievances, but turned to mass political strikes. The decisive part the general strikes played in the Revolution of 1905 raised the credibility of the general strike in the eyes of working-class agitators, and, particularly, Marxists. Some socialists advocated the use of the general strike as a means of stopping wars between capitalist nations.

The most significant general strike in history occurred in Great Britain in 1926. Although this was a sympathy strike, the government saw it as the first step in a revolution. The government was well prepared for the strike, and effectively crushed it.

Capitalist countries have now enacted reforms that have defused the revolutionary fever that was building in the late nineteenth and early twentieth century. In capitalist countries, skepticism has replaced much of the revolutionary certainty that added thrust to the use of general strikes to achieve economic and political reform.

See also British General Strike of 1926.

References Phillip, G. A. *The General Strike: The Politics of Industrial Conflict* (1976); Ridley, F. *Revolutionary Syndicalism in France* (1970).

Genoa

For a short span of about 70 years, from 1557 to 1627, Genoa stood at the apex of the capitalist world. The Genoese merchant bankers managed Europe's capital, credit, payments, and transactions. As often happens, geography lent a hand in the development of a capitalist city. With a screen of mountains at its back, Genoa faced the sea, blessed with numerous rivers and inlets that made excellent ports.

The mountains weakened the hold of feudal and religious authorities on governance of Genoa, giving the bourgeoisie an edge in the struggle with the nobility and bishops for political control of the city. In 958, the joint kings of Italy, Berengariuss III and Adalbert, granted Genoa a charter of freedom from crown interference. In the twelfth century, Frederick I of Germany demanded that Genoa respect his sovereignty, and Genoa paid him 1,200 silver marks per year. By the mid-thirteenth century, however, Genoa's defiance of the crown was complete. Class warfare between the nobility and a bourgeois aristocracy, often drawing in the lower classes, continued to darkened the politics

of Genoa. In 1363, Genoa enacted a law prohibiting members of the nobility from holding public office. In 1383, butchers, armed with the tools of their trade, marched on the palace of the doge, and compelled a reduction in taxes. From 1390 to 1394, Genoa boasted of ten revolutions, and ten doges.

Genoa shared with England a bent toward piracy during the early stages of capitalist development. Genoese pirates preyed on the Saracens, who had hemmed in Genoa by occupying Sicily, Corsica, Sardinia, and the Balearics. By the eleventh century, Genoa and Pisa had mostly ousted the Saracens; Genoa became a major participant in the first crusade, and afterwards shared in the Levantine trade. Something of the skill of Genoa's sea captains can be gleaned from the explorations of the most famous Genoese mariner, Christopher Columbus.

The industry that made Genoa the leader of the capitalist world was banking. Genoese merchant bankers conducted business throughout Europe, making loans and transferring funds. During a war with Venice during the fourteenth century, the city had raised money from citizens in return for promissory notes. At the end of the war, Genoa pledged the customs dues from its port to redeem the notes. The creditors organized themselves into a bank, the House of St. George, appointed eight directors to watch after their investments, collected taxes, and made loans to the state. Modern central banks can trace their ancestry to the House of St. George.

In 1557, the bankruptcy of the Spanish crown dealt a heavy blow to German banking, and Genoese banking stepped forward to fill the vacuum. Genoese banks financed voyages to the New World, and provided financing to the Spanish government between shipments of gold and silver. The influx of gold and silver created a need for banking mechanisms for transferring funds. Genoese bankers made use of bills of exchange to transfer funds whenever funds were needed to pay the expenses of the Spanish government.

Genoa's control of European finances was brief. Repeated bankruptcies of the Spanish crown may have scared the Genoese bankers, or perhaps the Dutch and English demanded more involvement in the shipment and distribution of the precious metals from the New World. By 1647, Dutch ships carried Spanish silver directly to the Low Countries.

Genoa wore the aspect of a capitalist city in every respect, and rose to prominence in the European financial system. It did not necessarily make unique contributions to the development of capitalism, but it further contributed to the capitalist system of European banking.

See also Financial Crisis of 1557.

References Braudel, Fernand. *The Mediterranean and the Mediterranean World in the Age of Phillip II* (1972); Braudel, Fernand. *Civilization and Capitalism* (1984).

German Great Depression
(1873–1896)

In Germany, as in other western countries, historians designated the period from 1873 to 1896 the great depression. The German economy exhibited a pattern of falling prices and interest rates, agricultural abundance, and rising real wages. Profits felt the squeeze of falling prices, and the growth rate of capital investment fell off.

Some economic historians regard the great depression in the last quarter of the nineteenth century as a myth that should be dispelled. Although prices definitely fell, and workers had to accept cuts in money wages, Germany witnessed expansions in industrial output and overseas trade. Since retail prices tended to fall faster than money wages, real wages rose. Nevertheless, a feeling of economic pessimism pervaded the era, and the phases of prosperity were shorter and milder than the recessions. Two cyclical upswings, in 1879–1882 and 1886–1889, separated three cyclical downswings, in 1873–1879, 1882–1886, and 1890–1894. German industrialists found economic conditions less favorable than the conditions that prevailed in the 1850s and 1860s. The growth in industrial output fell below the trends of the previous prosperity, between 1849 and 1873, and the following prosperity, between 1897 and 1914. Part of the gloom of the era may have come from the stock market speculative frenzy of 1872 and 1873, which came to a crashing end. Never had so many suicides followed a speculative debacle in Germany.

During the depression, the focus of German politics changed from discussions about political freedom to a fight for economic security. At first, the government stood committed to the principles of laissez-faire individualism, counting on the rationality of market mechanisms, and believing in self-correcting market adjustments. After 1877, the government began to abandon principles of laissez faire, and subsidized private initiatives engaged in public works. The short-lived flirtation with free trade came to an end in 1879, when the government turned to a protective tariff as the chief source of revenue for the imperial government. The nationalization of railroads also became an aim of government policy.

As unemployment spread, the working-class movement grew in aggressiveness and discontent, becoming a threatening source of instability and agitation for socialist ideas. The government enacted the Antisocialist Law of 1878, to outlaw significant labor union involvement in politics. The official view was that trade union activities dampened business confidence and impaired economic recovery. To break the alliance between labor and socialism, the government initiated its own program of economic security, enacting laws for compulsory worker's insurance against illness, accidents, involuntary unemployment, and old age. The Industrial Code of 1891 regulated working conditions.

In the eyes of German industrialists, cutthroat competition often appeared as the cause of deflation and economic instability. After the mid-1880s, the government encouraged cartels in industry, banking, and the professions. Cooperation replaced competition among rivals, as these cartels coordinated output decisions to stem the tide of falling prices.

Germany's reaction to the great depression of 1873 to 1896 anticipated the reaction of other capitalist countries to later depressions. The vague outlines of Roosevelt's New Deal can be found in Germany's economic and social policy in the last quarter of the nineteenth century. Aside from the social security and unemployment programs, the National Recovery Act, which was later found unconstitutional, set out to achieve many of the same objectives as the cartels in Germany. The agricultural programs of the New Deal did restrict output to maintain prices. The demand for tariff protection of domestic industry also became a familiar theme heard in times of economic distress. In the United States, many of the Depression era policies that discouraged price competition have been dismantled since the mid-1970s.

See also Cartels, Finance Capitalism, Social Insurance, Unemployment Insurance, Employer Liability and Worker Compensation.

References Hoffmann, Charles. *The Depression of the Nineties: An Economic History* (1970); Rosenberg, Hans. "Political and Social Consequences of the Great Depression in Central Europe." *Economic History Review* (1943).

German Tariff of 1879

The Tariff of 1879 represented a sharp turn toward protectionism, and abandonment of the free-trade policies that Germany had enacted between 1865 and 1873. In the words of Prince Bismarck, "I propose to return to the time-honored ways of 1823 to 1865. We left them in the latter year."

Germany's flirtation with free trade ended after the commercial crises of 1873, when industry struggled against economic depression, and the iron industry in Germany found itself undersold by English iron manufacturers. The free-trade proponents lost a valuable ally when the agricultural interest went over to the cause of protectionism. In the early nineteenth century, agriculture was a stronghold for free-trade sentiment in many countries, including the United States. By the 1870s, the development of railways had increased agricultural exports from the United States and Russia, at the expense of German agricultural exports. Faced with rising competition from the United States and Russia, German agricultural interest now favored preference for German goods in the German market.

An additional factor favoring a return to protectionist trade policies lay in the need to reform the government's finances. Individual German states contributed revenue to finance an imperial government that was demanding ever-increasing contributions. Bismarck saw import duties as a form of indirect taxation that would induce less discontent than the current direct taxation.

In February 1879, Emperor Wilhelm II expressed his support for a new protectionist tariff by stating,

The Federal governments are considering legislative measures for the removal, or at least the diminution, of the economic evils from which we are suffering. The proposals which I have made, and still intend to make, to my allies aim, by providing the Empire with a new source of revenue, at placing the Governments in a position to desist from levying the taxes which they and their Legislatures recognize as the hardest to enforce. At the same time I am of opinion that the country's entire economic activity has a right to claim all the support which legislative adjustment of duties and taxes can afford.... I regard it as my duty to adopt measures to preserve the German market to national production...and our customs legislation must accordingly revert to the tried principles upon which the prosperous career of the Zollverein rested for nearly half a century, but which have in important particulars been deserted in our mercantile since.

The revised tariff passed into law in July 1879, designed on the philosophy that all domestically produced goods deserved preference in the home market. This approach was intended to diffuse the opposition often aroused when special protection is granted to individual industries. Referring to Germany's abandonment of the principles of free trade, Bismarck quipped that Germany ceased to be "the dupe of an honest conviction."

The German economy prospered under the new tariff. Employment in the iron industry increased 35 percent between 1879 and 1884. Prices stood steady, wages rose, and shipping prospered as exports climbed. In December 1884, Bismarck told the Reichstag that the new trade policy had "freed the country of its poverty of blood."

Agriculture continued to struggle against low prices. The Reichstag, in May 1885, approved another round of tariff increases targeting agricultural products.

The German economy rose to become the economic miracle of the late nineteenth century. Perhaps it was ripe to reap the benefits of protectionist trade policies. Bismarck had observed that England, a staunch free-trade country, "used to have high protective duties until the time came when she had been so strengthened under protection that she could come forward as a Herculean combatant, and challenge all the world with 'Enter the lists against me!'"

The apparent success of protectionist trade policies in Germany helped fuel protectionist sentiment in Austria, France, Russia, and the United States, all of whom enacted and strengthened protectionist policies in the last two decades of the nineteenth century.

Today, capitalist countries like the United States still feel the lure of protectionist trade policies during periods of unemployment and recession. Whatever advantages trade and specialization hold out, countries often reject them in the face of domestic unemployment and deflation. Nevertheless, for nearly two centuries now, the best thinkers in economics have clung to the view that free trade offers the safest prospect for rising living standards. Since World War II, the world has been reshaping itself upon the lines of free trade.

See also General Agreement on Tariff and Trade, McKinley Tariff, Meline Tariff.

References Dawson, William Harbutt. *Bismarck and State Socialism* (1890); Hoffmann, Charles. *The Depression of the Nineties: An Economic History* (1970); Percy, Ashley. *Modern Tariff History: Germany, United States, and France* (1970).

Glass-Steagall Banking Act of 1933 (United States)

The Glass-Steagall Banking Act was one of the acts of economic reform passed in the first 100 days of Franklin Roosevelt's administration. It sought to revive confidence in the banking system, and to reduce bank competition for deposits. The Glass-Steagall Banking Act, more than any other piece of banking legislation, shaped the development of the current banking system.

Bank suspensions had been averaging a high level of 634 banks per year before the depression. In 1931, the position of banks in the United States caught the attention of John Maynard Keynes, who described it as "the weakest element in the whole situation." The banking crisis deepened with the onset of the economic crisis. Depositors pulled money out of banks and sent funds abroad. Some money was hoarded in homes. Gold reserves declined. President Hoover saw the banks as a victim of a crisis in confidence. From 1929 to 1933, more than 5,000 banks suspended redemption of deposits. One-third of all U.S. banks failed during the depression. After his inauguration in March 1933, President Roosevelt declared all banks closed for a week, to prevent panic from spreading.

The Glass-Steagall Banking Act became the law of the land on 16 June 1933.

To help restore confidence in banks, the act banned deposit banks from providing investment bank services. Investment banks buy newly issued stocks and securities from corporations, and resell them to the public for a profit. This banking activity plays a key role in helping corporations raise capital. After the stock market crashed, banks who had invested depositors' money in stocks had no way to recover their investment, and were forced into bankruptcy. This provision of the act remains in effect today, but it has been weakened by innovations in the organization of the banking industry. This divorce between deposit banking and investment banking does not exist in many countries, including Germany, France, Switzerland, and the United Kingdom.

Another provision of the Glass-Steagall Banking Act prohibited interest-earning checking accounts. The payment of interest on checking accounts increased bank competition for deposits. This added competition may have driven some banks into bankruptcy. The act also gave the Federal Reserve System the power to regulate interest rates on savings and time deposits. This provision was known as Regulation Q. It helped keep the cost of funds down for financial institutions. The deregulation of financial institutions in the 1980s phased out Regulation Q.

The Glass-Steagall Banking Act established the Federal Deposit Insurance Corporation. This corporation insured deposits from bank failure, up to a maximum limit. All banks that are members of the Federal Reserve System must buy deposit insurance from the FDIC. Today, virtually all commercial banks insure deposits with FDIC. After the savings and loan crisis in the 1980s, FDIC took over responsibility for furnishing deposit insurance to thrift institutions. This measure went far toward restoring confidence in the banking system.

Karl Marx foretold that capitalism would die an agonizing death from recurring economic crises that "put the bourgeois on trial." The financial system has often been the point of breakdown in these crises. Many bank and thrift failures during the 1980s showed that financial institutions are still vulnerable to disinflation and recession. Deposit insurance, however, helped maintain the public's confidence in the system.

See also Depository Institutions Deregulation and Monetary Control Act of 1980, Great Depression.

References Baye, Michael R., and Dennis W. Jansen. *Money, Banking, and Financial Markets: An Economics Approach* (1995); Schlesinger, Arthur M., Jr. *The Age of Roosevelt* (1960).

Global Commons

The concept of global commons refers to world resources outside the jurisdiction of nations. It includes the atmosphere, Antarctica, the oceans, and outer space. It includes migrating birds and ocean mammals and fish, as well as, the electromagnetic environment created by wireless transmission.

History holds out many examples of resources held in common in capitalist environments that fell victim to destructive exploitation. The fate of the American buffalo serves as a grim reminder of what happens to resources not belonging to anyone. Individuals seeking their own self-interest have an incentive to mercilessly convert common resources into private gain, as quickly as possible. Nevertheless, common grazing lands enjoyed a long history, and management systems of commons evolved that preserved the use of these resources for future generations. The international community now appears to be in the early stages of developing rules for managing global commons.

The plight of the great whales stands as a fitting symbol of the vulnerability of the global commons. Like the American buffalo, the great whales belong to no one, and therefore everyone thought they had an equal right to them. The first international agreement to protect whales was signed in 1931, but Japan and the Soviet Union abstained from the agreement.

During the post-World War II era, these two countries harvested whales to near-extinction, and, in 1982, the International Whaling Commission voted for a five-year moratorium on commercial whaling, which lasted from 1986 to 1990. The survival of the whales remains a matter of international concern.

Concern for excessive exploitation of the atmospheric commons has centered around three issues. First, the depletion of the ozone, from the release of chlorofluorocarbons into the atmosphere, threatens to remove an important shield that protects life on earth from ultraviolet radiation. Studies have shown that ultraviolet radiation is a cause of skin cancer. There is now a widespread international consensus to phase out the production and use of clorofluorocarbons by the year 2000. Second, the rise of atmospheric carbon dioxide, caused by burning fossil fuels, poses a threat of global warming, called the greenhouse effect. The outcome of global warming remains uncertain, but includes such scenarios as melting polar ice caps and flooded coastal areas. A third area of concern is atmospheric pollution that causes acid rain in areas across international borders, and far from the origin of the airborne emissions causing the pollution.

The electromagnetic environment poses two problems related to the management of commons. One problem is the allocation of radio frequencies, which requires international cooperation. The other problem relates to the health effects of electromagnetic radiation, which may become an area of concern in the future.

Developing cooperative initiatives for managing the global commons stands forth as one of the most interesting and important issues facing a world economy dominated by capitalist economies. If some resources are beyond the reach of political jurisdictions and private ownership, world capitalism will have to adapt itself to cooperative systems of commons management. Systems of common management that evolved in the precapitalist era may serve as a useful guide in developing systems for managing the global commons.

See also Enclosures, International Whaling Commission.

References Imber, Mark. *Environment, Security, and UN Reform* (1994); Nanda, Ved P. *International Environmental Law and Policy* (1995).

Gold Standard

The gold standard became the world monetary standard for a relatively brief time, roughly from 1870 to 1914. The coinage of gold dates back to 700 b.c. in the Mediterranean world, and it continued during the Roman Empire. Florence popularized gold coinage among Italian cities in the thirteenth century. The influence of the Italian cities seems to have brought the practice of gold coinage to England, where it caught on, particularly after the mid-fourteenth century. Charles II introduced a new gold coin called a guinea in 1663. The trend toward gold would spread from England to the rest of Western Europe.

As late as the beginning of the nineteenth century, England was still officially on a sterling silver standard, and no European country was on a gold standard, or had developed a gold standard system. England and other countries coined both

The gold vaults at the New York Federal Reserve Bank

gold and silver, and set the conversion ratio at which gold could be exchange for silver. In the eighteenth century, the English government overvalued gold relative to silver, causing an outflow of silver and an inflow of gold. Gold became predominant as a means of payment.

By the French Revolution, bank notes (paper money) circulated alongside specie in most countries. Banks held reserves of precious metals, to redeem paper money on demand. During the wars with revolutionary France and Napoleon, the Bank of England suspended specie redemption of its paper money, with the approval of the government. In 1812, the government made the Bank of England's bank notes legal tender. The bank notes were still inconvertible into specie as a wartime measure.

The Coinage Act of 1816 established England on the Gold Standard, when the rest of Europe was still on a silver standard. In 1819, Parliament passed the Act for the Resumption of Cash Payments, which provided for the resumption, by 1823, of the convertibility of Bank of England bank notes into gold specie. By 1821, the gold standard was in full operation in England. The English banking system evolved toward the use of Bank of England bank notes as reserves for commercial banks, and the Bank of England became the custodian of the country's gold reserves. The Bank of England learned to protect its gold reserves by adjustments in interest rates, using its bank-rate and open-market operations to raise interest rates, and stem an outflow of gold. Higher interest rates attracted foreign capital that could be converted into gold. A gold inflow allowed the bank to lower interest rates.

Until the 1870s, most countries other than England operated bimetallic monetary systems, with both gold and silver circulating as legal tender mediums. The bimetallic system proved awkward, because official conversion ratios between gold and silver often differed from the ratio that existed in the precious metals market. Gold discoveries in California and Australia flooded markets for precious metals, and gold began to replace silver as the circulating medium in France and other European countries. The wars and revolutions of the mid-nineteenth again forced governments into issuing inconvertible paper money. Governments often restored convertibility by establishing the gold standard. By the end of the 1870s, France, Germany, Holland, Russia, Austro-Hungary, and the Scandinavian countries were on the gold standard. The currency of each country was defined in a fixed weight of gold.

If the gold standard had a golden age, it was between 1870 and 1914. The standard acted as a discipline on the issuance of paper money. If prices in country A rose faster than prices in country b, residents of A would start buying more goods from country B. Gold would flow out of country A into country B, increasing the money supply in country B, and decreasing it in country A. These money-supply changes lowered prices in country A, and raised prices in country B. These adjustments restored equilibrium and eliminated the need for further gold flows. The world enjoyed stable prices in the heyday of the gold standard.

During World War I, Britain unofficially went off the gold standard, and the export of gold was legally prohibited in 1919. It was not feasible to export gold after 1914. The end of World War I set the stage for an international scramble for gold, as countries tried to reestablish national gold standards. Britain and France kept their currencies overvalued in terms of gold, hurting their export industries, and causing recessions at home. The economic debacle of the 1930s spelled the end of the gold standard for domestic economies, because governments wanted the freedom to follow cheap money policies in the face of severe depression.

The United States Gold Reserve Act of 1934 authorized the U.S. Treasury to buy and sell gold at a rate of $35 per ounce of gold, in order to stabilize the value of the dollar in foreign exchange markets. This legislation laid the foundation for the world to return to the gold standard for international transactions after World War II. The value of the dollar was fixed in gold, and the value of other currencies was fixed in dollars. The system only became fully operational after World War II, when most countries lifted bans on the exportation of gold. This gold exchange standard for international transactions remained in effect until the early 1970s. After experiments with devaluation, the United States suspended the conversion of dollars into gold in 1971, to avoid a major outflow of gold.

Abandonment of the gold standard preceded the strong worldwide surge of inflation in the late 1970s, and critics attributed the inflation to the loss of discipline provided by the gold standard. The experience of the 1980s and 1990s suggests that countries can control inflation without the gold standard. The inflation of the 1970s can be attributed to many factors. In the absence of the gold standard, countries enjoy more flexibility to adjust domestic money supplies to meet the needs of domestic economies. Most economists see the gold standard as a relic of history.

See also Dollar Crisis of 1971.

References Bordo, Michael D., and Forrest Capie. *Monetary Regimes in Transition* (1993); Davies, Glyn. *A History of Money* (1994).

Goldsmith Bankers

The goldsmiths of seventeenth-century London developed banking in its modern form. The goldsmiths united, in one business activity, functions such as safe storage of gold, silver, and deposits of money, loaning out deposits of money (as well as their own money), transferring money holdings from town to town or person to person, trading in foreign exchange and bullion, and discounting bills of exchange. Before the goldsmith bankers, these activities were scattered, often as sidelines or byproducts of other trading activities. Around 1633, goldsmith banking arose as an indigenous form of banking in England. Before the goldsmiths, banking in London was the province of Italians, Germans, and, particularly, the Dutch.

The first step in the goldsmith evolution toward banking began when some goldsmiths became dealers in foreign and domestic coins. Goldsmiths who specialized as coin dealers became known as exchanging goldsmiths, as opposed to working goldsmiths. The seizure of the mint in 1640, and the outbreak of civil war in 1642, sent people to goldsmiths in search of safety for jewelry, gold, silver, and coins. The civil war interrupted the normal goldsmith business of forging objects from gold and silver. Instead, goldsmiths became a safe haven for holding demand deposits of gold and silver. The goldsmiths maintained a running account of each depositor's holdings. They also conducted a profitable business in loaning out depositors' gold, silver, and coins to government and private customers. To meet the demands from borrowers, goldsmiths turned to paying interest on deposits, and offering time deposits.

The paperwork and recordkeeping of these activities laid the foundation for important innovations in banking. The bank note (paper money) evolved out of receipts for deposits at goldsmiths. The depositor got a receipt with the depositor's name and the amount of the deposit. These receipts soon became negotiable, like endorsed bills of exchange. Modern banking began when these receipts were issued, not just to those who had deposited money, but also to those who borrowed money. Instead of bearing the name of a particular depositor or borrower, soon the receipts were issued to the bearer. Thus the modern bank note came to life. The Promissory Notes Act of 1704 ratified the practice of accepting notes in exchange.

The goldsmiths first developed checks. The British form, "cheques," came from the word "exchequer," the British term for treasury. The cheques were named after the Exchequer Orders to Pay. The first cheques evolved out of bills of exchange, and were called notes or bills. The courts confirmed the negotiability of endorsed bills and notes in 1697.

The paper records of credit transactions and transfers of funds evolved into a considerable supplement of the metallic money supply. By the time of Adam Smith's *Wealth of Nations* in 1776, bank notes in circulation exceeded metallic coins. The money supply of the capitalist economic system was no longer limited to the supply of precious metals.

See also Seizure of the Mint, Stop of the Exchequer.

References Challis, E. *The Tudor Coinage* (1978); Davies, Glyn. *A History of Money* (1994).

Gompers, Samuel (1850–1924)

Samuel Gompers stands as the most towering of American labor leaders. He presided over the formation of the American Federation of Labor, whose delegates reelected him president every year but one, until his death in 1924.

Gompers was born in January 1850, the eldest son of Jewish Dutch parents who had immigrated to London from Amsterdam in the 1840s. Sent into the labor force at the age of 10 by his father, Gompers soon followed his father's footsteps, by apprenticing himself to a cigarmaker. The hardships of child labor first turned Gompers's mind to the poverty and exploitation of workers, and set his thinking along lines of social rebellion.

In 1863, the Gompers family migrated to New York City. There, Samuel attended lectures and night school, and worked as a cigarmaker, joining the cigarmaker union at the age of 14. Despite his youth, he became a leader in the union, rising to the presidency of a local in 1875. During the depression of the 1870s, the union struck and lost, leaving Gompers blacklisted and unable to find work for four months. Gompers weathered the hardships and steadily grew in determination.

Many early battles were fought against radicals and socialists for control of union organizations. In 1881, Gompers, after suffering an election defeat at the hands of a socialist, refused to be ousted as president, because the new president-elect employed apprentice cigarmakers, which qualified him as an employer. Years later, in one of the early conventions of the American Federation of Labor, Gompers ruled against seating a socialist delegate representing the Socialist Labor Party, because the delegate had no affiliation with a trade union. Before court battles frustrated Gompers after the turn of the century, he stood steadfastly against political partisanship.

The radicalism and socialist sympathies of the leaders of the Knights of Labor, and their high-handed leadership, held no charm for Gompers. In 1881, he participated in a conference in Pittsburgh that led to the formation of the Federation of Trades and Unions, the precursor of the American Federation of Labor. The Federation wobbled along without success until 1886, when Gompers took advantage of dissension in the Knights to hold a conference on the same date and in the

Samuel Gompers, 1916

same city where the Knights were holding a conference. Insurgent Knights joined with the members of the Federation to form the American Federation of Labor (AFL). The AFL adopted a conservative trade-union policy, excluded unskilled workers, and adopted a platform calling for political neutrality. The delegates elected Gompers president, a position he would hold until 1894, when he lost an election to a socialist. He was reelected president the following year and held that office until his death.

Gompers devoted his full energy to making the American Federation of Labor the dominant trade union in the United States, refusing to cooperate with the Knights of Labor, or with the International Workers of the World, and becoming increasingly bitter toward socialists. After the turn of the century, employers won several key court battles against unions, nearly sending Gompers to jail for violating an injunction. As the courts became the battleground for union rights, and as the Republican party became more reactionary, Gompers changed his attitude toward political neutrality. He persuaded Woodrow Wilson to support legislation protecting unions from antitrust legislation, strongly supported Wilson's reelection, and abandoned his pacifist philosophy to support America's participation in World War I. Remaining true to his individualistic spirit, he testified in Congress against a proposal for social insurance, because it would sap citizens of "their independence of spirit and virility." Proposals for minimum wage laws also met with Gomper's disapproval.

Labor made great strides during the presidency of Woodrow Wilson, and particularly during World War I. But, after World War I, business became more militant in dealing with trade unions, and the AFL's membership plummeted from 4,078,740 in 1920 to 2,936,468 in 1923. Gompers made matters worse by not anticipating the role of mass-production workers in the future labor movement.

He presided over his last AFL convention in the fall of 1924, and died in December of that year.

Gompers's leadership helps explain why the U.S. labor movement never developed a political party, such as arose in other capitalist countries. The Labor Party in Britain is a prime example. He envisioned a philosophy of unionism that withstood implacable hostility from employers and the courts, and won for labor the right to make its influence felt.

See also American Federation of Labor, Boycott, *Buck's Stove and Range* Case, *Danbury Hatters* Case, Knights of Labor.

References Kaufman, Stuart B. *Samuel Gompers and the Origin of the American Federation of Labor, 1848–1896* (1973); Madison, Charles A. *American Labor Leaders* (1950).

Government Bailouts

Few government actions strike harder against the spirit of capitalism than government bailouts of failing private sector firms. Capitalism has a survival-of-the-fittest strain in its philosophy, and governments violate that philosophical strain when they selectively bailout private sector firms verging on the brink of bankruptcy.

During the Great Depression of the 1930s, the governments of Germany and Italy resorted to government bailouts and buyouts to save from bankruptcy and liquidation firms failing in the private sector, and the U.S. government made low interest loans available to failing firms through the Reconstruction Finance Corporation.

During the stagflation era of the 1970s, several countries turned to government aid to prevent failures of major corporations. In 1974, the British government bought a majority interest in British Leyland, and infused additional capital to keep that company in operation. British Leyland turned to the government after bankers refused to extend further credit, and the government rescued the company without requiring sacrifices from employees or creditors.

In Japan, Toyo Kogyo, the manufacturer of Mazda automobiles, encountered difficulty in the mid-1970s, when soaring gasoline prices made its gas-guzzling rotary engine unattractive. The Japanese government played a quiet role in this rescue, using the central bank of Japan to funnel funds to banks engaged in financing Toyo Kogyo. The management of Toyo Kogyo came under the control of banks, which imposed an austerity program and streamlined manufacturing operations. The bailout stirred no debate from a public that hardly knew what was happening.

During the 1970s, the U.S. government engaged in several high-profile bailouts that provoked debates about the propriety of government bailouts in capitalist societies.

In 1970, Penn Central Railroad faced bankruptcy, and the Federal Reserve Bank of New York let the word out that banks should stand by Penn Central, and meet its credit requirements. Congress eventually took over the freight lines of Penn Central and five other bankrupt eastern railroads, creating Consolidated Rail Corporation, or Conrail, a quasi-government corporation. The passenger lines became part of Amtrak, another government corporation.

A second important bailout in the United States occurred when the federal government came to the aid of Lockheed Corporation, a major defense contractor and employer. Lockheed suffered from massive cost overruns on the C-5A military transport, which, coupled with the winding down of Vietnam War defense spending, pushed Lockheed over the edge of bankruptcy. The U.S. government provided loan guarantees that could not exceed $250 million at any time, and used its position to get financial concessions from Lockheed's creditors and customers. Lockheed beat the deadline for repaying its loans underwritten by the government. Its position as a big employer, possessing sensitive defense technology, helped win a timely government bailout. Nevertheless, critics called the Lockheed bailout a dreadful precedent that would encourage other ailing firms to seek government help, instead of making the tough decisions necessary to set their financial house in order.

The bailout that set important precedents in the United States was the Chrysler guaranteed loan that committed the federal government to repay $1.5 billion in loans to that beleaguered company. Chrysler had difficulty in adjusting to the era of fuel-efficient automobiles, and blamed new government regulations for many of its financial difficulties. The uniqueness of the Chrysler bailout lay in the number of concessions that the federal government extracted from creditors, local governments, employees, and suppliers. Virtually every constituency that had a vested interest in the preservation of Chrysler was required to make concessions. Chrysler had to sell off some of its assets, and the union had to agree to pay cuts. Suppliers had to buy Chrysler stock, in addition to infusing additional capital into Chrysler, and nonunion workers had to accept pay cuts and pay freezes. Creditors were required to extend substantial sums in additional credit, and state and local governments had to contribute $250 million to help save the company. In summary, the government, in addition to underwriting loans, used its power to extract concessions, forcing flexibility from Chrysler constituencies whose rigidity was part of the problem. Chrysler repaid its government-guaranteed loans ahead of schedule, and remains one of the major corporations in the United States.

According to capitalist doctrine, the market should decide which firms survive, guaranteeing the preservation of firms that are most successful in pleasing consumers. The sheer magnitude of the modern giant corporations, however, creates vast constituencies that political processes cannot ignore. Often, in the name of preserving jobs, governments bend to pressure to bailout large corporations. The bailouts raise equity questions, because small businesses will never receive that level of consideration from their government.

Remaining committed to the principles of free enterprise requires discipline in the face of depression and mounting business failures. On the other hand, the era of big government and giant corporations may have rendered obsolete the concept of government as only an umpire on the economic playing field. There might be a bit of truth to a statement attributed to a chief executive officer of General Motors to the effect that "What is good for General Motors is good for the country." Nevertheless, in the 1980s, inflation and low productivity replaced fear of unemployment as economic problems that aroused the most concern, and bankrupt companies met with less favor from voters and government officials, who often regarded bankruptcy as a symptom of inefficiency and inflated costs. Therefore, there is no trend favoring government bailouts in capitalist countries today.

See also Great Stagflation of the 1970s.

References Reich, Robert B. "Why the United States Needs an Industrial Policy." *Harvard Business Review* (1982); Reich, Robert B., and John D. Donahue. *New Deals: The Chrysler Revival and the American System* (1985).

Grand National Consolidated Trade Union (England)

The Grand National Consolidated Trade Union was one of the first efforts in England to unite workers of all trades into one trade union movement.

Just as the Industrial Revolution started in England, workers of England became pioneers in the trade union movement. A burst of trade union agitation followed the repeal of the Combination Acts in 1824. By 1829, a national spinners conference gave birth to the first national trade union of the modern type—The Grand General Union of All the Operative Spinners of the United Kingdom. The leader of the spinners union, John Doherty, was the first to act on the vision of a general union of all trades. In 1830, he launched

the National Association of United Trades for the Protection of Labor. This organization soon split into different groups, several of which later merged with the Grand National Consolidated Trade Union. In 1832, the Operative Builders Union leaped into the top ranks of national trade unions. The Builders Union organized all trades within one industry. This union let itself be commandeered by the followers of Robert Owen, who proposed that the Builders Union be converted into a guild that would displace the existing construction industry.

After a parliament of the Operative Builders Union embraced his ideas, Owen attended a national conference of trade unions held in 1833. At this conference, he unfolded a plan for extending his model for the Builders Union to a grand national union, which would unite all trade unions and other associations devoted to the improvement of the working classes. The delegates eagerly endorsed the plan, and scheduled a second conference, held in February 1834, which drew up a constitution, and named the organization the Grand National Consolidated Trade Union. Its mission, other than raising wages and reducing working hours, was to

prevent the ignorant, idle, and useless part of Society from having that undue control over the fruits of our toil, which, through the agency of a vicious money system, they at present possess; and that consequently, the Unionists should lose no opportunity of mutually encouraging and assisting each other in bringing about "A Different Order of Things," in which the really useful and intelligent part of society only shall have direction of affairs, and in which well-directed industry and virtue shall merit their just distinction and reward, and vicious idleness its merited contempt and destitution.

The formation of the Grand National sparked a feverish round of local trade union activity. Membership in the Grand National rose to a half million, and total union membership reached one million.

The Grand National aroused important opposition that sealed its fate. Several of the big national unions, such as the Builders Union, refused to merge with the grand union, and membership consisted mostly of local craft unions and societies. More importantly, the rash of strikes and union activity that followed formation of the union alarmed government officials and employers. The government prosecuted union leaders under laws that prohibited oaths of secrecy. Two brothers who formed a lodge of agricultural workers received seven-year sentences. Union members preferred secrecy in those early days, to avoid employer reprisals. Employers at Derby locked out workers who refused to sign documents promising not to join the union. For four months, the Grand National gave financial support to locked-out workers, but when the Grand National ran out of money, the workers were compelled to sign the documents.

The Grand National began and ended in 1834. Unions gave up for a time the ambitious goal of changing society with a sudden mass movement. The path to social and political acceptance for unions would be more torturous than the leaders of the Grand National envisioned.

See also Combination Acts.

References Cole, G. D. H. *A Short History of the British Working Class Movement, 1789–1947* (1948); Foster, William Z. *Outline History of the World Trade Union Movement,* 1956.

Great Debasement

From 1542 to 1551, the English crown, under Henry VIII and Edward VI, pursued a policy of currency debasement that became known as the Great Debasement. Before the era of paper money, governments reduced the amount of precious metals supporting domestic money supplies by reducing the value of precious metal in coins relative to face values. This stratagem was called debasement, because each coin was worth less in terms of its precious metal contents. During the gold standard era, governments achieved the same purpose by increasing the paper money in circulation, relative to the gold bullion held in reserves. Today, industrialized countries are on inconvertible paper standards, completely removing precious metals from domestic money supplies. Debasement, like printing excess paper money, was a secret form of taxation that monarchs could often impose, without receiving the approval of representative bodies, such as Parliament. The secret tax made itself felt by increasing prices relative to measures of income and wealth.

The crown of England, like many governments, held an exclusive monopoly on the privilege to coin money from precious metals. Normally, the face value of the coined money exceeded production cost, including the cost of precious metals. This difference the crown earned as a profit was called seigniorage, which, under debasement, rose to unreasonable levels. In March 1542, the value of the silver content of each coin averaged 75 percent of each coin's face value. By March 1545, the value of the silver content had fallen to 50 percent, and, by March 1546, to 33.33 percent. After debasement had run it course in 1551, each

A Henry VIII silver shilling of 1543

coin was worth 25 percent of its face value in silver content.

In 1551, under Elizabeth I, the English government instituted a plan to retire the debased currency and replace it with currency whose face value corresponded with its precious metal content. Retiring the debased currency was a tricky affair, because households and businesses tend to hoard good currency, and to pay debts with bad currency. Bad currency drives out good currency in an economic mechanism called Gresham's Law. To retire the debased currency, the government enacted laws forbidding the outflow of good currency to foreign markets, and ending the legal tender status of the debased currency beyond a certain date.

An apologist for the debasement policies of the English crown might point to the need to build up the English navy, and to finance other public defense expenditures. Critics would answer that Henry VIII was fond of building palaces. Whatever the driving force of debasement, the public gradually lost faith in the ability of governments to manage money supplies without oversight from private financial sectors that are affected by monetary mismanagement. In the United States, the money supply is regulated by a quasi-public–private agency, the Federal Reserve System, which is independent of the executive and legislative branches of government. Studies have shown that, in the 1970s, countries with independent monetary authorities experienced lower inflation rates than countries with monetary authorities dominated by government authority.

See also Central Banks and Free Banking.

References Davies, Glyn. *The History of Money* (1994); Gould, D. *The Great Debasement* (1970).

Great Depression (1929–1939)

For the development of capitalism, the decade of the 1930s was the most influential decade in the twentieth century. The world economy suffered a large-scale breakdown, lasting until World War II, which is known as the Great Depression.

To combat depression, Western governments turned to greater state intervention in economic affairs.

The first signs of economic deterioration appeared in the United States, in the aftermath of a major stock crash in October 1929. From 1929 to 1933, real output in the United States contracted 29 percent. That compares with a long-run average rate of 3-percent growth per year. It took until 1937 for real output to regain the lost ground. Gross investment spending (combined annual expenditures on plant and equipment, housing, and inventories) fell to 1 percent of real output in 1932 and 1933. The long-run share of real output devoted to gross investment stood close to 15 percent. Gross investment spending remained in a slump until World War II rearmament. Between 1932 and 1934, investment goods wore out and depleted faster than they were replaced, leaving net investment spending negative. More than one-third of the banks in existence at the close of 1929 had failed by 1933. Wholesale prices of commodities, on average, declined 23 percent from 1929 to 1932.

The employment statistics expose the human side of the economic tragedy. In 1919, the unemployment rate in the United States stood at 3.2 percent. By 1933, the unemployment rate had climbed to 25 percent, increasing the number of unemployed Americans, from 1.5 million in 1929, to 12 million. As late as 1940, the unemployment rate had only dropped back to 14 percent.

The depression spread worldwide. The number of unemployed in Western Europe rose from 3.5 million in the mid-1920s to over 15 million at the end of 1932. In Germany, the unemployment rate stood at 43 percent in 1932. The United States embroiled the world in a trade war, with the Smoot-Hawley Tariff of 1930. From 1931 to 1935, world trade averaged 20 percent lower than it averaged for the decade of the 1920s.

Economists have yet to pinpoint the exact cause of the Great Depression. It

Hooverville, a shantytown on the outskirts of Seattle, in 1934. This was just one of many such areas that sprang up across the United States during the Great Depression.

may have been primarily a U.S. phenomenon that spread to the rest of the world. Perhaps the return of Europe to full peacetime production, coupled with technological advances during World War I, led to considerable increases in world production that were trapped in an inflexible regime of international trade. During the Depression, several countries drastically depreciated their currencies to make home goods cheaper in foreign markets, and foreign goods more expensive at home. Another explanation points to investment spending, which, perhaps, had run its course from recent technological innovations. When investment spending sputtered, a ripple effect propagated the decrease in demand for capital goods to a decrease in demand for all goods.

The monetarist school of economists in the United States lay the blame for the Great Depression at the feet of the Federal Reserve System. According to this argument, the Federal Reserve pressed a bit too hard on the monetary brakes to tame a speculative frenzy in the stock market. A falling supply of money, followed by falling prices and bankruptcies, sent the United States into an economic tailspin.

During the Great Depression, many socialists and communists regarded the capitalist economic system in much the same way free-market economists regard socialism and communism today. They saw it as a failed system, one that could be safely relegated to the ash heap of history. Rather than give up private property, however, the free-market countries preferred to accept reforms of capitalism. Capitalism revived, and today dominates the world economy.

See also Agricultural Adjustment Act of 1933,

Glass-Steagall Banking Act of 1933, National Recovery Administration Act, Stock Market Crash of 1929.

References Atack, Jeremy, and Peter Passell. *A New Economic View of American History from Colonial Times to 1940* (1994); Biles, Roger. *A New Deal for the American People* (1991); Kindleberger, Charles P. *The World in Depression, 1929–1939* (1986).

Great Stagflation of the 1970s

During the 1970s, the free-market economies experienced a marked slowdown in economic growth, and a simultaneous increase in unemployment and inflation rates. An economic malaise spread over the world capitalist system; reliable empirical data was not as readily available for the communist countries.

The inflation rate for the United States, which averaged 3.4 percent for 1960–1973, rose to an average of 7.9 percent for 1973–1981. Over the same time periods, average inflation rates in the United Kingdom rose from 5.2 to 15.8 percent; in Japan, from 5.5 to 7.9 percent; in France, from 4.9 to 10.8 percent; and, in Italy, from 5.5 to 17.6 percent. West Germany, disciplined by the memory of the hyperinflation of the 1920s, kept the lid on its inflation, which only increased from 4.2 to 4.7 percent.

The unemployment figures show a similar upward drift. From 1965 to 1973, West Germany's unemployment rate averaged .8 percent, compared to an average unemployment rate of 3.4 percent from 1974 to 1981. A comparison of U.S. unemployment rates over the same time periods shows an increase from 4.5 to 6.9 percent. The average unemployment rate of West Germany, France, United Kingdom, Italy, Belgium, and Netherlands combined, over similar time periods, shows an increase from 2.9 to 5.4 percent.

The simultaneous increase in inflation and uncmployment puzzled observers, at the time. Inflation is usually a symptom of excess demand for goods and services, leading to a booming economy, and making it easy for businesses to raise prices. Unemployment more often accompanies an economic recession, when businesses lay off workers because of slack demand, and slash rather than increase prices. The phenomenon of rising unemployment, coupled with rising inflation, was called stagflation, because output and employment stagnated, while inflation accelerated. Stagflation posed a dilemma to policymakers, because government policies that slowed inflation raised the unemployment rate, and policies that lowered the unemployment rate fueled inflation. In other words, policies directed at inflation worsened unemployment, and vice versa.

Numerous theories purported to account for the stagflation of the 1970s. One theory cited the accelerated birthrate from 1946 to 1960, known as the baby boom, which increased the number of entrants to the labor market in the 1970s, nudging up the unemployment rate. Governments stimulated economies to create extra jobs, and produced inflation as a consequence. Another theory put the blame for stagflation at the feet of the huge oil price increases in the 1970s. The price of crude oil quadrupled during 1972–1973, increasing the cost of operating equipment, and sending an inflationary tidal wave throughout the price structure. Still another theory points to irresponsible monetary growth, after the world severed all ties with the gold standard in 1972. Unions and powerful corporations, rightly or wrongly, shared part of the blame for the stagflation, by constantly pushing up prices and wages.

During the 1980s, governments began focusing exclusively on taming inflation, and ignoring unemployment rates. Unemployment rates soared in the 1980s, and inflation came down. In the second half of the 1980s, unemployment rates began to fall, and, by the mid-1990s, inflation and unemployment rates had fallen below their 1970s levels. Although the era of stagflation appears to be over, it left a legacy of fear that high inflation and high interest rates will return. Financial markets still tremble at news of rising inflation or interest rates.

Although some observers saw stagflation as a crisis of capitalism, it may have, instead, strengthened capitalism. It discredited many government policies enacted in the aftermath of the Depression of the 30s, when laissez-faire capitalism was seen as flawed. Public and political support for unions declined substantially, and government regulation of prices was cut back. Government policies that were enacted in the 1930s to shore up prices were causing inflation in the 1970s. Just as the Depression of the 30s discredited the laissez-faire government policies then in vogue, the stagflation of the 1970s discredited policies emphasizing government regulation that were popular in the post-World War II era. The philosophy of laissez-faire capitalism is more influential in the counsels of government today than it was before the episode of stagflation.

See also Oil Price Revolution.

References Blinder, Alan S. *Economic Policy and the Great Stagflation* (1979); Bruno, Michael, and Jeffrey D. Sachs, *Economics of World Wide Stagflation* (1985).

Greenbacks (United States)

During the Civil War, the U.S. government issued a fiat money called greenbacks. Fiat money is money that cannot be converted or redeemed into a precious metal, such as gold or silver. By the close of the Civil War, greenbacks and related U.S. government notes accounted for about 75 percent of the money in circulation, mostly displacing bank notes of state banks as the principle currency in circulation.

During the first three months of Lincoln's presidency, the federal government took in less than $6 million, and its expenses were $25 million. The new secretary of the treasury, Salmon Portland Chase, who came to the office without financial experience, began his service with a naïve faith in hard money. The government borrowed heavily from banks, and demanded payment in specie, which was not redeposited in banks. Fears about the ultimate success of the war led the public to hoard specie. On 30 December 1860, banks in New York suspended specie payments on bank notes and deposits, and

banks in other parts of the country soon followed. The government began paying its bills with demand notes.

The first proposal for issuing legal tender notes to defray government expenses came before Congress on 30 December. Bankers raised protests about the government issuing fiat money, and dispatched a delegation to advise the secretary of the treasury and Congress on ways to finance the war. In place of issuing inconvertible paper money, declared legal tender by Congress, this delegation recommended a program of heavy taxation and borrowing in long-term capital markets.

Government officials weighed the alternatives of issuing legal tender fiat money or selling long-term bonds. Given the poor credit of the government, the paper money was bound to depreciate, and the bonds would only sell at large discounts (high interest rates). Issuing fiat money appeared the preferred alternative, and the remaining question for debate was whether the fiat money should be legal tender.

Congress took action on 25 February 1862, by adopting an act that provided for the issuance of notes that were "lawful money and a legal tender in payment of all debts public and private." Two exceptions to the legal tender provision were import duties and interest on the public debt. The government demanded payment of import duties in gold coin, which it used to pay interest on the government debt. The government issued $150 million of these notes, $50 million of which went to retire demand notes the government had already issued.

To vent inflationary pressures from such an issue of fiat money, the new greenback notes could be used to buy Treasury bonds that paid 6-percent interest, redeemable after 5 years, and maturing after 20 years. As another anti-inflationary measure, the Treasury accepted deposits of greenbacks, paying 5-percent interest, and redeemable with ten days notice. The option of converting greenbacks to Treasury bonds was removed in subsequent bills that authorized the issuance of additional greenbacks. In June 1864, Congress set a limit of $450 million on the issuance of greenbacks, a limit that was never exceeded.

After the Civil War, the question of a resumption of specie payments arose, because most of the world was on the gold standard. Various interest groups dreaded the deflation that would likely follow the reduction of the supply of fiat money in circulation. Prices had more than doubled during the Civil War. It was 1879 before the federal government began redeeming greenbacks with specie.

The greenback experience was an important precursor of the widespread adoption of inconvertible paper money in the twentieth century. Capitalist societies learned to prevent inflation from taking off by giving government a monopoly on the issuance of fiat money, and limiting its supply.

See also Bank of England.

References Barrett, Don C. *The Greenbacks and Resumption of Specie Payments* (1931); Nugent, Walter T. K. *Money and American Society, 1865–1880* (1968).

Greenmail (United States)

Greenmail, as in blackmail, was a form of financial warfare that aroused much public concern in the 1980s. At the dawn of the era of downsizing and restructuring, stock prices were low, in the sense that assets owned by corporations were valued by the stock market well below replacement costs. Put differently, the stock shares of the corporations owning the assets sold at low prices, relative to the replacement cost of the corporate assets. Presumably, if the assets of the corporations came under the control of strong, streamlined management, stock market evaluation of the shares of stock would rise.

Greenmail occurred when an investor or group of investors bought a large block of shares in a corporation, positioning themselves to make a tender offer to buy up controlling interest in the corporation. The corporation management saw the risk of a hostile corporate takeover, probably leading to downsizing and restructuring of management, and termination of many top managers. To ward off a hostile takeover, the management offered to buy back the block of shares that had been bought up, paying a price per share substantially above the market price, and above the price that other investors could get for their stock in the same corporation. The investor or group of investors, who were threatening management with a hostile takeover, sold their stock back to the management at exorbitant prices, receiving greenmail for giving up the threat of a hostile takeover.

The management of Texaco paid greenmail when Bass Brothers acquired a large block of Texaco stock. Texaco's management bought back 13 million shares of Texaco stock from them at $50 per share, when the same shares sold in the stock market for $40 per share. This $10-per-share premium to the Bass Brothers was the greenmail.

Stockholders and management reacted angrily to greenmail, seeing it as a form of financial piracy that put short-term greed above business activities that created jobs, produced goods and services, and contributed to the long-term development of corporations. Greenmailers defended themselves, saying resources should flow to stronger managers, and the threat of greenmail was a natural force in a capitalist economic system that mercilessly crushes inefficient users of resources.

See also Insider Trading.

References Gaughan, Patrick A. *Mergers and Acquisitions* (1991); *Mergers, Acquisitions, and Corporate Restructuring* (1996).

Gresham, Thomas
See Royal Exchange.

Hamilton's Tariff of 1789 (United States)

In 1789, Alexander Hamilton, first secretary of the treasury of the United States, proposed the enactment of a tariff to generate public revenue, pay the debts of the federal government, and to promote domestic manufacturing. Congress adopted a tariff chiefly to generate revenue, but which incorporated measures favoring domestic manufacturing.

The Constitution of 1787 bestowed upon Congress the power:

> to lay and collect taxes, duties, imposts, and excises, to pay the debts and provide for the common defense and general welfare of the United States; but all duties, imposts, excises shall be uniform throughout the United States;...to regulate commerce with foreign nations, and among the several States, and with the Indian tribes;...to make all laws, which shall be necessary and proper for carrying into execution the foregoing powers.

The first tax Congress enacted under its constitutional authority was the Tariff of 1789, which began a practice of depending upon tariff revenue to finance the federal government. Tariff revenue would account for 80 percent of the government's revenue collected in the pre-Civil War years.

The tariff levied a tax of a fixed amount on 36 articles. Liquors paid a tax of 8–10 cents per gallon, tea paid 6–20 cents per pound, and steel paid 56 cents per hundredweight. Other goods that paid fixed amounts were salt, sugar, molasses, cordage, and nails. The tariff levied an ad valorem tax of 15 percent on carriages; 10 percent on a group of goods that included glass, china, earthenware, and lace; 7.5 percent on paper, gloves, leather, buttons, clothing, hats, and metal wares; and 5 percent on most other imports. Seventeen raw materials useful for manufacturing paid no import duties, including salt peter, wool, cotton, hides, fur, and dyestuffs. Goods reexported from the United States within one year of entry only paid 1 percent, after the government, in effect, refunded the duties. Goods transported in vessels owned entirely by American citizens benefited from a 10-percent tax abatement.

The following year tariff rates rose to meet the financial requirements of the new government. In 1791, Hamilton wrote his *Report on Manufactures*, in which he marshalled virtually every argument favoring protectionism. Tariff policies became one of the battlegrounds that split northern and southern states. Southern states, producing raw materials for a world market, favored free trade; northern states, nurturing a young manufacturing sector, argued for protectionist policies.

The economic history of the United States suggests that tariffs may aid the process of industrialization in capitalist countries that supply mostly agricultural products and raw materials to world markets. Citing cases such as the United States, many less-developed countries of the world argue that free-trade policies work against them, and that less-developed countries should remain protectionist, while more-developed countries pursue free-trade policies.

See also Constitution of the United States, Continental System.

References Ashley, Percy. *Modern Tariff History* (1970); Parks, Robert J. *European Origins of the Economic Ideas of Alexander Hamilton* (1977).

Hanseatic League

The Hanseatic League was a loosely organized group of towns in Northern Germany that controlled Baltic trade during the fifteenth century, just as the Venetians controlled Adriatic trade. Although a rather vague association of towns engaged in Baltic trade stretched back into medieval times, officially the Hanseatic League came into existence in 1356. The word "Hanse" meant "group of merchants." Lubeck served as headquarters, but the league had no official assembly of representatives that set policy. The membership in the league fluctuated, at any time embracing from 70 to 170 towns, but Lubeck, Bremen, and Hamburg were its ranking members.

The purpose of the Hanseatic League lay in the need to coordinate maritime and commercial policies with the less-developed parts of the world, which included feudal Europe and Asia. The league set up trading posts, called kontors, and negotiated with local governments. The league's four major kontors were at Bruges, Bergen, Novgorod, and London.

The Hanseatic League used its bargaining power to monopolize trade in less-developed areas. The kontor at Bergen, Norway, negotiated trade concessions that gave the league a virtual monopoly on trade with Norway, the Orkney Islands, Iceland, Greenland, and the Shetland Islands. The inhabitants of these areas bought their necessities from the Hanzers at high prices, and sold them their fish, furs, and raw materials at low prices. The same monopoly exploitation prevailed at Novgorod until the Russians expelled the Hanzers at the end of the fifteenth century. The London kontor won many trade concessions but never controlled local trade on the same scale as the kontors in Bergen and Novgorod. The kontor at Bruges enjoyed a few trade concessions, but chiefly functioned to trade the raw products from the North for goods from the Levant. Closing a kontor meant instant depression for many areas, giving great power to threats by the league.

The kontors were walled-in and guarded compounds, usually accommodating around 3,000 residents, with their own residences, recreational facilities, warehouses, government, and justice system; the residents of the kontors did not fraternize or intermarry with the natives. The kontors were shared by merchants from all the towns that were members of the League.

The Dutch effectively challenged militarily the Hanseatic League's monopoly in the North Sea and Baltic, extracting, in 1534, the right to trade in the Baltic for four years. Native merchants, gradually gaining more influence with feudal governments, demanded the same commercial privileges as the Hanzers enjoyed. Feudal governments also became more sophisticated in fending off the hard bargains driven by the Hanzers. The Hanseatic League effectively came to an end in 1611, when Hamburg withdrew in favor of direct trade with England.

The Hanseatic League foreshadowed the trend of capitalist development to pass beyond the city-state, and to organize into larger economic units that could wield more bargaining power. The era that saw the decline of the Hanseatic League also saw the rise of England at the first capitalist nation-state.

See also Bruges.

References Fernand Braudel, *Civilization and Capitalism*, Vol. 3 (1984); Cox, Oliver C. *The Foundations of Capitalism* (1959); Dollinger, Philippe. *The German Hansa* (1970).

Haymarket Riot

See General Strike, Knights of Labor.

Henry the Navigator

See Da Gama, Vasco.

Holding Companies

Holding companies are corporations that hold shares of stock of other corporations. The holding company is sometimes referred to as the parent corporation. The corporation whose stock is owned by the parent company is called a subsidiary. A subsidiary may be a wholly owned subsidiary, if the parent company owns 100 percent of its stock, but ownership of substantially less than 50 percent of the subsidiary's stock often is sufficient to allow parent corporation control of a subsidiary corporation.

After enactment of the Sherman Antitrust Act of 1890, holding companies supplanted trusts in the United States as a means of pulling together firms in the same industry, and monopolizing markets. New Jersey paved the way in May 1889, when it amended its corporation law to provide the legal foundation for the formation of holding companies. This amendment enabled any corporation chartered under New Jersey laws to acquire the stock of any company or companies, and to pay for the acquisition with its own stock. In 1892, the Standard Oil Trust reorganized itself as a holding company under the laws of New Jersey. The new holding company, Standard Oil Company of New Jersey, owned a controlling interest in the firms of the former Standard Oil Trust. It acquired controlling interest by issuing its own stock in trade for the stock of former members of the Standard Oil Trust. According to a Bureau of Corporations report in 1906, Standard Oil controlled 91 percent of the refining industry. Section 7 of the Clayton Act of 1914 forbade one corporation from acquiring the stock of another corporation, if the effect was to lessen competition.

The 1920s saw the rise of holding-company pyramids as a means of acquiring extreme degrees of financial leverage. Financial leverage lets a small amount of stock ownership control a great amount of financial assets. A subsidiary at the base of the pyramid might own $100 million in assets, with 50 percent financed by stock and 50 percent financed by debt. The $50 million in stock would be owned by a first-tier holding company, which would finance $25 million in debt, and issue its own stock for the remaining $25 million. A second-tier holding company would acquire the $25 million in stock of the first-holding company, again financing 50 percent with debt. Such a pyramid might rise to four or more tiers. Even a second-tier system enables the second-tier company to control $100 million in assets with only $12.5 million in its own stock. The remainder is financed by debt, and the holders of debt have no voting control in a corporation. The dependence upon debt financing is what spelled the end of these pyramid holding companies in the 1930s. Interest on debt, unlike stock dividends, had to be paid, regardless of the state of the economy. The pyramid holding companies were an important weakness in the corporate structure in the 1920s, and accentuated the spiral of bankruptcies and deflation of the 1930s.

A species of holding companies rose to importance in the Japanese economy from the 1870s to World War II. These holding companies, called zaibatsu, were usually family-owned, and they controlled firms in a wide range of industries. After World War II, the Allied occupation authorities dissolved the zaibatsu, because of their close alliance with the military.

Holding companies have remained important in the United States in public utilities and banking. Organization into subsidiaries can be a useful means of separating the government-regulated portion from the rest of a business. Holding companies became widespread in the banking industry, because they allowed banks to circumvent laws against branch banking. Federal and state laws prevent banks from opening branches across state lines. A holding company, however, can legally own controlling interest in a bank located in another state. Today, more than 90 percent of bank deposits are kept by bank holding companies through their subsidiaries.

Something of a checkered past haunts the history of holding companies. The justification for large-scale enterprise is added efficiency, which is hard to measure. The rise of international competition has lessened concern about economic concentration among domestic companies, helping holding companies to elude public scrutiny. Nevertheless, AT&T was a large holding company in the telecommunications industry. The Bell operating companies and Western Electric equipment firm were wholly owned subsidiaries of AT&T until the mid-1980s. The U.S. Justice Department brought suit, and forced AT&T to divest itself of the Bell operating companies.

See also Cartels, Corporation, Mergers, Trusts, Zaibatsu.

References Atack, Jeremy, and Peter Passel. *A New Economic View of American History* (1994); Brigham, Eugene F. *Fundamentals of Financial Management* (1989).

Hyperinflation in Post-World War I Germany

The German hyperinflation of the early 1920s stands as a constant reminder of the monetary insanity lurking beneath the surface of modern systems of money and banking. The German money supply grew during and after World War I. In June 1914, German marks in circulation stood at 6,323 million; by December 1918, the number of marks in circulation had grown to 33,106 million. Prices over the same time span more than doubled. Germany had financed the war principally by monetizing government debt, rather than by raising taxes or borrowing in capital markets. After the armistice in 1918, German marks in circulation continued to expand, and, by December 1921, German currency in circulation stood at 122,963 million marks. Prices then were slightly over 13 times the 1914 level. Prices began to catch up with money growth. By June 1922, German marks in circulation had risen to 180,716 million, but prices were now over 70 times the 1914 level. The Reichsbanks abandoned all pretense of monetary control, as marks in circulation rose to 1,295,228 million by December 1922. By June 1923, the number had increased to 17,393,000 million.

After June 1922, price increases broke into runaway inflation. By December 1922, prices stood at 1,475 times their 1914 level; by June 1923, they were 19,985 times their 1914 level. Prices were rising so fast that workers were paid at half-day intervals, and rushed to spend their wages before they lost their value. Customers at restaurants would negotiate prices in advance, because prices could change before the meal was served. Grocery shoppers rolled to the store wheelbarrows laden with sacks of money, which was also bailed up and used for fuel. Prices continued to rise into November 1923. A newspaper, which sold for 1 mark in May 1922, rose in price to 1,000 marks in September 1923. By 17 November 1923, the newspaper sold for 70 million marks.

In December 1923, the money supply and prices stabilized. The German government reformed its monetary affairs, issuing a new unit of currency called the rentenmark, which was declared equal to 1 trillion marks. The new currency was issued by the Rentenbank, which replaced the Reichsbank as the note-issuing bank. The only asset of the new bank was a mortgage on agricultural and industrial land, and the paper-money issue of the new bank was strictly limited.

The inflation began with the stress of wartime finance. After the war, Germany needed to restock its warehouses with imported raw materials, and to pay war reparations. This led to an outflow of German marks, and to a depreciation of the German mark in foreign exchange markets. This depreciation caused inflation in the prices of imports, and the inflation spread to the rest of the economy. The Reichsbank kept the money supply rising faster than prices, to ward off unemployment. The French occupation of the Ruhr aggravated the matter considerably. The German government encouraged passive resistance, banned reparation payments, and printed money to pay striking miners. The French blockaded the area, and Germany lost the tax revenue.

The German experience with hyperinflation was the most spectacular the world had seen. Since World War II, Germany can boast of one of the best records for controlling inflation of any advanced industrialized country. John Maynard Keynes saw the inflation trends and commented in the *Economic Consequences of Peace* (1920):

> By a continuing process of inflation, the governments can confiscate, secretly and unobserved, an important part of the wealth of their citizens.... While the process impoverishes many, it actually enriches some. The sight of this arbitrary rearrangement of riches strikes not only at security, but at confidence in the equity of the existing distribution of wealth.

Many observers blame the episode of German hyperinflation for creating the political conditions that led to the rise of Hitler to power. Partly because of the German experience, modern capitalist societies consider price stability an important ingredient of social stability.

See also Hyperinflation of the Continental Currency, Hyperinflation of the French Revolution, Hyperinflation of the Russian Revolution.

References Kindleberger, Charles P. *A Financial History of Western Europe* (1984); Parsson, Jens D. *Dying of Money: Lessons from the Great German and American Inflations* (1974).

Hyperinflation of the Continental Currency (United States)

Hardly had the smoke cleared at Bunker Hill when the First Continental Congress, on 22 June 1775, authorized the issuance of $2 million in bills of credit. Congress had neither the power to tax nor to borrow money, and it chose to meet the financial crisis by issuing bills of credit that were to be redeemed by individual states according to an apportionment based upon population. The only other option, which Congress chose not to follow, was to apportion a certain amount of funds that each state was to raise by issuing its own state notes. By the close of

1775, Congress had issued $6 million in bills of credit, for redemption between 1779 and 1786. Benjamin Franklin's suggestion that the bills of credit bear interest fell on deaf ears. Each bill of credit was supposed to be signed by two members of Congress. Eventually, Congress hired 28 individuals to be bill signers. Between 22 June 1775 and 29 November 1779, Congress authorized the issuance of $241,552,780 in bills of credit. In 1779, Congress voted to limit the circulation to the $200 million in bills of credit outstanding at that time. No bills of credit were issued after 1779. The bills of credit became known as continentals.

The unwillingness of the states to levy taxes to finance the war necessitated the issuance of the continentals. Taxation had helped spark the revolt against the English government, and the state governments felt a need to tread lightly on taxes. Between 1775 and 1780, state governments issued $210 million of their own notes, further fueling the inflationary spiral.

To support the continentals, Congress asked the states to declare the continentals legal tender. Most states complied with this request, which was easier than levying taxes to redeem the continentals. Complementing this state action, Congress passed resolutions denouncing individuals who refused to accept the continentals. After hearing of one instance of such disloyal behavior, Congress, on 23 November 1775, resolved "That if any person shall hereafter be so lost to all virtue and regard for his country as to refuse..., such person shall be deemed an enemy of his country."

The increases in prices remained moderate until the end of 1776, but then the tempo of inflation accelerated, and became strident in 1779. At the beginning of 1779, the ratio between the face value of continentals and specie stood at eight to one. By the end of 1779, the ratio was over 38 to one.

New England held a price convention in Providence in December 1776. In addition to calling for more taxation and less paper money, it formulated a set of prices for farm labor, wheat, corn, rum, and wool. The New England states enacted these recommendations into law, and Congress recommended that other states follow suit. Congress also suggested that states give themselves the authority to confiscate hoarded goods. Anger over price increases was aired in mass meetings in some towns, and irate women raided shops where goods were reportedly hoarded. Merchants found themselves in court. Philadelphia protesters hanged in effigy a specie dollar in answer to the refusal of dealers to receive paper money.

A second price convention, held in 1778, compiled another list of approved prices. Congress was about to enter the act of legislating prices, authorizing the calling of a price convention in 1780, asking that states formulate price recommendations. These recommendations were to assume that prices were 20 times higher than they were in 1774. The idea of legislating prices, however, was abandoned, and, in March 1780, Congress asked states to repeal punitive legislation against those who refused to accept continentals.

The continentals continued to depreciate after 1779. By January 1781, the ratio of continentals to specie stood at 100 to 1. That became the official ratio at which the continentals could be converted into interest-bearing, long-term bonds, under the funding act of 1790.

The experience of the continental became a lesson in the evolution of paper money. Governments learned, and sometime relearn, that the supply of money must be restricted, to maintain its value. Today, the issuance of inconvertible paper money, made legal tender by government, is the custom worldwide.

See also Hyperinflation in Post-World War I Germany, Hyperinflation of the French Revolution, Hyperinflation of the Russian Revolution.

References Hepburn, Barton. *A History of Currency in the United States* (1967); Dewey, Davis R. *Financial History of the United States* (1903); Myers, Margaret G. *A Financial History of the United States* (1970).

Hyperinflation of the French Revolution

The English economist John Maynard Keynes, commenting upon an observation by Lenin, wrote,

> Lenin is said to have declared that the best way to destroy the Capitalist System was to debauch the currency.... Lenin was certainly right. There is no subtler, no surer means of overturning the existing basis of society than to debauch the currency. The process engages all the hidden forces of economic law on the side of destruction. And does it in a manner which no one man in a million is able to diagnose.

Perhaps Lenin or Keynes, or both, were familiar with the role of inflation during the French Revolution.

In October 1789, the National Assembly found itself in a desperate situation. Tax revenue fell far short of expenses, and the government survived day by day from advances from the Bank of Discount, a bank that primarily loaned funds to the government. The bank declared itself out of funds, and the Assembly needed resources to complete the Revolution. The Assembly met the financial crises with two important and interrelated measures. It confiscated Church lands, and it created an extraordinary treasury, charged with raising 400 million livres by selling assignats, which were certificates of indebtedness bearing 5-percent interest. The government announced its intention to sell the church property, and take assignats in payment. The church property, in effect, served as collateral for the assignats.

Assignats met with less than a hearty reception, because it was not clear which lands would be sold to creditors. In August 1790, the Assembly made assignats bank notes, and added an extra 800 million livres to the issue. The decree specified that the total number of assignats in circulation should never exceed 1,200 million livres. The new assignats bore no interest, and could be acquired by anyone, whereas the first issue was available only to creditors of the government. Instead of just liquidating the national debt, the government took to issuing assignats to pay for deficit spending.

By mid-1792, inflation was rising rapidly; prices rose 33 to 50 percent, while wages lagged far behind. In January 1793, a mob stormed stores in Paris; in February, a scarcity of soap sparked further riots. Mobs also obstructed grain shipments. In 1794, the government implemented a system of price controls, known as the Law of the Maximum. People who refused to accept assignats in payment, or accepted them (or paid them) at a loss, could be fined 3,000 livres and imprisoned for six months for the first offense. The fine and imprisonment could be doubled for the second offense. Speculation in specie and assignats could bring six years imprisonment, and forestalling was punishable by death. A forestaller was defined as a person who withheld necessary commodities from circulation. Nevertheless, farmers and manufacturers hoarded goods, and the specter of famine rose up for the spring. In December 1794, the government abandoned price controls, prices soared, and assignats fell to less than 3 percent of their face value.

The Convention, the governing body at that stage of the Revolution, acknowledged the fall of the assignats in June 1795. The nominal value of each successive issue was reduced according to a scale of proportions. In July of the same year, the Convention ordered in-kind payments for half of the land tax and rents. Peasants stopped bringing produce to market, to avoid accepting assignats. Speculation became rampant, and inflation ruined creditors and savers. As prices outpaced wages and workers suffered, speculative profits created a new class of ostentatious rich, who stood in stark contrast to the destitution of the lower classes. Inflation reached its peak as the Directory took power in November, 1795. Each day saw prices rise hourly, and

each night paper money came off the press for issuance the following day. Paper money issues doubled in four months, for a total of 39 billion livres.

In February 1796, the Directory discontinued the assignats. It tried an issue of land warrants, which were good for the purchase of national property at an estimated price without competitive bidding. The sale would be to the first taker. The public had lost faith in paper money, however, and in July 1796, the government decided to return to specie. Inflation continued to ravage the economy, until the advent of Napoleon in 1799. Apparently his wars brought in more than they cost, and his government improved the efficiency of taxation, ending the government's need to promiscuously print paper money.

Since the experience of the French Revolution, hyperinflation has been associated with revolutionary change. It played a role in the rise of Hitler to power in Germany, the Communist Revolution in China, and the Bolshevik Revolution in Russia. The American Revolution also had a hyperinflation episode.

See also Hyperinflation in Post-World War I Germany, Hyperinflation of the Continental Currency, Hyperinflation of the Russian Revolution.

References Lefebvre, Georges. *The French Revolution* (1961); Theirs, M. A. *The History of the French Revolution* (1844).

Hyperinflation of the Russian Revolution

The imperial Russian government resorted to inflationary finance to sustain itself through World War I. This wartime finance led to monstrous price increases, and the Bolsheviks continued the policy to accelerate the Revolution.

On the eve of World War I, Russia boasted the largest gold reserves in Europe, with gold reserves backing 98 percent of the Russian bank notes in circulation. The treasury held large gold reserves to back paper rubles. Revenue from taxes levied on the manufacture and sale of alcohol, which was one-fourth of the treasury's revenue, fell, because of a newly enacted law against alcohol consumption. Tariff revenue also dropped significantly with the onset of war. Instead of direct taxes and internal war-bond financing, the government turned almost exclusively to paper money and foreign loans to finance the war.

On 27 July 1914, the government suspended specie payments on paper rubles. The gold reserve requirement for the issuance of bank notes also came to an end. The government doubled the supply of paper money at the beginning of the war, when it issued an additional 1.5 billion rubles. The issuance of paper money continued until the supply had increased fourfold by January 1917. The issuance of paper money increased 100 percent in France and 200 percent in Germany over the same time frame.

Inflation forces remained dormant through the first half of 1915, because the war blocked exports, which increased domestic supplies. Toward the end of 1915, inflation began to accelerate rapidly, and by the end of 1916 prices were four times higher than the 1913 level. The cost of living grew two or three times faster than wages, and food and fuel shortages were common in urban areas. The government helped maintain order by threatening to induct into the army anyone who caused trouble. From 1913 to October 1916, the price of wheat flour rose 269 percent, buckwheat by 320 percent, salt by 500 percent, meat by 230 percent, and shoes and clothes by 400–500 percent. Workers formed cooperatives to purchase food and other necessities at lower prices.

The anger of the workers mounted as food and fuel became scarce. Long lines of people waited to buy bread, and by the time workers were off work the bread was gone. Strikes were common in Petrograd, the largest industrial center. Worker discontent became the political base that drove the Revolution.

In 1917, the Revolution began in earnest. Nicholas I abdicated in March 1917, followed by the Bolsheviks' seizure of power in October 1917. Throughout 1917, prices rose more rapidly. By October 1917, prices were 7.55 times the 1913 level. The supply of rubles in circulation was 19.6 billion, compared to 2.4 billion in the first half of 1914. After the October coup, the tax system fell apart, and the new government turned to the printing presses. By October 1918, prices had grown to 102 times the 1913 level, and to 923 times in October 1919.

In May 1919, the government completely unleashed the supply of paper money. The only restriction upon printing of fresh paper money was the supply of ink and paper. The government used gold holdings to buy printing supplies abroad. Nearly 50 percent of the treasury's budget went for the cost of printing paper money. In 1919, the supply of paper money in circulation grew to 225 billion rubles. In 1920, it reached 1.2 trillion rubles, and doubled again in the first half of 1921. By 1923, prices were 648.23 million times their 1913 level.

In *The Economic Consequences of Peace* (1920), John Maynard Keynes wrote:

Lenin is said to have declared that the best way to destroy the Capitalist System was to debauch the currency. By a continuing process of inflation, governments can confiscate, secretly and unobserved, an important part of the wealth of their citizens. By this method they not only confiscate, but they confiscate arbitrarily; and, while the process impoverishes many, it actually enriches some. The sight of this arbitrary rearrangement of riches strikes not only at security, but at confidence in the equity of the existing distribution of wealth.... Lenin was certainly right. There is no subtler, no surer means of overturning the existing basis of society than to debauch the currency.

The Russian revolutionaries were perhaps rather consciously borrowing a page from the history of the French Revolution. After the experience of the Russian

Revolution and post-World War I Germany, price stability has been considered important for maintaining social stability in capitalist societies.

See also Hyperinflation in Post-World War I Germany, Hyperinflation of the Continental Currency, Hyperinflation of the French Revolution.

References Pipes, Richard. *The Russian Revolution* (1991); Hasegawa, Tsuyoshi. *The February Revolution: Petrograd, 1917* (1981).

Import Duties Act of 1932 (England)

With the Import Duties Act of 1932, England abandoned a policy of free trade that had been the foundation of its commercial policy for nearly a century. With this act, England's commercial policy changed from a free-trade regime to a protectionist regime.

England had resisted the trend toward protectionist trade policies that was evident in many countries during the last three decades before World War I. After World War I, Britain made a few token concessions to the advocates of protectionist trade policies, but remained a free-trade country. In the 1920s, however, the British pound was overvalued, hurting British exports, and favoring imports. The forces of protectionism began to gather strength.

With the onset of the worldwide depression in 1929–1930, the pressures for trade barriers swept away all opposition. John Maynard Keynes, the most famous economist of the twentieth century, advocated tariffs and export bounties to shore up England's ailing economy. The Depression brought in its wake widespread unemployment, falling internal and export demand for domestic goods, and a widening balance-of-payments deficit. Tax revenue fell, while government outlays on such things as unemployment relief increased. The iron and steel industry, and several other major industries, felt the Depression very directly. Other countries combated the Depression by raising trade barriers. In 1930, the United States enacted the Smoot-Hawley tariff. A shift to protectionist trade policies seemed to meet the needs of the time. It increased the demand for domestically produced goods at the expense of foreign goods, and it generated extra revenue for the government.

The Import Duties Act exempted many food items and raw materials from import duties. For goods not exempted, the act placed a general ad valorem tax of 10 percent. The act also provided for the formation of an Import Duties Advisory Committee. This committee made recommendations for additional duties, targeting specific industries in need of protection. It was to take into consideration "the advisability in the national interest of restricting imports into the United Kingdom." Individual industries appealed to this committee for protection. The pig-iron industry persuaded the committee to recommend a 33-percent tariff on imported pig iron. The committee remained active throughout the duration of the Depression. In 1939, the committee recommended a 30-percent import duty on elastic goods of lace or lace net. The Exchequer, as the final arbiter, had to act upon the recommendations of the committee. After 1933, the Exchequer was empowered to grant concessions to individual countries, and this authority paved the way for the British government to extract trade concessions from foreign countries.

After World War II, the world's trading partners began multilateral negotiations to reduce trade barriers. Except for England's fall from grace in the 1930s, the nation had been the most faithful defender of free trade. After Adam Smith, England's economists never ceased praising free trade. More than any other capitalist country, England had remade the economic world in its own image.

See also General Agreement on Tariffs and Trade, Smoot-Hawley Tariff of 1930.

References Ashley, Percy. *Modern Tariff History: Germany, United States and France* (1970); Hutchinson, Sir Herbert. *Tariff-Making and Industrial Reconstruction* (1965); McCord, Norman. *Free Trade* (1970).

Imprisonment of Debtors

Governments enacted laws sanctioning the imprisonment of debtors in the Middle Ages. Imprisonment for debt became a humanitarian issue in the nineteenth century.

In the Middle Ages, falling hopelessly into debt could bring unwanted repercussions. According to one report, a merchant in Barcelona found himself beheaded for bankruptcy in 1360. In England, statutory authority for the imprisonment of debtors began in 1283, with the Statute of Anton Burnell, under which merchants could have debtors declare the amount and terms of their debt to the mayor. If the debtor defaulted on the due date, the creditor could seize goods belonging to the debtor as an indemnity for the debt, or have the debtor imprisoned. In 1285, the enactment of the Statute of Merchants enabled creditors to have a debtor imprisoned immediately upon showing proof that the debtor had defaulted on the day the debt was due. The Statute of 1352 strengthened the hand of creditors, dismissing the requirement for the debtor to declare his debt before the mayor. The creditor could demand the imprisonment of the debtor, until the debt had been settled. The Statute of 1352 put persons defaulting on debts to private creditors on the same footing as persons defaulting on debts to the crown. According to Ralph B. Pugh, "From this statute sprang all the imprisoning for debt, all the debtors' prisons or debtor's wards, and all the lamentations which they brought in their train."

The colonies in North America, highly dependent upon England for capital, followed the English practice of imprisoning debtors. In the eighteenth century, England enacted bankruptcy laws that allowed merchants and traders to declare bankruptcy and avoid imprisonment. Their assets were divided among their creditors. Some of the colonial governments enacted bankruptcy laws that protected the merchant class. Imprisonment remained a likely possibility for commercial bankrupts who concealed property from creditors, or engaged in any action to defraud creditors. The line drawn between honest and dishonest bankrupts was often blurred. Colonial governments often allowed debtors to avoid debtors' prison by pledging an oath of poverty, or by relinquishing all their belongings.

In the nineteenth century, the abolishment of imprisonment of debtors became a humanitarian issue. By the 1870s, most states in the United States had done away with debtors' prisons. States proceeded gradually, by first prohibiting imprisonment of petty debtors, veterans, and females. In northern New England, states defined debtors' prison as the area within the state boundary.

The practice of imprisoning debtors met a similar fate in Europe. In 1869, England abolished the imprisonment of debtors except in cases of fraud or disobedience to a court order. In 1793, the Convention of the French Revolution abolished imprisonment of debtors, but the revolutionary Assembly brought it back. France abolished the practice in 1867, and the North German Confederation and Austria abolished imprisonment of debtors in 1868. In 1877, the Code of Civil Procedure for the German Empire put an end to imprisonment of debtors.

Few issues stand closer to the heart of capitalism than the relationship between creditors and debtors. Capitalism channels the resources of savers into the best possible investment opportunities. The laws protecting the rights of creditors and debtors set the ground rules for this process. The practice of imprisoning debtors was probably a symptom of poor societies, in which capital was in short supply, and too valuable to be wasted. As the supply of capital grew in abundance, and lenders discovered better methods of securing loans and collecting information about borrowers, threat of imprisonment for defaulters no longer served a purpose. At that point, the humanitarian issue became paramount.

See also Bankruptcy Acts of 1543–1624.

References Coleman, Peter J. *Debtors and Creditors in America* (1974); Pugh, Ralph B. *Imprisonment in Medieval England* (1968).

Income Tax

The income tax constitutes the largest source of revenue in capitalist countries today, raising between 30 and 40 percent of total tax revenue in most industrialized countries.

One of the first advocates of an income tax was the Marquis de Vaudon, a French military engineer, who wrote on economics in the time of Colbert. He proposed a sort of personal income tax, based upon income from all sources. He envisioned a progressive tax with an upper limit of 10 percent on the highest incomes. Vaudon's book elucidating these ideas came to the attention of Louis XIV, who saw to it that a hangman burned the ignominious book in public. Vaudon died in disgrace.

During the Napoleonic Wars, England turned to the income tax as a temporary wartime measure to raise revenue. This episode gave England the dubious honor of being the first country to embrace the income tax. In a speech asking for the income tax, William Pitt, the prime minister, proposed that the "presumption founded upon the assessed taxes be laid aside, and that a general tax be imposed upon all the leading branches of income." Pitt's income tax had a 10-percent bracket for incomes above a certain level. No taxes were levied on incomes below a threshold level, and various rates were charged intermediate levels. Nonresidents paid taxes on income-earning property held in England. Residents paid taxes on income from inheritances in England or elsewhere, and on property, wages, professions, pensions, stipends, trades, and offices. Pitt's tax exempted corporate income, and allowed deductions for children.

Parliament repealed this first English income tax during a brief peace in 1802. In 1803, Parliament imposed the tax again, with a maximum rate of 5 percent.

The maximum rate rose to 10 percent before the end of the Napoleonic Wars. One member of Parliament mentioned 10 percent as the "natural limit of the tax." The public accepted the income tax as a grievous burden of war that would be repealed when war ended. In 1816, Parliament repealed the income tax, but in 1842 Parliament reimposed it, with a maximum rate of 3 percent. A commissioner was appointed to investigate claims for allowances. The tax was originally approved for three years, but was renewed in 1845. During Gladstone's service as prime minister, Parliament raised the rate to 6 percent, to help finance the Crimean War.

The British income tax reported income in five branches, known as schedules A, B, C, D, and E. Income from specific sources was reported in each schedule. Karl Marx cites figures derived from these schedules in his arguments and reasoning in his work *Das Kapital.* The *Communist Manifesto* specifically recommends a "heavy progressive or graduated income tax." The French first adopted an income tax in 1916.

The U.S. Congress first enacted an income tax at the beginning of the Civil War, in 1861. It taxed income at a rate of 3 percent on all income above $800 per annum. By 1865, incomes above $5,000 were taxed at 10 percent, and incomes from $600 to $5,000 at 5 percent. The tax remained in effect until 1872, but exemptions increased and rates declined after the Civil War. In 1894, Congress approved another income tax, which proposed to levy a 2-percent rate on personal and corporate income above $4,000. Congress exempted interest income on U.S. bonds. In a split five-to-four decision, the Supreme Court ruled this tax unconstitutional, because the Constitution required such a tax to be levied proportional to population among the states. Class consciousness among the lawyers was much in evidence during the debate.

The Sixteenth Amendment to the Constitution reads: "The Congress shall have the power to lay and collect taxes on incomes, from whatever source derived, without apportionment among the States, and without regard to any census or enumeration." A Republican Congress adopted the Sixteenth Amendment in 1909, perhaps hoping the states would never ratify it. The states ratified the amendment, and an income tax was enacted in 1913. It provided for graduated rates from 1 to 6 percent for the highest income bracket. Income below $3,000 was exempted for an individual.

The rates rose during World War I, but fell back to prewar levels after the war. Since the enactment of the income tax, virtually every Congress has modified the tax in some way. Income from capital gains was added later. During World War II, the rates became very progressive, and the rates on corporate income taxes rose to high levels. The rate on the highest bracket of personal income rose to 91 percent.

Wars in the twentieth century helped spread the use of the income tax. The income tax enabled capitalist countries to avoid the inflationary finance that often accompanied war. Hyperinflation plays pranks on social cohesion, and often leads to revolution. Russia experienced strong inflation during and after World War I. The income tax is one of many examples of innovations in capitalist economic systems that emerged under the pressure of a wartime mobilization of resources.

Beginning in the 1960s, the rates became much less progressive in the United States. The Revenue Act of 1964 reduced the marginal tax rate of the highest personal income bracket from 91 to 70 percent. The act reduced the maximum rate on corporate income from 52 to 48 percent.

Despite these rate reductions, a growing chorus of criticism pinned part of the blame for the stagflation of the 1970s on the income tax. First, it was said that the income tax was a tax on production, rather than consumption. It taxed people for earning income, rather than for spending it, thus contributing to a low rate of savings and investment. Second, the high tax rate on corporate income encouraged business purchases of consumer goods. Businesses bought airplanes, yachts, expensive automobiles, and other luxury goods, and counted them as expenses against the calculation of profits. Although these purchases were treated as business expenses, they were really consumer purchases for business owners and management. High business tax rates substantially reduced the impact of these consumer expenses on after-tax profits.

The Economic Recovery Act of 1981 reduced the highest marginal tax rate on personal income from 70 to 50 percent. Proponents of the major tax cut expected the economy to receive a major boost from the added incentives of additional after-tax income, even suggesting that tax revenue might rise, instead of fall, because of an anticipated burst of economic growth. Although the economy's performance remained disappointing, the movement for lower tax rates as a spur to economic growth continued. By 1995, the highest marginal tax rate on personal income was 39.5 percent, and the basic rate on corporate income was 35 percent. Accompanying the downward movement of tax rates has been the closing of loopholes, or the removal of tax-deductible expenses. Tax reform, including tax reduction and simplification, may deserve part of the credit for U.S. economic prosperity of the mid-1990s.

See also Economic Recovery Act of 1981, Excess Profits Tax, Revenue Act of 1964.

References Dowell, Stephen. *A History of Taxation and Taxes in England* (1888); Myers, Margaret G. *A Financial History of the United States* (1970); Stein, Herbert. *The Fiscal Revolution* (1996); Webber, Carolyn, and Aaron Wildavsky. *A History of Taxation and Expenditure in the Western World* (1986).

Indentured Servitude

Indentured servants entered into labor contracts binding them to work for a certain length of time in British colonial America. In return, the indentured servants, who could not pay their own way, had the transportation cost of their trip to America paid in full. Creditors in England were unwilling to make loans against future earnings for individuals headed for America. Collecting from someone 3,000 miles away could be difficult. Indentured servitude met a need for financing migration that capital markets at the time were unable to meet.

Around 1620, a decade after the settlement at Jamestown, the practice of indentured servitude arose in the colony of Virginia. According to one estimate, indentured servants accounted for one-half to two-thirds of all immigrants who came to pre-Revolutionary America after the wave of puritan migration in the 1630s. The practice in the eastern part of the North American mainland continued on a smaller scale into the 1840s. Just as indentured servitude ceased to exist on the mainland of North America, it became widely practiced in the West Indies and South America.

Indentured servants were bound under contract to work for a fixed number of years in their new land, but after their arrival in America, the indentured servants had little incentive to work. Although the law protected indentured servants from excessive corporal punishment and murder, it often winked at masters who beat their servants. To provide incentives, masters sometimes paid wages and struck bargains that held out the hope of early release. Indentured servants were known to run away and live with native tribes.

A market developed in the contracts for indentured service. Terms were set by the attractiveness of the destination and the skills, literacy, and age of the individual. Masters could buy or sell the unexpired terms of indentured servants already in America. Initially, the indenture system was a method of drawing unskilled labor to the plantations in the South. After the American Revolution, the indenture system became a means of importing skilled labor.

Rising wages in England, perhaps because of the Industrial Revolution, ended the migration of white indentured servants to North America. As contracts of indenture rose in price, the plantations in the South turned to slave labor, which was cheaper and able to withstand the harsher working and living conditions on the plantations.

The abolition of slavery in the 1830s, in the British West Indies, kept the practice of indentured servitude alive on the sugar plantations in that area. Sensitive to the charge of slavery, the British Colonial Office only permitted contracts of indenture for fixed terms, and with specific employers. Asia supplied most of the indentured servants on the sugar plantations. South America also imported Asian indentured servants. The Caribbean sugar islands and South America abolished servitude in 1917.

In the latter portion of the nineteenth century, indentured servitude experienced a revival in the western United States. The Act to Encourage Immigration of 1864 allowed immigrants to pledge their labor for up to one year, to repay an advancement on transportation cost. Chinese were brought in as indentured servants to work on mines and building railroads. In the United States, contracts of indenture remained legal until 1885.

Under the capitalist economic system, profits and wages lure capital and labor to those regions and occupations in which rewards are the highest. Colonial America faced a chronic labor shortage. Land was virtually in unlimited supply, and Europe had capital looking for opportunities in the New World. Under such ideal conditions, the productivity of a worker in America was substantially higher than in Europe. The supply of labor was the resource that put a limit on production, and indentured servitude was a method of attracting workers who could not afford to finance migration to America. The alternative would have been higher wages in America, which would have substantially reduced the profits of capital.

See also Slavery.

References Galenson, David W. "The Rise and

Fall of Indentured Servitude in the Americas: An Economic Analysis." *Journal of Economic History* (1984); Northrup, David. *Indentured Labor in the Age of Imperialism: 1834–1922* (1995).

Industrial Revolution

The essence of the Industrial Revolution was the replacement of human labor with mechanical power. It was an economic transformation that began in England in the latter third of the eighteenth century, spread to the rest of the world, and continues to the present day.

The revolution itself came to England first for several reasons. Control of the seas and possession of colonies gave England a ready supply of raw materials and foreign markets that needed manufactured goods. England's constitutional government gave business and economic interests a voice in government policy. Profits from English mercantile monopolies in colonial trade created a surplus of capital that needed an outlet.

The textile industry led the Industrial Revolution thanks to inventions like this carding machine, built in 1775 to separate cotton from debris and straighten the cotton once cleaned.

English nobility felt free to participate in commerce and industry, and scientific discovery took a practical turn in England, while it remained predominantly abstract on the continent. England kept itself free from invasion and war's devastation.

Several inventions paved the way for the industrial transformation of England. Abraham Darby and John Smeaton developed blast furnaces in 1754 and 1760, respectively. Smeaton's furnace applied a constant high-pressure blast that raised daily iron production from 12 to 40 tons per furnace. These new furnaces made iron affordable for uses never thought of before.

In 1763, Richard Reynolds laid the first known railway of iron tracks, allowing cars to move coal and ore faster than pack animals. John Wilkinson and Abraham Darby II built an iron bridge across the River Severn (1779), and Wilkinson built the first iron ship. England's iron industry turned out tools and machines for factories that were more durable and cheaper than ever before.

The textile industry led the Industrial Revolution in developing inventions to accelerate production. The transformation of the textile industry began with John Kay's invention of the flying shuttle (1733). Before Kay's invention, the width of material a single worker could weave, throwing the shuttle from one hand to the other, depended upon the length of the worker's arms. Kay developed a mechanism that threw the shuttle from one side of the loom to the other. Not only could the width of the material be broadened, but the weaving process sped up substantially. With Kay's invention, weavers could weave the thread much faster than the thread could be spun. Thread became in short supply, and the price soared. In 1769, James Hargreaves developed the spinning jenny (named for his wife Jenny), to replace the spinning wheel. Hargreaves linked eight spindles mechanically, so that a worker could spin eight threads at once, instead of one. With power to drive the system, the number of spindles could be increased without limit. In 1769, Richard Arkwright developed a water frame that used water power to pull and stretch fibers into a tighter and harder yarn than the most skilled spinner could produce using a spinning wheel. Around 1774, Samuel Crompton developed a machine humorously named Crompton's Mule. This machine used an alternating backward and forward motion to rotating spindles to stretch, twist, and wind the thread, producing a finer and stronger thread. In 1787, Edmund Cartwright built a 20-loom factory, driven first by animal power, and, after 1789, by steam power. His construction of a steam-powered factory operating 400 looms came to an end when workers rebelled and burnt the unfinished factory.

The Industrial Revolution reached its stride with the development of the steam engine to drive machines and factories. James Watt applied for his first patent for a steam engine in 1769. The patent was good until 1783. The engine was designed to use steam to create a vacuum in the barrel of a pump, rather than harness steam as a motive power. Watt had difficulty completing the development of his engine, because parts could not be manufactured with the tolerances and precision needed for efficient operation of the engine. In 1775, John Wilkinson invented a method for boring out a hollow cylinder. This development enabled Watt to produce steam engines with the efficiency and power needed for general use. Watt's machines still needed work. In 1781, he patented the device that converted the back-and-forth motion of the piston into rotating motion for driving machinery. One of Watt's employees, William Murdock, saw that steam power could replace animal traction, and built a model locomotive in 1784.

The expansion in production and trade and output put greater demands on the communication and transportation systems. In 1777, the Grand Trunk canal connecting the Trent and Mersey was fin-

ished. One canal connected Hull and Liverpool, and another canal connected them both with Bristol. In 1792, the Grand Junction canal cut a waterway from London through Oxford, on to the major midland towns. The years between 1818 and 1829 saw more than 1,000 additional miles of turnpike roads built. The first railroad began service in 1830.

As cottage production gave way to factories increasing in size and number, the factory system was born. As plants and machinery became ever more costly, the individuals and institutions that could raise great amounts of capital grew in power and influence, and capitalism became an economy dominated by entrepreneurs.

The exploitation of factory workers was the darker side of the Industrial Revolution. A workday in a factory lasted 12 to 14 hours, and a workweek was six days. Workers no longer owned the tools of the trade, and could take no pride in the quality of the finished product. Guild regulations, municipal ordinances, and justices of the peace no longer controlled wages and working conditions as they had in the past. After 1793, real wages sank, as prices rose faster than wages, when England's long war with revolutionary France brought shortages. Women and children filled many of the unskilled positions in the factories. Parish authorities sent orphans and pauper children to the factories to avoid supporting them under the Poor Laws. Child laborers worked from ten to 14 hours per day, and discipline in the factory was severe.

Workers were forbidden to form labor unions for collective bargaining. They tried to revive laws that in the past had given local justices of the peace control over wages. Workers rioted, wrecked machines, held strikes, and petitioned Parliament for help, all to no avail. Employers convinced Parliament that supply and demand should determine wages. The hands-off approach, leaving the economy free from government regulation, became the new dogma of the day. In 1799, Parliament outlawed associations organized for the purpose of obtaining higher wages, or shorter hours, or introducing any other regulation. Employees entering into such combinations were punishable by a minimum of three months imprisonment. The captains of industry triumphed completely.

See also Factory System, Machine-Smashing, Steam Engine.

References Ashton, S. *The Industrial Revolution, 1760–1830* (1964); Mantoux, Paul. *The Industrial Revolution in the Eighteenth Century* (1961); Stearns, Peter, and John H. Hinshaw. *The ABC-CLIO World History Companion to the Industrial Revolution* (1996).

Industrial Workers of the World

The Industrial Workers of the World (IWW) was an early twentieth-century union devoted to the unionization of unskilled and casual workers. Its creation was an important step in the unionization of industrial workers in the United States.

The American Federation of Labor (AFL) had steered clear of efforts to unionize unskilled workers, who could be easily replaced in a strike. The AFL contented itself with working for the betterment of skilled workers, within the context of the existing economic and political order. The radical elements of the labor movement found the vision embodied in the philosophy of the AFL too narrow, given their interpretation of the way the capitalist system worked.

The IWW emerged from a meeting in Chicago (1904) called by the Western Federation of Miners, the American Labor Union, and leaders of socialist groups. A letter sent out in 1905, inviting participants to a secret meeting in Chicago, expressed the philosophy of its founders. The letter asserted,

confidence in the ability of the working class, if correctly organized on both po-

Striking silk workers from Paterson, New Jersey, march up Fifth Avenue to Madison Square Garden on 5 June 1913.

litical and industrial lines, to take possession of and operate successfully...the industries of the country; Believing that working-class political expression, through the Socialist ballot, in order to be sound, must have its economic counterpart in a labor organization builded as the structure of the socialists society, embracing within itself the working class in approximately the same groups and departments and industries that the workers would assume in the working-class administration of the Co-operative Commonwealth....

The members of the IWW came to be known as Wobblies. William D. Haywood, president of the Western Federation of Miners, emerged as the leader. Syndicalism best describes the prevailing philosophy of the IWW. In the words of the leaders of the IWW, "No genuine democracy is possible in industry until those who do the work in a business (from hired president to hired common laborer) control its management."

Some of the idealism of the organization can be seen in the integrated organization of African-American and white lumber workers in the southern states. In 1907, however, the IWW conducted several strikes and demonstrations in the South that turned violent. It also held strikes of northeastern textile workers in 1912 and 1913. Although these strikes raised the public's awareness of the poverty and suffering of unskilled workers, they rarely led to the formation of a permanent union. The IWW mostly gained nationwide attention.

The overall distrust of organizations embedded in the philosophy of the IWW may have stunted its growth. A stable leadership and centralized bureaucracy never arose from the organizational efforts of the IWW. The IWW's opposition to U.S. involvement in World War I turned the federal government against the organization, and it arrested scores of IWW leaders and members, and won convictions under state criminal syndi-

calism laws. The red scare of 1919 finished driving the Wobblies underground. By the mid-1920s, the organization was no longer a force in the U.S. labor movement.

See also Syndicalism.

References Cartter, Allan M., and F. Ray Marshall, *Labor Economics: Wages, Employment, and Trade Unionism* (1967); Dubofsky, Melvyn. *We Shall Be All: A History of the Industrial Workers of the World* (1988).

Inflation and Deflation

Inflation is an overall rise in the general price level. It means the average level of all prices is rising, rather than the prices of a few select goods and services. Deflation is the reverse: a falling of the average level of prices. History appears to be inflationary, although episodes of deflation are numerous.

Although, on the surface, inflation appears to be an overall increase in prices, it can be interpreted as a decrease in the value of money. It leaves each unit of money capable of buying fewer goods and services.

Inflation is measured by price indices that are weighted averages of the growth in prices of a spectrum of goods and services. In the United States, the Consumer Price Index measures the inflation rate for goods and services that are associated with the basic cost of living, including food, gasoline, utilities, housing, clothes, etc. Another index, the Gross Domestic Product Deflator, measures the overall inflation rate for all goods and services, including factory equipment and other goods bought by businesses, luxury goods, and goods bought by the government.

Inflation often accompanies wartime expenditures. During World War II, the United States enacted wage and price controls to contain inflation. The price controls were lifted at the end of World War II, and inflation remained a problem throughout the Cold War era. Inflation tends to become a problem whenever governments do not want to levy taxes at a rate to support government expenditures. In the 1980s, a prolonged reduction in the growth of the money supply ended the inflationary inertia in the U.S. economy.

Economists often see controlling inflation as a problem in maintaining the value of money, which rises in value as the supply is restricted. A slow, steady rate of inflation that is easily anticipated causes less disruption than a high inflation rate showing substantial volatility. Inflation in the range of 300 percent annually, or higher, is called hyperinflation. This brand of galloping or runaway inflation is often associated with the complete breakdown of society.

The United States and several European countries saw deflation during the last quarter of the nineteenth century. Deflation puts a burden on debtors, who find it harder to raise the money to repay their debts. In the United States, debtor hardship helped fuel a populist revolt in the late nineteenth century that nearly propelled Willian Jennings Bryan to the presidency. One of the epochal moments in political oratory in the United States occurred in Bryan's Cross of Gold speech, in which he said, "You shall not press down on the brow of labor this crown of thorns, you shall not crucify mankind on this cross of gold." The cross of gold was the gold standard, which was seen as the culprit causing the deflation. Bryan wanted to monetize silver to increase the money supply and end deflation.

See also Hyperinflation in Post-World War I Germany, Hyperinflation of the Continental Currency, Hyperinflation of the French Revolution, Hyperinflation of the Russian Revolution.

References McCallum, Bennett T. *Monetary Economics: Theory and Policy* (1989); Weintraub, Sidney. *Capitalism's Inflation and Unemployment Crisis* (1978).

Injunction

See Buck's Stove and Range Case, Clayton Act of 1914, Norris-LaGuardia Act of 1932.

Insider Trading (United States)

Insider trading involves the use, for the purposes of speculation, of information obtained from company insiders, but which is not available to the vast bulk of shareholders. It allows stock traders to earn speculative profits at the expense of less-informed investors. The Securities Exchange Act of 1934 made it "unlawful for any person to engage in any act that operates as a fraud or deceit upon any person, in connection with purchase or sale of any security." Scandals of insider trading ranked among the major business stories during the 1980s. Corporate executives, lawyers, accountants, and relatives were implicated in insider trading. A typist at a law firm made $50,000 in one day, by trading in the stock market on inside information. Between 1980 and 1984, the Securities and Exchange Commission (SEC) brought 51 cases of insider trading to court.

The most famous insider trading scandal of the 1980s centered around Ivan Boesky, king of the arbitrageurs. He began buying up the stock of companies he considered good targets of takeovers. As corporate raiders entered the market, the prices of these stocks, with the aid of Boesky's own speculation, began a climb that paved the way for the takeover. When a price reaches a point at which owners of a majority of the stocks are willing to sell out to the corporate raiders, Boesky would sell out, reaping huge profits. Stock speculation of this sort became illegal when Boesky either had advanced inside knowledge that a company was about to be a takeover target, or intentionally spread rumors that a company was a takeover target.

In 1986, Boesky was caught in an insider trading investigation. He paid a fine of $50 million to the U.S. government, and put up another $50 million in an escrow account to compensate investors who were victimized by his illegal trading. Boesky not only squealed to the authorities about the role of insider trading in stock deals, but allowed them to tap his telephone conversations about his business dealings. Among those brought down by Boesky's cooperation with the authorities were some of the most prominent names in the corporate takeover business. The investigation implicated Carl Icahn, chairman of TWA, in helping Boesky spread takeover rumors to drive up the price of Gulf and Western's stock, of which, together, they owned a 50-percent share. Another famous corporate raider, Victor Posner, spent $80 million buying up a big electrical contractor, while Boesky held 13.4 percent of the stock.

The biggest name drawn into the Boesky scandal was Michael Milkin, senior executive vice president of Drexel, Burnham, and Lambert, of New York. Milkin's name in financial circles is forever linked to the low-grade, high-interest bonds, known as junk bonds. Corporate raiders used these bonds to raise vast sums of capital to finance corporate takeovers. Milkin's role in arranging financing for corporate takeovers gave him inside information, which he shared with Boesky. In turn, Boesky secretly held stock for Drexel, at Milkin's request, allowing Drexel to speculate in stock with inside information. In September 1988, the SEC brought charges against Drexel and Milken for manipulating the market in 16 different takeover situations. Drexel was using Boesky to bid up the prices of stocks that were takeover targets. Drexel and Milkin faced heavy fines and penalties.

In response to insider-trading scandals, Congress passed the Insider Trading Sanctions Act of 1984, and the Insider Trading Securities Enforcement Act of 1988. The latter act codifies previous insider-trading law, and more clearly defines insider trading as a breach of trust and confidence. Strengthening insider-trading laws reduces the risk for the average investor, making stocks more attractive to holders of financial capital, and improving the mobilization of savings in a capitalist society.

See also Greenmail, Mergers.

References Alkhafaji, Abbass F. *Restructuring American Corporations: Causes, Effects, and Implications* (1990); Frantz, Douglas. *Levine and Co.: Wall Street's Insider Trading Scandal* (1987).

Insurance

Insurance pools the risks of a great number of individuals or organizations, reducing the risk exposure of each member of the pool by spreading the loses over a considerable group. The group pays premiums into a fund that covers the loses of individual members of the group. Insurance schemes are founded in the law of large numbers. Applying this law to fire insurance, insurers can predict how many houses per 100,000 will be destroyed by fire each year, although they cannot predict which individual houses will burn. For risks to be insurable, losses must be predictable within a large group.

Perhaps one of the earliest forms of insurance was marine insurance. In ancient Greece, lenders financed commercial shipping ventures, and charged extra premiums that insured both ship and cargo. Laws existed during the Renaissance that governed marine insurance, and determined how long a ship had to be missing before its owners could collect insurance. In 1574, England enacted a law that provided for the creation of a Chamber of Insurance that sold marine insurance. Lloyd's of London, dating back to the eighteenth century, and the oldest insurance organization still in business, was devoted almost exclusively to marine insurance, until the twentieth century. Insurers became known as underwriters, because they signed their names under contracts on which they bore a share of the insurable risks.

The first life insurance policy dates back to the early sixteenth century, and the first fire insurance company came into existence after the Great Fire of London in 1666.

Businesses face two sorts of risks: insurable and uninsurable. Insurable risks can be insured against, reducing the individual risk linked to the private ownership of vast amounts of capital. The profits that businesses earn are compensation for the uninsurable risk that entrepreneurs and business owners must bear in the operation of a business. An example of an uninsurable risk is the risk that a technological development will render an existing product obsolete. Insurance for insurable risk makes private ownership of capital much more feasible. In a capitalist economic system, insurance is a convenience that helps households and businesses act on their own initiative.

See also Lloyd's of London.

References Athearn, James L., and S. Travis Pritchett. *Risk and Insurance* (1984); Hodgson, Godfrey. *Lloyds of London* (1984).

Interest Rate

An interest rate can be regarded as the cost of money, expressed as a percentage. If the annual interest rate is 10 percent, an individual borrowing $100 for a year pays $10 interest. Alternatively, an individual who holds $100 for a year gives up the opportunity to loan out the money, and earn interest. Theoretically, in a capitalist economic system, interest rates adjust to a level at which the interest income earned from loaning $100 of money equals the income earned from owning capital goods (tools, machinery, buildings, etc.) worth $100.

During the early development of capitalism, religious authorities regarded charging interest as a sinful means of earning income. Governments either banned interest, or put a legal ceiling on interest rates. In the United States, state usury laws limiting interest rates were common as late as the 1970s. Most have now been repealed.

During the recovery phase of the business cycle, interest rates tend to rise as capital goods become more productive, and, in the recession phase, interest rates tend to fall. Governments may act to purposely reduce interest rates, as an antidote to depression. Historically, the highest peaks in interest rates have often occurred during wartime. Interest rates reached historical peak levels during the Napoleonic Wars, and during World War I. The legacy of the Depression, and wage and price controls, helped keep a lid on interest rates during World War II, but the era of the Cold War, from 1946 to 1983, saw the longest upswing in interest rates since the beginning of the eighteenth century. Wars are often the occasion for heavy government borrowing and high inflation, both of which are enemies to low interest rates.

See also English Usury Laws, French Usury Laws.

References Barro, J. Robert. "Government Spending, Interest Rates, Prices, and Budget Deficits in the United Kingdom, 1701–1918." *Journal of Monetary Economics* (1987); Homer, Sidney. *A History of Interest Rates* (1977).

Interlocking Directorates (United States)

Interlocking directorates arise when individuals sit on the boards of directors of two or more corporations, and are in a position to encourage cooperation and reciprocity, and to discourage competition.

In the United States, interlocking directorates were instrumental in the growth of finance capitalism in the latter portion of the nineteenth century. In 1912, a Congressional committee investigating the banking industry cited the widespread involvement in interlocking directorates. Investment bankers sought representation on the boards of directors of corporations in which they held stock, and justified this practice in the name of protecting their investment, but they had an incentive to discourage serious competition between their customers. The Congressional committee saw the interlocking directorates as a force for restricting competition.

In 1912, the investment banking house of John Pierpont Morgan had placed one or more of its members on the boards of directors of 32 corporations. Morgan himself could be found in the ranks of directors or voting trustees for the New York Central Railroad; the New

York, New Haven and Hartford Railroad; the Southern Railway Company; the Philadelphia and Reading Railroad; the International Mercantile Marine Company; Adams Express; International Harvester; General Electric; and Western Union. In addition, J. P. Morgan and Company either owned or controlled a number of banks. By 1920, Morgan and Company could boast that 167 representatives of the banking house served as directors in 2,450 interlocking directorates. About one-fourth of the total corporate assets in the United States fell within J. P. Morgan's sphere of control.

Section 8 of the Clayton Act of 1914 forbade interlocking directorates that link two competing corporations. Section 8 has not been a powerful weapon in practice. It prohibits the same individual from serving on the boards of directors of two companies producing the same products. It does not prevent a high-level executive of one company from sitting on the board of directors of a competing company. Two companies who are potential competitors, but who have not actually entered into competition, are beyond the pale of section 8. Section 8 allows interlocking directorates between buyers and sellers, manufacturers and bankers, and between other corporations producing related, but not the same, products.

Interlocking directorates remained a touchy issue in the governance of corporate America in the post-World War II era. A study in 1968 found that 49 commercial banks participated in a total of 768 interlocking directorates with 286 of the 500 biggest industrial corporations.

See also Cartels, Clayton Act of 1914, Corporation, Finance Capitalism, Mergers.

References Neale, Allan D., and D. G. Goyden. *The Antitrust Laws of the United States of America* (1980); Schnitzer, Martin C. *Contemporary Government and Business Relations* (1978).

International Monetary Fund

John Maynard Keynes referred to the International Monetary Fund (IMF) and the World Bank as the "Bretton Woods' twins." Both institutions were born of the Bretton Woods Conference in 1944, which put foreign exchange markets under a system of fixed exchange rates—a system that lasted until 1971. Although the mission of the World Bank lay in financing development and reconstruction projects, the IMF bore responsibility for furnishing short-term credit for countries suffering balance-of-payments difficulties.

Countries experience balance-of-payments deficits when their outflow of money, from imports and foreign investment, exceeds their inflow of money from exports and capital borrowed abroad. A country can prevent currency depreciation, caused by excess money outflow relative to inflow, by borrowing funds from the IMF, and using these funds to support the value of its currency. Under the fixed exchange rate system, the IMF loaned funds to countries who needed to intervene in foreign exchange markets to maintain the values of their currencies at the fixed rates. Under the current system of floating exchange rates, the IMF has shifted its emphasis to helping less-developed countries maintain stable exchange rates that are necessary to attract foreign capital.

The funds of the IMF came from subscriptions of member countries, who contributed on the basis of such variables as national income and foreign trade. Each country contributed sums of its own currency, which serve as the IMF's lending capital. Out of these funds, the IMF might make foreign currency loans to countries who use the proceeds to buy up excess amounts of their own currency in foreign exchange markets. The borrowing country puts up its own currency as collateral for such a loan. Perhaps the greatest economic innovation of the IMF during the period of fixed exchange rates was the development of special drawing rights (SDRs), sometimes referred to as paper gold. By international agreement, the SDRs are exchangeable for other currencies, just as gold reserves.

The end of the fixed exchange rate

system in 1971 cast doubt on the future need for the IMF. The oil price revolution, however, not only pushed the fixed exchange rate system to the breaking point, but also put a heavy burden on the less-developed countries of the world, who responded by incurring great amounts of debt to foreign lenders. During the 1980s, high interest rates increased the cost of servicing this debt, and reduced exports to the recession-ridden United States, decreasing the inflow of dollars needed to service this debt. Many less-developed countries also turned to inflationary policies at home, further endangering the investments of foreigners. Under these conditions, the IMF assumed the thankless task of requiring these countries to follow responsible monetary and fiscal policies as a condition for receiving additional IMF credit. The IMF usually required policies of high interest rates, depreciated currencies, and smaller budget deficits, which means less social spending. Private lenders refused credit to countries who failed to follow IMF adjustment programs.

Under the floating exchange rate system, the industrially developed countries have little need of the resources of the IMF. The IMF has turned its attention to the less-developed countries, making longer-term loans to finance balance-of-payments deficits, and granting soft loans to the poorest of the world's countries. These balance-of-payments deficits allow these countries to import capital.

Some observers believe that the world capitalist economy will eventually develop a world central bank that oversees a world monetary system. In the activities of the IMF can been seen the faint glimmerings of a world central bank.

See also Bretton Woods System, Dollar Crisis of 1971, World Bank.

References Polak, Jacques J. *The World Bank and the International Monetary Fund: A Changing Relationship* (1994); Myers, Robert J., ed. *The Political Morality of the International Monetary Fund* (1987).

International Whaling Commission
See Environmental Regulation (International).

International Workingmen's Association (First International)

The International Workingmen's Association (IWA) was the first organization of the working-class movement that transcended national boundaries. In 1862, two French delegates visiting the London Industrial Exposition met with British trade unionists. The French delegation discovered that the British were receptive to the idea of an international organization, and, on 28 September 1864, the IWA was officially launched in London. Karl Marx attended this meeting, and delivered an important address that helped shape the mission of the organization. From the beginning, Marx was an influential member of the IWA. In the inaugural address, he urged that: "Proletarians of all countries, Unite." Marx also wrote the rules that set up the organization. The philosophy of the organization can be gleaned from general principles such as,

That the emancipation of the working classes must be conquered by the working classes themselves; that the struggle for the emancipation of the working classes means not a struggle for class privileges and monopolies, but for equal rights and duties, and the abolition of all class rule;

That the economical subjection of the man of labor to the monopolizer of the means of labor, that is the source of life, lies at the bottom of servitude in all its forms, of all social misery, mental degradation, and political dependence....

That all efforts aiming at that great end have hitherto failed from the want of solidarity between the manifold divisions of labor in each country, and from the absence of a fraternal bond of union between the working classes of different countries.

The IWA held its first congress in Geneva in 1866. Marx wrote a resolution that was adopted by this congress that voiced support for the traditional trade union struggles for better wages and working conditions, but put the unions to task for narrowness. In the words of the resolution, unions "have not yet completely realized their power to attack the very system of wage slavery and present day methods of production.... In addition to their traditional task, the trade unions must now learn how to act as focal points for organizing the working class in the greater interest for their complete emancipation...."

Between 1864 and 1870, the IWA established branches in nearly all European countries and the United States. London was the home of a 55-member general council that was entrusted with central administration. Branches elected London residents of their own nationality to sit on the council. Important leaders in British unions sat on the council and participated in the IWA, but British trade unions mostly stood aloof. The IWA enjoyed the strongest support in France, Denmark, and Belgium.

In 1871, the workers of Paris revolted and set up the Commune. Workers were enraged by what they saw as the reactionary government of the Republic that replaced the Second Empire, after the defeat of the French in the Franco-Prussian War of 1870. The Commune lasted two and one-half months, from 15 February to 28 May. The government deployed troops to crush the rebellion.

After the Commune fell, the French government suppressed trade unions and imprisoned many trade union leaders. IWA membership in England and other European countries fell away. The IWA congress of 1872 moved the organization to New York to prevent anarchists from taking over. The organization survived until 1876.

The revolutionary agenda of the IWA drew its inspiration from the class-struggle interpretation of history. Many economic reforms, enacted after the effects of universal manhood suffrage and women's suffrage were felt in political processes, diffused much class antagonism that expressed itself in organizations such as the IWA.

See also Marx, Karl; Paris Commune of 1871; Second International.

References Foster, William Z. *Outline History of the World Trade Union Movement* (1956); Morgan, Roger P. *The German Social Democrats and the First International* (1965).

Interstate Commerce Commission (United States)

See Deregulation of Trucking.

Iron Act of 1750 (United States)

The British Parliament enacted the Iron Act of 1750 to stifle the growth of iron-related industries in the American colonies. The Iron Act represents the kind of exploitative economic policies that forced colonies into the role of raw materials suppliers for the manufacturing interest of the parent country. Critics of capitalism cite legislation such as the Iron Act to show how parent countries stifled economic development in colonies to favor their own economic interest. In the 1700s, the exhaustion of charcoal timber in Britain almost brought the British iron industry to a stop. In 1773, imported bar iron in Britain tripled the amount of bar iron produced domestically. Since the British iron industry had a stronger voice in the British Parliament than the American colonists, Parliament saw fit to cap the development of iron industries in the colonies.

The law provided that "no mill or other engine for slitting or rolling of iron, or any plating forge to work with a tilt hammer, or any furnace for making steel, shall be erected." The law allowed Britain to import colonial pig iron duty-free, and the City of London to import colonial bar iron duty-free. After 1757, colonial bar iron entered duty-free in all British ports.

American colonists built iron works in

defiance of the Iron Act. During the American Revolutionary War, the iron industry helped supply the colonists with military armaments to fend off the British. Iron works were a favorite target of the British army.

Laws such as the Iron Act turned the colonists against the British government. In the nineteenth century, critics of capitalism fully exposed the openly oppressive nature of colonial policies such as the Iron Act, which seemed to be proof of the selfish purposes that lay behind the desire to acquire colonies. Restrictions on iron industries appeared particularly odious to a later generation, who equated economic development with iron-intensive industrialization. Third-world governments felt that these types of policies contributed to the legacy of poverty that many of them had inherited. In hindsight, colonial policies were contrary to the spirit of competition, and disappeared as a feature of capitalist development.

See also Colonial Policy, New Imperialism.

References Fisher, Douglas Alan. *The Epic of Steel* (1963); Nash, Gerald D., ed. *Issues in American Economic History: Selected Readings* (1964).

Jeffersonian Embargo of 1807 (United States)

From 1807 to 1809, the U.S. government banned all trade to Great Britain and Europe. America's foreign trade fell off drastically, only to return to its pre-embargo level in the 1840s.

The Jeffersonian embargo was born of the economic warfare that attended the Napoleonic Wars. In 1806 and 1807, England, unable to match Napoleon's strategy on land, blockaded European ports and required all neutral ships bound for continental ports to stop first in English ports for licensing and inspection. In turn, Napoleon established the Continental System, which kept out British goods from markets on the European continent. England restricted the types of cargoes that neutral ships could carry to Europe, and gave itself the right to board and seize neutral ships. France let it be known that neutral shipping cooperating with England's control of shipping would be seized if caught.

The United States was caught in the middle of this struggle between the economic titans of Europe, and did not command the military strength to enforce the rights of neutrals. Rather than force a military showdown, Jefferson chose the route of an embargo in an effort to force England to loosen its grip on neutral shipping.

The embargo brought on economic depression in coastal areas and port cities in the United States, and aroused an angry opposition. The price of American raw materials soared in England, and English manufactures ordinarily destined for American markets suffered falling prices. The embargo failed to induce England to change its policy toward neutral shipping, and, in that regard, was a failure.

The Embargo of 1807 is important in the history of capitalism, because it launched the United States on a path of industrial development. The United States was more than self-sufficient in food and raw material production, but had depended on England for manufactured products. The embargo created an opportunity in the United States to build what economists call import-substituting industries. The United States had been importing manufactured goods, mostly textiles, from England. The absence of English textiles in American markets substantially raised the demand for domestically produced textiles, and the financial capital that had gone to finance international trade was idle and ready to be drawn into manufacturing enterprises. The number of incorporations of factory businesses grew from seven in 1808 to 26 in 1809, and the faster pace of domestic industrialization continued until the end of the War of 1812. The embargo accomplished for the United States what Alexander Hamilton had wanted to accomplish with high tariffs. Although the United States is one of the staunchest defenders of free trade today, the industrialization process in the United States received its first stimulus from a trade embargo.

See also Continental System.

References Atack, Jeremy, and Peter Passell. *A New Economic View of American History* (1994); Malone, Dumas. *Jefferson and His Time* (1974).

Joint Companies Act of 1856 (England)

The Joint Companies Act of 1856 established the principle of limited liability in English company law. The principle of limited liability exempts stockholders from liability for the debts of the corporation. In bankruptcy, stockholders stand to lose only the value of the stock owned in the corporation. In the event of liquidation, stockholders receive what is left after the claims of creditors have been satisfied. The principle of limited liability reduces the risk for investors, and is an added incentive to finance risky ventures.

In England, corporations formed on the principle of limited liability date back at least to 1553. These early corporations received a special charter, either from the crown or by special act of Parliament. English law specifically forbade an ordinary partnership from functioning as a corporation. The government made sparing use of its power to charter corporations. Partnerships applying for a charter found the process expensive, cumbersome, and without assurance of success. A general movement to grant the privileges of incorporation to a wide range of business enterprises began in the nineteenth century.

At the beginning of the nineteenth century, large-scale businesses operated as unincorporated partnerships. These businesses were owned by many partners, who neither knew each other nor played any role in the management of the corporation. Partnership law required that a third party suing a business cite the name of each individual partner. Businesses organized as partnerships could frustrate lawsuits by concealing the names of some of the partners, or by keeping some partners living outside the country. As some partners sold out and others bought in, the legal complexities escalated. Also, the law made no provision for settling disputes between partners. Some partners tried to pass themselves off as creditors to the company. The liability of the partners extended to their personal property.

In 1834 and 1837, Parliament adopted legislation that enabled a board of trade to confer the ability to sue or be sued, and the protection of limited liability. In practice, this board of trade was reluctant to grant these special powers. In the Registration Act of 1844, Parliament established companies as legal entities that could sue and be sued, but withheld the protection of limited liability. This act also provided for a registration procedure

that required a minimum paid-up capital and a registration of prospectuses, which was intended to protect unwary investors from schemes to raise money for fraudulent business ventures.

The Joint Companies Act of 1856 provided that seven or more persons could incorporate with the privileges of limited liability by filing a "memorandum of association." This act significantly simplified and streamlined the process of forming a company. The memorandum had to state the name and purpose of the company, and whether liability was limited. The company could either adopt a standard set of rules or it could propose its own set of rules. The standard rules required that a balance sheet be presented at annual stockholder meetings. One-fifth of the stockholders in number and in value could demand that the Board of Trade appoint accountants to inspect a company's books. The safeguards provided by the Registration Act of 1844 were dropped. The following decade saw a surge in the growth of corporations.

The emergence of limited liability was a great leap forward in the development of the capitalist economic system. It enabled risky, large-scale undertakings to marshal capital from a diversified range of unrelated sources. Modern large-scale industrial undertakings are too sizable to be financed by a handful of investors who are connected by personal relationships, and who can share in the management of the corporation. If stockholders were not protected by limited liability, they would demand higher profits, and companies lower on the profitability scale could not raise capital.

See also Bubble Act of 1720, Corporation, Joint-Stock Companies.

References Hannah, Leslie. *Rise of the Corporate Economy* (1976); Shannon, A. "The Coming of General Limited Liability." *Essays in Economic History* (1954).

Joint-Stock Companies

The English mercantile monopolies were organized as either regulated companies or joint-stock companies. The regulated companies operated as an umbrella organization of separate merchant traders who did not pool their capital. The joint-stock companies operated as modern corporations.

The establishment of a joint-stock company required a royal charter or an act of Parliament, either of which described in detail the activities the enterprise could engage in. According to Adam Smith's description of the joint-stock company, "no member can demand payment of his share from the company; but each member can, without their consent, transfer his share to another person, and thereby introduce another person." A market set the prices of these shares, and, according to Smith, the price a share will bring in the market "may be greater or less, in any proportion, than the sum which its owner stands credited for in the stock of the company."

A court of directors managed the business of the joint-stock company. The shareholder was only bound for the company's debts to the extent of the value of the holder's stock. That is, the stockholders enjoyed the protection of limited liability. As in modern corporations, the shareholders usually contented themselves with accepting the dividend yields decided by the court of directors. According to Smith's analysis, "This total exemption from trouble and risk, beyond a limited sum, encourages many people to become adventurers in joint-stock companies who would, upon no account, hazard their fortunes in any private co-partnery." Smith went on to argue that joint-stock companies were only rarely successful, unless they held a monopoly. He explained that the directors of such companies were the directors of other people's money rather than their own, and therefore did not exercise the same vigilance.

Elizabeth I granted the old English East India Company a charter in 1600. The company traded as a regulated company, with separate traders using company ships until 1612, when the company united as a joint-stock company. At one time, value of the stock totaled £744,000, at a rate of £50 per share. The company's charter was not confirmed by an act of Parliament, which left some question about the legality of its monopoly privilege. The company's charter bestowed an exclusive privilege or monopoly on trade in its territories. The company was empowered to make and enforce laws, and maintain forts and garrisons in its territories.

The wave of speculative fever that preceded the South Sea Bubble led Parliament to pass the Bubble Act of 1720, which outlawed the sales of stock from companies operating without a charter from Parliament. The act also made it more difficult for companies to obtain a charter. The financial panic was a setback for joint-stock companies as a means for mobilizing capital. Unincorporated joint-stock companies, however, remained a form of business organization and were officially sanctioned in the Joint Companies Act of 1856. This act made incorporation a simple matter of registration and complying with a uniform set of standards. Incorporation no longer required a private act of Parliament or royal charter.

See also Bubble Act of 1720, South Sea Bubble.

References Daunton, Martin. *Progress and Poverty: An Economic and Social History of Britain* (1995); Lawson, Phillip. *The East India Company: A History* (1993); Smith, Adam. *An Inquiry into the Nature and Causes of the Wealth of Nations* (1776).

Judaism and Capitalism

Scholars have speculated that Judaism may have been one of the cultural forces that helped the spirit of capitalism break through the hampering shell of the medieval world. Judaism is not the only religion that may have aided the development of capitalism. Max Weber, in his book *The Protestant Ethic and the Spirit of Capitalism*, attributed the advanced economic development of the predominately Protestant countries of the Western world to values nurtured by Protestantism. These theories have to be weighed carefully, because

Confucianism was once thought to be a regressive force in the development of Asia, and, now that the Asian economies have bloomed, Confucianism is receiving credit for its positive role. These theories easily degenerate into stereotyping, but they have been advanced as possible factors in the development of capitalism.

In the words of Werner Sombart, an influential writer on the history of capitalism, "Now, whatever increased Jewish influence—and be this noted once and for all—that also extended the spirit of capitalism in its highest form...." Writing before the formation of the modern state of Israel, Sombart expressed a theory that takes generalization a bit too far:

> The Jews may be taken as the most perfect type of a trading people. But how did they become such? Surely no small reason was that Fate for 2,000 years deprived them of any need of cultivating warlike activities. The warlike natures among them thus gradually disappeared.

Sombart holds out another explanation that appears more plausible, but that is nevertheless quite abstract:

> I can account for the fact that one reason the Jews were so eminently prepared for capitalism as that they had been money-lenders from the days of Solomon, while in the Middle Ages it

A man stops to buy pretzels from a woman's small street cart in New York early in the twentieth century.

was a calling which they practically monopolized.... Money lending was one of the well-springs of the capitalist spirit.... [I]t is an intellectual economic procedure, no more and no less.

According to the same author, Judaism rivaled Puritanism for inculcating values congenial to capitalist development. Judaism found no virtue in poverty, and was more receptive to wealth than was Christianity, excepting perhaps the Puritan denomination. It encouraged the "rationalization of life," referring to the suppression of appetites and emotions in favor of long-term goals.

Jewish ethics established one code of behavior governing conduct toward other Jews, and another code of behavior governing conduct toward non-Jews. This twofold code of morality became a molding force in capitalistic development. According to Sombart,

> the differential treatment of non-Jews in Jewish commercial law resulted in the complete transformation of the idea of commerce and industry, generally in the direction of more freedom. We have called the Jews the Fathers of Free Trade, and therefore of capitalism. They were prepared for this role by the free-trading spirit of their commercial and industrial law.

In Spain, Jews controlled the Levant trade, until the Spanish government expelled them at the end of the fifteenth century. They migrated to Holland, bringing the Levant trade with them, and Holland became the first state to practice complete toleration of Jews. In 1654, Oliver Cromwell lifted the policy excluding Jews from England.

The role of Jews in capitalist development stands among the most fascinating and speculative topics in economic history. One study of merchant bankers in Europe found that, of the 31 merchant bankers who died millionaires between 1809 and 1939, 24 were Jewish. Jewish populations in capitalist societies invariably produced a disproportionate share of entrepreneurs and financiers.

See also Confucianism, Merchant Bankers, Puritanism.

References Braudel, Fernand. *Civilization and Capitalism*, Vol. 2 (1982); Sombart, Werner. *The Quintessence of Capitalism: A Study of the History and Psychology of the Modern Business Man* (1967).

July Monarchy (France)

The July Revolution of 1830 brought to power a new government in France: the July Monarchy, sometimes called the bourgeois monarchy. It placed Louis-Philippe on the throne of France, replacing Charles X, the king of France under the restoration government that succeeded Napoleon. Louis-Philippe's father had sided with the revolutionists during the French Revolution and had died on the guillotine.

In the eyes of the growing capitalist class in France, the restoration government favored landed interests at the expense of industrial capital, a preference arising from the restoration government's ties with pre-Revolutionary, feudal France, and its allies. A popular uprising drove Charles X from the throne, but control of the revolution remained in the hands the wealthy business classes. Symbolizing the transition to middle-class values, Louis-Philippe clothed himself in the attire of a businessman, rather than in military dress. He grew rich saving and investing his earnings, and replaced die-hard aristocrats at court with businessmen, intellectuals, and progressive nobles.

The July Monarchy presided over rapid economic development in France. The Industrial Revolution got under way in France, harnessing mechanical power, increasing the division of labor, producing ready-made products, and erecting a substantial industrial structure. The July Monarchy created the Ministry of Commerce and Public Works. Later it created a separate Ministry of Public Works.

The July Monarchy was shamelessly pro-business. It enforced hardline policies against working-class agitation, merci-

The Battle in the Rue, 28 July 1830

lessly suppressing strikes and unions, and following the spirit and letter of the law that required the courts to accept the word of employers over workers. In contrast, the government winked when businesses colluded in violation of the law. A liberalization of bankruptcy law allowed nonfraudulent bankrupts to evade prison and be rehabilitated. The July Monarchy enacted a patent law conferring upon inventors the sole privilege to profit from their inventions and innovations. A primary education act aimed to substantially reduce illiteracy in the French population and work force. The high tariffs inherited from the restoration government were fine-tuned, to help businesses import necessary raw materials and machinery.

Unlike the restoration government, the July Monarchy opened up the purse strings on public expenditures, substantially adding to the social overhead capital of France, and running budget deficits throughout the 1840s. Railroad, highway, and canal development were special beneficiaries of public works expenditures.

One piece of ineffective reform legislation belongs to the July Monarchy. Over the objections of manufacturers, the government adopted a child labor law that included a requirement of primary education for children workers.

The Revolutions of 1848 put an end to the July Monarchy. The combined dissatisfaction of the working class and the proponents of republican government pulled down the monarchical government of Louis-Philippe. A short-lived republican government replaced the July Monarchy, and lasted until Louis Napoleon's coup d'etat in 1851.

Perhaps the greatest contribution of the July Monarchy to capitalist development in France was the image of the bourgeois monarchy, and the culture of confidence in economic progress that helped draw entrepreneurs into risk-taking enterprises.

See also Uprising of the Lyon Silk Workers, Revolutions of 1848.

References Collingham, H. A. C. *The July Monarchy: A Political History of France, 1830-1848* (1988); Johnson, Christopher H. "The Revolution of 1830 in French Economic History." *France* (1975).

Kennedy Tax Cut
See Revenue Act of 1964.

Keynes, John Maynard
See Keynesian Revolution.

Keynesian Revolution

The Keynesian revolution refers to the ascendancy of the macroeconomic theories of John Maynard Keynes among economists and policymakers in the mid-twentieth century. Keynesian macroeconomics became the most widely accepted paradigm in macroeconomics, displacing classical macroeconomics, which had held sway in most of the nineteenth and early twentieth centuries.

Keynes's theories portrayed the capitalist economic system as unstable, and prone to depressions, but amenable to stabilization with a foresighted government fiscal (budgetary) policy. Classical theories saw the capitalist economic system as a stable, self-correcting economic system that more often suffered from the destabilizing effects of government actions. Classical economists argued that government budgetary policy should aim at balancing the public sector budget, helping to strengthen the confidence of the private sector, and minimizing the risk of government policy destabilizing an otherwise stable economy. Keynes proposed using the public sector budget as a balance wheel to offset fluctuations in private sector spending, particularly investment spending.

Keynes saw the capitalist economic system buffeted by shifts in long-term expectations, causing repercussions amplified by rigidities in prices. Fluctuations in demand caused fluctuations in production, instead of fluctuations in prices. In recessions, consumers lost jobs, instead of benefiting from lower prices, causing the market for goods and services to shrink further as unemployment rose, in a process that fed on itself. The key to stabilizing the economy lay in planning government spending countercyclically. That is, when the private sector subsides into a slump, the government should swim against the tide and spend more, even if government tax revenue is down because of the slump. When the private sector expands, government should resist the temptation to spend more, even if tax revenue is rising with private sector growth. Government should increase spending when tax revenue is down because of an economic cycle, leading to a budget deficit. When tax revenue is rising because of an economic upswing, the government should spend less rather than more. Put differently, the government should plan to build post offices, highways, and public buildings when the private sector is in a recession, offsetting the effects of the private sector recession on unemployment.

Keynesian economics is sometimes called depression economics, because its inflationary side effects are unlikely to materialize in a depression. The steady growth in living standards during the first three decades after World War II, which coincided with the growth in government spending, seemed to vindicate Keynesian economics. As an added attraction, Keynesian economics sanctioned the high level of government spending needed to finance defense expenditures stemming from the Cold War.

The high inflation rates of the 1970s discredited Keynesian economics, just as the Depression of the 1930s had discredited classical economics. The economic upswings became ever more inflationary, as government refused to cut back when the private sector was expanding. By the

1980s, a new school of modern-day classical economists, called monetarists, had mostly displaced the Keynesians as the leaders in economic thought. Monetarists usually argued that stabilizing the rate of growth of the money supply stabilized the economy, without the aid of compensating government spending; this argument falls back on the idea that the economy is basically stable, except when government actions are destabilizing.

The rise of the Monetarist school of economics, at the expense of the Keynesian school, helped inspire a renewed faith in the superiority of the capitalist economic system as a system that functions well independent of government action. Nevertheless, many Keynesian features remain in current economic policy, such as unemployment compensation expenditures that rise and fall automatically with the economic cycle.

See also Classical School of Economics.

References Heilbroner, Robert. *The Worldly Philosophers* (1953); Klein, Lawrence. *The Keynesian Revolution* (1950); McConnell, Campbell R., and Stanley R. Brue. *Economics* (1993); Stein, Herbert. *The Fiscal Revolution in America* (1996).

Knights of Labor

The Knights of Labor preceded the American Federation of Labor (AFL) as the largest national federation of trade unions in the United States. The Noble Order of the Knights of Labor began as a secret society in 1869, when workers were not eager to tell employers of their union membership. Their secrecy proved a handicap, because the public was fearful of radical and revolutionary activities, and it aroused opposition from the Catholic Church.

In 1878, the Knights dropped the secrecy and took on the aspect of a public organization with a program. Terrance V. Powderly, a machinist and twice mayor of Scranton, became the leader.

The Knights embraced workers of any craft or industry, as long as they worked for a living. In the eyes of the Knights, this requirement left out bankers, bootleggers, bartenders, Pinkerton detectives, and lawyers. The Knights proposed the education of workers and development of producer cooperatives to combat the "evils of wealth." They favored self-improvement, rather than militant activities, to improve the lot of the working class. Membership rose from 20,000 in 1879 to a peak of 702,000 in 1886.

The Knights of Labor reached the apex of its influence and prestige in 1885, when it won public sympathy in a strike against the Wabash railroad. The union succeeded in preventing a wage cut. The year 1886 saw over 1,600 strikes, and the results, for the Knights, were disastrous. About half of the strikes began on May Day. One of the strikes was against the McCormick Harvesting Machine Company in Chicago, where the picket line became a scene of fighting and disorder. When police injured several strikers in an effort to maintain order, the union staged a protest meeting at Haymarket Square. As the meeting came to a close, a group of anarchists made use of the occasion to deliver inflammatory speeches. When police intervened, a bomb exploded, killing and wounding several policemen. The public blamed the unions for the violence, and union membership declined.

The structure of the Knights of Labor brought together diverse groups who found it difficult to agree on any cooperative initiative. In 1881, some independent national unions, with defections of craft unions from the Knights, organized the Federation of Organized Trades and Labor Unions (FOTLU). In 1886, the FOTLU became the AFL. The Knights of Labor never recovered from 1886, and the AFL gradually overshadowed the Knights. The AFL limited its membership to skilled workers who could effectively use strikes and boycotts to improve wages and hours.

See also American Federation of Labor.

References Brooks, Thomas R. *Toil and Trouble: A History of American Labor* (1971); Cartter, Allan M., and F. Ray Marshall. *Labor Economics: Wages, Employment, and Trade Unionism* (1967); McLaurin, Melton A. *The Knights of Labor in the South* (1978).

Kontratieff, Nokolai
See Kontratieff Cycles.

Kontratieff Cycles

The term "Kontratieff cycles" came from the Russian-born economist Nikolai Dmitrievich Kontratieff, who claimed to have discovered long waves in the development of capitalist economies. Born in 1892, Kontratieff founded and directed the Moscow Business Conditions Institute. Between 1919 and 1928, he studied price and production trends in capitalistic economies, and concluded that capitalistic economies generate long waves in economic activity.

Kontratieff's theory was out of step with the prevailing Soviet orthodoxy of that time. Contrary to Karl Marx, the theory predicted a return to prosperity in capitalistic economies, rather than a permanent downfall. In 1928, Kontratieff lost his position as head of the Business Conditions Institute. In 1930, a charge of heading the Working Peasants Party earned him deportation to Siberia without trial. He apparently remained in detention the remainder of his life.

According to Kontratieff, the long wave in European capitalist economies goes through one complete cycle every 50 years. In the data Kontratieff analyzed, he dates the beginning of an upswing in the 1780s, a turning point during the 1810–1817 period, and a downswing ending during the 1844–1851 period. An upswing for a second long wave begins during the 1844–1851 period, and lasts until the turning point during the 1870–1875 period. The downswing begins in the 1870–1875 period, and ends during the 1890–1896 period. A third upswing begins during the 1890–1896 period, and reaches a turning point during the 1914–1920 period. Kontratieff's data ended around 1920.

The timing of the peaks and troughs for the European capitalistic economies are synchronized, according to Kontratieff. In other words, the long waves are international in scope.

Kontratieff's work is mostly empirical. His theories about the process generating the long waves appear vague and suggestive. He observed that the downswings are particularly hard on agriculture, but appear to stimulate innovations. The cluster of innovations that occurs in the downswing finds its way into application in the upswing. Wars and revolutions break out in the upswing phases. Kontratieff seemed to agree that the replacement cycle of capital goods (expensive factories, transportation facilities, etc.) is a driving force in long-wave propagation.

Kontratieff's ideas enjoyed a resurgence in the popular press in the 1980s. If the 1930s represented the tail of the downswing that began in the 1914–1920 period, the 1980s would see the final stages of another downswing, based on a 50-year cycle. In October 1987, the stock market fell 1,000 points on the Dow Jones Industrial Average, but fears that the stock crash could be the beginning of another 1930s style calamity have not been borne out.

Professional economists are generally skeptical of Kontratieff's theories. An economic cycle with a fixed periodicity of 50 years entails more precision than is generally found in the social sciences. There are no economic theories to justify an economic cycle recurring with such predictability. Contemporary researchers have not been able to verify the existence of the Kontratieff cycle in rigorous statistical tests.

References Coghlan, Richard. "The Wave Is Your Friend." *Barons* (1993); Garvy, G. "Kondratieff's Theory of Long Waves." *Review of Economics and Statistics* (1943); Kondratieff, N. D. "The Long Waves in Economic Life." *Review of Economics and Statistics* (1935).

Labor Exchange Act of 1909 (England)

The British labor exchanges were forerunners of the modern state employment commissions in the United States, which serve as clearing houses of information about employment vacancies, for unemployed workers. Later, industrialized countries married the concept of the labor exchange to systems of unemployment compensation. Britain adopted such a system in 1911, Germany in 1927, and the United States in the 1930s.

According to the act that Parliament passed in 1909 to establish labor exchanges, "In this Act the expression 'labor exchange' means any office or place to be used for the purpose of collecting and furnishing information, either by the keeping of registers or otherwise, respecting employers who desire to engage work people and work people who seek engagement or employment."

The act also authorized "advances to be made by way of loan toward meeting the expenses of work people traveling to places where employment has been found for them through a labor exchanges...." The act authorized the Board of Trade to establish labor exchanges wherever it saw a need, or to assist private labor exchanges that were already in existence.

The establishment of labor exchanges fits in with the philosophy that government policy should help people help themselves. One of the major hindrances to the functioning of free markets is the lack of information. Workers do not know where to find the best jobs, and employers do not know where to find the best workers. Households and businesses must invest time shopping around in product markets and job markets to get the best deals. The purpose of the labor exchange is to improve the operation of the labor market, by collecting information for workers and businesses. Readily available information about job opportunities reduces the time individual workers spend out of work. Providing financial aid to workers, who must migrate to areas with jobs, further improves the operation of the labor market. Direct government regulations, such as minimum wage laws, replace market-clearing (supply and demand) solutions with government mandates.

Labor exchanges improve, rather than distort, the operation of capitalist labor markets.

See also Unemployment Insurance.

References Court, H. B. *British Economic History, 1870–1914* (1965); De Schweinitz, Karl. *England's Road to Social Security from the Statute of Laborers in 1349 to the Beveridge Report of 1942* (1961).

Labor Party (England)

The British Labor Party was born of the trade union and socialist agitation of the late nineteenth century, and it grew to become one of the major political parties in the British Parliament. In the latter portion of the nineteenth century, workers and artisans in Britain came to view themselves as members of a separate class in society, the working class. Class consciousness replaced vague feelings of belonging to an all-embracing middle class. By 1884, virtually all the manual workers in Britain enjoyed the voting franchise.

The General Election of 1892 saw the first electoral successes of labor representatives. This success at the polls encouraged socialist organizations and labor leaders to form the Independent Labor Party in 1893. The second choice for a name was the Socialist Labor Party. This party avowed an openly socialist program, including the collective ownership of the means of production. The name of the new party signaled its intention to woo non-socialist members of the working class.

Meanwhile, the Trade Union Congress had rebuffed suggestions to assess on its affiliates a political levy, to pay election expenses of members running for seats in Parliament, and to support members serving in Parliament. In 1899, the delegates of a Trade Union Congress meeting adopted a resolution to hold a special conference of representatives from "Co-operative, Socialist, Trade Union, and other working-class organizations," with the prime objective to "devise ways and means for the securing of an increased number of Labor Members in the next Parliament." The origin of the Labor Party can be traced to this beginning. When the delegates met, they formed a new body, called the Labor Representation Committee (LRC), composed of an independent federation of trade unions, trades councils, and cooperative and socialist societies. The socialist societies included the Independent Labor Party, the Social Democratic Federation (a Marxist group), and the Fabian Society. These societies played an influential part in the leadership of the new organization.

Within six months of its inception, the LRC entered the fray in the General Election of 1900. It endorsed 15 candidates for seats in Parliament, and two of them won. The LRC aligned itself with the Liberal Party, in which some members were already called Lib-Labs, because of their connection with trade unions.

At first, trade unions were slow to affiliate themselves with the LRC. The turning point came in 1892, with the *Taff Vale* case. After this court case, union leaders and officers lay under the risk of suits for civil damages because of strike actions. Trade unions turned to the political process to meet this challenge flung down by the judicial process. From 1902 to 1903, affiliated membership in the LRC doubled, rising to 861,000.

Before the General Election of 1906, the leadership of the LRC and the Liberal Party secretly negotiated an agreement to withhold liberal opposition from LRC candidates standing for election. The LRC scored a major success, sending 29 representatives to Parliament. After the election, the LRC renamed itself the Labor Party.

By the end of World War I, the Labor Party was the second-largest party in Parliament. It openly avowed a socialist program. In this early period, its representatives in Parliament came from the ranks of the working class. As a minority party with liberal support, it formed its first government in 1924. This government was short-lived, but the Labor Party organized another government in 1929, which lasted until 1931. In the general election of 1945, the Labor Party won a major victory on a program of nationalization.

In the post-World War II era, members of Parliament belonging to the Labor Party are more often university graduates than manual workers, though the Labor Party still depends on working-class support in elections.

In the mid-1970s, high inflation and slow growth discredited the economic policies espoused by Labor governments, and many observers put the blame of inflation at the feet of unions.

In 1979, British voters turned to the Conservative Party to address Britain's economic problems. The Labor Party remained out of power for 18 years. On May 1, 1997 a rejuvenated Labor Party, shorn of socialist ideology and close affiliation with labor unions, returned to power under the leadership of the young and stylish Tony Blair, the current Prime Minister of Britain.

See also *Taff Vale* Case, Thatcherism, Trade Union Congress.

References Cook, Chris, and Ian Taylor, eds. *The Labor Party: An Introduction to its History, Structure, and Politics* (1980); Pelling, Henry. *A Short History of the Labor Party* (1976).

Labor Unions

Labor unions are working-class associations devoted to advancing the economic interest of the workers. In some societies, labor unions have sought revolutionary change, but in the United States unions have focused on improving wages, hours, and working conditions. These unions achieve their goals by bargaining collectively with employers, and their chief weapon is the strike, a collective refusal to work.

Early in the development of capitalism, an unpropertied working class surfaced that possessed skills but no education, owned no stake in factories, wielded virtually no political power, and feared displacement by machines manned by women and children. Labor unions were one of the most enduring institutions that grew out of working-class discontent. In continental Europe, working-class discontent was ruthlessly suppressed or manipulated as a pawn in the struggle between business classes and aristocracy. In England, however, labor unions sank roots and survived in the face of opposition from employers, government, and judiciary.

Labor unions fall into two different groups. The first unions to establish themselves, against the angry opposition of employers and governments, were the craft unions. These unions organized workers with particular skills, such as carpenters or cobblers. Craft unions have clout, because they can control the number of new workers trained in the craft. Also, when skilled workers strike, there are no workers waiting on the sidelines to replace them.

A second group of unions is called industrial unions, which organize workers according to industry, for example, all the miners in coal mines, or all the production workers in the steel industry. These unions organize unskilled workers in particular industries, which become vulnerable in strikes. Usually, there is a reservoir of unskilled workers waiting to cross picket lines when well-paid unskilled workers go on strike. In the United States, industrial unions grew rapidly in the 1930s, after the government enacted legislation tilting the balance in favor of industrial unions at the expense of management.

The largest union organization in the United States is the AFL-CIO. The American Federation of Labor, or AFL, was formed in 1886, under the leadership of Samuel Gompers. The AFL dominated the labor moment in the United States until the 1930s, and set the pattern for conservative unionism, by emphasizing direct bargaining with employers, rather than promoting a political agenda. The philosophy of the AFL helps explain why working-class agitation in the United States never led to the formation of a labor political party, as it did in England.

In 1936, the AFL expelled a group of insurgent unions who wanted to launch an aggressive unionization program among unorganized industrial workers. The traditional leadership of the AFL saw industrial unions as weak, and showed little initiative in trying to organize the vast numbers of manufacturing workers in America's industrialized sector. Also, efforts to unionize the steel industry had failed. The insurgent unions organized themselves as the Congress of Industrial Organizations, or CIO, and entered a phase of aggressive and successful organization of industrial workers, particularly in the automobile and steel industry.

In the 1950s, labor found itself again on the defensive in the political area; in 1955, the AFL and the CIO merged, forming the AFL-CIO. Since the 1950s, the percentage of the U.S. labor force belonging to unions has fallen from 25 to 15 percent. The growth of the white-collar work force and the service industry, migration of industry to the less-unionized South, and the rise of women and part-time workers, all help explain the decline of unionization in the United States. Government policy has also been less friendly to unions since the 1950s. The Canadian government has been more prounion, and the percent of the labor force unionized in Canada is twice as big as in the United States.

The labor policies of the Reagan presidency in the United States, and of Margaret Thatcher in England, sent labor unions reeling in both countries, and unions have not recovered the political clout they possessed, even in the 1970s. Unions are now soul-searching, trying to assess their place in the modern economic landscape, and hoping to find new strategies that will propel them to leadership of a modern labor movement.

See also American Federation of Labor, Congress of Industrial Organizations, Grand National Consolidated Trade Union, Industrial Workers of the World, Knights of Labor, Labor Party, Trade Union Congress.

References Brooks, Thomas R. *Toil and Trouble: A History of American Labor* (1971); Clark, Gordon. *Unions and Communities Under Siege* (1989); Cole, G. D. H. *A Short History of the British Working Class Movement: 1789–1947* (1948, reprint 1960); Masters, Marick F. *Unions at the Cross Roads* (1997).

Landrum-Griffin Act of 1959 (United States)

The Landrum-Griffin Act, officially termed the Labor-Management Reporting and Disclosure Act, targeted antidemocratic practices in union governance and misuse of union funds.

Before the passage of Landrum-Griffin, the public often saw labor organizations as prey to venal and corrupt labor leaders. Even labor leaders such as John L. Lewis, whose integrity was not an issue, exerted dictatorial control over the unions they led. Public skepticism about the leadership and organization of labor unions, whether justified or a figment of employers' imaginations, moved Congress to act on the issue.

Landrum-Griffin is organized into five titles. Title I sets forth a bill of rights for union members, and requires that all members of a union have the right to nominate candidates, vote in elections and referendums, attend membership meetings, and share in the discussions and voting at such meetings. Title I also shields union members from unfair disciplinary action, and protects the rights of members to sue unions.

Title II requires unions to disclose in a report to the secretary of labor information covering the salaries to union officers, loans to union officers and members, and activities of officers that involve possible conflicts of interest. Title V also requires that employers report interaction with union officers.

Title III requires unions to file reports when the governance of particular locals is placed under trusteeship. Legitimate reasons for placing a local under trusteeship include such things as restoration of responsible financial practices, democratic procedures, or compliance with collective bargaining agreements.

Title IV sets forth election procedures that require secret ballots and the safeguarding of participation of opposing voices. The secretary of labor can ask a federal district court to set aside the results of a dishonest election.

Title V addresses the issue of the misuse and theft of union funds. Union members handling union funds have to be bonded. Embezzlement of union funds is a federal offense, and offenders are subject to fines and imprisonment. Certain felons and Communist Party members are banned from holding a union office for five years after their conviction or lapse in membership.

By the 1950s, union leaders had won a more powerful voice in economic affairs, but their credibility had not grown proportionately in the eyes of the public. Capitalist interest in the United States still remembered the role that unions had played in the Russian Revolution and other revolutionary endeavors. Landrum-Griffin was a price unions had to pay to earn the legitimacy and political acceptance needed to play an effective role in interest-group politics.

See also National Labor Relations Labor Act, Taft-Hartley Act of 1947.

References McLaughlin, Doris B. *The Landrum-Griffin Act and Union Democracy* (1979); Northrup, Herbert R., and Gordon F. Bloom. *Government and Labor: The Role of Government in Union–Management Relations* (1963).

Law, John (1671–1729)
See Mississippi Bubble.

Le Chapelier Law (France)

The Le Chapelier Law of the French Revolution banned trade corporations of masters and journeymen, including any worker association resembling in membership and mission the modern trade union. The law owed its authorship to Isaac Rene Guy Le Chapelier, one of the influential members of the National Assembly.

The French Revolution swept away the guilds and trade corporations. Before the Revolution, the skilled artisans within urban areas were members of trade corporations, who had an exclusive franchise from the king to practice that trade within a local area, allowing these organizations to monopolize the supply of skilled artisans. Masters and journeymen had their own separate corporations. In addition to regulating each trade, these corporations provided social and mutual-aid services, such as arranging funerals.

The trade corporations soon came under the scrutiny of the National Assembly. In March 1791, the National Assembly enacted a new tax, called a patent. In an amendment to the law establishing the patent, the assembly added a provision that stated, "Beginning on the coming April first, it shall be free to every citizen to engage in whatever commerce, or to exercise whatever profession, art or trade he may wish, after having provided himself with a patent and paid its price, according to the rates thereafter determined."

Any sort of privilege was suspect during the Revolution. The National Assembly abolished trade corporations, without a whimper from either masters or journeymen. In May 1791, the carpenter compagnons, or journeymen's corporations, asked the master carpenters to share in the writing of rules to govern their trade. By then, trade corporations no longer existed legally, and the masters would not cooperate in writing the rules. When the journeymen tried to impose on the masters trade regulations of their own making, masters petitioned the National Assembly. The journeymen's actions moved the National Assembly to adopt the Le Chapelier Law, which specifically banned worker associations and strikes. According to the discussion in the Assembly, even worker associations mainly engaged in helping sick and unemployed workers of the same trade should be proscribed, because they "tend to bring about the rebirth of corporations; they require frequent meetings of individuals of the same profession, the naming of syndics and other officers, the formation of regulations, the exclusion of those who do not submit themselves to these regulations. It is thus that privileges, masterships, etc. will be reborn."

The passage of the Le Chapelier Law provoked no memorable opposition. According to the wording of the law, citizens of the same trade are prohibited

when they find themselves together, to name for themselves a president or secretary syndic, to maintain registers, to form regulations on their supposed common interest.... If, against the principles of liberty and of the constitution, citizens attached to the same professions, arts and trades, should make deliberations, should made agreements among themselves tending to refuse in concert, or to accord only at a determined price the aid of their industry or of their labors, the said deliberations and agreements...are declared unconstitutional and an assault against liberty and against the declaration of the rights of man, and of null effect.

Punishment for violating the Le Chapelier law took the form of fines and suspensions of citizenship. Although the Le Chapelier law forbade coalitions of employers to lower wages, as well as coalitions of workers to raise wages, in practice, it was used mostly against workers; the interpretation of the law betrayed a class bias. Associations of workers and strikes were banned, but the law was never brought to bear on business organizations such as chambers of commerce. The effect was to strengthen employers relative to employees.

Mutual aid societies managed to survive in spite of the law; many of these became front organizations to circumvent laws against strikes. The repression of workers' associations, with added legal remedies and varying degrees of intensity, continued until 1864. The French government, under Emperor Napoleon III, began to relax the laws against worker associations. The rights of workers to organize trade unions were hard won rights in all capitalist countries of the nineteenth century.

See also Combination Acts.

References Lefebvre, Georges. *The French Revolution* (1964); Sewell, William H., Jr. *Work and Revolution in France: The Language of Labor from the Old Regime to 1848* (1980).

Leveraged Buyouts (United States)

A rash of leveraged buyouts changed the face of corporate America in the 1980s. The essence of a leveraged buyout lies in company management's use of outside borrowing to acquire the publicly held shares of company stock. The management arranges financing, often by selling junk bonds, and makes an offer, called a tender offer, to purchase, at a set price, stock not owned by the management, and turns a public corporation into a private company. Firms specializing in arranging leveraged buyout financing can take the initiative to identify a firm that would be an excellent target for a leveraged buyout, and to contact the management and offer to arrange the financing.

The term "leveraged" arises from the high ratio of debt to total assets that characterizes those firms newly formed by leveraged buyouts. These firms will have between 80 and 98 percent of their assets financed by debt. The dependence on debt financing allows the remaining stockholders to control vast amounts of assets. Put differently, the investment of the remaining stockholders has more leverage, because it controls more assets.

The 1980s saw over 2,800 firms involved in leveraged buyouts, when there were only about 1700 firms listed on the New York Stock Exchange. One attraction of the leveraged buyout was the protection it afforded against hostile takeovers, which occurred when outside investors bought out controlling interest in companies, with plans for replacing much of the management.

Leveraged buyouts were popular with shareholders, who appreciated the opportunity to sell their stock holdings at premium prices. Lenders and existing bondholders objected, because the new-formed firms were saddled with high-interest expenses, which, unlike dividends, had to be paid regardless of the level of profits. Consequently, firms formed out of leveraged buyouts were vulnerable to recessions, and were often forced into bankruptcy and reorganization. In the face of recession-level sales and high-interest costs, these firms turned to downsizing employees as a matter of survival. On the positive side, leveraged buyouts may have helped firms become meaner and leaner and, therefore, more productive.

Leveraged buyouts were associated with the seedier side of capitalist development in the 1980s. In the public's mind, they are probably associated with the abuse of insider information, junk bonds, downsizing, and bankruptcy. It is too soon, however, to evaluate their future role in the development of the capitalist economic system.

See also Greenmail, Insider Trading.

References Barmash, Isadore. *A Not-So-Tender Offer: An Insider's Look at Mergers and Their Consequences* (1995); Spiro, George W. *The Legal Environment of Business: Principles and Cases* (1993).

Lewis, John L. (1880–1969)

John L. Lewis, perhaps the greatest American labor leader, spearheaded the organization of the Congress of Industrial Organizations (CIO), and successfully launched a campaign to organize the basic industries of steel, automobiles, rubber, and electrical products. Under his leadership as president of the United Mine Workers (UMW), miners achieved the highest pay and best benefits of any group of workers in the United States. Perhaps most revealing about Lewis was his rhetoric, which gave full rein to the frustration and rage felt by the mass of low-wage and unskilled workers in manufacturing and mining.

Lewis was born on 12 February 1880, the eldest son in a mining family in Lucas, Iowa. His father suffered the fate of a blacklisted miner, engendering in Lewis a deep sympathy for miners and a resentment against mine operators. He went to work in the mines when he was 17, and became active in the union, representing his local as a delegate to a convention of the UMW in 1906. In 1907, he married Myrta Edith Bell, a school teacher who encouraged him to read widely in the classics. In 1909, Lewis moved his family to Panama, Illinois, where he soon became president of the union local. In 1911, Lewis's talent came to the attention of Samuel Gompers, who made him a field representative for the American Federation of Labor (AFL). At the 1916 convention of the UMW, he was appointed to the position of statistician. A period of rapid turnover in the UMW's leadership helped lift Lewis to the position of acting president. He served as acting president until the end of World War I, when he became the duly-elected president of the UMW.

Lewis's leadership was combative and aggressive at the outset; he angered President Wilson by calling for a nationwide strike for higher wages, before peace was formally declared at the end of World War I. Characteristic of Lewis, the UMW was demanding higher wages despite an existing contract. In 1921, Lewis unsuccessfully challenged Samuel Gompers for the presidency of the AFL.

In the aftermath of World War I, the coal industry suffered from excess capacity and fierce competition. Lewis waged an energetic and confrontational struggle to protect the miners from the depressed conditions of the coal industry, but the UMW lost membership, as mine after mine turned nonunion: In one Pittsburgh district, UMW membership dropped from 45,000 to 293. Dissident members of the UMW described Lewis's leadership as "an unbroken series of defeats."

With the election of Franklin Roosevelt and his prolabor policies, Lewis rightly perceived the new opportunities for organizing workers, and he launched the most successful organizing crusade in the history of unions. In 1933, mine operators in Appalachia signed the first Appalachian Joint Wage Agreement with the UMW. Membership in the UMW jumped from 150,000 to 515,000.

Lewis rose to inspired leadership in his efforts to organize mass-production workers in heavy industry. Conservative leadership in the AFL would have no part in organizing manufacturing workers in separate industrial unions. Lewis and other insurgent union leaders formed the Committee for Industrial Organizations, for the purpose of organizing industrial workers. When the AFL refused to accept the new unions, they formed the CIO, with John L. Lewis as the first president. The CIO succeeded beyond the most optimistic expectations, counting among its organizing successes General Motors and United States Steel. Lewis resigned his position as president of the CIO in protest of Franklin Roosevelt's election to a third term as president, in 1940.

Lewis reaffiliated the UMW, which had been a member of the CIO, with the AFL. He waged forceful battles to improve wages and benefits for miners, doubling the average pay of miners between 1939 and 1949. Miners became the best-paid and best-pensioned workers in the United States. When the AFL refused to support a campaign to repeal the Taft-Hartley Act, which Lewis called the "slave labor law," he withdrew the UMW from the AFL. Lewis remained president of the UMW until 1960, and he died in 1969.

Lewis was intelligent, ferociously aggressive, and brooked no opposition within the UMW. He started as a Republican, became a New Dealer, and became a Republican again. His harsh rhetoric reflected the true thoughts of the rank and file of the workers in his day. Since the days of Lewis, the capitalist economic system has found a synthesis of the interests of workers and employers that has vented some of the frustration that inspired Lewis's leadership.

See also Congress of Industrial Organizations, Unionization of the Steel Industry.

References Madison, Charles A. *American Labor Leaders* (1962); Ziegler, Robert H. *John L. Lewis: Labor Leader* (1988).

Livret (France)

The livret was a worker passport or identification booklet that workers were legally required to carry in nineteenth-century France. The origin of the livret lies in the laws for the surveillance and social control of labor enacted during the Napoleonic era. The French Revolution set the example of economic improvement achieved by revolution. Middle-class and capitalist interests ultimately controlled the Revolution and reaped its benefits. One legacy of the Revolution was the fear that the working classes might follow the example of revolution to redress grievances.

A worker's livret contained information from his employer about the terms of his employment, his conduct and behavior, and debts owed his employer. Loans to workers and wage advances were common during hard times. The requirement of the livret tightened employer control over workers. Workers leading or participating in protests or strikes against an employer could expect that activity to be noted in their livret. Other reasons why a worker might make a bad risk to an employer would also be cited. A worker could only change jobs after his employer and the mayor had signed his livret. This practice kept workers on their good behavior, and made it more difficult to change jobs or to engage in working-class agitation.

In most trades, masters required journeymen to keep a livret. In the silk industry, merchants required the master weavers to keep a livret d'aquit for each of their looms, in which the terms of weaving contracts were shown, and merchants could refuse contracts to a master weaver based upon the contents of these livrets d'aquit.

In addition to obliging workers to carry a livret, early nineteenth-century French labor law outlawed unions and strikes, and required courts to accept an employer's word against an employee's word. That is, an employer's word was acceptable evidence, but an employee needed physical evidence.

The liberal reforms of Napoleon III virtually put an end to the livret as a means for controlling workers, and the livret was abolished in its entirety in 1890.

The repressive labor law in the aftermath of the French Revolution lends some credibility to Marx's interpretation of history as the history of the class struggle. Despite France's revolutionary tradition, England pioneered the modern trade union movement.

See also French Revolution and Napoleon, Le Chapelier Law, Lyon Uprising of 1834

References Bezucha, Robert J. *The Lyon Uprising of 1834: Social and Political Conflict in the Early July Monarchy* (1974); Clough, Shepard B. *France: A History of National Economics, 1789–1939* (1964).

Lloyd's of London

Lloyd's of London is a famous insurance market of historical importance. It is not a company office, but an insurance market composed of a large number of insurance underwriters functioning under one roof. In 1890, a Lloyd's underwriter described it to a lady visitor this way: "Individually, madam, we are underwriters. Collectively, we are Lloyd's." Lloyd's began as a market for marine insurance, and grew to worldwide fame as a place to insure anything.

The first insurance contracts apparently stemmed from the need to insure against maritime losses. Marine insurance developed early in antiquity; a Roman edict of 533 A.D. mentions marine insurance. In 1432, the city of Barcelona adopted a statute that entitled the owner of a vessel to collect insurance, if the vessel had not been heard from in six months.

In the fourteenth century, a group of Hanseatic merchants began underwriting marine insurance in London. The oldest English marine insurance policy extant was issued in 1547. The number of underwriters steadily grew in number, with the growth of English maritime trade during the Elizabethan period. Late in the seventeenth century, London underwriters began to frequent and conduct business at Edward Lloyd's coffeehouse on Tower Street. In 1692, Lloyd moved his coffeehouse to Lombard Street. Lloyd himself was not in the marine insurance business, but he sent runners down to the wharves to get news about casualties or the arrival of ships. By 1696, Lloyd was publishing *Lloyd's News*, containing maritime news of interest to underwriters. This short-lived newspaper became the predecessor of *Lloyd's List*.

The speculation associated with the South Sea Bubble spawned a proliferation of new insurance ventures organized as joint-stock companies. Among the new insurable risks these companies proposed to insure was fire, death from gin drinking, or being lied to by one's business partners. One policy insured against a loss of what was carefully described as "female chastity."

In 1720, the government chartered the London Assurance Company and the Royal Exchange Assurance Corporation. These corporate charters conferred monopoly privileges to sell marine insurance, but left private individuals free to underwrite policies. These two companies focused on fire insurance and left marine insurance to Lloyd's.

The Bubble Act stopped the proliferation of small insurance companies without official charters. The way was paved for the private individuals at Lloyd's to take over the market for marine insurance.

After the death of Edward Lloyd, the coffeehouse was operated by sons-in-law, until it came into the hands of Thomas Jemson in 1727. He was the first to publish *Lloyd's List*. Extant copies of this publication of shipping news date back to 1740. A passion for gambling in England during the eighteenth century infected the insurance market, and threatened to cast a shadow over the integrity of Lloyd's. A group broke away and formed the New Lloyd's Coffee House, located on Pope's Head Alley. The breakaway group became the nucleus of the Lloyd's that signed an agreement in 1773 to move to the Royal Exchange. The underwriters of Lloyd's had now clearly organized themselves, independent of the owner of a coffeehouse. This time period marks the beginning of the modern Lloyd's of London.

Lloyd's framed its first formal constitution in 1811, giving it a formal corporate existence, and, in 1871 Parliament enacted Lloyd's Act, which gave a legal sanction to a governing committee. This act made it illegal for a nonmember to write a Lloyd's policy, and gave the governing committee power to expel members for bankruptcy or fraud. Parliament passed another Lloyd's Act in 1911, specifically authorizing Lloyd's expansion into nonmarine insurance.

Late in the nineteenth century, Lloyd's developed two classes of underwriters. An active group of underwriters wrote policies for a larger number of other underwriters, called Names, many of whom knew little about insurance, and never came near Lloyd's. By the 1980s, Lloyd's boasted of over 20,000 member underwriters, each one liable for underwriting losses to the full extent of their personal and business assets. Lloyd's was left free to conduct business as a relatively unregulated private organization during the post-World War era, despite Britain's sharp turn toward socialism. Britain earned valued foreign exchange from Lloyd's international insurance, making Lloyd's a favored organization in the eyes of government officials.

In the mid-1970s, Lloyd's was rocked by scandal. Underwriters balked at their own unlimited liability for underwriting losses, after learning that some insurance policies did not follow Lloyd's own rules. Despite calls for public regulation, Parliament passed the Lloyd's Act of 1982, which established a governing council, with increased power to discipline members who did not follow Lloyd's rules for underwriting insurance. This act adhered to the principle of self-regulation, and gave council members immunity from law suits. Scandals continued to shadow the most famous insuring organization, but the most damaging blow came from a series of natural and manmade disasters between 1987 and 1991. In 1992, Lloyd's reported that 1988 was the first year since 1961 that Lloyd's had sustained a loss. Losses continued to mount, and the Names underwriters virtually rose in rebellion. Unlimited liability meant that whole estates were held hostage until insurance claims were settled. Meanwhile, Lloyd's lost much of its reputation for prompt payment of insurance claims. So far the conservative trend in British government has spared Lloyd's from detailed government oversight, despite pleas from policyholders and member underwriters, whose confidence has been severely shaken.

From a historical perspective, Lloyd's met an important need in a capitalistic economic system in which insurance, like credit, is convenience that helps households and businesses act on their own initiatives. Insurance reduces the risk borne by entrepreneurs in the large-scale private undertakings that distinguish the capitalist economic system.

See also Royal Exchange.

References Brown, Anthony. *Lloyd's of London* (1974); Luessenhop, Elizabeth, and Martin Mayer. *Risky Business: An Insider's Account of the Disaster at Lloyd's of London* (1995).

London Dock Strike of 1899

The strike of the London dockers in 1899 marks a turning point in the annals of the English working-class movement. The dockers stood within the ranks of the un-skilled general laborers, most of whom had been turned out of doors by the English trade union movement. The older trade unions in England had emphasized organization of workers with a particular skill, such as carpenters. In addition to representing skilled workers to employers, these unions provided such things as old-age benefits. This merging of skill and benefits helped maintain the loyalty and financial support of union members in good times and bad. It also made these unions cautious about expending union funds to finance strikes, and favored resolution of disputes through negotiation, arbitration, and conciliation. Only skilled workers could be counted on to afford the financial support these unions needed.

Left-wing militant socialist leaders spearheaded the organization of the general laborers in England. Their first success came early in 1899, with the formation of the Gasworkers and General Laborers Union. The gasworkers negotiated an eight-hour day for many of its workers before the year was out, which strengthened aspirations of the general laborers, just at the time when a strike started over a wage dispute at the West India Dock. The strike spread dockside, and within a week the strikers brought the port of London to a standstill. Ten thousand workers joined in the strike. Ben Tillet, Tom Mann, and John Burns led the struggle. Two years before, Ben Tillet had founded the General Laborers Union, a union of dock workers. Tom Mann and John Burns, engineers by trade and members of the Almagamated Society of Engineers, rose to prominence as effective union organizers. Eleanor Aveling, the daughter of Karl Marx, served as secretary of the strike committee.

The dockers asked for a wage of six pence an hour (not an increase), a bonus for overtime, the end of subcontracting and piece work, and a guarantee of four hours pay for coming to work.

This strike caught the attention of the world more than any other labor dispute up to that time. Contributions to a strike fund poured in from unions as far away as Australia. The English middle class had just learned of the plight of the casually employed dock workers from Charles Booth's *Life and Labor of the People of London*. With public support, the strike fund rose to nearly £50,000.

The docker strike lasted a month. Public sympathy and solidarity among the trade unions helped the dockers win. Cardinal Manning assisted in the mediation of the dispute, and employers accepted most of the dockers' demands.

The victories of the gasworkers and the dockers led to a burst of union-organizing activity, particularly of general laborers. During the strike, the battle cry of the new unionists was "Trade Unionism for All." The Tea-Porters Union became the Dock, Wharf, Riverside, and General Workers Union. The Gasworkers Union became a national organization that organized general laborers from every field. Within three years, union membership in Great Britain doubled. The new unions brushed aside the friendly benefit activities of the older unions, and focused on raising funds to support workers in strikes and lockouts. They emphasized class solidarity and were closely allied with socialism.

See also British General Strike of 1926, Congress of Industrial Organizations.

Reference Cole, G. D. H. *A Short History of the British Working-Class Movement: 1789–1947* (1948, reprint 1960); Hunt, Edward, *British Labor History: 1815-1914* (1981).

London Stock Exchange

The early English mercantile trading companies, such as the East India Trading Company, sold transferable shares of stock as a means of raising capital. As public interest in buying shares grew, and the needs for capital of the merchant trading ventures increased, a market in these shares arose. The dealers in stocks were called stockjobbers, and, in the beginning, they plied their trade in the Royal Exchange, built in 1556 by Sir Thomas Gresham. In 1698, the stockjobbers removed themselves to the coffeehouses of Exchange Alley. On 26 March 1714, a list was available in the proprietor's office, near Jonathan's coffeehouse, on which could be found price quotes for East India stock, bank stock, the South Sea loan, and the African Company.

Early stockjobbers hardly held a position in society. Dr. Samuel Johnson defined a stockjobber as "a low wretch who gets money by buying and selling shares in funds." During the reign of William III (1689–1702), an act of Parliament addressed the allegations levied against the stockjobbers, referring to diverse brokers and stockjobbers, or pretended brokers, who sell and discount "Talleys, Bank Stock, Bank Bills, Shares, and Interest in Joint Stock and other Matter and Things." These groups had combined to "raise or fall from time to time" the values of these investments.

After 1 May 1697, no one could practice the trade of stockjobber in London, in Westminster, or within the Bills of Mortality, without a license from the lord mayor and aldermen. The license certified the individual to have ability, honesty, and good fame. The licensee took the following oath:

I doe sincerely promise and sweare That I will truly and faithfully execute and performe the Office and Employment of a Broker between Party and Party in all things appertaining to the Duty of the Said Office and Employment without Fraud or Collusion to the best of my Skill and Knowledge and according to the Tenour and Purport of the Act intituled an Act to restraine the number and ill Practice of Brokers and Stock Jobbers. So help me God.

Despite regulation, the public continued to hold the stock market in suspicion. In 1711, Jonathan Swift wrote, "Bank stock is fallen 3 or 4 percent by the whispers about the town of the Queen's being ill, who is, however, very well. This may ruine the Creditt of the Nation and endanger the Government it selfe." In 1719, Daniel Defoe portrayed the manipulation as follows:

> If Sir Josiah Child had a mind to buy, the first thing he did was to commission his brokers to look sour, shake their heads, suggest bad news from India;...and perhaps they would actually sell for ten, perhaps twenty, thousand pound. Immediately, the Exchange...was full of sellers; nobody would buy a shilling, till perhaps the stock would fall six, seven, eight, ten percent, sometime more. Then the cunning jobber had set of them employed...to buy, but with privacy and caution, till by selling ten thousand pound at four or five percent loss, he would buy a hundred thousand pound stock at ten or twelve percent under price; and in a few weks, by just the contrary method, set them all a-buying, and then sell them their own stock again at ten or twelve percent profit.

The stockjobbers became an exclusive club meeting at Jonathan's coffeehouse, which served as the Stock Exchange. Dealers in foreign stocks remained at the Royal Exchange, and the rotunda of the Bank of England housed the market in government securities. In 1802, the Stock Exchange moved to its present location. The building was constructed to house the Stock Exchange at a location close to the Bank of England. The Bank of England drove out the dealers in government securities in 1837. The railroad building boom of the mid-1800s brought with it an enormous increase in stock speculation, and membership on the London Stock Exchange took a great leap forward. By 1875, it boasted of 2,000 members.

Today, the London Stock Exchange is the largest stock exchange in the world, in terms of number and variety of issues traded. It remains a private organization, with its own operating rules and constitution. The membership elects a council that administers the Exchange. Gradually, a clear distinction grew between brokers and jobbers. The broker buys and sells for customers, and charges a commission. The stockjobber is a dealer who sells to brokers and other members of the house, but not to the public. The broker and jobber make up a unique system of trading that is different from the auctions of most stock exchanges.

See also New York Stock Exchange, Royal Exchange, Sir John Bernard's Act, South Sea Bubble.

References Beard, Miriam. *History of the Business Man* (1938); Goldberg, Susan. *Trading: Inside the World's Leading Stock Exchanges* (1986); Michie, Ranald C. "The London and New York Stock Exchanges, 1850–1914," *Journal of Economic History* (1986); Powell, Ellis T. *The Evolution of the Money Market, 1385–1915* (1966).

Ludlow Massacre (United States)

The Ludlow Massacre stands at the heart of one of the most vicious clashes between capital and labor in the history of the United States. It lent support to the socialist propaganda that, in every country, including the United States, government protects the ruling class.

In September 1913, 9,000 miners struck the Colorado Fuel and Iron Company, a corporation under the control of John D. Rockefeller. The strike lasted 15 months. A blow-by-blow account of this strike belongs in the chronicles of naked class warfare. The striking miners and their families, evicted from company dwellings in the company camps, erected a colony of tent dwellings at the edge of the southern Colorado coal fields.

One of the irreconcilable differences that led to the strike was the company's refusal to recognize the United Mine Workers union as the miners' bargaining agent. The miners agreed to put all other issues on the table for arbitration, and the mine operators offered to let the governor of Colorado settle every issue, except for recognition of the union. In part, the miners were rebelling against company intrusion in every aspect of their life. The list of the miners' demands included the right to select their own doctor, trade at stores of their own choosing, and live in

A lone man surveys the aftermath of the great fire that swept through the tent colony in Ludlow, Colorado, in April 1914.

boarding places chosen by themselves. The miners also wanted a 10-percent increase in wages, an eight-hour day, and a payment for "dead work," which took time, but drew no compensation. They asked to elect their own check-weighmen.

Local law enforcement officials deputized armed thugs that the company brought in from Texas, New Mexico, and West Virginia. Machine guns and searchlights became part of the landscape, and a company-owned armored automobile earned the nickname Death Special. Miners armed themselves in self defense. After sporadic violence claimed a few lives on both sides, the State of Colorado sent in the Colorado National Guard and imposed martial law. A fragile peace returned to the coal mines and National Guard units withdrew, except for Company A and Troop B, which had strong connections with the mine operators.

In April 1914, the tent colony at Ludlow was virtually besieged by the remaining state militia. Rumors spread that the militia planned to level the colony of striking miners. Each side blames the other for firing the first shot. With or without provocation, the militia sprayed the tent colony with machine gun and rifle fire. One boy and three men died in a 12-hour battle. That night, which was Easter night, the militia entered the tent colony and drenched the tents with oil. The miners had dug pits for protection. When the militiamen put a match to the oil-drenched tents, women and children were huddling in these pits for protection. Most of them fled, but, in one pit, 13 children and one pregnant woman burned to death. Six men were shot to death.

The massacre at Ludlow incited an uprising of miners in surrounding districts, prompting President Wilson to send federal troops to restore order. The government sought the aid of Rockefeller, but he refused to use his influence with the mine operators to bring a settlement. President

Wilson wrote a letter to Rockefeller expressing his "profound regret" regarding Mr. Rockefeller's stance.

After the complete suppression of the strike, Rockefeller sponsored a plan for a company union that gave workers some opportunity to air their grievances. He visited the mines to promote the company union, dancing with as many of the women as possible at social gatherings. The miners voted to accept the company union.

The history of capitalism would not be complete without describing the bullying tactics that captains of industry exhibited in instances such as the Colorado coal strikes. History now shows that these tactics were not in step with the long-term trends of capitalist development. In the 1930s, workers in the United States won their right to choose their own unions in secret ballot elections.

See also Class Struggle; Pullman Strike; Rockefeller, John Davison.

References Baker, Ray Stannard. *Woodrow Wilson: Life and Letters*, Vol. 4 (1938); Brooks, Thomas R. *Toil and Trouble: A History of American Labor* (1971); McGovern, George, and Leonard Guttridge. *The Great Coal Field War* (1972).

Machine Smashing

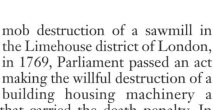

Invention of labor-saving devices raised the question of the future of workers who were thrown out of work by the new machines. Workers often saw machines as a new source of competition that drove down wages.

Several inventors felt the resentment of workers against this new force in the marketplace. In 1598, the stocking-frame invention of William Lee drew the hostility of workers, who saw their livelihood threatened. Lee left England to find refuge in France, but was forced to return to England. Dud Dudley received a patent in 1621 on a method for making iron with pit coal. His ironworks aroused the jealousy of ironmasters, who incited workers to break in and sack Dudley's ironworks. In 1753, rioters broke into and sacked the house of John Kay, the inventor of the flying shuttle. When James Hargreaves, who invented the spinning jenny, built a few of the machines for sale in 1767, workers broke in and wrecked them. Edmund Cartwright designed a steam-powered mill with no less than 400 looms. In 1792, the buildings were constructed, and the first machine had just been installed when violence broke out with local weavers: The place was burnt to the ground.

Concern about the impact of machinery on the livelihood of workers extended beyond the workers themselves. In 1634, Charles I ordered the demolition of a newly constructed sawmill, because it threw sawyers out of work. Ten years before Hargreaves, Lawrence Earnshaw built a cotton-spinning machine, but destroyed it rather than take bread out of the mouths of the poor.

In the second half of the eighteenth century, workers turned their resentment against the manufacturers. In response to mob destruction of a sawmill in the Limehouse district of London, in 1769, Parliament passed an act making the willful destruction of a building housing machinery a felony that carried the death penalty. In 1779, machine-smashing riots broke out in Lancashire. An armed mob numbering as many as 8,000, with colors flying and drums beating, stormed and destroyed mills valued at £10,000. On the following day, rioters professed their plan to take Bolton, Manchester, Stockport, and Cromford, destroying all the engines along the way, and even throughout England. Disturbances broke out in other localities. Rioters stormed Peel's cotton-printing factory in Altham, wrecked the engines, and tossed them into the river. The government sent troops from Liverpool to suppress the riots. A few rioters ended up on the gallows, but most escaped punishment. In 1796, the government garrisoned certain spinning mills in Yorkshire. In 1802, the use of the gig mill met with serious disturbances in Wiltshire and Somerset.

In 1811, separate bands of angry weavers, called Luddites, after an obscure individual named Ned Ludd, invaded district after district, and destroyed textile frames. From Nottinghamshire to Lancashire, Derbyshire, and Leicestershire, angry bands wrecked machines, but avoided injury to persons. The rebellion continued into 1812. Parliament sent a regiment to suppress the revolt. The leaders were tried in a mass trial in 1813, and were either hanged or deported.

Some efforts were made to engage the government in protecting workers from displacement by machines. In 1552, Parliament passed an act prohibiting the use of the gig mill. A royal proclamation in 1623 forbade the use of the needle-making machine.

In 1802, Wiltshire shearman not only attacked cloth-finishing machinery, but appealed to the courts to make the machinery illegal. These appeals for government protection were often made in the name of maintaining the quality of the finished product.

Machine smashing was not limited to England. According to Karl Marx, in *Das Kapital*, "In the seventeenth century nearly all Europe experienced revolts of the workpeople against the ribbon-loom, a machine for weaving ribbons and trimmings...."

We now know that wages rise with increases in output per worker, and that labor-saving machinery is a necessary part of rising living standards for workers. The adoption of labor-saving machinery is a necessary process, in which workers are freed from producing one product to join the production efforts of new products. The first workers, however, thrown out on the street and replaced by machinery, found little comfort in a rational perspective on the matter.

See also Factory System, Industrial Revolution.

References Daunton, Martin. *Progress and Poverty: An Economic and Social History of Britain 1700–1850* (1995); Mantoux, Paul. *The Industrial Revolution in the Eighteenth Century* (1961); Sale, Kirkpatrick. *Rebels against the Future: The Luddites and Their War on the Industrial Revolution* (1995).

Magellan, Ferdinand
See Circumnavigation of the Earth.

Marine Mammal Protection Act of 1972
See Environmental Regulation (International).

Maritime Insurance
See Lloyd's of London.

Marshall Plan
The Marshall Plan was a substantial U.S. foreign aid program for Western Euro-

Secretary of State George Marshall (right) walks with President Harry Truman to Blair House after a conference on foreign policy in 1948.

pean countries, to assist in economic reconstruction following World War II.

After World War II, preventing the spread of communism became a major objective of the United States, and economic assistance was an important weapon in that struggle. With material support from neighboring communist countries, Greek Communists revolted against the Greek government in 1946, and Turkey also felt internal and external pressure from communist forces. The post-World War I experience had taught Europe that wartorn and economically exhausted countries can be fertile ground for political instability, with governments raising to power that could embroil the world in wars, and terrorize civilian populations. With communism the likely beneficiary from political instability in Europe, the United States sought to aid economic recovery in Western Europe as a means of promoting political stability in democratic countries.

The Marshall Plan received its name from George C. Marshall, who was U.S.

secretary of state when the plan was formulated and implemented. From 1947 to 1950, the United States infused over $13 billion into Western European countries, excluding Soviet-bloc countries and Spain. The U.S. government asked European governments to draw up a plan that showed the need for financial assistance, and how assistance would be used. Western European countries formed the Organization for European Economic Cooperation (OEEC), which encouraged coordination and prevented national plans from defeating the major goals of American aid. The aid was given in the form of credits that did not have to be repaid.

The sometimes-not-too-peaceful competition between capitalism and communism during the post-World War II era served as a backdrop for one of the largest foreign aid programs in history, of which the Marshall plan was only a part. Between 1945 and 1967, the United States gave away $56.1 billion to foreign countries, hoping that economic development and prosperity was the best defense against a communist ideology that taught that democracy was a sham substitute of equality of votes for equality of wealth, and that equality of wealth was the best hope for people held in the bonds of mass economic misery.

References Donovan, Robert J. *The Second Victory: The Marshall Plan and the Post-War Revival of Europe* (1987); Kindleberger, Charles P. A *Financial History of Western Europe* (1984).

Marx, Karl (1818–1883)

During the twentieth century, Karl Marx's name became synonymous with revolutionary fervor against capitalism. His writings furnished the intellectual foundation for the socialist critique of capitalism that gathered momentum late in the nineteenth century.

Marx was born on 5 May 1818, in Trier, Germany, the eldest son of Heinrich Marx, a provincial lawyer, and Henriette Marx. Marx's unique personality emerged early in life. He attended the Trier gymnasium for five years, where his teachers noted his lack of discipline and tendency toward exaggeration. Poetry seems to have been his main interest at school.

In 1835, at the age of 17, Marx entered Bonn University, and became a leader in a regional fraternity. He indulged in such riotous revelry that his father pulled him out after the second semester, and sent him to the University of Berlin, a school with a reputation for sober study. To please his father, Marx studied jurisprudence, in preparation for a career in law, but his true interest lay with literature and art. The philosophy of the young Hegelians won him over during this time. The young Hegelians flirted with atheism, and were leftist republicans in politics. In 1838, his father died, and Marx abandoned all thought of becoming a lawyer. He read widely on his own, studied Greek philosophy, and wrote a dissertation, which he submitted to Jena University, entitled "Difference between the Democritean and Epicurean Philosophy of Nature."

Since Marx's adherence to the young Hegelians ruled out hopes of an academic appointment, he took up a career of radical journalism. In 1842, he became editor of the *Rheinische Zeitung*. In 1843, the cen-

The grave of Karl Marx in London

sors suppressed this paper, and Marx, after marrying Jenny von Westhalen, moved to Paris, where he became active in the socialist movement, and formed a lifelong working friendship with Frederick Engels. His radical journalism earned him the hatred of the Prussian government, which ordered his arrest if he returned to Prussia, and which apparently instigated his expulsion from Paris. He was allowed to live in Brussels, on condition that he stay out of Belgian politics. He remained in Brussels for three years, mostly under police supervision. Marx and Engels joined the secret Communist League, which, in 1847, commissioned Marx and Engels to write the *Manifesto of the Communist Party* for its second congress. In the *Manifesto*, Marx put forth in stirring rhetoric his ideas of the class struggle and the coming dictatorship of the proletariat.

With the outbreak of the Revolutions of 1848, Marx and Engels, expelled from Belgium, returned to Prussia, after a brief stay in Paris. They started a radical newspaper that lasted nearly a year, before the Prussian government closed it down, and expelled Marx and Engels. In the aftermath of political reaction, Marx settled in London. England was the only country that left its radicals unmolested. He spent the next 34 years of his life in London, studying at the British Museum, and receiving financial help from Engels. In 1864, he formed the International Workingmen's Association (the First International).

Marx's chief work in his later years was the writing of *Das Kapital*. The first volume was published during Marx's life; two volumes came out after he had died. In this work, Marx not only developed a theory of capitalist development, but wrote in eloquent words of the plight of the proletariat. Marx felt that periodic industrial crises of growing intensity were necessary features of capitalism, and would eventually destroy it.

Only in the past few years has the Marxian critique of capitalism lost its hold in much of the noncapitalist world. Marx's imagination and genius created a powerful vision of capitalism, but history has not vindicated it. In fairness, many of the abuses that aroused Marx's indignation were addressed when working people won the right to vote in democratic countries.

See also International Workingmen's Association, Manifesto of the Communist Party, Revolutions of 1848.

References Foner, Philip S. *When Karl Marx Died: Comments in 1883*. Revised ed. (1983); Raddatz, Fritz J. *Karl Marx: A Political Biography* (1979).

Masters and Servants Acts (England)

The Masters and Servants Acts established important legal obligations of employees to employers in nineteenth-century Britain. The British trade unions vigorously objected, because of the bias in the acts against workers.

The law of masters and servants was founded upon a whole series of acts, including the Statute of Artificers in 1563, the Masters and Servants Act of 1824, and the Masters and Servants Act of 1867. As the law stood in 1867, workers committed a criminal offense if they broke a contract with an employer, or left work unfinished. The verdict of a single justice could send an employee to prison for violating criminal sanctions against these and similar actions. Only after 1848 might a justice summon an employee to court, rather than issue an arrest warrant for these crimes. The court could not hear evidence the worker gave in his own defense, or against his employer, but employers could give evidence against a worker. Workers faced imprisonment for breaking a contract with an employer, but an employer was only liable for civil damages for breaking a contract with an employee. Striking workers could easily find themselves arrested and imprisoned because of the law of masters and servants. In labor disputes, this area of the law became a powerful weapon in the hands of employers.

In 1864, a conference of trade unions met in London to discuss the problem, and to organize agitation for changing the law. Parliament took up the issue in 1867, and passed the Masters and Servants Act of 1867. This act took important steps to level the playing field between employer and employee, but still left employees facing criminal penalties and imprisonment before trial. Summons to appear in court replaced summary arrest warrants, unless justices had good reason to believe a worker might flee. Justices could and did easily abuse this provision. Nevertheless, justices had to hear the case in open court, rather than in their private residence, and more than one justice was necessary for court action. Workers could give evidence in their own defense, and were only subject to imprisonment in cases involving serious injury to persons and property. Fines and restitution usually satisfied the court. Despite the act's shortcomings, trade unions won a great victory in the act of 1867.

The general election of 1868 was the first time the mass of propertyless workers exercised the privilege to vote. The Liberal Party and the Conservative Party wooed the new addition to the electorate. The Conservative Party was able to go further to reform labor law in favor of the workers. With the Conservative Party in power, Parliament passed the Employers and Workmen Act of 1875, to replace the Masters and Servants Act of 1867. This new act ended imprisonment for breach of contract, except in unusual cases involving vital public services, and for endangerment of life or valuable property. Employers and workers stood on equal footing before the law. Either party could seek civil damages if the other party failed to live up to contractual obligations.

See also Trade Union Act of 1871.

References Cole, G. D. H. *A Short History of the British Working Class Movement: 1789–1947* (1948, reprint 1960); Hunt, Edward. *British Labor History, 1815–1914* (1981).

McKinley Tariff of 1890
(United States)

The McKinley Tariff of 1890 ranks as the most protectionist tariff the U.S. government had enacted up to that time. The tariff took its name from William McKinley, who served as chairman of the House Ways and Means Committee when the bill passed the House, and who later became president of the United States.

During the latter portion of the nineteenth century, opinion on tariffs in the United States split mostly along party lines: Republicans stood staunchly in favor of protectionist trade policies, and Democrats advocated tariff reduction. The ratio of tariff revenue to the value of imports subject to tariffs averaged around 45 percent. Protest against high tariffs mounted, and Congress appointed a tariff commission in 1882, to make recommendations. The commission recommended tariff reductions on the order of 20 to 25 percent. With the enactment of the Tariff Act of 1883, Congress conceded a symbolic 4-percent reduction to the demand for tariff reform. Grover Cleveland, a Democrat, succeeded to the presidency in 1884, and advocated tariff reduction, but Congress never acted. In 1887, Cleveland described the tariff as a "vicious, inequitable, and illogical source of tax revenue." In the 1888 presidential election, the Republicans uncompromisingly championed the cause of protectionist trade policies, and attributed the agitation for free trade to the whiskey trust and the agents of foreign manufacturers. The Republicans won the election, and spearheaded the passage of the McKinley tariff.

In debate, Congress heard the protectionist philosophy urged upon its members, without qualification. No longer were tariffs advocated as temporary measures to shield infant industries from foreign competition. They were defended as a permanent and necessary feature of the economic landscape.

The McKinley tariff increased rates on some fabrics to over 100 percent. For the first time, travelers paid duties on goods brought home from foreign countries. Agricultural products were subjected to tariff protection, to soften the objections of farmers, but, since the United States was an exporter of agricultural products, the inclusion of agricultural products was without significance. High tariff rates on farm machinery remained in place.

The most innovative feature of the tariff was the provision for reciprocal agreements. This provision authorized the executive branch to strike treaties for reciprocal tariff reductions with individual countries, without asking for Senate approval. Congress repealed this provision in 1894, but the idea resurfaced in legislation enacted in 1934. Congress revised the tariff slightly in 1894, and adjusted the rates upward in 1897. The tariff rates, as revised in 1897, remained in effect until the eve of World War I.

The United States was not unique in turning to protectionist trade policies in the last quarter of the nineteenth century. France, Germany, and Russia are prominent examples of countries that took up the banner of protectionism. England remained committed to free trade until the Depression of the 1930s. The explosion in output caused by the advancement of technology bears part of the responsibility for the trend toward trade barriers in the late nineteenth century. Also, many economies of the world, including the United States, labored under a trend of deflation. At the end of World War II, the major trading partners began in earnest to find ways to reduce trade barriers.

See also Meline Tariff.

References Ashley, Percy. *Modern Tariff History* (1970); Myers, Margaret G. *A Financial History of the United States* (1970).

Medici Bank

The Medici Bank of Florence rose to become the most important financial institution in fifteenth-century Europe. The Medici set up a system of branch banks, any one of which could be declared independent by rearranging accounts. Such arrangements protected the parent bank from the bankruptcy of individual branches caused by localized economic difficulties. The Medici Bank was the chief bank for the Roman Catholic curia, and it had branches in the major cities of Italy, as well as in London, Lyon, Geneva, Bruges, and Avignon.

Members of the Medici family became involved in Florentine banking in the latter 1300s. In 1393, Giovanni di Bicci de Medici (1360–1429) took ownership of the Roman branch of a bank owned by one of his Florentine cousins. He removed the headquarters of his bank to Florence in 1397, the official founding date for the Medici Bank. At the time, Rome was a source of funds, but Florence offered more investment opportunities. By 1402, the Medici Bank had opened a branch bank in Venice, which was also an important outlet of investment opportunities. In the same year, the bank employed a total of 17 people at its headquarters in Florence; five were clerks.

The wool and cloth industries were the export mainspring of the Florentine economy in the fourteenth and fifteenth centuries. In 1402, the Medici Bank loaned 3,000 florins (nearly one-third of its original capital) to finance a Medici family partnership to produce woolen cloth. In 1408, a second and more successful shop for producing woolen cloth was begun. The Medici diversified their risk by engaging in the trade of a large number of commodities, including wool, cloth, alum, spices, olive oil, silk stuffs, brocades, jewelry, silver plate, and citrus fruit.

In 1429, Giovanni di Medici died, and management of the bank passed into the hands of his eldest son, Cosimo. In 1435, the bank opened its first branch beyond the Alps, in Geneva. The Medici opened another woolen-cloth manufacturing shop, and in 1438 they acquired a silk shop. The Medici Bank opened a branch in Bruges in 1439, branches in London and Avignon in 1446, and the Milan branch in 1452 or 1453; the Geneva branch was transferred to Lyon in 1464. The Medici Bank was organized as a partnership, with the Medici family as the largest investor in the parent company, and the parent company as the largest investor in the branch partnerships. The parent company functioned like a modern holding company. Under Cosimo's leadership, the Medici Bank became the largest banking house of its time.

The Medici accepted time deposits that were several times greater than the invested capital. Unlike some of the exchange banks of the time, which were primarily involved in fund transfers associated with international trade, the Medici Bank was a lending institution. Openly charging interest (usury) was prohibited, but interest charges were hidden in bills of exchange, by which foreign currency was purchased for delivery at a future date. Profit was at the mercy of the foreign exchange markets. What was called a dry exchange involved no transfer of goods or foreign exchange, and effectively guaranteed interest to the lender. In 1429, dry exchanges were outlawed in Florence, but the law was suspended at least temporarily in 1435, just after the Medici became the defacto, if not legal, rulers of Florence.

When Cosimo died in 1464, the bank had passed its peak. An invalid son, Piero de' Medici, assumed the management of the bank. According to Machiavelli, he began calling in loans, causing a contraction in credit and numerous business failures. Piero died in 1469. Piero's son, Lorenzo the Magnificent, was a great statesman. He had a humanistic education without business training or experience. A line written in capital letters in his diary may throw light on Medici involvement in government. He wrote: "One cannot live in wealth in Florence without the state." He turned the management of the bank over to managers, and the bank gradually lost ground. On Lorenzo's death in 1492, his son, Piero di Lorenzo, assumed control of Medici political and business interests in Florence, but he had neither business nor political acumen. In 1494, the Medici were ousted from Florence. The bank, already tottering on bankruptcy, was confiscated, and was not successful under its new owners.

The Medici Bank contributed little to economic growth. Too many of its funds were used to finance conspicuous consumption of royal courts or wars such as the War of the Roses, or the exploits of the Italian condottieri, captains of mercenary armies who sometimes rose to political prominence. These loans often led to scenarios of sending good money to rescue bad money.

The Medici family produced three popes, and continued to furnish Florence with rulers into the 1700s. They represent one of the early examples of capitalist families rising to social and political power.

See also Florentine Industrial Capitalism.

References Bullard, Melissa M. *Filippo Strozzi and the Medici: Favor and Finance in Sixteenth Century Florence and Rome* (1980); de Roover, Raymond. *The Rise and Decline of the Medici Bank, 1397–1494* (1966).

Meiji Era (Japan, 1868–1912)

The Meiji era transformed the Japanese economy from a dysfunctional feudal system to a dynamic capitalistic economy with imperialistic ambitions.

In the early nineteenth century, Japan stood, in economic development, where western Europe stood in the late Middle Ages. More than 90 percent of the population were impoverished feudal peasants bound to the land. A primitive, but self-sufficient, agricultural system devoted its energies to the production of rice. Since the 1600s, the emperor had been a symbolic figure in a land fragmented by territorial lords paying allegiance to the ruling shogun of a great military family. Artisans and tradesmen boasted no political or social rights, but there were rudiments of a guild system. Political restrictions and regulations suppressed commerce. A ban on foreign intercourse was calculated to petrify Japanese society in a static medieval state.

After 1750, the shogunate found itself invariably embarrassed by financial difficulties, leading to higher taxes, borrowings, and currency debasements. The pride of a modest but growing merchant class resented the arrogance of a military aristocracy. The treaties that Western powers forced upon Japan in the 1850s caused the shogunate to further lose face. A rising tide of revolt swept aside the bankrupt shogunate, which could not marshal the resources to resist. After a brief military struggle during 1867 and 1868, the shogunate fell beneath the onslaught of a group of feudal clans that rallied around the emperor.

The new government abolished the fiefs and proprietary rights of the lords. It lifted restrictions on freedom of movement, internal trade, and entry into new occupations. Property rights in land became transferable, and internal tariffs and tolls were removed. All citizens enjoyed the same rights before the law. A new land tax, levied according to the assessed value of land, brought order to public finance. Within the span of a few years, Japan changed from a society that shunned Western influences to a society that hungered for Western knowledge and methods.

Between 1870 and 1872, British capital helped finance the first railroad. It connected Tokyo with Yokohama. By 1893, Japan had 2,000 miles of railroads, 100,000 tons of steam vessels, and 4,000 miles of telegraph lines. The government established the Bank of Japan in 1882, which issued paper money convertible into silver. In 1897, Japan went on the gold standard, putting Japan in good stead with foreign capital markets. A war indemnity extracted from China supplied the gold to support the gold standard.

Raw silk, which quadrupled in production from 1868 to 1893, led the list of Japanese exports to the rest of the world. In the 1890s, the textile industry brought the Industrial Revolution to Japan, replete with low-wage female labor.

The Japanese government lent a helping hand to the development of large-scale industry. Ocean shippers received a government subsidy. An added premium was paid for Japanese ships. Government acted on its own initiative to build iron works.

See also Bank of Japan, Unequal Treaties, Zaibatsu.

References Halliday, Jon. *A Political History of Japanese Capitalism* (1975); Lockwood, William W. *The Economic Development of Japan: Growth and Structural Change, 1868–1938* (1954); Wiley, Peter B. *Yankees in the Land of the Gods* (1990).

Meline Tariff of 1892 (France)

The Meline Tariff of 1892 signaled a clear shift toward protectionism in French commercial policy, and gave added momentum to a trend that was evident in most economies of that era, which may have been a reaction to the trade policies of the German Zollverein—a free-trade union of German states. By 1879, the Zollverein had turned the German states into a sizable protectionist trading block, and the rapid growth of German industrial output seemed to vindicate protectionist trade policies. The deflation of commodity prices, a trend that France shared with many other countries, may have contributed to protectionist sentiment in many countries.

The tariff took its name from Felix Jules Meline, secretary general of a tariff commission, who played an important role in enactment of the tariff. A longtime advocate of protectionism, Meline argued in 1880 that "the more capital increases, the higher salaries will be; and the higher they are, the more the working class, for which we have so much solicitude, gains in well-being and morality."

The rise of Germany as a competitor in manufacturing helped push France toward protectionism. A treaty between France and Germany assured that most-favored-nation treatment governed trade between the two countries, but the two countries remained rivals. For example, Germany struck a commercial treaty with Switzerland that reduced tariffs on livestock raised at 1,000 meters or above in altitude, which excluded French farmers from the concession.

The Meline tariff set up a minimum tariff that applied to all countries that enjoyed most-favored-trade status with

France, and a maximum tariff that applied to all other countries. The French government could change these rates at will, without renegotiating commercial treaties with individual countries. In contrast to previous French tariffs, agriculture won a significant measure of protection under the Meline tariff, which was a reaction to the competition of American and Australian agriculture. A member of the Chamber of Deputies exclaimed, "Never forget that industry and agriculture are twin sisters which push with their robust shoulders the imperishable chariot of the nation along the infinite route of progress."

The tariff became law on 12 January 1892. It increased tariff rates an average of 80 percent over the old rates. The rates on manufactured goods were higher than the agricultural rates. Prosperity followed the enactment of the Meline tariff, vindicating its proponents. It also sparked a round of tariff wars, particularly with Italy and Switzerland. In the last two decades of the nineteenth century, France, Germany, Russia, and the United States became more protectionist. Great Britain remained a free-trade country in a world of protectionism, until the Depression of the 1930s.

After World War II, the forces of protectionism gave way to a worldwide sentiment for freer trade. Trade barriers were seen as contributing to the friction that led to military conflict. Developed countries have periodically engaged in multilateral negotiations to reduce trade barriers, and in the capitalist world the vision of competition has expanded to the global market. The achievement of competition within isolated national markets was an important achievement of the early phase of capitalism.

See also McKinley Tariff of 1890, Zollverein.

References Ashley, Percy. *Modern Tariff History* (1970); Clough, Shepard B. *France: A History of National Economics, 1789–1939* (1964).

Mellon Tax Cut of 1921
See Excess Profits Tax.

Mercantilism

The laissez-faire capitalism that flowered in the nineteenth century was a reaction to the state-regulated economies that evolved with the centralization of political power in the European nation-states. The antithesis of laissez-faire capitalism was the mercantilist policy consciously practiced by nation-states in the seventeenth and eighteenth centuries.

Before the consolidation of political power in the state, towns regulated local economic activity in detail. The rules of each guild had the force of law, and wages, hours, and prices were set by law. Monopolies and speculative hoarding were prohibited, and standards were set for quality of products. With the rise of the nation-state, the administrative economic regulation of the guilds and towns gave way to the equally complex and detailed regulation of the state economy. Nations self-consciously strove to develop capitalism, with the aid of a maze of rules and regulations. The French finance minister Colbert gave the name Colbertism to the thorough mercantilist regulation of industry.

The first principle of mercantilism can be found in the idea that the greatness and power of a state are determined by the abundance of money (precious metals). This stock of money grew with what is now called a favorable balance of trade. The exports of home commodities should exceed in value the imports of foreign commodities, and this positive balance of trade was settled with the importation of money or precious metal. This domestic supply of gold and silver made it easier for monarchs to raise funds, either by loans or taxes. An edict by Henry IV of France, in 1603, states that arts and manufactures are encouraged as "the sole means of avoiding the transportation out of the kingdom of the precious metals and the consequent enrichment of our neighbors."

Adam Smith, in his *An Inquiry into the Nature and Causes of the Wealth of Nations*, discussed mercantilism at length. He described the "restraints on importation," along with the "encouragements of exports," by which a nation could turn the balance of trade in its favor. Restraints on imports, in the form of duties or prohibitions, were applied to the imports of such foreign goods as could be produced domestically. They could also be directed to the imports from countries with which an unfavorable balance of trade was unwanted. Goods that were imported for the purpose of re-exportation could enter duty-free, and the encouragements to exports took the form of subsidies for the production of exportable goods, advantageous commercial treaties, and the establishment of colonies. Countries sometimes prohibited the export of a raw material that was needed for a domestic industry. Mercantilist policy struck down barriers to free trade within the borders of the nation, such as internal tariffs and tolls. In Germany, the barriers between the various states did not come down until the Zollverein—a free-trade union of German states—was formed (1834).

In mercantilist policy, the opportunity to engage in economic activity was a privilege. The prince granted privileges and imposed duties, as the interest of the state (or ruler) dictated. Granting monopoly privileges was common; the great trading companies, such as the East India companies of England, France, and Holland, enjoyed monopoly privileges on the importation and exportation of certain commodities. Patents of monopoly were granted for the introduction of new industries.

National governments continued the practice of the guilds in the minute regulation of industry. English industry remained the most free from regulation. Nevertheless, in 1630, English regulation covered these and similar matters:

Only Spanish black shall be used to dye silk. Cloth shall be made only from native wool. No tobacco shall be planted in England. Cloths for export must meet certain requirements for length, breadth, and weight. A commission will conduct an investigation to see why the fishing industry is not flourishing. No dye can be made of logwood or blackwood. No new houses can be constructed in London. No one will import foreign thread. Eating bread on Fridays and other fast days is prohibited.

The French government regulated the size of tools used in weaving. The state displaced the authority of guilds, but embodied the same spirit of detailed regulation of industry, which was partly directed at raising the quality of domestic goods, making them more attractive in foreign markets.

Mercantilist policies also promoted improvements in transportation. Roads and canals were built to facilitate internal transportation, and shipbuilding was subsidized to encourage transportation to foreign countries.

Adam Smith strongly attacked the logic of the mercantilist system. He argued that a high per-capita output played a much larger role than the stock of domestic precious metal in determining a nation's economic welfare. John Maynard Keynes, in *The General Theory*, referred to "what now seems to me to be the element of scientific truth in mercantilist doctrine.... At a time when domestic authorities had no direct control over the domestic interest rate..., the effect of a favorable balance of trade on the influx of precious metals was their only indirect means of reducing the domestic rate of interest and so increasing the inducement to home investment." In modern times, Japanese economic policy has been described as mercantilist policy. The Japanese have maintained a favorable balance of trade, and have enjoyed above-average economic growth.

See also Colonial Policy; Smith, Adam.

References Gomes, Leonard. *Foreign Trade and the National Economy: Mercantilist and Classical Perspectives* (1987); Nussbaum, Frederick. *A History of the Economic Institutions of Modern Europe* (1935).

Merchant Adventurers (England)

The Merchant Adventurers was a guild of English merchants that monopolized English foreign trade in the Baltic and North Sea during the sixteenth and seventeenth centuries. Unlike the joint-stock companies, which were the precursors of the modern corporation, the Merchant Adventurers was an organization of individual merchants that was not incorporated as a single company. The prime of the Merchant Adventurers preceded the era of the large joint-stock companies, such as the East India Company. They were the English rivals of the Hanseatic League. The Merchant Adventurers was what Adam Smith called a regulated company. According to Smith, "When those companies do not trade upon a joint stock, but are obliged to admit any person, properly qualified, upon paying a certain fine, and agreeing to submit to the regulations of the company, each member trading upon his own stock, as at his own risk, they are called regulated companies." Among those who were not properly qualified were shopkeepers, retailers, and non-Englishmen.

The Merchant Adventurers received a royal charter in 1564 that ratified their long practice of regulating membership and ground rules for English trade with Europe. England's prime export at the time was wool and woolen goods, which the Merchant Adventurers commanded the sole privilege to market in the major trading centers of Europe; they also controlled English imports from Europe. The trading body of the Merchant Adventurers chartered ships for trade missions, and set shipment quotas for each member. Quotas, restricted to 400 cloths per year for new members, rose to 1,000 cloths per year after 15 years of membership.

Governance of the Merchant Adventurers rested in the hands of a governor and a court of 24 assistants, usually headquartered in the Netherlands. In Antwerp, the Merchant Adventurers was a self-governing political body of English residents, empowered to imprison members, adjudicate disputes involving trade or moral conduct, and levy fines on non-members caught trading.

Adam Smith assailed the regulated companies for their monopolistic spirit:

The usual corporation spirit, wherever the law does not restrain it, prevails in all regulated companies. When they have been allowed to act according to their natural genius, they have always, in order to confine the competition to as small a number of persons as possible, endeavored to subject the trade to many burdensome regulations.... The object, besides, of the greater part of the bye-laws of all regulated companies, as well as of all other corporations, is not so much to oppress those who are already members, as to discourage others from becoming so.... The constant view of such companies is always to raise the rate of their own profit as high as they can; to keep the market, both for the goods they export, and for those which they import, as much understocked as they can: which can be done only by restraining the competition, or by discouraging new adventurers from entering into the trade.

The free-trade movement put an end to the monopoly privileges of the Merchant Adventurers. In spite of monopolistic practices, the Merchant Adventures deserve credit for wresting English foreign trade from the hands of the Hanseatic League, and demonstrating to England the profits to be had from foreign trade. These profits would finance larger ventures, requiring more capital and longer voyages, eventually lifting England to leadership of the world capitalist economic system.

See also Joint-Stock Companies, Hanseatic League.

References Cox, Oliver C. *The Foundations of Capitalism* (1959); Carus-Wilson, Eleanora M. *Medieval Merchant Venturers: Collected Studies* (1967); Smith, Adam. *An Inquiry into the Nature and Causes of the Wealth of Nations* (1776).

Merchant Bankers

The prestigious private banking houses, such as Rothschilds, Morgan, and Baring Brothers, belonged to a class of banks called merchant bankers. They traded in commodities and financial securities on their own account, but often served as middlemen, buying commodities for wholesalers and manufacturers, and floating loans and stocks for railroads, canals, and other vast undertakings. Governments and kings courted merchant bankers to float loans to fight wars, and to transfer funds to armies in foreign countries. The Rothschilds raised more than £100 million for the Allied governments in the war against Napoleon. Merchant bankers were not deposit banks, although some held large deposits for regular customers.

Surrounding merchant bankers was an impressive aura of integrity, trust, and loyalty that forbade taking short-term advantage of insider information. Developing long-term relationships with customers, based on long experience of fair dealing, and standing by one's word, enabled merchant bankers to mobilize capital for vast projects in foreign countries. Otherwise, these projects would not have found financing at reasonable interest rates.

The British merchant bankers began as foreigners, often from Germany, but also from Holland and the United States. The Barings, Rothschilds, and Warburgs came to Britain from Germany. The Morgans came from the United States, and the Hopes and Raphaels from Holland. Jews were well represented in the ranks of merchant bankers. Of 31 merchant bankers who died millionaires between 1809 and 1939, 24 were Jewish. The Barings and Morgans were among the few leading merchant bankers who were not Jewish. The extensive Jewish involvement may account for the international outlook of the merchant bankers.

The impeccable reputation of merchant bankers aided in the development of the London market for bills of exchange. An endorsement from a merchant banker made it much easier to discount bills of exchange at low interest rates. By endorsing bills of exchange, merchant bankers played a vital role in facilitating international trade.

Perhaps unfairly, critics of sizable European capital exports in the latter part of the nineteenth century laid a portion of the blame on the merchant bankers. British merchant bankers arranged much of the European financing for building railroads and canals in the United States during the nineteenth century. Similar projects in remote parts of the world would draw investors and capital, once a prominent merchant banking house undertook to arrange the financing. The principal complaint against foreign financing was that the capital could have been put to better use at home. Critics accused merchant bankers of having a bias toward foreign financing, because most of their connections were foreign. Although there may be a bit of truth to this criticism, probably much foreign investment was simply attracted by higher interest rates abroad.

In 1890, nearly half of Britain's foreign investment was in Argentina, mostly arranged by Baring Brothers. When a political revolution broke out in August 1890, Britain barely escaped a financial debacle, and Barings tottered on the brink of bankruptcy. The other merchant bankers of London, and several banks, including the Bank of England, helped Barings weather the storm.

The growth of government-sponsored and large corporate banks has diminished the importance of banking dynasties such as Barings and Rothschilds. Barings continues as a merchant bank managed by members of the Baring family, which has controlled the firm since before 1800. In the nineteenth century, merchant bankers held a strategic position in international capital flows, and assisted in the mobilization of finances for far-flung capitalist projects.

See also Baring Brothers and Company, Limited; Rothschild Banking Family.

References Carosso, Vincent P. *The Morgans: Private International Bankers* (1987); Cowles, Virginia. *The Rothschilds: A Family of Fortune* (1973); Davies, Glyn. *A History of Money: From Ancient Times to the Present Day* (1994); Wechsberg, Joseph. *The Merchant Bankers* (1966).

Mergers (United States)

A merger is a combination of two business organizations into one business organization, either because one business acquires the stock of another, or because one business acquires the assets of another. At the turn of the century, mergers replaced trusts as the primary legal vehicle for industrial consolidation.

The Sherman Antitrust Act of 1890 outlawed trusts, price-fixing agreements, and other restraints of trade that lessened competition, but mergers remained legal. As an alternative source of tax revenue, the government of New Jersey conceived the idea of encouraging corporations to establish legal residence in the state, which enabled the state to raise revenue from incorporation fees and franchise taxes.

In 1889, New Jersey amended its corporation laws to enable corporations chartered in New Jersey to purchase and hold the stock of other corporations, and to pay for the stock with issues of their own stock. As amended in 1893, New Jersey corporations could buy and own the stock of corporations chartered in other states, and exercise all rights of ownership. Delaware soon adopted New Jersey's corporation law virtually verbatim, except for a lower tax rate, and became another popular haven for corporations. Other states, including New York, entered the fray with less success.

The Sherman Act, coupled with the liberalization of corporation laws, touched off a merger wave in the United States. The year 1895 saw four mergers. The number rose to six in 1897, and jumped to 16 in 1898. The merger wave reached a peak in 1899 with 63 mergers. The number of mergers per year trailed off to 19 in 1901, and to five in 1905. The nation's industrial structure felt the impact more than these numbers reveal. Consolidations put an end to 1,800 firms, and substantially reduced the number of firms controlling output in basic industries, such as oil, steel, and tobacco. According to the 1900 census, 0.5 percent of the nation's manufacturing establishments owned 15 percent of the industrial capital, and produced 8 percent of the industrial output.

The U.S. government sought to outlaw mergers as a means of evading the Sherman Act. Section 7 of the Clayton Act of 1914 forbade the acquisition of the stock of one company by another company when the effect was to "restrain commerce." In 1926, the Supreme Court ruled that the acquisition of the assets, as opposed to the stock, of another company was not a violation of the Clayton Act. The Celler-Kaufer Act of 1950 amended section 7 of the Clayton Act to cover mergers through the acquisition of assets, as well as stock.

Another merger wave gathered force in the 1920s, when the boom in the stock market aided the financial consolidation of industries in utilities, automobiles, and communications. In the 1950s, mergers to consolidate firms in the same industry were clearly illegal in the United States, because of the effects on competition. A third wave of mergers in the 1960s brought a new type of corporation, the conglomerate, into prominence. A conglomerate is a corporation formed out of mergers of several firms in unrelated industries.

Some observers saw the fourth wave of mergers in the 1980s as merger mania. A combination of high inflation and low stock prices meant that replacement costs of assets held by firms were much higher than the stock market evaluation of the firms owning the assets. Purchasing the stock of companies became an inexpensive way of acquiring expensive assets, such as oil reserves. The development of the junk bond market in the 1980s also made it easier to finance mergers with debt.

These conditions, combined with a government sympathetic to big business, sparked the wave of merger mania.

The latest merger waves proved that antitrust laws have not stopped the growth of big business. Although competition is preserved in individual markets, huge corporations can exert more than their share of political influence. To regulate big business, government also must become big, a trend that may not favor capitalism. These are issues that remain unresolved.

See also Cartels, Corporation, Sherman Antitrust Act of 1890, Trusts.

References Brigham, Eugene F. *Fundamentals of Financial Management* (1989); Gaughan, Patrick A. *Mergers and Acquisitions* (1991); Lamoreaux, Naomi R. *The Great Merger Movement in American Business, 1895–1904* (1986).

Military–Industrial Complex (United States)

The military–industrial complex refers to the close cooperation of the Pentagon and the defense industry, and its major role in the U.S. economy during the post-World War II era, which led some critics to talk of Pentagon capitalism. The soul-searching that has taken place in the United States over Pentagon capitalism might seem a bit squeamish to more militaristic societies of the past, such as Nazi Germany.

In his farewell address, President Dwight Eisenhower warned, "In the councils of government we must guard against the acquisition of unwarranted influence whether sought or unsought, by the military-industrial complex. The potential for the disastrous rise of misplaced power exists and will persist." Ironically, in 1946, then-General Eisenhower had written a memorandum, as chief of staff of the U.S. Army, calling for close cooperation between the army and civilian scientists, industry, and universities. Arguing for civilian assistance in military planning, General Eisenhower stated in the memorandum: "Effective long-range military planning can be done only in light of predicted developments in science and technology." President Eisenhower was the architect and one of the first critics of the military–industrial complex.

According to critics, the military–industrial complex represents the most dangerous extension of that modern industrialized state, in which important decisions are made neither by stockholders, consumers, or public officials. The real decisions are made by the technostructure, the bureaucratic layers of educated, technical elites, who possess the real power in corporations, because of their superior knowledge. The technostructure of the defense contractors govern the technological development of weaponry, and market these products through close working relationships with planners and decision-makers in government agencies, such as the Defense Department, Atomic Energy Commission, NASA, etc. Decisions about military planning and the choice of weapons are based not on the national interest, but on the interest of private companies in the defense industry.

The growth in the influence of this defense-related technostructure can be traced to several factors. First, following the Depression of the 1930s, government committed itself to the maintenance of full employment. Important interest groups of both business and labor accepted the concept of using high levels of government expenditures to maintain full employment. Heavy industry in the United States would only undertake long-range planning under the expectation that government would maintain a prosperous economy. Maintaining a high level of demand, with big government expenditures, seemed necessary. Second, the Cold War made defense preparedness a popular issue with the voters. Third, the military-industrial complex won the support of the scientific community, since the government became a major financial contributor for research and technological development in areas with defense applications. In summary, vast economic interests in the United States acquiesced in the growth of the military–industrial complex.

Critics charge that the military–industrial complex represents a concentration of economic and political force that has a vested interest in maintaining tension in the world, or even in causing wars. The excessive influence of this interest in government is a threat to peace. In addition, the political influence of this interest draws too great a share of resources into the production of defense goods, at the expense of important social goals. Education, housing, and medical care stand in need of tax revenue earmarked for expensive high-tech weaponry.

The growth of the military–industrial complex coincided with a high level of government taxation to support defense expenditures. Many of the defense contractors were spared the competitive pressures of the private sector, and became inefficient, and cost overruns continually plagued the development of major weapon systems.

Criticism of the military–industrial complex reached a peak in the 1970s. With the end of the Cold War in the late 1980s, U.S. defense manufacturers turned to foreign governments to find buyers for their products. By 1995, foreign governments bought more than half of the jet fighters produced in the United States.

According to some critics, the subject of the military–industrial complex raises important questions about the ability of gigantic corporations in modern capitalism to plan and manage the demand for products, such as the big defense firms have been able to do. Sheer bigness itself becomes a fault when huge corporations find ways to manage the demand for their product through effective advertising and other means, creating desires in the minds of consumers that would not have developed on their own, and drawing resources away from more pressing needs.

References: Galbraith, John K. *The New Industrial State* (1967); Melman, Seymour. *Pentagon Capitalism: the Political Economy of War* (1970).

Miller-Tydings Act of 1937 (United States)

The Miller-Tydings Act exempted price-maintenance agreements from the Sherman Antitrust Act. The 1930s witnessed a severe round of deflation. Deflation puts pressure on businesses with debt, and usually induces a burst of bankruptcies. Government policies of the New Deal leaned toward discouraging downward price flexibility.

Manufacturers found that retailers and distributors stood reluctant to carry brand-named and trademarked products that could be purchased much cheaper in discount stores. The Miller-Tydings Act authorized manufacturers to enforce resale-price agreements with distributors. These price agreements committed retailers to selling brand-named and trademarked products at prices set by manufacturers. Instead of suggested retail prices, manufacturers set prices.

Price-fixing agreements between retailers, or between manufacturers and distributors, ran afoul of the Sherman Act. With the growth of chain stores and discount stores, the small independent retailers began to support fair-trade legislation that legalized price-maintenance agreements. Manufacturers may have felt that maintaining the price of their product helped protect its image as a quality product. Numerous state governments also passed fair-trade legislation before the federal government acted. The Miller-Tydings Act amended the Sherman Act to exempt goods sold in interstate commerce. It authorized resale-price agreements of brand-named and trademarked goods involved in interstate commerce, when the state where the goods were sold had a fair-trade law. The law did not protect resale-price agreements in states without fair-trade laws. It protected brand-named and trademarked products that faced competition from similar products.

The Miller-Tydings Act came under criticism for interfering with price competition. As inflation rose to the forefront of economic problems in the 1970s, government began to repeal some of the Depression era legislation that put an inflationary bias in the economy. The Miller-Tydings Act made an easy target for the deregulation trend of the 1970s, and Congress repealed it in 1976.

See also Great Depression, Sherman Antitrust Act of 1890.

References Schnitzer, Martin C. *Contemporary Government and Business Relations* (1978); Waldman, Don E. *The Economics of Antitrust* (1986).

Minimum Wages

A minimum wage sets a legal floor on wages. Under a minimum-wage law, employers are legally bound to pay individual employees a wage equal to, or above, the minimum wage. Probably the earliest effort to legislate a minimum wage floor occurred in England. In 1805, a group of weavers in England organized, not to strike, but to petition Parliament to pass a minimum-wage bill. In 1808, a minimum-wage bill came before the House of Commons, where it failed to pass by a significant margin. Efforts to set legal minimum wages first met with success in New Zealand in 1894. The New Zealand government created district conciliation boards, with authority to supervise collective bargaining, and to set minimum wages when appropriate. Two years later, the State of Victoria, in Australia, formed special boards for specific low-wage industries. These boards combined equal numbers of employers and employees under the leadership of an outside chair that represented the public interest. These boards acted as independent wage-fixing agencies. The success of the system recommended it to other industries. Other states in Australia followed the precedent set by Victoria, and the system spread to England with the Trade Boards Act of 1909.

The State of Massachusetts was the first governmental entity in the United States to enact minimum-wage legislation. In 1911, the governor appointed the Commission on Minimum Wage Boards to study the matter. This commission drafted a bill calling for the formation of trade boards, after the English model. The Massachusetts legislature approved the bill, with important modifications. First, the authority of the boards extended only to women and minors. Second, recommendations of the board were not legally binding upon employers. The recommendations were publicized to bring the pressure of public opinion to bear on the employers.

A year after the Massachusetts legislature took action, eight other states passed minimum-wage legislation. Oregon was the next state to enact minimum-wage legislation, with a law that included provisions for fines and imprisonment for violators. Again, boards in each industry determined a minimum wage that applied only to women and minors. The law read, in part,

> It shall be unlawful to employ women in any occupation...for wages which are inadequate to supply the necessary cost of living and to maintain them in health and it shall be unlawful to employ minors...for unreasonably low wages.

After lengthy litigation, the Oregon law was upheld by a split opinion of the Supreme Court.

Other states abandoned the approach of using boards and commissions, and enacted minimum-wage laws that set a flat rate applicable to all industries. In Arizona, Arkansas, and Utah, minimum-wage laws set minimum wages between $9 and $10 per week.

In 1938, the federal government took a stand on the minimum wage, with the enactment of the Fair Labor Standards Act, which set a federal minimum wage of 25 cents per hour for workers in industries engaged in interstate commerce. The act also required that non-supervisory employees receive one and a half times their regular hourly rate on hours worked in excess of 40 hours per week. Over time, Congress expanded its coverage to occupations initially exempt. Congress increased the minimum wage over the years to keep pace with inflation, but between 1981 and 1989 the minimum wage remained at $3.35 per hour while inflation eroded away its purchasing power. In 1989 the minimum wage increased to $4.25 per hour, and in August 1996 Congress passed and President Clinton approved legislation phasing-in a $.90 increase in the minimum wage, putting it at $5.15 per hour in January 1998.

The minimum wage as a weapon for combating poverty draws mixed reviews. Critics observe that labor groups most affected by the federal minimum wage, such as teenagers, report high unemployment rates. Also, the federal minimum wage may discourage the employment of unskilled and inexperienced workers. A provision in the legislation lifting the minimum wage in 1989 allowed employers to pay teenagers a reduced minimum for a 90-day training period. When the minimum wage was $4.25 per hour, the training wage was $3.61 per hour, but employers failed to take advantage of the training wage on a significant scale and the program expired in 1993. So far the federal minimum wage law has both weathered criticism and continued to enjoy widespread support.

According to a strict theoretical understanding of the operation of the capitalist system, a minimum wage should be counterproductive. The difficulty with the minimum wage lies in its interference with a market mechanism for setting wages. Nevertheless, most workers support the minimum wage, because they regard the market mechanism as amoral, believing that it ignores questions of fairness. Workers find the view that they should have absolute faith in the judgment of the market too cynical for their hopes.

See also Trade Boards Act (England).

References Cartter, Allan M. F., and Ray Marshall. *Labor Economics: Wages, Employment, and Trade Unionism* (1967); Douglas, Paul H., Curtis N. Hitchcock, and Willard E. Atkins, *The Worker in Modern Economic Society* (1923); Hart, Vivien. *Bound by Our Constitution: Women, Workers, and the Min-* *imum Wage* (1994); Mankiw, Gregory. *Macroeconomics* (1992); Nordlund, Willis J. *The Quest for a Living Wage* (1997)

Ministry of International Trade and Industry (Japan)
See Asian Capitalism.

Mississippi Bubble (France)
According to Adam Smith, "The idea of the possibility of multiplying paper money to almost any extent was the real foundation of what is called the Mississippi scheme, the most extravagant project of banking and stock-jobbing that perhaps the world ever saw." The author of the Mississippi scheme was John Law, a Scottish financier, who felt that Scottish industry languished from a lack of money. He conceived the notion that a bank could issue paper money equal in value to all the land in a country. The Scottish

Street speculators during the collapse of the Mississippi Company in 1720, which caused an economic disaster in France known as the Mississippi Bubble

Parliament was not interested, but the new regent of France, Philippe d'Orleans, saw Law's theories as a way out of the bankrupt finances of France. Philippe authorized Law to establish the Banque Generale (1716), which was the first bank to issue legal tender paper money. It accepted deposits, paid interest, and made loans. The value of its paper money was defined in terms of a fixed weight of silver. In April 1717, taxes were made payable in the bank's paper money.

In 1717, Law secured a royal charter to launched the Mississippi Company. This was a trading company organized to exploit the Mississippi basin. Law sold 200,000 shares of this new company to the public. The price stood at 500 livres per share, but three-fourths of the payment could be made with government notes at face value. These government notes were then worth one-third of their face value. The shares found a ready market in holders of depreciating government notes eager for a piece of a profit-making enterprise. Law became bolder with success, and instructed his bank to buy the royal tobacco monopoly and all French companies devoted to foreign trade. These companies he combined with the Mississippi Company, for the complete monopolization of French foreign trade.

In 1718, Law's bank was reorganized as the Banque Royal, and the government made the bank's paper money legal tender. By 1720, the combination of trading companies, known as the Mississippi Company, was amalgamated with the bank. The Banque Royal bought up the national debt by exchanging it for shares in the Mississippi Company. Turning the national debt into shares of the Mississippi Company set an example that was soon copied by the South Sea Company in England. The prices of the shares in the Mississippi Company rose to fantastic heights, on a wave of speculative frenzy. Law's bank continually increased the supply of paper money, much of which was used to bid up the shares in the Mississippi Company. When prices of commodities rose 100 percent, and wages 75 percent, between 1716 and 1720, the public lost faith in the value of paper money.

In the meantime, things were not going well for the Mississippi Company. There were no precious metals to be found, and no attraction could induce families to emigrate to the Mississippi basin. Profits fell far short of expectations.

In 1719, the price of the stock peaked, and the downward spiral began. Those who knew sold their stock at the peak, and redeemed their bank paper money in gold. As the sell-off gained momentum, Law's bank issued paper money to buy the shares of stock. Holders of paper money besieged the bank, demanding silver or gold, and several people were killed in the confusion.

The Mississippi Bubble left a deep distrust of paper money and big banks in the mind of the French people. Nearly a century elapsed before France was willing to try paper money again. Learning the pitfalls of paper money has been a slow process in modern capitalist countries. Angola, Argentina, and Bolivia rank among the countries that have experienced hyperinflation in the post–World War II era.

See also South Sea Bubble.

References Durant, Will, and Ariel Durant. *The Age of Voltaire* (1965); Minton, Robert. *John Law: The Father of Paper Money* (1975); Schumpeter, Joseph. *Business Cycles*, Vol. 1 (1939); Smith, Adam. *Inquiry into the Nature and Causes of the Wealth of Nations* (1776); Spiegel, Henry W. *The Growth of Economic Thought* (1971).

Mitterrand's Capitalist Revival (France)

A member of the French Socialist Party, Francois Mitterrand, came to power in France in 1981, with a coalition of socialist and communist voters, presumably on a mandate to nudge France closer to socialism. Instead, he presided over a revival of capitalism, leaving the socialist and communist parties weakened and disoriented.

Mitterrand's predecessor, Valery Giscard D'Estaing, put France through the rigors of an austere monetary and fiscal policy to combat inflation. Mitterrand ran for election promising faster growth and full employment. During the first two years of Mitterrand's presidency, the socialists made some headway, enacting socialist policies, shortening the work week, adding worker holidays, boosting the minimum wage and welfare benefits, and imposing a wealth tax. The banking system and five big industrial groups were nationalized.

Mitterrand's policies caused higher inflation and a depreciating franc, without compensating improvement in unemployment. In March 1983, a monetary crisis brought Mitterrand's socialist agenda to an end. The Bank of France ran out of reserves, and Mitterrand chose to abandon socialist policies, in order to maintain the standing of France in the European Community. After the crisis of 1983, Mitterrand mostly left running the French economy to government ministers, some of whom were right wingers.

Mitterrand's government imposed anti-inflation policies, which were necessary to keep France in the European Monetary Union. Perhaps Mitterrand's greatest bow to capitalism was acquiescence in the privatization of nationalized industries. The French government ran up huge budget deficits during the 1980s, and was in no position to inject much-needed capital into state-owned enterprises. To acquire additional capital, the government allowed state-owned enterprises to sell stock in the private sector. In some cases, the government sold off shares in state-owned companies to raise revenue for itself. The government's stated policy sought to maintain 51-percent ownership in state-owned enterprises.

The capitalist economic system experienced a resurgence during the 1980s. The United States, United Kingdom, France, and Spain saw conservative governments come to power that were intent on strengthening capitalist forces in their respective economies. In addition, strongholds of socialism and communism crumbled under the pressure of the economic difficulties of the 1980s. The capitalist revival in France is unique, in that Francois Mitterrand, who won election to enact a socialist program, abandoned socialism in the face of economic realities, and watched over a return to a procapitalist economic program. He was elected to a second term of seven years as president in 1988, and continued a leadership spiced with left-wing rhetoric, while France moved away from socialism.

See also Felipe Gonzalez and Spain's Capitalist Revolution, Thatcherism.

References Saseen, Jane. "Farewell to Never Never Land." *International Management* (1991); Singer, Daniel. *Is Socialism Doomed: The Meaning of Mitterrand* (1988).

Mogul Steamship Case (England)

In 1891, the House of Lords rendered a decision in the *Mogul Steamship* case that significantly undermined the ancient common law doctrines prohibiting restraints of trade. After this decision, English courts increasingly turned a blind eye to monopolistic trade practices, until the post–World War II era.

The last quarter of the nineteenth century saw the ocean freight rates enter a phase of falling prices. The British liner companies, operators of ocean liners, developed the conference system to shore up prices and share markets. Shipping lines serving particular routes and regions of the world held regular conferences to formulate agreements on rates. Customers were bound to remain loyal to these companies by a plan of deferred rebates that could be granted or withheld.

In 1888, the Mogul Steamship Company brought suit against a group of British liner companies, alleging that these companies had conspired to monopolize trade between China and Europe. This group of companies had just renewed an agreement among themselves to grant a 5-percent rebate to shippers who used their ships exclusively. The clash between the Mogul Steamship Company and the conference of companies began in May 1885, when two Mogul ships sailed to Hankow to load cargo for a return voyage. Mogul dispatched these two ships, independent of the conference. On receiving word of Mogul's action, the conference dispatched two of its own vessels to Hankow and slashed its freight rates below cost. Mogul only secured cargo at a similar low rate. In the suit filed against the conference companies, Mogul asked for civil damages, and for an injunction against the conspiracy to exclude Mogul from trade with the Far East. The court dismissed Mogul Steamship Company's plea, and the decision was upheld at every stage of the appeal process. One of the appeals court judges, who sided in favor of the defendants in the case, reasoned as follows:

> The offering of reduced rates by the defendants in the present case is said to have been "unfair." This seems to assume that, apart from fraud, intimidation, molestation, or obstruction, of some other personal right in rem or in personam, there is some natural standard of "fairness" or "reasonable" (to be determined by the internal consciousness of judges and juries) beyond which competition ought not to go. There seems to me to be no authority, and I think, with submission, that there is no sufficient reason for a such a proposition. It would impose a novel fetter on trade.

Governments in capitalistic countries began to act against monopolistic practices, as the science of economics delineated in further detail its effects on economic efficiency. The United States was the first to ban monopolistic practices with the Sherman Antitrust Act of 1890. European governments tolerated monopolistic collusion until the end of World War II. In 1948, Parliament passed the Monopolies and Restrictive Practices Act. Parliament took more forceful action with the passage of the Restrictive Trade Practices Act of 1956.

The trend toward economic concentration and monopolistic collusion was evident in all capitalistic countries in the later portion of the nineteenth century. The trend was strongest in Germany, and Russia followed in Germany's steps. Lenin saw Russian capitalism evolving into a form of state monopoly capitalism, whose logical sequel was socialism.

See also Restrictive Trade Practices Act of 1956, Sherman Antitrust Act of 1890.

References Court, H. B. *British Economic History, 1870–1914* (1965); Macrosty, Henry. *The Trust Movement in British Industry* (1968).

Molestation of Workmen Act of 1859 (England)

This important contribution to British trade union law legalized peaceful picketing and reinforced the workers' right to organize. This was the first important piece of trade union legislation after Parliament repealed the laws relating to the combination of workers in 1825. Section 1 of the act read as follows:

> That no workman or other person, whether actually in employment or not, shall, by reason merely of his entering into an agreement with any workman or workmen, or other person or persons, for the purpose of fixing or endeavoring to fix the rate of wages or remuneration at which they or any of them shall work, or by reason merely of his endeavoring peaceably, and in a reasonable manner, and without threat or intimidation, direct or indirect, to persuade others to cease or abstain from work in order to obtain the rate of wages or the altered hours of labor so fixed or agreed upon or to be agreed upon, shall be deemed or taken to be guilty of "molestation" or "obstruction," within the meaning of the said Act, and shall not therefore be subject or liable to any prosecution or indictment for conspiracy. Provided always, that nothing herein contained shall au-

thorize any workman to break or depart from any contract or authorize any workman to break or depart from an contract or authorize any attempt to induce any workman to break or depart from any contract.

Trade unions were not to savor this victory for long. The Criminal Law Amendment Act of 1871 brought back sanctions against picketing, and, in 1875, Parliament adopted the Conspiracy and Protection of Property Act, which legalized peaceful picketing. This act enabled workers to picket for the purpose of communicating and exchanging information, but prohibited peaceful persuasion directed to workers crossing picket lines. Subjecting workers crossing picket lines to peaceful persuasion remained illegal until the Trade Disputes Act of 1906 protected this right. The Trade Disputes and Trade Unions Act of 1927 almost turned back the clock on picketing to pre-1859. In 1946, Parliament repealed the act of 1927.

In the eyes of employers, who valued the sanctity of private property, the practice of picketing seemed particularly unfair. On picket lines, striking workers were not only refusing to work, but were trying to prevent employers from hiring other workers. On the other hand, striking workers felt a strong sense of betrayal toward workers crossing picket lines, and demanded an opportunity to apply social pressure. The issue was pregnant with symbolic value, aside from the effectiveness of the tactic from the unions' perspective.

See also Trade Disputes Act of 1906, Trade Disputes and Trade Unions Act of 1927.

References Cole, G. D. H., and A. W. Filson, *British Working Class Movements: Selected Documents* (1965); Pelling, Henry. *A History of British Trade Unionism* (1963).

Monarchical Capitalism
See Portuguese Colonial Empire.

Money

Money serves four basic functions in an economic system. It acts as a medium of exchange, a store of value, a unit of account, and a standard of deferred payment. To serve as a medium of exchange, whatever acts as money must be universally acceptable in trade. Money has to be a durable good, somewhat immune to corrosion and natural deterioration, to meet the need for a wealth-preserving store of value, and maintain a stable value to fulfill the role of a unit of account and standard of deferred payment. Money acts as a unit of account when goods are priced in terms of money, and as a standard of deferred payment when long-term credit agreements are defined in terms of money.

Since ancient times, the most advanced countries have struck coined money from precious metals. Gold and silver were not only immune to corrosion, and aesthetically appealing, but may have been regarded as metals of the gods, and of unlimited demand as suitable contributions to religious temples to placate the gods. Transporting precious metals, however, was difficult and hazardous. It became simpler to keep gold stored at goldsmiths, with an account that could be transferred to other parties in payment of goods. These goldsmiths began to issue receipts for deposited gold, and these receipts evolved into paper money.

Goldsmiths evolved into banks that accepted gold and silver deposits, and issued paper money or bank notes redeemable in gold and silver. Early in the eighteenth century, Europe experienced its first disastrous experience with paper money, when John Law's bank in France issued paper money on an extravagant scale, exceeding the bank's resources for redeeming the paper money, and the money depreciated rapidly in a bout of inflation. Banks issuing their own paper money survived in the United States until the Civil War. These banks accepted gold and silver specie deposits, and issued paper money redeemable in specie.

During the nineteenth century, governments began establishing or acknowledging central banks that enjoyed a monopoly on the privilege to issue bank notes. An institution that monopolized the issuance of paper money could restrict its supply, helping to maintain its value. These central banks stood ready to redeem their bank notes in gold or silver specie with the same face value.

The twentieth century saw the widespread adoption of fiat money; that is, paper money not convertible into gold, silver, or another commodity. Governments used their power to adjudicate disputes to make government-sanctioned paper money legal tender for all debts. Central banks slowly learned to restrict the supply of paper money, maintaining its value and avoiding inflation, without the support of a gold or other commodity standard.

See also Bank of England, Central Banks and Free Banking, Gold Standard, Goldsmith Bankers, Greenbacks, Mississippi Bubble.

References Davies, Glyn. *A History of Money* (1994); McCallum, Bennet T. *Monetary Economics: Theory and Policy* (1989).

Monopoly

A monopoly exists when only one company produces and sells a product for which there are no close substitutes. A monopolist commands a certain degree of market power that can be exploited at the expense of its customers. It will charge a higher price than a group of competitive firms producing the same product would charge, and will restrict production below what a group of competitive companies would produce. The monopolist's formula for profits is to charge a higher price, and produce less output. A group of sellers can combine and monopolize an industry, acting cooperatively, as though they were a single seller, fixing prices at a higher level, and restricting output. This sort of behavior is illegal in most capitalist countries.

Monopolies may exist because government protection outlaws competition, for various reasons, or because the monopolist controls an industry in which the advantages of large-scale production prohibit smaller firms from effective competition, or because of the ownership of an essential raw material.

Governments in capitalist societies have generally become less tolerant of monopolies. During the sixteenth and seventeenth centuries, governments sold patents of monopoly to raise revenue. The development of the patent system limited these government-granted monopolies to inventors. In the United States, an inventor can patent a new invention for 17 years.

Governments also grant monopolies to public utilities, for example, electric and gas companies, telephone and cable service, or mass transit. These industries are called natural monopolies, because the cost advantages and convenience of having only one seller outweigh the disadvantages of monopoly. To enjoy the privileges of a monopoly, public utilities have to submit to government regulation of prices and quality of service.

De Beers Diamond Company of South Africa monopolizes the market for diamonds by virtue of ownership of 50 percent of the world's supply of diamonds. De Beers also controls the diamond output of other diamond mines, putting it in command of 80 percent of the world's diamonds. De Beers maintains the price of diamonds by restricting output.

Monopolies never last forever. Until the early 1980s, American Telephone and Telegraph (AT&T) had a government-protected monopoly over long-distance telephone service in the United States. AT&T's monopoly originated from the original Bell patents for the invention of the telephone, and was also a public utility monopoly, because it was not feasible to have more than one set of telephone wires crossing the country. Technological developments allowing the microwave transmission of telephone made competition feasible in the market for long-distance telephone calls. The U.S. Justice Department brought an antitrust suit against AT&T, and broke up its monopoly on long-distance telephone service.

See also American Telephone and Telegraph Monopoly, Patent System, Statute of Monopolies of 1624.

References Brock, Gerald W. "The Regulatory Change in Telecommunications: The Dissolution of AT&T." *Regulatory Reform: What Actually Happened* (1986); McConnell, Campbell R., and Stanley L. Brue. *Economics* (1993); Solo, Robert A. *The Political Authority and the Market System* (1974).

Morgan, John Pierpont (1837–1913)

John Pierpont Morgan Sr. was the most distinguished member of an American banking dynasty of the nineteenth and twentieth century. As world financiers, the Morgans rivaled the great European banking dynasties of Rothschild, Baring, and Hope.

The Morgans, like the Rothschilds, were private international investment bankers. These banks were private partnerships, and not government-chartered corporations subject to banking regulations. They held deposits for only a few large business clients, and handled the financial transactions associated with international trade and the settlement of international debts. They marketed issues of government bonds and corporate stock. Governments floating bond issues, and corporations floating stock issues, sought private investment bankers to buy the issues and place the issues with other investors.

John Pierpont Morgan's father, Junius S. Morgan, was an American citizen who found success as an investment banker in London. He began as a junior partner in George Peabody and Company, in 1854. Much of the partnership's business was selling American railroad corporation stocks to British investors. The partnership also bought and sold stocks and bonds for American clients. In 1864, Peabody withdrew from the partnership, and the firm became J. S. Morgan and Company. The firm rose in wealth and influence. It handled a bond issue for the French government during the Franco-

Prussian War, after more established institutions, such as Rothchilds, shrank from the task.

John Pierpont Morgan started his first firm, J. P. Morgan and Company, in New York, in 1861, with himself as the sole owner. His father's contacts sent him business, and the Civil War helped speed things along. In 1871, J. P. Morgan became a partner in the firm of Drexel, Morgan, and Company. The firm had partnerships in New York, Philadelphia, London, and Paris. The firm arranged most of the financing for the U.S. government. It also arranged loans for foreign governments, and was heavily involved in railroad securities.

In 1890, Junius S. Morgan died, and J. P. Morgan succeed his father as head of the London partnership. In 1893, Drexel died, which left Morgan as the senior partner. In 1895, the firm became J. P. Morgan and Company.

In the two decades before World War I, J. P. Morgan became one of the most powerful financiers in the world. His firm arranged financing for governments and railroads around the globe. He cooperated with the State Department, and refused foreign loans that raised objections from the U.S. or British governments.

Morgan used his power to consolidate railroads and manufacturing firms. One of his greatest accomplishments was the consolidation of several steel firms into United States Steel, which then became the largest corporation in the world. Morgan wielded vast power over railroad and industrial corporations. As a condition for securing investment credit, Morgan placed his associates on boards of directors, ostensibly to protect investors' interests. The result was a system of interlocking directorates that placed enormous economic power in the hands of Morgan. These interlocking directorates stifled competition.

By the eve of World War I, J. P. Morgan had become a symbol of the money trust. In the eyes of the public, the money trust ran the economy for the benefit of the bankers. When a business fails because of competition, banks are left holding defaulted loans. When bankers have too much power, they protect their investments by destroying competition among their clients. The public had had enough, and, in 1912, a congressional committee conducted hearings on the power that bankers like J. P. Morgan held over their clients. Morgan himself testified before the committee, and tried to dispel the country's fear of Wall Street domination. His testimony aroused further controversy. Apparently to help revive his spirits, he took a transatlantic voyage. He died in Rome on 31 March 1913.

J. P. Morgan was an expression of the trend toward finance capitalism evident in capitalist countries toward the end of the nineteenth century. This trend led to fears that the world was in the grip of a great international conspiracy of bankers. Walter Page, ambassador to Great Britain under President Wilson, was referring to J. P. Morgan when he said, "A revision of the currency and banking laws, if a wise revision be made, will prevent any other such career, even if another such strong personality were to arise. The possession of such great power—or the possibility of its possession—does not fit into the American scheme of life or business." The Federal Reserve Act of 1913, and subsequent antitrust and banking legislation, render another J. P. Morgan unlikely.

See also Finance Capitalism, Rothschild Banking Family.

References Carosso, Vincent P. *The Morgans: Private International Bankers, 1854–1913* (1987); Wechsberg, Joseph. *The Merchant Bankers* (1966).

Multinational Corporations

Multinational corporations operate production and marketing facilities on a global scale, forming strategies that transcend the boundaries of national governments. They are controlled by multinational management and are financed by multinational stockholders. Corporations involved in international trade have been around as long as corporations themselves. Early corpora-

tions were dependent on home governments for special charters. Their loyalty belonged to the country of origin, with whom they remained identified. In the modern multinational corporation, the country of origin only houses the corporate nerve center for a global business network, whose economic power makes it an influential constituent of many national governments. Multinational corporations are often oligopolistic participants in the markets they serve.

The mercantile trading companies of the seventeenth and eighteenth centuries pioneered the development of multinational corporations. These firms often employed their own military forces to subjugate countries who were trading partners. The Industrial Revolution gave rise to even bigger corporations that needed to exploit the world's resources of minerals, oil, and ore deposits. Around the turn of the century, U.S. multinational corporations made themselves known in Latin America. The United Fruit Company propped up governments in Central America with the help of the U.S. government. In 1957, the United Fruit Company owned 147,770 acres in Cuba.

In 1918, Congress passed the Webb-Pomerene Act, which exempted from antitrust laws American firms joining together for export. Multinational corporations grew in the 1920s, but depression and war disrupted the growth of the multinational corporations. The post–World War II era saw a marked growth in multinational enterprises. For the United States, the book value of foreign investments, mostly by domestically based multinational corporations, more than doubled in the 1960s. Of the 50 largest industrial corporations in the world in 1974, 24 were headquartered in the United States, 20 in Europe, and the remainder in Japan, Brazil, and Iran. Exxon was the largest of these multinational corporations, with a total of $42.1 billion in sales, an amount that is more than the gross national product of Belgium, Denmark, and most South American countries. IBM, with sales totaling $13 billion, ranked thirteenth in size, comparable to the gross national product of Austria. As industrial corporations have spread across the globe, the banks have followed their clientele. Big banks, such as Chase-Manhattan, have formed consortia with banks from other countries to make international loans. Industries well represented in a list of multinational firms include automobiles, machinery, tools, chemicals, oil, drugs, electrical equipment, electronics, and high technology.

Concern about the emergence and implications of multinational corporations grew in the post-World War II era. Multinational corporations can shop around for countries with favorable environmental and labor laws, putting workers in the developed countries at a disadvantage. Also, these corporations are suspected of meddling in the political affairs of countries where they have investments. For example, the U.S.-based company, ITT, helped to overthrow the democratically elected president of Chile in 1973. A military dictatorship replaced the democratically elected government.

Growth of foreign trade and reduction of trade barriers have kept the multinational corporations in the spotlight. Revelations of U.S. multinational corporations paying bribes to officials of foreign governments led to the passage of the Foreign Corrupt Practices Act in 1977. A controversial section of this act banned the payment of bribes, or giving "anything of value" to foreign officials to influence a government decision. Multinational corporations complained that payments to government officials was a necessary part of conducting business in some countries, and that the act put U.S. companies at a disadvantage. The act was revised in 1988 to allow certain types of payments, giving corporations more flexibility in dealing with foreign governments.

Not all multinational businesses are gigantic corporations. As the growth in foreign trade has drawn in many smaller businesses, business scholars have adopted the term "multinational enterprise," signifying that proprietorships and partnerships, in addition to corporations, are engaged in multinational business. Each year, about 4,000 to 5,000 businesses join the ranks of new multinational enterprises, or MNEs. Most of these new MNEs are smaller companies that arouse less concern in host countries.

The government regulation of MNEs will remain an issue in capitalist economies, because the power of the largest MNEs rivals the power of many smaller governments. Nevertheless, the MNEs are key players in the globalization of business, forcing home countries and host countries to find ways of accommodating their needs.

See also Conglomerates, Corporation.

References Aliber, Robert Z. *The Multinational Paradigm* (1993); Clegg, Jeremy. *Multinational Enterprise and World Competition* (1987); Daniels, John D., and Lee H. Radebaugh. *International Business* (1998).

National Association of Manufacturers (United States)

The National Association of Manufacturers (NAM) has become a powerful lobbying organization for business interests in the United States. Something of the spirit of the organization appears in its 1908 constitution. Section 1 of article II reads:

> The general objects and purposes for which the said corporation is formed are, the promotion of the industrial interest of the United States, the fostering of domestic and foreign commerce of the United States, the betterment of the relations between employer and employee, the protection of the individual liberty and rights of employer and employee, the education of the public in the principles of individual liberty and ownership of property, the support of legislation in furtherance of those principles and opposition to legislation in derogation thereof.

The stated objectives in the constitution do not quite do justice to the organization's ardent opposition to the growth of union power in the United States.

Credit for first proposing a national organization of manufacturers belongs to Thomas H. Martin, the editor of a southern industrial journal, the *Dixie Manufacturer* of Atlanta. In 1894, the editorials in Martin's journal broached the idea of a national organization. Martin faded from the picture rather quickly, and Thomas P. Egan presided over the first national meeting of manufacturers in Cincinnati in 1895. The new organization elected Thomas Dolan from Philadelphia as its first president.

The early years of the association reveal little of the passionate hostility to organized labor that marked its later history. From 1895 to 1902, tariff reform and promotion of foreign trade absorbed the association's interest. One of the successes of the association during this early phase was persuading the federal government to establish the cabinet-level Department of Commerce.

In 1902, the secretary of the NAM became a full-time Washington, D.C. lobbyist while Congress was in session, appearing before congressional committees, and arguing for the causes of the association.

Between 1903 and 1913, the NAM set to work to thwart the lobbying efforts of the American Federation of Labor, which was seeking legislation to exempt unions from antitrust laws, and limit the power of federal courts to issue injunctions against strike actions. Early in the Wilson administration, when legislation favoring unions was enacted, the NAM came under sharp criticism for its corrupt lobbying tactics, including allegations of a $200,000 slush fund for influencing legislators.

In the 1920s, the NAM commanded substantial power as a lobbying organization. In the 1930s, the association shared in the overall decline in the prestige of business leaders, but its membership swelled as the business community looked for organized leadership to oppose the New Deal. It stood firmly against the Wagner Act, corporate taxes, deficit spending, and adding justices to the Supreme Court. During the post-World War II era, the NAM appeared a bit reactionary in its refusal to accept the welfare state, which many saw as the wave of the future.

In the 1980s, the association found a friendlier environment in Washington, where it remains a powerful and influential voice of business interests. Aside from promoting individual free enterprise, the association has also worked to support copyrights and patent rights.

Like all lobbying organizations, the NAM has at times lost objectivity in its effort to promote the interest of its members. It remains, however, remarkably consistent in promoting the ideas of laissez-faire capitalism laid down by Adam Smith.

References Hrebenar, Ronald, and Ruth K. Scott. *Interest Group Politics in America* (1990); Steigerwalt, Albert K. *The National Association of Manufacturers, 1895–1914* (1964).

National Labor Relations Act (United States)

The National Labor Relations Act (1935), also known as the Wagner Act, is a landmark piece of labor legislation in the United States. The act protected the right of workers to organize into unions, and to bargain collectively with employers.

The philosophy of the Wagner Act assumed that employers must share the blame for strikes and business recessions by refusing to bargain collectively. The act specified several unfair labor practices committed by employers, including an employer's refusal to bargain collectively with a union representing a majority of their employees, employer interference with the workers' right to organize, and formation of company-dominated unions. The U.S. Supreme Court upheld the constitutionality of the Wagner Act in 1937, citing the federal government's right to regulate interstate commerce.

The Wagner Act created the National Labor Relations Board (NLRB). The NLRB consists of five members, appointed by the president, and a general council. The NLRB has the power to investigate unfair labor practices, and to order employers to cease and desist. Federal courts enforce these orders. The NLRB conducts secret-ballot elections that decide if workers at a company want to organize a union, or which union they want to represent them.

The act declares as unfair labor practices company efforts to "interfere with, restrain, or coerce employees in the exercise of the rights" to organize and join a union. Exactly what actions are covered by this portion of the act is open to interpretation, but a company clearly violates the act by terminating a worker for joining a union. The act also requires that companies bargain in good faith with unions certified to represent workers under provisions of the NLRB Act.

The act deserves much of the credit for the rapid growth of unions, particularly industrial unions, in the 1930s and 1940s. The representation election procedures may have encouraged rivalry between the AFL and the CIO. These two union organizations found it easier to raid each other's membership than to organize nonunion workers. These raids proved costly, however, and few workers wanted to change affiliation. These organizations eventually merged. The act may have reduced fragmentation in the labor market by requiring that a union representing the majority of workers in a bargaining unit represent all of the workers in that unit.

After World War II, a feeling grew that the Wagner Act had strengthened unions too much. The act was subsequently amended to balance the strength of unions with employers.

References Gregory, Charles O. *Labor and the Law* (1958, with 1961 supplement); Gross, James. *The Making of the National Labor Relations Board: A Study in Economics, Politics, and the Law* (1974).

National Recovery Administration (United States)

The National Recovery Administration (NRA) was the New Deal's experiment with government-sanctioned cartels to combat deflation, and to coordinate industry production with consumer demand. The policies of the NRA assumed that the cure for the Great Depression lay in the proper mixture of competition and coordination between firms of the same industry. President Franklin D. Roosevelt signed the enabling legislation, which was part of the National Industrial Recovery

Act, on 16 June 1933. The staff of the NRA grew from 400 in 1933 to 4,500 in 1935, its last year of operation.

The NRA facilitated the negotiation of industrial codes that regulated output, prices, and labor policies. The enabling legislation granted these codes a two-year exemption from antitrust laws. The head of the NRA, Hugh Johnson, an energetic leader prone to excesses in speech and behavior, first sought to draft industrial codes in critical industries such as steel, petroleum, automobile, textiles, lumber, and coal.

Success came first in the textile industry. The mill owners approved a plan limiting workers to 40 hours per week, and machines to 80 hours of weekly operation. By limiting production, the NRA sought to bolster prices, and the reduced work week helped make room for unemployed workers in the textile mills. The mill owners agreed to a minimum weekly wage of $11 for northern workers, and $10 for southern workers, and accepted the workers' right to organize and bargain collectively.

Other industries put up a bit more resistance than the textile industry. The petroleum industry, which had seen the price of petroleum drop from $2.28 to 10 cents per barrel, split between the big producers and the small independents. The NRA finally imposed a code providing for production quotas and price-fixing, but limited the government's role to making recommendations. The steel and iron and the automobile industries resisted the adoption of codes that strengthened the hand of the workers, or raised wages and reduced working hours.

An approved industry code usually began as a recommendation submitted by a trade association. The NRA then sponsored a conference of representatives from the Industrial Advisory Board, the Labor Advisory Board, and the Consumer Advisory Board. The Industrial Advisory Board outranked the other two boards, which left the finished code mostly an agreement between business owners and government officials. By the end of 1933, the NRA had codes in place for 541 industries, which practically finished the task of negotiating codes.

The NRA came under attack for promoting monopoly, and compliance became a difficult public relations problem. In Jersey City, a tailor ran afoul of the NRA for charging 35 cents for pressing a suit when the Tailor Industry Code called for 40 cents. This infraction of the code brought the tailor a penalty of 30 days imprisonment, coupled with a $100 fine. The tailor only served three days of the sentence. Critics of the NRA began to call it the No Recovery Act or the National Run-Around.

Roosevelt asked Congress to extend authorization for the NRA for two more years beyond the expiration date in June 1935. Before the two houses of Congress could come to an understanding, the U.S. Supreme Court struck down the National Industrial Recovery Act.

When he first approved the National Industrial Recovery Act, President Roosevelt observed that "history probably will record the National Industrial Recovery Act as the most important and far-reaching legislation ever enacted by the American Congress." The act might have merited some of Roosevelt's praise, if the NRA had proven successful. The apparent success of cartels in Germany made the purposes of the NRA credible in the best-trained eyes in business and government. Its failure meant that capitalism in the United States reverted to development along competitive lines.

See also Cartels, Great Depression.

References Biles, Roger. *A New Deal for the American People* (1991); Himmelberg, Robert F. *The Origins of the National Recovery Association: Business, Government, and the Trade Association Issue, 1921–1933* (1993).

National Stabilization Plan of 1959 (Spain)

Spain's National Stabilization Plan of 1959 marked a significant departure from policies of economic isolationism and heavy-handed government intervention. In June 1959, the government of Spain sent the plan as a memorandum to the International Monetary Fund and the Organization for European Economic Cooperation. The plan was enacted into law in July 1959, and enumerated various economic reforms that the government adopted to help Spain qualify for financial assistance from these organizations.

The preamble was revealing as much for what it left out as for what it included. It brushed aside the Francoist propaganda that put blame for Spain's economic difficulties at the feet of "evil foreign conspiracies," boycotts by foreign countries, and international Jewish plots aimed at "Christian Spain." In the words of the preamble, "The Spanish government feels that the time has arrived to formulate economic policy so as to direct the Spanish economy in conformity with the policies of the nations of the western world and to liberate it from public interventions, inherited from the past, which no longer support the needs of the present situation."

The National Stabilization Plan addressed four fundamental areas: the public sector, monetary policy, and flexibility of internal and external economic markets. The first two areas were addressed in light of Spain's high rate of inflation. The government proposed to put a ceiling on government spending, and to end the government's ability to borrow without limit from the Bank of Spain. Before the National Stabilization Plan, the government sold bonds that were immediately redeemable at the Bank of Spain.

The third area addressed in the plan made mention of the need to remove rigidities in the operation of internal markets, noting that "there will also be a tendency to eliminate the rigidities imposed by labour legislation, as well as those originating in restrictions of competition." Perhaps more important, the government committed itself to ending Spain's policy of economic isolationism and self-sufficiency, which the government had adopted in 1939 to promote internal industrialization. The government liberalized restrictions on imports and foreign investment in Spain, and developed an exchange rate regime consistent with the principles of the Bretton Woods System.

With the National Stabilization Plan, Spain began to move away from a closed, highly regulated economy, and toward an open, market-driven economy. The Spanish economy had stagnated during the 1940s and 1950s, discrediting economic policies that were based on rigid controls and aimed at economic self-sufficiency. In the 1960s, Spain experienced an unprecedented 7-percent rate of growth, exceeding anything Spain had experienced in the past. Imports grew as firms purchased modern equipment abroad, and foreign investment flowed in. Exports grew along with the European economy during the decade of the 1960s.

Like Italy, Spain lost its economic footing early in the evolution of European capitalism, by clinging to its feudal past, perhaps as a negative reaction to the excesses of the French Revolution and Napoleon's invasion of Spain. In the eyes of the Spanish aristocracy, the rebellion against monarchy and religion during the French Revolution was the cause of bloodshed and wars. Because of the conservative influence of the landed aristocracy and the Church, the capitalist spirit was slow to develop in Spain. Since the National Stabilization Plan, Spain has cautiously gravitated toward the market-driven model of capitalism that is now spreading throughout the world.

References Lieberman, Sima. *Growth and Crisis in the Spanish Economy, 1940–1993* (1995); Wright, Alison. *The Spanish Economy, 1959–1976* (1977).

Nationalization

In a process of nationalization, the government secures ownership or controlling interest of privately owned industries. Modern socialist economies were formed out of a program of widespread nationalization of land, mines, and basic industries. Widespread nationalization usually followed political revolutions in countries without deeply rooted capitalist institutions. In the mid-twentieth century, however, the trend toward nationalization engulfed Great Britain, the very birthplace of laissez-faire capitalism. Perhaps the greatest challenge capitalism faced in the twentieth century lay in the trend toward nationalization in advanced capitalist countries.

In 1933, Italy, in the clutches of an economic crisis propagated by a worldwide depression, nationalized about one-fourth of the total financial and industrial assets of the country. The nationalization plan extended to major commercial banks, communications, major airlines, shipping lines, iron and steel industries, and engineering and shipbuilding plants. The Italian government established a holding company, the Institute of Industrial Reconstruction, to disentangle the close relationship between banking and industry, and to acquire the assets of industry. At first, nationalization took the form of assuming the industrial securities portfolios of the three largest commercial banks, including the majority of the stock of these banks. Private stockholders continued to own interest in the nationalized companies, and these companies retained the names of their private sector predecessors.

The Italian government implemented its program of nationalization without public discussion, and out of fear that the economic crisis would significantly damage the public credibility of the government. In France, nationalization wore the aspect of a popular movement. At the end of World War II, politicians, scholars, and propagandists saw the nationalization of industry as a means of reforming French political and economic life. French nationalization may have been a partial response to the Nazi policy of nurturing economic concentration. France nationalized many of the same industries as the Italians, including the commercial banks, but France also nationalized the coal industry, which was mostly absent in Italy, and public utilities. In the case of Renault motor works, the French government established a profit-sharing arrangement with the workers that split profits evenly between the government and the workers.

Immediately after World War II, the British Labor Party won an election on a platform of nationalization. Acting on this expression of public support, between 1946 and 1951, Parliament passed eight measures of nationalization. The Bank of England was the first target, becoming nationalized in March 1946. The British acted a bit more thoughtfully than the French and Italians, and only reached a decision to nationalize the pivotal iron and steel industry in February 1951.

France and Britain sold long-term bonds at market interest rates to compensate the stockholders of the nationalized industries. The Italian government bought the nationalized industries at 1933 prices, but a subsequent round of violent inflation wiped out the government's debt.

While governments continued to experiment with institutional machinery to improve the operation of nationalized industries, the stagflation of the 1970s damaged the public enterprises' reputation for productivity. Historically, charges of inefficiency have more often than not haunted public enterprises. On coming to power in the late 1970s, the British Conservative Party led Britain on a course of denationalization, or privatization. With the economic failure of the Soviet-bloc countries in the 1980s, the trend favoring privatization became worldwide in scope, and the world saw a rebirth of capitalism closer to the U.S. model.

See also Expropriation, Privatization, Welfare State.

References Einaudi, Mario, Maurice Bye, and Ernesto Rossi. *Nationalization in France and Italy* (1955); Tivey, Leonard, ed. *The Nationalized Industries since 1960: A Book of Readings* (1973).

Navigation Acts (England)

Adam Smith stated, in *An Inquiry into the Nature and Causes of the Wealth of Nations*, "As defence...is of much more importance than opulence, the Act of Navigation is, perhaps, the wisest of all the commercial regulations of England." That is high praise from one of history's most forceful proponents of free trade. Smith cited the shipping industry as an example of an industry that merits protection from free trade for reasons of national defense. Smith favored departures from free trade to protect industries that are either essential for national defense, or in an infant stage of development.

Dutch shipping carried the bulk of world trade in goods in the seventeenth century. The linkages of the shipping industry with other economic sectors made it a strategic industry. In addition to the freight revenue, it created a demand for shipbuilding, marine insurance, warehousing facilities, and other industries related to the storing and further processing of goods.

Parliament passed Navigation Acts in 1651, 1660, 1662, and 1663. Animosity toward the Dutch was running high in 1651; war broke out in 1652, and continued intermittently until 1674. Parliament intended to cripple the Dutch shipping and transshipment trade, and to bring the economic benefits of those activities to England. The acts provided that only English-owned ships, manned by a crew that was three-fourths British subjects, could carry goods in the coastal

Sailing ships used by the English during the eighteenth century are depicted in this undated engraving by Thomas Baston.

trade of Great Britain. Trade with British settlements and plantations fell under the same rule. Imports of an enumerated list of bulky goods had to be transported either in English ships, or in ships from the country of origin, defined the way English ships were defined. These imports from a specific country could not be carried in ships from a third country. Last, neither English ships nor ships from any other country could bring the enumerated list of bulky goods to English ports from any other country, except the country where the goods originated. This provision was to sidetrack points of reshipment. Violators of any provision of the act faced confiscation of ships and goods.

The Navigation Acts survived into the early nineteenth century. After 1783, Parliament amended the acts to ease restrictions on trade with the United States. The acts drew criticism from advocates of free trade. They were amended in 1822 to exempt goods that were imported into England to be re-exported later to another country. This provision aided England's entrepot trade. The distinction between goods produced in a specific country, as opposed to being merely imported from that country, was also dropped in 1822. Other countries began to ask for exemptions. Despite the weight carried by Adam Smith's defense of the Navigation Acts, in 1849, Parliament repealed the acts, with the exception of the provision regarding coastal trade.

The Navigation Acts fit the mercantilist policy of government regulation. They probably could have been defended on the basis of the infant industry argument. The acts deserve some credit for paving the way for English control of the seas in the nineteenth century.

See also Navigation Acts (France).

References Daunton, Martin. *Progress and Poverty: An Economic and Social History of Britain, 1700–1850* (1995); Harper, Lawrence A. *The English Navigation Laws: A Seventeenth Century Experiment in Social Engineering* (1964).

Navigation Acts (France)

European governments enacted navigation acts that gave a virtual monopoly to domestic shipping over foreign shipping in the conduct of foreign trade. On 21 September 1793, the revolutionary government of France enacted the first French navigation act, patterned after the English Navigation Act. In *An Inquiry into the Nature and Causes of the Wealth of Nation*, Adam Smith, referring to the English Navigation Act, said, "It is not impossible, therefore that some of the regulations of this famous act may have proceeded from national animosity. They are as wise, however, as if they were all been dictated by the most deliberate wisdom." For reasons of national defense, Smith exempted navigation acts from his usual harsh judgments against trade restrictions.

If animosity toward the Dutch inspired the English Navigation Act, animosity toward the English motivated the French to enact their own navigation act. England and France were at war, and the French Navigation Act helped satisfy the French shipping industry. Otherwise, that industry would have suffered harm by the high tariffs that became French policy during and after the Revolution. When the act became law, French-owned ships accounted for only 3,763 of the 16,255 ships that carried French sea commerce, and British ships carried two-fifths of French sea trade. When England enacted its Navigation Act, Dutch ships carried one-half of England's sea commerce. By 1791, only one-fourteenth of England's sea trade was in the hands of foreigners.

The French Navigation Act of 1793 required that all French sea commerce travel in French ships. In the case of imports, an exception was made for the foreign ships of the country where the goods originated. The foreign ships that met this exception still had to pay a surtax. This act held out the prospect of a thriving merchant marine and shipbuilding industry. It encouraged the domestic consumption of French-produced goods over imports. The Convention saw itself as removing the linchpin of English prosperity. The act was suspended for a time during the Revolution, but it became the basis for regulating French shipping from 1814 to 1861.

In April 1816, the French government relaxed the restrictions by enabling foreign ships to import goods into France from any country. The government, however, levied a special tax on non-European goods imported into France from other European countries. This tax encouraged the importation of goods directly to France. The act provided that coastal trade and trade with French colonies travel in French ships exclusively.

From 1793 to 1845, ships of French registry had to be constructed in France, and owned entirely by Frenchmen. After 1845, the government broadened the ownership provision to one-half or more ownership by Frenchmen.

The government of the Second Empire, under Napoleon III, began liberalizing trade restrictions. The Anglo-French Commercial Treaty of 1860 abolished the requirement that only ships built in France could fly the French flag. By paying a special levy, ships built in England could be nationalized French. By 1866, foreign-built ships could become French by paying relatively insignificant sums. By 1869, all the privileges of protection granted to the French merchant marine and shipbuilding industries fell beneath the brief laissez-faire tide that arose under Napoleon III's government. The French government returned to a policy of protectionist trade restrictions, but not for the shipping industry.

The French Navigation Acts reflected the political power of capitalist interests in France, which had been suppressed under the ancien regime. They represented the types of restrictions that many countries put in place during phases of rapid industrial and capitalist development. Today, Japan most often has to defend protectionist trade policies, and also happens to be the newest member to the ranks of highly industrialized countries.

See also Anglo-French Commercial Treaty of 1860, Navigation Acts (England).

References Clough, Shepard B. France: *A History of National Economics* (1964); Dunham, Arthur L. *The Anglo-French Commercial Treaty of 1860 and the Progress of the Industrial Revolution in France* (1971).

New Imperialism: 1880–1914

Toward the end of the nineteenth century, the world saw a burst of European imperialistic fervor. European powers vied for colonial possessions, until most countries and areas of the nonwestern world belonged to the sphere of influence of one European power. Areas in Africa and the Far East fell under direct political control of various European countries.

The reasons for this fervor for territorial possessions may lie in the competition of the various European governments for power and prestige. At mid-nineteenth century, only Britain and Holland boasted of colonial empires. Britain's colonial possessions had helped that small country remain a formidable player in European politics. Many of these governments raised higher tariff walls in the latter nineteenth century, which may have forced them to look for colonies that could make their economies self-sufficient.

According to influential critics of capitalism, the surge of imperialism was born of the dynamic logic of the capitalism system in its mature stage of development. In the words of Lenin,

Imperialism is capitalism in that stage of development in which the dominance of monopolies and finance capital has established itself; in which the export of capital has acquired pronounced importance; in which the division of the world among the international trust has begun; in which the division of all the territories of the globe among the great capitalist powers has been completed.

The theory of imperialism that shaped the thinking of Lenin argues that the capitalist system is designed to favor the accumulation of capital. The skewed distribution of income puts many consumer goods beyond the reach of most households. The upper-income groups can afford to save a large proportion of their income, and their savings are borrowed to finance capital goods. As an economic system matures, profitable investment ventures dry up, at the same time that savings reach high levels. This may happen because there are no new lands or mineral deposits to develop. At this point, the economy is generating a surplus of savings (capital) that must look beyond national boundaries for opportunities to exploit. According to Lenin, the advanced capitalist countries export capital to underdeveloped countries and colonial possessions, where "profits are usually high, for capital is scarce, the price of land is relatively low, wages are low, raw materials are cheap."

Toward the end of the nineteenth century, several European countries reached the advanced stage in which capital is exported. Armed with surplus capital, these countries rushed to colonize the remainder of the world. Once the world had been partitioned among the major capitalist powers, these countries could only invest additional surplus capital by capturing colonial possessions of rival powers. One of the purposes of the two world wars in the twentieth century was to redistribute colonial possessions.

The theory that a surplus of capital can lead to imperialism is an important insight. Today, Japan generates a surplus of capital that it invests in foreign countries, particularly in the United States. The phenomenon of imperialism, however, predates the modern capitalist system. In the post-World War II era, communist countries also sought to dominate the economies of satellite countries. Imperialism is not unique to the capitalist system.

In mentioning the positive traits of capitalism, Karl Marx states that it "has conducted expeditions that put in the shade all former migrations of nations and cru-

sades." This productive energy might have been the driving force behind the new imperialism.

See also Finance Capitalism.

References Blaisdell, Donald C. *European Financial Control in the Ottoman Empire* (1966); Davis, Clarence B., and Kenneth E. Wilburn Jr., eds. *Railway Imperialism* (1991); Fieldhouse, D. K. *Economics and Empire: 1830–1914* (1973); Keay, John. *Empire's End: A History of the Far East from High Colonialism to Hong Kong* (1997)

New York Stock Exchange

The New York Stock Exchange is the largest, and one of the oldest, organized stock exchanges in the United States.

Trading in financial instruments began in New York after the American Revolution and the establishment of the new national government under the Constitution. The new national government refunded, with new 6-percent federal bonds, the state bonds issued during the Revolutionary War. These federal and state bonds, issued to finance internal improvements, became the speculative grist for the new financial mill developing under a tree in front of 68 Wall Street. In 1792, a group of 24 brokers specializing in financial instruments organized themselves, with minimum rates, and an agreement to favor each other. The following year, the market took up residence at the Tontine Coffee House, at the northwest corner of Wall Street and Williams. The trade in stocks and bonds grew rapidly. Brokers, seeing a need for a more formal organization, established the New York Stock and Exchange Board in 1817. This organization functioned as a private club with initiation fees. New admissions could be blackballed with three negative votes. Membership started with eight firms and 19 individual traders.

The term "board" came from the blackboard on which securities were listed (today, the New York Stock Exchange is sometimes referred to as the Big Board). There were no requirements for listing stock. At a set time, the names of stocks were called out and offers to buy or sell determined the price. In the 1830s, trades rose to 1,000 shares per day.

Time settlements encouraged speculation in the early stock market. Many contracts provided for payment six months to 12 months after a trade was made. This practice enabled brokers to operate with little capital of their own. The limit on time settlements was reduced to 60 days, in 1840. Settlement on the following day gradually became customary.

In 1837, Wall Street saw its first great panic. The economic difficulties started with disorganization in the banking system. Banks and railroad companies accounted for most of the stocks listed at that time, and government securities were still the mainstay of financial trading. The stock exchange in Philadelphia suffered a severe blow when the State of Pennsylvania suspended interest payments on state bonds, which Pennsylvania banks held. New York was able to maintain interest payments on its bonds. From that time, New York gained ground, and Philadelphia, its rival as a financial center, lost ground. In the 1840s, the development of the telegraph encouraged centralization in financial markets.

By the 1850s, the stocks of railroad companies dominated the listing on the New York Stock and Exchange Board. In 1857, another serious panic rocked the market. The Civil War made this panic short-lived, but it revealed a weakness in the financial system that showed up in future panics. Many country banks kept funds on deposit in New York. These deposits earned interest, and brought assurance that bills of the country banks would be accepted without discount. New York banks loaned these funds to speculators financing stock purchases. In 1857, the Ohio Life Insurance and Trust Company, a bank with a reputation for conservative banking, failed because its New York office had been investing in railroad stocks, whose prices had been falling. This event caused banks outside New York to withdraw their deposits out of fear of more bank failures. New York banks called in loans from speculators and the market crashed.

In 1863, the New York Stock and Exchange Board changed its name to the New York Stock Exchange. The ticker tape made its appearance in 1867, and the telephone in 1878. On 15 December 1886, more than 1 million shares changed hands in one day, for the first time.

The New York Stock Exchange was more restrictive in its membership than the London Stock Exchange, encouraging the growth of rival exchanges. In 1868, a restriction on membership of 1,060 members came with the provision that the memberships could be sold. Up to 1914, this number had only increased by 40. In 1870, seats were selling in the $4,000 to $4,500 range. By 1987, the price had risen to $1.1 million. At the turn of the century, the Consolidated Stock Exchange and the New York Curb Market were two important rivals. The Curb Market became the American Stock Exchange, which is today's other major national stock exchange.

In 1873, once again Wall Street was the scene of a major panic. As in 1857, trouble in railroad stock set the stage when railroad companies, finding their stock depressed, turned to bank financing. Defaults among the railroads crippled the banks, and the stock exchange closed for ten days. Banks were holding $60 million of stock as collateral when the exchange closed.

Panics buffeted the stock market again in 1884 and 1893. The panic of 1907, which began with a series of bank failures, was the first to lead to a government investigation. John Pierpont Morgan Jr. organized an effort to raise funds to stem the tide of the panic. By then, the public was suspicious of stock market manipulations, causing both the State of New York and Congress to investigate abuses in stock market trading. Morgan answered questions before a congressional committee. The committee made recommendations, but WW I began before anything could be done.

The stock crash of 1929 led to the first government regulation of stock exchanges. A congressional inquiry found evidence of manipulation of stock prices, which led to the passage of the Securities Exchange Act of 1934, prohibiting manipulation of stock prices. This act created the Securities and Exchange Commission that regulates stock exchanges today.

From the first organization in 1792, until 1975, minimum brokerage commission fees were set by the exchange. In 1975, the Securities and Exchange Commission forced the New York Stock Exchange, and other exchanges, to abandon this practice. Commission rates fell dramatically, and major brokerage firms went bankrupt. Discount brokers have been growing in number as deregulation and computers are changing the brokerage industry rapidly.

During the 1980s, computerized program trading became an important tool of stock market investors. Program trading makes use of computer programs that automatically trigger buy or sell orders, under certain market conditions. Stock index options—options to buy or sell a measure of a stock market index (for example, Standard and Poor's 100 index)—figured mostly in program-trading strategies. When the stock market suffered another headline-making crash on 19 October 1987, sending the Dow-Jones index tumbling 598.32 points, many observers pointed the finger of suspicion at program trading. In 1990, Congress enacted legislation that strengthened the hand of the Securities and Exchange Commission to control wide swings in stock prices and put restrictions on program trading,

The stock exchange is the ideal vantage point for observing the pulse beat in the capitalist economic system. Expectations about the future are registered instantaneously in the stock market. Prices on the New York Stock Exchange are probably the most widely followed economic statistics in the world.

See also Securities Exchange Act of 1934, Stock Market Crash of 1929.

References Dalton, John M. *How the Stock Market Works* (1993); Gordon, John Steele. *The Scarlet Woman of Wall Street* (1988); Thomas, Dana L. *The Plungers and the Peacocks* (1967).

New World
See Columbus, Christopher; Commercial Revolution; Dutch Capitalism; Financial Crisis of 1557; Price Revolution of Sixteenth- and Seventeenth-Century Europe; Spanish Colonial Empire.

Norris-LaGuardia Act of 1932 (United States)
The Norris-LaGuardia Act governs the role and use of federal courts in labor disputes. The act is shaped by the philosophy that the government has aided employer organizations by providing for incorporation and other forms of business organization, and, therefore, government interference in the workers' right to organize and bargain collectively raises questions of unfair partiality in public policy. That government interference often took the form of court-ordered injunctions against the activities of labor unions. A court issues an injunction to restrain a person from doing or not doing certain things in order to prevent damage to property. The American courts expanded the applicability of the injunction beyond the British practice, by interpreting the right to do business as a property right. Union activities such as picketing damaged the employer's right to do business.

The Norris-LaGuardia Act made life easier for the unions, by making it extremely difficult for employers to obtain a federal-court-ordered injunction against a union. The act also struck at yellow-dog contracts, by rendering them unenforceable in federal courts.

See also Yellow-Dog Contracts.

References Gould, William B. *A Primer on American Labor Law* (1986); Gregory, Charles O. *Labor and the Law* (1958, with 1961 supplement).

North American Free Trade Agreement

In 1993, the North American Free Trade Agreement (NAFTA) established a free-trade area embracing Canada, Mexico, and the United States. A free-trade area abolishes tariffs and quotas between member trading partners. It is a modest step in the process of economic integration. It lets members set their own tariffs on goods from outside the free-trade era, and does not give resources such as labor the right to migrate across country borders within the free-trade area.

The fundamental purpose of NAFTA lay in the progressive removal of all tariffs on North American goods traded between Canada, Mexico, and the United States. For most goods, tariff protection either ended with the enactment of NAFTA, or was scheduled for a gradual phasing out over five to ten years. Quotas and prohibitions on trade met with a similar treatment, either ending immediately, or subject to gradual elimination over a ten-year period. NAFTA defined North American goods in various ways. Automotive goods qualify under NAFTA, when the percentage of North American content meets a certain percentage standard, ranging from 60 to 62.5 percent.

NAFTA is the first free-trade area encompassing both industrial and nonindustrial countries. With a combined GDP of $6 trillion, and 360 million consumers, NAFTA rivals the European Community as one of the world's biggest consumer markets. The U.S. economy is clearly the dominant trading partner, generating an output ten times that of Canada, and 25 times that of Mexico. The average wage also varies substantially among the trading partners.

In addition to establishing a free-trade area, NAFTA lifted barriers on foreign investment from member countries, and also set up machinery for resolving disputes between investors and NAFTA countries.

At its inception, NAFTA came under sharp criticism in the United States, on several accounts. Critics feared that NAFTA would export jobs to Mexico; cause U.S. companies to relocate in Mexico; swamp the U.S. markets with Mexican goods, displacing domestic manufacturers; accelerate Mexican immigration; and give an advantage to Mexico, because of its lax environmental standards. So far, however, NAFTA has not led to an economic slowdown in the United States.

Agreements like NAFTA appear to strike a blow for free trade, letting the world capitalist economic system fully exploit the advantages of country specialization. Some economists worry about a trend toward rival trading blocs, such as NAFTA and the European Community. Although NAFTA represents a trend toward free trade, a gradual reduction of trade barriers worldwide is the ideal goal.

See also European Union, Zolleverein.

References Daniels, John D., and Lee H. Radebaugh. *International Business* (1998); Lustig, Nora, Barry B. Bosworth, and Robert Z. Lawrence, eds. *North American Free Trade* (1992).

Occupational Health and Safety Act of 1970 (United States)

The Occupational Health and Safety Act is one of the more important results of the wave of social regulation that began in the 1960s, which was not concerned with prices or quality of goods and services in specific industries, like earlier industrial regulation, but, instead, sought to protect the quality of life for the public at large. The purpose of the Occupational Health and Safety Act lay in the protection of workers against occupational injuries and illnesses. The act provided for the creation of the Occupational Health and Safety Administration (OSHA), which is a federal agency within the Department of Labor responsible for insuring that workplaces meet health and safety standards.

Evidence of concern about occupational diseases developed early in the history of capitalism. In 1473, Ulrich Ellenbog published a pamphlet referring to the "poisonous wicked fumes and smoke" that attend the goldsmith occupation. In 1556, Georgius Agricola published a treatise on diseases that afflict miners. In 1700, Bernardino Ramazzini, the grandfather of occupational medicine, published the first systematic treatment of occupational medicine.

Before the creation of OSHA, state agencies bore responsibility for enforcing health and safety standards in workplaces. President Johnson included an occupational health and safety bill in his 1968 legislative program, but his withdrawal from the presidential race, combined with only modest support from organized labor, left the bill stalled in Congress. In November 1968, a mine exploded in Farmington, West Virginia, killing 78 miners, and fueling support for stricter enforcement of mine safety laws. Coincidental with renewed concern for miner safety was a grassroots effort to raise awareness of the victims of black lung disease. By 1970, organized labor had put occupational health and safety at the top of its list of legislative priorities. Congress passed a bill the same year, and President Nixon, who had already vetoed one piece of labor legislation that year, approved the Occupational Health and Safety Act.

To meet its congressional mandate, OSHA sets health and safety standards for workplaces, inspects employer premises for violations, and levies fines and issues citations to violators. OSHA's regulations soon drew fire from businesses, who resented rules on such matters as the height of fire extinguishers from the floor. In 1978, OSHA rescinded many of its detailed regulations, and turned more of its attention to health hazards that cause fatal or near-fatal diseases, such as cancer.

During the 1970s, work-related accidents declined slightly. During the 1980s, the Reagan and Bush administrations cut OSHA's budget by one-third, which may have contributed to an increase in the number of workplace injuries, sparking debate of possible revisions to the Occupational Health and Safety Act. One proposal has been to provide for criminal penalties for violators. OSHA represents the kind of government regulation that finds little favor among strong adherents of laissez-faire capitalism. According to the theory of the labor market in the capitalist system, employers who offer workers the most favorable combination of wages and work-related risks will get the best workers, and be more competitive. Employers who offer workers a less-attractive combination of wages and work-related risks will lose the best workers, and stand a smaller chance of surviving. The problem with this theory was that workers often do not have all the information needed to make wise choices. Furthermore, the number of work-related injuries and fatalities was at a socially unacceptable level. "During World War II, while 292,000 U.S. servicemen were killed in battle, 300,000 U.S. workers were killed in industrial accidents." more lives were lost from industrial accidents in the United States than from military combat. Also, workplaces are often contaminated with chemicals, and other secret killers, that arouse little concern among uninformed workers. Government regulation was needed to improve employer performance in the area of occupational safety and health.

See also Environmental Protection Agency.

References Mendeloff, John. *Regulating Safety: An Economic and Political Analysis of Occupational Safety and Health Policy* (1979); Starling, Grover. *The Changing Environment of Business: A Managerial Approach to Business* (1984); Spiro, George W. *The Legal Environment of Business* (1993).

Oil Price Revolution

The 1970s saw the price of crude oil increase more than 1,000 percent, sending a wave of inflation reverberating throughout the world economy. Much of the increase was concentrated in two major price shocks. In 1972, the price of a barrel of oil stood at $2.50. In 1973–1974, the price of a barrel of oil quadrupled, and, in 1979–1980, the price doubled again, to finish the decade at $34 per barrel. In 1986, the price of oil fell by one-half, marking a clear end of the oil price revolution.

The two major oil price shocks were triggered by political crises in the Middle East. A fourth Arab–Israeli war in 1973 brought an oil embargo against the United States. The embargo prompted the Organization of Petroleum Exporting Countries (OPEC)—an international cartel of oil-exporting countries that controlled oil prices during the 1970s—to curtail production and inflate the price of oil. In 1979, the Iranian revolution stopped the flow of Iranian oil to the world oil market, touching off another round of oil price increases. In the 1980s, a worldwide recession threw OPEC into disarray, and the price of oil began to slide, crashing in 1986.

Many observers credit the oil revolution for the worldwide episode of stagflation during the 1970s. Stagflation denotes slow growth and rising inflation and unemployment. The rising price of oil increased the operating cost of capital equipment, increasing the cost of using labor-saving machinery and equipment, relative to the cost of labor itself. The high price of oil either stalled or reversed the process of substituting machinery and equipment for labor, virtually ending growth in output per worker. Governments around the world set in place anti-inflation policies that caused recessions and high unemployment. After the oil market crashed in 1986, inflation has remained surprisingly tame, and productivity has shown improvement.

The riddle of high inflation and high unemployment, combining symptoms of boom and recession at a point in time, created a crisis of skepticism in economic policy, and opened minds to new policies. Most of the prevailing economic orthodoxy was born of the Depression of the 1930s, when surplus production was the problem. In the 1970s, shortages replaced surpluses as the chief threat to the economic system, and the emphasis in economic policy changed from increasing demand to increasing supply. As supply-side economic policies displaced demand–management policies, capitalism experienced a revival in countries that had become socialist in all but name, including England and France.

See also Economic Recovery Act of 1981, Great Stagflation of 1970s, Mitterrand's Capitalist Revival, Thatcherism.

References Blinder, Alan S. *Economic Policy and the Great Stagflation* (1981); Schneider, Steven A. *The Oil Price Revolution* (1983).

Old Poor Laws of England

A series of Poor Laws, drawn up and enacted between 1536 and 1601, set English policy toward the poor until the nine-teenth century. The Poor Laws provided that every parish levy a tax to care for the unemployable poor, and to put the em-ployable to work in state-managed work-houses. The need to suppress growth of beggary and vagrancy occasioned the laws, as much as the acknowledgment of a state responsibility to keep its people above starvation. Every recipient of parish relief, excepting widows, orphans, the el-derly, and the sick, had to work. Among the penalties for those avoiding work was whipping or branding. As the workhouses began to resemble prisons, only the most destitute could be found on the rolls of public relief.

Gilbert's Act of 1792 permitted parishes to support the able-bodied poor without sending them to workhouses. Parish officers placed the able-bodied un-employed on farms, and supplemented their wages with public relief. This prac-tice evolved to the point that public relief became a subsidy to aid wages. The Speenhamland system extended this prac-tice by subsidizing wages up to a min-imum standard, based on the price of bread and the number dependents of the recipient. This system enabled farmers to employ surplus labor below market rates of wages. These are the features that dominated debate on the Poor Laws in the early nineteenth century.

The English economist Thomas Malthus, among others, criticized the Poor Laws as they had evolved in the late eighteenth century. To Malthus, the first obvious tendency of the laws was to

increase the population without in-creasing the food for its support. A poor man may marry with little or no prospect of being able to support a family without parish assistance. They may be said, therefore, to create the poor which they maintain; and as the provisions of the country must, in con-sequence of the increased population, be distributed to every man in smaller proportions, it is evident that the labor

of those who are not supported by parish assistance will purchase a smaller quantity of provisions than before, and consequently more of them must be driven to apply for assistance.

A harsher criticism came from the Se-lect Committee on Labourers' Wages of 1824, who concluded that "a surplus pop-ulation is encouraged; men who receive but a small pittance know that they have only to marry, and that pittance will be augmented in proportion to the number of their children."

Criticisms of the Poor Laws led to the enactment of the Poor Law Amendment Act of 1834. This amendment ended the practice of subsidizing wages. Once again, able-bodied recipients of public relief were placed in workhouses under condi-tions that made them worse off than the lowest class of independent laborers. The administration of public relief was taken out of the hands of local parishes. A board of guardians, elected by large-property owners, oversaw the administration of public relief. The administration of public relief became the responsibility of salaried workhouse masters and relief officers, rather than parish officials. A more imper-sonal and mechanical process replaced local discretion in granting public relief. Appeals from personal considerations were made to a central authority in London.

See also Poor Law Amendment Act of 1834.

References Blaug, Mark. *Economic History and the History of Economics* (1986); Daunton, Martin. *Progress and Poverty: An Economic and Social History of Britain 1700-1850* (1995).

Organization for European Economic Cooperation
See Marshall Plan.

Organization of Petroleum Exporting Countries (OPEC)
See Deregulation of the Oil Industry, Oil Price Revolution.

Panic of 1893
See Depression of the 1890s.

Paper Money
See Bank of England, Bank of Japan, Goldsmith Bankers, Hyperinflation in Post-World War I Germany.

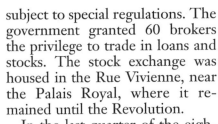

Paris Bourse
The Paris Bourse is the major stock exchange in France. The chronological dates for the beginning of the European bourses remain uncertain. In 1141, King Louis VII created the changeurs on the Pont du Change in Paris. This early market was a place to trade bills of exchange. In 1557, a Venetian ambassador to Paris, alluded, in a report to his government, to the Pont au Change, where business people met in the morning and afternoon. In 1572, dealers in securities were first required to obtain royal permission. In this early period, Lyon overshadowed Paris as a financial center. Until the eighteenth century, the Paris Bourse traded in bills of exchange and various forms of government bonds. Speculation in stocks of private companies made its appearance early in the eighteenth century. Only in the eighteenth century could France boast of a proper stock market.

The first speculative mania to seize Parisian speculators occurred between 1716 and 1720. John Law formed a company with the privilege to issue unlimited paper money, and to monopolize the development of the Mississippi basin. The banking side of the business supplied paper money to fuel the speculation in stock. As holders of the paper money began to demand redemption in gold, the speculative bubble collapsed. For a half century, the Paris stock market felt the weight of this unhappy debacle. In the aftermath, government showed more interest in the stock market. In 1724, the king decreed the establishment of an official exchange, which became a legal entity subject to special regulations. The government granted 60 brokers the privilege to trade in loans and stocks. The stock exchange was housed in the Rue Vivienne, near the Palais Royal, where it remained until the Revolution.

In the last quarter of the eighteenth century, gambling fever spread throughout French high society. Playing the lottery, horse racing, chess, and dominoes were ways of placing wagers. The gambling fever also infected the stock market with a frenzy for speculation. In 1785, Catherine the Great's ambassador to Paris wrote the following description of stock market speculation on the Paris Bourse:

> There has been introduced into the capital a type of deal or compromise as dangerous for the sellers as for the buyers, whereby one man promises to provide at some distant date effects he does not possess, and the other commits himself to paying for them with money he does not have, with the option of being able to demand delivery before the deadline, allowing for discounting.... Such undertakings occasion a series of insidious manoeuvres tending to have a temporary effect on the nature of prices of public bonds, giving some an exaggerated value, and using others in such a way that they are cried down.... The result is a disorderly kind of unscrupulous speculation, of which any wise businessman disapproves, that puts at risk the fortunes of those imprudent enough to dabble in it, diverts capital from more solid investment which would benefit national industry, excites cupidity in chasing after immoderate profits...and might compromise the reputation the Paris market so justly enjoys in the rest of Europe.

In 1807, Napoleon confirmed the rights of the traders, and ordered the construction of the Palais Brongiart, which has been the home of the stock exchange

Armed Parisians attend a meeting of the Commune in 1871, as depicted in Harper's Weekly.

since 1827. Over time, the Paris exchange rose to complete supremacy over other security markets in France, including the one at Lyon. William Parker, in a study of the Paris Bourse published in 1920, claimed a "money trust" manipulated the market.

Today, an exchange commission governs the Paris Bourse. The head of the commission is the governor of the Banque of France, and the minister of finance chooses the other members. Stockbrokers do not own a seat on the exchange, but are public officials appointed by the minister of finance. The Paris Bourse has remained an innovative stock market. In 1973, brokers were given permission to trade outside official business hours.

The growth of securities markets served a valuable service to the development of capitalism. Before the development of securities markets, the power of banking and financial magnates, such as the Fuggers, had achieved dangerous proportions. The lure of speculation significantly raises the amount of capital that a society can mobilize, and circumvents the powerful financial magnates.

See also Amsterdam Exchange, Antwerp Bourse, London Stock Exchange, Mississippi Bubble, New York Stock Exchange.

References Braudel, Fernand. *Civilization and Capitalism: 15th–18th Century*, Vol. 2 (1982); Ehrenberg, Richard. *Capital and Finance in the Age of the Renaissance* (1928).

Paris Commune of 1871

Socialist thinkers and writers came to view the Paris Commune of 1871 as the first dictatorship of the proletariat in history.

In December 1851, Napoleon III had secured the reins of power in a coup d'etat, less than three years after the Revolutions of 1848. He had been elected president in December 1848, by a wide margin, but the conservative elements dreaded the outcome of the election coming up in 1852. During his government, liberal republicans (nonsocialists) and republican socialists shared a common disapproval for the status quo. Both groups wanted a return to republican government. The liberal republican candidates to the National Assembly courted working-class support. The republican socialists strove to form a coalition of peasants and urban workers.

The Franco-Prussian War broke out in July 1870. Napoleon III remained in power until September 1870, when news reached Paris that he had been captured in the battle of Sedan. Republican socialist militants stormed the National Assembly and demanded that it proclaim a republic. The National Assembly obliged the militants by forming a provisional government of moderate republicans, and proclaiming a republic. The Prussians besieged Paris, but the new government, called the Government of National Defense, was more fearful of a militant republican socialist insurrection than of the Prussians. The Paris National Guard had a major working-class contingent. As the government met with further military reverses, and betrayed its eagerness for an armistice, it aroused heavy opposition among patriotic Parisian republicans. Radical republicans staged demonstrations to protest the government's policies. The government banned demonstrations, and announced that there would be no election until the siege was raised. An attempted insurrection at the end of October was defused by negotiation, but the government later broke an agreement to grant amnesty to the leaders.

The Government of National Defense signed an armistice on 28 January 1871, and scheduled a National Assembly election in February. This National Assembly was to negotiate the peace terms, and the election turned on the issue of war and peace. The royalists, favoring peace, won a majority of the seats. After negotiating the peace treaty, the new Assembly enacted several laws directed at the republican socialists and their working-class supporters in Paris. It abolished payments for service in the National Guard, made all overdue rents and debts payable in four months, with interest, and sentenced two working-class revolutionaries to death for involvement in the October uprising. Leaders in the Assembly talked of restoration of monarchy.

On 18 March, popular resistance blocked an effort of government troops to secure cannons held by the Parisian National Guard. Since many middle-class members of the National Guard had fled Paris, the working class now controlled that organization. The government troops had to withdraw from Paris. The National Guard officers held municipal elections on 26 March, and turned the city over to an elected government. The republican socialists carried the election and the new government became known as the Paris Commune. It lasted from 26 March to 28 May, when government troops from Versailles recaptured Paris after four days of bloody streetfighting and massacres. The government discontinued the National Guard units throughout France, because of the role these organizations had played in revolutionary uprisings.

The Paris Commune was the second time that the working class had bid for power in France. The episode became an inspiration to socialist revolutionaries for its living demonstration of a proletarian dictatorship. The Commune showed little hint of socialism, but it did give the working class a strong voice in government. It restored pay for service in the National Guard, prohibited night work in bakeries, assisted with debts for rents, and extended the time for payment of other debts. Employer fines on factory workers were abolished. Some government contracts were given to worker associations, and other labor organizations received assistance. Factories whose owners had left the city were turned into worker cooperatives. The Commune never sought to nationalize the banks, mines, or railroads.

The experience of the Paris Commune kept hope alive for a proletarian victory in the class struggle. As workers learned to exert their influence in democratic elec-tions based upon universal suffrage, they became reconciled to the capitalist system.

See also Uprising of the Lyon Silk Workers, Revolutions of 1848.

References Aminzade, Ronald. *Class, Politics, and Early Industrial Capitalism: A Study of Mid-Nineteenth Century Toulouse, France* (1981); Hicks, John, and Robert Tucker. *Revolution and Reaction: The Paris Commune, 1871* (1973).

Patent System

In 1859, Abraham Lincoln delivered a talk entitled "A Lecture on Discoveries and Inventions," outlining six great steps in the history of liberty. The last step on his list was the law of copyrights and patents. Such was the importance Lincoln attached to the patent system. A patent confers upon an inventor the exclusive privilege to make and market a new invention for a certain length of time. It gives the inventor the right to prevent others from making and marketing the same product, granting a monopoly privilege for a fixed duration, usually 14 to 20 years.

During the Italian Renaissance, the city-states of Florence and Venice granted patents to inventors. Venice adopted a statute governing patents. The practice of granting patents to inventors spread to Europe. The monarchies of Europe made grants of monopoly of any sort a royal prerogative, including monopolies on patented new inventions. A patent of monopoly was granted to the glass industry in France in 1551. In 1567, the English government granted a patent of monopoly for the glass industry in England.

England, more than any other European country, pioneered the development of the patent system. The Clerks Act of 1536 described the steps that an applicant for a patent had to follow. As many as ten government offices had authority in the request for a patent. Gratuities were expected at each step, and the system was vulnerable to industrial espionage. The Statute of Monopolies of 1636 banned monopolies that were purely creatures of royal prerogative, but it made an important exception for monopolies of patented inventions. According to section six of the 1636 statute, patents were permissible only for the "sole working and making of new manufacture." Abstract knowledge and philosophical principles were not entitled to patent protection. An invention that was corporeal, tangible, vendible, and practical met the criteria. The Statute of Monopolies permitted patents for a term of 14 years. The patent system was widely utilized in England during the Industrial Revolution.

Early in the nineteenth century, many European countries took patents out of the hands of the royal prerogative and enacted formal patent statutes. The French revolutionary government in 1791 adopted a patent law based on the argument that individuals have a natural right to own the property of their own ideas. Patent laws were adopted in Russia (1812), Spain (1826), Netherlands (1809), and Sweden (1826), among others. England only adopted a formal patent statute in 1852.

Prior to the American Revolution, state governments enacted patent laws. Article 1, Section 8, of the Constitution of the United States states that "the Congress shall have Power...[t]o promote the Progress of Science and useful Arts, by securing for limited times to Authors and Inventors the exclusive right to their respective Writings and Discoveries."

The U.S. Congress adopted the first federal patent law in 1790, which led to numerous infringement suits. It encouraged duplication and frivolous patents, but court cases arising from this law settled one important issue: The courts ruled that federal patent law took precedence over state patent laws. The Congress passed a new patent law in 1836, which laid the foundation for the modern patent system. It established the Patent Office as a separate federal bureau, and created the position of commissioner of patents. The process of reviewing a patent application now followed a series of methodical steps. U.S. patent laws were amended by the Patent Act of 1952, which allowed inventions to be patented if they were not obvious to the person of ordinary skill in the area. These more subjective criteria opened the door to more litigation.

The important issue in patent law today is worldwide protection of intellectual property rights (IPRs), referring to what might be called intangible property. IPRs include inventions, trademarks, and copyrights. Countries vary substantially in the protection afforded IPRs: Less-developed countries typically protect IPRs to a lesser extent, because they have fewer domestic companies with vested interests in IPRs. Pirated goods are goods sold without the permission of the holder of a patent, trademark, or copyright. One study found that 70 percent of the software sales in the Middle East, Africa, and Latin America involved pirated copies. The low cost of copying much copyrighted material has contributed to the problem of piracy.

As early as 1883, several countries in the West struck a treaty providing for more cooperation in patent matters. The World Intellectual Property Organization was created by treaty in 1967, and is working toward uniform patent laws, and laws protecting IPRs. The United States has used its trade laws to encourage countries to cooperate in the protection of IPRs. The Trade and Tariff Act of 1984 authorized the president to consider these issues when countries ask for special tariff privileges.

Countries have experimented with other ways of rewarding inventors, such as cash prizes, honors, etc. In capitalist economic systems, the patent system has survived as a means of rewarding inventors. The patent system assures that only those inventions will be rewarded that prove themselves in the marketplace.

See also Statute of Monopolies of 1624.

References Daniels, John D., and Lee H. Radebaugh. *International Business* (1998); Dutton, I. *The Patent System and Inventive Activity during the Industrial Revolution* (1984); Warshofsky, Fred. *The Patent Wars: The Battle to Own the World's Technology* (1994).

Peter the Great (1682–1725)

Peter the Great was perhaps the first statesman to launch a program of state capitalism in an effort to modernize a less-developed country. He ruled as czar of Russia from 1682 until his death in 1725. When he acceded to the throne, Russia was a landlocked country without significant industry, producing mostly agricultural commodities on feudal estates.

Before the advent of railroads, access to the sea was a necessity for capitalist development. Capitalism flourished in Venice and Amsterdam, where access to the sea was the principle resource. Peter was sufficiently conscious of the importance of sea power and shipbuilding that he spent time as a carpenter in the shipyards of the Dutch East India Company in Holland, and in the Royal Navy's dockyard in England. After a defeat at the hands of the Swedes while trying to push the frontiers of Russia to the Baltic coast, Peter realized that Russia's military had to have the support of a modernized economic system.

To accelerate industrialization in Russia, the Russian government became the entrepreneur and the financier. Naturally, Peter favored industries that were necessary to support armies, particularly mining and iron production. He also favored textile industries because armies need uniforms. Soon, the state-owned factories were producing paper, buttons, and woolen and linen stockings. Sometimes, the government recruited private entrepreneurs to take ownership and control of firms that the government had started. Leather, tapestries, flints, glass, and mirrors were among the products produced in factories initiated by the state.

To pay for industrialization and war, Peter taxed the peasants to the point of revolt, of which there were several under

The equestrian statue of Peter the Great at St. Petersburg, with St. Isaac's Cathedral in the background, from a nineteenth-century painting by Vorobyev

his reign. Merchants also suffered from taxes and proliferation of state monopolies that took business out of their hands. The Russian government became directly involved in importing and exporting goods at the expense of the Russian merchant class. State monopolies became another source of revenue for the government, which gave itself a monopoly on the sale of salt, and doubled the price; it also developed a tobacco monopoly, and profits grew 800 percent.

In 1721, Peter brought the war with Sweden to a successful conclusion, and signed a treaty that ceded to Russia the eastern shores of the Baltic coast, at last securing Russia access to the sea. As early as 1703, the foundation of a fort was laid on what was to become St. Petersburg, a city whose Neva River opened onto the Baltic coast. Peter conscripted serfs to build the city, forcibly redirected Russian shipping and foreign trade through St. Petersburg, moved the czar's residence to the new city, and made it the capital of Russia. Peter envisioned St. Petersburg as a "second Amsterdam," and the city became known as the Venice of the North.

Because of Peter the Great's vision, Russia experienced a burst of industrialization between 1700 and 1725 that was unprecedented at a time when mercantilist policies were promoting industrialization in many countries in Europe. The tradition of public initiative rather than private initiative, however, may have helped put Russia on the road that led to communism in the twentieth century. The absence of democratic traditions must also share the blame for communism in Russia, since the Bolshevik Revolution replaced one authoritarian government with another.

References Anisimov, Evgenii V. *The Reforms of Peter the Great: Progress Through Coercion in Russia* (1993); Massie, Robert. *Peter the Great: His Life and World* (1980).

Political Business Cycle (United States)

Economists in the United States claim to have found a correlation between phases of the business cycle and the cycle in presidential elections. This correlation is called the political business cycle.

Cyclical fluctuations are apparently an inevitable part of the capitalist economic system, and stand among its riddles that await further elucidation. One famous economist, Henry Stanley Jevons, thought sunspot activity accounted for economic fluctuations on Earth. Other economists submitted evidence of periodicity in economic fluctuations: Studies reported 50-, ten-, and three-year cycles. But theories of sunspot cycles and periodic cycles have not survived rigorous examination. The political business cycle holds out more promise than these theories for explaining the smaller cycles.

Although the necessity of these fluctuations remains a riddle, economists have learned how government can help stabilize them. A government's control over its budget and the money supply, theoretically, enables it to speed up or slow down the economy from any point, by regulating the levels of unemployment and inflation. Government should strive to stabilize the economy, or, at least, not to destabilize it. Given that economic fluctuations are inevitable, however, elected officials have an incentive to rig the cycle, that is, time the cycle in order that good news will arrive around election time. Good news translates as low unemployment and control over inflation.

A study of economic growth (GNP growth) during Democratic and Republican administrations, from Truman through Reagan, has shown that recessions are most likely to occur in the second year of Republican administrations, which can boast of five of the seven economic recessions that occurred during that time period. The second year of Democratic administrations is most likely to see rapid economic growth, which has an average growth rate of 6.2 percent, compared with –0.4 percent for the second year of a Republican administration. This wide gap in economic growth rates closes by the fourth year of presidential terms.

Republicans averaged 4.1 percent for the fourth year; the Democrats averaged 3.3 percent. Of the seven recessions during this period, only one occurred during the fourth year of a term. The average growth rate for the first year of the presidential term was 3.3 percent for the Democrats and 3.1 percent for the Republicans.

This evidence suggests that voters elect Democrats to bring down unemployment; hence, the high growth rate in the second year. Republicans are elected to put a lid on inflation, and their assault on inflation shows up as negative growth in the second year.

Karl Marx saw economic fluctuations as evidence that the capitalist system would collapse. The same knowledge that enabled governments to prime the pump in depressions also put in the hands of government the power to time upswings with elections. Public officials might argue that stable economic conditions are necessary for voters to make good decisions in orderly elections. Critics could say that the political business cycle is a symptom of the excessive power of government in modern capitalism.

See also Kontradieff Cycle.

References Mankiw, Gregory. *Macroeconomic Economics* (1992); Stein, Herbert. *Presidential Economics* (1994).

Poor Law Amendment Act of 1834 (England)

The Poor Law Amendment Act of 1834 overhauled the English system of poor relief that had been in place since the sixteenth century. The new Poor Law was conceived in the spirit of the new free-market economics.

Among the critics of the old Poor Law could be found some of the most prominent economists of the day. Thomas R. Malthus felt that public relief for the able-bodied poor encouraged early marriages, which in turn added to the population growth rate. In Malthus's thought, economic considerations are the main restraint on family formation and the birthrate. His thought was shaped by classical economists such as Adam Smith and David Ricardo. They believed real wages adjusted to a level just sufficient for the population to reproduce. An increase in real wages increased the population birthrate, which increased the supply of labor and brought real wages back down. Malthus's work on population growth helped earn him the title of father of the new Poor Law.

Under the old Poor Law, public relief was administered by local parish officials, and its administration wore some of the aspects of patronage. The system provided what was called outdoor relief, which had evolved into a subsidy for wages. Laborers qualified for relief payments proportional to the price of bread and the number of their dependents. Farmers hired laborers at wages below what a consideration of the laborers' productivity would justify. Public relief made up the difference between the wage the farmers paid and the amount the laborers needed to subsist. Critics claimed that men could improve themselves by marrying and having children. Local parishes impatiently bore the cost of the local poor relief system.

In 1830, riots broke out in southern England among agricultural laborers. Local officials granted more generous public relief to quell the public disorder, which was a policy that had worked in the past. This time, however, grants of more generous relief seemed to cause disaffected laborers to press for more concessions. Nassau Senior, a classical economist who served on a Poor Law commission, wrote,

The riots, and still more the fires, of 1830 were a practical lesson on the rights of the poor and the means of enforcing them.... That wages are not a matter of contract but a matter of right, that they depend, not on the value of the laborer's services, but on the extent of his wants, or of his expectations...all these monstrous and anarchical doctrines were repeated not only by the rioters themselves but by the farmers, the clergy, the magistrates, in short by all the ignorant and timid throughout the country.

The new Poor Law embodied two principles that were supposed to remedy the evils of the old Poor Law. One principle was less eligibility. The amount of relief available to an able-bodied individual could only be enough for mere subsistence. The second principle was the workhouse test. The minimal relief available had to be earned in a workhouse. The system was set up to make earning relief in a workhouse the least attractive alternative an individual could choose. Only workers who had no alternatives in the labor market would turn to public relief.

Advocates of the new Poor Law felt it would restore the deficiencies in character that led to poverty. They argued wages would rise and poverty diminish. The difficulty of this optimistic assessment lay in a misunderstanding of the source of much of the poverty. The rapid mechanization of agriculture threw unskilled agricultural workers out of work. Dislocated workers from agriculture and industry continued to supply the ranks of the destitute. Early in the twentieth century, England enacted social legislation that superseded the Poor Law. Programs providing unemployment compensation and old-age pensions represented a complete break with the nineteenth-century Poor Law.

See also Old Poor Laws of England, Welfare State.

References Daunton, Martin. *Progress and Poverty: An Economic and Social History of Britain, 1700–1850* (1995); Rimlinger, Gaston V. *Welfare Policy and Industrialization in Europe, America, and Russia* (1971).

Portuguese Colonial Empire

At the beginning of the sixteenth century, Portugal established itself as an imperial power of the first rank among European countries. For 150 years, it dominated European trade with India and the East Indies. The Portuguese empire survived into the twentieth century with the aid of British support, long after Portugal ceased to play a major role on the stage of world trade.

Portugal spent the fifteenth century preparing itself for oceanic exploration, collecting nautical knowledge, colonizing islands such as the Azores, inching down the western coast of Africa, and rounding the southern tip of Africa in 1486. Portugal's aim was control of the spice and pepper trade. Venice had managed to monopolize that trade with the Moslem world at the expense of the other Christian states in Europe. Portugal sought to share in the trade and to deprive the infidel countries of the revenue. The religious motives of weakening the infidels reinforced, or perhaps overshadowed, the economic motives.

After Vasco Da Gama rounded the Cape of Good Hope and visited India in 1497, Portugal acted swiftly to destroy Moslem naval power and shipping in the Indian Ocean. By 1509, the Portuguese had fortified themselves in India, and had appointed the first governor of Portuguese India. By 1512, the Portuguese controlled the exports of the Moluccas, or Spice Islands; by 1540, it was trading with Japan and China. In the New World, Portugal colonized Brazil.

Portuguese imperialism has been called monarchical capitalism, or royal mercantilism. Portugal never established chartered private companies, such as the English East Indies Company, or the Dutch East Indies Company. The Portuguese government opened up trade with the Indies, and the Portuguese crown maintained a high level of involvement. Royal ships carried the cargo from the Indies. In addition to a government-paid salary, the captains of royal ships controlled a small share of the cargo space to load with their own goods. The goods in the remainder of the cargo space belonged to the royal merchant capitalists.

Portugal was one of the early conscious practitioners of mercantilism. According to mercantilism, colonies were exploited for the benefit of the mother country, and the mother country regulated trade to maintain an excess of exports over imports, leading to an accumulation of precious metals. In mercantilist thought, the accumulation of precious metals measured a country's wealth.

Individualistic entrepreneurial capitalism never developed in Portugal on the scale that it later developed in Holland and England. Domestic manufacturing and agriculture languished without stimulus from Portugal's colonial trade. The overly rigid application of mercantilist principles may have restricted capitalist development in Portugal. The heavy involvement of the government in colonial trade may also bear a portion of the blame. Portugal could not make the transition from a military spirit, with its search for plunder and tribute, to a commercial spirit, with its lust for profits. Its contribution to capitalist development lay in opening up direct trade between Europe and the East, and in pioneering transoceanic exploration.

See also Da Gama, Vasco; Mercantilism; Spice Trade.

References Hart, Henry H. *Sea Road to the Indies* (1950); Kindleberger, Charles P. *World Economic Primacy, 1500–1900* (1996); Subrahmanyam, Sanjay. *The Portuguese Empire in Asia, 1500–1700: A Political and Economic History* (1993).

Price Revolution in Sixteenth- and Seventeenth-Century Europe

Price Revolution is the conventional term referring to the wave of inflation that swept Europe during the sixteenth and seventeenth centuries. The inflation acquired the status of a revolution for the following reasons: It followed a long period of stable prices, and the prevailing view at the time was that prices and wages should be matters of fairness and justice, rather than functions of supply and demand.

Inflation struck Spain the hardest, quadrupling prices within a century. The acceleration in prices reached a peak in most countries between 1540 and the 1570s. Wages fell behind prices. In England, from 1580 to 1640, prices of necessities rose 100 percent, while wages inched up 20 percent. England's first series of humane Poor Laws came into being in the midst of the Price Revolution. By the mid-seventeenth century, the inflation had ceased in most countries, followed by a century of stable or even falling prices.

Economists have mostly credited the influx of gold and silver from the New World for causing the inflation. An increase in the supply of anything, including money, relative to its demand, causes its value to go down. A reduction in the value of a unit of money translates as inflation to the public. Scholars in other areas seem less satisfied with this single explanation. The timing of the beginning, peak, and end of the inflation only roughly corresponds with timing of comparable dates for the influx of gold and silver. The economist Jean Bodin (1530–1596) listed five reasons for the inflation: (1) abundance of gold and silver, (2) monopolies, (3) scarcity of goods caused by exports and waste, (4) luxury of kings and nobleman, and (5) debasement of coin. He regarded the abundance of gold and silver as the principal reason.

The Price Revolution became an important stimulus in the development of capitalism. Wages and rents lagged behind prices. Price increases went straight to profits. Entrepreneurs ploughed these profits into new industries and new ventures of trade, speculation, and building. Profit inflation, as a result of lags in costs, bid up the price of capital goods relative to consumer goods. The increase in the production of capital goods, relative to consumer goods, laid the foundation for further economic expansion.

See also Spanish Colonial Empire.

References Davies, Glyn. *A History of Money* (1994); Hamilton, J. *American Treasure and the Price Revolution in Spain, 1501–1650* (1934).

Private Property

Although private property ownership is of ancient origin, rights of ownership were often restricted. Under feudal societies, nobles owned hunting rights on virtually all land. Portions of the land were available for communal pasturage, forage for fuel, and other agricultural uses. With the rise of capitalism, the most abstract philosophers vied with theologians, legislators, and judges to see who could defend private property most eloquently. The nineteenth century saw the high tide of the individualistic concept of private property. During the twentieth century, governments have shown more willingness to sacrifice the rights of property in favor of social reform.

King John of England signed the Magna Carta in 1215. This charter of English liberty abounds with statements protecting the rights of property. It required justice for individuals wrongfully dispossessed of property by monarchs or assessed illegal fines. Constables and bailiffs were forbidden from taking a person's corn or chattel without immediate compensation, or from taking a citizen's horses or carriages for public use. The king could not take timber from another man's land for royal use. Creditors could not seize the land of a defaulting debtor, if the debtor owned chattel to pay the debt. Land could not be taken from a debtor who was able to pay, and land put up as surety for debts could only be seized and held by creditors as long as the debtor was unable to pay.

The absolute monarchs of the seventeenth century clung to the theory that the monarch owned all the land. In practice, however, they guarded private property from confiscation. Political philosophers who defended absolute monarchy, such as Jean Bodin and Thomas Hobbes, insisted that monarchs were bound by higher laws to secure the rights to private property.

Toward the end of the seventeenth century, private property found one of its most eloquent defenders in John Locke, who is also one of the great figures in the history of philosophy. Locke cited property as a necessity for human progress, civilization, and peace between individuals and nations. Locke enshrined property as a natural right, conferred by natural law. Natural rights took precedence over rights granted by the generosity of governments. The influence of Locke can be seen in the *Declaration of Independence*. Locke referred to life, liberty, and the pursuit of property as natural rights. Jefferson wrote of the inalienable rights of life, liberty, and the pursuit of happiness.

David Hume, one of the great philosophers of the generation after Locke, defended private property solely upon its utility to society. In Hume's words:

> Who sees not that whatever is produced or improved by a man's art or industry, ought, for ever, to be secured for him in order to give encouragement to such useful habits and accomplishments? That the property ought also to descend to children and relations, for the same useful purpose? That it may be alienated by consent, in order to beget that commerce and intercourse which is so beneficial to human society? And that all contracts and promises ought carefully to be fulfilled, in order to secure mutual trust and confidence, by which the general interest of mankind is so much promoted?

Montesquieu, one of the most famous political philosophers of the eighteenth century, also preferred practical considerations over abstract concepts of natural rights. Rejection of natural rights did not, however, lower his esteem for private property. Said Montesquieu, "Let us, therefore, lay down a certain maxim, that whenever the public good happens to be a matter in question, it is not for the advantage of the public to deprive an individual of his property, or even to retrench the least part of it by law, or a political regulation."

The Constitution of the United States makes numerous references to the protection of property. Article 4 of the Bill of Rights protects individuals from unreasonable searches of themselves, or their houses and papers. Article 5 provides that no person "shall be deprived of life, liberty, or property, without due process of law." The Fourteenth Amendment to the Constitution states, "nor shall any State deprive any person of life, liberty, or property without due process of law."

The Declaration of the Rights of Man and of the Citizen, the human rights document of the French Revolution, treated property rights as among the inalienable rights of man. Article 2 states that the purpose of political associations was to secure natural rights—liberty, property, security, and resistance to oppression. The last article describes the right to property as "inviolable and sacred."

During the nineteenth century, the courts reinforced the constitutional protections for private property. Private property enjoyed greater protection than ever before, or since.

In the twentieth century, the courts have given governments more authority to regulate the use of private property. The concept of property has expanded over time to include such things as rights. An important concern in recent years has been the protection of intellectual property rights.

The protection of property rights rose to become a major cultural theme inspired by the growth of capitalism. Private property is still regarded as the cornerstone of the capitalist system.

References Dietze, Gottfried. *In Defense of Property* (1963); Ely, James W., Jr. *The Guardian of Every Other Right* (1992).

Privatization Revolution

Privatization occurs when the government divests itself of property and activities that can be owned and operated by the private sector. The sale of a state-owned enterprise in a public market is the type of thing meant by privatization. Since the 1980s, privatization as economic policy has gained ground rapidly in the United States and Europe.

In the United States, state and local governments have been among the most aggressive in privatizing government activities and services. The easiest candidates for privatization have been housekeeping services, building maintenance, vehicle fleet management, lawn care, data processing, and engineering services. Several cities have taken on the larger task of privatizing major services, such as garbage collection, street sweeping, emergency ambulance service, and even fire protection and law enforcement. Some of the big investment activities that have not escaped the privatization trend include water systems, waste-water treatment plants, hospitals, and highways. Private companies are now in the business of running jails and prisons for state and local governments. The private sector is supplying judges for the resolution of disputes. Judge Wapner's "People's Court" of television fame is a good example of judges drawn into private practice.

A 1985 study, comparing ten cities supplying various services, in-house, with another ten cities that made use of private contractors for the same services, found that street repair was 37 percent more expensive when conducted by the government; street cleaning and lawn care were 43 percent more expensive; signal maintenance, 56 percent more expensive; building maintenance, 73 percent more expensive; and asphalt, 96 percent more expensive. The private sector and the public sector were about evenly matched in the area of data processing. Another study by the New York Department of Education reported the cost per student for a college degree was higher in public universities than in private universities. In an era of fiscal tightness, the attractiveness of privatization speaks for itself.

Perhaps the sale of Conrail is the most revealing symbol of the commitment of the U.S. government to privatization. Conrail was a non-profit government corporation formed in the mid 1970s out of the bankrupt railroads of the northeastern United States. In 1987, the government put its 85-percent stake in Conrail up for sale in a public stock offering that raised $1.65 billion before underwriting fees. By the end of March, 1987, Conrail was a publicly traded corporation on the New York Stock Exchange.

In 1987, the federal government formed a commission to target government activities that could be more efficiently provided by the private sector. Some possibilities that surfaced as prime candidates included air traffic control, postal service, low-income housing, housing finance, federal loan programs, educational programs, military commissaries and prisons, Medicare, and urban mass transit. The Defense Department has also been aggressively looking for opportunities for privatization.

The English prime minister, Margaret Thatcher, launched a major program of privatization. In England, the appropriate term is denationalization, because the British government had nationalized much of its industry. The British government sold to the private sector such enterprises as Jaguar, British Rail Hotels, English Channel Ferry Service, British Petroleum, British Aerospace, Britoil, British Telecom, British Gas, and British Airport Authority. Jaguar's profits increased 142 percent within two years after becoming a private company. The sale of British Gas constituted the largest stock offering in British history.

The vitality of contemporary capitalism speaks very clearly in the movement toward privatization. Just as the trend of nationalization was discredited by slow growth and inflation, some unimagined economic problems may raise questions about the wisdom of privatization. Presently, privatization appears the answer to improving efficiency in public services.

See also Thatcherism.

References Alkhafaji, Abbass F. *Restructuring American Corporations: Causes, Effects, and Implications* (1990); *International Finance Corporation. Privatization Principles and Practice* (1995).

Proletariat

According to critics of capitalism, the proletariat is an oppressed working class born of the capitalist economic system. In the words of Karl Marx, in the *Manifesto of the Communist Party,*

> In proportion as the bourgeoisie, that is, capital, is developed, in the same proportion is the proletariat, the modern working-class, developed—a class of laborers, who live only so long as they find work.... These laborers, who must sell themselves piecemeal, are a commodity like any other article of commerce, and are consequently exposed...to all the fluctuations of the market.... Owing to the extensive use of machinery and to division of labor, the work of the proletarian loses all individual character.... He becomes an appendage of the machine...in proportion as machinery obliterates all distinctions of labor and nearly everywhere reduces wages to the same low level.... [T]he cost of production of a workman is restricted almost entirely to the means of subsistence that he requires for the...propagation of his race. With its [proletariat's] birth begins its struggle with the bourgeoisie.... They direct their attacks...against the instruments of production themselves; they destroy imported wares that compete with their labor, they smash machinery to pieces, they set factories ablaze, they seek to restore by force the vanished status of the workman of the Middle Ages.... [T]he more or less veiled civil war raging within existing society...breaks out into open revolution, and...the violent overthrow of the bourgeoisie lays the foundation for the sway of the proletariat.

Just what is the process by which capitalism gave birth to the germ of its own destruction? Before the capitalist mode of economic organization became dominant, industrial workers were organized in guilds. These workers owned their own tools, bought raw materials, and sold the finished product. Workers entered a guild as journeymen and rose to the level of master. The guilds maintained wages by limiting the number of new journeymen recruited and trained in the craft.

The beginnings of the proletariat lie in the economic differentiation of the guilds. Wealthy masters gained control over the sale of the final product, and the supply of raw materials. These wealthy masters developed the putting-out system, under which they contracted with smaller craftsmen (weavers, carders, spinners, etc.) to supply raw materials, and to purchase the finished product. The putting-out system gave rise to cottage industry in rural areas beyond the jurisdiction of the guilds. The smaller craftsmen, unable to keep up with the rising cost of tools and machines, found themselves in the ranks of an underclass of proletarians, who owned nothing of value but their own labor.

The agricultural revolution in rural areas brought an infusion of fresh recruits into the ranks of the proletarians. The emergence of scientific, and, later, mechanized, farming reduced the share of the population needed to produce food. In England, the enclosure movement consolidated land holdings into larger farms. Villagers who lost communal rights to the use of land had to become wage earners. On the continent, governments granted freedom to peasants and serfs, but the newly freed peasants and serfs often received a small bit of land, not big enough to take advantage of the most efficient methods of production. They had to rent equipment and borrow capital from the larger farmers and landlords. When they sank too deeply in debt, as they often did, they became wage earners.

The regulations of the guild barred the rural refugees from becoming skilled craftsmen in the towns. Aside from guild regulations, wealthy masters were driving the small craftsmen into the swelling ranks of the unskilled proletarians. The factory system leveled the death blow to the guild system. Only the wealthy could afford the machinery, and the workers needed modest skills at best.

The nineteenth century saw the spread of democratic governments and universal manhood suffrage in capitalist economic systems. The proletariat acquired a voice in government. As these propertyless voters made their influence felt, the economic ground rules were being adjusted to give the laboring classes a level playing field. Much of the revolutionary discontent of the proletariat, as Marx called the working class, has vanished.

See also Agricultural Revolution, Class Struggle, Enclosures.

References Dobb, Maurice. *Studies in the Development of Capitalism* (1947); Hamilton, Richard F. *The Bourgeois Epoch* (1991); Marx, Karl, and Friedrich Engels. *The Manifesto of the Communist Party* (1848).

Promissory Notes Act of 1704
See Goldsmith Bankers.

Public Debt

In his book *The Spirit of Laws*, published in 1748, the French philosopher Montesquieu states, "Some have imagined that it was for the advantage of a state to be indebted to itself: they thought that this multiplied riches by increasing the circulation."

Apparently, circulation increased if the public was willing to hold government debt, instead of hoarding gold and silver. No less an apostle of capitalism than Alexander Hamilton, in his *First Report on the Public Credit*, cited advantages of a public debt:

First,—Trade is extended by it, because there is a larger capital to carry it on, and the merchant can, at the same time, afford a trade for smaller profits; as his stock, which, when unemployed, brings him an interest from the Government, serves him as money when he has a call for it in his commercial operations.

Secondly,—Agriculture and manufactures are also promoted by it, for the like reason....

Thirdly,—The interest of money will be lowered by it; for this is always in a ratio to the quantity of money, and to the quickness of circulation. This circumstance will enable both the public and individuals to borrow on easier and cheaper terms.

Historically, governments have needed access to great sums of money to fight wars. Before governments acquired the credibility to borrow funds, they had to save in prosperous times to garner the financial resources to wage war. As governments became independent entities, separate from particular rulers, and earned reputations for fairly enforcing contracts, they acquired the ability to borrow funds. Now governments turn exclusively to borrowing to finance wars and other extraordinary activities.

During the sixteenth century, the Spanish crown became the biggest debtor in European financial markets. Bankers loaned funds to Spain at double-digit rates on a short- and long-term basis. On occasion, the Spanish government forced bankers to accept low-interest, long-term loan agreements in payment for short-term loans paying higher rates of interest. The Spanish government wracked European financial markets by suspending interest payments six times within a century, and declaring bankruptcy in 1557, 1575, 1596, 1607, 1627, and 1647.

During the seventeenth and eighteenth centuries, French finance ministers struggled with managing a heavy public debt. Turgot, the finance minister under Louis XVI, stated his policy in 1774:

No bankruptcy, either avowed or disguised.... No increase in taxes, the reason for this lying in the condition of your people.... No loans,...because every loan necessitates, at the end of a given time, either bankruptcy or the increase of taxes.... To meet these three points there is but one means. It is to reduce expenditure below revenue, and sufficiently below it to insure each year a saving of twenty millions, to be applied to the redemption of the old debts. Without that, the first gunshot will force the state into bankruptcy.

France again turned to loans to finance a war. In 1797, the government of the French Revolution repudiated two-thirds of the public debt of France. In 1800, the remainder of the public debt was refunded with new securities.

Records of the public debt of the British government date back to the seventeenth century. Over the long term, the British public debt, like that of other European countries, continued to rise.

By the latter portion of the nineteenth century, most of the governments of advanced industrialized nations boasted of public debts. During the course of World War I, public debt in Western countries soared to unprecedented levels. In the United States, the public debt increased from $1,191 billion to $24.299 billion from 1915 to 1920. Early in the 1920s, Germany repudiated its public debt with massive inflation, virtually destroying the middle class. France wiped out much of its World War I debt with inflation over a longer span of time, with less drastic results for the middle class.

In capitalist countries, public debts increased during World War II and continued to rise in the postwar era. Central banks hold government bonds as assets to offset the paper money and reserve deposits that are carried as a liability on their accounts. Contemporary economists debate the burden public debts place on future generations. It is a thorny issue, when one considers that public debts may contribute to current prosperity.

A public debt clearly puts a burden on future generations, if the government borrows funds that the private sector needs to finance factories and other facilities and equipment. In contrast, a public debt may contribute to the welfare of future generations, if government initiatives reflect a lack of initiative in the private sector, which may be the case in an economic depression.

See also Financial Crisis of 1557, French Revolution and Napoleon, Hyperinflation in Post-World War I Germany.

References Dickson, G. M. *The Financial Revolution in England: A Study in the Development of the Public Credit, 1688–1756* (1967); Durant, Will, and Ariel Durant. *Rousseau and Revolution* (1967); Homer, Sidney. *A History of Interest Rates* (1977); McConnell, Cambell R., and Stanley R. Brue. *Economics* (1993).

Pullman Strike of 1894
(United States)

On 11 May 1894, the workers at the Pullman Palace Car Company in Pullman, Illinois, called a strike that became one of the most famous clashes between labor and capital in the United States. The strike rose to historical importance after the American Railway Union orchestrated a boycott in support of the striking workers. One authority on labor history described it as "the only attempt ever made in America of a revolutionary strike on the Continental European Model."

Pullman, Illinois, was a company town. The employer was the Pullman Palace Car Company, a manufacturer of passenger cars for trains. George Pullman built the company and the town. Workers rented houses from the company, bought food and supplies from the company store, and sold their labor to the company. Pullman bought water from Chicago for four cents per thousand gallons, and sold it to the residents of Pullman for ten cents per thousand gallons. The company charged rents 20 to 25 percent above the amounts charged in Chicago and sur-

National Guardsmen fire into the crowd of rioting railway workers in Chicago, 1894.

rounding areas. The economy of Pullman made no room for competition.

During the Panic of 1893, the company slashed wages by one-fourth, without making cuts in rent, fuel, or other components of the cost of living. By the spring of 1894, many workers had joined the American Railway Union. In May 1894, the workers organized a grievance committee to negotiate with the company, and to encourage the company to alleviate their miseries. Despite pledges to the contrary, the company dismissed three members of the grievance committee on 10 May. On the following day the workers walked out.

On 12 June, the American Railway Union opened its first convention in Chicago. The delegates were in sympathy with the striking workers at Pullman and wanted the union to take action. Eugene Debs, president of the American Railway Union, urged caution, and persuaded the convention to appoint a committee to negotiate with George Pullman, but this committee met with a rebuff. After delegates from the striking workers addressed the convention, sympathy for the union ran high. The delegates gave the company four days to accept mediation or face a boycott of all trains with Pullman cars attached.

George Pullman and the Pullman Palace Car Company stood firm, and the union made good on its threat of a boycott. By the end of June, 125,000 workers had joined the boycott. The railroad companies set out to break the strike by attaching Pullman cars to trains carrying U.S. mail. The U.S. attorney general was a former railroad corporation lawyer. Interference with the delivery of the U.S. mail gave the federal government cause to enter the dispute. President Cleveland sent federal troops, who opened fire on a crowd of strikers, killing some 30 people. The federal courts granted an injunction against the strike and the activities of the leaders of the American Railway Union. As an interesting aside, the injunction was granted under the provisions of the Sherman Antitrust Act of 1890, which was enacted to outlaw the kind of monopolistic practices found in Pullman, Illinois. Eugene Debs went to jail for violating the injunction, and the American Railway Union called off the boycott on 2 August. Eugene Debs later ran for president as the candidate for the Socialist Party.

The case of Pullman, Illinois, stands as a warning of the degree of capitalist exploitation that can be expected when competition is missing. The fruits of capitalism are withheld from some members of society when competition between buyers and sellers breaks down. Monopolistic markets surrounded the workers at Pullman on all sides, in the labor, housing, and fuel markets.

See also London Dock Strike of 1899, Ludlow Massacre.

References Brooks, Thomas R. *Toil and Trouble: A History of American Labor* (1971); Laidler, Harry W. *Boycotts and the Labor Struggle: Economic and Legal Aspects* (1913); Lindsey, Almont. *The Pullman Strike* (1964).

Puritanism

One might wonder why any religious sect, necessarily concerned with discovering and obeying eternal divine laws, should have any connection with the rather transitory economic phenomenon of human history. European history after the sixteenth century, however, reveals a correlation between the countries in which Protestantism displaced Catholicism and countries where merchant capitalism, and, later, industrial capitalism, got an early start, and flourished. Amsterdam and London come to mind as two shining examples of this correlation. Either the correlation is a coincidence, or the Protestant Reformation acted as a spur to the development of capitalism.

The Puritan religion held sway in the early history of New England. It can lay claim to being the most influential religion in the early history of the United States. Some scholars claim that the Puritan religion helped lay the foundation for the development of capitalism in the United States. Poverty found no glorification in the Puritan religion. According to Cotton Mather (1663–1728; the famous Puritan minister who figured prominently in the Salem witch trials), each person has two callings: a calling to serve god, and a personal calling to a particular employment. This second calling makes a person useful to his neighbors. Success in one's calling is a sign of divine approval. Business is a calling like any other employment. God will bless your efforts with success, if you are where God wants you to be. Success on earth became a sign of divine approval, an indication that one is numbered among the elect.

Benjamin Franklin admired Cotton Mather, and had visited him, as a youngster. On theological questions, Franklin was something of a free thinker. The moral austerity of the Puritans, however, left a strong imprint on him. His list of virtues included temperance, silence, order, resolution, frugality, sincerity, justice, moderation, cleanliness, tranquillity, chastity, and humility. Franklin's *Poor Richard's Almanac* tirelessly sang the praises of industry, saying, for example, "God gives all things to industry." The keys to worldly success were summed up in two words: industry and frugality. Franklin saw that Puritan values had a tremendous utilitarian value.

Timothy Dwight's (1752–1817; the influential intellectual leader and President of Yale from 1795 until his death) preaching reflected the latter-day Puritanism embodied in the form of Congregationalism. He spoke of idleness as "not only a gross vice in itself, but the highway to all other vices." He too lauded the virtue of industry.

The Puritans approved of the pursuit of wealth, but they disapproved of living ostentatiously. John Winthrop (1588–1649), first governor of the Massachusetts Bay Colony, scolded Thomas Dudley for building an unnecessarily elaborate house, thus setting a bad example for the community. According to *Poor Richard*, "A penny saved is a penny earned." Richard Baxter, a preacher in Cromwell's England, warned against using wealth for luxurious living—this was the path of damnation.

The Puritan religion may have provided some of the social discipline needed to maintain a high level of goods production, while keeping consumer goods production at modest levels. This is the kind of social priority that paved the way for a high level of capital formation. In addition, John Calvin defended charging interest in levels up to 5 percent. The tenets of the Puritan religion lifted the burden of anxieties and scruples that bore down on the conscience of many people in business and moneymaking pursuits.

In 1895, a statistical study of Baden, Germany reported that Protestants are more likely to be wealthy than Catholics. The author of the study reasoned that "The Catholic...is of a calmer disposition, with less thirst for profit; he prefers a safe existence, even with a small income, to a life of risks and excitement, even if the latter would bring him wealth and honor."

The thesis that Puritanism laid the framework for the capitalist spirit to flourish has drawn criticism. It fails to explain the economic exuberance of the Italian city-states in the fourteenth and fifteenth centuries. Christopher Columbus was not averse to risk. The Protestant countries may yet lose their economic leadership, just as the Italian states lost it in the sixteenth century. Puritan values have lost much of their hold, even in Protestant countries. The thesis does not enjoy a consensus among scholars, but it is thought-provoking concerning the kinds of values that foster economic development.

See also Judaism and Capitalism.

References Griswold, Whitney. "Three Puritans on Prosperity." *New England Quarterly* (1934); Weber, Max. *The Protestant Ethic and the Spirit of Capitalism* (1930).

Putting-Out System

In the chronological development of capitalism, the putting-out system lies between guild organization and the factory system. It represented a pure form of cap-

The Art of STOCKING-FRAME-WORK-KNITTING.

Engraved for the Universal Magazine 1750 for J. Hinton at the Kings. Arms in S.t Pauls Church Yard LONDON.

Workers often labored in their own homes under the putting-out system, as seen in this eighteenth-century English engraving titled "The Art of Stocking Frame Work Knitting."

italism. A putter-out, often a merchant, supplied a worker with raw materials, equipment, and other things requiring capital. The worker often performed the work in his own house, where he entirely controlled the management of the work. The putter-out supplied only capital, and the worker only labor.

Before the capitalist era, the guild system was the predominant form of industry organization. The master craftsmen stood at the apex of the production process, owning his own tools, purchasing the raw materials, and marketing finished products. A worker entered the craft as an apprentice, rose to journeyman, and then to master craftsman. In each town, guild

regulations governed everything from how many years a worker served as an apprentice to the price of finished products. The guilds controlled the number of workers in each craft, and the supply and quality of output. Because the guild system led to monopoly control, the costs of finished goods were high.

The putting-out system was a means of dodging the high cost of production of the guild system. Guild regulations were only effective in towns. A putter-out could contract with a head of household in a rural area to supply raw materials and equipment, and pay piecework rates for the finished product. The households often had other sources of income, probably from agriculture. Since guild regulations did not reach into the homes of rural families, women and children often figured significantly in the work. The textile industry adapted itself well to the putting-out system. Weaving and spinning could easily be conducted in the homes of workers in rural areas.

The putting-out system may have originated with impoverished master craftsman who mortgaged their machinery to creditors, and promised to repay in finished product. Others may have purchased machines on credit, giving the lender control over the use of the machine. An English law enacted in the mid-sixteenth century declared that "rich clothiers do oppress the weavers...by engrossing of looms into their hands and letting them out at such unreasonable rents as the poor artificers are not able to maintain themselves by and much less their wives and families."

Under the putting-out system, worker specialization significantly entered into the production process for the first time. In the textile industry, a merchant putter-out might own a bleachery that could meet the needs of a large number of weavers. The production of needles gives the best example of specialization in the putting-out system. One putter-out would lead the production of needles, through the hands of 72 workers, most of whom were domestic workers. These fledgling steps toward specialization led to the detailed specialization on the factory assembly line.

The ability to generate considerable power in one location led to the congregation of workers under one roof, and thus the factory system was born. Nevertheless, the putting-out system has survived in some industries into the twentieth century. In the southwestern United States, saddles are still produced with a form of the putting-out system. Under the guild system, human capital and financial capital merged in one person: the master craftsmen. With the putting-out system, a new player rose to prominence in the production process, whose contribution to the production process lay in the ownership of financial capital.

See also Factory System.

References Daunton, Martin. *Progress and Poverty: An Economic and Social History of Britain, 1700–1850* (1995); Nussbaum, Frederick L. *A History of the Economic Institutions of Modern Europe* (1935).

Railroads

If one industry fully reflects the history of nineteenth-century capitalism, it is railroads. Such issues as private versus public initiative, state regulation versus private enterprise, free competition versus monopoly, imperialism, tariff wars, and economic cycles, in one way or another, all touched on the development of the railroads. Railroad issues dominated early stock market speculation in the United States.

Railroads, powered by steam locomotives, appeared in England at the dawn of the nineteenth century. The first great pioneer of railroad and locomotive building, George Stephenson, finished the construction of the first public railroad line in 1825. It connected Stockton and Darlington, and carried freight and passengers. In 1829, a much-improved railroad opened, connecting Liverpool and Manchester. In the United States, the first public railroad, carrying passengers and freight, opened in 1830.

In the 1830s, governments in the United States and Europe—particularly England and Germany—began granting charters for railroad companies on a significant scale. Charters were usually for short lines, perhaps 15 miles long, and sometimes included provisions prohibiting competition with other forms of public transportation. Only in Belgium did the government take the lead in laying out a logical system of railroads.

In the 1850s, the railroad companies entered a period of consolidation. Between 1847 and 1862, the number of railroad companies in England decreased from several hundred to only 12. In France, the number decreased from 33 in 1847 to six in 1859. In the United States, the line connecting the Hudson and Lake Erie was formed from a union of 16 different companies.

The 1850s also saw railroad construction pushing into areas barely accessible by other forms of transportation. The first railroad crossing the Alps, connecting Semmering, Vienna, and Trieste, opened in 1854. In 1867, the Brenner railroad connected Munich with Italy. The construction of the railroad from Lyon to Turin required cutting a tunnel 7.5 miles in length. It was completed in 1871. In 1882, another railroad was completed that tunneled nine miles through the heart of the Alps. In the United States, the Union and Central Pacific route opened in 1869. The miles of railroad track in the world rose from 20,000 in 1850 to 225,000 in 1880.

Railroads opened international trade to parts of the world formerly connected by the most primitive communication. The rise of trade barriers in the latter nineteenth century was probably a reaction to lower transportation costs.

Governments began to support and sometimes control the development of railroads. In the United States, state and federal governments granted large subsidies to encourage railroad expansion. England mostly contented itself to leave railroad development to free enterprise. The governments of Germany and Prussia turned to a system of complete state ownership. On a smaller scale, state ownership developed in France, Austria, and Italy. Government support and control, but not ownership, was evident in Spain, Portugal, and, especially, Russia. In England, Parliament created a commission to regulate railroads. In the United States, Congress adopted the Interstate Commerce Commission to regulate railroads in 1887. Widespread government ownership of the railroads may have helped Lenin to form his theory that capitalism was evolving toward a form of state monopoly capitalism.

Construction of railroads in non-European countries led to a period of railroad imperialism. Foreign governments needed European financial capital to construct railroads. British investors were active in financing railroad construction in India, China, South America, and Canada. Governments helped arrange financing and tried to influence the routes of railroads. Non-European governments, needing foreign capital, often had to bow to the wishes of European governments.

The multiplication of automobiles and trucks, and the rapid improvement of the airplane, overshadowed the railroad industry during the twentieth century. Suddenly, the days when railroad issues dominated the New York stock market seemed like ancient history, and railroads were no longer an energizing force in capitalist development. After 1970, intercity passenger service in the United States survived only with a government subsidy.

Toward the end of the twentieth century, however, railroads seemed poised to experience a revival. In a world conscious of environmental, safety, and quality-of-life issues, railway transportation began to take on the luster of a modern technology. Railway transportation outperformed alternative forms of transportation in terms of energy efficiency, air pollutants, greenhouse emissions, traffic congestion, injuries and fatalities, and land usage. Even the car-dependent United States has talked of turning to high-speed train service for important, high-volume routes. Europe has already laid plans to connect major cities with 30,000 kilometers of high-speed rail lines. U.S. cities are expanding urban rail systems to combat traffic congestion and air pollution.

The railroads favored the capitalist tendency toward aggregation. When roads were the main method of transportation, the supply of food in nearby areas restricted the growth of cities. The development of railroads significantly widened the area supplying food. As cities grew, business grew, with large shippers de-manding lower transportation rates than small shippers. Businesses grew bigger as the world grew smaller.

See also Age of Steel, Finance Capitalism.

References Davis, Clarence B., and Kenneth E. Wilburn Jr., eds. *Railway Imperialism* (1991); Hadley, Arthur T. *Railroad Transportation: Its History and Its Laws* (1885); Lowe, Marcia D. *Back on Track: The Global Rail Revival* (1994).

Refeudalization

Refeudalization, meaning a return to feudal forms of economic organization, contributed to Italy's retreat from capitalist expansion in the seventeenth century. Feudalism, like slavery, tended to thrive on the periphery of capitalism, where regions, trying to meet the growing demand for raw materials from capitalist nations, struggled with limited supplies of labor.

During the seventeenth century, refeudalization was evident in peripheral areas, where capitalism had not sunk deep roots. Italy, often regarded as the birthplace of capitalism, also experienced a process of refeudalization, as economic leadership of the capitalist world passed to Holland and England. According to the historian Rosario Vallari:

Widely accepted now is the notion that in the seventeenth century Italy experienced a far reaching process of refeudalization, which, if it did not entirely obliterate the achievements of earlier centuries, nonetheless, caused a clear break on the path of expansion that Italy had trodden since the days of the Comuni. [Refeudalization] manifested itself, as is well known, in the stoppage of that commercial and industrial growth that had been at the root of the civilization of the city-states; but in the countryside too, property and production relationships underwent a process of involution, as ecclesiastical and noble privileges in economic, social, and political matters gained fresh ground.... This was a time of consolidation and expansion for the large church and feudal estates...and of the reappearance of a whole set of privileges, prerogatives, abuses, and shackles that the feudal system imposed on productive activity.

The process of refeudalization involved a defection of the bourgeoisie, who took its wealth and purchased offices and titles, government bonds, and fiefs, preferring to cultivate the aristocratic arts of leisure, rather than undertake the hazards and risks of commercial enterprise. As city governments fell into the hands of landed wealth, the urban mercantile class faced a less friendly, and certainly less understanding, political environment.

Some scholars attribute the defection of the bourgeoisie to Spanish influence. Treasure from the New World had made Spain the most prosperous and powerful country in Europe, and the most powerful political influence in Italy. Lombardy was under Spanish rule, and the Spanish government sold fiefs as a means of raising money. The Spanish extolled the military virtues, and put a stigma on commercial vocations. Nineteenth-century historian Carlo Cattaneo put it in these terms:

Those families that, in keeping with our native traditions, had continued to practice honest and noble trades even after they had achieved great wealth, now, finding themselves outranked by the least Spanish captain, began to despise the labors of their forefathers and strove to purify their blood by a life of sloth.... Then vast sums of capital that had been invested in business in Lyons, Paris, Antwerp, London, and Cologne were withdrawn and were sunk in land and titles, in aristocratic ostentation, in alms which corrupted the industrial populace.

Recently, scholars have spread the blame more widely, citing the Renaissance revival of the study of law and humanistic studies that required leisure. The pageantry of the French court, and infatuation with ideas of chivalry and honor,

may also have added inspiration to the process of refeudalization.

Capitalism thrives on the values of the urban business classes, which the landed aristocracy often finds debasing. Napoleon derisively referred to the English as a "nation of shopkeepers." Such aristocratic values seem incomprehensible in a country such as the United States, where the number of self-made millionaires exceeds the number of millionaires by inheritance. Whether a culture of capitalism is a prerequisite for the emergence of capitalism remains uncertain. Clearly, where capitalism prospers, business occupations are accorded the highest ranks of social prestige.

See also Judaism, Puritanism.

References Braudel, Fernand. *The Mediterranean and the Mediterranean World in the Age of Philip II*, Vol. 2 (1973); Sella, Domenico. *Crisis and Continuity: The Economy of Spanish Lombardy in the Seventeenth Century* (1979).

Reform Act of 1832 (England)

The Reform Act of 1832 altered the composition of Parliament in favor of the industrial capitalists and middle classes, at the expense of the landowning aristocracy, artisans, and craftsmen. It extended the voting franchise to the middle classes.

Before 1832, the House of Commons bore little resemblance to a representative body of a democratic government. Geographical representation in the House of Commons betrayed no relationship to population or number of eligible voters. Newspapers printed advertisements for the seats of rotten boroughs. Voters also put their votes up for sale, and elections became contests of bribery.

The Industrial Revolution shifted population to different areas and spurred the growth of new towns. Rich merchants and financiers could often buy their way to power and influence in Parliament, but the industrial employers and tradesmen had little voice in government. The voting franchise favored the owners of land. The growing middle class, living in the underrepresented large towns, had little share in government. Because of wartime taxes and debt, the cry for business government rose from the middle class.

The driving power of the reform movement drew strength from a temporary alliance of the middle classes and the working classes. Both groups counted themselves as outsiders in the political process, and the working classes called for universal male suffrage. When the Whig party championed the cause of reform, the leadership of the reform movement clearly passed into the hands of the middle class. When the Whigs came to power in 1830, they put reform at the head of their agenda.

In March 1831, Lord John Russell introduced a bill that abolished the rotten boroughs, extended the voting franchise to include most of the middle class, and redistributed geographical representation in Parliament to mirror population distribution. Manual workers in some boroughs enjoyed wide suffrage under existing laws, but lost out on the right to vote in the new proposal. Russell's measure never passed the House of Commons. After a general election strengthened the hand of the Whigs, a second measure passed the House of Commons, only to die in the House of Lords.

After this second failure, the Whig party seemed slow to act again. By then, the radical members of the working class felt betrayed. Francis Place, who had spearheaded the drive to repeal the Combination Acts, helped organize the National Political Union, which included, but was not limited to, the local unions in the big towns and cities. Moderate members of worker organizations came around to support the Whig proposal. The slogan, "The whole bill, and nothing but the bill," came to symbolize workers' support of the bill, in spite of the absence of wider suffrage. Working-class agitation, and the fear it inspired, supplied the political momentum to carry the third bill over the top. The bill received the royal assent in June 1832.

The new Reform Act increased the number of the male population who could vote from 14 percent to 18 percent, and it extended the right to vote to the propertied middle class, but took it away from many artisans. On balance, it increased the correlation between property and the right to vote, and shifted the emphasis away from landed property, to include industrial and commercial wealth. The definition of property was widened to include such things as mortgages and bills of exchange.

The reins of government now rested clearly in the hands of employers. Workers began to see government less as a seat of corruption, and more as a weapon in the hands of capitalist oppressors. The disillusioned workers had learned how to organize politically, and would now try to seek their goals without an alliance with the middle class.

See also Class Struggle.

References Cole, G. D. H. *A Short History of the British Working-Class Movement: 1789–1947* (1948); Woodward, E. L. *The Age of Reform: 1815–1870* (1962).

Reform Bill of 1867
See Trade Union Act of 1871.

Registration Act of 1844
See Joint Companies Act of 1856.

Regulation Q (United States)
Regulation Q referred to the code of Federal Reserve restrictions governing the maximum interest rates that banks and other depository institutions could pay on various types of deposits. It grew out of Depression-era banking regulations. The Depository Institutions Deregulation and Monetary Control Act of 1980 phased out Regulation Q.

The outline of a marked trend toward rising bank failures came into focus before the Depression of the 1930s, but an alarming rate of bank failures rose to crisis proportions between 1930 and 1933. Congress gave part of the blame for the rash of bank failures to interest-bearing checking accounts, which were symptomatic of the keen competition between banks for depositors' money. They may also have reflected a lack of confidence in banks. In the Banking Act of 1933, Congress prohibited the payment of interest on checking accounts, and empowered the Federal Reserve to set interest-rate ceilings for savings and time deposits at banks.

The Interest Control Act of 1966 brought thrift deposits under interest-rate regulation. Rising interest rates in the 1960s squeezed thrifts whose revenue came from long-standing mortgages negotiated when interest rates were much lower. The purpose of this act lay in the desire to protect those thrifts that faced insolvency if interest rates on thrift deposits were bid up beyond what low-interest mortgages could pay.

Regulation Q grew into an elaborate schedule of interest-rate ceilings. It allowed thrift institutions to pay one-fourth percent more than commercial banks on passbook accounts. This discrepancy was justified on grounds that thrift customers needed an added incentive to compensate for the absence of checking privileges at thrift institutions. These kinds of differentials existed for the size and length of the deposits, and for the type of institution.

Rising interest rates in the 1970s induced an outflow of funds from thrift institutions. To protect thrifts, the Federal Reserve raised the minimum denomination of Treasury bills from $1,000 to $10,000. Treasury bills were safe as federally insured deposits, and paid interest rates above the ceilings of Regulation Q. This action of the Federal Reserve was intended to stem the tide of thrift depositors turning to Treasury bills to escape Regulation Q. The Federal Reserve also lifted interest-rate ceilings on deposits at, or above, $100,000.

As interest rates climbed to giddy heights in the 1970s, financial innovation found ways for small investors to sidestep Regulation Q. A prime example is the creation of the money market mutual fund accounts. These accounts technically represented ownership of shares of stock whose values always remained at $1 per share. In turn, money market mutual fund companies invested depositors' funds only in Treasury bills, making the funds as safe as federally insured accounts. Although money market mutual fund accounts were secure, they were exempt from Regulation Q, and often paid very high rates of interest. Commercial banks and thrifts faced unbearable competition from the money market mutual fund companies. With these institutions clamoring for freedom to compete, Congress abolished interest-rate ceilings, and the ban on interest-bearing checking accounts.

The history of Regulation Q illustrates the organic resourcefulness of the capitalist system to develop innovations that elude government regulations. Money market mutual fund accounts were born of government regulation. As the legacy of the Depression of the 1930s faded from public memory, fear of competition in the banking industry subsided. Congress acted to remove a portion of the government regulation, but the banking industry remained highly regulated.

See also Depository Institutions Deregulation and Monetary Control Act of 1980.

References Baye, Michael R., and Dennis W. Jansen. *Money, Banking, and Financial Markets* (1995); White, Lawrence J. "The Partial Deregulation of Banks and other Depository Institutions." *Regulatory Reform: What Actually Happened?* (1986).

Restrictive Trade Practices Act of 1956 (England)

The Restrictive Trade Practices Act ended the toleration in English law of monopolistic trade practices by members of a trade. England had fallen well behind the United States in developing antitrust laws to protect competition. Congress passed the Sherman Antitrust Act of 1890. Restraints on trade were illegal under ancient common law in England. Common law doctrines, however, were hardly ever invoked in cases involving monopolistic practices after the House of Lords decision in the *Mogul Steamship Company* case in 1891. From that time on, monopolistic practices and collusive agreements often enjoyed the approbation of the law. In 1937, the House of Lords decided, in the *Thorton v. Motor Trade Association* case, that industry price agreements were lawful and enforceable under law. In defense of this decision, Lord Wright wrote: "[T]he interest of the combination is to promote and protect the legitimate trade interests of the respondent Association and its members and is not a combination willfully to injure."

The passage of the Monopolies and Restrictive Practices (Inquiry and Control) Act of 1948 signaled a change in English attitudes toward restrictive trade practices. This act provided for inquiries into monopolistic practices, to determine the existence and the implications of conditions of monopoly. The act's major accomplishment was to use the power of inquiry to collect information. Its provisions "for dealing with mischiefs" were amended by the Restrictive Trade Practices Act of 1956.

The Restrictive Trade Practices Act required the registration of all agreements limiting the freedom to sell and buy on terms agreeable to the parties of transactions. In addition to the prices at which sales are transacted, the act covered agreements involving the amount of sales or purchases between parties, or the amounts or kinds of production parties could undertake: Price fixing and production quotas had to be reported.

The act established the Restrictive Practices Court to evaluate agreements from the perspective of the public interest. Judges and laypeople compose this court. The laypeople outnumber the judges on this special court, but a judge presides. This court will declare a restrictive agreement against the public interest, unless the agreement meets special criteria elucidated in the act. The court must render a judgment on exceptions under these criteria, and may uphold agreements of collusion and restrictive prac-

tices if (1) the agreement is necessary to protect the public from injury, or gives the public some other positive benefit; (2) if the agreement is necessary to counteract the monopoly power exerted by others; (3) if removal of the agreement may cause unemployment in an industry or area; or (4) if removal of the agreement may cause a loss in export trade.

The Restrictive Practices Act gave more latitude for justifying monopolies and restrictive agreements than U.S. antitrust laws permit. The courts in the United States have tended to rule against any activity that tends to monopolize an industry. The rather tardy interest of England and other European countries in preserving competition enabled the United States to pioneer this area of capitalist development.

See also Clayton Act of 1914, Sherman Antitrust Act of 1890.

References Bernhard, Richard C. "English Law and American Law on Monopolies and Restraints of Trade." *Journal of Economics and Law* (1960); Macrosty, Henry. *The Trust Movement in British Industry* (1968).

Revenue Act of 1964 (United States)

The Revenue Act of 1964 is commonly called the Kennedy tax cut, because President Kennedy proposed the tax cut before his assassination. It was important in the history of capitalism, because it was proposed solely to stimulate the U.S. economy. Its proponents were not advocating a plan to downsize government spending, or to grant relief to discontented tax payers.

The justification for the tax cut lay in the idea that income tax revenue represents a leakage from the spending stream, which occurs whenever recipients of income do not use it to directly buy goods and services. Economists in the Kennedy administration concluded that the U.S. economy was suffering from fiscal drag, a situation in which tax revenue leakages reached excessive levels as the economy approached full employment, acting as a drag that stunted economic recoveries. The cure for this economic ailment called for either cutting taxes or adding compensating injections to the spending stream, such as greater government spending, investment spending, or consumer spending.

Before the tax cut, the scale of marginal tax rates on income ranged from 20 to 91 percent. After the tax cut, the scale ranged from 14 to 70 percent, which added up to an average tax reduction of about 25 percent. The tax rate on corporate income declined from 52 to 48 percent.

The bill was advanced as a $11.5 billion cut in taxes. Tax revenue dropped about $10 billion the first year, but quickly rose above the level that existed before the tax cut. Between 1963 and 1967, tax revenue rose at the same rate as it did between 1959 and 1963.

The tax cut achieved its prime objective, which was to spur the economy to higher levels of growth and prosperity. By 1968, the high levels of government spending associated with the Vietnam War threatened to send a prosperous U.S. economy into an inflationary boom. Since fear of inflation eclipsed the concern for fiscal drag, the Johnson administration proposed a 10-percent surtax, dampening the expansionary forces in the economy.

Economists who designed the tax cut of 1964 saw it as a means of stimulating the economy by increasing consumer demand for goods and services. In the 1980s, supply-side economists attributed the success of the tax cut of 1964 to the incentives it provided for working, saving, and taking risk by advancing the after-tax rewards for these activities. The success of the tax cut of 1964 reinforced the concern that high tax rates have harmful effects in capitalist economic systems, and decreased the likelihood that high marginal rates on income would survive the World War II and Cold War eras, when government spending was necessarily high.

See also Economic Recovery Act of 1981, Income Tax.

References Okun, Arthur M. "Measuring the Impact of the 1964 Tax Reduction." *Perspectives on Economic Growth* (1968); Stein, Herbert. *The Fiscal Revolution in America* (1996).

Revocation of the Edict of Nantes (France)

In 1598, Henry IV of France issued the Edict of Nantes, which protected the right of Huguenots to practice their faith within France, under strict limitations. Huguenots were a Protestant minority in predominantly Catholic France. This edict granted the right of Huguenots to practice their faith on their own estates, or within towns that had traditionally been Protestant before 1597. It also protected the rights of Huguenots to membership in guilds, professions, and employments, to representation in courts of law, and to educational opportunities. The Huguenots were prominent in banking, trade, and industry, particularly silk, glass, and paper making.

In 1685, Louis XIV revoked the Edict of Nantes. In the persecution that led up to the revocation, and its subsequent enforcement, many Huguenots emigrated from France, taking valuable skills and capital with them. An influx of Huguenot immigrants helped lift Holland to world leadership in silk, linen, and paper making. The French economy stagnated from 1684 until 1717, inducing speculation at the time that the departure of the Huguenots acted to retard economic development in France. Today, scholars are unsure of the actual impact on French economic development, because many Huguenots remained behind, benefiting from the trade contacts with Huguenots who had emigrated to other countries.

The Revocation of the Edict of Nantes, and the subsequent speculation about its repercussions, is suggestive of why capitalism has thrived in countries that practice religious toleration. Theoretically, capitalism rewards individuals exclusively on the basis of productivity, rather than religious affiliation, pedigree, or other traits. When unpopular minorities are judged on factors other than productivity, the more productive members of those minorities migrate to capitalist countries, where natural aptitudes are rewarded. Some scholars have also argued that the spirit of Protestantism, unlike the spirit of Catholicism, is conducive to the development of capitalism. For these reasons, capitalist countries, such as Holland and England, which practiced religious toleration, benefited from the influx of Huguenots, at the expense of countries, such as France, that practiced religious persecution.

See also Puritanism.

References Braudel, Fernand. *Civilization and Capitalism*, Vols. 1–3 (1984); Scoville, Warren C. *The Persecution of Huguenots and French Economic Development: 1680–1720* (1960); Stankiewicz, J. *Politics and Religion in Seventeenth Century France* (1960).

Revolutions of 1848

A wave of revolutionary uprisings surged through continental Europe in 1848. Only Russia stood above the revolutionary chaos that shook the thrones of Europe. Middle-class businessmen, lawyers, journalists, intellectuals, and students yearned for democratic institutions. Artisans saw machinery replacing skilled workers, and felt at the mercy of a free market that had no respect for the concept of a living wage. The urban working class added the momentum to a revolutionary movement shaped by middle-class proponents of constitutional government. The same year that saw simultaneous uprisings of workers taking to the streets also saw the publication of the *Manifesto of the Communist Party*. The memory of workers throwing up barricades and fighting in the streets supplied the raw material for the communist vision of a proletarian revolution.

The Revolutions of 1848 began in Paris, and spread to Germany and Prussia, Austria, and Italy. In France, the Revolution of 1848 gave birth to the Second Republic. The Parisian working class played a vital role in supporting the revolt against the monarchy, but the new government turned against the workers in a bloody repression.

The agitation that sparked the revolution in Paris favored expanding the suffrage. The republican and working-class groups held reform banquets to help gather petition signatures for expanding the suffrage. The government ordered the cancellation of a reform banquet planned for 22 February. On 23 February, protesters took to the streets, and raised 24 barricades in popular areas of Paris. Efforts to put down the insurrection by force were ineffectual. On 24 February, Louis Philippe abdicated and sought refuge in England. Later on the same day, a provisional government of moderate and radical republicans proclaimed itself the government of France.

The new government in Paris decreed freedom of the press, legalized worker associations, established universal male suffrage, and called for the election of a National Assembly. It also made all adult male citizens eligible for the National Guard, and adopted the tricolor flag. To quell fears of another reign of terror reminiscent of the French Revolution, the new government put an end to the death penalty for political offenses. The Hotel de Ville served as the headquarters of the new government. The pressure of a crowd of working-class protesters waiting outside influenced early decisions of the government.

The worker demonstrators demanded the organization of labor and the right to work. The new government announced that National Workshops would provide work for the unemployed, whose numbers were growing. The government also established a commission on labor to meet the need for the "organization of labor." The decree creating this commission stated:

Considering that the Revolution, made by the people should be made for it: That it is time to put an end to the long and iniquitous sufferings of the laborers; That the question of labor is of a supreme importance; That there are no more lofty, more dignified preoccupation of a republican government; That it is particularly suitable to France to study ardently and to resolve a problem posed today in all the industrial nations of Europe; That the ways of guaranteeing to the people the legitimate fruits of their labor must be considered without delay; The Provisional Government of the Republic decrees: A permanent commission, which will be entitled: Commission of Government for the Laborers, will be named, with the express and special mission of considering their destiny.

All the trades in Paris had representation on the commission, which was headed by two members of the new government. The commission met in the Palais de Luxembourg, and became known as the Luxembourg Commission. Worker associations founded on democratic principles sprang to life. Although their primary purpose was the regulation of individual trades, they also served as political clubs. For a while, the Luxembourg Commission was the only elected body in Paris. It acquired a status in the eyes of the workers that exceeded its mandate from the government. Those were days of rapturous enthusiasm for the workers.

The election of the National Assembly on 23 April became a major setback for the workers' movement. Peasants in rural areas helped return conservative representatives to the new assembly. Earlier in April, the government had lined the streets with guards during one of the worker demonstrations. The candidates of the working-class movement even lost in Paris.

The government turned more hostile to the initiatives of the worker associations. On 15 May, the workers made a feeble effort to pull off another revolution. The National Assembly disbanded the Luxembourg Commission, and pressed charges against working-class leaders in the government. On 21 June, a government decree announced the end of the National Workshops. The workers felt a deep sense of betrayal, a common

theme of the Revolutions of 1848, and staged an armed insurrection. The army spent four days quashing the uprising, which cost the lives of 15,000 insurgents; another 12,000 faced imprisonment.

Like the Paris insurrection that began a few weeks earlier, the German Revolution of 1848 began as an unstable alliance of the middle and working classes against the existing government. Demonstrations over food shortages and petitions for parliamentary reform marked the autumn of 1847 in Germany. Political reformers argued for a national parliament, universal suffrage, freedom of the press, and basic human rights. Despite the rising current of discontent, an insurrection in Germany would probably not have happened in the absence of an uprising in France, because the protesters in Germany were not as sophisticated. Some thought freedom of the press meant freedom from being pressed by high taxes; others thought it meant the privilege to put notices in the classified ads free of charge.

Frederick Wilhelm IV, king of Prussia, made military preparations in Berlin as protection against an uprising. Protesters and troops met in the streets, shots rang out, protesters accused the soldiers of an unprovoked attack, and the fighting began. The protesters barricaded streets and fought for control of Berlin. Many of the streetfighters were young handicraftsmen and artisan journeymen, which was the portion of the working class suffering most from the Industrial Revolution. Frederick Wilhelm voluntarily disengaged the troops, and ordered them to leave the city. He unwittingly fell into the hands of leaders of the uprising, became the head of a civilian government, and provided for the election of a parliament to enact constitutional reforms. Fear of continued working-class agitation drove the members of this parliament into to the arms of Frederick Wilhelm, the proponents of monarchy, and the army. In November 1848, Frederick Wilhelm abolished the Prussian parliament.

In the meantime, liberal forces were

preparing to unite Germany under one national legislature. The National Parliament was elected, and convened in Frankfurt on 18 May 1848, with the purpose of drafting a constitution for a united Germany.

The working class was feeling its power in society, and started to organize. Workers' associations sprouted up everywhere, and the National Parliament received an influx of petitions from worker groups asking for laws or programs to address their plight. One common concern of these petitions was fear of free trade, which meant, to the workers, unbridled competition. Workers felt shorn of the protection of the rules and regulations of the guilds, and they felt pressured by foreign goods produced with machines. Workers also wanted the right to vote. As the new parliament moved closer to the older dynastic governments, the workers rioted.

The National Parliament wrote a constitution that created a federal government responsible to a national parliament representing a united Germany. The new constitution had few democratic features other than universal suffrage. The National Parliament offered the crown to Frederick William as the head of the new government, but he refused, and the Parliament had no army to support it. The Parliament disbanded in failure, workers rioted, and troops enforced order. The German revolution was a failure in its larger goals.

The repression of the worker associations may have encouraged the growth of socialist organizations in Germany. The *Manifesto of the Communist Party* of Marx and Engels came out in February 1848. Marx was not an influential player in the worker associations during the Revolutions of 1848, but the *Manifesto* was written as a platform for the Communist League, which was one of the worker associations that was suppressed after 1848. Several of its members were arrested and imprisoned. Regardless of the suppression of worker associations, working-class consciousness had been raised in Germany, and workers, who saw the middle class as part of the enemy, were susceptible to socialist theories.

Although the spark and inspiration of the Revolutions of 1848 came from the February uprising in Paris, the first tremors of the revolutionary quake were felt in southern Italy and Sicily. In January 1848, the citizens of Sicily drove out the forces of King Ferdinand of Naples. The populace took control of the city, set up a provisional government, and declared Sicily an independent state. As word spread to Naples of the events in Sicily, the people led a revolt that forced King Ferdinand to grant a constitution. The spirit of revolt spread to Venice, Florence, Milan, and Rome. In 1849, the Hapsburg monarchy reestablished itself in northern Italy, and Naples recaptured Sicily. The revolutionaries of 1848 could boast of few victories.

From Berlin, the revolution spread like a chain reaction to the four major centers of the Habsburg Empire—Vienna, Budapest, Prague, and northern Italy. In Vienna, unruly mobs sacked food stores, butcher shops, bakeries, and tobacco shops. They burned and looted factories, and smashed machines. The government agreed to constitutional reforms to placate the middle class, including freedom of the press, which was used to fan the flames of revolutionary fervor. On 15 May, the government quelled a fresh insurrection by supporting the election of a constituent assembly by universal suffrage. This assembly abolished serfdom in Austria, which became one of the few accomplishments of the Revolutions of 1848. The emperor and the court fled Vienna. The middle class yearned for an assembly composed of property owners. Bursts of rioting continued to threaten property throughout the summer. Most of the members of the assembly were moderates who wanted law and order. In October, a frenzied mob butchered Count Latour, the minister of war, and hung his mangled corpse to a lamppost. The court, which had returned in August, again fled the city, along with many aristocrats, capitalists, and middle-class property owners. Radical students, factory workers, and artisans took control of the city. They manned the city walls and barricaded the streets. Imperial troops recaptured the city on 31 October. By the end of 1849, the Hapsburg monarchy had reinstated itself in Vienna, Hungary, and northern Italy.

Karl Marx, in *Das Kapital*, described the results of the Revolutions of 1848 in the following terms:

[T]he June insurrections in Paris and its bloody suppression united, in England as on the Continent, all the factions of the ruling classes, landlords and capitalists, stock exchange wolves and shopkeepers, Protectionists and free-traders, government and opposition, priests and freethinkers, young whores and old nuns, under the common cry for the salvation of Property, Religion, the Family, and Society. The working class was everywhere proclaimed, placed under a ban, under a virtual law of suspects.

Invariably, the Revolutions of 1848 ended in failure. The working class emerged from the revolutions with a clearer identification of itself as a separate class engaged in a class struggle. The stress of these revolutions opened the hidden seam in the coalition between middle-class supporters of democratic institutions and members of the working class demanding economic improvement. Important elements of the working class began to separate itself from the agitation for democratic institutions, and to think in terms of a dictatorship of the proletariat. The energizing factor in these uprisings lay in the desire of a middle class for parliamentary government and a working class seeking relief from economic woes. These revolutions left the monarchical governments in power in every country but France, led to a suppression of the working-class movement, and left working-class agitators feeling betrayed and used by the middle class.

See also Paris Commune of 1871, Uprising of the Lyon Silk Workers.

References Noyes, P. H. *Organization and Revolution: Working Class Associations in the German Revolutions of 1848–1849* (1966); Sewell, William H., Jr. *Work and Revolution in France: The Language of Labor from the Old Regime to 1848* (1980); Sperber, Jonathan. *The European Revolutions, 1848–1851* (1994).

Right to Work (Prussia)

The Prussian common law, as promulgated by King Frederick William II in 1794, recognized the responsibility of the government to provide work, and to protect the poor. The Prussian Landrecht (Civil Code) contained the following clauses:

1. It is the duty of the State to provide for the sustenance and support of those of its citizens who cannot...procure subsistence themselves.
2. Work adapted to their strength and capacities shall be supplied to those who lack means and opportunity of earning a livelihood for themselves and those dependent upon them.
3. Those who, for laziness, love of idleness, or other irregular proclivities, do not choose to employ the means offered them by earning a livelihood, shall be kept to useful work by compulsion and punishment under proper control.
4. The state is entitled and bound to take such measures as will prevent the destitution of it citizens and check excessive extravagance.
5. The police authority of every place must provide for all poor and destitute persons, whose subsistence cannot be ensured in any other way.

In these clauses, we sense the germ of the idea that the state is responsible for the social protection of the individual. The idea passed from Prussia to Germany. In the 1880s, Germany pioneered social legislation that became a prototype for unemployment compensation, workers' compensation, old-age assistance, and medical insurance programs. From Germany these programs passed to France, England, the United States, and most industrialized countries. The Depression of the 1930s saw governments experiment with public employment programs that made government the employer of last resort. After World War II, the U.S. government officially accepted the responsibility to promote a full-employment economy.

In 1884, Chancellor Bismarck, speaking to the Reichstag in favor of social insurance for workers, made a famous declaration of the workingman's "right to work." Bismarck made this statement in light of the foregoing clauses. By a curiosity of history, in the twentieth century, the phrase "right to work" came to refer to the right to work without joining a union.

See also Employer Liability and Worker Compensation, Social Insurance, Unemployment Insurance.

References Dawson, William Harbutt. *Bismarck and State Socialism* (1890); De Schweinitz, Karl. *England's Road to Social Security from the Statute of Laborers in 1349 to the Beveridge Report of 1942* (1961); Rimlinger, Gaston V. *Welfare Policy and Industrialization in Europe, America, and Russia* (1971).

Right-to-Work Laws (United States)

In the United States, federal labor law allows individual states to enact state laws, called right-to-work laws, that ban union shops. A union shop exists where an employer hires an individual who works as a nonunion employee during a probationary period, which rarely lasts longer than six months, when the worker must join a union, or pay union dues, as a condition of employment.

In 1947, Congress passed the Taft-Hartley Act, amid widespread concern about a rash of strikes and growing union power. John L. Lewis labeled the Taft-Hartley Act the "slave labor law," because of its antiunion tenor: It outlawed various unfair labor practices and the closed shop. Without outlawing the union shop, it authorized individual state governments to outlaw union shops.

States that enacted right-to-work statutes are located mostly in the South, Midwest, and West, and included Alabama, Arizona, Arkansas, Florida, Georgia, Iowa, Louisiana, Mississippi, Nebraska, Nevada, North Carolina, North Dakota, South Carolina, South Dakota, Tennessee, Texas, Utah, Virginia, and Wyoming. Right-to-work laws are concentrated in those areas where labor unions had most difficulty establishing themselves. Many of these states are in regions that lag in per capita income and regard unions as inimical to economic development. Unions point to the job growth in right-to-work states as a factor that accounts for declines in the percent of the labor force that is unionized. Unions also complain that right-to-work laws create a class of free-riders, who enjoy the same rights to union representation as dues-paying union members. State right-to-work elections have been hotly contested. Kansas repealed a right-to-work law in 1982; Louisiana enacted its right-to-work law only in 1977.

See also Taft-Hartley Act of 1947.

References Clark, Gordon. *Unions and Communities Under Siege* (1989); Masters, Marick F. *Unions at the Crossroads* (1997).

Riksbank (Sweden)

The Riksbank, or Bank of Sweden, the oldest central bank in the world, was the first European bank to issue bank notes. Goldsmiths had issued receipts that circulated as money, but the Riksbank was the first bank to issue paper money.

The Riksbank came into being in 1656 as a private bank, split into two departments. One department was an exchange, or deposit, bank, organized along the lines of the Bank of Amsterdam. It accepted deposits of coins and precious metals, and issued bank deposits that served as money, and that were back up by 100-percent reserves of precious metals. The second department was a lending bank.

The Riksbank issued its first bank notes in 1661. Other banks had already pioneered the use of bills of exchange and bank deposits as circulating mediums that supplemented the circulation of coins. Sweden turned to bank notes as a medium of exchange, because payments in copper, which served as money in Sweden, were bulky and heavy, even for domestic transactions. Sweden adopted copper as the basis for money in 1625, perhaps because Sweden boasted the largest copper mine in Europe, and the Swedish government owned a share of it. Copper mines paved the way for bank notes, when, for convenience and utility, they began paying miners in copper notes. These notes were preferable to copper coins and traded at a premium.

In 1668, ownership of the Riksbank passed into the hands of the government, making it the oldest central bank in operation today. By the early 1700s, bank notes were no longer a rarity in Europe. The Bank of England was chartered in 1694, for the purpose of making loans and issuing bank notes, and, by 1720, France was learning the disastrous consequences of issuing bank notes without discipline. The threat of hyperinflation from issuing bank notes without discipline continues to haunt the capitalist countries today.

See also Central Banks and Free Banking.

References Kindleberger, Charles P. *A Financial History of Western Europe* (1984); Samuelsson, Kurt. *From Great Power to Welfare State: 300 Years of Swedish Social Development* (1968).

Rio Declaration on Environment and Development

The Rio Declaration on Environment and Development was adopted at a conference of the United Nations Committee on Environment and Development held in Rio de Janeiro in June 1992. The final language of the declaration revealed the chasm that separates developed and developing countries on environmental issues. Participants even disagreed on the name of the declaration: Representatives from the developed countries wanted to call the declaration the Earth Charter, patterned after the Universal Declaration of Human Rights of 1948. Representatives of developing countries, where environmental goals are more often sacrificed in favor of economic development, found fault with the heavy environmental connotation of in "Earth Charter." The title was changed to the Rio Declaration of Human Rights of 1992.

From the outset, the Rio Conference was planned as a 20-year anniversary commemoration for the Stockholm Conference of 1972. The Rio Declaration reaffirmed an important principle enunciated in the Stockholm Declaration, which acknowledged the sovereignty of governments to control the exploitation of resources within their jurisdictional boundaries, but placed upon them the "responsibility to ensure that activities within their jurisdiction or control do not cause damage to the environment of other States or areas beyond the limits of their national jurisdiction." The Rio Declaration, echoing another important principle of the Stockholm Declaration, called for the development of a body of international environmental law that could force violators to accept liability and make compensation.

Several principles of the Rio Declaration emphasize the importance of the economic development of the Third World as a part of the solution to global environmental and economic problems. One principle states that, "in order to achieve sustainable development, environmental protection shall constitute an integral part of the development process and cannot be considered in isolation from it." References are made to decreasing disparities in living standards, and to promoting a supportive and open international economic system. One passage in the Rio Declaration reads:

> States shall cooperate in a spirit of global partnership to conserve, protect and restore the health and integrity of the Earth's ecosystem. In view of the different contributions to global environmental degradation, States have common but differentiated responsibilities. The developed countries acknowledge the responsibility that they

bear in the international pursuit of sustainable development in view of the pressures their societies place on the global environment and of the technologies and financial resources they command.

The Rio Declaration drew some criticism for not putting enough emphasis on conservation of resources. The developed capitalist countries, such as the United States, pressed the hardest for conservation and environmental measures to protect resources, such as the atmosphere and ocean, that are shared by all nations. These are wealthy countries who can afford to exercise some restraint, but also have experience with what can happen to resources that are not privately owned, and are shared with many on a first-come, first-served basis.

Nevertheless, the developing countries obviously feel their poverty much more keenly than their environmental degradation. With socialism now in disarray, the world capitalist system must find a way to deal with the mounting environmental crisis. Maurice Strong, the secretary-general of the United Nations Committee on Environment and Development during the Rio Conference, compared the situation of the world environment in 1992 with what it had been during the Stockholm Conference in 1972, in these words:

As I traveled to every region of the world, retracing my steps of twenty years ago, the extent and nature of this environmental degradation and its tragic human consequences were everywhere. The cities of the developing countries, growing at rates beyond anything ever before experienced, are now among the world's most polluted, many of them headed for environmental and social breakdown. The appalling destruction of natural resources, loss of forest cover, erosion and degradation of soils, and deterioration of supplies and quality of water are visible throughout the developing world. Economic losses in agriculture, fisheries, and tourism are tragically manifested in diminished livelihoods for already impoverished and struggling people. This forbidding drama is unfolding throughout the developing world, threatening a massive human eco-tragedy beyond any ever before witnessed, the grim portents of which can be seen in the recurring famines in Africa.

See also Global Commons, Stockholm Declaration.

References Nanda, Ved P. *International Environmental Law and Policy* (1995); Panjabi, Ranee K. L. *The Earth Summit At Rio: Politics, Economics, and the Environment* (1997).

Robinson-Patman Act of 1936 (United States)

The Robinson-Patman Act is also known as the Chain Store Act, because its major purpose is to prevent chain stores from extracting discounts from suppliers that small businesses could not extract. These discounts were thought to give the chain stores an unfair cost advantage over the smaller businesses.

Section 2(a) of the act reads:

That it shall be unlawful for any person engaged in commerce, in the course of such commerce, either directly or indirectly, to discriminate in price between different purchasers of commodities of like grade and quality, where either or any of the purchasers involved in such discrimination are in commerce...and where the effect of such discrimination may be substantially to lessen competition or tend to create a monopoly in any line of commerce, or to injure, destroy or prevent competition with any person who either grants or knowingly receives the benefit of such competition, or with customers of either of them:

PROVIDED, That nothing herein contained shall prevent differentials which make only due allowance for differences in the cost of manufacture, sale, or delivery resulting from the differing methods or quantities in which such commodities are to such purchasers sold or delivered:

PROVIDED HOWEVER: That the Federal Trade Commission may, after due investigation and hearing to all interested parties, fix and establish quantity limits, and revise the same as it finds necessary, as to particular commodities or classes of commodities, where it finds that available purchasers in greater quantities are so few as to render differentials on account thereof unjustly discriminatory or promotive of monopoly in any line of commerce; and the foregoing shall not then be construed differentials based on differences in quantities greater than those so fixed and established....

The controversial nature of the Robinson-Patman Act lies in the emphasis on protecting individual competitors, rather than the competitive process. Other antitrust statutes restrict business practices that lessen competition. The Robinson-Patman Act restricts price discrimination when the effect is to lessen competition, or to injure a particular competitor. Critics of the act contend that discounts to big buyers are justified because of efficiency, and that the act protects small companies that are no longer efficient. The Supreme Court never held quantity discounts illegal per se, but quantity discounts have not fared well as a defense.

The Robinson-Patman Act has been most useful in prosecuting cases in which price discrimination is related to geography, or to cases where only one buyer benefits from price discrimination. Policymakers have gradually judged the act with more skepticism, and it is not widely enforced.

See also Clayton Act of 1914, Sherman Antitrust Act of 1890.

References Kintre, Earl W. *A Robinson-Patman Primer* (1979); Spiro, George W. *The Legal Environment of Business* (1993); Waldman, Don E. *The Economics of Antitrust: Cases and Analysis* (1986).

Rockefeller, John Davison (1839–1937)

John D. Rockefeller, who ranks among the greatest of the American capitalists during the late nineteenth century, employed various monopolistic practices to build one of the first giant corporations.

Born in 1839 in Richford, New York, Rockefeller was one of several children of William and Eliza Rockefeller. Apparently, his father traveled from town to town as a doctor, selling patent medicine. When the father was home, the family enjoyed some relief from the financial hardship that it learned to accept during his absence.

When Rockefeller was 18 years old, a $1,000 loan from his father helped establish him as a commission merchant in Cleveland, Ohio. The firm prospered, and, in 1860, he traveled to the oil fields of Pennsylvania to evaluate the attractiveness of oil as an investment. (In 1859, the oil fields of western Pennsylvania had seen the first gusher in American history.) The commission house of Clark and Rockefeller invested in a refinery. In 1864, Rockefeller married, sold his interest in the commission house, bought out Clark's share of the refinery, and threw himself wholeheartedly into the oil industry. Rockefeller had two partners in his refinery: Sam Andrews, who had developed an improved method of refining, and Henry Flagler, a nephew-in-law.

Rockefeller soon formed a strategy to monopolize the oil refining business in Cleveland. The cornerstone of this strategy lay in a secret rebate that Rockefeller extracted from the railroads, which was 15 times greater than the rebate received by any of his competitors. The other refineries in Cleveland either went out of business or joined with Rockefeller and his associates, who, in January 1870, incorporated Standard Oil Company of Ohio, with outstanding stock valued at $1 million.

Under the guise of a corporation innocently named the Southern Improvement Corporation, Rockefeller interests nego-

John D. Rockefeller, 1910

tiated deals with railroads that awarded rebates on shipments for Standard Oil, as well as rebates on shipments of competitors. As an added sweetener to this arrangement, the railroads gave Standard Oil information on competitor prices and discounts, and the names of customers of competitors.

Agents secretly associated with Rockefeller bought out competing refineries, and Rockefeller brought some competitors to their knees in price wars that he could win because of his alliance with the railroads. By 1878, Rockefeller and his allies controlled 95 percent of all pipelines and refinery capacity in the United States. In the 1880s, Standard Oil was organized as a trust. The stocks of the affiliated companies were put in the hands of nine trustees, one of whom was Rockefeller. In 1890, Congress passed the Sherman Antitrust Act, with the direct intention of abolishing combinations such as Standard Oil. The Standard Oil trust was coming under closer government scrutiny and harassment, when the State of New Jersey, as a revenue-raising measure, amended its corporate law, which allowed one corporation to own stock in another corporation; this gave birth to modern holding companies. The Standard Oil trust was reorganized as Standard Oil of New Jersey, which was a holding company for the stock of all the companies affiliated with Standard Oil. This giant corporation dominated the oil industry, until the Justice Department sued for its dissolution in 1911.

Rockefeller retired in 1896. His fortune more than quadrupled after his retirement, because of the development of the internal combustion engine that burned gasoline, a distillate of petroleum. He died in 1937, at the age of 98. As knowledge of the workings of the economic system grew in sophistication, Rockefeller's brand of business ethics failed to meet the public's standards of fair play. His monopolistic business practices are now illegal in many capitalistic countries.

See also Holding Companies, Mergers, Sherman Antitrust Act of 1890.

References Hawke, David D. *John D: The Founding Father of the Rockefellers* (1980); Nevins, Allan. *John D. Rockefeller: The Heroic Age of American Enterprise* (1941).

Rothschild Banking Family

The House of Rothschild was the reigning family among European bankers and financiers during the first half of the nineteenth century. Other banking houses rose to prominence later in the nineteenth century, and, after World War II, Rothschild banks in London and Paris continued to hold positions of prominence in financial circles.

The first Rothschild to make a name in banking was Mayer Amschel Rothschild, who was born in 1743 to a poor Jewish family in Frankfurt am Main. He found success managing the finances of German states, and lending to the nobility. He had five sons. The eldest son, Mayer Amschel, remained in Frankfurt, which was the headquarters for the House of Rothschild before it moved to Paris. He sent his other sons to establish branches of the House of Rothschild in the leading capitals of Europe. Nathan went to London, James to Paris, Solomon to Vienna, and Karl to Naples. Formally, the branches were separate organizations, but the brothers consulted on big deals, and undertook cooperative initiatives.

Nathan was one of the most gifted of the many financial geniuses to come from the Rothschild family. During the Napoleonic Wars, he found means to transfer British subsidies to Prussia and Austria, who were allies in the war against France. He could also deliver money to armies in the field in the right mix of currencies. The London branch of Rothschilds arranged £100 million in credit for the Allied governments.

The Paris branch of Rothschilds was unable to do much until after the fall of Napoleon. In 1817, Nathan decided it was time to establish a full-fledged institution in Paris. By 1820, the Paris branch of Rothschilds had replaced the Frankfurt branch as the flagship institution.

Nathan underestimated the future of railroads at first, and the Rothschilds refused to take part in the first boom in English railroad construction, but after seeing the value of railroads in England, the Rothschilds aggressively participated in railroad financing on the continent. Nathan became the railway king of Europe, and the Rothschilds advanced credit to various governments for financing railroad construction.

The Rothschilds adapted to the Industrial Revolution by becoming investment bankers. In cooperation with other houses, they bought large blocks of stock of newly formed companies, and, once these companies turned a profit, the Rothschilds sold the shares to the public at handsome prices. From these kinds of transactions, the Rothschilds built their fortune.

The Rothschilds continued to assist governments in financial markets. In 1871 and 1872, they placed the loans that France floated to pay its war indemnity after the Franco-Prussian War. In 1875, they raised the £4 million the British government needed to become the principal stockholder of the Suez Canal Company.

The House of Rothschild was a genuine international business. Part of the secret of their success lay in the stress upon broad consultation among family members, and in aiming for modest profits. Like the House of Morgan in the United States, they helped mobilized the capital needed to finance the vast undertakings of railroads and industrial enterprises of the Industrial Revolution. Bankers wielded enormous power in nineteenth century capitalism. It was said that owners of machinery ruled workers, and bankers ruled owners of machinery.

See also Merchant Bankers.

References Cowles, Virginia. *The Rothschilds: A Family of Fortune* (1973); Wechsberg, Joseph. *The Merchant Bankers* (1966).

Royal Exchange (England)

An early indication of England's determination to develop its own financial institutions came with construction of the Royal Exchange. Early in the sixteenth century, Antwerp rose to dominate the European market in bills of exchange, but when Antwerp lost its position as a European financial center after the 1570s, Amsterdam and London stood to gain most of its business as a financial center.

An English adventurer, Sir Richard Gresham, visited Antwerp early in the 1500s. The Antwerp Bourse impressed Sir Richard, and put into his mind the idea of constructing a similar facility in London. The king was won over, but a site was never procured.

Sir Richard's son, Thomas Gresham, of Gresham's law fame, received a royal appointment (1552) as the king's merchant in Antwerp. Thomas was equally awestruck by the Antwerp Bourse, and decided to erect a similar trading center in London. Construction got under way in 1566, and was finished within two years. The architecture borrowed heavily from the Antwerp Bourse. In 1570, Queen

The Royal Exchange in London, from an undated engraving

Elizabeth visited the structure and proclaimed it the "Royal Exchange."

In its early history, the Royal Exchange housed virtually the whole commercial activity of London. Traders in foreign exchange, stocks, and commodities congregated in the Exchange. The points of assembly for traders in different markets were called walks: There was a Brokers Walk, a Hamburg Walk, a French Walk, etc. One observer said that the confusion of traders speaking so many different languages reminded one of Babel.

Gresham's Royal Exchange burned in the Great Fire of London (1666), but a larger structure was built, which opened in 1669.

The Stock Exchange apparently wore out its welcome, and moved out of the Royal Exchange in 1698. Stock traders were held in low esteem at the time. Commodity markets became specialized and broke away. The insurance business made the Royal Exchange its home: The Royal Exchange Assurance Corporation received its royal charter in 1720, and Lloyd's, which had begun in Lloyd's coffeehouse, moved to the Royal Exchange in 1774.

In 1838, the second Royal Exchange fell victim to fire, and the third exchange opened in 1844. This structure still stands, though it ceased to function as a trading center in 1939. The Guardian Royal Exchange Assurance Company still keeps its headquarters at the Royal Exchange.

References Bell, Walter G. *The Great Fire in London in 1666* (1971); Davies, Glyn. *A History of Money* (1994); Powell, Ellis. *The Evolution of the Money Market, 1485–1915* (1915).

Russian Industrial Society

The Russian Industrial Society was the first national organization in Russia committed to the encouragement of capitalist development. The society served as the chief forum for public discussion of policies fostering private enterprise. It vigorously lobbied the czarist state to implement its recommendations for stimulating the Russian economy. In addition to industrialists and wholesale merchants, journalists, engineers, and a few bureaucrats could be found in the ranks of its leadership.

The Russian Industrial Society was born of the protectionist sentiment that grew out of the trade liberalization policies of the 1850s. In February 1867, a banquet attended by 250 Russian manufacturers, traders, sympathetic bureaucrats, and journalists led to the formation of the society. In November 1867, the czar granted the charter, which authorized the society to petition the government "on all question of Russian industry and trade." The society set for itself a goal of representing all classes of people engaged in productive activity, diffusing innovations helpful to economic development, and petitioning, when necessary, for the removal of government impediments to economic progress. The society was fervent about Russian nationalism, and excluded most non-Russians from membership.

Although a protective tariff was the cornerstone of the society's economic program, its views were enlightened, even on this matter. The society saw the tariff as a temporary measure. It said in 1892,

There is no doubt that with the development of transportation, the easing of credit, reforms in factory and commercial legislation, the spread of technical education, improvements in the condition of the working class, etc. the need for protective measures will decline, and free competition—this mighty engine of all industry—will make it strong....

The society opposed monopolies and other special privileges, often without success. It successfully recommended a ban on factory labor for children under 12. The government adopted its recommendation for accident insurance for workers. The society's tariff recommendations usually met with a friendly reception, and the government acted on the society's recommendation to develop a system of industrial statistics.

The society failed to persuade the government to reform its corporate law. In czarist Russia, a charter of incorporation required the approval of the interested ministries, and the signature of the czar himself. In Europe and the United States, new companies only needed to register with the appropriate government agency. In Russia, the outdated process of incorporation encouraged political favoritism and corruption.

Between 1892 and 1903, the government favored the growth of cartels, despite a law against price fixing. Heavy industry remained dependent upon government purchases. The government usually opted for bureaucratic policies, rather than market-oriented capitalism. Government aid kept the capitalists loyal to the monarchy. On the eve of the Russian Revolution, the economy could be described as a form of state socialism, unfriendly to private enterprise.

The Russian Industrial Society succumbed to internal strife. Different regions of the country were affected differently by some of the tariff recommendations. By 1905, the society was defunct.

Lenin felt that socialism was the next logical step after the state-monopoly capitalism fostered by the czarist government. The Russian Industrial Society advocated reforms that would give Russia a form of free-market capitalism, similar to that in the United States and England, but the czarist government was unable to see the necessity for these reforms.

See also Witte System.

References Laue, Theodore H. Von. *Sergei Witte and the Industrialization of Russia* (1963); Owen, Thomas C. "The Russian Industrial Society." *Journal of Economic History* (1985).

Russian Revolution of 1917
See Hyperinflation of the Russian Revolution.

Russian Tariff of 1891
The enactment of the Tariff of 1891 generalized and ratified the trend toward protectionism that had been mounting in Russia since the late 1870s. A wave of protectionism surged through Europe during the last two decades of the nineteenth century; for example, in 1879, Germany made a significant turn toward protectionism, raising tariffs levied on imports, and making tariff revenue an important source for government. With the Tariff of 1891, the Russian government took up the cause of protectionism, and exceeded anything that a European government had enacted up to that time.

Russia had shared with Europe a trend toward free trade that lasted from mid-century to the 1870s, but, one by one, European countries raised the banner of protectionism. Each country had reasons of its own for adopting protectionism, in addition to economic difficulties common to all the countries.

Periodic bouts of chronic currency debasement marked Russian financial history, dating back to the seventeenth century. In 1839, the Russian government adopted a silver standard. During the Crimean War (1853–1856), the government suspended the convertibility of paper money into silver. After the war, the value of the silver ruble fluctuated, partly because the rest of the world was moving to the gold standard. The Russian government realized that only a stable ruble could assure foreign investors that capital invested in Russia could be safely returned to the country of origin, without a capital loss. To establish the value of the ruble in the confidence of foreign exchange markets, the Russian government elected to work toward the adoption of the gold standard. To build up gold reserves, the government needed to reduce the outflow of gold caused by imports.

The government took the first step toward protectionism in 1877, when it required the payment of tariff duties in gold. The government increased tariff duties in 1881 and 1885, and the epochal tariff of 1891 increased tariffs to levels that virtually prohibited imports in many industries.

The tariff played a strategic role in the government's plan for economic development. The exclusion of foreign manufactures from the Russian market created a strong incentive for building factories on Russian soil. The suppression of imports created an excess of exports that enabled Russia to build up its gold reserves. After the establishment of the gold standard in 1897, foreign capital flowed into Russia in great quantities. Gold reserves assured foreign investors that interest payments could be redeemed in gold. The tariff also generated tax revenue that the government used to promote public works and economic development.

In summary, in the late nineteenth century, Russian formulated a mercantilist plan of economic development reminiscent of France and England during the seventeenth and eighteenth centuries. Despite Adam Smith's ridicule of mercantilism a century before, Russian found it expedient to follow a similar commercial policy. Industrialization accelerated in Russia, and capitalistic development was flourishing when it was aborted by the Bolshevik Revolution.

See also German Tariff of 1879, McKinley Tariff, Meline Tariff.

References Knowles, L. C. A. *Economic Development in the Nineteenth Century* (1932); Laue, Theodore H. Von. *Sergei Witte and the Industrialization of Russia* (1963).

Russian Uprising of 1905
The 1905 uprising led to the introduction of democratic reforms, and marked the beginning of open trade union organization in Russian. The czarist government conceded to a form of constitutional government, under the pressure of a general strike waged by the working class. Lenin

saw the uprising of 1905 as a dress rehearsal for the Russian Revolution of 1917, because it showed the power of the general strike as a weapon in the hands of the working class.

Like the Russian Revolution of 1917, the uprising of 1905 began in disaffection with a war that the Russian people neither understood nor supported. The Russian military had fought 11 months against Japan, suffering one catastrophic defeat after another, when an outbreak of worker protests shook the foundations of the Russian government. On 22 January 1905, 200,000 protesters, among whose numbers were women and children, marched on the White Palace in Petrograd. The leader of the protest had sent word to Czar Nicholas II, asking him to receive the petitions of the protesters, but the czar took his departure from Petrograd, and an armed palace guard awaited the protesters. The protesters sang "God Save the Czar," and bore petitions asking for an eight-hour day, a minimum wage of one ruble per day, and constitutional reform. The palace guard fired on the demonstrators at close range, killing more than 500 people, and wounding several thousand. Blood-stained snow became a vivid memory for the survivors of Bloody Sunday. A swelling wave of strikes, demonstrations, and assassinations swept through Russia.

In September 1905, the Russian government signed a humiliating peace treaty with Japan. In October, a dispute in the printing trade sparked a general strike, called the comma strike, because printers, paid by piecework, wanted to be paid for punctuation marks. The outpouring of sympathy strikes for the printers escalated into one of the most complete general strikes in history. In Petrograd, groups of 500 factory workers each elected a delegate to a central council, or Soviet, to direct the strike, distribute arms, and issue supplies. At the end of October, Czar Nicholas agreed to a constitutional government of a limited form, including a representative assembly called a Duma.

In December 1905, the czar began to move against the Soviet, arresting its president, whom Trotsky replaced. Rather than calling for an armed uprising, Trotsky called for workers to stop paying taxes, and to make a run on the banks. Workers were asked to withdraw their savings, and to demand gold in payment. The czar relented, granting more of the workers' demands. Nevertheless, the revolutionary fervor spent itself before the year was out. A call for a general strike on 16 December met with little enthusiasm. The government arrested Trotsky, and the uprising subsided.

Despite such government repression, Russian trade unions developed significantly in the uprising of 1905. In September 1905, Moscow was the site of the first national trade union conference in Russian history. In February 1906, Russia saw its second national trade union conference. By some estimates, union membership had grown to 250,000 by 1907.

In Marxist theory, the uprising of 1905 fit the pattern of the bourgeois revolutions that wrenched much of Europe in 1848. The period from 1896 until 1914 brought rapid economic development to Russia, but, of course, the development of capitalism in Russia came to a sudden halt with the Revolution of 1917.

See also General Strike, Revolutions of 1848.

References Foster, William Z. *Outline History of the World Trade Union Movement* (1956); Moorehead, Alan. *The Russian Revolution (1958);* Shanin, Teodor. *Russia, 1905–1907*, Vols. 1–2 (1986).

Savings and Loan Bailout (United States)

Between 1988 and 1991, more than 1,000 savings and loan (S&L) institutions failed, putting out of business approximately one-third of all the S&Ls in the United States. Deposits at these failed institutions were insured by the Federal Savings and Loan Insurance Corporation (FSLIC), whose resources fell short of the amount owed depositors at failed institutions. Put differently, the S&L collapse bankrupted the FSLIC. Congress stepped in and passed a bill supplying funds for redeeming insured deposits at failed institutions, and establishing the Resolution Trust Corporation, with authority for liquidating the assets of the failed S&Ls. The bailout was expected to cost the federal government $160 billion over a ten-year period, and maybe as much as $500 billion over 40 years.

As the U.S. economy was in transition from inflation to disinflation, the S&L industry also changed from a highly regulated industry to a deregulated industry. During the period of rising inflation in the United States, S&Ls faced strict legal limits on the interest rates that depositors could earn on S&L deposits. S&Ls paid low interest rates on deposits, and made relatively low interest loans on home mortgages. The deregulation of the S&Ls lifted the interest-rate ceilings of S&L deposits, and allowed S&Ls to enter the business for consumer and commercial loans. Interest rates escalated rapidly in the early 1980s, under the pressure of a tight, anti-inflation monetary policy, which squeezed S&Ls that held low-interest mortgages, but paid high interest rates on current deposits. Mortgages held by S&Ls earned interest rates well below the market interest rates that had to be paid to keep current depositors. S&Ls tried to save themselves by turning to riskier consumer and commercial loans that paid higher interest rates, but, when depression struck in the oil and real estate industries in the last half of the 1980s, S&Ls began to fail rapidly.

Financial crises have plagued capitalist economies from the outset, leading Karl Marx to suggest that capitalism would destroy itself from crises that reflect internal contradictions. Recognizing the vulnerability of the economic system to financial crises, the U.S. government established a system of deposit insurance in the 1930s, which removed an important source of instability in the capitalist economic system. The S&L collapse in the United States uncovered the following weakness in deposit insurance: Fully insured depositors had no incentive to favor S&Ls with conservative investment policies over S&Ls with risky investment portfolios. That is, depositors had no incentive to keep track of investment practices of individual S&Ls, which allowed them a free rein to finance risky business ventures.

S&Ls are now insured by the Federal Deposit Insurance Corporation (FDIC), the agency that has always insured commercial bank deposits. The FDIC is devising a plan to vary the insurance premiums that financial institutions pay according to the riskiness of loan portfolios. Under such a plan, financial institutions that carry high-risk loan portfolios pay higher deposit insurance premiums.

See also Glass-Steagall Banking Act of 1933.

References Barth, James R. *The Great Savings and Loan Debacle (1991)*; Long, Robert Emmet, ed. *Banking Scandals: The S&Ls and BCCI* (1993).

Say's Law

See Classical School of Economics.

Second Bank of the United States

The Second Bank of the United States met the needs for a central bank in the United States between 1816 and 1836. During the War of 1812, state banks suspended the conversion of their bank notes into specie. At that time, each bank issued its own paper money and held specie (gold and silver coins) to redeem its paper money. Today, banks issue checking accounts and hold paper money to redeem the checking accounts. When the banks suspended specie payments in 1814, six months before the war ended, the federal government had no way to pressure them to return to convertibility. Critics of the First Bank of the United States softened their constitutional objections. The Jeffersonian Republicans, instead of the New England Federalists, were supporting such a bank. Congress approved the charter for the Second Bank of the United States early in 1816, and President Madison signed the bill on 10 April.

The Second Bank of the United States bore a strong resemblance to the First Bank of the United States. The Second Bank was capitalized at $35 million, and the government owned one-fifth of the stock and appointed five of the 25 directors. Shares of stock were sold at a price to attract broadly based ownership. Foreign-owned stock had no voting rights, and large shareholders were limited to 30 votes. Subscribers could pay as little as one-fourth in specie and the remainder in government securities.

The Second Bank got off to a wobbly start. In 1818, a House committee investigated the bank. It then had $2.4 million in specie to support $22 million in demand liabilities, and was on the verge of suspending specie payments itself. The investigating committee discovered that the Second Bank had extended loans to its own stockholders, who used stock in the bank as collateral. This practice enabled speculators to buy stock in the Second Bank using the bank's money. Furthermore, the officers of the bank had speculated in its stock, and the Second Bank had also been slow in demanding specie payments on notes issued by state banks.

The Second Bank's poor management bore fruit in the economic contraction in 1818, and the bank's effort to bring its own house in order hastened the economic downturn. The Baltimore branch failed after it had made bad loans, and its officers had speculated in its stock. The president of the Second Bank resigned, and Langdon Cheves assumed the leadership of the bank (1819). His conservative administration put the bank on firm financial footing. Nicholas Biddle succeeded Cheves in 1823. Biddle's understanding of the role of a central bank put him ahead of his time. He placed the public responsibilities of the bank above the private interest of its stockholders. In 1834, a French traveler termed the Second Bank the "banque centrale."

The Second Bank forced the state banks to maintain specie payments for their bank notes, and accumulated specie to reduce money in circulation. The bank increased the money in circulation by making more loans. The bank's practices made enemies of state banks in the West and South, who resented its regulation of state bank notes. These banks tended to expand the supply of bank notes in circulation beyond what their reserves of specie could be counted on to redeem.

The state banks had a powerful ally in President Andrew Jackson. Biddle and his advisors saw the hostility to the bank gathering momentum, so, rather than wait for the Second Bank's charter to expire in 1836, they asked Congress for a renewal of the charter in 1832. The bill for rechartering the bank passed the House and the Senate, but President Jackson vetoed it.

Critics charged that the bank put too much power in the hands of officials who were neither elected directly by the people nor responsible to elected officials. In addition, paper money had not yet established itself in the confidence of the voters. President Jackson himself was a hard-money person. The public saw paper money as the culprit in depressions. In his veto message, President Jackson stated,

> Equality of talents, of education, or of wealth cannot be produced by human institutions...but when the laws undertake to add to these natural and just advantages artificial distinctions...to make the rich richer, and the potent more powerful, the humble members of society—the farmers, mechanics, and laborers—who have neither the time nor the means of securing like favors to themselves, have a right to complain of the injustice of their Government.

Jackson's rhetoric may bear the stamp of the demagoguery of the frontier politician, rather than the best thinking of the time. Thomas Jefferson, perhaps the best-educated and most cosmopolitan of the early presidents, described his opinion of banks in this way:

> I have ever been the enemy of banks; not of those discounting cash; but of those foisting their own paper into circulation, and thus banishing our cash. My zeal against those institutions was so warm and open at the establishment of the [First] bank of the U.S. that I was derided as a Maniac by the tribe of bank-mongers, who were seeking to filch from the public their swindling and barren gains.

With the establishment of the Federal Reserve System in 1913, the United States finally came to terms with the idea of a central bank. By then, the role of central banks in maintaining economic stability was better understood. Banks were better accepted than they were in Jefferson's day.

See also Bank of England, Bank of France, Central Banks and Free Banking, Federal Reserve System, First Bank of the United States.

References Myers, Margaret. *A Financial History of the United States* (1970); Schlesinger, Arthur M., Jr. *The Age of Jackson* (1945); Timberlake, Richard

H. *The Origins of Central Banking in the United States* (1978).

Second International

The Second International was formed in 1889 as an international organization, composed mostly of trade unions and socialist organizations with Marxist philosophies. An important element in the Marxist message was contained in the slogan "Proletarians of all countries, unite." As the nineteenth century drew to a close, working-class consciousness was maturing in most capitalist countries. International conferences were held in 1877 (Ghent), 1881 (Chur, Switzerland), 1883 (Paris), 1886 (Paris), and 1888 (London). An international conference held in Paris in 1889 led to the formation of an unnamed international organization, which came to be known as the Second International.

By the time of the formation of the Second International, Marxist philosophy had won the battle for the mind of European socialism. Socialist political parties espousing Marxist ideology had come into being in all major European countries.

One of the recurring themes at the annual congresses of the Second International was the problem of war. Marxist ideology saw wars as a product of capitalist imperialism. The congresses of the Second International passed resolutions urging workers of the world to unite to stop wars that were fought by the proletariat for the benefit of the capitalists. Some of the proposals discussed included arbitration of international disputes, refusal of socialist parties to vote for war credits for governments at war, arms limitation agreements, nationwide referendums on declarations of war, and replacement of armies with citizen militia.

One proposal repeatedly voted down by successive congresses suggested the use of the general strike as a measure to stop war. Belligerent countries, paralyzed by simultaneous general strikes of the workers in each country, could not prosecute a war. At the congress of the Second

International held in Stuttgart in 1907, Vladimir Lenin proposed the following amendment to an antiwar resolution:

> If war threatens to break out, it is the duty of the working class and of its parliamentary representatives in the country involved, supported by the consolidating activity of the International (Socialist) Bureau, to exert every effort to prevent the outbreak of the war by means they consider most effective, which naturally vary according to the accentuation of the class struggle and of the general political situation. Should war break out nonetheless, it is their duty to intervene in favor of its speedy termination and to do all in their power to utilize the economic and political crisis caused by the war to rouse the peoples and thereby to hasten the abolition of the capitalist system.

The resolution passed after some amendments. During World War I, Lenin acted on his proposal, and overthrew the Russian government.

The outbreak of world war dispelled the illusions of the Second International. The workers in the belligerent countries saw their own country fighting a defensive war, and rallied to the cause. Socialist parties in France and German voted war credits, despite a pledge not do so. At the suggestion of Lenin and radical socialists, the Second International held a conference in Stockholm in 1917, to discuss ways to pressure the warring governments to end hostilities. Britain and France refused passports to their delegates, and the effort failed.

One of the legacies of the Second International is the designation of 1 May as May Day, a day set aside to honor the struggles of the working class in most countries of the world. The United States chose, instead, the first Monday in September as Labor Day, because of the influence of conservative unionism. May Day was chosen by the Second International, however, because 1 May 1886 marked the beginning of a historic strike in Chicago for the eight-hour day.

See also International Workingmen's Association.

References Abraham, Richard. *Rosa Luxemburg: A Life for the International* (1989); Foster, William Z. *Outline History of the World Trade Union Movement* (1956); Haupt, Georges. *Socialism and the Great War: The Collapse of the Second International* (1972).

Securities Exchange Act of 1934 (United States)

The Securities Exchange Act of 1934 is the Depression-era legislation that still forms the basis for the regulation of stock exchanges and stock trading today. The act was intended to protect investors from the speculative practices that led to the stock market crash of 1929.

The House version of the bill came under consideration in February 1934, and addressed three areas of concern: First, the bill aimed to put a stop to insiders rigging market prices; second, the bill sought to protect investors from inaccurate information, by requiring the registration of new and existing securities traded on the stock exchanges; third, the bill put margin sales under federal regulation. Margin sales involved the purchase of stock with borrowed money, using the stock certificate as collateral.

Wall Street lobbied hard against the bill. One opponent of the bill described it as "along the road from democracy to communism." Richard Whitney, then president of the New York Stock Exchange, told critics, "The Exchange is a perfect institution." In Senate Banking Committee testimony, he said, "I claim that this country has been built by speculation, and further progress must be in that line."

To placate critics, the final version of the bill removed the Federal Trade Commission from involvement in the regulation of securities, and established a new commission to implement and oversee federal regulation of stock trading. The discretion of the new Securities and Exchange Commission (SEC) tended to replace the mandatory statutes in earlier versions of the act. The Federal Reserve Board was given the authority to set margin requirements, which set the fraction of a stock purchase that cannot be borrowed, and which must be paid with the purchaser's own money. President Roosevelt signed the bill on 6 June 1934. The commission is composed of five members and a chairperson. To help win acceptance on Wall Street, President Roosevelt chose Joseph P. Kennedy to serve as the first chairperson of the SEC.

Today, any company whose stock is listed on one of the 13 largest U.S. stock exchanges must file detailed financial reports to the commission. Unlisted companies with assets of $1 million, and a minimum of 500 stockholders, must also file the same report. Newly issued securities must be registered with the SEC, before they are publicly offered. SEC accountants compare the registration statement with the proposed prospectus that will be used to sell the stock, and the SEC can stop the sale of the stock if the prospectus is misleading.

The SEC regulates the stock exchanges. Companies are required to disclose information to the exchanges that aid in tracking trading patterns that might reveal manipulation of stock prices or price rigging. The SEC prohibits aggregations of funds (pools) to manipulate prices artificially. It also prohibits sales between members of the same group to register artificial transaction prices (wash sales). Also, the SEC regulates stock trades of corporate insiders. The stock transactions of insiders (officers, directors, and major stockholders) are reported monthly to the SEC, and short-term profits belong to the corporation. The form and use of the proxy to solicit votes for the board of directors are also subject to SEC regulation.

The stock market crash of 1929, and the following Depression, damaged the credibility of market systems and laissez-faire capitalism. Markets do not work well when some participants are much better informed than others. The wisdom of a wary consumer was not always a match for the complexities of modern goods and marketing methods. The public supported regulation in the stock market, to prevent the better-informed from taking advantage of the less-informed.

See also New York Stock Exchange, Stock Market Crash of 1929.

References Brigham, Eugene F. *Fundamentals of Financial Management* (1989); Schlesinger, Arthur M., Jr. *The Age of Roosevelt*, Vol. 2 (1959); Seligman, Joel. *The Transformation of Wall Street: A History of the Securities and Exchange Commission and Modern Corporate Finance* (1982).

Seizure of the Mint (England)

Charles I, reigning king of England from 1625 to 1649, was always in need of money, despite a treaty with Spain that assured him abundant supplies of bullion. Minting coins became such a booming royal business that the Tower mint could not keep up, prompting Charles to open branch mints throughout the kingdom.

The machinery of public finance was a bit primitive during Charles's reign. On one occasion, he forced the East India Company to sell him its entire stock of pepper on credit, payable after two years. Charles bought the pepper at a price of 2s. 1d. per pound, and then sold it for 1s. 8d. per pound, raising instant cash in a roundabout credit transaction that angered the merchants of London. On two occasions, the Privy Council blocked proposals that Charles advanced to increase the mint profits by debasing the coins, which was a favorite stratagem of monarchs for squeezing more resources from subjects. Debasing the coin meant watering down the precious metal content in coins with a given face value.

The government's creditors, mainly goldsmiths and merchants, claimed freshly minted coins when they became available. In 1640, Charles stopped the flow of coins from the mint, planning to uses the coins for his own expenditures, and, instead, promised to pay the crown's creditors 8-percent interest on his outstanding debt. A howl rose from gold-smiths and merchants, who wanted their money immediately, causing Charles to let two-thirds of the coins go to the crown's debtors. Charles kept one-third of the coins, and promised to pay his creditors 8 percent for six months.

Charles eventually paid the creditors in full, but only after the merchants and goldsmiths had lost faith in the government's management of monetary affairs. Already, there was talk of setting up a national or public bank, and the incident of the mint seizure convinced influential people that the government could not be trusted with direct power over such a bank. The Bank of England came into being in 1694, and developed as a private institution that, nevertheless, enjoyed close ties with the government.

See also Bank of England, Financial Revolution.

References Craig, J. *The Mint: A History of the London Mint from AD 287 to 1948* (1953); Davies, Glyn. *A History of Money: From Ancient Times to the Present Day* (1994).

Sherman Antitrust Act of 1890 (United States)

The Sherman Antitrust Act of 1890 was the first major legislative initiative aimed at outlawing trusts and other contracts and combinations that serve to monopolize trade and commerce. Long before antitrust issues arose in the United States, English common law had considered void all contracts in restraint of trade. The English courts had refused to uphold the grants and patents of monopoly that the English crown bestowed on the mercantile trading companies. The Sherman Act represents the first time a nation legislated antitrust policy.

The Sherman Act was born of the political pressures created by monopolies squeezing farmers, and national producers invading local markets and undercutting local producers. The farmers felt the squeeze from two directions: the monopoly power of the railroads in high shipping costs for grain; and companies that supplied life's necessities to the farmers were controlled by trusts, who charged monopoly prices. In the presidential election of 1888, both Democrats and Republicans wrote in platform planks directed against trusts.

The Sherman Act bears the name of John Sherman, who first introduced a Senate antitrust bill in 1888. The bill occasioned some debate in the Senate, but Congress was not ready to deal with the issue. Senator Sherman introduced his bill again in 1889. The bill went to the Senate Finance Committee, where it was amended. The Judiciary Committee took up the bill, and rewrote it. Although Senator Sherman did not write the final version of the bill, he supported its passage. In Finance Committee hearings, Senator Sherman argued:

If we would not endure a king as a political power we should not endure a king over the production, transportation, and sale of any of the necessities of life. If we would not submit to an emperor we should not submit to an autocrat of trade, with power to prevent competition and fix the price of any commodity.

The Senate passed the bill 52 to 1, and the House passed it 242 to 0. President Harrison signed this landmark legislation, probably unaware of its significance.

Sections 1 and 2 of the Sherman Act embody the major thrust of the act. Section 1 reads, in part:

Every contract, combination in the form of a trust or otherwise, or conspiracy, in restraint of trade or commerce among the several states, or with foreign nations, is hereby declared illegal. Every person who shall make any such contract or engage in any such combination or conspiracy, shall be deemed guilty of a misdemeanor, and, on conviction thereof, shall be punished by fine not exceeding five thousand dollars or by imprisonment not exceeding one year, or by both said punishments, in the discretion of the court.

Section 2 reads, in part:

Every person who shall monopolize, or attempt to monopolize, or combine or conspire with any other person or persons to monopolize any part of the trade or commerce among the several states, or with foreign nations, shall be deemed guilty of a misdemeanor.

Section 3 expands the coverage of section 1 to embrace U.S. territories and the District of Columbia. Section 4 gave federal courts jurisdiction over violations of the act, and empowered the attorney general to enforce the act, as well as to institute proceedings to prevent and restrain violations. For example, the attorney general can ask for dissolution and divestiture as a remedy in civil antitrust proceedings. Section 6 enables the government to seize property involved in any combination in violation of the Sherman Act. The government rarely makes use of this provision. Section 7 provided for treble damage awards, in addition to attorney fees in civil suits filed under the provisions of the act. The cases are argued in federal circuit court.

The Sherman Act fell short of striking a lethal blow at monopolies, and actually added momentum to a wave of mergers, around the turn of the century. It only outlawed persons combining to fix prices, without attacking mergers per se. The Supreme Court emphasized the verb form "monopolize," which tended to leave the status quo intact. Labor leaders were disappointed that the courts applied the act to unions. In 1912, all three presidential candidates (Roosevelt, Taft, and Wilson) saw a need for new antitrust legislation.

See also United States v. Aluminum Company of America, United States v. Standard Oil Co. of New Jersey, United States v. Trans-Missouri Freight Association, United States v. United Shoe Machinery Corporation.

References Spiro, George W. *The Legal Environment of Business* (1993); Waldman, Don E. *The Economics of Antitrust: Cases and Analysis* (1986).

Sir John Barnard's Act of 1733 (England)

Sir John Barnard's Act of 1773 was an act to "prevent the infamous practice of Stock-Jobbing." The act refers to the "inconveniences" occasioned by the "wicked, pernicious, and destructive" trade of the stockjobber. Industry and trade supposedly suffered from the practice of stockjobbing. The act outlaws all "all wagers, puts and refusals." It struck at transactions in which there was no delivery of stock. Wagers had to do with betting on future prices of stock. Puts and refusals were concerned with buying or selling stock for delivery at some future date. These transactions are now known as futures. Speculators would sell stock for future delivery, if they believed stock prices were falling. At the time of delivery, the stock would be bought at the lower prices, and instantly sold for a profit. If speculators believed stock prices were rising, then they would buy stock in the present for delivery in the future, when the stock could be immediately sold for a premium. Puts were options to sell stock at a future date. All brokers, agents, scriveners, and other persons involved in negotiating and writing such contracts were subject to a penalty of £500. The act also levied a penalty of £500 against the "frequent and mischievous practice for persons to sell and dispose of stocks of which they are not possessed."

Court cases quickly whittled away the effectiveness the act. In the beginning, it mostly had the effect of making dealers careful of whom they dealt with. The act was repealed in 1868 as long obsolete, and the practices cited in the act are now widely accepted tools for stock market speculation in the New York stock market. This act, nevertheless, represents one of the first government efforts to regulate stock market speculation. The regulation of option trading is a live issue even today.

Early English experiences in the stock market had left many investors with the feeling that stock price fluctuations were rigged. The government tried to address the issue with Sir John Bernard's Act, but without success.

See also Amsterdam Exchange, London Stock Exchange.

References Dos Passos, John Randolph. *A Treatise on the Law of Stock-Brokers and Stock-Exchanges* (1882); Powell, Ellis. *The Evolution of the Money Market, 1385–1915* (1915).

Slater, Samuel (1768–1835)

In 1833, President Andrew Jackson visited Samuel Slater, addressing him as the father of American manufacturing. He was the first industrial capitalist produced by the new nation.

Slater was born in England in 1768, the fifth child of a prosperous farm family. A year later Richard Arkwright patented his machine for spinning cotton. Cotton mills sprung up, and soon Slater's town of Belper became home to a cotton mill. His father assisted Arkwright's partner, Jedediah Strutt, in securing land and water privileges in a nearby town. Strutt let Arkwright place Samuel as an apprentice in the Belper mill. He was 14 when he signed his own indenture for seven years.

During the first six months, Slater spent Sundays studying the machinery, rather than visiting his mother, who had just become widowed. These early mills were crude affairs, made of wooden cog wheels and powered by water. By the end of his seventh year, Slater managed a cotton mill.

The rapid expansion of the British textile industry may have encouraged Slater to look for new opportunities. He kept his decision to immigrate to America a secret, only writing his mother before his ship departed for America. Slater faced some risk, because Parliament had forbade skilled workers in the textile industry from immigrating. In November 1789, Slater reached America. He took a ship from New York to Providence, Rhode Island, met Moses Brown, and signed a contract to build a complete set of Arkwright machinery. His mill began operation in December 1790. His partners marketed their product, and Slater focused on management of the mill. Nine children, ranging in age from seven to 12, composed the work force at Slater's mill. These children worked 12 hours a day, at $6 a day.

The factory system spread after Slater's achievement. In 1827, Slater helped design and construct a steam-powered mill. His business prospered until the panic of 1829, and he even benefited from the shakeout, by acquiring financially troubled mills, and increasing by seven the number of mills he owned. When Slater died, he was operating textile mills in three states.

At one time, Slater either owned or shared interest in 13 textile mills. His mills were formed as partnerships with close friends, relatives, or trusted business associates, and were located in mill villages, which furnished housing for the families. Whole families worked for the mill, or perhaps the men worked on farms. Men were warned against depending too much on their children for family support.

The textile industry led the industrialization process in the United States. Other leading sectors would eventually dominate the industrial economy, such as steel and automobiles.

See also Company Towns, Entrepreneurship, Industrial Revolution.

References Gies, Joseph, and Frances Gies. *The Ingenious Yankees* (1976); Tucker, Barbara M. *Samuel Slater and the Origins of the American Textile Industry, 1790–1860* (1984).

Slavery

Slavery was the most oppressive of the systems of forced agricultural labor that flourished in European colonies during the eighteenth and nineteenth centuries. The rights to the energy, skills, and talents of slaves belonged to slave owners, who deployed them without regard to the best interest or preferences of individual slaves. Enslavement was a lifetime proposition. The ownership of slaves was transferable, and auction markets developed, where

A slave auction in Virginia, as depicted in Harper's Weekly

slaveholders bought and sold slaves.

Systems of forced labor arose everywhere in western European capitalism during its early stages of development. The rise and fall of slavery in the United States mirrored the rise and fall of serfdom in Russia. Eastern Europe witnessed a trend of re-enserfment during the early phase of Western capitalistic development. The spread of forced labor systems in peripheral areas stood in marked contrast to the abandonment of forced labor systems in the European countries at the forefront of capitalist development.

Spanish colonies successfully enslaved the indigenous Indian population. The English colonies enslaved Indians, but without much success. Runaway Indians could count on support from friendly tribes, making enslavement difficulty. In the 1600s, white indentured servants filled the need for forced labor. African slaves appeared in Virginia as early as 1619. To-

ward the end of the seventeenth century, the flow of white indentured servants dropped off significantly, because of improved economic conditions in Europe. In addition, a fall in the mortality rate among inhabitants of the southern colonies made investment in the lifetime productivity of a slave more feasible. Given these factors, coupled with growing European demand for agricultural stables, the colony of Virginia saw a fourfold increase in the importation of enslaved Africans at the end of the seventeenth century. The charter of the Royal African Company in 1672 included a grant of monopoly on the slave trade. In the eighteenth century, Britain dominated the world's slave trade.

Slavery, like other systems of forced labor, became widespread in areas where limitations on the supply of labor acted as a severe bottleneck on production. A planter in Virginia had vast land holdings on which to raise tobacco, which enjoyed strong demand in Europe. The amount of tobacco a planter could raise and sell depended on the number of workers he could command. Later, the development of the steam engine, and the mechanization of the textile industry, created similar conditions for southern cotton planters. New England farms were self-sufficient economic organizations, in which farmers consumed most of what they produced. Without a strong export market, farmers saw no need to import labor to increase production.

As white forced labor disappeared, society began to separate whites and Africans. Laws were passed prohibiting marriages between whites and Africans. In 1667, Virginia passed a law assuring slave owners that they did not have to emancipate slaves who had converted to Christianity.

Slavery in the United States, and serfdom in Russia, ended in the 1860s. The expansion of forced labor at the outposts of capitalism reveals the power of the economic forces unleashed by capitalism. As the population density increased in these areas, the added profit from forced labor diminished, and the moral repugnance at the practice became a prime consideration. The emphasis on free competition between individuals in capitalist doctrine, including open competition in labor markets, softened the burden of guilt that capitalism might bear for the rise of forced labor in the seventeenth and eighteenth centuries.

See also Indentured Servitude, Serfdom.

References Curtin, Phillip D. *The Atlantic Slave Trade* (1969); Kolchin, Peter. *Unfree Labor: American Slavery and Russian Serfdom* (1987).

Smith, Adam (1723–1790)

Adam Smith's book, *An Inquiry into the Nature and Causes of the Wealth of Nations*, furnished the intellectual underpinnings for laissez-faire capitalism.

Smith was born in Kirkcaldy, Scotland, near Edinburgh, in 1723. His father, who had been comptroller of the customs, died before Smith was born, leaving him as the only child in the care of his mother, whom he would outlive by only six years. Smith excelled at school, despite spells of abstraction that became a memorable personality trait in later years. After completing the Kirkcaldy grammar school, Smith, at the age of 14, entered the University of Glasgow. Mathematics and natural philosophy interested him, but the ideas of Francis Hutcheson, an eminent moral philosopher, became a creative force in the intellectual development of Smith. Hutcheson subscribed to the theory that the end of moral actions was the "greatest happiness for the greatest number." When Smith was 17, Oxford admitted him with a scholarship, where he spent the next six years. He barely escaped expulsion from Oxford for having a copy of David Hume's *A Treatise on Human Nature.*

In 1751, Smith accepted an offer from the University of Glasgow to fill the chair in logic. In April 1752, he moved to a more lucrative post as chair in moral philosophy. In 1759, Smith became a person to be reckoned with in the intellectual world, when he published *The Theory on Moral Sentiments.* In this book, Smith worked out the foundations of human nature that shaped his future work in economics.

In 1763, Smith left his university appointment to become the tutor, on a tour of France, to the stepson of Charles Townsend, the person whose policies as chancellor of the Exchequer helped to drive the American colonists to revolt. Smith's new responsibilities meant a pay raise and a lifetime pension. He met Voltaire in Geneva, and visited the fashionable salons of Paris, where he met Turgot, D'Alembert, Helvetius, Marmonted, and Rochefoucauld. He became attached to the physiocrats, who were propagating the philosophy of laissez faire (hands-off government policy). Smith wanted to dedicate his famous book, *Wealth of Nations*, to the eminent physiocrat, Francois Quesnay, and would have done so if Quesnay had not died before

Smith finished his book. In 1766, an assassination in the streets of Paris took the life of a member of Smith's party, abruptly ending Smith's stay in Paris. Smith returned to Kirkcaldy, lived with his mother, and devoted his time to study and occasional visits to London and Edinburgh. He began writing his great treatise on the wealth of nations. On his visits to London, he visited the most celebrated literary figures of the day, including Edward Gibbon, Samuel Johnson, and Edward Burke.

The first edition of the *Wealth of Nations* came out in 1776; the book went through five editions during Smith's life. In 1778, Smith accepted a position as commissioner of the customs of Scotland. He spent the remainder of his life in Edinburgh, living with his mother and a cousin. He died on 17 July 1790.

In the *Wealth of Nations*, Smith depicted a picture of a harmoniously functioning economic system harnessing the self-interested passion of individual participants. In the words of Smith:

It is not from the benevolence of the butcher, the brewer, or the baker that we expect our dinner, but from their regard to their own interest. We address ourselves not to their humanity but to their self-love, and never talk to them of our own necessities but of their advantages.

In Smith's vision, the regulating mechanism was competition and free markets, which channeled the energy of self-interest toward socially useful ends, as if an invisible hand was directing society's activities. Smith was against monopolies granted as government favors, and government intervention in markets, including barriers to foreign trade. He observed that "people of the same trade seldom meet together but the conversation ends in a conspiracy against the public, or in some diversion to raise prices."

Smith's message fell on receptive ears in early nineteenth-century England. Mercantilist economic policies had put industrial capitalists in a straitjacket of government regulations. These regulations extended so far as to give local justices of the peace jurisdiction to set wages. Smith's vision of free competition, extending so far as free international trade, became a vital idea that to this day is still shaping the development of capitalism.

See also Classical School of Economics.

References Heilbroner, Robert. *The Worldly Philosophers* (1972); Ross, Ian Simpson. *The Life of Adam Smith* (1995).

Smoot-Hawley Tariff of 1930 (United States)

The Smoot-Hawley Tariff of 1930 was the most protectionist tariff ever enacted by the United States. The tariff met with retaliation from trading partners, causing a drop in the volume of world trade that helped drive the world economy into a deep depression.

In the United States, agriculture had never recovered from the otherwise brief depression that followed World War I. Protectionist sentiment in agriculture awaited an opportunity to raise tariff duties on agricultural products. President Hoover, normally sympathetic to liberal trade policies, saw higher tariffs as part of a strategy to restore business confidence in the aftermath of the stock market crash the previous October. Senator Reed Smoot of Utah and Congressman Willis C. Hawley of Oregon were committed protectionists. The bill they drew up began as a measure to raise duties on imported agricultural products. Tariff fever gained momentum, with legislators adding a wider variety of goods, including manufactured goods, to the tariff bill. The level of protection also rose.

The final version of the bill raised duties on raw Cuban sugar, cattle, mutton and lamb, corn milk, lemons, hides, flax, hemp cotton, wool, clothing, lumber, boots and shoes, silk and woolen goods, hydraulic cement, and bricks. The average ad valorem tax levied on the affected imports rose from approximately 26 percent to approximately 50 percent.

A thousand members of the American Economic Association signed a statement denouncing the Smoot-Hawley legislation. Senator Jim Watson of Indiana predicted that enactment of the bill would mean "this nation will be on the upgrade, financially, economically, and commercially within thirty days, and within a year from this date we shall have regained the peak of prosperity." The bill became law on 17 June 1930. President Hoover signed the bill with six gold pens. A British economist of the time, perhaps realizing the new tariff would seal the fate of the gold standard, described it as "a turning point in world history." Australia and Argentina, exporters of primary products to the United States, were the first to go off the gold standard.

Before retaliation made itself felt, the tariff may have slightly strengthened the U.S. economy. In 1930, prices fell slower in the United States than in other countries. The balance of payments turned from deficit to surplus, and the stock of monetary gold rose, but retaliation set in almost immediately. Great Britain raised tariffs in 1931; Canada, Cuba, Mexico, France, Italy, Spain, and a number of smaller countries raised duties on some products. The following year saw a second round of retaliation. Worse than higher tariffs were quantitative restrictions and quotas on imports that some countries imposed. World trade fell into a vicious downward spiral, falling in volume by about one-third of its value in 1929.

The Smoot-Hawley Tariff backfired for the United States. Exports fell faster than imports as the rest of the world raised trade restrictions on U.S. products. Net U.S. exports fell from $842 million in 1929 to $225 million in 1933.

Most capitalist countries came out of World War II realizing the destructive effects of the Smoot-Hawley tariff. These countries, including the United States, began to ignore domestic pressures for protective tariffs, and negotiations for mutual reductions of tariffs became an important agenda item for trade policy in the post-World War era.

See also Import Duties Act of 1932.

References Ashley, Percy. *Modern Tariff History: Germany, United States, and France* (1970); Atack, Jeremy, and Peter Passel. *A New Economic View of American History from Colonial Times to 1940* (1994); Schlesinger, Arthur, Jr., *The Age of Roosevelt* (1957).

Social Insurance (Germany)

Modern programs of social insurance, such as Social Security in the United States, originated in the social insurance programs inaugurated in Germany late in the nineteenth century. In the 1880s, Bismarck's Germany enacted a trio of laws that laid the foundation for a system of social insurance: The Accident Insurance Law and the Sickness Insurance Law passed the Reichstag in May, 1883, and went into force in December 1884; the Reichstag approved the Old Age Insurance Law in June 1889.

The Reichstag first framed an accident insurance bill in 1881, but a federal council rejected this bill after it passed. Although the bill never became law, the wording of its introduction is revealing. It reads:

That the State should interest itself to a greater degree than hitherto in those of its members who need assistance, is not only a duty of humanity and Christianity...but a duty of state-preserving policy, whose aim should be to cultivate the conception—and that, too, amongst the non-propertied classes...that the state is not merely a necessary but a beneficent institution. These classes must, by the evident and direct advantages which are secured to them by legislative measures, be led to regard the State not as an institution contrived for the protection of the better classes of society.... The apprehension that a Socialistic element might be introduced into legislation if this end was followed should not check us.

The leadership that the Reichstag got

from both the emperor and Chancellor Bismarck supported the establishment of a national system of insurance. At first, Bismarck favored a government insurance program against sickness, accident, and old age. In his proposal for a national insurance system, he argued,

> The corollary of compulsion is, in my opinion, insurance through the State...without that [there is] no compulsion. I should not have courage to exercise compulsion if I had nothing to offer in return.... If compulsion is enforced it is necessary that law provide at the same time an institution for insurance, which shall be cheaper and securer than any other. We cannot expose the savings of the poor to the danger of bankruptcy...[and] we cannot compel insurance in private companies which might go bankrupt, even with good management, because of conjunctures or great calamities.

After the rejection of the first accident bill, the emperor, in a famous declaration, reiterated his government's commitment to the general concept of social insurance. He mentioned no particulars, except the inclusion of sickness insurance. It read in part,

> In February of this year, we expressed our conviction that the cure of social ills must be sought exclusively in the repression of Social Democratic excesses, but simultaneously in the positive advancement of the welfare of the working classes. We regard it as our imperial duty to urge this task again upon the Reichstag.... [The aged and infirm working people are entitled to] greater state care than has hither to been accorded them.... The finding of the proper ways and means for the latter is a difficult task.

In the enactment of the laws for accident, sickness, and old age, the Reichstag departed from the purely government program that Bismarck had envisioned.

Bismarck came to regard his first proposal as too bureaucratic. The laws did provide for compulsory insurance that covered all the working classes. Employers paid all the premiums for accident insurance. For the sickness insurance, employers paid one-third and the workers paid two-thirds. For old-age insurance, employers and workers paid an equal share, and the government added a subsidy. The insuring institutions were nonprofit agencies organized for the specific purpose of providing accident, or sickness, or old-age insurance. Associations providing accident insurance were organized by industry, and regional associations provided sickness insurance.

Workers received compensation for all accidents, even when the injured worker was the negligent party. Women received compensation for three weeks after giving birth, except in cases of illegitimacy. A person could be treated in a hospital with the consent of his spouse or members of his household. The standard period of contribution for old-age insurance was 30 years. If a worker died after contributing for five years, his surviving spouse or orphaned children received half of his annuity. If a female worker died after contributing for 15 years, her children received half of her annuity.

It is remarkable that one of the least democratic and revolutionary of the capitalist countries of the nineteenth century was the most innovative in the area of social insurance. The democratic governments of the nineteenth century, and the revolutionary monarchies of France, often pandered to the most powerful economic interest of the day, but Germany's patriarchal traditions came to the aid of its working class. By the mid-twentieth century, all the major industrialized societies had enacted systems of social insurance.

See also Employer Liability and Worker Compensation, Social Security Act, Unemployment Insurance.

References Dawson, William Harbutt. *Bismarck and State Socialism* (1890); Rimlinger, Gaston. *Welfare Policy and Industrialization in Europe, America, and Russia* (1971).

Social Security (United States)

The Social Security Act of 1935 ushered in the age of social insurance in the United States. Social insurance originated in Germany in the late nineteenth century. The British Parliament legislated old-age pensions in 1908. A strong patriarchal tradition paved the way for social insurance in Germany, and a spirit of egalitarianism made Britain receptive to ideas of social insurance. In the United States, patriarchal traditions and egalitarian views held little sway, and a tradition of individual responsibility seemed incompatible with social insurance. The Depression of the 1930s taught Americans that economic destitution can even overtake those committed to hard work, thrift, and planning for the future. The economic system can be at fault, rather than the personal characteristics of individuals, or the management of businesses.

In his social security message to Congress, President Roosevelt buttressed his arguments with an appeal to the Constitution:

> If, as our Constitution tells us, our Federal Government was established among other things "to promote the general welfare," it is our plain duty to provide for that security upon which welfare depends.... Our task of reconstruction does not require the creation of new and strange values. It is rather the finding of the way once more to known, but to some degree forgotten, ideals and values.... I believe that the funds necessary to provide this insurance should be based upon contributions rather than by an increase in taxation.

Economic insecurity caused by unemployment and old age was the prime concern of President Roosevelt and his administration. The Social Security Act incorporated provisions to induce state governments to establish unemployment insurance programs. It established public assistance to aged and blind persons, and to dependent children.

The most significant of its measures provided for the creation of an old-age insurance program. This program bore a greater resemblance to private insurance systems than its European brethren. Equal contributions from worker and employer financed the social insurance. The contributions from workers earned them a contractual right to the benefits. No reference to paternalism was made in justifying the employer's contribution. Instead, a rather unconvincing argument referred to it as "an automatic method of meeting the depreciation charges on the human factor cooperating in production similar to the usual accounting charges for depreciation of plant and equipment."

Benefits were proportional to contributions, and ranged from $10 to $80 per month. In 1939, the program was amended to entitle a contributor's aged wife, widow, parents, and children under 18 to receive benefits. In 1950, the coverage was expanded from 65 to 89 percent of the work force. After the passage of the original act, future amendments introduced more features to redistribute income.

The most significant change to the social security system came in 1965, with passage of the Medicare program. This program provides hospital and medical care for persons 65 years and older. In his first message on social security, President Roosevelt had observed that he was not recommending health insurance "at this time."

The Depression of the 1930s reminded Americans of the economic insecurity lurking in the background of the capitalist economic system. Economic destitution can be the result of a failure of the entire economic system, rather than of individual initiative and management. The virtues of hard work, thrift, and planning are no match for the downdraft of a major depression. In addition, the glut of unemployment during the Depression gave the American people an incentive to enact programs encouraging older workers to retire.

See also Social Insurance, Unemployment Insurance.

References Biles, Roger. *A New Deal for the American People* (1991); Light, Paul. *Artful Work: The Politics of Social Security Reform* (1985); Rimlinger, Gaston V. *Welfare Policy and Industrialization in Europe, America, and Russia* (1971).

Socialized Medicine
See Welfare State.

Societe Generale de Credit Mobilier (France)

The Societe Generale de Credit Mobilier, usually called the Credit Mobilier, was the first joint-stock bank in France, and it furnished a model for joint-stock banks that was widely followed on the Continent. Founded in 1852, the Credit Mobilier owed its origin to the chilly greeting the regime of Louis Napoleon received from the financiers of France, including the House of Rothschild.

From the outset, the Credit Mobilier was conceived as a financial institution that would centralize long-term financing for railroads and heavy industry. By controlling access to long-term financing, the Credit Mobilier would shape industrial development, and remove competition between client firms. Although control of the bank rested with the Ministry of Finance, the management of the bank fell to Isaac and Emile Pereire, two brothers who were among the bank's largest investors. The bank had authorization to accept deposits; to advance credits against securities; to issue, purchase, or sell shares of stock; to finance railroads and industrial undertakings; and to sell bonds equal to ten times its joint-stock capital in value. The plan called for selling bonds to raise revenue that would go to purchasing stock of railroad and industrial enterprises. As it turned out, the Credit Mobilier was able to raise an abundance of capital by selling its own shares, which sold at premium prices. Its deposit business consisted of large deposits from major enterprises.

The Credit Mobilier shared in financing new railroad companies in France, Spain, Northern Italy, Austria, Russia, and Switzerland. By 1860, financing from the Credit Mobilier had paid for the construction of 10,000 kilometers of railroad outside of France. The French coal and steel industry, and the Silesian zinc industry, received financing from the Credit Mobilier, which also purchased sizable shareholdings in new credit-mobilier-type banks formed abroad.

The Rothschilds were the most aggressive in opposing the expansion of the Credit Mobilier abroad, and in seeking authorization to establish rival joint-stock banks in France. In 1864, the French government relented and granted permission to establish a competing joint-stock bank that could hold deposits and issue shares of stock. By then, the Credit Mobilier was beginning to face difficulties. The economic crisis in 1866–1867 caused the value of the Credit Mobilier's assets to fall in value. The Banque of France injected funds into the Credit Mobilier, sparing it from bankruptcy, but leaving it only able to honor existing business commitments. The Credit Mobilier lasted in this downsized condition until 1902.

Despite its failure, the Credit Mobilier became a prototype for the big commercial banks in Central Europe. These banks not only held deposits and granted short-term credit, but also held shares of stock, and provided long-term financing for big businesses. The precedents established by the Credit Mobilier began the trend toward close association between banks and industry that characterized late nineteenth-century German capitalism.

See also Finance Capitalism, Rothschild Banking Family.

References Born, Karl Erich. *International Banking in the 19th and 20th Centuries* (1983); Cameron, Rondo, et al. *France and the Economic Development of Europe, 1800–1914* (1961).

South Sea Bubble (England)

The South Sea Bubble was the first English experience with what, in today's terminology, would be called a major stock market crash. The English government began granting charters for joint-stock companies before 1600. It took an act of Parliament, or a grant from the crown, to charter a joint-stock company, and the charter usually came with monopoly trading privileges. The companies operated like modern corporations, selling stock to raise capital, paying dividends, and issuing stock certificates that could be transferred from one individual to another. By 1698, London had a stock exchange for trading stock. As the market developed, it began to exhibit waves of speculation and contraction. The South Sea Bubble of 1720 was the most serious of the contractions, affecting future confidence in joint-stock companies.

In 1711, the South Sea Company received a royal charter, confirmed by an act of Parliament. The charter granted the company a monopoly on English trade with Spanish colonies in America and the Pacific Isles. In 1719, the South Sea Company conceived a plan, with government backing, that extended an invitation to holders of government obligations to exchange them for stock in the South Sea Company, which would hold the government obligations, and charge the government less interest than it was currently paying. King George I became the governor of the South Sea Company, and the government helped to spread the word of the profits expected from the company's monopoly privileges. Within six days of the company's offer to exchange stock for government debt, two-thirds of the holders of government obligations took advantage of the offer. Other investors became infatuated with shares of South Sea stock, and the price increased from £77 to £123.5 (1719).

On 7 April 1720, both Houses of Parliament approved the proposals of the company. As the price of the stock rose, the company continued to raise cash by floating new issues of stock. On 12 April, the company announced a new stock offering at £300 per share. "Persons of all ranks crowded to the house" to buy the new shares. In a few days, the price rose to £340. On 21 April, the company announced a summer dividend of 10 percent. This announcement helped fuel the speculative fever, and the company floated another stock issue at £400 per share on 23 April. The new shares were bought up in a few hours. In June, the price had risen to over £800 per share.

In the meantime, other companies were caught up in the mania. The public rushed to buy stock in companies organized for such things, as in the words of Walter Bagehot in his *Lombard Street*.

Wrecks to be fished for on the Irish coast–Insurance of Horses and other Cattle (two millions)–Insurance for loses by servants–To make Salt Water Fresh–For building of Hospitals for Bastard Children, For building of Ships against Pirates–For making of Oil from Sunflower Seeds–For Improving Malt Liquors–For recovery of Seaman's Wages–For extracting of Silver from Lead–For making of Iron with Pitcoal–For importing a Number of large Jack Asses from Spain–For trading in Human Hair–For fatting of Hogs–For a Wheel of Perpetual Motion.

Perhaps the strangest was "for an Undertaking which shall in due time be revealed." The undertaking could be learned by purchasing two guineas' worth of stock. The promoter sold 1,000 of the subscriptions in the morning, and disappeared in the afternoon. These excesses led to the passage of the Bubble Act of 1720, which outlawed all stock issues, except by companies with government charters, and also made it more difficult to obtain these charters. The South Sea Company supported the Bubble Act, because these companies were drawing investors away from their stock.

In July, a new issue of South Sea Company stock sold for £1,000 per share. The boom began to lose steam when word spread that Spain was dampening the company's trade with America. Lesser companies were failing, and the Mississippi Bubble burst in France. In August, the price of shares fell to £700. In September, the market crashed, and South Sea Company shares tumbled to £131 per share. The collapse caused a wave of bank failures and bankruptcies, and, in September, the Bank of England announced it would absorb shares of South Sea stock, to ease the crisis. After this announcement, the Bank of England had to defend itself from a run on its bank.

The South Sea Bubble signaled the climax of the commercial revolution that began with growth in the joint-stock trading companies. A long period of prosperity had generated great amounts of capital that needed investment opportunities. As opportunities waned for earning profits from the creation of joint-stock trading companies with monopoly trading privileges, speculators turned to riskier and more desperate ventures. The collapse of the South Sea Bubble haunted the market in joint-stock company shares for a century. The pace of economic development and innovation leveled off until the Industrial Revolution.

See also Bubble Act of 1720, Mississippi Bubble.

References Bagehot, Walter. *Lombard Street: A Description of the Money Market* (1873); Carswell, John. *The South Sea Bubble* (1960); Erleigh, Viscount. *The South Sea Bubble* (1933); Kindleberger, Charles P. *Manias, Panics, and Crashes: A History of Financial Crises* (1978).

Spanish Colonial Empire

Columbus's voyage to America gave Spain claim to what turned out to be one of the biggest surprises in history—the vast stretch of land of the Americas. Explorers under the Spanish flag soon conquered a colonial empire that extended to the East Indies. It was the undeveloped lands of America, however, that constituted an unprecedented challenge for a colonial power.

Spain began conducting its trade with the West Indies along the lines of the Portuguese colonial trade with the East Indies, which the King of Portugal carried on as a royal monopoly. He bore the risk, owned the ships, and conducted the trade

on his own account. The Portuguese model met the needs of trade with the highly civilized societies of the East, where trade and commerce had a long history.

Spain soon discovered that the Portuguese model was unfit for the West Indies and the Americas. The quantities of capital and labor needed to exploit those areas were more than even the Spanish crown could marshal. In 1495, the Spanish government set conditions that enabled all Castilian subjects to travel to America for settlement, exploration, or trade. This freedom lasted eight years, before Spain established a house of trade, called the Casa de Contratación, and began a policy of highly restricted and regulated colonial trade.

All colonial trade had to be conducted by Spaniards, and had to begin and end in the port of Seville, granting the merchants of Seville a valuable monopoly that they jealously guarded. Initially, the Casa de Contratación was run for the private profit of the crown, but colonies complained that they were not getting sufficient provisions from Spain. As private initiative replaced government initiative, the Casa de Contratación became an elaborate customs house. The government collected detailed information on cargoes to and from the New World, set standards for ships, and required all ships to travel in fleets guarded by royal ships.

The crown took special interest in precious metals. Until 1584, all mines belonged to the crown. The crown began demanding a two-thirds share of mine output, but, early in the sixteenth century, the crown's share dropped to one-fifth, where it remained until the eighteenth century. All gold had to be brought to the royal smelter to be taxed and stamped. Gold without the royal stamp could not be shipped to Spain.

The Spanish mercantile system has won little applause from economists. Adam Smith, in the *Wealth of Nations*, never tires of pointing the finger of reproach at the failed economic policies of

Slaves work near a fancifully depicted harbor in Florida, where Spanish ships sit at anchor.

Spain and Portugal. He claimed that Portugal and Spain were the only two European countries that had lost ground since the growth of trade with the American colonies. It was the eighteenth century before Spanish joint-stock companies, similar to the English East India Company, came into existence, to assist in the exploitation of the new colonies. The influx of gold and silver from the New World drove up prices in Europe, and strengthened the demand for manufactured goods from northern Europe. Spanish manufacturing and agriculture felt little of the stimulus of trade with the New World, and, according to Smith, deteriorated. Apparently, Spain contented itself with infusing Europe with fresh supplies of precious metals, counting itself a wealthy country, because of its bullion reserves. The crown placed too much emphasis on enriching itself, on granting monopoly privileges, and on detailed regulations, and too little emphasis on economic development at home.

Spain's experience with the colonies demonstrated that the task of exploiting the vast resources of the New World was too much for a government without the incentives and initiative of private enterprise. In a few centuries, the New World would become a political sanctuary for the capitalist spirit of private enterprise. At home, the aristocratic and feudal society of Spain either could not or would not redirect the resources of the American colonies toward capitalist development. Colonial trade, which two centuries later would help inspire an Industrial Revolution in England, seemed to enervate Spanish manufacturing with the influx of precious metals.

See also Colonial Policy; Columbus, Christopher; Mercantilism; Portuguese Colonial Empire.

References Haring, Clarence Henry. *Trade and*

Navigation Between Spain and the Indies (1918); McAlister, Lyle N. *Spain and Portugal in the New World, 1492–1700* (1984).

Spanish Monetary Disorder and Inflation of the Seventeenth Century

At the beginning of the seventeenth century, Spain's revenues from gold and silver mines in the New World began trailing off, and its government budget was bloated after years of financing wars and royal pomp necessary for a great world power. To pay for numerous wars and heavy government expenditures during the seventeenth century, the Spanish crown minted copper coins, and opened a period of monetary disorder that contributed to Spain's economic deterioration.

During the first quarter of the seventeenth century, the government's unbridled coinage of copper coins spawned a wave of inflation that drew public protest. The face value of the copper coins exceeded their intrinsic value, yielding the government a profit from minting the coins. By 1627, public anger over wheat and livestock shortages, coupled with widespread inflation, pressured the government to switch to a deflationary monetary policy. The nominal values of the copper coins were cut in half, without compensating the holders of the devalued copper coins. The government began a practice of making solemn promises not to tamper with the currency, but which seemed to be promises only meant to be broken.

The government resumed a policy of inflationary finance in 1634. Rather than incurring the expense of supplying copper to the mints, the government restamped the existing copper coins to increase their face value. Coins were called in several times and restamped, often doubling or tripling their nominal value. Between 1627 and 1641, copper coins were inflated three times and deflated four times. In 1641, inflation reached a peak, and silver was selling at a premium of 190 percent. In 1642, the government undertook a brutal deflationary devaluation, reducing the face value of copper coins by 70–80 percent.

In 1651, the government, again needing money for military outlays, called in copper coins of one denomination, and restamped them at quadruple their value. In 1652, the government returned to a deflationary monetary policy, and devalued copper coins. This time, however, the government compensated holders of the devalued copper coins with interest-bearing bonds.

Counterfeiting contributed significantly to depreciating the value of the copper currency. After 1660, counterfeiting was punishable with the death penalty, and burning at the stake awaited those participating in the importation of counterfeit coins. About 92 percent of the money in circulation was copper, and the remaining gold and silver coins were clipped.

Monetary disorder continued, until it reached a crisis in 1680, with silver selling at a premium of 275 percent. The government issued a decree devaluing copper currency by one-half, which was equivalent to one-fourth its 1664 value. Prices plummeted 45 percent in a few months, forcing a harsh adjustment. The government began to reduce the supply of copper coins, and had ceased minting copper by 1693. Spain enjoyed monetary stability throughout the first half of the eighteenth century.

The Spanish economy showed the effects of nearly a century of monetary disorder. The woolen industry in Toledo, and the number of cargo ships sailing between Spain and the Indies, shrank by three-fourths. Some industrialized areas lost half their population. Spain's dependence upon foreign treasure had perhaps already sapped vitality from some domestic industries, rendering inflationary policies tempting in an economy that could not generate sufficient tax revenue to finance its government. Nevertheless, monetary chaos stifled private initiative and capitalist development, contributing to Spain's economic deterioration.

References Hamilton, Earl J. *War and Prices in Spain. 1651–1800* (1947); Vives, Jaime Vicens. *An Economic History of Spain* (1969).

Spice Trade

Today, with spices easily affordable, it is hard to imagine that handsome profits from the spice trade once stirred mariners to heroic enterprises, and that empires rose and fell with control of their trade.

During the fourteenth and fifteenth centuries, Venice dominated the trade of eastern spices with Europe. The Mamelukes, who governed Egypt, shared with Venice a common enemy, the Turks. Through its connection with Egypt, Venice exercised a virtual monopoly on the East–West spice trade, and control of Mediterranean trade made Venice one of the wealthiest and most powerful city-states of its day.

The lure of monopoly profits from the spice trade spurred Portugal to a century-long quest for a sea route to the Indies. In 1418, a Portuguese prince, Henry the Navigator, established a naval college at Sagres, attracting the best navigators and astronomers, and searching for the routes of trade in spices, gold, ivory, and slaves. The king of Portugal sent one overland expedition through Arabia to India, to discover the source of the spice trade and the trade routes to the Middle East. Portuguese mariners explored the western coast of Africa, and rounded the Cape of Good Hope in 1487. In 1498, Vasco da Gama sailed around the Cape of Good Hope and up the eastern coast of Africa, to Malindi, and from there to Calicut. Da Gama's expedition opened up the spice trade to Portugal. Portugal wrestled control of the spice trade between India and Africa from the hands of the Arabs and Persians, and began the century-long Portuguese monopoly of the eastern spice trade with Europe. By 1511, the hegemony of Portugal had extended to the Malabar coast of India, Ceylon (now Sri Lanka), Malacca on the Malay Peninsula, Java, and Sumatra. The Spice Islands soon afterwards fell within Portugal's sphere of control. The price of pepper soared in Europe, as Portugal exploited its monopoly on the spice trade.

Venice's lucrative monopoly of the spice trade had tempted Portugal, whose monopoly profits, in turn, attracted rivals. Britain, Spain, and the Dutch sent expeditions in search of cargoes of spices. Spain sent Ferdinand Magellan to find a western route to the East Indies around the southern tip of South America. One of Magellan's ships returned after circumnavigating the globe. It had picked up enough cloves, nutmegs, mace, and cinnamon in the East Indies to pay for the entire expedition. When Francis Drake's Golden Hind ran aground, three tons of cloves were thrown overboard to raise the ship out of the water.

The Dutch sent expeditions to the East Indies early in the seventeenth century, and, by the end of the seventeenth century, had driven the Portuguese out, and contained England, to trade with India. The Dutch took full advantage of their monopoly position, restricting supplies to drive up prices. They ordered the destruction of clove and nutmeg trees on all islands, except Amboyna and Ternate in the Moluccas, and the Banda group. The production of cloves and nutmeg fell to one-fourth of its pre-Dutch level. The Dutch also burned much of the bark that cinnamon came from.

During the eighteenth century, the British and the French were determined to break the Dutch monopoly on the spice trade. By 1796, many Dutch possessions in the East Indies had fallen into English hands. In 1824, the British and the Dutch signed a peace treaty that gave the East Indies to the Dutch, except for the northern part of Borneo, which fell to the British, along with India, Ceylon, and Malaya. Also, the French and the British smuggled plants from the Dutch East Indies, and transplanted them to islands under French and British control. By the opening of the nineteenth century, no one country monopolized the trade of any one spice.

The Portugese conducted the spice trade as a government enterprise. The British and the Dutch formed joint-stock companies, precursors of modern corporations, to profit from the spice trade. Virtually all elements of modern capitalist enterprise, such as bearing risks, mobilizing vast sums of capital, and pursing profits, are exhibited by the spice trade.

See also Colonial Policy, Dutch Capitalism, Portuguese Colonial Empire.

References Israel, Jonathan. *Dutch Primacy in World Trade, 1585–1740* (1989); Parry, John W. *The Story of Spices* (1953); Subrahmanyam, Sanjay. *The Portuguese Empire in Asia, 1500–1700* (1993).

Statute of Artificers of 1563 (England)

The Statute of Artificers became the law of the land in England during the time of Elizabeth I. This statute represents the kind of laborious governmental regulation of the economy that laissez-faire capitalism swept way in the eighteenth and nineteenth centuries. It remained the law until 1815.

The most interesting feature of this statute was the power given to justices of the peace to set maximum and minimum wages for every type of employment in their territory. Justices took into consideration changes in the level of prices in making periodic reassessments of wages. A kind of yearly contract guaranteed workers an annual wage. Employers dismissing workers without just cause paid fines of 40 shillings. Workers unlawfully quitting their jobs went to jail. A worker leaving his town or parish without permission of his employer and local magistrate could be punished. Hours of work lasted from dawn to dark in winter and for 12 hours in summer. The statute forbade strikes of any kind, on pain of imprisonment or heavy fines. The justices could force any willfully unemployed man to take employment, if he was under age 30 and had an income of less than 40 shillings per year. In rural areas, men under 60, in good health, could be put to work harvesting.

Parliament repealed the wage-fixing clauses of the Statute of Artificers in 1813. In most employments, the assessment of wages fell into disuse and virtually disappeared by the beginning of the nineteenth century. Some especially regulated industries kept the practice alive in certain areas.

The Spitalfields Act, renewed by an act of 1792, gave Middlesex justices of the peace, and the authorities of the City of London, the power to fix wages for silk weavers. The Arbitration Act of 1800 required that two arbitrators hear all disputes about wages, payments for accessories, or delivery or quality of goods. Each party appointed one arbitrator. The arbitrators had three days to reach a decision before the matter went to the justice of the peace. Arbitration was compulsory, but employer hostility rapidly made the act inoperative.

The Statute of Artificers also regulated the terms and conditions of apprenticeships. The statute provided that no person could practice a trade without first serving as an apprentice for seven years. Limits on the number of apprenticeships, relative to the number of adult workers, helped control the supply of labor, and to keep wages up in some trades. The cutlers of Hallamshire allowed one apprenticeship for each master, excepting a master's son. Apprentices whose parents were not in the trade often paid high entrance fees. The apprenticeship regulations gave monopoly power to members of a trade. The apprenticeship clause of the statute was repealed in 1814.

With the onset of the Industrial Revolution, workers tried to revive the Statute of Artificers to protect themselves against employers. Employers wanted to take on as many apprentices as possible. Specialization in the workplace took away the need for skilled workers. Workers saw the movement of unapprenticed worker into industry as the cause of low wages. In weighing these issues, Parliament came down on the side of laissez faire, striking a fatal blow to laborious government regulation of the labor market.

See also Depression of the Late Sixteenth Century.

References Daunton, Martin. *Progress and Poverty: An Economic and Social History of Britain 1700–1850* (1995); Durant, Will, and Ariel Durant. *The Age of Reason Begins* (1961); Mantoux, Paul. *The Industrial Revolution in the Eighteenth Century* (1961); Palliser, David M. *The Age of Elizabeth: England under the Late Tudors, 1547–1603* (1983).

Statute of Monopolies of 1624 (England)

At the beginning of the seventeenth century, English sovereigns could not impose taxes without the approval of Parliament, but they could grant monopolies without Parliament's approval. Given the lack of tax revenue, patents of monopoly became a way to reward persons who rendered valuable services to the crown, either in military or civilian employment. Prior to the reign of Elizabeth I, the English crown had exercised this power in moderation, but Elizabeth carried this practice to an extreme. A partial list of the commodities assigned to monopolies during her reign included salt, iron, powder, cards, calf skins, ox-shin bones, train oil, lists of cloth, potashes, vinegar, steel, brushes, pots, bottles, saltpeter, lead, calamine stone oil, oil of blubber, glasses, paper, tin, and sulfur. When the complete list was read in Parliament, a member expressed surprise that bread was not on the list, and expressed the view that, "if affairs go on at this rate, we shall have bread reduced to a monopoly before next parliament." In addition to exorbitant price increases, monopolists were granted wide and arbitrary powers to protect themselves from those, who, attracted by the high profits, tried to infringe upon their monopoly. The patentees of saltpeter had the power to enter and search every house, stable, cellar, or wherever they suspected saltpeter was being stored. The patentees often extorted money from those who wanted to be spared the trouble. Recognizing that feelings were running high in Parliament, Elizabeth rescinded the more odious and grievous patents of monopoly. Parliament accepted Elizabeth's gesture, and never asked that she renounce the royal prerogative to grant monopolies.

James I granted patents of monopoly, and annulled them, when he needed help from Parliament. The House of Commons determined to remedy this practice, and forced the king's assent to the Statute of Monopolies of 1624, which declared null and void monopolies created by royal prerogative.

With one blow, the Statute of Monopolies struck down the vast vested interest of the royal monopolies. A century and a half later, Adam Smith observed of Englishmen that they were "to their great honor of all peoples, the least subject to the wretched spirit of monopoly." The statute provided for two important exceptions to the ban on monopolies granted by the crown. First, organizations such as the East India Company could maintain monopolies in areas of foreign trade. Second, inventors could receive patents for new inventions. Under these exceptions, the crown could still sell patents of monopoly to raise revenue. In 1631, a company bought from Charles I a patent on the manufacture of soap.

The patent system outlined by the statute received mixed reviews as a stimulant to invention and innovation in industry. Critics charged it protected the inventor for extended periods of time. James Watt was reportedly able, for a quarter of a century, to forestall the development of new types of steam engines. Supporters of the patent system point to rapid technological development, beginning with the Industrial Revolution, perhaps aided by the patent system. The practice of granting patents of monopoly for new inventions has stood the test of time, surviving into the modern era.

See also Patent System.

References Ashton, S. *The Industrial Revolution: 1760–1830* (1964); Donald, Maxwell B. *Elizabethan Monopolies: The History of the Company of Mineral and Battery Works from 1565 to 1604* (1961); Hume, David. *History of England* (1752–1762). Reprint, 1985.

Statute of Westminster of 1931 (England)

See Disimperialism.

Steam Engine

The invention of the steam engine stands forth as an epochal event in the process of economic industrialization. With steam power available, access to water power no longer dictated the location of factories. Large-scale factories, not possible with water or animal power, rose in urban areas, close to labor, resources, and consumer markets.

Although accounts of steam engines date back to Hero of Alexandria in a.d. 200, steady development of the steam engine began in the seventeenth century. The steam engine originated as a mutation of a steam pump. The first scientific analysis on the expansion of steam began in the late 1600s. In 1698, Thomas Savery built a steam pump for drawing water out of flooded mines. In Savery's pump, alternations in the temperature of steam in a container caused alternations in atmospheric pressure, which first drew water up under vacuum conditions, and then pushed it up when pressured returned. Cold water was poured on the container to change temperature. Around 1708, Thomas Newcomen built an atmospheric pump, in which a container was sealed by a piston at the top and connected at the bottom to a source of steam accessed by a valve. When cold water was poured on the container, the steam cooled, creating a vacuum, and drawing down the piston. The piston at the top was connected to a lever with a counterweight at the opposite end. Therefore, when fresh steam entered the container, the vacuum disappeared and the counterweight pulled the piston back up. These early efforts at steam power were inefficient, because too much energy was wasted in cooling down and reheating the condensing chamber.

James Watt's genius as an inventor was worthy of the task of turning these mongrel devices into workable steam engines. Watt's minor inventions for improving the steam engine are almost too long to list. His first contribution came in 1764, with the development of a condensing chamber separate from the cylinder that held the piston. In Watt's engine the cylinder holding the piston remained hot continuously. His most important contribution was the use of steam to propel the piston. Earlier engines used steam as an indirect power to create a vacuum in a cylinder. It was 1781 before Watt patented the device that converted the alternating action of the piston into the rotary motion of a wheel.

In 1767, Watt formed a partnership agreement with John Roebuck to build steam engines. In 1769, Parliament granted Watt a patent until 1783. He and Roebuck set up a steam engine near Edinburgh, but the lack of precision in the tolerances doomed the project to failure. In 1773, Roebuck sold his interest to Matthew Boulton, a wealthy manufacturer who owned the Soho factory north of Birmingham. The Soho factory built bronzes, vases, chandeliers, tripods, watch chains, and shoe buckles, among other things. Boulton saw that skilled workmanship could correct the imprecision of the engine that Watt and Roebuck had built. It helped a bit when John Wilkinson, in 1775, invented a device for boring out cylinders, significantly improving the tolerances between the piston and the cylinder. Watt and Boulton now produced engines that measurably outperformed any other source of power. Manufacturers and mine owners from all over England put in orders for steam engines. Parliament granted a patent extension from 1783 to 1800.

Watt continued to improve his steam engine. In 1781, he patented a device that converted the back and forth action of the piston to the rotary action of a wheel. In 1782, he patented an engine with a piston propelled by alternating pressure from both ends. In 1788, he patented the fly-ball governor, which smoothed the flow of steam, and stabilized engine speed. Watt paid off his debts in 1783, retired when his patent expired in 1800, and lived until 1819.

The steam engine transformed factories and transportation. In 1784, William Murdock, the foreman at the Soho factory, built a model locomotive. Steam engines soon saw service in flour mills, malt mills, and flint mills for earthenware and china. The first steam spinning mill was set up in 1785.

The steam engine became a powerful force for capitalist expansion, increasing output per worker, and placing greater demands for the mobilization of capital. World trade expanded, and business ventures took on a larger dimension.

See also Factory System, Industrial Revolution.

References Mantoux, Paul. *The Industrial Revolution in the Eighteenth Century* (1962); Rolt, T. C. *The Steam Engine of Thomas Newcomen* (1977).

Stock Market

A stock market is where currently outstanding stocks of corporations are bought and sold under highly competitive conditions. Currently outstanding stock is stock that has already been issued, or, put differently, stock that might be regarded as second-hand stock. Since stock markets trade in previously issued shares of stock, they are regarded as secondary markets. Corporations float a new stock offering in the primary markets. An example of a primary market transaction is when a corporation sells a new issue of stock to an investment banker, such as Merrill Lynch, which then resells the stock to investors. In the United States, stock markets are auction markets.

Historically, stock markets began spreading at the beginning of the eighteenth century. One of the first speculative manias, followed by a crash, occurred in London around 1720. Stock markets evolved as an offshoot of markets that traded mostly in government bonds.

In the United States, stock markets fall into two basic categories: organized exchanges and over-the-counter markets. The New York Stock Exchange and the American Stock Exchange and national exchanges; the Midwest Stock Exchange, Pacific Stock Exchange, Philadelphia Stock Exchange, Boston Stock Exchange, and Cincinnati Stock Exchange are regional exchanges; all of these are organized exchanges. The over-the-counter market consists of a network of computers that connects dealers in specific securities

with thousands of brokers, who act as agents. The dealers always make known the price at which they will buy or sell stock in a particular company.

The organized exchanges have a tangible location, often in their own building, and are governed by a board elected from the membership. Members are said to have seats on the exchanges, which are also bought and sold. The privilege to trade on the exchange comes with owning a seat.

Before the stock of a corporation can trade on an exchange, the stock must be listed with the exchange. For the big exchanges, such as the New York Stock Exchange, only the largest corporations can qualify for listing.

Stock markets are only one of several markets for financial assets that help mobilize savings and channel them into the most productive enterprises. Corporate bonds, government bonds, and even home mortgages are traded in secondary markets. Indices of average stock prices, however, rank among the most influential indicators of financial conditions. Many observers mark the beginning of the Depression of the 1930s with the stock market crash of 1929.

See also Amsterdam Exchange, Bubble Act of 1720, Dow Jones Industrial Average, London Stock Exchange, New York Stock Exchange, Securities Exchange Act of 1934, South Sea Bubble, Stock Market Crash of 1929.

References Brigham, Eugene F. *Fundamentals of Financial Management* (1989); Keown, Arthur J., et al. *Foundations of Finance* (1998).

Stock Market Crash of 1929 (United States)

The stock market crash of 1929 signaled the beginning of the Great Depression of the 1930s. The national experience of these events shaped the development of capitalism in the United States in the twentieth century.

John Maynard Keynes, in the *General Theory of Money, Interest, and Employment*, describes the cyclical process in these words:

By a cyclical movement we mean that as the system progresses in, e.g., the upward direction, the forces propelling it upwards at first gather force and have a cumulative effect on one another but gradually lose their strength until at a certain point they tend to be replaced by forces operating in the opposite direction.... There is, however, another characteristic of what we call the Trade Cycle..., namely, the phenomenon of the crisis—the fact that the substitution of a downward for a upward tendency often takes place suddenly, and violently, whereas there is, as a rule, no sharp turning point when an upward is substituted for a downward tendency.

The stock market crash that sounded the first notes of economic crisis occurred in October 1929. In his inaugural address six months before the crash, President Herbert Hoover shared his view on the national economy in the words, "I have no fears for the future of our country. It is bright with hope." Signs of trouble began arising by the summer of 1929, when the Federal Reserve reported that its measure of industrial production had nosed over for a 5-percent decline. Investment spending, covering expenditures on plant and equipment, housing, and inventories, was subsiding from a peak in 1926. The Federal Reserve had begun tightening the monetary reins in 1928. It sold bonds in the open market, and, in three separate moves, raised the discount rate from 3.5 to 5 percent. Between April 1928 and November 1929, the money supply fell at an annual rate of more that 1 percent. That rate compares with a 3.8-percent growth rate between 1927 and 1928.

Standard and Poor's Composite Stock Index crested on 7 September 1929. The

Panic and confusion reign on Wall Street following the stock market crash of October 1929.

discovery of fraud on the London Stock Exchange, and Bank of England moves to raise interest rates, gave the New York stock market the jitters. Prices drifted down about 10 percent without signs of panic. The Federal Reserve, citing signs of economic weakness, loosened its grip on the monetary reins. The market rallied, recovering 8 percent of its loss.

On 15 October, Irving Fisher, one of the most famous economists of the era, assured stock investors that stock prices stood on "what looks like a permanently high plateau." That same day, stock prices fell 3.5 percent. Prices continued to fall steadily, followed by a mild rally on Tuesday, 22 October.

On Wednesday, the sell-off accelerated, as brokers called customers who had borrowed funds to buy stock. The customers had to either sell the stock or add more collateral to their loans. On 24 October, Black Thursday, the sell-off—almost 13 million shares—overtook the technology. Only late in the evening did sellers discover the prices they received for their stock.

A group of prominent bankers had met on Wednesday in the offices of J. P. Morgan and Co. and formed a pool to support the market. As word spread that the pool was bidding on stock, prices stabilized. The panic on Wall Street set off a round of crashes of foreign stock markets, beginning in London, and rippling through Berlin, Paris, and Tokyo. The following day, President Hoover tried to improve the psychology, saying "the fundamental business of the country—that is the production and distribution of goods—is on a sound and prosperous basis."

On Monday, 28 October, the market opened lower, and again the sell-off gained momentum. On Tuesday, the market fell 23 percent, and more than 16 million shares traded hands. The downward spiral drew in the stocks of blue-chip corporations such as AT&T and U.S. Steel. This time, the bankers reached no agreement to stem the tide, and prices continued to fall.

By mid-November, stock prices had lost 40 percent of their value.

One important factor contributing to the stock crash of 1929 was the practice of buying stock on borrowed money, and then using the stock as collateral. Investors sometimes put up as little as 10 percent of their own money. These sales were called margin sales. When stock prices fell, investors were obliged to increase the down payment. A downward spiral that fed on itself began, as investors sold stock to raise funds for larger down-payment margins. Also, investment trusts of that day sold bonds to raise money for stock purchases. Financial leverage from margin sales and investment trusts drove the market into a tight downward spiral.

The stock market crash left the impression that capitalist economic systems often float on a thin film of confidence. Much of the economic legislation of the 1930s was intended to make the system more stable.

See also Security Exchange Act 1934.

References Atack, Jeremy, and Peter Passell, A *New Economic View of American History* (1994); Galbraith, John Kenneth. *The Great Crash: 1929* (1961).

Stockholm Declaration

The Stockholm Declaration represented the first international recognition that a global environmental challenge was looming that could only be avoided by concerted action from the world community. The Stockholm Declaration was adopted by the United Nations Conference on the Human Environment, held in Stockholm, Sweden, in 1972. The call for a world conference on the human environment had come from a resolution passed by the U.N. General Assembly in 1968.

The Stockholm Declaration was worded as 26 environmental principles that were legally nonbinding. They represented a consensus of opinion that the world community needed to do better in protecting the global environment. The preamble of the declaration emphasized the need to protect the environment for future generations. It also emphasized a goal that can conflict with environmental protection, which is worldwide economic and social development. The preamble states that reaching the environmental goals "will demand the acceptance of responsibility by citizens and communities and by enterprises and institutions at every level, all sharing equitably in common efforts."

The declaration's first principle puts an "environment of quality" on the level of an individual right, but states that each individual must share the burden of protecting the environment for future generations. Principle 19 cites the role that education must play in training environmentally responsible individuals, companies, and communities.

Other principles of the declaration refer to the need to conserve natural resources "for the benefit of present and future generations through careful planning and management," and to increase "the capacity of the earth to provide vital renewable resources." Referring to nonrenewable resources, one principle cites the need to "guard against the danger of their future exhaustion, and to ensure that benefits from such employment are shared by all mankind." The principles make mention of controlling ocean pollution, protection of wildlife and their habitat, and protection from toxic substances.

The principles emphasize the need for social and economic development in the developing world, the importance of sharing scientific and technological advances helpful in solving environmental problems, and the special needs of developing countries for financial and technological assistance to "incorporate environmental safeguards into their development and planning."

Perhaps the most famous principle is Principle 21, which recognizes the right of individual countries to exploit their own resources, but on condition that "activities within their own jurisdiction or control do not cause damage to the environment of other States or of areas be-

yond their national jurisdiction." On a related subject, Principle 22 states that "States shall co-operate to develop further the international law regarding liability and compensation for the victims of pollution and other environmental damage caused by activities within the jurisdiction or control of such states to areas beyond their jurisdiction."

With the first discovery of the New World, the ability of capitalism to mobilize the exploitation of resources was one of its principle advantages. Capitalist countries in the New World rose to unprecedented levels of prosperity and wealth. The world is now faced with a different problem, requiring the conservation of resources that can never be privately owned, such as whales, and clean air and water. One of the greatest challenges of world capitalism today, which evolved in an environment of underutilized resources, is to adapt to an economic environment in which restraint and cooperation must temper unbridled competition in the use of the world's resources.

See also Global Commons.

References Nanda, Ved P. *International Environmental Law and Policy* (1994); Panjabi, Rance K. L. *The Earth Summit at Rio: Politics, Economics, and the the Environment* (1997).

Stop of the Exchequer (England)

In January 1672, Charles II issued a proclamation that suspended payment on tallies and Exchequer orders to pay, an action that became known as the Stop of the Exchequer. The British treasury is called the Exchequer, because, during the Middle Ages, transactions with the British treasury took place in a room with tables covered by checkered cloth. The modern term "check" is a derivative of "exchequer."

During the reign of Charles II, the Exchequer discounted tallies and Exchequer Orders to Pay to goldsmith bankers, paying interest rates above 6 percent. Tallies were wooden sticks that represented a debt of the government, and Exchequer Orders to Pay were paper orders that were replacing the wood tallies that were a holdover from the Middle Ages. The goldsmith bankers paid 6-percent interest on near-money accounts, in order to raise funds for discounting tallies and paper orders from the government. The government pledged to redeem the tallies and paper orders in a rotating order.

When the goldsmith bankers had loaned out all they could, and were no longer able to discount tallies and paper orders, Charles stopped payment on the tallies and paper orders. This stop of the Exchequer initially caused a run on the goldsmith bankers, and many were eventually ruined by this action. Later, the government honored about half of its debt to the goldsmith bankers.

The Stop of the Exchequer reminded people of the Seizure of the Mint, creating more doubt about government involvement in banking. It also cast a shadow on paper money, and postponed the development of an institution like the Bank of England for another 20 years. The credibility of government money suffered a severe setback from this experience, and, in England, issuing paper money became the province of banks.

See also Bank of England, Financial Revolution, Seizure of the Mint, Tallies.

References Davies, Glyn. *A History of Money: From Ancient Times to the Present Day* (1994); Horsefield, K. "Stop of the Exchequer Re-Visited." *Economic History Review* (1982).

Subsidies

Subsidies are government-sponsored financial support for the production of particular goods and services. In a subsidized industry, each unit of a good that a firm produces draws a direct payment from the government. By defraying a portion of the costs of production, subsidies either raise income to producers, lower prices to consumers, or are some combination of the two.

Governments may subsidize certain activities to make them more affordable to consumers. Higher education in the United States benefits from government subsidies that are designed to make edu-

cation more affordable to lower- and middle-income families. Medical care is also subsidized.

Governments have turned to subsidies to raise income among producers, particularly farmers, who have suffered from low incomes, as mechanization has dramatically increased agricultural production. Subsidies in agriculture may be tied to programs to limit production.

One of the more controversial uses of subsidies seeks to make domestic industries more competitive in foreign markets. Countries experiencing high levels of unemployment may try to export the unemployment to other countries, by subsidizing the production of domestic industries producing goods with international markets. Subsidies allow domestic industries to sell goods below cost in foreign markets, which is a practice that is sometimes called dumping. Firms located in countries where the goods are dumped find themselves undersold, perhaps forcing them to close plants and to lay off workers. Therefore, the unemployment problem shifts from the country with the subsidized industry to the country where the goods are dumped.

Issues involving subsidies in foreign trade are not always easy to unravel. The U.S. government inevitably subsidizes the development of commercial aircraft, because of payments for the development of military aircraft. England and France openly subsidize Concorde's supersonic transportation with the United States.

See also European Union, General Agreement on Tariffs and Trade.

References Appleyard, Dennis R., and Alfred J. Field Jr. *International Economics* (1992); Daniels, John D., and Lee H. Radebaugh. *International Business* (1998).

Sweat Shops
See Trade Boards Act.

Swiss Banks
Swiss banks enjoy a worldwide reputation for protecting the identity of depositors.

This important characteristic helped Switzerland grow to be one of the world's major banking centers in the twentieth century. Another factor contributing to the growth of Swiss banking is Switzerland's position of neutrality. On 20 May 1815, the Vienna Congress established the permanent neutrality of Switzerland among the European powers—a position the superpowers of the world honored through two great wars in the twentieth century.

Switzerland was not a pioneer in early European banking. Geneva was the first of the Swiss cities to become a banking center, and, by 1709, Geneva boasted of a dozen bankers who left a name in Swiss financial history, and Louis XIV floated loans in Geneva to finance his wars. Geneva bankers kept close ties with France, and remained involved in financing French public debt until the end of the nineteenth century.

Basel only developed a significant banking industry in the nineteenth century. In 1862, the Basel Register listed 20 banks, nine of which were exclusively devoted to banking.

Financial activity of various sorts appeared in Zurich during the sixteenth century. In 1679, an injunction from the city council prohibited a reduction of interest rates from 5 to 4 percent. Merchant bankers, who accepted deposits for investment in securities, appeared in the middle of the eighteenth century. Zurich did not see the formation of a bank, in the broad sense, until 1786. In 1805, the official register of Zurich reported two banks devoted exclusively to banking.

By the eve of World War I, Switzerland ranked as one of the international financial centers. Six large banks (Swiss Credit Bank, Swiss Bank Corporation, Union Bank of Switzerland, Trade Bank of Basel, Federal Bank, and Swiss People's Bank) controlled a system of branches throughout Switzerland. These banks floated international loans for European governments, and to railroad and other industrial concerns in the United States. After World War I, inflation in the currencies of the former belligerents made Switzerland more attractive as a safe haven.

In the post-World War II era, three of the big banking houses remained: the Swiss Credit Bank, the Swiss Bank Corporation, and the Union Bank of Switzerland. There was also a widespread network of smaller banks, rural loan associations, and branches of foreign banks. In 1968, Switzerland had a population of 6 million people and 4337 banking offices, which added up to one banking office for every 1,400 individuals.

In the 1930s, Switzerland enacted laws that strengthened the anonymity protection of depositors in Swiss banks. During that time, some countries prohibited citizens from holding assets abroad on pain of criminal penalties, and even sent agents into Switzerland to track down assets owed by their own citizens. On the other hand, some people wanted to keep deposits in Switzerland, in case they had to make a hasty departure from their homeland for political or racial reasons. Swiss banks began opening the so-called numbered accounts, which substantially reduced the number of bank employees who knew the name of a depositor. Also, the Swiss government claimed no right to pry into bank accounts, either to collect information on its own citizens or on the citizens of foreign countries. Governments around the world have lodged complaints against Swiss banks for holding deposits of foreigners evading taxes.

Switzerland's strong tradition of respect for the rights of private property gave it a unique position in the world banking system, and in the capitalist economic system. Without raw materials or sea ports, Switzerland achieved economic success with a thriving banking industry favored by customs and laws.

References Fehrenbach, T. R. *The Swiss Banks* (1966); Ikle, Max. *Switzerland: An International Banking and Finance Center* (1972).

Syndicalism (France)

Syndicalism refers to a revolutionary phase of the French trade union movement that manifested itself during the decade before World War I. Although syndicalism surfaced in other countries, it was a unique product of French history, and rose to its fullest expression in France. Its methods bore aspects of revolution, and its goal lay in the vision of an economic system organized around unions, called syndicats, in French. An exact definition of syndicalism remains elusive, because of the movement's emphasis upon spontaneity of action. Detractors would say that the movement was neither pragmatic nor theoretical, but proponents of syndicalism regarded the movement as pragmatic.

The French Revolution set the precedent of revolution as a method of redressing grievances, achieving social change, overthrowing a socially dominant class, and addressing issues in the context of class warfare. The legend of the Revolution inspired social reformers and shaped their thinking. It also set the example of revolutionaries using working-class agitation to add momentum to a revolution, and then turning against the working class. The governments of the French Revolution enacted repressive policies against unions and working-class organizations. Subsequent revolutions in 1830 and 1848 brought new governments to power. These governments followed a pattern of rising to power with the aid of working-class agitation, and then turning against the working class with harsh repression. When the French government legalized unions in 1884, workers found no charm in a political power that employers could always count on as an ally. In the eyes of workers, the state was

as much the enemy as were the employers.... The apparatus of political democracy and universal suffrage was a trumpery, and parliamentary action at best a diversion. The state blinded the working class with the notion of patriotism, while using its troops to shoot down strikers, and training workers to be cannon fodder in imperialist wars. The political parties who claimed to represent the workers only turned the workers' energies from the real struggle. The Socialist parties were run by bourgeois intellectuals and professional people; only the unions were pure working-class organizations.

Syndicalists led the General Confederation of Workers (CGT) between 1902 and 1914. This organization was founded in 1895, and had unified the French working-class movement under its leadership in 1898. Under the leadership of the syndicalists, the CGT raised the banner of the general strike as the principal weapon for achieving the emancipation of the working class. It made one of its favorite themes the international solidarity of the working class, and forbade involvement in political parties.

Although syndicalism can claim credit for popularizing the general strike and formulating a strategy for its use, a general strike never materialized in France. CGT support of the French government during World War I dispelled the myth of international working-class solidarity, and marked the end of the syndicalist stage of the French labor movement.

Syndicalist leaders were genuine proletarians, who saw victory in terms of control of a work area. They were inspired with resentment, and displayed a will to fight. During the first half of the twentieth century, most governments of capitalist countries enacted reforms that strengthened the hand of the workers in the labor market, and defused much of the working-class resentment.

See also General Strike.

References Lorwin, Val R. "France." *Comparative Labor Movements* (1952); Ridley, F. *Revolutionary Syndicalism in France* (1970).

Taff Vale Case (England)

The *Taff Vale* case struck at the legal foundation of British trade unions at the turn of the century. This court decision made trade unions liable for damages caused by strikes.

The union involved was the Amalgamated Society of Railway Servants. In 1900, a local dispute sent the railwaymen of the Taff Vale Railway Company out on strike, without approval from the Amalgamated Society. With few exceptions, the railway companies had warded off unionization, reasoning that trade unions were incompatible with the quasi-military discipline needed for quality service. The Taff Vale Railway Company, sharing the opinions of most railway companies, greeted the strike with militant opposition. The Amalgamated Society of Railway Servants strongly supported the workers, when Taff Vale hired strikebreakers to replace striking workers. The Amalgamated Society made the striking workers eligible for strike pay, and sent a union official to dissuade the strike breakers from going to work. The strikers on the picket lines became unruly, and violence attended the workers' action. The Amalgamated Society neither authorized nor incited acts of violence.

The Taff Vale Company sought legal action against individual strikers, and, more important, for the future of trade unions, against the Amalgamated Society itself. The company got an injunction that restrained officers of the Amalgamated Society from actions that harmed the company's business, such as persuading strike-breakers not to cross picket lines. The company asked for civil damages against the Amalgamated Society itself, for the actions of its officers and members, and won an award of £23,000 from the Amalgamated Society. The House of Lords upheld the judgment after several appeals. This court decision shook the trade union world. Strikes always damaged business in some fashion. Now, whether or not authorized by a union, strikes put union funds at risk for civil damages. These were funds that unions held for payments to striking workers, and for payments of benefits. Although there had been acts of violence, the civil liability of the union in no way hinged upon the commission of criminal acts.

This case jeopardized the right to strike for the first time since 1875. The Trade Union Act of 1871 and the Conspiracy and Protection of Property Act of 1875 had supposedly left unions and union funds immune from liability in the conduct of industrial disputes. The attorneys for Taff Vale are reported to have advised against the action of seeking civil damages, on the strength of existing trade union law. The law had evolved since the passage of those acts in the 1870s, and unions now had to seek fresh legislation. Parliament passed the Trade Disputes Act of 1906, which, among other things, protected British trade unions against civil actions.

The legal system in most countries was slow to accept the legitimacy of unions. The *Taff Vale* case is a good example of the hurdles the British legal system put in the path of the development of modern unions.

See also Molestation of Workmen Act of 1859, Trade Union Act of 1871.

References Cole, G. D. H. *A Short History of the British Working-Class Movement, 1789–1947* (1948); Hunt, Edward H. *British Labor History, 1815–1914* (1981).

Taft-Hartley Act of 1947 (United States)

John L. Lewis, President of United Mine Workers, called the Taft-Hartley Act the "slave labor law." Also known as the

Labor Management Relations Act, it was the first piece of major legislation in the twentieth century to strike at union power. A wave of strikes and work stoppages at the end of World War II swung the pendulum of public opinion away from labor unions. Strikes had become highly publicized disputes over wages and hours, rather than heroic struggles against domineering employers who refused to recognize and bargain with unions. With feelings running high, Congress brushed aside President Truman's veto, and made Taft-Hartley the law of the land.

Union members and sympathizers found fault, particularly, with the sections prohibiting various "unfair labor practices" on the part of unions and union organizers. The act banned, as an unfair labor practice, any sort of strong-arm tactics that unions might use to intimidate workers into joining a union, or supporting union causes.

Another unfair labor practice banned under Taft-Hartley was employer discrimination against nonunion employees. Related to this provision was the ban on closed shops, which make union membership a condition of employment. A union shop forces an employee to join a union after a period of probationary employment. Taft-Hartley banned closed shops as part of a collective bargaining agreement, and empowered states with the right to outlaw union shops. In states where union shops remained legal, Taft-Hartley allowed employers to concede to the request for a union shop, but protected employees in nonunion shops from discrimination.

According to Taft-Hartley, a union refusal to bargain in good faith with an employer falls into the category of an unfair labor practice, and is illegal. Refusing to bargain could take the form of take-it-or-leave-it demands, reflecting a union's readiness to use the strike weapon.

Other important areas of unfair labor practices prohibited by Taft-Hartley were secondary boycotts and sympathy strikes. A secondary boycott could be a situation in which employees strike and picket an employer, not for higher wages, but because the employer is doing business with another employer of whom the union disapproves. Perhaps this other employer refuses to come to terms with its own employees in a labor dispute.

Taft-Hartley also put excessive initiation fees and featherbedding under the heading of unfair labor practices that are illegal.

Under Taft-Hartley, employers could sue unions for civil damages when no-strike clauses were broken, or when secondary boycotts and sympathy strikes were waged, against the law. The internal process of unions came under closer scrutiny under Taft-Hartley, requiring submission of detailed financial reports, safeguarding of administration of pension funds, and abstaining from making political contributions in elections for federal offices.

Taft-Hartley set up a procedure for government intervention in strikes having important repercussions for the entire economic system. The president can ask for an injunction against the strike for a period of 80 days. The 80-day interval serves as a cooling-off period, and gives the government time to poll the workers on the acceptability of the last offer made by the employer.

With Taft-Hartley, the U.S. version of capitalism tried to strike a balance between the rights of unions to organize workers for cooperative initiatives, and the rights of employers and nonunion employees to exercise freedom of speech and action.

See also Closed Shops and Union Shops, National Labor Relations Act.

References Clark, Gordon. *Unions and Communities under Siege* (1989); Gould, William B. *A Primer on American Labor Law* (1986); Northrup, Herbert R., and Gordon F. Bloom. *Government and Labor: The Role of Government in Union–Management Relations* (1963).

Tallies (England)

In England, tallies were wooden sticks that functioned as instruments of credit and exchange in public finance. The Exchequer (treasury) began using tallies in the Middle Ages, and, by the humor of history, the use of tallies survived into the early nineteenth century.

A tally was a wooden stick with notches denoting various sums of money. A notch the length of a man's hand denoted £1,000, and a notch the width of a man's thumb denoted £100. A simple v-shaped notch represented £20. The handle of a tally remained notchless. In a credit transaction, the notched segment of the wooden tally was split lengthwise down the middle and the handle remained with one half of the tally. The creditor kept the larger half with the handle, and the debtor kept the smaller half, called the foil. The two halves would match, or tally. The tallies were assignable, meaning creditors could transfer ownership of tally debts to third parties. In this connection, tallies circulated as money.

Tallies entered into the British public finance system in two ways. First, a citizen owing taxes to the government might hand the Exchequer a tally, signifying a debt of taxes. The government would use the tally to pay for goods and services. The recipient of the tally presented it to the taxpayer, who had the other half (the foil) and demanded payment. A second use of tallies in public finance occurred when the government issued tallies in payment for goods and services. In this instance, the government was the debtor, and tallies originating from the government could be used in payment of taxes. Originally, the government pledged future tax revenue from specific sources earmarked for redemption of these tallies. Later the government issued tallies to be redeemed from the general revenue. Tallies used as an instrument of government debt paid interest.

It was this second use of tallies that contributed to the growth of a primitive money market in London. Purveyors of goods to the government received tallies, and discounted them at goldsmith bankers, rather than using them in exchange. This practice reached its zenith in the seventeenth century. Later, the Bank of England also discounted tallies, creating an even more ready market in tallies, and adding to their acceptability in exchange.

By the seventeenth century, tallies were already an anachronism, but they were not officially discontinued until 1834. In addition to assisting the emergence of the London money market, tallies reduced the need for money minted from precious metals, and eased pressure on the English government to debase the coinage to finance excess government expenditures.

See also Financial Revolution.

References Davies, Glyn. *A History of Money: From Ancient Times to the Present Day* (1994); Dickson, P. G. M. *Financial Revolution in England* (1967); Feavearyear, Sir Albert. *The Pound Sterling: A History of English Money* (1963).

Tariffs

Tariffs are taxes on goods imported from foreign countries. Until the twentieth century, tariff revenue was an important source of tax revenue for the leading governments of the world.

Tariffs aimed to achieve two purposes at once. First, tariffs generated revenue to pay government expenditures. Second, tariffs protected domestic industry from foreign competition. Tariffs levied solely to raise revenue were usually rather modest, but tariffs levied to protect domestic industry were at times prohibitively high, and acted to retard trade significantly.

Governments defended protective tariffs, considering that new start-up industries needed protection from foreign competition until they were further developed. Governments also sought protection from foreign competition for industries vital to national defense.

During times of severe economic depression, governments have enacted prohibitive tariffs to boost business confidence, and to protect domestic jobs. During the severe depression of the 1890s, France, Germany, the United

States, and Russia are among the big countries that raised high tariff walls to protect domestic industry from foreign competition. England was the only major trading nation that stood committed to free trade (foreign trade without restrictions, including tariffs) during the last half of the nineteenth century. At the onset of the Depression of the 1930s, the United States enacted a strongly protectionist tariff, provoking a swift and strong retaliation from major trading partners, including England, who finally gave up its staunch defense of free trade. These countries retaliated with high tariffs of their own, and the resulting trade war was credited with adding to the depth and length of the Depression.

During the post-World War II era, major trading partners of the world have sponsored multilateral negotiations for the purpose of mutually scaling down tariffs. In the long term, tariffs can lower a country's living standard by protecting inefficient industries from foreign competition. Also, the effects of retaliation invariably mitigate any positive effects of tariffs on domestic employment. For these reasons, governments try to resist enacting tariff barriers to protect domestic firms from foreign competition.

See also Anglo-French Commercial Treaty of 1786, Anglo-French Commercial Treaty of 1860, General Agreement on Tariffs and Trade, German Tariff of 1879, Hamilton's Tariff of 1789, Import Duties Act of 1932, McKinley Tariff of 1890, Meline Tariff of 1892, Russian Tariff of 1891, Smoot-Hawley Tariff of 1930.

References Appleyard, Dennis R., and Alfred J. Field Jr. *International Economics.* (1992); Ashley, Percy. *Modern Tariff History: Germany, United States, and France* (1970).

Taxation

According to Jean Baptiste Colbert, Louis XIV's finance minister, "the art of taxation consists in so plucking the goose as to obtain the largest possible amount of feathers while provoking the smallest possible amount of hissing." Taxes are the levies that governments place on its citizens to raise the revenue required to defray the cost of government operations.

A list of the things governments have taxed would not be short. The broad categories would include imported goods, luxury goods, necessary goods, addictive goods, personal property, income-earning property, wages, interest, profits, corporation profits, and profits from sale of tangible or financial assets, such as stocks and bonds.

Adam Smith, the most famous apostle of laissez-faire capitalism, suggested that taxes should be levied proportionate to the ability to pay (income), that payment should be convenient to the taxpayer, that taxpayers should know precisely what they owe and when it is due, and that the government's cost of collecting the tax should be small relative to the taxes collected.

Adam Smith also mentioned low taxation as a factor contributing to the prosperity of the English colonies. In the words of Smith, in the *Wealth of Nations,*

the labor of the English colonists is not only likely to afford a greater and more valuable produce, but, in consequence of the moderation of their taxes, a greater proportion of this produce belongs to themselves, which they may store up and employ in putting into motion a still greater quantity of labor.

The mercantilist economies emphasized taxes on imported goods as a means of increasing national wealth. The U.S. government depended primarily on taxes on imported goods until the enactment of the income tax during World War I.

Given the emphasis on production in capitalism, governments in capitalist economies have shied away from taxes that retard incentives, or that act as a crushing burden on enterprise and risk-taking. Falling into the category of taxes that are believed to impact economic performance is the capital gains tax, which sets the tax on profits earned from selling stock held longer than one year. Currently the capital gains tax in the United

States is capped at 28 percent, substantially below the highest tax levied on wage income. The purpose of holding down the capital gains tax is to promote investment in business enterprise, which in turn promotes growth in employment and living standards.

See also Economic Tax Recovery Act of 1981, Excess Profits Tax, Income Tax, Revenue Act of 1964.

References Kimzey, Bruce W. *Reagonomics* (1983); Webber, Carolyn, and Aaron Wildavsky. *A History of Taxation and Expenditure in the Western World* (1986).

Thatcherism (England)

Margaret Thatcher came to power as prime minister of Britain in 1979, and, through extraordinarily forceful leadership, launched a capitalist revolution. Thatcher and her supporters saw themselves as trying to resurrect the spirit and substance of capitalism amidst the ruins and decay of socialism. In the words of Thatcher, "I came to office with one deliberate intent. To change Britain from a dependent to a self-reliant society—from a give-it-to-me to a do-it-yourself nation; to a get-up-and-go instead of a sit-back-and-wait-for-it Britain." Nigel Lawson, a member of Thatcher's cabinet, wrote in his memoirs, "We were not seeking simply to remove various controls and impositions, but by so doing to change the entire culture of a nation from anti-profits, anti-business, government-dependent lassitude and defeatism, to a pro-profit, pro-business, robustly independent vigour and optimism."

Thatcher's policies were a multi-pronged attack on Britain's slide toward socialism, marking a sharp break with the past, and took on the aspect of a revolution. Her policies sought to reinvigorate the British economy by reducing the power of trade unions, privatizing many of the nationalized industries, enacting supply-side tax policies, taming inflation, lifting government controls, and fostering a culture of enterprise.

Thatcher's government refused to cave in to striking workers. The coal miners, who historically had played a radical role in Britain's labor history, stayed out on strike for a year, without winning major concessions. The Employment Act of 1980 and the Employment Act of 1982 imposed restrictions on unions, and removed the immunity of trade unions from civil damages for unlawful activities. The Trade Union Act of 1984 tried, without success, to reduce the political activity of trade unions. New legislation, aided by a severe recession, brought an end to much of the union militancy that marked British industry in the 1970s.

The list of nationalized companies that were sold to the private sector, or privatized, included British Rail Hotel, English Channel Ferry Service, Jaguar, British Petroleum, British Aerospace, Britoil, British Telecom, British Gas, and British Airport Authority.

Thatcher's first budget reduced the tax rate on the highest tax bracket from 83 to 60 percent. The tax rate on the lowest tax bracket fell from 33 percent to 30 percent, a rather modest decrease. The first budget planned for cuts in government spending and borrowing. However, a deep recession in the mid-1980s imposed heavy demands on social programs, frustrating attempts to reduce government spending. The reduction in rates for the higher brackets improved the incentives for entrepreneurial action.

Unlike previous British governments that had combated inflation with wage and price guidelines, Thatcher's government relied solely upon reductions in the monetary growth rate to bring down inflation. This reliance on monetary discipline to banish inflation squared with Thatcher's philosophy of not interfering with free markets.

Whether Thatcher's capitalist revolution will stem the tide of economic decline in Britain remains unclear. Her reputation for stubbornness and insensitivity cost her the support of her party in 1990, but the Conservative Party stayed in power under different leadership until

May 1, 1997, preserving the capitalist revolution that she led. The Labor Party was able to return to power only after shedding its socialist ideology and close affiliation with labor unions.

The capitalist revolution that began in Britain became a world capitalist revolution. It spread to the United States in 1980, with the election of Ronald Reagan as president, and to Europe, when the socialist leaders of France and Spain took unexpected turns to the right. It culminated in the collapse the communist economies of Russia and Eastern Europe.

See also Trade Union Act of 1984.

References Dellheim, Charles. *The Disenchanted Isle: Mrs. Thatcher's Capitalist Revolution* (1995); Riddell, Peter. *The Thatcher Decade* (1989).

Tokyo Bubble (Japan)

The Nikkei Index of the Tokyo stock market stood at 12,000 in 1986, and spiraled upward, reaching 27,000 in 1988. In 1989, the Nikkei peaked at 39,000; then the market faltered, dropping to 15,000 by 1992. The market began a gentle recovery in 1993.

The cause of the bubble can be found in international agreements to stabilize the U.S. dollar. In the second half of the 1980s, the value of the dollar steadily fell in foreign exchange markets, increasing the cost of foreign goods to American consumers. The United States and its trading partners in the Louvre Agreement of 1987 sought to reverse the downward trend of the dollar. To help prop up the dollar, the Bank of Japan lowered its discount rate to an all-time low of 2.5 percent. The discount rate is the interest rate at which commercial banks can borrow from the Bank of Japan. Also, the Bank of Japan gave the money supply free rein to grow at 10–12 percent a year, roughly double Japan's growth in real income. Relatively tame inflation rates allowed the bank to pursue such a policy without fueling inflationary expectations. When the U.S. stock market crashed in October 1987, the Bank of Japan became even more willing to inject additional liquidity into the Japanese monetary system.

Banks and insurance companies incurred heavy losses, primarily because the bubble in stock prices was mirrored in a bubble in real estate prices. The *Houston Chronicle*, on 27 May 1997, reported that "some leading banks were still struggling and that the gap between the strong and the weak is widening as they continue to dispose of problem loans—the legacy of aggressive lending in the 1980s 'bubble' era."

The inevitable scrutiny in the aftermath of a crash brought to light several shady financial practices of the sort that bubbles seem to invite, including the manipulation of securities prices, making good the losses of big investors, and imaginative accounting that hid real losses. Shady dealings had also infected the political process.

The economic recession that followed the crash sparked a broader debate about national goals and priorities, taking note of air and water pollution, respiratory disease, cadmium and mercury poisoning, and noise. Some political and business leaders suggested that Japan should lay less emphasis on global economic expansion, and more emphasis on domestic goals related to education, welfare, wages, medical services, urban infrastructure, and family and community issues.

The seemingly endless Japanese economic expansion during the post-World War II era may have begun to taper off. Karl Marx prophesied that recurring economic crises would be the end of capitalism. In today's political environment, however, economic crises are as likely to prompt reforms favoring laissez-faire capitalism as reforms with socialist leanings. Japan's economic difficulties do not seem to have dampened a trend toward deregulation and less bureaucratic guidance.

See also Stock Market Crash of 1929.

References Kindleberger, Charles P. *World Economic Primacy: 1500 to 1990* (1996); Wood, Christopher. *The End of Japan INC* (1994).

Totalitarian Monopoly Capitalism (Germany)

Whether the economy of National Socialism belonged to a species of capitalism is open to some doubt. Franz Neumann, in his book *Behemoth: The Structure and Practice of National Socialism, 1933–1944*, coined the term "totalitarian monopoly capitalism" to refer to Nazi capitalism. The German economy of the Nazi era was capitalistic in the sense that joint-stock corporations were a fundamental business unit, and these corporations earned profits that were distributed to stockholders. The substitution of cartel coordination and government regimentation for free product and labor markets, however, represented important departures from the model of laissez-faire capitalism.

The Nazis came to power in the aftermath of a period of deflation and excess capacity. To help meet the crisis caused by worldwide depression, government enacted a statute in 1933 that empowered the federal minister of economics to implement a policy of compulsory cartellization, compelling firms to either join existing cartels or create cartels where none existed. The statute also empowered the federal minister of economics to prohibit the opening of new enterprises and expansion of existing enterprises, and to regulate the capacity of existing enterprises.

Another statute increased the power of cartels to squeeze out inefficient producers, defined as producers that, among other things, engaged in price cutting. In 1939, the government enacted a statute that legalized the compulsory liquidation of small retailers and artisans whose businesses were too small to be efficient. From independent business owners, these individuals often sank to the level of manual workers. These actions were taken in the name of increasing efficiency. An implicit assumption of Nazi economic policies was the notion that large-scale businesses were necessarily more efficient than small-scale businesses. Joint-stock corporations were not immune to the weeding-out process. Under Nazism, the number of joint-stock corporations declined, but the average capital invested in each corporation rose. Price controls kept a lid on prices in markets that were not subject to cartel price fixing, and the government held tight reins on the banking system and on access to credit.

The Nazi regime was not prone to nationalization of private industries, and even made some efforts to privatize firms that had been acquired by government bailouts in the past. Several business combines, owned and controlled by the hierarchy of the Nazi party, however, arose, to provide an economic basis for the government.

The departure from laissez-faire capitalism was most drastic in labor markets. The law forbade strikes and lockouts, restricted the ability of workers to change jobs, and workers could not be fired without the approval of a local labor exchange. Workers had to carry a workbook showing the worker's occupation, apprenticeship, training, and former employer.

Following the German occupation of Europe, German combines and cartels set to work bringing the economies of the occupied and satellite countries under the domination of the German economy. Some of the tactics for extending control over these areas included confiscation of "non-Aryan" and enemy businesses, and state-owned enterprises, control of commercial banks with large industrial investments, forced sale to German enterprises or mergers with German cartels and combines, and buying up issues of new stock.

The outcome of World War II was a severe setback for the species of monopoly capitalism that reached its fullest development in Germany during the 1930s and World War II. The emphasis on efficiency at the expense of fairness and justice may have been a part of a world view that led the Nazis to break nearly every human and divine law that binds societies together, casting a shadow on German innovations in the development of capitalism. During the post-World War II era, the American and British models of capitalism gained ascendancy, emphasizing domestic competition, free markets, and free international trade. The 1980s saw a virtual capitalist revolution in the revival of free-market economies throughout the world.

See also Fascist Capitalism.

References Allen, James S. *World Monopoly and Peace* (1946); Braum, Hans-Joachim. *The German Economy in the Twentieth Century* (1990); Neumann, Franz. *Behemoth: The Structure and Practice of National Socialism, 1933–1944* (1942).

Trade Boards Acts (England)

The plight of workers in the sweating industries in England caught the attention of the British public around 1885. The sweating industries employed the poorest and most helpless class of workers. Subsistence wages, unsanitary working conditions, and long hours ranked at the top of the job descriptions in the labor market niche these workers filled. Parliament authorized the creation of trade boards to assure that these workers received fair treatment at the hands of employers. The first Trade Boards Act passed Parliament in 1909, and the second in 1918.

The Trade Boards Act of 1909 provided for the establishment of boards to set a fixed minimum wage in exceptionally low-wage industries. The act identified four specific industries as low-wage industries in need of a trade board. The industries were paper box-making, chain making, machine lace-finishing, and ready-made and bespoke (made to order and custom-made) tailoring. In addition to a certain number of independent members, the membership of each board included an equal number of employer and employee representatives. Employers violating the wage rates fixed by its board faced the rigors of the criminal justice system. A recommendation of the minister of labor, with Parliament's approval, was necessary to bring new trades under the coverage of the Trade Boards Act. The minister of labor could order the inclusion of an additional trade if he was "satisfied that the rate of wages prevailing in any branch of the trade is exceptionally low as compared with that in other employments." (In 1913, additional industries related to clothing trades were classified in the low-wage catagory.)

The Trade Boards Act of 1918 amended the act of 1909 in certain important respects. First, a special order of the minister of labor was all that was needed to subject another trade to the provisions of the Trade Boards Act. The act of 1918 made no requirement that Parliament confirm the coverage of a new trade. Second, the minister of labor could make a special order if he was "of opinion that no adequate machinery exists for the effective regulation of wages throughout the trade and that accordingly, having regard to the rates of wages prevailing in the trade or any part of the trade, it is expedient that the principal Act should apply to that trade." Third, employers no longer enjoyed a six-month grace period to implement wage recommendations made by a trade board.

After the passage of the act of 1918, the number of trade boards steadily increased. Sixty-three trade boards were in existence by 1921. The wording of the act of 1918 enabled the minister of labor to establish trade boards in industries in which collective bargaining was not practiced. In time, trade boards became less involved in protecting workers in the sweating industries, and more involved in the general regulation of wages. In some trades, the boards overtly addressed the scale of wages, rather than the minimum wages.

At first, the effect of the trade boards was to push up wages. In the 1920s, the trade boards began to incur the wrath of employers for holding wages up, while the economy sank into depression. The trade boards came to realize that, in some circumstances, wages had to fall.

The practice of establishing minimum wages spread to other capitalistic countries. The United States has a minimum wage law that applies to firms in all industries that meet certain criteria. Economists often interpret minimum wages as price floors that lead to surplus market conditions. In the labor market, this surplus may translate as unemployment among teenagers or other groups, who often work for minimum wages.

See also Minimum Wages.

References Douglas, Paul, Curtis N. Hitchcock, and Willard E. Atkins. *The Worker in Modern Economic Society* (1923); Schmiechen, James A. *Sweated Industries and Sweated Labor: The London Clothing Trades, 1860–1914* (1984).

Trade Disputes Act of 1906 (England)

The most important section of the Trade Disputes of 1906 shielded the financial resources of trade unions from suits for civil damages.

The decision in the *Taff Vale* case of 1901 set a precedent for securing civil damages from unions for the interference caused by strikes. This decision effectively checkmated union use of the strike as a weapon in labor disputes. Trade unions turned their attention to the political process for legislative relief. Unions who did not already have a political fund started raising one, and working-class resentment made itself felt at election time. The Labor Representation Committee in Parliament boasted of 29 members after the general election of 1906. That group changed its name to the Labor Party after the election. The Liberals swept the general election of 1906 by a wide margin. The Labor Party made common cause with the Liberal Party on most issues, but stood firm on the issue of legislation reversing the effects of the *Taff Vale* case.

A royal commission, appointed by a Conservative government in 1903, issued its report after the election of 1906, and suggested that the civil liability of trade unions be limited to actions approved by the union, or at least actions the union had refused to repudiate. The report also suggested that individuals receive immunity from civil actions, based on interference caused by strikes and the leadership responsibilities associated with organizing strikes. Actions that workers could take individually without violating criminal law were not to become illegal when individuals acted in combination. "Peaceful persuasion" could attend the picketing process, according to the recommendation of the commission's report. An act of 1859 had protected peaceful persuasion, but further legislation in 1871 had banned it, and legislation in 1875 had not fully restored its legality.

The government introduced a bill based on the recommendations of the commission. Trade unions had lobbied hard in the election to persuade candidates to pledge support for complete reversal of the results of the *Taff Vale* decision. The government relented, and section 4 of the act read:

An action against a trade union, whether of workmen or masters, or against any officials thereof on behalf of themselves and all other members of the trade union, in respect of any tortious act alleged to have been committed by or on behalf of the trade union, shall not be entertained by any court.

In other respects, the Trade Disputes Act of 1906 followed closely the proposals in the government's original bill. Lawyers found fault with the sweeping protection that unions received from civil proceedings. In the eyes of the legal community, unions now stood in a privileged position relative to other organizations in society. They possessed the right to commit civil wrongs without fear of legal action. Parliament, directly influenced by working-class voters, was willing to move faster than the legal community in approving and protecting workers.

See also Masters and Servants Acts, Molestation of Workmen Act of 1859, *Taff Vale* Case.

References Cole, G. D. H. *A Short History of the British Working-Class Movement, 1789–1947* (1948); Robertson, Norman, and K. I. Sams. *British Trade Unionism* (1977).

Trade Disputes and Trade Unions Act of 1927 (England)

The Trade Disputes and Trade Unions Act of 1927 took away hard-won rights of trade unions in Britain. Parliament passed the act in reaction to the General Strike of 1926.

After Britain's return to the gold standard at 1914 parity, the British economy faced deflationary pressure. Miners struck to resist demands for wage cuts. Employers across industry expressed the opinion that high wage costs were aggravating the economic situation. Unions in other industries felt that if the miners gave in to wage cuts, they would next be asked to take wage cuts. The trade unions called a general strike in sympathy with the struggle of the miners. In the minds of government leaders, the striking workers evoked images of the Bolshevik Revolution. The Conservative government stood militantly on the side of the mine owners. When the general strike failed, the government turned to thoughts of weakening the power of unions. One issue the government wanted to settle was the legality of general strikes.

The Trade Disputes and Trade Unions Act of 1927 banned general strikes and other sympathetic strikes that, in the eyes of the courts, were held to force the government to certain action. Participants in illegal strikes subjected themselves to fines, or to imprisonment for up to two years. The right to picket, which British workers had enjoyed since 1859, came under strong restrictions. The act prohibited state employees from joining trade unions affiliated with trade unions of workers in the private sector. The ability of unions to raise funds from union members to support political actions also suffered a blow. Before the act, the majority of a union could vote for financial support of a political cause. A union member had to expressly request that funds from his contributions not be used for political causes. Under the act of 1927, each union member had to give written consent before their contributions could be put into a political fund. The act put union funds within reach of civil suits for damages. Unions also faced more restrictions on their ability to discipline strikebreakers.

The trade unions saw this act as vicious, and worked for its repeal. In 1946, Parliament repealed the Trade Disputes and Trade Unions Act of 1927.

See also Taff Vale Case, Trade Union Act of 1871.

References Cole, G. D. H. *A Short History of the British Working-Class Movement, 1789–1947* (1948); Robertson, Norman, and K. I. Sams. *British Trade Unionism* (1977).

Trade Union Act of 1871 (England)

The Trade Union Act of 1871 secured for British trade unions a safe legal status, but left some union activities, such as picketing, outside the protection of the law. The Combination Act of 1825 had given unions the right to negotiate wages and hours, but their legal status stood in doubt. Some judges withheld from trade unions and their funds the full protection of the law, regarding them in violation of common law prohibitions against trade restraints.

The Reform Bill of 1867 extended the voting franchise to a major portion of the working class. With the general election of 1868, Members of Parliament began to pledge support of trade union rights. At first, the liberal government of Gladstone was reluctant to take action, but the unions urged that the government press ahead, and, in 1871, the government introduced a bill. The first version of the bill displeased unions, because it contained provisions against all forms of molestation, obstruction, and intimidation. Picketing of premises was expressly prohibited. These provisions effectively repealed the Molestation of Workmen Act of 1859. The unions pressed the government on the issue and the government met the union's objections by splitting the bill into two bills. One bill granted full legal status to trade unions, entitling unions and union funds to the full protection of the law. This bill passed as the Trade Union Act of 1871. The second bill contained penal provisions against molestation, obstruction, and intimidation, and passed as the Criminal Law Amendment Act of 1871. Unions opposed the passage of the Criminal Law Amendment Act, and began agitating for its repeal.

In strikes and labor disputes, the government began to prosecute union leaders under the Criminal Law Amendment Act. The Liberal government, who had refused to amend the Criminal Law Amendment Act, fell from power in 1874. The Conservative government established a royal commission to examine the operation of the labor laws, and it proposed a comprehensive bill for friendly societies, which would cover trade unions. A howl of protest rose from union leaders, who objected to the provision that repealed the Trade Union Act of 1871. The Conservative government, perhaps hoping to establish itself in the confidence of this new working-class electorate, yielded. It made only minor amendments to the Trade Union Act of 1871, and it replaced the Criminal Law Amendment Act of 1871 with the Conspiracy and Protection of Property Act of 1875. This act made peaceful picketing lawful, and provided that no act committed by workers in combination would be illegal, unless the same act was illegal when committed by a single individual. The offensive words, such as molestation, obstruction, and intimidation, were struck out of the new legislation. The same government also replaced the Masters and Servants Act of 1867 with the Employers and Workmen Act of 1875, which was another change that pleased the trade union lobby.

The legislation reforming labor law in the 1870s was a sweeping victory for the trade unions. They still faced occasional legal resistance, but had become legitimate players in the nation that pioneered laissez-faire capitalism.

See also Combination Acts, Master and Servants Acts, Molestation of Workmen Act of 1859.

References Cole, G. D. H. *A Short History of the British Working-Class Movement, 1789–1947* (1948); Robertson, Norman, and K. I. Sams. *British Trade Unionism* (1977).

Trade Union Act of 1984 (England)

The Trade Union Act of 1984 required trade unions to hold elections every ten years, to determine if union members supported the maintenance of political funds. All unions who already had political funds were required to hold elections within 12 months of 1985, to determine if their membership still wanted to maintain political funds. Political expenditures became illegal if no election was held, or if a majority of union members voted against maintaining a political fund.

The act also expanded the coverage of activities that had to be paid for out of political funds. This portion of the act was intended to curtail the political activities and electioneering of unions that operated without political funds. This expanded coverage required that only political-fund monies could be used to pay for materials used to sway elections. Unions without political funds had spent much money to block Thatcher's reelection in 1983 as prime minister.

The union elections held within the 12-month interval came down on the side of keeping the political funds, sending Thatcher one of the few defeats she received at the hands of the unions. By 1987, six additional unions had voted to establish political funds, reflecting the political climate among union members.

Thatcher is reported to have said that she would like to see an American-type arrangement in Britain, in which labor unions are not affiliated with a particular political party. In Britain, the Trade Union Congress and the unions are affiliated with the Labor Party. In the aftermath of the Conservative government's failure to touch the political funds, some observers speculated that the issue should have been the appropriateness of the affiliation of unions with a particular political party. This question was raised because union members, who overwhelmingly voted in favor of having political funds, were not throwing their support with such hardiness in favor of the Labor Party at the polls.

The Trade Union Act of 1984 reflects the return of public skepticism about useful roles for unions in capitalist societies. Historically, unions have more often been perceived by the public as hampering the capitalist economic system, rather than contributing to its smooth operation. Perhaps the proper balance of power between unions and employers still eludes the modern capitalist economic system. Alternatively, the declining importance of blue-collar manufacturing in the work force might have doomed unions to a much-diminished role in the political process.

See also Thatcherism.

References Dellheim, Charles. *The Disenchanted Isle: Thatcher's Capitalist Revolution*, 1995; McIlroy, John. *Trade Unions in Britain Today* (1988); Riddell, Peter. *The Thatcher Decade* (1989).

Trade Union Congress (England)

The Trade Union Congress (TUC) is a national federation of unions in England comparable to the AFL-CIO in the United States. The TUC traces its origin to an 1868 conference of trade societies organized by the Manchester and Salford Trades Council. The organization was first conceived as a workingmen's social science association that would hold annual conferences, at which papers would be read on subjects pertinent to workers and union members, and would be published in proceedings. The original idea of the annual conferences wore the aspect of an academic conference, rather than a union meeting. The first congress did hear papers; however, the pressing issues facing workers and unions held the attention of most delegates. The future development of the TUC was fixed when the first congress endorsed a resolution that read "that it is highly desirable that the trades of the United Kingdom should hold an annual congress for the purpose of bringing the trades into closer alliance, and to take action on all parliamentary matters pertaining to the general interest of the working classes."

The second congress appointed a committee to oversee the enactment of legislation improving safety for miners. The third congress elected a parliamentary committee that became a permanent lobbying arm of the TUC. The organization became strictly a trade union federation, rather than a debating organization for radical ideas. In 1895, the constitution of the TUC was amended to prevent unions from nominating prominent nonmembers as delegates to TUC Congresses. These prominent nonmembers were often socialist agitators. Only full-time union officials, and members working in trades, were allowed to attend a congress. Until 1916, the staff of the TUC consisted of a secretary and a clerk.

The parliamentary committee created the Labor Representation Committee, which evolved into the Labor Party in the British Parliament, ending Labor's alliance with the Liberal Party. In 1921, the parliamentary committee was replaced by a general council. It was the general council that called the General Strike of 1926.

In 1986, unions affiliated with the TUC had over 9.2 million members, approximately 40 percent of the work force, which was down from 50 percent in 1979. The percentage of the British work force unionized remains much higher in Britain than the United States. Adding to the woes of declining membership, the TUC, which had close ties to the Labor Party until the 1980s, has lost political clout. Concern over the political power of unions was one of the issues that made Margaret Thatcher prime minister. In a bid to regain favor with the electorate, the Labor Party began to emphasize its independence from unions. The affiliates of the TUC have also demanded more decentralization of decision-making, and have questioned the costs of the £10-million bureaucracy that the TUC supports.

The TUC in England is on the defensive for much the same reasons as unions in the United States are finding themselves in difficulty. The decline in the percentage of the work force engaged in manufacturing had robbed labor unions of the heart of their support. Unions, however, have been on the defensive in the past, particularly between the world wars, when membership plummeted. Since unions in Britain and the United States won back the ground lost in the 1920s, they may pull off another comeback, perhaps becoming more white-collar than they have been in the past.

References McIlroy, John. *Trade Unions in Britain Today* (1988); Roberts, B. C. *Trade Union Government and Administration in Great Britain* (1956).

Treaty of Versailles

After the Armistice of 1918, the leaders of the Allied nations—principally Woodrow Wilson, Lloyd George, and Georges Clemenceau—negotiated the terms of a treaty for restoring order and stability to Europe and keeping the peace with Germany. Germany had no voice in the terms of the treaty, and found its terms objectionable, but signed the treaty out of necessity.

The Treaty of Versailles imposed heavy war-reparation payments on Germany and forced territorial concessions that impaired Germany's productive potential. Some critics argued that the treaty should have done more to crush Germany, preventing a resurgence of German power. Other critics argued that the vindictive

Georges Clemenceau rises and asks the German delegates to come forward for the signing of the peace treaty at Versailles in 1919.

provisions of the treaty ignored important economic realities in Europe, and that the treaty imposed a heavy debt on Germany, and at the same time destroyed her ability to pay.

Prior to World War I, Germany had become a highly industrialized nation that was dependent upon food imports. The return of Alsace-Lorraine to France, and other territorial concessions, reduced Germany's industrial capacity, and its ability to export industrial goods. Exports were necessary for Germany to pay for food imports, raw material imports, and war reparations.

British economist John Maynard Keynes criticized the treaty. According to Keynes, in his book *The Economic Consequences of Peace*,

The Treaty includes no provisions for the economic rehabilitation of Europe,—nothing to make the defeated Central Europe into good neighbors, nothing to reclaim Russia; nor does it promote in any way a compact of economic solidarity amongst the Allies themselves; no arrangement was reached at Paris for restoring the disordered finances of France and Italy, or to adjust the systems of the Old World and New.

Aside from unrealistic demands on Germany for war reparations, Keynes observed the sad fiscal condition of the budgets of most of the governments in Europe. Keynes saw serious disruption of the movement of finished goods and raw materials in Europe, because of depreciated currencies, destruction of transportation facilities, redrawing of national boundaries, and breaking up of empires into nation-states. He recommended suspending war reparations, cancellation of debts among Allied governments, and the formation of a European free-trade union to facilitate trade across new national boundaries.

Keynes attributed to the wartime inflationary policies of the European governments a rising tide of hatred against the entrepreneurial class in Europe. In the words of Keynes:

We are faced in Europe with the spectacle of an extraordinary weakness on the part of the great capitalist class, which has emerged from the industrial triumphs of the nineteenth century, and seemed a very few years ago our all-powerful master. The terror and personal timidity of the individuals of this class is now so great, their confidence in their place in society and in their necessity to the social organism so diminished that they are the easy victims of intimidation. This was not so in England twenty-five years ago, any more than it is now in the United States.... Now they tremble before every insult; call them pro-Germans, international financiers, or profiteers, and they will give you any ransom you choose not to speak of them so harshly.

During the 1920s, Austria, Hungary, Germany, and Poland experienced episodes of hyperinflation, and, in France, prices increased sixfold from 1913 to 1927. After the inflation of the 1920s, the 1930s saw the world economy plunge into depression.

Not all observers agreed with Keynes's criticism of the terms of the Treaty of Versailles, which turned out to be unenforceable. Nevertheless, after World War II, the United States established the Marshall Plan, which supplied grants rather than loans to finance the reconstruction of Europe. Also, during the post-World War II era, Europe created the European Economic Community, a free-trading bloc composed of European countries.

See also Hyperinflation in Post-World War I Germany, Marshall Plan.

References Baruch, Bernard M. *The Making of the Reparation and Economic Sections of the Treaty* (1970); Keynes, John Maynard. *The Economic Consequences of Peace* (1920); Watt, Richard M. *The Kings Depart, the Tragedy of Germany: Versailles and the German Revolution* (1969).

Trusts (United States)

Trusts became an important vehicle of industrial consolidation and control of competing firms in the nineteenth-century United States. The trusts gave their name to the antitrust legislation that outlawed monopolies, price fixing, and marketing agreements between competitors.

Before the development of trusts in the late 1800s, firms of the same industry formed pools and associations that fixed prices and divided market shares. These pools and associations were not always able to control recalcitrant members, and were not well suited for organizing large-scale industries. Trust agreements were a new kind of combination that, unlike pools and associations, were designed to meet the needs of large-scale industry. In trust agreements, the stockholders accepted trust certificates in exchange for stock holdings in member corporations. In this arrangement, the stockholders turned their right to control the member corporations over to a group of trustees. The trust certificates entitled each stockholder to receive a share of the earnings proportionate to the share of ownership contributed to the trust. The trust certificates conferred upon stockholders the right to elect the trustees. They traded like shares of stock. In 1899, trust certificates were more actively traded than shares of stock.

The Standard Oil Company organized as the first industrial trust in 1879. Its revised trust agreement of 1882 became the model for future trust agreements. This second trust agreement came into being because of recognition that some of the refineries belonging to the 40 businesses in the Standard group were inefficient, and should be closed. The new trust agreement created an office of nine trustees to "exercise general supervision over the affairs of the several Standard Oil Companies." The new trustees reduced the number of operating refineries under the trust's supervision from 53 to 22.

Over 70 mills producing cottonseed oil formed the American Cotton Oil Trust in 1884. The year 1885 saw the formation of the National Linseed Oil trust, and also trusts in whiskey production, sugar refining, lead, rope, and cordage. Several states passed laws against trusts and combinations; others initiated legal proceedings. The Sherman Antitrust Act of 1890 outlawed trusts.

Another form of business combination, the holding companies, which are often referred to as trusts in popular discussion, took the place of trusts as a means of consolidating control of several large enterprises. New Jersey changed its corporation law to allow one corporation to hold the stock of another. In 1892, the 64 members of the Standard Oil trust voted to dissolve the trust, and to transfer the ownership of the stock of the 20 companies to one particular company. Standard Oil underwent reorganization as a holding company under the New Jersey laws of incorporation.

The trend toward centralized control of large-scale industries was a worldwide trend in the latter portion of the nine-

A political cartoon published in 1888 depicts Standard Oil as a python threatening to crush the Tide Water Pipe Line.

teenth century. The advantages of mass production were held out to justify this trend. The United States was the first of the capitalist countries to mount legislative efforts to protect competitive markets from business combinations of large-scale industrial enterprises.

See also Mergers; Rockefeller, John Davison; Sherman Antitrust Act of 1890.

References Atack, Jeremy, and Peter Passell. *A New Economic View of American History* (1994); Solo, Robert A. *The Political Authority and the Market System* (1974).

Tulipmania (Low Countries)

Tulipmania, the tulip speculative boom, stands as the first well-documented speculative frenzy in European history. The tulip had come to Vienna in the sixteenth century from Turkey, where the flower had caught the eye of travelers who were struck by its beauty. Cultivation of the tulip migrated to Germany, then to Belgium, and then to Holland. The tulip became fashionable in Paris and in English court circles, and public interest in the tulip rose to a passion. Some of that passion infected the tulip market, where traders began buying and selling futures in tulips.

Speculative fever in tulips received an added boost from anxiously awaited mutations that arose if a virus had infected tulips. The public was hungry for new specimens of tulips, and a variation of the tulip bloom, if it was beautiful, could expect to bring high prices from growers who would use it as breeding stock.

By the 1630s, tulipmania had spread to every level of Dutch society, and most cultivable land was devoted to tulip production. Virtually the entire population took up speculating in tulips, as prices soared. Rare specimens sold for thousands of florins, and, at one point, a single rare bulb was traded for a successful brewery in France.

Originally, speculators sold and traded tulip bulbs over the winter. As the frenzy spread, speculators took contracts year-round for deliveries in the spring. One of the earliest known futures markets developed to further entice and challenge the wits of tulip speculators. What are now called puts and calls make their first documented appearance in this speculative drama. A put is an option to sell a commodity or stock at a future date. A call is an option to buy a commodity or stock at a future date. Speculators often never planned to take delivery on what they bought, but they planned to resell their contract for a profit. The term "windhandel," meaning trading in air, was coined to describe such speculative maneuvers.

Families mortgaged estates to buy tulip contracts. Speculators sold tulips they did not own, but promised to acquire in the future. In 1637, the market crumbled, and many wealthy families and old merchant firms met with financial ruin, as lawsuits swamped the courts. Dutch commercial activity entered into a prolonged slump.

Buying and selling in futures remains a common practice in commodity and stock markets in modern capitalistic markets, where earning income by bearing risk is a legitimate activity, allowing speculators to specialize in bearing risks that many firms want to avoid. Tulipmania demonstrates how speculative practices can contribute to destabilizing commodity and financial markets, which is a problem that still exists today, despite substantial regulation.

See also Amsterdam Exchange, Antwerp Bourse, London Stock Exchange.

References Garber, M. "Tulipmania?" *Journal of Political Economy* (1989); Houte, J. A. van. *An Economic History of the Low Countries, 800–1800* (1977); Train, John. *Famous Financial Fiascos* (1985).

Unemployment Insurance

Unemployment insurance pays benefits to unemployed workers, and is usually based on a scheme financed by contributions from workers and employers.

Contributory schemes to aid workers who were unemployed, because of illness or incapacity, began in Germany during the latter 1800s. Unemployment insurance began in Britain with the enactment of the Unemployment Insurance Act of 1911. Compulsory unemployment insurance became law in Germany in 1927. When the provinces of Alsace-Loraine returned to French sovereignty in 1928, the workers demanded the same social insurance they enjoyed under German rule. The French government enacted a program of social insurance that included state participation in an unemployment insurance program.

In the United States, the Social Security Act of 1935 provided for the establishment of a combined federal and state unemployment insurance system. As an incentive to states to establish unemployment insurance programs, employers in states with acceptable unemployment insurance programs received an exemption from 90 percent of the Federal Unemployment Tax.

All 50 states have an unemployment insurance system. A modest payroll tax finances the state programs. In most states, the payroll tax is levied on the employer only, which is at variance with the practice of most countries. Currently, the program insures about 90 percent of civilian workers. An unemployed worker usually qualifies for benefit payments after one week of unemployment. The level of compensation varies proportionately, up to a fixed limit, to an unemployed worker's former salary. The exact size and duration of the payments depend on the state, and some states are more generous than others.

Critics of capitalism saw unemployment as the paradox of individual destitution in the midst of a wealthy and sophisticated society. The apparently inherent cyclical fluctuations of capitalism bore the blame for unemployment, rather than inadequacies in individuals who lacked employment. Unemployment insurance seemed one way to rectify this burden of insecurity placed on the labor force. In addition to aiding unemployed workers, unemployment insurance commended itself as a means of restricting the propagation of cyclical fluctuations by smoothing out fluctuations in household expenditures.

In the 1970s and 1980s, the unemployment rate showed a stubborn refusal to drop below 5 percent, regardless of the level of economic prosperity evidenced by other measures. Many economists asked if unemployment insurance could be increasing unemployment by subsidizing the time invested in searching for new jobs. Researchers observed that Britain sustained high unemployment levels, averaging 14 percent, between World War I and World War II. British unemployment benefits were generous during that time, and the unemployment rates varied with the generosity of the benefits. During the same time, teenagers, who were ineligible for unemployment benefits, reported low unemployment rates. When the benefits for married women fell in 1932, the unemployment rate of married women, compared to men, also fell.

In summary, unemployment insurance helps to stabilize the cyclical fluctuations of the capitalist system. The downside is that unemployment insurance may encourage unemployed workers to extend job searches.

References Benjamin, Daniel, and Levis Kochin.

"Searching for an Explanation of Unemployment in Interwar Britain." *Journal of Political Economy* (1979); Cartter, Allan M., and F. Ray Marshall. *Labor Economics: Wages, Employment, and Trade Unionism* (1967); Rimlinger, Gaston V. *Welfare Policy and Industrialization in Europe, America, and Russia* (1971).

Unequal Treaties (Japan)

In the aftermath of Commodore Matthew Perry's second expedition, Japan signed so-called unequal treaties with several Western powers. These treaties were called unequal because of a lack of reciprocity in the provisions, and because they put Japan in a colonial relationship with the Western powers.

Japan clung to a policy of self-imposed isolation from the 1600s to the mid-nineteenth century. Beginning in the 1790s, Western powers sought to pry open Japanese ports to foreign trade. The Japanese rebuffed all advances by foreigners until 1853, when the U.S. government officially commissioned Perry to lead a squadron of four ships on an expedition to open relations with Japan. The squadron arrived in Uraga at the southern end of Tokyo bay.

Perry demanded that the Japanese strike an agreement with the United States. The provisioning of U.S. ships, the treatment of shipwrecked U.S. sailors, and the establishment of official relations led the list of key issues. To receive the Japanese answer, Perry returned in the spring with a fleet of nine ships. The agreement Perry struck opened two ports of refuge, arranged for returning shipwrecked sailors, and promised an exchange of consuls in the future. Trade issues were tabled for future discussion. Britain and Russia soon negotiated similar treaties. In 1856, Townsend Harris, the first U.S. consul to Japan, took up residence and pressed for a commercial treaty. In 1858, the United States signed a treaty of amity and commerce with Japan. Several Western powers signed treaties soon afterward. These treaties are collec-

An 1840 Japanese woodblock print depicts Nahonbashi, traditionally the very center of the country, bustling with activity.

tively referred to as the unequal treaties, because of the imperialistic note they sounded.

The terms of the treaties provided that Western traders reside in foreign settlements and other prescribed areas. One of the inequitable provisions of the treaty exempted Western traders from Japanese law, even in disputes involving Japanese. The consul of the country of the offending party presided as judge. This provision was unequal, since Japanese nationals in Western countries were not accorded the same protection. Later agreements put a 5-percent tariff ceiling on goods imported into Japan. A most-favored-nation clause entitled these Western powers to any trade concessions granted to other nations in the future.

The terms of the unequal treaties that Western powers imposed upon Japan were less restrictive than the ones imposed on China. The treaties provided for revisions as early as 1872, but it was the turn of the century before Japan shook off the restrictive measures, and it was 1911 before Japan gained control over its own tariff structure.

Under the unequal treaties, Japan became an importer of heavy manufactured goods produced in the United States and Europe, and an exporter of raw silk, tea, coal, and other raw materials. Unable to protect domestic industry with import tariffs, Japan built industry on the foundation of low wages and governmental support. The absence of tariff protection also forced Japan to specialize from the beginning of its industrialization.

The opening of trade with the West, and the assault on Japanese sovereignty, discredited the existing government, and brought a new government to power. In 1871, Japan sent a top-level delegation to the United States and Europe, with instructions to negotiate better treaty terms for Japan. The delegation failed in its primary mission, and returned to Japan awestruck with Western technology, and the economic and social development of Western countries. The Japanese govern-

ment committed itself to a program of industrialization along Western lines, and consciously strove to westernize Japanese technology and economic institutions.

The history of the opening of Japan to the West reveals the powerful urge for expansion that capitalism has exhibited since Columbus discovered America. Few non-Western countries responded to the challenge flung down by Western capitalism as effectively as Japan. Rather than becoming a victim of imperialism, Japan soon rivaled other imperialistic powers in its drive for expansion.

See also Meiji Era.

References Halliday, Jon. *A Political History of Japanese Capitalism* (1975); Wiley, Peter B. *Yankees in the Land of the Gods* (1990).

Unification of Italy

Before the political unification of Italy during the nineteenth century, Italy was composed of a collection of small states bullied by the European powers, particularly Austria and France. After unification, the new government embarked upon a policy of government-assisted capitalist development, which had Italy well on the road to industrialization by the eve of World War I.

During the Renaissance, capitalism flourished in Italian city-states such as Florence, Venice, and Genoa. Some scholars credit the birth of modern capitalism to these city-states, which dominated world trade during their zenith, but they lost ground as the center of world trade migrated from the Mediterranean to the Atlantic seaboard. Also, as capitalism sunk its roots in the nation-states, beginning in England, economic supremacy passed from the city-states to national economies. At the end of the eighteenth century, while England was caught in the coils of the Industrial Revolution, Italy was what today would be called an economically backward country. Napoleon's army ran over Italy at will, and Italy emerged from the Napoleonic Wars under the thumb of Austria.

Italy's glorious past, however, was a

strong spur to nationalism. After the Napoleonic Wars, Italian statesmen took up the issue of strengthening Italy economically and politically. Italian writers and thinkers cited the necessity of economic strength as a foundation of political strength. Following the theories of English and French economists, they saw the key to economic development lying in a larger market that could support larger and more economical industrial establishments, and a greater division of labor. One of these thinkers, Carlos Cattaneo, called for a federation of Italian states that would lead to a United States of Europe, thus anticipating the European Economic Community.

The prime minister of the Kingdom of Sardinia, Count Camillo Benso di Cavour, supplied the political and diplomatic leadership that, coupled with an indigenous liberation movement, unified the small Italian states freed from Austrian domination. Much of the unification occurred in 1860 and 1861, but Venetia was annexed in 1866, and Rome in 1870. The tariff policy of the Kingdom of Sardinia was extended to the new unified state, and the Piedmont lira was established as the national currency.

The new government began an aggressive program of economic development, particularly constructing railroads, assisting the development of shipbuilding, and promoting industrialization. The government entered upon a policy of massive government deficits to finance development, and soon had to suspend the convertibility of the lira into gold. Cavour defended the policy in these words:

> We have adopted a policy of action—a policy of progress. Instead of attempting to balance expenditures with receipts by economies, which would mean renouncing any idea of betterment or of great enterprise, we have preferred to promote works of public utility, to develop every factor of growth, which our State possesses, to develop in all parts of the country every possible industrial and economic activity of which the nation is possible.

Until the 1890s, economic growth remained slow in Italy, but much of the necessary infrastructure for supporting growth was put in place. The Italian economy was held back by a worldwide slump in economic conditions during much of that time. Another factor was a tariff policy that leaned toward free trade, which the new state had adopted from the Kingdom of Sardinia. In 1887, the Italian government enacted a protectionist tariff policy, raising customs duties to 40 percent on some items. This high tariff touched off one of the most famous tariff wars in history, between France and Italy.

During the three decades prior to World War I, Italy made significant economic progress, though less dramatic than the progress of Germany, Japan, or the United States. Like Germany, Italian nationhood came from the work of statesmen who were ambitious for economic development, and felt a keen rivalry with the advanced capitalistic nations. Because of these nationalistic ambitions, the governments in these countries have played a more active role in developing capitalistic institutions in their national economies.

References Clough, Shepard B. *The Economic History of Modern Italy* (1964); Hall, Edgar. *Risorgimento: The Making of Modern Italy* (1970).

Unionization of the Steel Industry (United States)

In 1937, union organizers discovered the crack in the antiunion armor of the steel industry in the United States. That armor had turned back major union offensives in 1892, 1902, 1909, 1919, and 1934. Such a series of defeats at the hands of the steel industry had become a psychological barrier to the union movement. The steel industry was important to labor, because of its symbolical value as a citadel of antiunionism, and its place at the cornerstone of heavy American industry.

The Steel Workers Organizing Committee (SWOC) of the Congress of Industrial Organizations launched its drive to organize the United States Steel Corporation during the summer of 1936. The SWOC organizers pointed to the victories of Roosevelt and the New Deal Democrats to raise hopes among the hesitant steel workers.

The company unions played a pivotal role that U.S. Steel could hardly have anticipated, when, in 1933, it acted on the recommendations of its personnel director to form company unions, which then succeeded in hampering the efforts of the CIO to attract dues-paying members. About 90 percent of the workers belonged to the company unions, and only about 3 percent joined the CIO.

The elected leadership of the company unions effectively checkmated company officials, by raising the specter of the CIO. They emphasized the importance of protecting the integrity of the company unions against the charge of company manipulation and domination. Company officials found themselves unwelcome at meetings of company unions. The minutes of some of these meetings accurately reported speeches of labor union activists.

The SWOC turned its efforts toward gaining control of the company unions. Labor union activists at the head of company unions took credit for concessions extracted from company officials, and, when company officials rejected pleas from company unions, the leaders fed the flames for a real union. Company unions themselves split between prounion and antiunion sympathizers.

U.S. Steel saw productivity fall off, as activists in the company unions made themselves heard. A casual encounter between CIO president John L. Lewis and U.S. Steel president Myron Taylor led to an agreement between the CIO and U.S. Steel. Taylor apparently read the political tea leaves, and saw the CIO as an unorthodox means of restoring order to the work force in the steel industry. Over the weekend of 27–28 February, Lewis and Taylor finalized a settlement. The union won a 5-percent wage increase, the 40-hour work week, and time-and-a-half pay for overtime. The settlement was unique in labor history, because workers never had an opportunity to approve, reject, or amend the agreement.

The SWOC signed contracts with 51 other companies, including five U.S. Steel subsidiaries, within a month of its victory. The smaller steel companies were a bit harder to crack. A successful strike brought Jones and Laughlin to the bargaining table in the summer of 1937. Weirton, Youngstown, Republic, and Inland held out until World War II. To fend off unionization, these companies granted the wages and working conditions won by the unions at U.S. Steel. Some of the most violent clashes in labor history arose out of the strikes against the Little Steel companies in 1937. Shots were fired on Memorial Day in Chicago, killing 10 people, when a group of peaceful, unarmed marchers encountered a group of Chicago city police who were housed and fed by Republic Steel.

With organization of the steel and automobile industries, the unskilled workers established themselves in the heart of the labor movement. Bringing this group under the banner of organized labor eased much of the political unrest directed toward the capitalist system. It neutralized an important segment of the work force that had added much of the momentum to socialist agitation in European countries.

See also Congress of Industrial Organizations; Lewis, John L.; London Dock Strike of 1899.

References McDonald, David. *Union Man* (1969); Ziegler, Robert H. *The CIO, 1935–1955* (1995).

United States Gold Reserves Act of 1934
See Gold Standard.

United States Steel Corporation
See Morgan, John Pierpont.

United States v. Aluminum Company of America (Alcoa) (1945)

United States v. Aluminum Company of America (Alcoa) (1945) stands as a landmark antitrust case that led to a stricter interpretation of section 2 of the Sherman Antitrust Act of 1890, which reads, "Every person who shall monopolize, or attempt to monopolize, or combine or conspire with any other person or persons to monopolize any part of the trade or commerce among several states, or with foreign nations, shall be deemed guilty of a misdemeanor."

Alcoa produced 100 percent of the primary aluminum in the United States, and controlled 90 percent of the domestic market. The exclusive ownership of important patents and essential raw materials formed the basis of Alcoa's monopoly position. The company embraced all stages of production, from bauxite ore, through alumina and aluminum ingots, to fabrication. This vertical integration, coupled with the advantages of mass production and moderate prices, bolstered Alcoa's domination of the market.

Because of a large secondary market in scrap aluminum, the first district court to hear the case ruled that Alcoa enjoyed only a 33-percent market share. The second court to hear the case ruled, however, that Alcoa was the original source of the aluminum in the secondary market, and that the proper definition of the market was the primary aluminum market. Alcoa enjoyed a 90-percent market share of the primary aluminum market.

The *Alcoa* case marks a turning point in the burden of proof placed on the government in antitrust cases. Prior to the *Alcoa* case, the Supreme Court had ruled that only unreasonable attempts to monopolize violated the Sherman Act. The New York Court of Appeals heard the *Alcoa* case, when the Supreme Court could not, because too many justices had to excuse themselves, because of prior involvement in the case. Judge Learned Hand of the New York Court of Appeals wrote the opinion on the case, in which he argued,

> Many people believe that possession of unchallenged economic power deadens initiative, discourages thrift and depresses energy; that immunity from competition is a narcotic, and rivalry is a stimulant, to industrial progress; ...Congress...did not condone "good trusts" and condemn "bad" ones. ...[C]ontinued control did not fall undesigned into "Alcoa's" lap.... It could only have resulted from a persistent determination to maintain the control.... It insists that it never excluded competitors; but we can think of no more effective exclusion than progressively to embrace each new opportunity as it opened, and to face every newcomer with new capacity already geared into a great organization; having the advantage of experience, trade connections, and the elite of personnel..., no monopolist monopolizes unconscious of what he is doing.

In the *Alcoa* case, the Court ruled that a monopoly is a violation of section 2 of the Sherman Act, unless market share has been thrust upon the monopolist and was virtually unavoidable. A monopoly is illegal without evidence of aggressive and exclusionary practices designed to undermine competitors.

In modern capitalism, competition is seen as an important regulating force that minimizes conflict between individual and public interest. In antitrust cases, such as the *Alcoa* case, we see the legal system growing in its comprehension of competition and free markets as something it should defend.

See also Sherman Antitrust Act of 1890, *United States v. Standard Oil.*

References Neale, Allan D., and D. G. Goyden. *The Antitrust Laws of the United States of America* (1980); Shenefield, John H. *The Antitrust Laws: A Primer* (1993); Waldman, Don E. *The Economics of Antitrust: Cases and Analysis* (1986).

United States v. Standard Oil Co. of New Jersey (1911)

The *Standard Oil* case ranks among the most famous antitrust cases. During the latter portion of the 1800s, John D. Rockefeller and associates aggressively sought control of the oil refining industry. Standard Oil stood in control of 90 percent of the market share after absorbing over 100 competitors. It often paid premium prices for the stock of competitors. Sometimes it acquired competitors with the aid of predatory pricing. It also controlled the major pipelines, which controlled competitor's access to crude oil supplies. The company succeeded in extracting freight rebates from railroad companies, extending this practice so far that Standard Oil received rebates for the shipments of its competitors.

The Supreme Court unanimously found Standard Oil in violation of the antitrust laws. This landmark decision of the Supreme Court set forth the famous Rule of Reason, which interpreted section 2 of the Sherman Antitrust Act to mean that only unreasonable attempts to monopolize should be held in violation of the law. Chief Justice Edward White wrote the Court's opinion, in his own special legal language. He wrote:

[We] think no disinterested mind can survey the period in question without being irresistibly driven to the conclusion that the genius for commercial development and organization which it would seem was manifested from the beginning soon begot an intent and purpose to exclude others which was frequently manifested by acts and dealings wholly inconsistent with the theory that they were made with the single conception of advancing the development of business power by usual methods, but which, on the contrary, necessarily involved the intent to drive others from their right to trade, and thus accomplish the master which was the end in view.

In this opinion, the Court took the position that monopoly power in and of itself is not necessarily illegal. Standard Oil was faulted for transcending the bounds of normal business methods in its drive for monopoly power. The Court held against monopolizing actions, or actions that lead to monopoly, rather than monopoly per se.

Justice John Marshall Harlan concurred with the ruling against Standard Oil, but dissented on the rationale. He found no indication in the Sherman Act that Congress intended to exempt monopolies acquired by reasonable business practices.

Standard Oil split up into 34 different companies. Initially, Standard Oil's stockholders held stock in each of the 34 companies. Some of the companies failed. Standard Oil of New Jersey eventually became Exxon, one of the big competitors in the industry. Chevron grew out of Standard Oil of California. Amoco started as Standard Oil of Indiana. During the 1930s, the industry felt competition had gone too far, which is a common perception during times of deflation. Ironically, the government became involved in trying to prop up prices.

Many critics of capitalism saw replacing monopoly power with competition as an answer to problems of capitalism. The protection of competitive markets is consistent with the preservation of private property, while avoiding the worst abuses of capitalism. Enforcement of the antitrust laws in the United States remains an important force in the development of capitalism.

See also Sherman Antitrust Act of 1890.

References Neale, Allan D., and D. G. Goyden. *The Antitrust Laws of the United States of America* (1980); Shenefield, John H. *The Antitrust Laws: A Primer* (1993); Waldman, Don E. *The Economics of Antitrust: Cases and Analysis* (1986).

United States v. Trans-Missouri Freight Association (1897)

The *Trans-Missouri Freight Association* case was the first price-fixing case brought before the Supreme Court. In March 1889, 15 western railroads organized themselves as the Trans-Missouri Freight Association. Three other railroads joined later. The association stated its purpose as establishing freight rates for its members. It held meetings to set rates, penalized members who violated its rate agreements, and even set penalties for members who failed to show up at a rate-setting meeting. In 1892, two years after the passage of the Sherman Antitrust Act of 1890, the association itself dissolved, but a seven-member committee continued to set rates.

The Justice Department filed suit under section 1 of the Sherman Act, which reads:

Every contract, combination in the form of a trust or otherwise, or conspiracy, in restraint of trade or commerce among the several states, or with foreign nations, is hereby declared to be illegal. Every person who shall make any such contract or engage in any such combination or conspiracy, shall be punished by fine not exceeding five thousand dollars, or by imprisonment not exceeding one year, or by both said punishments, in the discretion of the court.

In defense of its practices, the association argued that railroads were regulated by the Interstate Commerce Commission, and were therefore exempt from the Sherman Act. The association also argued that its rates were reasonable, and that the alternative was cutthroat competition that would destroy the industry.

The Supreme Court overturned the lower court rulings, and ruled in favor of the government. The Court turned a deaf ear to the arguments of the association. Justice Rufus Peckham wrote the opinion, which suggested that price-fixing agreements were illegal per se, and that the fact that the rates were reasonable was irrelevant. He went on to argue that the consequences of competition may be unpre-

dictable, but that only Congress could amend the law to make allowances for destructive competition.

Although the Supreme Court wavered in early cases, by the 1930s price fixing was definitely illegal in the United States. Price-fixing agreements, as well as agreements to alternate the position of lowest bidder in bids, may be made in secret and therefore difficult to detect and prosecute. The trend in favor of price competition is so strong in the United States that many industries, whose prices were formerly regulated by government boards, have now undergone a process of deregulation. The government deregulated the airline industry, whose fares were set by a government board, and competition lowered prices. Soon after deregulation, a price war broke out that perhaps met the criteria of destructive competition. In the long run, however, the industry stabilized with lower prices.

See also Sherman Antitrust Act of 1890.

References Neale, Allan D., and D. G. Goyden. *The Antitrust Laws of the United States of America* (1980); Shenefield, John H. *The Antitrust Laws: A Primer* (1993); Waldman, Don E. *The Economics of Antitrust: Cases and Analysis* (1986).

United States v. United Shoe Machinery Corporation (1954)

In 1954, the U.S. Supreme Court affirmed a district court decision that found the United Shoe Machinery Corporation guilty of monopolizing the shoe machinery industry. United Shoe had cleverly used patent rights to extend monopoly power to the market for nonpatented machinery. The source of United Shoe Machinery Corporation's monopoly power lay in a legal patent on a machine essential for making shoes. The holder of patent rights enjoys the exclusive privilege to monopolize the market of a patented product. United Shoe refused to sell patented machinery outright. It only leased patented machinery under these conditions: (1) Lessees had to sign a "tying agreement," promising to lease all machinery, patented and unpatented, from United Shoe; (2) machines were leased for a minimum of ten years; (3) lessees paid a substantial financial penalty for returning machines before the expiration of the lease.

United Shoe's business arrangements restricted competition on a number of fronts. First, the lease arrangement for marketing the machinery preempted the development of a market of used machines. A market for used goods can be an important source of competition in durable goods industries, such as automobiles and business equipment. Second, the lease arrangement enabled United Shoe to extrapolate a legal monopoly on patented machinery into a monopoly on unpatented machinery. Third, the ten-year duration of the lease increased the capital requirements for new firms in the shoe manufacturing industry.

In 1917, the Justice Department unsuccessfully brought suit against United Shoe Machinery Corporation under the Sherman Antitrust Act of 1890. At that time, the Supreme Court acquitted United Shoe under the principle of the Rule of Reason. The Court attributed United Shoe's 90-percent market share to an "efficiency that was beneficial to the shoe industry." When the Justice Department brought suit again in 1947, the Court had become less tolerant of monopolistic practices.

United Shoe fit the description of a "good trust." Its profits were normal. The cost of machinery accounted for only 2 percent of the average wholesale price of shoes. The lessees had no complaints about the reliability of the machinery or the service.

In ruling against United Shoe, District Court Judge Charles E. Wyzanski, Jr., stated,

> In one sense, the leasing system and the miscellaneous activities just referred to...were natural and normal.... Yet, they were not practices which can be properly described as the inevitable consequences of ability, natural forces,

or law.... They are contracts, arrangements, and policies which, instead of encouraging competition based on pure merit, further the dominance of a particular firm. In this sense, they are unnatural barriers; they unnecessarily exclude actual and potential competition; they restrict a free market....

At first, the Court contented itself with requiring United Shoe to shorten its lease to five years, to abolish penalties for returning machines after one year, and to offer its machines for sale. Within a decade, the market share of United Shoe had decreased from 90 to 60 percent. In 1968, the Supreme Court ordered a divestiture of sufficient assets to reduce United Shoe's market share to 33 percent.

As the concept of competition has evolved, business practices that were well within the bounds of honesty and propriety 100 years ago are now outside of the law. Competition replaces government regulation in a capitalist economic system. That is why the legal system, politicians, and scholars have devoted a good deal of time and effort to refining the concept of competition, and increasing the level of competition in markets.

See also Sherman Antitrust Act of 1890.

References Neale, Allan D., and D. G. Goyden. *The Antitrust Laws of the United States of America* (1980); Shenefield, John H. *The Antitrust Laws: A Primer* (1993); Waldman, Don E. *The Economics of Antitrust: Cases and Analysis* (1986).

Unlawful Oaths Act of 1797 (England)

The Unlawful Oaths Act became a legal weapon for the suppression of labor unions in early nineteenth-century England. Parliament passed the legislation as the Act for more Effectually Preventing the Administering or Taking of Unlawful Oaths, in response to mutinies in the navy. Contrary to its original purpose, the government later used it to suppress working-class agitation and trade union activity.

To protect members from hostile employers and government, early unions kept their activities enveloped in a cloak of secrecy. Merely supplying knowledge that a worker was a member of a union could cost that worker his job. Elaborate rituals and ceremonies of initiation reinforced the commitment of individual members to secrecy. The building trades were particularly known for elaborate initiation practices. The common ancestry that unions share with Freemasons also explained traditions of initiation and secrecy.

Portions of the act read as follows:

WHEREAS divers wicked and evil-disposed persons, have of late attempted to seduce persons serving in his Majesty's services by sea and land, and others of his Majesty's subjects, from their duty and allegiance to his Majesty, and to incite them to acts of mutiny and sedition, and have endeavored to give effect to their wicked and traitorous proceedings, by imposing upon the persons whom they have attempted to seduce the pretended obligations of oaths unlawfully administered; be it enacted...that any person or persons who shall, in any matter or form whatsoever, administer or cause to be administered, or be aiding or assisting at, or present at and consenting to, the administering or taking of any oath or engagement purporting or intended to bind the person taking the same to engage in any mutinous or seditious purpose...shall, on conviction thereof by due course of law, be adjudged guilty of a felony, and may be transported for any term of years not exceeding seven years; and any such person who shall take any such oath or engagement, not being compelled thereto, shall, on conviction thereof by due course of law, be adjudged guilty of a felony, and may be transported for any term of years not exceeding seven years.

In 1825, Parliament had repealed the Combination Acts that had been enacted specifically to suppress trade unions. In 1833, the agricultural workers at Tolpuddle, in Dorset, led by two brothers named Loveless, organized a lodge called the Friendly Society of Agricultural Labourers. This was part of the burst of union organizing activity that followed the organization of the Grand National Consolidated Trade Union. The agricultural workers planned to affiliate their lodge with the Grand National, and had adopted initiation ceremonies associated with that organization.

The government was then opening a campaign to crack down on unions. Without ever making any plea for higher wages, or any threat of strike action, the Lovelesses and four other members of the Friendly Society were arrested and put in jail. The only charge against them involved administering and taking oaths. After a brief trial, the judge handed down a seven-year sentence to each defendant. The trade unions organized a vigorous public protest, but the government refused to admit that the sentences were excessive. The unions kept up the protests against the sentences, and, after four years, the defendants returned to England.

The other trade unions of the Grand National acted to abolish the rituals and initiation ceremonies. Robert Owen, who had proposed the formation of the Grand National, had always opposed oaths and ceremonies as "relics of barbarism."

The English government twisted the Unlawful Oaths Act into a repressive measure against unions, after Parliament had repealed its own antiunion legislation. That the government would resort to this expedient says something of the menace that employers saw in unions in the early days of capitalism.

See also Grand National Consolidated Trade Union.

References Cole, G. D. H., and A. W. Filson, *British Working Class Movements: Selected Documents, 1789–1875* (1965); Firth, Majorie M. *The Tolpuddle Martyrs* (1974); Webb, Sidney, and Beatrice Webb, *The History of Trade Unionism* (1920).

Uprising of the Lyon Silk Workers (France)

In 1831, and again in 1834, the silk workers of Lyon led a bloody uprising against local authorities. The silk workers' rallying cry was "Live working or die fighting." A young Karl Marx regarded the revolt of the silk workers as the beginning of the class war of the proletariat against the capitalists.

In 1830, Lyon, France, ranked among the leading manufacturing centers in the world. More than half of the city's commercial income arose from silk and silk-related industries. The Industrial Revolution had not yet invaded the silk industry. Master weavers owned small shops of looms that were operated by journeymen. Silk merchants purchased raw silk, let it out to the weavers for weaving, and marketed the finished product. Silk was a luxury good whose demand fluctuated sharply with changing economic conditions. The master weavers and journeymen felt squeezed by the merchants, as economic pressures forced merchants to find ways to slash costs. The silk workers were highly literate, elite workers; Lyon was the only city in Europe that could boast of two working-class newspapers.

The French Revolution had destroyed the traditional corporate structure of the silk industry. Associations among merchants, such as chambers of commerce, were lawful, but worker associations were banned, as were strikes. Coalitions of workers to raise wages were forbidden. Equally forbidden were coalitions of employers to lower wages, but the law fell more heavily upon the workers. After 1803, courts had to accept the word of any employer against the word of a worker; after the Revolution and the First Empire, the merchant capitalists wielded more economic power relative to the workers. In Lyon, secret worker associations formed as mutual-aid societies, and functioned in the face of these legal restrictions. These associations were connected by pyramids of associations, with each layer of the pyramid interlocking the membership of the lower layers.

The masters and journeymen saw the merchants as the parasites in the silk industry. The masters wanted to reorganize the industry without the merchants, and the merchants sought ways to circumvent the masters. One plan of the master weavers proposed the formation of cooperatives, with elected leadership, fixed wages of workers, and shared profits.

In October 1831, a group of workers, aided by the pressure of mass rallies and petitions, persuaded local officials to form a commission empowered to negotiate a citywide rate for weaving. With several thousand workers waiting outside, a panel of merchants and master weavers negotiated a set rate, but, instead of implementing the negotiated rate according to plan, the merchants appealed to government officials in Paris, and complained about the intervention of local officials. On 17 November, the silk workers received word from Paris that the agreement was not legally binding, and was null and void. Feelings ran high, and, on the following Monday, a general strike and protest march were held. Local officials brought out the National Guard, who turned its guns on the protesters, killing and wounding several. When workers throughout the city joined the fight, the local garrison proved no match for the number of workers. The army evacuated, and the workers seized control of Lyon. Local officials defused the rebellion by putting the city in the hands of 16 wealthy and influential masters. Workers safeguarded the municipal treasury and silk warehouses, and later the army returned unopposed. This short-lived insurrection made a deep impression on contemporaries. J. B. Monfalcon, a local historian who wrote a firsthand account of the insurrection, observed,

The moral influence of the November insurrection will be immense: Their victory, so singularly the result of a succession of accidents and the incapacity

347

of the authorities, will make them [the workers] more demanding.... Perhaps for a hundred years the marvelous tale of the defeat of the National Guard and the garrison of Lyon by the unarmed workers will charm the leisure of the workshop; this tradition will pass from generation to generation; a son will say with pride..., "My father was one of the conquerors of Lyon."

The government resolved not to intervene again between merchants and masters, and gravitated to a more repressive stance toward worker associations. In February 1834, the workers called another general strike, again to support a citywide rate for weaving. This strike also ended in failure, and some of the leaders were put on trial. The day of the verdict became the occasion for another workers'

rebellion. The government had enacted a law giving police special power to suppress any unwanted associations. Workers protested the new law against associations on the same day that the trial reconvened. Fighting again broke out between soldiers and protesters: The army lost more than 300 soldiers, and many more workers were presumed killed.

The workers' uprising in Lyon helped give birth to the messianic hope of a working-class revolution that would put the workers at the helm of the state. It is a hope that must be foreign to our present white-collar work force.

See also Class Struggle, Proletariat, July Monarchy.

References Bezucha, Robert J. *The Lyon Uprising of 1834: Social and Political Conflict in the Early July Monarchy* (1974); Collingham, A. C. *The July Monarchy* (1988).

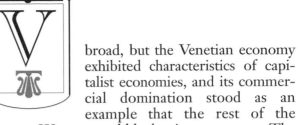

Venetian Capitalism

At the dawn of the capitalist era, Venice monopolized East–West trade for geographical and political reasons, and controlled an empire that stretched along her trading route to the Levant.

Some historians have credited Venice with giving birth to capitalism. This far-reaching generalization may be a bit broad, but the Venetian economy exhibited characteristics of capitalist economies, and its commercial domination stood as an example that the rest of the Western world had to improve upon. The voyages of Christopher Columbus, Vasco de Gama, and Ferdinand Magellan were efforts to tap the trade with the East that Venice dominated.

Venetian merchants and bankers gather at the Rialto—a forerunner of the modern stock exchange—in a 1489 painting by Vittore Carpaccio.

The government of Venice was in the hands of an aristocratic merchant class long enriched by commercial activities. None of the feudal disdain for commercial activities, such as was evident in the aristocracy of France under the ancien regime, was found in Venice. In 1423, the Doge Thomas Mocenigo, in a farewell testament typical of the commercial spirit of Venice, observed that trade was more effective than arms for maintaining a preeminent position in Christendom.

Business activity in Venice was conducted mostly by temporary associations of merchants, usually involving two or three partners. Long-term companies with substantial capitalization, such as the East India Company in England, did not appear in Venice. These temporary partnerships of merchants financed ships on merchant ventures, and, when the ship returned, the partnership dissolved. At the end of the voyage, one-fourth of the profits went to the ship, and the remaining three-fourths to the capitalists who financed the voyage. If the capitalists put up three-fourths of the financing and the ship one-fourth, the profits were split equally between the ship and the capitalists. Even Venetians of modest means committed funds to financing ships.

Merchants and bankers met at a special place each day, similar to a stock exchange, in front of the Rialto. As merchants made deals, bankers stood by and settled transactions, shifting funds between accounts. Commodity prices, long-term interest rates, and maritime insurance premiums were set at the Rialto meetings.

In addition to its preeminent position in international trade, Venice was the most industrialized city of its time. Its list of manufactured goods included glass, silk, playing cards, and chess pieces. The government set strict standards of quality for Venetian manufactured goods, determining acceptable raw materials, dyes, and weave densities. The guilds felt pressure from the merchants to put up financing for wages and raw materials to

workers outside the guilds. The guilds nevertheless maintained their power. When Venice entered an era of decline in the sixteenth century, merchants complained that the guilds held up wages.

Venice also boasted a sizable number of unskilled workers, an urban proletariat, outside the guilds, who were employed as sailors, rowers, and porters. These unskilled workers were recruited in a labor market in front of the Doge's palace. Signs of labor unrest drew severe penalties.

Perhaps Venice became a victim of its own success. It remained a simple form of capitalism. Its bankers never opened branches in other cities or countries. As capitalist institutions progressed in city-states and countries answering the challenge that Venice posed, Venice failed to adapt, and was eclipsed at an early stage in capitalist development. Nevertheless, the Venetian model of capitalism, with its monopoly profits from the Eastern trade, acted as the carrot that stirred Western Europe to heroic explorations, soon followed by large-scale capitalist enterprises.

See also Bank of Venice.

References Braudel, Fernand. *Civilization and Capitalism: 15th–18th Century*, Vol. 3 (1979); Lane, Frederic C. *Venice: A Maritime Republic* (1973).

Venture Capital

Venture capital is the high-risk financing that is needed to launch a new start-up company, and sustain that company from incubation until it can reach a plateau of high growth. Venture capitalists rank second only to entrepreneurs in importance for the creation of new companies and industries.

Historically, venture capitalists were wealthy individuals who could afford to sustain major losses on risky investments without substantially impairing their financial position. During the post-World War era, venture capitalist firms began operating on the fringes of Wall Street. These firms have contacts with people who have financial capital, and are willing to take high risk. Although these firms account for a minute fraction of the total amount of financial capital raised on Wall Street, they supply capital to individuals who hold entrepreneurial promise, and who are developing innovations on the cutting edge of advanced technology. Compared to other financiers, venture capitalists are the most likely to raise capital for a start-up firm in an area that is likely to blossom into a new industry. Recently, biotechnology, computer hardware and software, telephone and data communications, and medical and health care have been popular industries engaging the attention of venture capitalist.

Venture capitalists are much more than financiers passively waiting for an entrepreneur to translate a business idea into a profitable enterprise. They look to back entrepreneurs in whom they have confidence, and they are aware of the pitfalls that new businesses encounter. Venture capitalists develop substantial in-house expertise on the problems and challenges of taking a new firm from start-up to steady growth, and they stand ready to provide advice and assistance to their new entrepreneurs. On a specific deal, they may seek partners from other venture capitalist firms, who have special expertise in that area. The fledgling entrepreneur will receive help honing his business plan, and in selecting his management team. In return for financial backing, the venture capitalists will usually own a significant share of a new firm, and they have been known to fire an entrepreneur in whom they have lost confidence, leaving the entrepreneur feeling that the venture capitalists stole the business.

The venture capitalists will sell their interest when a company passes the threshold of rapid growth, enabling it to sell stock to the public to raise capital. They are financial catalysts who make things happen, because of a combination of high-risk capital and expertise in identifying promising business proposals. By infusing high-tech firms with capital during an incubation period, they belong to those dynamic and innovative forces that push an economic system to the frontiers of technological sophistication.

See also Entrepreneurship.

References Doerflinger, Thomas M., and Jack L. Rivkin. *Risk and Reward* (1987); Chakravarty, S. N. "What It Takes To Be An Entreprenuer," *Forbes*, March 2, 1984.

Wage and Price Controls

Wage and price controls freeze wages and prices at a certain point, and perhaps establish procedures for gradually adjusting wages and prices. Episodes of hyperinflation and wars have most often laid the groundwork for the enactment of wage- and price-control programs.

In 1793, the government of the French Revolution initiated a system of price controls that became known as the Law of the Maximum. A decree of 29 September 1793 empowered district administrations with the authority to set commodity prices at rates one-third higher that the levels of 1790. The decree granted municipal authorities the responsibility for setting wages at 50 percent higher than the 1790 level. In 1794, the Committee on Provisions issued an enormous schedule of the national Maximum, or price list. Each district added transportation costs, 5-percent profit for the wholesaler, and 10 percent for the retailer, and then published a catalogue of prices. Hoarding commodities to avoid selling at controlled prices was punishable by death. Despite the government's involvement in the forcible requisitioning of supplies, the controlled economy of the Revolution broke down. In December 1794, the government suppressed the Law of the Maximum.

The American colonies experimented with wage and price controls to cope with shortages in commodities and labor. In 1623, the governor of Virginia issued a proclamation fixing prices and profit rates on a list of goods ranging from Canadian fish to wine vinegar. A war with Indians apparently created a shortage of goods that led to the controls. The colonial government lifted the controls in 1641. In 1630, the Massachusetts Bay Colony enacted a schedule of wages for skilled workers, coupled with a limit on the markup for finished goods. In 1633, a law banning all "excessive wages and prices" displaced the scale of wages and limitation on markups.

The colonists turned again to wage and price controls to protect themselves from the wave of hyperinflation that struck the colonial economy during the War of Independence. The Continental Congress did not have the power to impose wage and price controls, and remained split on the efforts of state governments. The New England colonies enacted legislation to control prices, but the southern colonies demurred. Goods flowed to regions were prices remained free to rise with market conditions, and state efforts to control prices failed.

During the U.S. Civil War, inflation surged in the northern states, and reached hyperinflation proportions in the Confederacy. Neither the North nor the South enacted a system of wage and price controls during that conflict, which perhaps reflects the ascendancy of laissez-faire economics during the nineteenth century.

During World War I, virtually all the belligerent powers resorted to systems of wage and price controls. By then, inventions such as the typewriter had increased the administrative efficiency of governments. In the United States, wholesale prices had risen 60 percent above their 1914 level when Congress declared war on Germany. The U.S. government made use of as many as eight government agencies to control prices; for example, the War Industries Board controlled the prices of many basic raw materials, and the Food Administration set the prices for many staple foods, such as wheat and livestock. Inflation slowed substantially, contributing to a general feeling that the controls were a success. The controls were lifted at the end of the war, amid some talk that the controls should be extended to the peacetime economy.

In 1936, Germany imposed a comprehensive system of wage and price controls that remained in effect for 12 years. This system of controls was part of Germany's centrally planned economy that was directed toward military mobilization. When the Allied occupation governments kept the controls in place at the end of World War II, black markets sprang up to meet the needs for certain supplies. Germany's rapid economic growth began after the controls were lifted in 1948.

During World War II, many countries established some form of wage and price controls to contain inflation. The United States went to a comprehensive system of wage and price regulation in 1942. The Office of Price Administration had to approve price increases, and a National War Labor Board approved wage increases. The main effect of the controls in the United States lay in the postponement of inflation until after the war. The United States briefly turned again to wage and price controls during the Vietnam War.

In a capitalist economic system, wage and price controls are most successful when governments use them to reduce inflationary expectations, while actual inflation is brought down by monetary restraint. The use of wage and price controls to suppress inflation runs the risk that black markets will emerge, and that producers will secretly reduce the quality of products to save money. The reduction in the quality of products, forcing consumers to buy them more frequently, defeats the purpose of the controls. Economists in the capitalist world mostly condemn the peacetime use of controls. The experience of Germany suggests that the prolonged use of controls becomes a drag on productivity.

See also Hyperinflation of the Continental Currency, Hyperinflation of the French Revolution.

References Blinder, Alan S. *Economic Policy and the Great Stagflation* (1979); Rockoff, Hugh. *Drastic Measures: A History of Wage and Price Controls in the United States* (1984).

Wall Street
See New York Stock Exchange.

Watt, James
See Steam Engine.

Weavers Act of 1555 (England)

The Weavers Act of 1555 prohibited any weaving, clothmaking, and "engrossing of looms" outside "a city, borough, town corporate or market town or else in such a place or places where such cloths have been used to be commonly made by the space of ten years." The act was intended to combat the reconfiguration of the cloth industry along the lines of the merchant-employer model. Merchant-employers circumvented the craft guilds by putting out work directly to craftsmen living outside town boundaries. Craftsmen within a town were organized into craft guilds, which effectively controlled the supply of craftsmen and wages by limiting the number of apprentices, much like a modern-day craft union. The city of Northampton complained of the practice as early as 1464. Norwich and other cloth centers banned any burgess from employing weavers living beyond the city boundaries. In 1534, Parliament passed an act to prohibit clothmaking in the county of Worcestershire beyond the boundaries of the five principal towns. The Weavers Act of 1555 extended the ban on rural clothmaking to other parts of the kingdom. The Statute of Artificers of 1563 further barred the involvement of the rural population in the clothmaking industry. A provision of this act prohibited anyone from practicing the craft of weaver without first serving as an apprentice, and further specified that only the sons of at least £3 freeholders (private owner of a piece of land worth £3) could qualify to enter apprenticeships.

The Weavers Act represented the resistance to a new merchant-employer class that was becoming an oligarchy in clothmaking towns. They represented a richer, capitalistic element among the craftsmen, who wished to organize their capital in the employment of other craftsman. This legislation seems to have temporarily stemmed the growth of rural domestic industry.

See also Statute of Artificers of 1563.

References Bowden, Peter J. *The Wool Trade in Tudor and Stuart England* (1962); Dobb, Maurice. *Studies in the Development of Capitalism* (1947); Fisher, F. J. "Commercial Trends and Policy in Sixteenth Century England." *Essays in Economic History* (1954).

Welfare State

The welfare state appeared to be the ultimate goal of capitalist evolution during the first three decades after World War II. The welfare state is an economy in which government spending is not only at a relatively high level, but a large share of that spending is earmarked for social programs. A trend toward the welfare state manifested itself in most of the advanced capitalist societies, but was perhaps most evident in Great Britain.

The state-directed British economy of World War II had mobilized resources quite successfully, raising hopes that a managed economy could compete with, or outperform, a laissez-faire economy. The Labor Party, out of power since 1931, participated in Churchill's "National Government" and won a heady victory over the Conservative Party in the general election of 1945, signaling the public's desire to continue social reform that had begun during World War II. The government nationalized basic industries, including steel, coal, electric power, railroads, and gas, and government planning commissions supplied a guiding hand to all sectors of national production.

The British government enacted a new National Insurance Act in 1946, which provided for more generous benefits for recipients of old-age and unemployment insurance. Perhaps more importantly, in the same year, the government enacted a program of socialized medicine, known as the National Health Service. Financing for these social programs came from a system of high taxes, with steeply graduated rates on income, and high tax rates on inheritances.

The United States did not go as far as Britain in developing a welfare state, balking particularly at socialized medicine and the nationalization of major industries. The welfare state reached it fullest maturity in the Scandinavian countries, perhaps because defense expenditures absorbed a smaller share of government spending in those countries.

Some observers have attributed the emergence of the welfare state to the political empowerment of women, including, but not limited to, the right to vote, in the early twentieth century. According to this theory, women historically managed families, and families are socialistic organizations, following the socialist principle, "From each according to his ability, to each according to his needs." That is, children's needs are met as they arise, without regard to their ability to produce. The voice of women in politics, therefore, forced governments to pay more attention to the needs of families, tipping the balance in favor of socialistic policies that working-class movements had been promoting without success.

The 1980s experienced a "capitalist revolution", as governments around the world backed away from the public commitments of the welfare state. Declining productivity, budget deficits, unemployment, and inflation in the 1970s had helped open the debate on the wisdom of the welfare state. Also, private retirement programs and private medicine in the United States seemed to outperform their public sector counterparts. By 1980, privatization, deregulation, tax cuts, and less government spending led the agenda of democratically elected leaders in the United States and England.

One of the more troubling aspects of welfare programs was the adverse effects public subsidies had on work incentives, an important consideration in the value system of capitalism. Poor people who found low-paying jobs often could expect no significant improvement in living standards, because of lost welfare benefits. An important theme of welfare reform has been the search for ways to help families meet basic needs, without reducing incentives to take employment. "Workfare", rather than welfare, has been the keynote of proposals for welfare reform.

Perhaps the swelling ranks of women in the work force contributed to the idea that welfare recipients, often poor women with dependent children, should be expected to work. The Welfare Reform Act of 1988, enacted by the U.S. Congress, emphasized the workfare approach. This act required states to provide educational opportunities, job training, and job placement to recipients of Aid to Families with Dependent Children (AFDC). States must also provide one year of child care and medical coverage to families leaving the welfare rolls for the work force, and must extend welfare benefits to families with two parents when the primary income earner is unemployed. Formerly, most recipients to AFDC were single mothers.

In August 1996, a Republican-controlled Congress enacted, and President Clinton approved, another major welfare reform bill, the Work and Responsibility Act of 1996, that limits the number of years a person can receive welfare. Under this bill families must give up most of their benefits within two years unless the head of the family begins to work.

The emergence of the welfare state may have been a product of the competition between socialism and capitalism during the twentieth century, since many of the programs of the welfare state extended the advantages of socialism to the less-productive members of society. Another factor contributing to the growth of the welfare state lay in increased power of working classes in wartime economies that put a premium on cooperation. The tendency of societies to periodically redistribute income, to peaceably defuse class warfare, may also have played a role in the rise of the welfare state.

See also Social Insurance, Social Security, Thatcherism, Unemployment Insurance.

References Bruce, Maurice. *The Coming of the Welfare State* (1966); Koven, Seth, and Sonya Michel, eds. *Mothers of a New World: Maternalist Politics and the Origins of the Welfare States* (1993); McConnell, Campbell R., and Stanley L. Brue. *Economics* (1993); Mankiw, N. Gregory. *Principles of Economics* (1997).

Whitney, Eli (1765–1825)

Eli Whitney owes his fame to his invention of the cotton gin, but perhaps his greatest contribution to the development of capitalism lay in pioneering the development of interchangeable parts and mass production.

Whitney was born in Westborough, Massachusetts, on 8 December 1765, to a prosperous farm family. The oldest of four children, he attended local schools and spent much time in his father's shop, where he found a lathe and other tools for repairing farm implements. His interest in learning led him, at the age of 17, to become a schoolmaster. Since his education to that time had been primarily in the three Rs, he stayed up at night studying to keep ahead of his students, and learned enough arithmetic, Greek, and Latin to win admittance to Yale.

After graduation from Yale in 1792, Whitney took a position on the plantation of the late General Nathanael Green in Georgia. His work on the Greene plantation raised his awareness of the problem of separating cotton from cotton seed, and Whitney set to work to develop a machine that would perform this task. His efforts met with such success that, on 27 May 1793, he signed an agreement with the manager of the plantation to share the profits from his cotton gin. He built a shop in New Haven, Connecticut, to manufacture his cotton gins, and the Patent Office granted him a patent on 15 October 1793.

Although Whitney stood unchallenged as the inventor of the cotton gin, the device was too simple to enforce patent rights. Any smith or carpenter could easily manufacture a gin, and pirated copies were readily available. Litigation and legal fees absorbed what profits came to Whitney.

A quarrel between the United States and France in 1798 forced the U.S. government to take measure of its woefully inadequate facilities for manufacturing guns. Whitney made a proposal to the government to substantially increase the production of guns, using water-powered machinery. Until then, gunsmiths fashioned each gun separately, which was a slow process that made extensive use of skilled labor. Whitney proposed to develop machines that manufactured large numbers of each part separately, and with sufficient uniformity to make the parts interchangeable. Individual parts could then be chosen indiscriminately for assembly. Progress was slow. In 1801, two years beyond the contracted time, Whitney delivered 500 of the 4,000 muskets he owed the government. The government was pleased with the result, because of the convenience of interchangeable parts, making Whitney's guns easily disassembled, repaired, and reassembled.

Whitney's guns did not immediately eclipse traditional handcrafted guns, which, for a while, enjoyed a greater reputation for reliability. Even his interchangeable parts fell far short of modern standards of precision. They often needed a little hand-finishing in the assembly stage of production.

The impact of Whitney's achievement was soon felt in other industries. The New England clock industry found that water-powered lathes and other machinery could produce interchangeable parts for clocks, displacing the handicraft methods that had dominated clock manufacture. The accomplishments of large-scale capital enterprises seemed without end, because the production process was freed from the supply of skilled labor. Building on Whitney's accomplishment, Henry Ford built an automobile for the great multitudes, and capitalism entered a stage of mass consumption.

See also Entrepreneurship; Factory System;

Ford, Henry.

References Gies, Joseph, and Frances Gies. *The Ingenious Yankees* (1976); Green, Constance M. *Eli Whitney and the Birth of American Technology* (1956).

Wildcat Banks (United States)

During the pre–Civil War era, wildcat banks, although technically legal, abused the bank-note-issuing authority of state banks, issuing bank notes or paper money under circumstances that discouraged, or rendered impossible, conversion into gold and silver specie. The wildcat banks emerged in a banking system that allowed each bank to issue its own bank notes, which legitimate banks stood ready to redeem into gold and silver specie. As security for outstanding bank notes, state banking laws required banks to own federal or state government bonds and keep them on file at a state auditor's office. The First Bank of the United States and the Second Bank of the United States had helped maintain an honest currency by forcing western banks and country banks to redeem their bank notes in specie.

In 1833, the demise of the Second Bank of the United States left the banking system without an important safeguard against the temptation of bankers to issue bank notes in excess. Bank notes from distant localities circulated at varying discounts, depending on the likelihood of redemption into specie. Newspapers published lists of good notes and bad notes, and periodicals appeared that were exclusively devoted to the values of bank notes.

Wildcat banks were usually formed without buildings, offices, or furniture, and required minimal amounts of capital. A group of investors would purchase bonds, often state bonds selling at a discount, and file the bonds with a state auditor, who authorized the investors to start a bank. The investors possessed the engraved plates and dies that were used to print the bank notes, and often printed bank notes equaling two or three times the amount of the bonds filed with the state. In practice, the legal requirement that the state auditor countersign each bill did not act as a brake on the issuance of bank notes.

Investors were known to start up wildcat banks with only enough money to buy engraving plates and dies, and to pay the cost of printing up the bank notes. Investors arranged through brokers to pay for the bonds after they were delivered to the state auditor's office. The investors then brought the freshly printed bank notes to the auditor's office, had them countersigned, and used them to pay for the bonds.

Although bank notes were theoretically convertible into gold and silver specie, wildcat banks were put in places difficult to find. In some cases, an Indian guide was necessary to find what was no more than a shanty located on an Indian reservation. The accessibility of a wildcat bank determined the discount at which its bank notes traded. Brokers dispatched carpetbaggers to find remote banks and to demand the redemption of bank notes into specie. Some of the wildcat banks stationed lookouts that threatened and intimidated strangers who might be seeking redemption of bank notes.

In the early state of American capitalism, the supply of capital necessarily fell short of what was needed to exploit the virtually endless supply of natural resources. Wildcat banks contributed to mobilizing much-needed capital, but they cost the banking industry a bit of credibility with the public. Understanding the history that the banking industry has had to live down helps explain why the banking industry remains highly regulated.

See also Second Bank of the United States.

References Knox, John Jay. *A History of Banking in the United States* (1903); Rockoff, Hugh. "The Free Banking Era: A Reexamination." *Journal of Money, Credit and Banking* (1974).

Witte System (Russia)

Named for Sergei Witte, the Witte system stands among the first government-sponsored industrial revolutions in a poor, less-developed country. Witte is said to have "resembled the Bolsheviks in ruthlessness and his optimism." He promoted a form of state capitalism while serving as czarist minister of finance in late nineteenth-century Russia. Between 1890 and 1900, Russian industrial output doubled in value.

Sergei Witte took office as minister of finance on 11 September 1892. Russia was just recovering from a serious food famine, in 1891. His predecessor left a legacy of starving peasants and balanced budgets. A combination of high taxes and fiscal parsimony kept the budget balanced, but the famine of 1891 brought to light the heavy burden of taxation.

Witte outlined his views in his first budget report:

Government economy has its limits; refusing justified claims upon government can inflict serious difficulties upon the normal development of the civil and economic life of the country. Our fatherland overflows with all kinds of natural riches, but it has not yet utilized those riches in any desirable degree for the increase of its wealth. Financial policy should not fail to pay attention to the undesirable effects of excessive economy in meeting the growing demand, but should consider as its task giving reasonable assistance to the development of the productive forces of the country. Such a policy should give better results also in regard to the finance of the government and raise not only the welfare of the population but also its paying powers and increase the sources of government revenue.

The cornerstone of Witte's policy was the protectionist tariff of 1891. The tariff protected domestic manufactures from foreign competition, and discouraged imports. Reducing imports helped Russia to accumulate the gold reserves needed to adopt the gold standard, and the gold standard made Russian investments safer and more attractive in the eyes of foreign investors. Railroad construction was the mainspring in Witte's policies. The Siberian railroad was one among many railroad projects started and completed during Witte's tenure.

In a memorable budget report for 1893, Witte set the stage for national planning in industry. In 1897, a Marxist decried Witte's "bourgeois-bureaucratic-socialist" planning as "trespassing on socialist ground." In a secret memorandum to the czar in 1899, Witte wrote,

> The solicitude shown to various branches of industry, a new railroad, the discovery of a new field of enterprise—these and other measures, even if partial and of local application only, touch the entire ever more complicated network and upset the established equilibrium. Every measure of the government in regard to trade and industry now effects the entire economic organism and influences the course of its further development. In view off these facts, the Minister of Finance concludes that the country, which in one way or the other is nurtured by the commercial and industrial policy of the government, requires above all that this policy be carried out according to a definite plan, with strict system and continuity.

In the face of strong opposition, Witte put Russia on the gold standard in 1897. Once the ruble was convertible into gold, foreign capital flowed in. Opponents accused Witte of turning Russia into a colony of Europe. In a secret memorandum to the czar, Witte referred to the foreign investments as "a small leaven introduced in order to stimulate the sluggish energies of the Russian industrial community."

Witte drew further criticism for raising the heavy burden of taxation on an already overtaxed population. Various indirect taxes, such as taxes on sugar, matches, and kerosene, were raised by sizable percentages. In the name of discouraging alcohol consumption, the government gave itself a monopoly on the sale of vodka. Criticism of Witte's policies grew, until he had to resign as minister of finance in August 1903. The world by then was in the clutches of an industrial slump that struck Russia particularly hard. The inflow of foreign capital to finance railroad construction and internal improvements trailed off.

The government, which was the major consumer of Russian industrial products, reduced its orders. Critics charged that the domestic market could not sustain the enlarged industrial capacity. Witte had ignored agriculture, and agricultural income had shown no improvement under his policies, but the rural population bore the brunt of his extreme taxation.

The failures of the Witte system can be traced to the unbalanced growth between manufacturing and agriculture, the crushing burden of taxation, and the excessive dependence on government rather than individual initiative. The Witte system revealed the problems of forcing rapid industrialization within the framework of a capitalistic economy with backward agriculture and little savings.

See also Russian Industrial Society, Russian Tariff of 1891.

References Shann, Teodor. *Russia, 1905–1907* (1986); Laue, Theodore H. Von. *Sergei Witte and the Industrialization of Russia* (1963).

Works Progress Administration (United States)

The Works Progress Administration (WPA) was the largest of the programs of public employment during the Great Depression years in the United States. The high unemployment rates of the 1930s, ranging from 25 percent at the depths of the Depression to 17 percent on the eve of World War II, demonstrated to public officials the need for an employer of last resort. The WPA was the federal government's answer to that need.

British economist John Maynard Keynes, in his book *The General Theory of Employment, Interest, and Money*, wrote of the contribution programs of public employment make to economic prosperity:

> If the Treasury were to fill old bottles with bank notes, bury them at suitable depths in disused coal mines which are then filled up to the surface with town rubbish, and leave it to private enterprise on well-tried principles of laissez-faire, to dig the notes up again...there need be no more unemployment and, with the help of its repercussions, the real income of the community, and its capital wealth, also, would become a good deal greater than it is.... Ancient Egypt was doubly fortunate, and doubtless owed to this its fabled wealth, in that it possessed two activities, namely, pyramid-building as well as the search for the precious metals.... Two pyramids...are twice as good as one..., but not so two railways from London to York.

By 1935, the Roosevelt administration saw that some form of economic relief remained necessary, but hesitated to continue programs of cash relief. In the words of Roosevelt: "To dole out relief in this way is to administer a narcotic, a subtle destroyer of the human spirit." Congress passed the Emergency Relief Appropriation Act in 1935, which earmarked $4.8 billion for federal works projects. Roosevelt selected Harry Hopkins to direct the new Works Progress Administration program. Hopkins began with the philosophy that as much of the money as possible should be spent on wages, as opposed to raw materials and other costs.

The WPA lasted until 1943, and spent $11 billion, $8.8 billion of which went to bricks-and-mortar projects. Among the WPA accomplishments were 40,000 new buildings, 85,000 repaired buildings, 572,000 miles of improved rural roads, 78,000 new bridges, 67,000 miles of paved city streets, 24,000 miles of sidewalks, 350 new airports, and 8,000 landscaped parks. Sewage systems, water treatment plants, and drainage facilities also made popular WPA projects. WPA activities could be seen in virtually every community in the nation.

Perhaps the most controversial and innovative programs of the WPA provided support for artists, actors, musicians, and writers who met the criteria for relief. The Federal Arts Project adorned public buildings and community arts centers with 2,566 murals and 17,794 pieces of sculpture. The Federal Writers Project lent support to such budding authors as Saul Bellow, Richard Wright, Ralph Ellison, John Cheever, Nelson Algren, and Eudora Welty. It also collected folklore, and recorded the recollections of 2,000 ex-slaves. Hundreds of musicians found employment giving free public concerts with the Federal Musicians Project. The Federal Theater Project entertained 350,000 people per week with plays performed by needy actors.

The WPA kept up to 3 million people employed at a time. When the arms buildup of World War II caused a labor shortage, and unemployment fell to 1 percent, the government no longer felt public employment projects filled a need, and programs like the WPA disappeared. In the post–World War II era, the government experimented with modest public employment efforts, but the trend was away from programs that could not pass the private sector's test of profitability. By the mid-1980s, these programs had disappeared. If the world capitalist economic system suffers another major collapse like the 1930s, the government may again be needed as an employer of last resort.

See also Great Depression.

References Badger, Anthony J. *The New Deal: The Depression Years, 1933–1940* (1989); Biles, Roger. *A New Deal for the American People* (1991).

World Bank

The World Bank (officially the International Bank for Reconstruction and Development) plays a major role in mobilizing capital for development projects in Third-World countries, serving as a clearinghouse of ideas for promoting economic development, and publishing statistical data and research on the state of the world economy.

In addition to negotiating a fixed exchange rate system for international trade, the Bretton Woods Conference of 1944 organized the World Bank as an arm of the United Nations. The delegates of the Bretton Woods Conference had in mind the reconstruction needs of wartorn Europe and Japan, and the development needs of the less-developed areas of the world. On 25 June 1946, the bank opened its headquarters in Washington, D.C. Member countries furnished subscriptions of capital to the World Bank, which also raises capital by selling bonds in private capital markets. Since the bonds are guaranteed by member governments, they bear relatively low interest rates, lowering the cost of capital to the bank.

The first quarter-century of the bank saw an emphasis on financing basic economic infrastructure needed to support industry. Between fiscal years 1961 and 1965, electric power and transportation projects accounted for 76.8 percent of the bank's lending. The bank continued to extend substantial loans to developed countries until 1967. After Robert McNamara assumed the presidency in 1968, the bank began to channel more resources into projects that directly relieve poverty, increasing bank lending on agriculture and rural development projects, from 18.1 percent in fiscal year 1968 to 31 percent in fiscal year 1981.

In 1960, the International Development Association (IDA) was created as a division of the bank. This organization makes soft loans (loans that charge modest interest in light of the risks), and interest-free loans to the poorest countries that cannot qualify for loans from the World Bank, whose lending philosophy is more conservative. Also affiliated with the World Bank is the International Financial Corporation (IFC), created in 1956 to raise private capital for financing private-sector projects. The loans of the IFC are structured on a commercial basis, with maturities ranging from seven to 12 years.

During the 1960s and 1970s, the World Bank financed public enterprises, but, in the 1980s, the bank reaffirmed its commitment to financing private-sector projects. The bank has used its leadership to strengthen the private sector in Third-World countries, and to promote privatization of public enterprises.

The World Bank is perhaps the foremost leader on economic development issues. In 1978, the World Bank began publishing the influential *World Development Report*, combining articles on current development issues and a statistical report of economic indicators for the nations of the world.

In the past, businesses and governments in less-developed areas enlisted the services of prestigious merchant bankers, such as Morgan, Barings, or Rothchild, to meet their financing needs. The World Bank and similar organizations are not only necessary to mobilize the volume of capital needed in less-developed areas, but are also more disinterested and public-spirited in their motives. Although they pressure governments to follow economically sound policies, they are free from the suspicion of using the power of finance for political advantage or private gain.

See also Bretton Woods System, Merchant Bankers.

References Ayres, Robert L. *Banking on the Poor: The World Bank and World Poverty* (1983); Polak, Jacques J. *The World Bank and the International Monetary Fund: A Changing Relationship* (1994).

Yellow-Dog Contracts

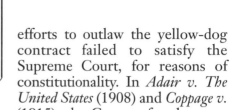

The term "yellow-dog contract" came to represent agreements that workers made with employers not to join a union. Employers made these contracts a condition of employment. The purpose of the contracts was not to give employers grounds for firing workers who joined unions; employers did not need a reason for firing nonunion workers. However, yellow-dog contracts put union organizers in the position of persuading workers to break a contract. Employers found in these contracts a powerful lever for putting union organizers on the wrong side of the law. Yellow-dog contracts ranked among the more effective antiunion weapons in the hands of employers in the United States before 1932.

In 1898, Congress passed the Erdman Act, which prohibited yellow-dog contracts with railroad workers. Numerous states passed laws to protect union organizers from yellow-dog contracts. Early efforts to outlaw the yellow-dog contract failed to satisfy the Supreme Court, for reasons of constitutionality. In *Adair v. The United States* (1908) and *Coppage v. Kansas* (1915), the Court refused to uphold the constitutionality of anti-yellow-dog contracts. These contracts were interpreted as infringements of the freedom of contract. In the 1917 *Hitchman Coal and Coke* case, the Supreme Court upheld the issuance of injunctions against unions organizing workers bound by yellow-dog contracts. The use of injunctions where yellow-dog contracts were involved became a powerful weapon for thwarting the organizing efforts of unions.

The Norris-La Guardia Act, passed in 1932, effectively ended the use of the yellow-dog contract.

References Brooks, Thomas R. *Toil and Trouble: A History of American Labor* (1971); Gregory, Charles O. *Labor and the Law* (1958, with 1961 supplement).

Zaibatsu (Japan)

The Japanese word *zaibatsu* translates as "money-clique." The zaibatsu were the huge financial combines that grew to economic prominence in late nineteenth-century Japan. These combines dominated the advanced-capitalistic sector of the Japanese economy until the end of World War II, when the Occupation forces dissolved them. The zaibatsu in Japan belong in the same class of business organizations as trusts and other monopolistic combinations that marked the era of finance capitalism in Germany and the United States.

In the 1930s, four zaibatsu (Mitsui, Mitsubishi, Sumitomo, and Yasuda) penetrated, and often dominated, every sector in the Japanese economy. Despite a corporate organization, zaibatsu were family businesses. At the apex of the zaibatsu was a family partnership that owned all the capital in a holding company. This holding company controlled a group of subsidiaries. In the case of Mitsui, the largest zaibatsu, 11 families, all descended from the founder of the firm, shared ownership. The securities of the subsidiary businesses constituted the assets of the zaibatsu. In turn, the zaibatsu controlled the appointment of directors and managers in the subsidiary businesses. The Mitsui zaibatsu owned all, or controlling, interest in Mitsui Bank, Mitsui Bussan, Mitsui Mining, Mitsui Trust, Toshin Warehouse, and Mitsui Life Insurance. Each of these concerns owned controlling interest in many companies. Again, control was exercised through the appointment of directors and managers. For instance, Mitsui Bussan owned subsidiaries from the following industries: rayon, flour-milling, cotton merchanting, engineering, electrical apparatus, loom, condensed milk, marine and fire insurance, and oil refining. Each of these companies also owned and controlled subsidiaries, giving the zaibatsu a pyramid organization.

All zaibatsu boasted one or more important subsidiaries engaged in banking and finance. In Japan of the 1930s, the public invested primarily in fixed-interest bank deposits, rather than corporate securities. Large-scale enterprises could only raise capital by selling securities to banks and other financial institutions. By controlling banking and financial subsidiaries, zaibatsu mobilized capital to finance undertakings of industrial and commercial subsidiaries. Zaibatsu controlled four of the six major banks in Japan in the 1930s. Zaibatsu trust companies held nearly 70 percent of all Japanese trust deposits. The influence of the zaibatsu banks and financial institutions was very directly felt on the industrial development of Japan. Zaibatsu gained control over small companies by extending credit, in return for receiving monopoly rights to market their product.

Government aided the rise of the zaibatsu, conferring important benefits and concessions. On the other hand, the zaibatsu stood ready to raise capital and other resources the government needed in times of war and stress. Whenever Japan went to war, the zaibatsu won huge profits.

In post-World War II Japan, the Occupation authorities created the Holding Company Liquidation Commission, which was charged with terminating family ownership of the zaibatsu, and dissolving the holding companies. Nineteen of the largest holding companies in Japan were dissolved. The Anti-Monopoly Law of 1947 was intended to block any tendencies toward monopolistic concentration. After the Peace Treaty of 1952, Japan repealed the Anti-Monopoly Law, and industrial combinations emerged again, each affiliated with a favored bank. Close linkages between banks, government, and industry have remained a trademark of Japanese capitalism.

See also Finance Capitalism; Holding Companies; Morgan, John Pierpont.

References Allen, G. C. "The Concentration of Economic Control in Japan." *The Economic Journal* (1937); Fruin, Mark. *The Japanese Enterprise System: Competitive Strategies and Cooperative Structures*

(1992); Halliday, Jon. *A Political History of Japanese Capitalism* (1975); Lockwood, William. *The Economic Development of Japan* (1954).

Zollverein (Germany)

The German Zollverein was a nineteenth-century free-trade union of German states. Free trade prevailed between members of the Zollverein, and a common tariff wall protected member industries against imports from nonmember industries. The formation of the Zollverein puts Germany in a unique category in the history of capitalism. It is the only instance of a capitalist country achieving economic unification before political unification.

At the beginning of the nineteenth century, a medley of German states, dukedoms, and municipalities awaited political and economic unification into a modern nation-state. These were the last remnants of the Holy Roman Empire, which Voltaire described as being "neither Holy, nor Roman, nor an Empire." The flow of trade struggled against approximately 1,800 different customs barriers. Trade within Prussia suffered the constriction of 67 different local tariffs.

Prussia began moving toward free internal trade during the Napoleonic era, when European trade was controlled. In 1818, after the defeat of France, Prussia abolished internal trade barriers and erected an external tariff wall, which allowed agricultural products to enter duty-free, and placed an average of 10-percent tariff on imported manufactured goods. The protection afforded domestic manufactures was modest. Adam Smith's ideas of free trade were influential in Germany at that time.

The protectionist policies of England, France, and Russia may have been the driving force of the free-trade movement in Germany. These countries were turning away exports from German states, and German exports were in search of new markets. Also, petty German states could retaliate against the trade restrictions of the major powers by raising their own tariff barriers, but this policy was ineffective, because each state protected such a small market. Only an economically unified Germany could retaliate with trade restrictions that could force the other powers to come to terms.

In 1828, the smaller German states formed the South German Union. Also in 1828, Prussia signed a treaty with Hesse, combining those two countries into the Northern Customs Union. By 1834, an agreement was reached to unite these two unions and several individual states into the Customs Union (Zollverein). Additional states joined the union into the 1850s. By the 1840s, the Zollverein had acquired an international status.

The Zollverein followed a policy of tariff reduction until after the Franco-Prussian War. The economic unification of Germany then became official political unification. Under Bismarck's leadership, the Zollverein, in 1879, turned to a policy of protection, and tariffs went up to give manufactures more protection. Agriculture also enjoyed tariff protection.

Protectionist trends in Germany, along with more competition from America, gave impetus to protectionist sentiment in Austria, France, and Russia. Central Europe remained protectionist until the outbreak of World War I.

The history of the Zollverein and the unification of Germany give credence to the view that the rise of the nation-state and the rise of capitalism are closely related. In Germany's case, the economic unification led to political unification. The Zollverein was a trailblazer in the formation of customs unions, which is still an ongoing activity. The European Union and the North American Free Trade Agreement are current examples. These unions, however, are unlikely to lead to political unification.

See also European Economic Community.

References Ashley, Percy. *Modern Tariff History: Germany, United States, and France* (1970); Henderson, O. *The Zollverein* (1959); Knowles, L. C. A. *Economic Development in the Nineteenth Century* (1932).

Chronology

1492 Columbus discovers New World.

1494 First textbook treatment of double-entry bookkeeping.

1498 Vasco Da Gama reaches India.

1519 Ferdinand Magellan departs for circumnavigation of Earth.

1531 Antwerp builds a new bourse that becomes a model for bourses in Amsterdam and London.

1536 Poor Law in England requires local parishes to take care of the indigent.

Clerks Act in England describes the steps to be followed to obtain a patent.

1540 Peak in inflation from influx of precious metals from New World.

1542 Beginning of Great Debasement in England, which lasts until 1551.

1551 Beginning of English trade depression of late 1500s.

1557 European Financial Crisis of 1557 is sparked by bankruptcies of Spanish crown.

1563 Statute of Artificers subjects English labor market to detailed regulation.

1566 Construction begins on Royal Exchange in London.

1572 Dealers in financial securities are required to have royal approval in France.

1597 Dutch first reach East Indies.

1600 East India Company established in England.

1609 Bank of Amsterdam established.

1613 Amsterdam builds its own bourse.

1619 First African slaves are brought to colony of Virginia.

1620 Beginning of European Economic Crisis of 1600s.

1624 Statute of Monopolies in England bans monopolies created by royal decree, except for patented new inventions and monopolies of foreign trade.

1637 Tulip market crumbles in Holland, ending the tulipmania speculation.

1651 English Navigation Act restricts most English trade to English ships.

1661 Riksbank in Sweden becomes first European bank to issue paper money.

1673 French Code of Commerce imposes system of detailed mercantile regulations on industry.

1685 Revocation of Edict of Nantes causes many Huguenots to emigrate from France, taking valuable skills and capital with them.

1692 Edward Lloyd moves his coffeehouse, frequented by London insurance underwriters, to Lombard Street.

1694 Bank of England established.

1703 Peter the Great lays foundation for a fort in area that will become St. Petersburg.

1705 English Bankruptcy Act of 1705 recognizes concept of "honest bankrupts."

1714 London stockjobbers in coffeehouses of Exchange Alley begin posting lists of stock prices.

1717 In England, Sir Thomas Coke begins attracting visitors to his farm that uses scientific methods.

1719 Financial speculation and banking debacle in France known as Mississippi Bubble.

1720 South Sea Bubble bursts, ending speculative frenzy in London stock market.

Bubble Act in England restricts formation of joint-stock companies.

1733 Sir John Barnard's Act outlaws "wagers, puts, and refusals" on the London stock market.

1750 English enclosure movement enters most intensive phase.

1763 Beginning of depression of late eighteenth century.

1769 James Watt applies for first patent for steam engine.

English Parliament makes destruction of a building housing machinery a felony punishable by death.

1750 English Iron Act, intended to stifle iron industry in American colonies.

1775 Continental Congress authorizes issuance of continentals, which lead to hyperinflation in American Colonies.

1776 Adam Smith publishes *An Inquiry into the Nature and Causes of the Wealth of Nations*, which denounces government-regulated economies in favor of laissez-faire capitalism.

1786 Anglo-French Commercial Treaty substantially reduces trade barriers.

1787 Constitutional Convention drafts Constitution of the United States, and submits it to 13 states for ratification.

1789 Beginning of French Revolution that sweeps away feudalism in France.

Governing assembly of French Revolution begins issuing assignats, which become a source of hyperinflation.

U.S. government enacts tariff as main source of tax revenue.

1790 Samuel Slater's first textile mill begins operation in United States.

U.S. Congress enacts first patent act to protect inventors.

U.S. Congress charters First Bank of the United States.

1791 National Assembly in France enacts the Le Chapelier Law, banning worker coalitions.

1792 In New York, 24 brokers organize themselves as a group of traders specializing in financial instruments.

1793 French Navigation Act restricts most French trade to French ships.

Government in France initiates system of price controls to control hyperinflation, but without success.

1794 Prussian common law recognizes the responsibility of government to provide work and to protect the poor.

1797 Unlawful Oaths Act in England gives the government another legal weapon for the suppression of labor organizations.

1799–1800 English Combination Acts of 1799 and 1800 ban trade unions.

1800 Bank of France established.

1806 Napoleon inaugurates Continental System against England that lasts until 1815.

1807 Jeffersonian embargo in United States accelerates domestic industrialization.

1811 Luddites destroy textile frames in a machine-smashing riot.

1819 English Factory Act forbids employment of children under nine in cotton mills.

1824 English Parliament repeals Combination Acts.

1825 England claims credit for first public railroad.

1830 Beginning of bourgeois monarchy in France, which lasts until 1848.

1831 Uprising of Lyon silk workers helps give birth to idea of working-class revolution.

1832 Reform Act of 1832 changes composition of English Parliament in favor of industrial capitalists and middle classes, at expense of landed aristocracy.

President Andrew Jackson vetoes the charter renewal of Second Bank of the United States, beginning an era of free banking in the United States.

1834 Formation of Grand Consolidated Trade Union, the first effort to unite English workers of all trades into one movement.

Poor Law Amendment in England restricts relief to poor and demands that recipients work in workhouses.

Beginning of the Zollverein, a free-trade block of German states.

1842 England first enacts income tax on a permanent basis.

1844 Bank Charter Act of 1844 is first step in giving Bank of England monopoly on issuance of paper money.

1846 Repeal of Corn Laws in England begins an English policy of free trade that lasts to 1930s.

1848 Publication of Manifesto of the Communist Party.

Revolutions of 1848, which begin as unstable alliances of middle classes and working classes, and end with working classes feeling betrayed.

1853 Commodore Perry opens up Japan.

1854 In England, Sir Henry Bessemer applies for a patent on his new method of producing steel.

English Parliament abolishs usury law.

1856 Joint Companies Act establishes idea of limited liability in English company law.

1857 Financial Panic of 1857.

1859 Molestation of Workmen Act in England legalizes peaceful picketing.

1860 Anglo-French Commercial Treaty of 1860 marks a sharp break with protectionism.

Unification of Italy.

1861 Emancipation Edict in Russia ends serfdom.

1863 President Lincoln issues Emancipation Proclamation, freeing slaves in secessionist states.

England adopts first effective air pollution legislation, the Alkali Act.

1864 Organization of International Workingmen's Associations.

1868 Meiji era of rapid modernization begins in Japan.

1869 England abolishes imprisonment of debtors.

Knights of Labor begin as a secret society.

1870 Beginning of golden age of the gold standard, which lasts until 1914.

1871 Trade Union Act of 1871 gives English trade unions a safe legal status, but leaves some activities outside the protection of the law.

Employer Liability Act in Germany protects workers from work-related injuries.

In the Paris Commune of 1871, working class leaders briefly seize control of the government.

1873 Financial Panic of 1873.

Beginning of European depression in late 1800s.

1878 Germany enacts Anti-Socialist Law that virtually bans trade unions.

1879 German Tariff of 1879 ends a trend toward free trade in Europe.

1880 Beginning of the era of New Imperialism that lasts until 1914.

1882 Bank of Japan established.

1883 Accident Insurance Law and Sickness Insurance Law in Germany provides compulsory insurance of workers for injury and sickness.

1885 Contracts of indentured servitude outlawed in United States.

1886 Formation of American Federation of Labor in United States.

1889 Second International forms as an organization of trade unions and socialist organizations with Marxist philosophies.

1890 Sherman Antitrust Act bans trusts and monopolizing behavior in the United States.

French government ends use of the livret, a worker identification passbook required of all workers since the French Revolution.

McKinley Tariff in United States substantially increases tariff protection.

1891 Russian Tariff of 1891 generalizes trend toward protectionism in world economy.

Mogul Steam Ship case in England undermines common law prohibitions on restraints of trade, encouraging the growth of monopolistic business practices.

1892 Meline Tariff in France substantially increases tariff protection.

1894 New Zealand enacts minimum wage legislation.

Pullman Strike of railway workers that is ruthlessly quashed by federal authorities.

1895 First meeting of National Association of Manufactures in Cincinnati, Ohio.

1897 In *Trans-Missouri Freight Association* case, U.S. Supreme Court rules price fixing illegal under Sherman Antitrust Act.

1898 U.S. government adopts first permanent bankruptcy law.

Merger wave in United States reaches a peak, with 63 mergers in one year.

1899 London Dock Strike, a major victory for unskilled workers.

1903 Henry Ford launches Ford Motor Company.

1905 Russian Uprising of 1905 marks the beginning of major working-class agitation in Russia.

1906 Food and Drug Act marks major departure from laissez-faire in United States.

After winning 29 seats in Parliament,

the Labor Representation Committee renames itself the Labor Party, in England.

1909 Labor Exchange Act in England creates state employment offices.

1911 U.S. Supreme Court holds Standard Oil in violation of antitrust laws, leading to the breakup of Standard Oil into 34 different companies.

Unemployment Insurance Act in England provides for compensation to unemployed workers.

1913 Federal Reserve Act establishes central banking system in United States.

United States adopts income tax.

1914 Ludlow massacre of families of striking miners in southern Colorado.

1916 Beginning of hyperinflation in Russia that lasts through Revolution.

1918 United States adopts excess profits tax that lasts until 1921.

1922 Beginning of hyperinflation in Germany that lasts through 1923.

1929 New York stock market crash, and beginning of the Great Depression that lasts until beginning of World War II.

1930 Smoot-Hawley Tariff in United States sparks trade war.

1932 England ends nearly a century-old policy of free trade, with Import Duties Act.

Norris-La Guardia Act in United States ends use of yellow-dog contracts.

1933 Agricultural Adjustment Act in United States increases government intervention in agriculture.

Glass-Steagall Banking Act in United States increases regulation of banking.

1934 Securities Exchange Act in United

State subjects stock market to significant regulation to protect investors from speculative practices.

1935 Creation of Works Progress Administration, a Depression-era public works program in the United States.

Social Security Act begins era of social insurance in United States.

National Labor Relations Act protects right of workers to organize and bargain collectively in United States.

1936 Robinson-Patman Act in United States seeks to prevent large chain stores from extracting discounts from suppliers that small businesses cannot extract.

1937 Unionization of pivotal U.S. Steel Company in the United States.

1938 Fair Labor Standards Act in United States establishes minimum wage, and bans child labor.

Formation of Congress of Industrial Organizations in United States.

1944 Creation of Bretton Woods international monetary system, including International Monetary Fund and World Bank.

1946 British government establishes welfare state, with a far-reaching program of nationalization of basic industry, and expands social programs, including socialized medicine.

Full Employment Act of 1946 commits U.S. government to maintaining full employment.

Formation of International Whaling Commission, an organization committed to conserving whales.

1947 Taft-Hartley Act in United States bans unfair labor practices by unions and union organizers.

Formation of General Agreement on Tariffs and Trade, an international organization devoted to lowering trade barriers in foreign trade.

United States implements Marshall Plan to rebuild wartorn economies of Europe.

1956 Restrictive Trade Practices Act of 1956 marks end of English toleration of many monopolistic business practices.

1958 Formation of European Economic Community.

1959 Landrum-Griffin Act in United States targets antidemocratic practices in union governance.

1963 First Clean Air Act adopted in United States.

1964 Revenue Act of 1964 in United States slashes taxes as a measure of economic stimulation.

1970 First Clean Water Act adopted in United States.

Occupational Health and Safety Act in United States gives government authority to protect workers from unsafe work environments.

1971 Dollar crisis leads to end of gold standard in international trade.

1972 Consumer Products Safety Act in United States establishes agency to protect consumers from unsafe products.

Equal Employment Act in United States outlaws employment discrimination based upon age, race, religion, or sex.

Marine Animal Protection Act enacted in United States, largely to protect dolphins.

Stockholm Declaration calls for individual countries to refrain from activities that damage the environment of areas beyond their national jurisdiction.

1973 Beginning of era of stagflation that lasts until 1981.

1978 Airline Deregulation Act in United States brings free-market competition to airline fares.

1979 Margaret Thatcher elected prime minister in English Parliament, and begins a capitalist revolution in England.

1980 Depository Institutions Deregulation and Monetary Control Act in United States partially deregulates banking industry.

Motor Carrier Act in United States deregulates trucking freight rates.

1981 U.S. government decontrols domestic crude oil prices.

Economic Recovery Act in United States substantially scales down taxes.

1983 President Mitterand abandons socialist agenda and shifts to free-market, anti-inflation polices in France.

1987 President Reagan appoints Privatization Commission in United States to target public activities that could more efficiently be carried out by the private sector.

1988 Beginning of savings and loan debacle in United States.

1993 North American Free Trade Agreement establishes a free-trade area in Canada, Mexico, and United States.

1996 United States adopts welfare reform that limits the number of years a person can receive most welfare benefits.

1997 British Labor Party, shorn of socialist ideology and strong labor union connections, gains power for the first time in 18 years.

Great Britain hands over the colony of Hong Kong to the government of mainland China.

Bibliography

Abraham, Richard. *Rosa Luxemburg: A Life for the International.* New York: St. Martin's Press, 1989.

Acheson, A. L. K. *Bretton Woods Revisited.* Toronto: University of Toronto Press, 1972.

Addy, John. *The Agrarian Revolution.* London: Longman Group, 1972.

Alexander, John K. *The Selling of the Constitution: A History of Newspaper Coverage.* Madison, WI: Madison House, 1990.

Alkhafaji, Abbass F. *Restructuring American Corporations: Causes, Effects, and Implications.* New York: Quorum Books, 1990.

Allen, G. C. "The Concentration of Economic Control in Japan." *Economic Journal* 47, no. 186 (June 1937): 271–286.

Allen, James B. *The Company Town in the American West.* Norman, OK: University of Oklahoma Press, 1966.

Allen, James S. *World Monopoly and Peace.* New York: International Publishers, 1946.

Allen, Shelia, and Carole Truman, editors. *Women in Business: Perspectives on Women Entrepreneurs.* New York: Routledge, 1993.

Aminzade, Ronald. *Class, Politics, and Early Industrial Capitalism: A Study of Mid-Nineteenth Century Toulouse, France.* Albany, NY: State University of New York Press, 1981.

Anisimov, Evgenii V. *The Reforms of Peter the Great: Progress Through Coercion In Russia.* Translated by John T. Alexander. London: M. E. Sharp, 1993.

Appleyard, Dennis R., and Alfred J. Field, Jr. *International Economics.* Homewood, IL: Richard D. Irwin, 1992.

Ashley, Percy. *Modern Tariff History: Germany, United States, and France.* New York: Howard Fertig, 1970.

Ashton, T. S. *Economic Fluctuations in England, 1700–1800.* Oxford: Oxford University Press, 1959.

———. *The Industrial Revolution, 1760–1830.* New York: Oxford University Press, 1964.

Atack, Jeremy, and Peter Passel. *A New Economic View of American History from Colonial Times to 1940.* New York: W. W. Norton, 1994.

Ayres, Robert L. *Banking on the Poor: The World Bank and World Poverty.* Cambridge, MA: MIT Press, 1983.

Badger, Anthony J. *The New Deal: The Depression Years, 1933–1940.* New York: Hill & Wang, 1989.

Bagehot, Walter. *Lombard Street.* 1873. Reprint, Homewood, IL: Richard D. Irwin, 1962.

Baker, Ray Stannard. *Woodrow Wilson: Life and Letters.* Vol. 4, 1938. Reprint. New York: Greenwood Press, 1968.

Bibliography

Baklanoff, Eric N. *Expropriation of U.S. Investments in Cuba, Mexico, and Chile.* New York: Praeger, 1975.

Barnes, Donald G. *A History of the English Corn Laws,* 1930. Reprint. New York: Augustus M. Kelley, 1961.

Barrett, Don C. *The Greenbacks and Resumption of Specie Payments, 1862–1879.* Cambridge, MA: Harvard University Press, 1931.

Barth, James R. *The Great Savings and Loan Debacle.* Washington, DC: AEI Press, 1991.

Baruch, Bernard M. *The Making of the Reparation and Economic Sections of the Treaty,* 1920. Reprint. New York: Howard Fertig, 1970.

Batchelor, Ray. *Henry Ford, Mass Production, Modernism, and Design.* New York: St. Martin's Press, 1994.

Baumol, William J. "Entrepreneurship, Productive, Unproductive, and Destructive." *Journal of Political Economy* 98, no. 5 (October 1990): 893–921.

Baye, Michael R., and Dennis W. Jansen. *Money, Banking, and Financial Markets: An Economics Approach.* Boston: Houghton Mifflin, 1995.

Beales, H. L. "The 'Great Depression' in Industry and Trade." In *Essays in Economic History,* edited by E. M. Carus-Wilson, pp. 406–415. London: Edward Arnold, 1954.

Beard, Charles. *An Economic Interpretation of the Constitution.* New York: Macmillan, 1913.

Beard, Miriam. *History of the Business Man.* New York: Macmillan, 1938.

Bell, Walter G. *The Great Fire in London in 1666,* 1920. Reprint. Westport, CT: Greenwood Press, 1971.

Benjamin, Daniel, and Levis Kochin. "Searching for an Explanation of Unemployment in Interwar Britain." *Journal of Political Economy* 87 (June 1979): 441–478.

Berber, Peter L. *The Capitalism Revolution: Fifty Propositions About Prosperity, Equality, and Liberty.* New York: Basic Books, 1986.

Bernhard, Richard C. "English Law and American Law on Monopolies and Restraints of Trade." *Journal of Economics and Law* 3 (October 1960): 136–145.

Bezucha, Robert J. *The Lyon Uprising of 1834: Social and Political Conflict in the Early July Monarchy.* Cambridge, MA: Harvard University Press, 1974.

Biles, Roger. *A New Deal for the American People.* Dekalb, IL: Northern Illinois Press, 1991.

Blaisdell, Donald C. *European Financial Control in the Ottoman Empire.* New York: AMS Press, 1966.

Blaug, Mark. *Economic History and the History of Economics.* New York: New York University Press, 1986.

Blinder, Alan S. *Economic Policy and the Great Stagflation.* New York: Academic Press, 1979.

Board of Governors of the Federal Reserve System. *The Federal Reserve System: Purposes and Functions.* Washington, DC, 1984.

Bordo, Michael D., and Forrest Capie. *Monetary Regimes in Transition.* Cambridge, UK: Cambridge University Press, 1993.

Born, Karl Erich. *International Banking in the 19th and 20th Centuries.* Translated by Volker R. Berghahn. New York: St. Martin's Press, 1983.

Bowden, Peter J. *The Wool Trade in Tudor and Stuart England.* New York: St. Martin's Press, 1962.

Bowers, David A. *An Introduction to Business Cycles and Forecasting.* Reading, MA: Addison-Wesley, 1985.

Braudel, Fernand. *Civilization of Capitalism: 15th–18th Century,* 3 vols. Translated by Sian Reynolds. New York: Harper & Row, 1979.

———. *The Mediterranean: and the Mediterranean World in the Age of Phillip II.* Vols. 1–2. Translated by Sian Reynolds. New York: Harper & Row, 1972.

Braum, Hans-Joachim. *The German Economy in the Twentieth Century.* New York: Routledge, 1990.

Brigham, Eugene F. *Fundamentals of Financial Management*. 5th ed. Chicago: Dryden Press, 1989.

Brock, Gerald W. "The Regulatory Change in Telecommunications: The Dissolution of AT&T." In *Regulatory Reform: What Actually Happened*, edited by Leonard W. Weiss and Michael W. Klass., pp. 210–233. Boston: Little, Brown, 1986.

Brooks, Thomas R. *Toil and Trouble: A History of American Labor*. New York: Delacorte Press, 1971.

Brown, Anthony. *Lloyd's of London*. New York: Stein and Day, 1974.

Brown, Robert E. *Charles Beard and the Constitution: A Critical Analysis of "An Economic Interpretation of the Constitution."* Princeton, NJ: Princeton University Press, 1956.

Bruce, Maurice. *The Coming of the Welfare State*. Revised. New York: Schocken Books, 1966.

Bruck, W. F. *Social and Economic History of Germany from Wilhelm II to Hitler, 1888–1938*, 1938. Reprint. New York: Russell & Russell, 1962.

Bruno, Michael, and Jeffrey D. Sachs. *Economics of World Wide Stagflation*. Cambridge, MA: Harvard University Press, 1985.

Burns, Joseph M. *A Treatise on Markets*. Washington DC: AEI, 1979.

Burstein, Paul, editor. *Equal Employment Opportunity: Labor Market Discrimination and Public Policy*. Hawthorne, NY: Aldine de Gruyter, 1994.

Caldwell, Lynton Keith. *International Environmental Policy*. 2nd ed. Durham, NC: Duke University Press, 1990.

Calomiris, Charles W., and Larry Schweikart. "The Panic of 1857: Origins, Transmission, and Containment." *Journal of Economic History* 51, no. 4 (1991): 807–834.

Cameron, Rondo, in collaboration with Olga Crisp, Hugh Patrick, and Richard Tilly. *Banking in the Early Stages of Industrialization*. London: Oxford University Press, 1967.

Carosso, Vincent P. *The Morgans: Private International Bankers, 1854–1913*. Cambridge, MA: Harvard University Press, 1987.

Carswell, John. *The South Sea Bubble*. London: Cresset Press, 1960.

Cartter, Allan M., and F. Ray Marshall. *Labor Economics: Wages, Employment, and Trade Unionism*. Homewood, IL: Richard D. Irwin, 1967.

Chiu, Stephen W.K., K. C. Ho, and Tai-lok Lui. *City States in the Global Economy: Industrial Restructuring in Hong Kong and Singapore*. Boulder, CO: Westview Press, 1997.

Clapham, J. H. *An Economic History of Modern Britain*, 1930. Reprint, London: Cambridge University Press, 1951.

Clapp, B. W., H. E. S. Fisher, and A. R. J. Jurica. *Documents in English History: England From 1000–1760*. London: G. Bell & Sons, 1977.

Clark, Gordon L. *Unions and Communities Under Siege*. Cambridge, UK: Cambridge University Press, 1989.

Clough, Shepard Bancroft. *European Economic History: The Economic Development of Western Civilization*. New York: McGraw-Hill, 1968.

———. *France: A History of National Economics, 1789–1939*. New York: Octagon Books, 1964.

———. *The Economic History of Modern Italy*. New York: Columbia University Press, 1964.

Coghlan, Richard. "The Wave Is Your Friend." *Barons* 73, no. 23 (June 7, 1993): 18–19.

Cole, Charles Woolsey. *Colbert and a Century of French Mercantilism*. Hamden, CT: Archon Books, 1964.

Cole, G. D. H. *A Short History of the British Working Class Movement, 1789–1947*. 1948. Reprint, London: George Allen & Unwin, 1960.

Cole, G. D. H., and A. W. Filson. *British Working Class Movements: Selected Documents, 1789–1875*. New York: St. Martin's Press, 1965.

Bibliography

Cole, H. S. D., et. al., editors. *Models of Doom*. New York: Universe Books, 1973.

Coleman, Peter J. *Debtors and Creditors in America: Imprisonment for Debt, and Bankruptcy, 1607–1900*. Madison, WI: State Historical Society of Wisconsin, 1974.

Collingham, H. A. C. *The July Monarchy: A Political History of France, 1830–1848*. New York: Longman, 1988.

Constitution of the United States. 1789.

Court, W. H. B. *British Economic History, 1870–1914*. Cambridge, UK: Cambridge University Press, 1965.

Cowles, Virginia. *The Rothschilds: A Family of Fortune*. New York: Alfred A. Knopf, 1973.

Cox, Oliver C. *The Foundations of Capitalism*. New York: Philosophical Library, 1959.

Craig, J. *The Mint: A History of the London Mint from AD 287 to 194*. Cambridge, UK: Cambridge University Press, 1953.

Crumbly, D., and Craig E. Reese, editors. *Readings in the Crude Oil Windfall Profits Tax*. Tulsa, OK: PenWell Books, 1982.

Curran, Kenneth James. *Excess Profits Taxation*. Washington, DC: American Council on Public Affairs, 1943.

Curtin, Philip D. *The Atlantic Slave Trade*. Madison, WI: University of Wisconsin Press, 1969.

Daniels, John D., and Lee H. Radebaugh. *International Business*. 8th ed. Reading, MA: Addison-Wesley, 1998.

Dasgupta, A. K., *Phases of Capitalism and Economic Theory and Other Essays*. Oxford, UK: Oxford University Press, 1983.

Daunton, Martin. *Progress and Poverty: An Economic and Social History of Britain, 1700–1850*. Oxford, UK: Oxford University Press, 1995.

Davidson, Miles H. *Columbus Then and Now: A Life Reexamined*. Norman, OK: University of Oklahoma Press, 1997.

Davies, Glyn. *A History of Money from Ancient Times to the Present Day*. Cardiff, UK: University of Wales Press, 1994.

Davis, Clarence B., and Kenneth E.

Wilburn, Jr., editors. *Railway Imperialism*. Westport, CT: Greenwood Press, 1991.

Dawson, William Harbutt. *Bismarck and State Socialism*. London: Swan Sonnenschein, 1890.

De Roover, Raymond. *The Rise and Decline of the Medici Bank, 1397–1494*. New York: W. W. Norton, 1966.

De Schweinitz, Karl. *England's Road to Social Security from the Statute of Laborers in 1349 to the Beveridge Report of 1942*. New York: A. S. Barnes, 1961.

De Vries, Margaret Garritsen. *Balance of Payments Adjustment, 1945 to 1986: The IMF Experience*. Washington, DC: International Monetary Fund, 1987.

Dellheim, Charles. *The Disenchanted Isle: Mrs. Thatcher's Capitalist Revolution*. New York: W. W. Norton, 1995.

Dewey, Davis R. *Financial History of the United States*. New York: Longmans Green, 1903.

Dickson, P. G. M. *The Financial Revolution in England: A Study in the Development of Public Credit, 1688–1756*. New York: St. Martin's Press, 1967.

Dietze, Gottfried. *In Defense of Property*. Chicago: Henry Regnery, 1963.

Dobb, Maurice. *Studies in the Development of Capitalism*. New York: International Publishers, 1947.

Doerflinger, Thomas M., and Jack L. Rivkin. *Risk and Reward: Venture Capital and the Making of America's Great Industries*. New York: Random House, 1987.

Dos Passos, John Randolph. *A Treastise on the Law of Stock-Brokers and Stock-Exchanges*, 1882. Reprint. Westport, CT: Greenwood Press, 1968.

Douglas, Paul, Curtis N. Hitchcock, and Willard E. Atkins. *The Worker in Modern Economic Society*. Chicago: University of Chicago Press, 1923.

Dowell, Stephen. *A History of Taxation and Taxes in England*, 1888. Reprint, Vols. 1–3. New York: Augustus M. Kelley, 1965.

Durant, Will. *The Mansions of Philosophy*. New York: Simon & Schuster, 1929.

———. *The Reformation*. New York: Simon & Schuster, 1957.

Durant, Will, and Ariel Durant. *The Age of Reason Begins*. New York: Simon & Schuster, 1961.

———. *The Age of Voltaire*. New York: Simon & Shuster, 1965.

———. *Rousseau and Revolution*. New York: Simon & Schuster, 1967.

Dutton, H. I. *The Patent System and Inventive Activity during the Industrial Revolution, 1750–1852*. Manchester, UK: Manchester University Press, 1984.

Edmunds, Stahrl, and John Letey. *Environmental Administration*. New York: McGraw-Hill, 1973.

Edwards, George W. *The Evolution of Finance Capitalism*, 1938. Reprint. New York: Augustus M. Kelley, 1967.

Ehrenberg, Richard. *Capital and Finance in the Age of the Renaissance*. 1928. Translated by H. M. Lucas. New York: August M. Kelley, 1963.

Einaudi, Mario, Maurice Bye, and Ernesto Rossi. *Nationalization in France and Italy*. Ithaca, NY: Cornell University Press, 1955.

Ellis, Geoffrey James. *Napoleon's Continental Blockade: The Case of Alsace*. Oxford, UK: Clarendon Press, 1981.

Ely, James W., Jr. *The Guardian of Every Other Right*. Oxford, UK: Oxford University Press, 1992.

Ensign, Forest Chester. *Compulsory School Attendance and Child Labor*. North Stratford, NH: Arno Press, 1969.

Erleigh, Viscount, *The South Sea Bubble*. New York: Putnam, 1933.

Feavearyear, Sir Albert. *The Pound Sterling: A History of English Money*. 2nd ed. Oxford, UK: Clarendon Press, 1963.

Fehrenbach, T. R. *The Swiss Banks*. New York: McGraw Hill, 1966.

Ferris, William. *The Grain Traders*. East Lansing, MI: Michigan State University Press, 1988.

Fieldhouse, D. K. *Economics and Empire, 1830–1914*. Ithaca, NY: Cornell University Press, 1973.

Fisher, Douglas Alan. *The Epic of Steel*. New York: Harper & Row, 1963.

Fisher, F. J. "Commercial Trends and Policy in Sixteenth Century England." In *Essays in Economic History*, Vol. 1, edited by E. M. Carus-Wilson, pp. 152–172. London: Edward Arnold, 1954.

Fitzgibbons, Athol. *Adam Smith's System of Liberty, Wealth, and Virtue: The Moral and Political Foundations of the Wealth of Nations*. Oxford, UK: Clarendon Press, 1995.

Foster, William Z. *Outline of the History of the World Trade Union Movement*. New York: International Publishers, 1956.

Frank, Andre Gunder. *World Accumulation, 1492–1789*. New York: Monthly Review Press, 1978.

Fruin, Mark. *The Japanese Enterprise System: Competitive Strategies and Cooperative Structures* (1992).

Galbraith, John Kenneth. *Economics and the Public Purpose*. Boston: Houghton Mifflin, 1973.

———. *The New Industrial State*. Boston: Houghton Mifflin, 1967.

Galenson, David W. "The Rise and Fall of Indentured Servitude in the Americas: An Economic Analysis." *Journal of Economic History* 44, no. 1 (March 1984): 1–25.

Garber, P. M. "Tulipmania?" *Journal of Political Economy* 97, no. 3 (1989): 535–560.

Garnet, Robert W. *The Telephone Enterprise: The Evolution of the Bell System's Horizontal Structure, 1876–1909*. Baltimore: Johns Hopkins University Press, 1985.

Garvy, G. "Kondratieff's Theory of Long Waves." *Review of Economics and Statistics* 25, no. 4 (1943): 203–219.

Gaughan, Patrick A. *Mergers and Acquisitions*. New York: Harper Collins, 1991.

Gelderman, Carol. *Henry Ford: The Wayward Capitalist*. New York: Dial Press, 1981.

Gies, Joseph, and Frances Gies. *The Ingenious Yankees*. New York: Thomas Y. Crowell, 1976.

Gilbart, J. W. *The History, Principles, and Practice of Banking.* 1882. Reprint. Vols. 1–2. New York: Greenwood Press, 1968.

Gilder, George. *Recapturing the Spirit of Enterprise.* San Francisco: Institute for Contemporary Studies, 1992.

Goldberg, Susan. *Trading: Inside the World's Leading Stock Exchanges.* San Diego: Harcourt, Brace, & Jovanovich, 1986.

Gomes, Leonard. *Foreign Trade and the National Economy: Mercantilist and Classical Perspectives.* New York: St. Martin's Press, 1987.

Goodway, David. *London Chartism: 1838–1848.* Cambridge, UK: Cambridge University Press, 1982.

Gordon, John Steele. *The Scarlet Woman of Wall Street.* New York: Weidenfeld & Nicholson, 1988.

Gordon, Myron J., and Gordon Shillinglaw. *Accounting: A Management Approach.* 4th ed. Homewood, IL: Richard D. Irwin, 1969.

Gould, J. D. *The Great Debasement.* Oxford: Oxford University Press, 1970.

Gould, William B. *A Primer on American Labor Law.* Cambridge, MA: MIT Press, 1986.

Green, Constance M. *Eli Whitney and the Birth of American Technology.* Boston: Little, Brown, 1956.

Gregor, A. James. *Italian Fascisim and Developmental Dictatorship.* Princeton, NJ: Princeton University Press, 1979.

Gregory, Charles O. *Labor and the Law.* New York: W. W. Norton, 1958, with 1961 supplement.

Griswold, A. Whitney. "Three Puritans on Prosperity." *New England Quarterly* 7 (September 1934): 475–493.

Gross, Karen. *Failure and Forgiveness, Rebalancing the Bankruptcy System.* New Haven, CT: Yale University Press, 1997.

Hackett, Clifford P. *Cautious Revolution: The European Community Arrives.* Westport, CT: Praeger, 1990.

Hadley, Arthur T. *Railroad Transportation: Its History and Its Laws.* 1885. Reprint. New York: Johnson Reprint, 1968.

Hall, Edgar. *Risorgimento: The Making of Modern Italy.* London: Macmillan, 1970.

Halliday, Jon. *A Political History of Japanese Capitalism.* New York: Pantheon, 1975.

Hamilton, David E. *From New Day to New Deal: American Foreign Policy from Hoover to Roosevelt, 1928–1933.* Chapel Hill, NC: University of North Carolina Press, 1991.

Hamilton, Earl J. *American Treasure and the Price Revolution in Spain, 1501–1650.* Cambridge, MA: Harvard University Press, 1934.

———. *War and Prices in Spain, 1651–1800.* 1947. Reprint. New York: Russell & Russell, 1969.

Hamilton, Richard F. *The Bourgeois Epoch: Marx and Engels on Britain, France, and Germany.* Chapel Hill, NC: University of North Carolina, 1991.

Haring, Clarence Henry. *Trade and Navigation Between Spain and the Indies.* Cambridge, MA: Harvard University Press, 1918.

Harrison, Joseph. *The Spanish Economy: From the Civil War until the European Community.* Cambridge, UK: Cambridge University Press, 1995.

Hart, Henry H. *Sea Road to the Indies.* New York: Macmillan, 1950.

Hasegawa, Tsuyoshi. *The February Revolution: Petrograd, 1917.* Seattle, WA: University of Washington Press, 1981.

Haupt, Georges. *Socialism and the Great War: The Collapse of the Second International.* Oxford, UK: Clarendon Press, 1972.

Hauser, Henri. "The European Financial Crisis of 1559." *Journal of Economics and Business*, 1930. Reprint, Vol. 2, pp. 241–255. New York: Kraus Reprint Corporation, 1964.

Hawke, David D. *John D: The Founding Father of the Rockefellers.* New York: Harper & Row, 1980.

Heilbroner, Robert. *The Worldly Philosophers.* New York: Simon & Schuster, 1953.

Henderson, W. O. *The Zollverein.* London: Frank Cass, 1959.

———. *The Industrial Revolution in Europe, 1815–1914*. London: Frank Cass, 1961.

Hidy, Ralph W. *The House of Baring in American Trade and Finance: English Merchant Bankers at Work, 1763–1861*. Cambridge, MA: Harvard University Press, 1949.

Higgins, Benjamin. *Economic Development*. Revised ed. New York: W. W. Norton, 1968.

Hoffmann, Charles. *The Depression of the Nineties: An Economic History*. Westport, CT: Greenwood Press, 1970.

Homer, Sidney. *A History of Interest Rates*. 2nd ed. New Brunswick, NJ: Rutgers University Press, 1977.

Horsefield, K. "Stop of the Exchequer Re-Visited." *Economic History Review*, 2nd series, 35, no. 4 (November 1982): 511–528.

Houte, J. A. van. *An Economic History of the Low Countries, 800–1800*. New York: St. Martin's Press, 1977.

Hubbard, R. Glenn, and Robert J. Weiner. "Petroleum Regulation and Public Policy." In *Regulatory Reform: What Actually Happened?* edited by Leonard W. Weiss and Michael W. Klass, pp. 105–136. Boston: Little, Brown, 1986.

Hume, David, *The History of England, 1754–1762*. Reprint, Vols. 1–6. Philadelphia: Collins, 1985.

Hunt, Edward. *British Labor History: 1815–1914*. Atlantic Highlands, NJ: Humanities Press, 1981.

Hutchinson, Sir Herbert. *Tariff-Making and Industrial Reconstruction*. London: George G. Harrap, 1965.

Ikle, Max. *Switzerland: An International Banking and Finance Center*. Translated by Eric Schiff. Stroudsburg, PA: Dowden, Hutchinson, & Ross, 1972.

Ingram, George M. *Expropriation of U.S. Property in South America: Nationalization of Oil and Copper Companies in Peru, Bolivia, and Chile*. New York: Praeger, 1974.

Israel, Jonathan I. *Dutch Primacy in World Trade, 1585–1740*. Oxford, UK: Clarendon Press, 1989.

Jay, Anthony. *Management and Machiavelli*. New York: Holt, Rinehart, and Winston, 1967.

Johnson, Christopher H. "The Revolution of 1830 in French Economic History." In *1830 in France*, edited by John M. Merriman, pp. 139–189. New York: New Viewpoints, 1975.

Jones, W. J. "The Foundations of English Bankruptcy: Statutes and Commissions in the Early Period." *Transactions of the American Philosophical Society*, Vol. 69, pt. 3 (1979): 5–63.

Joyner, Tim. *Magellan*. Camden, ME: International Marine, 1992.

Kaplan, Daniel P. "The Changing Airline Industry." In *Regulatory Reform: What Actually Happened?* edited by Leonard Weiss and Michael W. Klass. Boston: Little, Brown, 1986.

Keown, Arthur J., et. al. *Foundations of Finance*. Upper Saddle River, NJ: Prentice Hall, 1998.

Keynes, John Maynard. *The Economic Consequences of Peace*. New York: Harcourt, Brace and Howe, 1920.

———. *The General Theory of Employment, Interest, and Money*. New York: Harcourt, Brace, 1936.

Kimzey, Bruce W. *Reaganomics*. New York: West Publishing, 1983.

Kindleberger, Charles P. *A Financial History of Western Europe*. London: George Allen & Unwin, 1984.

———. *Manias, Panics, and Crashes: A History of Financial Crises*. New York: Basic Books, 1978.

———. *World Economic Primacy, 1500 to 1990*. Oxford, UK: Oxford University Press, 1996.

———. *The World in Depression, 1929–1939*. 2nd ed. Los Angeles: University of California Press, 1986.

Kintre, Earl W. *A Robinson-Patman Primer*. 2nd ed. New York: Macmillan, 1979.

Klein, Lawrence. *The Keynesian Revolution*. New York: Macmillan, 1950.

Kline, Samuel. *The Laboring Classes in Renaissance Florence*. New York: Academic Press, 1980.

Knowles, L. C. A. *Economic Development in the Nineteenth Century*. London: Routledge & Kegan Paul, 1932.

Knox, John Jay. *A History of Banking in the United States*. New York: Bradford Rhodes, 1903.

Kolchin, Peter. *Unfree Labor: American Slavery and Russian Serfdom*. Cambridge, MA: Belknap Press, 1987.

Kondratieff, N. D. "The Long Waves in Economic Life." Translated by W. L. Stolpher. *Review of Economics and Statistics* 17, no. 6 (1935): 105–115.

Koven, Seth, and Sonya Michel, editors. *Mothers of a New World: Maternalist Politics and the Origins of the Welfare States*. New York: Routledge, 1993.

Kyong-Dong, Kim. "Confucianism and Capitalist Development in East Asia." In *Capitalism and Development*, edited by Leslie Sklair, pp. 87–106. London: Routledge, 1994.

Laidler, Harry W. *Boycotts and the Labor Struggle: Economics and Legal Aspects*. 1913. Reprint. New York: Russell & Russell, 1968.

Lamoreaux, Naomi R. *The Great Merger Movement in American Business, 1895–1904*. New York: Cambridge University Press, 1986.

Landy, Marc K., Marc J. Roberts, and Stephen R. Thomas. *The Environmental Protection Agency: Asking the Wrong Questions*. Oxford, UK: Oxford University Press, 1990.

Lane, Frederic C. *Venice: A Maritime Republic*. Baltimore: John Hopkins Press, 1973.

Laue, Theodore H. Von. *Sergei Witte and the Industrialization of Russia*. New York: Columbia University Press, 1963.

Lawson, Philip. *The East India Company: A History*. London: Longman, 1993.

Lefebvre, Georges. *The French Revolution*. Vols. 1–2. Translated by John H. Stewart and James Friguglietti. New York: Columbia University Press, 1964.

Lichtenstein, Nelson. *Labor's War at Home: The CIO in World War II*. Cambridge, UK: Cambridge University Press, 1982.

Lieberman, Sima. *Growth and Crisis in the Spanish Economy, 1940–1993*. New York: Routledge, 1995.

Light, Paul. *Artful Work: The Politics of Social Security Reform*. New York: Random Press, 1985.

Lindsey, Almont, *The Pullman Strike*. Chicago: University of Chicago Press, 1964.

Livesay, Harold C. *Andrew Carnegie and the Rise of Big Business*. Boston: Little, Brown, 1975.

Lloyd, Trevor Owen. *The British Empire, 1558–1983*. Oxford, UK: Oxford University Press, 1984.

Lockwood, William W. *The Economic Development of Japan: Growth and Structural Change: 1868–1938*. Princeton, NJ: Princeton University Press, 1954.

Long, Robert Emmet, editor. *Banking Scandals: The S & Ls and BCCI*. New York: H. W. Wilson, 1993.

Lorwin, Lewis L. *The American Federation of Labor*, 1933. Reprint. New York: AMS Press, 1970.

Lorwin, Val R. "France." In *Comparative Labor Movements*, edited by Walter Galenson, pp. 313–409. New York: Prentice-Hall, 1952.

Louis, Arthur. *The Anglo-French Commercial Treaty of 1860 and the Progress of the Industrial Revolution in France*, 1930. Reprint. New York: Octagon Books, 1971.

Lowe, Marcia D. *Back on Track: The Global Rail Revival*. Washington, DC: Worldwatch Institute, 1994.

Lustig, Nora, Barry B. Bosworth, and Robert Z. Lawrence, editors. *North American Free Trade*. Washington, DC: Brookings Institution, 1992.

Macaulay, Thomas B. *The History of England from the Accession of James II*, 1861. Reprint, Vol. 4. Chicago: Donohue, Henneberry, n.d.

Macleod, Roy M. "The Alkali Acts Administration, 1863–1884: The

Emergence of the Civil Scientist."
Victorian Studies 9, no. 2 (December 1965):
85–112.

Macrosty, Henry. *The Trust Movement in
British Industry*. New York: Agathon Press,
1968.

Madison, Charles A. *American Labor Leaders*.
New York: Frederick Ungar, 1950.

Malone, Dumas. *Jefferson and His Time*. Vol.
5. Boston: Little, Brown, 1974.

Mankiw, N. Gregory. *Macroeconomics*. New
York: Worth, 1992.

Mantoux, Paul. *The Industrial Revolution in
the Eighteenth Century*. New York: Harper
and Row, 1961.

Marx, Karl. *The Class Struggles in France:
1848–1850*, 1895. Reprint. New York:
International Publishers, 1964.

Marx, Karl, and Friedrich Engels. *Manifesto
of the Communist Party*, 1848. Reprint.
Translated by Samuel Moore. Chicago:
William Benton, 1952.

Massie, Robert. *Peter the Great: His Life and
World*. New York: Alfred A. Knopf, 1980.

Masters, Marick F. *Unions at the Cross Roads*.
Westport, CT: Quorum Books, 1997.

Matthews, George T., editor. *The Fugger
Newsletter*. New York: Capricorn Books,
1959.

McAlister, Lyle N. *Spain and Portugal in the
New World: 1492–1700*. Minneapolis:
University of Minnesota Press, 1984.

McConnell, Campbell R., and Stanley R.
Brue. *Economics*. 12th ed. New York:
McGraw Hill, 1993.

McIlroy, John. *Trade Unions in Britain Today*.
Manchester, UK: Manchester University
Press, 1988.

McLean, David. "Finance and 'Informal
Empire' before the First World War."
Economic History Review, 2nd series, 29, no.
2 (1976): 291–305.

McNally, David. *Political Economy and the
Rise of Capitalism: A Reinterpretation*. Los
Angeles: University of California Press,
1988.

Meadows, Donella H., Dennis L. Meadows,
Jorgen Randers, and William W. Behrens

III. *The Limits to Growth*. New York:
Universal Books, 1972.

Melman, Seymour. *Pentagon Capitalism: The
Political Economy of War*. New York:
McGraw-Hill, 1970.

Mendeloff, John. *Regulating Safety: An
Economic and Political Analysis of
Occupational Safety and Health Policy*.
Cambridge, MA: MIT Press, 1979.

Merivale, Herman. *Lectures on Colonization
and Colonies*, 1861. Reprint. New York:
Augustus M. Kelley, 1967.

Mingay, G. E. *The Agricultural Revolution:
Changes in Agriculture, 1650–1880*.
London: Adam and Charles Black, 1977.

Minton, Robert. *John Law: The Father of Paper
Money*. New York: Association Press, 1975.

Mittra, Sid. *Central Bank Versus Treasury: An
International Study*. Washington, DC:
University Press of America, 1978.

Moore, Geoffrey H., *Business Cycles, Inflation,
and Forecasting*. 2nd ed. Cambridge, MA:
Ballinger, 1983.

Moore, Thomas Gale. "Rail and Trucking
Deregulation." In *Regulatory Reform: What
Actually Happened?* edited by Leonard W.
Weiss and Michael W. Klass. pp. 14–39.
Boston: Little, Brown, 1986.

Moorehead, Alan. *The Russian Revolution*.
New York: Harper and Brothers, 1958.

Morison, Samuel Eliot. *Admiral of the Ocean
Sea: A Life of Christopher Columbus*.
Boston: Little, Brown, 1942.

———. *The Great Explorers*. New York:
Oxford University Press, 1978.

Myers, Margaret. *A Financial History of the
United States*. New York: Columbia
University Press, 1970.

Myers, Robert J., editor. *The Political
Morality of the International Monetary Fund*.
New Brunswick, NJ: Transactions Books,
1987.

Nanda, Ved P. *International Environmental
Law and Policy*. New York: Transnational
Publishers, 1995.

Nappi, Carmine. *Commodity Market and
Controls*. Lexington, MA: Lexington
Books, 1979.

Bibliography

Nash, Gerald D., editor. *Issues in American Economic History: Selected Readings.* Boston: D. C. Heath, 1964.

Nash, Roderick. *The Rights of Nature: A History of Environmental Ethics.* Madison, WI: University of Wisconsin Press, 1989.

Neale, Allan D., and D. G. Goyden. *The Antitrust Laws of the United States of America.* 3rd ed. London: Cambridge University Press, 1980.

Neumann, Franz. *Behemoth: The Structure and Practice of National Socialism, 1933–1944.* New York: Oxford University Press, 1944.

Nevins, Allan. *John D. Rockefeller: The Heroic Age of American Enterprise.* New York: Charles Scribner's Sons, 1941.

Northrup, Herbert R., and Gordon F. Bloom. *Government and Labor: The Role of Government in Union–Management Relations.* Homewood, IL: Richard D. Irwin, 1963.

Novak, Michael. *The Future of the Corporation.* Washington, DC: AEI, 1996.

Noyes, P. H. *Organization and Revolution: Working Class Associations in the German Revolutions of 1848–1849.* Princeton, NJ: Princeton University Press, 1966.

Nussbaum, Frederick L. *A History of the Economic Institutions of Modern Europe*, 1935. Reprint. New York: Augustus M. Kelley, 1968.

Okun, Arthur M. "Measuring the Impact of the 1964 Tax Reduction." In *Perspectives on Economic Growth*, edited by Walter Heller. pp. 25–50. New York: Random House, 1968.

Owen, Thomas C. "The Russian Industrial Society." *Journal of Economic History* 45, no. 3 (September, 1985): 587–606.

Palliser, D. M. *The Age of Elizabeth's England under the Late Tudors: 1547–1603.* London: Longman, 1983.

Panjabi, Ranee K. L. *The Earth Summit At Rio: Politics, Economics, and the Environment.* Boston: Northeastern University Press, 1997.

Parks, Robert J. *European Origins of the Economic Ideas of Alexander Hamilton.* New York: Arno Press, 1977.

Parrson, Jens D. *Dying of Money: Lessons from the Great German and American Inflations.* Boston: Wellspring Press, 1974.

Parry, John W. *The Story of Spices.* New York: Chemical Publishing, 1953.

Pelling, Henry. *A Short History of the Labor Party.* 5th ed. London: Macmillan Press, 1976.

Phillip, G. A. *The General Strike: The Politics of Industrial Conflict.* London: Weidenfield and Nicolson, 1976.

Ping, Martin J., editor. *The McGraw-Hill Handbook of Commodities and Futures.* New York: McGraw-Hill, 1985.

Pipes, Richard. *Russia under the Old Regime.* New York: Charles Scribner's Sons, 1974.

———. *The Russian Revolution.* New York: Alfred A. Knopf, 1991.

Polak, Jacques J. *The World Bank and the International Monetary Fund: A Changing Relationship.* Washington, DC: Brookings Institution, 1994.

Powell, Ellis. *The Evolution of the Money Market, 1385–1915*, 1915. Reprint. New York: August Kelley, 1966.

Prentice, Archibald. *History of the Anti-Corn Law League.* Vols. 1–2. 2nd ed., 1853. Reprint. New York: Augustus M. Kelley, 1968.

Price, Roger. *The Economic Modernization of France.* New York: John Wiley, 1975.

Pugh, Ralph B. *Imprisonment in Medieval England.* Cambridge, UK: Cambridge University Press, 1968.

Raddatz, Fritz J. *Karl Marx: A Political Biography.* Translated by Richard Barry. Boston: Little, Brown, 1979.

Reich, Robert B., and John D. Donahue. *New Deals: The Chrysler Revival and the American System.* New York: Times Books, 1985.

Riddell, Peter. *The Thatcher Decade: How Britain Has Changed during the 1980s.* Oxford, UK: Basil Blackwell, 1989.

Ridley, F. F. *Revolutionary Syndicalism in France.* Cambridge, UK: Cambridge University Press, 1970.

Rimlinger, Gaston V. *Welfare Policy and Industrialization in Europe, America, and Russia*. New York: John Wiley & Sons, 1971.

Roberts, B. C. *Trade Union Government and Administration in Great Britain*. Cambridge, MA: Harvard University Press, 1956.

Robertson, Norman, and K. I. Sams. *British Trade Unionism*. Vols. 1–2. Totowa, NJ: Rowman & Littlefield, 1977.

———. *Drastic Measures: A History of Wage and Price Controls in the United States*. Cambridge, UK: Cambridge University Press, 1984.

Rockoff, Hugh. "The Free Banking Era: A Reexamination." *Journal of Money, Credit and Banking* 6, no. 2 (May 1974): 146–157.

———. *Drastic Measures: A History of Wage and Price Controls in the United States*. Cambridge, UK: Cambridge University Press, 1984.

Rolt, L. T. C. *The Steam Engine of Thomas Newcomen*. Hartington, UK: Moorland, 1977.

Rose, J. Holland. "The Continental System, 1809–1814." In *Cambridge Modern History*, Vol. 9, edited by A. W. Ward, G. W. Prothero, and Stanley Leathes, pp. 361–389. New York: Macmillan, 1934.

Rosen, C., and K. Young. *Understanding Employee Ownership*. Ithaca, NY: International Labor Relations Press, 1991.

Rosenberg, Hans. "Political and Social Consequences of the Great Depression in Central Europe." *Economic History Review* 13 (1943): 58–73.

Ross, Ian Simpson. *The Life of Adam Smith*. Oxford, UK: Oxford University Press, 1995.

Roy, William G. *Socializing Capital: The Rise of the Large Industrial Corporation in America*. Princeton, NJ: Princeton University Press, 1996.

Ruggiero, Romano. "Between Sixteenth and Seventeenth Centuries: The Economic Crisis of 1619–1622." In *The General Crisis of the Seventeenth Century*, edited by Geoffrey Parker and Lesley M. Smith, pp. 165–225. London: Routledge & Kegan Paul, 1978.

Samuelsson, Kurt. *From Great Power to Welfare State: 300 Years of Swedish Social Development*. London: George Allen & Unwin, 1968.

Sargent, Arthur J. *The Economic Policy of Colbert*. New York: Burt Franklin, 1968.

Saseen, Jane. "Farewell to Never Never Land." *International Management* (Europe Edition) 46, no. 10 (December, 1991): 38–39.

Sayers, R. S. *The Bank of England, 1981–1944*. Cambridge, UK: Cambridge University Press, 1976.

Schlesinger, Arthur M., Jr. *The Age of Jackson*. Boston: Little, Brown, 1945.

———. *The Age of Roosevelt*. 3 vols. Boston: Houghton Mifflin, 1957–1960.

Schmiechen, James A. *Sweated Industries and Sweated Labor: The London Clothing Trades, 1860–1914*. Urbana, IL: University of Illinois Press, 1984.

Schneider, Steven A. *The Oil Price Revolution*. Baltimore: Johns Hopkins University Press, 1983.

Schnitzer, Martin C. *Contemporary Government and Business Relations*. Chicago: Rand McNally College Publishing, 1978.

Schroeder, Paul W. *The Transformation of European Politics, 1763–1848*. Oxford, UK: Clarendon Press, 1994.

Schumpeter, Joseph. *Business Cycles: A Theoretical, Historical, and Statistical Analysis of the Capitalist Process*. 2 vols. Philadelphia: Porcupine Press, 1939.

Scoville, Warren C. *The Persecution of Huguenots and French Economic Development, 1680–1720*. Los Angeles: University of Los Angeles Press, 1960.

Sella, Domenico. *Crisis and Continuity: The Economy of Spanish Lombardy in the Seventeenth Century*. Cambridge, MA: Harvard University Press, 1979.

Sewell, William H., Jr. *Work and Revolution in France: The Language of Labor from the Old Regime to 1848*. Cambridge, UK: Cambridge University Press, 1980.

Shanin, Teodor. *Russia, 1905–1907*. Vols. 1–2. New Haven, CT: Yale University Press, 1986.

Shannon, H. A. "The Coming of General Limited Liability." In *Essays in Economic History*, edited by E. M. Carus-Wilson, pp. 358–379. London: Edward Arnold, 1954.

Sheehan, James J. *German Liberalism in the Nineteenth Century*. Chicago: University of Chicago Press, 1978.

Shenefield, John H. *The Antitrust Laws: A Primer*. Washington, DC: AEI Press, 1993.

Smith, Adam. *An Inquiry into the Nature and Causes of the Wealth of Nations*, 1776. Reprint. Chicago: William Benton, 1952.

Smith, Vera C. *The Rationale of Central Banking*, 1936. Reprint. Indianapolis, IN: Liberty Press, 1990.

Snider, Delbert. *Introduction to International Economics*. 6th ed. Homewood, IL: Richard D. Irwin, 1975.

Sobel, Robert. *The Rise and Fall of the Conglomerate Kings*. New York: Stein and Day, 1984.

Solo, Robert A. *The Political Authority and the Market System*. Cincinnati, OH: Southwestern Publishing Company, 1974.

Sombart, Werner. *The Quintessence of Capitalism: A Study of the History and Psychology of the Modern Business Man*. Translated by M. Epstein. New York: Howard Fertig, 1967.

Spargo, John. *The Bitter Cry of the Children*. Chicago: Quadrangle Books, 1968.

Sperber, Jonathan. *The European Revolutions, 1848–1851*. Cambridge, UK: Cambridge University Press, 1994.

Spiegel, Henry W. *The Growth of Economic Thought*. Englewood Cliffs, NJ: Prentice-Hall, 1971.

Spiro, George W. *The Legal Environment of Business: Principles and Cases*. Englewood Cliffs, NJ: Prentice-Hall, 1993.

Stankiewicz, W. J. *Politics and Religion in Seventeenth Century France*. Berkeley, CA: University of California Press, 1960.

Starling, Grover. *The Changing Environment of Business: A Managerial Approach*. 2nd ed. Boston, MA: Kent Publishing, 1984.

Stearns, Peter. *The ABC-CLIO World History Companion to the Industrial Revolution*. Santa Barbara, CA: ABC-CLIO, 1996.

Steigerwalt, Albert K. *The National Association of Manufacturers, 1895–1914*. Grand Rapids, MI: University of Michigan, 1964.

Stein, Herbert. *Presidential Economics*. Washington, DC: AEI Press, 1994.

———. *The Fiscal Revolution in America*. 2nd ed. Washington, DC: AEI Press, 1996.

Stillman, Richard J. *Dow Jones Industrial Average: History and Role in an Investment Strategy*. Homewood, IL: Dow Jones-Irwin, 1986.

Strachey, John. *The End of Empire*. New York: Random House, 1960.

Strieder, Jacob. *Jacob Fugger the Rich, Merchant and Banker of Augsburg*. New York: Adelphi, 1931.

Subrahmanyam, Sanjay. *The Portuguese Empire in Asia, 1500–1700: A Political and Economic History*. London: Longman Group UK, 1993.

Supple, B. E. *Commercial Crisis and Change in England, 1600–1642*. Cambridge, UK: Cambridge University Press, 1959.

Taft, Philip. *The A. F. of L. in the Time of Gompers*. New York: Harper & Brothers, 1957.

Temin, Peter, with Louis Galambos. *The Fall of the Bell System*. Cambridge, UK: Cambridge University Press, 1987.

Theirs, M. A. *The History of the French Revolution*. 4 vols. Philadelphia: Carey Hart, 1844.

Thomas, Dana L. *The Plungers and the Peacocks*. New York: G. P. Putnam's Sons, 1967.

Thompson, Dorothy. *The Chartists*. New York: Pantheon Books, 1984.

Timberlake, Richard Henry. *The Origins of Central Banking in the United States*. Cambridge, MA: Harvard University Press, 1978.

Tivey, Leonard, editor. *The Nationalized Industries Since 1960: A Book of Readings.* Buffalo, NY: University of Toronto Press, 1973.

Train, John. *Famous Financial Fiascos.* New York: Charles N. Potter, 1985.

Trattner, Walter I. *Crusade for the Children.* Chicago: Quadrangle Books, 1970.

Trout, Andrew. *Jean Baptiste Colbert.* Boston: Twayne Publishers, 1978.

Tucker, Barbara M. *Samuel Slater and the Origins of the American Textile Industry, 1790–1860.* Ithaca, NY: Cornell University Press, 1984.

Turner, Michael E. *English Parliamentary Enclosure: Its Historical Geography and Economic History.* Hamden, CT: Archon Books, 1980.

U.S. Department of Health, Education, and Welfare. Food and Drug Administration. *Milestones in Food and Drug Law History.* Washington, DC, 1974.

Van Der Wee, Herman. *The Growth of the Antwerp Market and the European Economy.* Vols. 1–3. The Hague: Holland Nijhoff, 1963.

Van Horne, James C., and John M. Wachowicz, Jr. *Fundamentals of Financial Management.* 10th ed. Upper Saddle River, NJ: Prentice Hall, 1998.

Vives, Jaime Vicens. *An Economic History of Spain.* Princeton, NJ: Princeton University Press, 1969.

Waldman, Don E. *The Economics of Antitrust: Cases and Analysis.* Boston: Little, Brown, 1986.

Wall, Joseph Frazier. *Andrew Carnegie.* New York: Oxford University Press, 1970.

Ward, J. T. *The Factory Movement, 1830–1855.* New York: St. Martin's Press, 1962.

Warren, Kenneth. *World Steel: An Economic Geography.* New York: Crane, Russak, 1975.

———. *Triumphant Capitalism.* Pittsburgh: University of Pittsburgh Press, 1996.

Warshofsky, Fred. *The Patent Wars: The Battle to Own the World's Technology.* New York: John Wiley & Sons, 1994.

Watt, Richard M. *The Kings Depart, the Tragedy of Germany: Versailles and the German Revolution.* New York: Simon & Schuster, 1969.

Webber, Carolyn, and Aaron Wildavsky. *A History of Taxation and Expenditure in the Western World.* New York: Simon & Schuster, 1986.

Weber, Max, *The Protestant Ethic and the Spirit of Capitalism,* 1905. Reprint. Translated by Talcott Parsons. New York: Charles Scribner's Sons, 1930.

Webster, A. "The Political Economy of Trade Liberalization: The East India Co. Charter Act of 1813." *Economic History Review,* 2nd series, 43 (1990): 404–419.

Wechsberg, Joseph. *The Merchant Bankers.* Boston: Little, Brown, 1966.

Wee, Herman Van Der. *The Growth of the Antwerp Market and the European Economy.* 3 vols. The Hague, Netherlands: Nijhoff, 1963.

Weiss, Leonard W. Weiss, and Michael W. Klass. *Regulatory Reform: What Actually Happened?* Boston: Little, Brown, 1986.

Wendt, Lloyd. *The Wall Street Journal: The Story of Dow Jones and the Nation's Newspaper.* Chicago: Rand McNally, 1982.

White, Lawrence J. "The Partial Deregulation of Banks and other Depository Institutions." In *Regulatory Reform: What Actually Happened?* edited by Leonard W. Weiss and Michael W. Klass, pp. 169–209. Boston: Little, Brown, 1986.

Wiley, Peter B. *Yankees in the Land of the Gods.* New York: Viking, 1990.

Winston, Clifford. "Economic Deregulation: Days of Reckoning for Microeconomists." *Journal of Economic Literature* 31, no. 3 (September 1993): 1263–1289.

Wood, Christopher. *The End of Japan INC.* New York: Simon & Schuster, 1994.

Woodward, E. L. *The Age of Reform: 1815–1870.* Oxford, UK: Clarendon Press, 1962.

Wright, Alison. *The Spanish Economy: 1959–1976.* New York: Homes & Meier, 1977.

Bibliography

Yeo, Eileen, and Stephen Yeo, editors. *Popular Culture and Class Conflict, 1590–1914: Explorations in the History of Labor and Leisure.* Atlantic Highlands, NJ: Humanities Press, 1981.

Ziegler, Robert H. *The CIO, 1935–1955.* Chapel Hill, NC: University of North Carolina Press, 1995.

Illustration Credits

Index

Index